CONTEMPORARY SOCIOLOGICAL THEORY

CONTEMPORARY SOCIOLOGICAL THEORY

SECOND EDITION

GEORGE RITZER

UNIVERSITY OF MARYLAND

McGRAW-HILL PUBLISHING COMPANY

New York St. Louis San Francisco Auckland Bogotá Caracas Hamburg
Lisbon London Madrid Mexico Milan Montreal New Delhi
Oklahoma City Paris San Juan São Paulo Singapore Sydney Tokyo Toronto

CONTEMPORARY SOCIOLOGICAL THEORY

INTERNATIONAL EDITION

1 2 3 4 5 6 7 8 9 0 K K P F C P 9 4 3 2 1 0

Cover design by Sandra Josephson.
Composition by Delphian Typographers, Staten Island, New York.

Library of Congress Cataloging-in-Publication Data

Ritzer, George.
 Contemporary sociological theory / George Ritzer
  p.   cm.
 Bibliography: p.
 Includes index.
  1. Sociology.   2. Sociologist.   I. Title.
HM24.R4936   1988
301'.01—dc19   87-26027
                                                CIP

When ordering this title use ISBN 0-07-100889-6

Printed in Singapore

PERMISSIONS ACKNOWLEDGMENTS

Text

CHAPTER 3: Figures 3.1 and 3.3 from Talcott Parsons and Gerald Platt, *The American University*. Reprinted by permission of Harvard University Press.

Autobiographical sketch of Robert K. Merton. Copyright © 1981 by Robert K. Merton. Reprinted by permission of the author.

CHAPTER 7: Autobiographical sketch of George Caspar Homans. Reprinted by permission of the author.

Figures 7.1 and 7.2 from Don Bushell and Robert Burgess, "Some Basic Principles of Behavior." In Robert Burgess and Don Bushell (eds.), *Behavioral Sociology*. Copyright © 1969 by Columbia University Press. Reprinted by permission of the publisher.

Quotations from George Homans, *Social Behavior: Its Elementary Forms*. Copyright © 1961 by Harcourt Brace Jovanovich, Inc. Reprinted by permission of the publisher.

Quotations from Peter Blau, *Exchange and Power in Social Life*. Copyright © 1984 by Macmillan Publishing Co. Reprinted by permission of the publisher.

CHAPTER 8: Adaptation of Patricia M. Lengermann and Ruth A. Wallace, *Gender in America: Social Control and Social Change*, pp. 141–144. Copyright © 1985 by Prentice-Hall, Inc. Adapted by permission of Prentice-Hall, Inc., Englewood Cliffs, New Jersey.

CHAPTER 9: Quotations from Michel Foucault, *Madness and Civilization*, tr. Richard Howard. Copyright © 1965 by Pantheon Books. Reprinted by permission of Pantheon Books, a Division of Random House, Inc.

Quotations from Michel Foucault, *The History of Sexuality, Vol. I.: An Introduction*, tr. Robert Hurley. Copyright © 1980 by Pantheon Books. Reprinted by permission of Pantheon Books, a Division of Random House, Inc.

CHAPTER 10: Figure 10.2 from James Coleman, "Social Theory, Social Research, and a Theory of Action." *American Journal of Sociology* 91:1309–1335. Reprinted by permission of the University of Chicago Press.

Figure 10.3 from Ronald Burt, *Toward a Structural Theory of Action*. Copyright © 1982 by Academic Press. Reprinted by permission.

Photos

PAGE 7:   Culver Pictures

PAGE 15:   Culver Pictures

PAGE 26:   The Granger Collection

PAGE 29:   The Granger Collection

PAGE 31:   National Library of Medicine

PAGE 42:   Culver Pictures

PAGE 48:   Courtesy, University of Chicago

PAGE 52:   Courtesy, American Sociological Association

PAGE 60:   From Howard Press, C. W. Post College, Twayne Publishers, div. of
             G. K. Hall & Co., Boston

PAGE 80:   The Bettmann Archive

PAGE 98:   Courtesy, Robert K. Merton

PAGE 122:   The Granger Collection

PAGE 144:   UPI/Bettmann Newsphotos

PAGE 149:   Gamma-Liaison

PAGE 163:   Courtesy, Immanuel Wallerstein

PAGE 176:   Courtesy, University of Chicago

PAGE 189:   Courtesy, American Sociological Association

PAGE 210:   Courtesy, Mrs. Alfred Schutz

PAGE 260:   Photo: Christopher S. Johnson

PAGE 298:   Courtesy, Jessie Bernard

PAGE 308:   Courtesy, Dorothy Smith

PAGE 330:   The Granger Collection

PAGE 357:   Courtesy, Peter M. Blau

PREFACE

The second edition of this book, *Contemporary Sociological Theory,* is derived from, and is being published simultaneously with, the second edition of *Sociological Theory,* a book devoted to the entire history of the discipline's theory, both classic and contemporary. Although some historical background will be presented here, the main focus is contemporary theory.

It is a testimony to the vitality of sociological theory that this book is dramatically different from the first edition, published only a few years ago. Chapters 1 (the early years) and 2 (the later years) continue to provide an overview of the history of sociological theory, although many recent developments have been added. The rest of the book is devoted to the most important contemporary theories.

Chapter 3 begins with a discussion of structural functionalism, including this time an overview of the structural-functional theories of Talcott Parsons. (Parsons's thoughts on action theory are discussed in Chapter 9.) Also new to this edition is a discussion in Chapter 3 of the recent rise of neofunctionalism. Chapter 3 also includes a discussion of the conflict theory alternative to structural functionalism.

Chapter 4 deals with main varieties of neo-Marxian theory—economic determinism, Hegelian Marxism (with an expanded discussion of Antonio Gramsci), critical theory (with a significant expansion of the treatment of Jurgen Habermas), structural Marxism, neo-Marxian economic sociology (with a new discussion of recent works by Burawoy, Edwards, and Clawson), historically oriented Marxism, and a brief new section dealing with the rise of game-theoretic Marxism.

Chapter 5 deals with symbolic interactionism and includes such recent developments as the reassessment of the significance of Erving Goffman's theories and the work of Robert Perinbanayagam.

Chapter 6 is devoted to phenomenological sociology and ethnomethodology. This chapter now opens with a discussion of the theories of Alfred Schutz. The material on ethnomethodology is greatly changed as a result of an abundance of new work, especially by British ethnomethodologists and conversation analysts.

Chapter 7 deals with exchange theory and behavioral sociology and is little changed from the last edition.

Chapter 8 is an entirely new chapter on feminist theory written especially for this edition by two experts, Patricia Madoo Lengermann and Jill Niebrugge-Brantley. To my knowledge, this is the first time feminist theory has received full-scale coverage in a sociological theory text.

Chapter 9 is devoted to an array of recent developments in contemporary theory. Significant attention is devoted to the changing nature of action theory, systems theory, structuralism and poststructuralism (including a new, detailed treatment of the work of Michel Foucault), structural theory, a new discussion of network theory, and existential sociology.

Chapter 10 is an entirely new chapter devoted to a dramatic development in sociological theory in the 1980s—the rise of efforts to integrate macro and micro theories. A wide array of works is discussed here, the most notable of which are Anthony

Giddens's structuration theory, Jurgen Habermas's recent effort to integrate action and systems theory, Jeffrey Alexander's multidimensional sociology, Randall Collins's attempt to provide the microfoundations of macrosociology, and Michael Hechter's similar effort using rational-choice theory. This effort to integrate macro and micro theories is likely to be a dominant concern in sociological theory into the 1990s and beyond. It is currently occupying the attention of some of the best young theorists in the field.

The book concludes with an appendix which in addition to a discussion of the metatheoretical approach that undergirds the book as a whole, now also offers an overview of sociological metatheory.

A number of biographical sketches, held over from the previous edition, are presented throughout the text: Robert Park, Karl Marx, Emile Durkheim, Max Weber, Georg Simmel, Talcott Parsons, Alfred Schutz, Robert K. Merton, Louis Althusser, Immanuel Wallerstein, George Herbert Mead, George Caspar Homans, and Peter Blau. The number of such sketches has been greatly increased in this edition. New sketches deal with Ibn-Khaldun, Auguste Comte, Sigmund Freud, Herbert Spencer, Pitirim Sorokin, C. Wright Mills, Erving Goffman, Nicos Poulantzas, Jessie Bernard, and Dorothy Smith.

I would like to thank Pat Lengermann and Jill Brantley for their excellent, pathbreaking chapter on feminist theory. I would also like to thank Roger Reitman and David Walczak for their help in the first edition, contributions that continue to be manifest in this edition. I am especially grateful to Bob Antonio for his many useful ideas on improving this edition. Farid Alatas helped me greatly in preparing this new edition, and he was always a delight in challenging me to take on new theoretical perspectives.

CONTENTS

PART TWO: THE MAJOR THEORIES   75

/ Chapter Three: Structural Functionalism, Neofunctionalism, and the Conflict Theory Alternative   77

Chapter Four: Varieties of Neo-Marxian Sociological Theory   121

Chapter Five: Symbolic Interactionism   171

Chapter Six: Phenomenological Sociology and Ethnomethodology   202

Chapter Seven: Exchange Theory and Behavioral Sociology   249

Chapter Eight: Contemporary Feminist Theory   282

By Patricia Madoo Lengermann and Jill Niebrugge-Brantley

Biographical and
Autobiographical Sketches

PART ONE
INTRODUCTION

CHAPTER ONE
A Historical Sketch of Sociological Theory: The Early Years

SOCIAL FORCES IN THE DEVELOPMENT OF SOCIOLOGICAL THEORY
POLITICAL REVOLUTIONS
THE INDUSTRIAL REVOLUTION AND THE RISE OF CAPITALISM
THE RISE OF SOCIALISM
URBANIZATION
RELIGIOUS CHANGE
THE GROWTH OF SCIENCE

INTELLECTUAL FORCES AND THE RISE OF SOCIOLOGICAL THEORY
THE ENLIGHTENMENT AND THE FOUNDING OF SOCIOLOGY IN FRANCE
KARL MARX AND THE DEVELOPMENT OF GERMAN SOCIOLOGY
THE ORIGINS OF BRITISH SOCIOLOGY
ITALIAN SOCIOLOGY: PARETO AND MOSCA
TURN OF THE CENTURY DEVELOPMENTS IN EUROPEAN MARXISM

T HIS is a book about contemporary sociological theory. The bulk of it is devoted to well-established theories that continue to be relevant to this day and to theories that are just coming into their own. However, an adequate understanding of today's theories requires some familiarity with the history of sociological theory. Thus, this chapter and the next will be devoted to an overview of the major theorists and theories in the history of sociology.

Although sociological ideas are traceable to the early history of humankind, sociology as a distinctive discipline is not much more than a century old. Thus, while the material discussed in the first two chapters is not contemporary, it is not exactly ancient history either. From a long-range point of view, all of sociological theory is really relatively modern.

The material to be discussed is contemporary in still another sense: the theories and theorists discussed here are, in the main, those that continue to be relevant to this day. To take just a few examples, the ideas of major thinkers like Max Weber, Karl Marx, and Emile Durkheim are still very useful, and widely used, even though they were first developed in the 1800s and early 1900s.

We need to summarize the history of sociological theory too because many contemporary theories have been with us for some time, and to understand them we have to appreciate their early roots and the historical context in which they arose. Thus, in these first two chapters we will first encounter the theories that will occupy our attention throughout the rest of this book.

Although there are many definitions of the term *sociological theory*, this book is based on the simple idea that a sociological theory is a *wide-ranging* system of ideas that deals with the *centrally important* issues of social life.

This definition is in stark contrast to the formal, "scientific" definitions that often are used in theory texts. A formal definition might be that a theory is a set of inter-related propositions that allow for the systematization of knowledge, explanation and prediction of social life, and generation of new research hypotheses (Faia, 1986:134). Although such a definition has a number of attractions, it simply does not fit many of the sets of ideas to be discussed in this book. In other words, most sociological idea systems fall short on one or more of the formal components of a theory, but they are nonetheless considered theories by most sociologists.

Our focus is the important theoretical work of *sociologists* or the work done by those in other fields that has come to be *defined as important in sociology*. To put it succinctly, this is a book about the "big ideas" in sociology that have stood the test of time (or promise to), idea systems that deal with major social issues and are far-reaching in scope.[1]

Presenting a history of sociological theory is an enormous task, but because we devote only two chapters (Chapters 1 and 2) to that task, what we offer is a highly selective historical sketch.[2] The idea is to provide the student with a historical scaffold-ing on which the later discussions can be erected. As the reader proceeds through the later chapters that discuss specific theories and theorists, it might prove useful to return to these two overview chapters and place topics in their historical context. (Figure 1.1 is a schematic representation of the history covered in this chapter.) It also might be useful to reread these chapters after having finished the book. Much of the material in them then will be more easily comprehended.

One cannot really establish the date when sociological theory began. People have been thinking about, and developing theories of, social life since early in history. But we will not go back to the early historic times of the Greeks or Romans or even the Middle Ages. This is not because people in these epochs did not have sociologically relevant ideas, but because the return on our investment in time would be small; we would spend a lot of time getting very few ideas that are revelant to *modern* sociology. In any case, none of the thinkers associated with those eras thought of themselves, and few are now thought of, as sociologists. (For discussion of one exception, see the bio-graphical sketch of Ibn-Khaldun.) It is only in the middle and late 1800s that we begin to find thinkers who can be clearly identified as sociologists. These are the sociological thinkers we shall be interested in, and we begin by examining the main social and intel-lectual forces that shaped their ideas.

---

[1]There is also an elaborate metasociological schema that is the basis of Chapters 1 and 2 as well as the book as a whole. That schema is outlined in the Appendix at the end of this book.

[2]For a much more detailed historical sketch, see Jerzy Szacki (1979).

FIGURE 1.1 Sociological Theory: The Early Years

SOCIAL FORCES							
FRANCE							
Political revolutions	*Enlightenment* Montesquieu (1689–1755) Rousseau (1712–1778)	*Conservative Reaction* de Bonald (1754–1850) de Maistre (1753–1821)	Saint-Simon (1760–1825)	Comte (1798–1857)		Durkheim (1858–1917)	
	GERMANY						
Industrial Revolution and the rise of capitalism			Kant (1724–1804)	Hegel (1770–1831)	*Young Hegelians* Feuerbach (1804–1872)	Marx (1818–1883)	*Economic Determinists* Kautsky (1854–1938)	*Hegelian Marxists* Lukács (1885–1971)
						German Historicism Dilthey (1833–1911)	Weber (1864–1920)
Rise of socialism						Nietzsche (1844–1900)	Simmel (1858–1918)
	ITALY						
Urbanization						Pareto (1848–1923)	Mosca (1858–1941)
Religious change							
	GREAT BRITAIN						
Growth of science			*Political Economy* Smith (1723–1790)	Ricardo (1772–1823)		*Evolutionary Theory* Spencer (1820–1903)	

SOCIAL FORCES IN THE DEVELOPMENT
OF SOCIOLOGICAL THEORY

All intellectual fields are profoundly shaped by their social settings. This is particularly true of sociology, which is not only derived from that setting but takes the social setting as its basic subject matter. We will focus briefly on a few of the most important social conditions of the nineteenth and early twentieth centuries, conditions that were of the utmost significance in the development of sociology. We also will take the occasion to begin introducing the major figures in the history of sociological theory.

Political Revolutions

The long series of political revolutions ushered in by the French Revolution in 1789 and carrying over through the nineteenth century was the most immediate factor in the rise of sociological theorizing. The impact of these revolutions on many societies was enormous, and many positive changes resulted. However, what attracted the attention of many early theorists was not the positive consequences, but the negative effects of such changes. These writers were particularly disturbed by the resulting chaos and disorder, especially in France. They were united in a desire to restore order to society. Some of the more extreme thinkers of this period literally wanted a return to the peaceful and relatively orderly days of the Middle Ages. The more sophisticated thinkers recognized that social change had made such a return impossible. Thus they sought instead to find new bases of order in societies that had been overturned by the political revolutions of the eighteenth and nineteenth centuries. This interest in the issue of social order persists to this day as one of the major concerns of many sociologists and several sociological theories.

The Industrial Revolution and the
Rise of Capitalism

At least as important as political revolution in the shaping of sociological theory was the Industrial Revolution, which swept through many Western societies, mainly in the nineteenth and early twentieth centuries. The Industrial Revolution was not a single event but many interrelated developments that culminated in the transformation of the Western world from a largely agricultural to an overwhelmingly industrial system. Large numbers of people left farms and agricultural work for the industrial work offered in the burgeoning factories. The factories themselves were transformed by a long series of technological improvements. Large economic bureaucracies arose to provide the many services needed by industry and the emerging capitalist economic system. In this economy, the ideal was a free marketplace where the many products of an industrial system could be exchanged. Within this system, a few profited greatly while the majority worked long hours for low wages. A reaction against the industrial system and against capitalism in general followed and led to the labor movement as well as to various radical movements aimed at overthrowing the capitalist system.

The Industrial Revolution, capitalism, and the reaction against them all involved an enormous upheaval in Western society, an upheaval that affected sociologists greatly.

ABDEL RAHMAN IBN-KHALDUN: A Biographical Sketch

There is a tendency to think of sociology as exclusively a comparatively modern, Western phenomenon. In fact, however, scholars were doing sociology long ago and in other parts of the world. One example is Abdel Rahman Ibn-Khaldun.

Ibn-Khaldun was born in Tunis, North Africa, on May 27, 1332 (Faghirzadeh, 1982). Born to an educated family, Ibn-Khaldun was schooled in the Koran (the Muslim holy book), mathematics, and history. In his lifetime, he served a variety of sultans in Tunis, Morocco, Spain, and Algeria as ambassador, chamberlain, and member of the scholar's council. He also spent two years in prison in Morocco for his belief that state rulers were not divine rulers. After approximately two decades of political activity, Ibn-Khaldun returned to North Africa, where he undertook an intensive five-year period of study and writing. Works produced during this period increased his fame and led to a lectureship at the center of Islamic study, Al-Azhar Mosque University in Cairo. In his well attended lectures on society and sociology, Ibn-Khaldun stressed the importance of linking sociological thought and historical observation.

By the time he died in 1406, Ibn-Khaldun had produced a corpus of work that had many ideas in common with contemporary sociology. He was committed to the scientific study of society, empirical research, and the search for causes of social phenomena. He devoted considerable attention to various social institutions (for example, politics, economy) and their interrelationships. He was interested in comparing primitive and modern societies. Ibn-Khaldun has not had a dramatic impact on modern sociology, but that may change as scholars in general, and Islamic scholars in particular, rediscover his work and outline its relevance to contemporary sociology.

The four major figures in the early history of sociological theory—Karl Marx, Max Weber, Emile Durkheim, and Georg Simmel—were all preoccupied, as were many lesser thinkers, with these changes and the problems they created for society as a whole. They spent their lives studying these problems, and in many cases they endeavored to develop programs that would help solve them.

The Rise of Socialism

One set of changes aimed at coping with the excesses of the industrial system and capitalism can be lumped under the heading of socialism. Although some sociologists favored socialism as a solution to industrial problems, most were personally and intellectually opposed to it. On the one side, Karl Marx was an active supporter of the overthrow of the capitalist system and its replacement by a socialist system. Although he did not develop a theory of socialism per se, he spent a great deal of time criticizing various aspects of capitalist society. In addition, he engaged in a variety of political activities that he hoped would help bring about the rise of socialist societies.

However, Marx was atypical in the early years of sociological theory. Most of the early theorists, such as Weber and Durkheim, were opposed to socialism (at least as it was envisioned by Marx). Although they recognized the problems within capitalist society, they sought social reform within capitalism rather than the social revolution argued for by Marx. They feared socialism more than they did capitalism. This fear played a far greater role in shaping sociological theory than did Marx's support of the socialist alternative to capitalism. In fact, as we will see, in many cases sociological theory developed in reaction *against* Marxian and, more generally, socialist theory.

Urbanization

Partly as a result of the Industrial Revolution, large numbers of people in the nineteenth and twentieth centuries were uprooted from their rural homes and moved to urban settings. This massive migration was caused, in large part, by the jobs created by the industrial system in the urban areas. But it presented many difficulties for those people who had to adjust to urban life. In addition, the expansion of the cities produced a seemingly endless list of urban problems—overcrowding, pollution, noise, traffic, and so forth. The nature of urban life and its problems attracted the attention of many early sociologists, especially Weber and Georg Simmel. In fact, the first major school of American sociology, the Chicago school, was in large part defined by its concern for the city and its interest in using Chicago as a laboratory in which to study urbanization and its problems.

Religious Change

Social changes brought on by political revolutions, the Industrial Revolution, and urbanization had a profound effect on religiosity. Many early sociologists came from religious backgrounds and were actively, and in some cases professionally, involved in religion (Hinkle and Hinkle, 1954). They brought to sociology the same objectives as they had in their religious lives. They wished to improve people's lives (Vidich and Lyman, 1985). For some (such as Comte), sociology was transformed into a religion. For the rest, their sociological theories bore an unmistakable religious imprint. Durkheim wrote one of his major works on religion. Morality played a key role not only in Durkheim's sociology but in much of later sociological theory (for example, the work of Talcott Parsons). A large portion of Weber's work also was devoted to the religions of the world. Marx, too, had an interest in religiosity, but his orientation was far more critical.

The Growth of Science

As sociological theory was being developed, there was an increasing emphasis on science, not only in colleges and universities but in society as a whole. The technological products of science were permeating every sector of life, and science was acquiring enormous prestige. Those associated with the most successful sciences (physics, biology, and chemistry) were accorded honored places in society. Sociologists (especially Comte and Durkheim) from the beginning were preoccupied with science, and many wanted to model sociology after the successful physical and biological sciences. However, a debate soon developed between those who wholeheartedly accepted the scientific model and those (such as Weber) who thought that distinctive characteristics of social life made a wholesale adoption of a scientific model difficult and unwise. The issue of the relationship between sociology and science is debated to this day, although even a glimpse at the major journals in the field indicates the predominance of those who favor sociology as a science.

These are but a few of the major social factors that played key roles in the early years of sociological theory. The impact of these factors will become clear as we discuss the various theorists and theories throughout the body of the book. A variety of *other* social factors also have been important throughout the history of sociological theory, though it will not always be possible to point out their influence. For example, the radical movements of the 1960s and early 1970s led to a renewed interest, in the United States and in many other societies, in Marxian and other forms of radical theory. Although their impact varies in intensity, social factors *always* are implicated in the development of sociological theory.

Although social factors are important, the primary focus of this chapter is the intellectual forces that played a central role in shaping sociological theory. In the real world, of course, intellectual factors cannot be separated from social forces. For example, in the discussion of the Enlightenment that follows, we will find that that movement was intimately related to, and in many cases provided the intellectual basis for, the social changes discussed above.

INTELLECTUAL FORCES AND THE RISE OF SOCIOLOGICAL THEORY

The many intellectual forces that shaped the development of social theories are discussed within the national context where their influence was primarily felt. We begin with the Enlightenment and its influences on the development of sociological theory in France.

The Enlightenment and the Founding of Sociology in France

It is the view of many observers that the Enlightenment constitutes a critical development in terms of the later evolution of sociology (Hawthorn, 1976; Nisbet, 1967; Seidman, 1983; Zeitlin, 1981). The Enlightenment was a period of remarkable intellectual development and change in philosophical thought.[3] A number of long-standing ideas and beliefs—many of which related to social life—were overthrown and replaced during the Enlightenment. The most prominent thinkers associated with the Enlightenment

---

[3]This section is based on the work of Irving Zeitlin (1981). Although Zeitlin's analysis is presented here for its coherence, it has a number of limitations: there are better analyses of the Enlightenment, there are many other factors involved in shaping the development of sociology, and Zeitlin tends to overstate his case in places (for example, on the impact of Marx). But on the whole, Zeitlin provides us with a useful starting point, given our objectives in this chapter.

were the French philosophers Charles Montesquieu (1689–1755) and Jean Jacques Rousseau (1712–1778). The influence of the Enlightenment on sociological theory, however, was more indirect and negative than it was direct and positive. As Irving Zeitlin puts it, "Early sociology developed as a reaction to the Enlightenment" (1981:10).

The thinkers associated with the Enlightenment were influenced, above all, by two intellectual currents—seventeenth-century philosophy and science.

Seventeenth-century philosophy was associated with the work of thinkers such as René Descartes, Thomas Hobbes, and John Locke. The emphasis was on producing grand, general, and very abstract systems of ideas that made rational sense. The later thinkers associated with the Enlightenment did not reject the idea that systems of ideas should be general and should make rational sense, but they did make greater efforts to derive their ideas from the real world and to test them there. In other words, they wanted to combine empirical research with reason (Seidman, 1983:36–37). The model for this was science, especially Newtonian physics. At this point, we see the emergence of the application of the scientific method to social issues. At another level, not only did Enlightenment thinkers want their ideas to be, at least in part, derived from the real world, but they also wanted them to be useful to the social world, especially in the critical analysis of that world.

Overall, the Enlightenment was characterized by the belief that people could comprehend and control the universe by means of reason and empirical research. The view was that because the physical world was dominated by natural laws, it was likely that the social world was, too. Thus it was up to the philosopher, using reason and research, to discover these social laws. Once they understood how the social world worked, the Enlightenment thinkers had a practical goal—the creation of a "better," more rational world.

With an emphasis on reason, the Enlightenment philosophers were inclined to reject beliefs in traditional authority. When these thinkers examined traditional values and institutions, they often found them to be irrational—that is, contrary to human nature and inhibitive of human growth and development. The mission of the practical and change-oriented philosophers of the Enlightenment was to overcome these irrational systems.

CONSERVATIVE REACTION TO THE ENLIGHTENMENT

On the surface, we might think that French sociology was directly and positively influenced by the Enlightenment. After all, didn't French sociology become rational, empirical, scientific, and change-oriented? The answer is that it did, but not before it was also shaped by a set of ideas that was developed in reaction to the Enlightenment. In Seidman's view: "The ideology of the counter-Enlightenment represented a virtual inversion of Enlightenment liberalism. In place of modernist premises, we can detect in the Enlightenment critics a strong anti-modernist sentiment" (1983:51). As we will see, sociology in general, and French sociology in particular, has from the beginning been an uncomfortable mix of Enlightenment and counter-Enlightenment ideas.

The most extreme form of opposition to Enlightenment ideas was French Catholic counterrevolutionary philosophy, as represented by the ideas of Louis de Bonald (1754–1840) and Joseph de Maistre (1753–1821). These men were reacting against not only the Enlightenment but also the French Revolution, which they saw partly as a product of the kind of thinking characteristic of the Enlightenment. De Bonald, for example, was disturbed by the revolutionary changes and yearned for a return to the peace and harmony of the Middle Ages. In this view, God was the source of society; therefore, reason, which was so important to the Enlightenment philosophers, was seen as inferior to traditional religious beliefs. Furthermore, it was believed that because God had created society, people should not tamper with it and should not try to change a holy creation. By extension, de Bonald opposed anything that undermined such traditional institutions as patriarchy, the monogamous family, the monarchy, and the Catholic Church. To call de Bonald's position conservative is to understate the case.

Although de Bonald represented a rather extreme form of the conservative reaction, his work constitutes a useful introduction to its general premises. The conservatives turned away from what they considered to be the "naive" rationalism of the Enlightenment. They not only recognized the irrational aspects of social life but also assigned them positive value. Thus they regarded such phenomena as tradition, imagination, emotionalism, and religion as useful and necessary components of social life. In that they disliked upheaval and sought to retain the existing order, they deplored developments such as the French Revolution and the Industrial Revolution, which they saw as disruptive forces. The conservatives tended to emphasize social order, an emphasis that continues to be one of the central themes of a major portion of sociological theory.

Zeitlin has outlined ten major propositions that he sees as emerging from the conservative reaction and providing the basis for the development, at least initially, of French sociology.

1. Whereas Enlightenment thinkers tended to emphasize the individual, the conservative reaction led to a major sociological interest in, and emphasis on, society and other large-scale phenomena. Society was viewed as something more than simply an aggregate of individuals. Society was seen as having an existence of its own with its own laws of development and deep roots in the past.

2. Society was the most important unit of analysis; it was seen as more important than the individual. It was society that produced the individual, primarily through the process of socialization.

3. The individual was not even seen as the most basic element within society. A society consisted of such component parts as roles, positions, relationships, structures, and institutions. The individuals were seen as doing little more than filling these units within society.

4. The parts of society were seen as interrelated and interdependent. Indeed, these interrelationships were a major basis of society. This view led to a conservative political orientation. That is, because the parts were held to be interrelated, it followed that tampering with one part could well lead to the undermining of other parts and, ultimately, of the system as a whole. This meant that changes in the social system should be made with extreme care.

5. Change was seen as a threat not only to society and its components but also to the individuals in society. The various components of society were seen as satisfying people's needs. When institutions were disrupted, people were likely to suffer, and their suffering was likely to lead to social disorder.

6. The general tendency was to see the various large-scale components of society as useful for both society and the individuals in it. As a result, there was little desire to look for the negative effects of existing social structures and social institutions.

7. Smaller units, such as the family, the neighborhood, and religious and occupational groups, also were seen as essential to individuals and society. They provided the intimate, face-to-face environments that people needed in order to survive in modern societies.

8. There was a tendency to see various modern social changes, such as industrialization, urbanization, and bureaucratization, as having disorganizing effects. These changes were viewed with fear and anxiety, and there was an emphasis on developing ways of dealing with their disruptive effects.

9. While most of these feared changes were leading to a more rational society, the conservative reaction led to an emphasis on the importance of nonrational factors (ritual, ceremony, and worship, for example) in social life.

10. Finally, the conservatives supported the existence of a hierarchical system in society. It was seen as important to society that there be a differential system of status and reward.

These ten propositions, derived from the conservative reaction to the Enlightenment, should be seen as the immediate intellectual basis of the development of sociology in France. Many of these ideas made their way into early sociological thought, although some of the Enlightenment ideas (empiricism, for example) were also influential.

Although we have emphasized the discontinuities between the Enlightenment and the counter-Enlightenment, Seidman makes the point that there also are continuities and linkages. First, the counter-Enlightenment carried on the scientific tradition developed in the Enlightenment. Second, it picked up the Enlightenment emphasis on collectivities (as opposed to individuals) and greatly extended it. Third, both had an interest in the problems of the modern world, especially its negative effects on individuals.

We turn now to the actual founding of sociology as a distinctive discipline—specifically, to the work of three French thinkers, Claude Saint-Simon, Auguste Comte, and especially Emile Durkheim. There is general agreement that they were the founders of sociology.

CLAUDE HENRI SAINT-SIMON (1760–1825)   Saint-Simon was older than Auguste Comte, and in fact Comte, in his early years, served as Saint-Simon's secretary and disciple. There is a very strong similarity between the ideas of these two thinkers, and yet a bitter debate developed between them that led to their eventual split (K. Thompson, 1975). Because Comte is generally considered to be more important to the founding of sociology, we need say only a few words about Saint-Simon's thinking.

The most interesting aspect of Saint-Simon was his significance to the development of *both* conservative sociological theory (like Comte's) *and* Marxian theory, which was in many ways the opposite of conservative sociology. On the conservative side, Saint-Simon wanted to preserve society as it was, but he did not seek a return to life as it was in the Middle Ages, as did de Bonald and de Maistre. In addition, he was a *positivist* (Durkheim, 1928/1962:142), which meant that he believed that the study of social phenomena should employ the same scientific techniques as were used in the natural sciences. On the radical side, Saint-Simon saw the need for socialist reforms, especially the centralized planning of the economic system. But Saint-Simon did not go nearly as far as Marx did later. Although he, like Marx, saw the capitalists superseding the feudal nobility, he felt it inconceivable that the working class would come to replace the capitalists. Many of Saint-Simon's ideas are found in Comte's work, and we now turn to a brief examination of it.

AUGUSTE COMTE (1798–1857)   Comte was the first to use the term *sociology*. He had an enormous influence on early sociological theorists (especially Herbert Spencer and Emile Durkheim). And he believed that the study of sociology should be scientific, just as many contemporary sociologists do (Lenzer, 1975). Nevertheless, Auguste Comte is no longer a powerful influence on sociology.

Comte's work can be seen, at least in part, as a reaction against the French Revolution and the Enlightenment, which he saw as its main cause (1830–42/1974; 1851–54/1976). He was greatly disturbed by the anarchy that pervaded society and was critical of those French thinkers who had spawned both the Enlightenment and the Revolution. He developed his scientific view, "positivism," or "positive philosophy," to combat what he considered to be the negative and destructive philosophy of the Enlightenment. Comte was in line with, and influenced by, the French counterrevolutionary Catholics (especially de Bonald and de Maistre). However, his work can be set apart from theirs on at least two grounds. First, he did not think it possible to return to the Middle Ages; advances of science and industry made that impossible. Second, he developed a much more sophisticated theoretical system than his predecessors, one that was adequate to shape a good portion of early sociology.

Comte developed *social physics*, or what he was later to call *sociology,* to combat the negative philosophies and the anarchy that in his view pervaded French society. The use of the term *social physics* made it clear that Comte sought to model sociology after the "hard sciences." This new science, which in his view would ultimately become *the* dominant science, was to be concerned with both social statics (existing social structures) and social dynamics (social change). Although both involved the search for laws of social life, he felt that social dynamics was more important than social statics. This focus on change reflected his interest in social reform, particularly of the ills created by the French Revolution and the Enlightenment. Comte did not urge revolutionary change, because he felt the natural evolution of society would make things better. Reforms were needed only to assist the process a bit.

This leads us to the cornerstone of Comte's approach—his evolutionary theory, or the *law of the three stages.* The theory proposes that there are three intellectual stages through which the world has gone throughout its history. According to Comte, not only did the world go through this process, but groups, societies, sciences, individuals, and even minds went through the same three stages. The *theological* stage was the first, and it characterized the world prior to 1300. During this period, the major idea system emphasized the belief that supernatural powers, religious figures modeled after humankind, were at the root of everything. In particular, the social and physical world was seen as produced by God. The second stage was the *metaphysical* stage, which occurred roughly between 1300 and 1800. This era was characterized by the belief that abstract forces like "nature," rather than personalized gods, explain virtually everything. Finally, in 1800 the world entered the *positivistic* stage, characterized by belief in science. People now tended to give up the search for absolute causes (God or nature) and concentrated instead on observation of the social and physical world in the search for the laws governing them.

It is clear that in his theory of the world Comte focused on intellectual factors. Indeed, he argued that intellectual disorder was the cause of social disorder. The disorder stemmed from earlier idea systems (theological and metaphysical) that continued to exist in the positivistic (scientific) age. Only when positivism gained total control would social upheavals cease. Because this was an evolutionary process, there was no need to foment social upheaval and revolution. Positivism would come, although perhaps not as quickly as some would like. Here Comte's social reformism and his sociology coincide. Sociology could expedite the arrival of positivism and hence bring order to the social world. Above all, Comte did not want to seem to be espousing revolution. There was, in his view, enough disorder in the world. In any case, from Comte's point of view, it was intellectual change that was needed, so there was little reason for social and political revolution.

We have already encountered several of Comte's positions that were to be of great significance to the development of sociology—his basic conservatism, reformism, and scientism, and his evolutionary view of the world. Several other aspects of his work deserve mention because they also were to play a major role in the development of sociology. For example, his sociology does *not* focus on the individual but rather takes as its basic unit of analysis larger entities such as the family. He also urged that we look at *both* social structure and social change. Of great importance to later sociological theory, especially structural functionalism, is Comte's stress on the systematic character of society—the links among and between the various components of society. He also accorded great importance to the role of consensus in society. He saw little merit in the idea that society is characterized by inevitable conflict between workers and capitalists. In addition, Comte emphasized the need to go out and do sociological research rather than engage in abstract theorizing. He urged that sociologists use experimentation and comparative historical analysis. Finally, Comte was an elitist; he believed that sociology ultimately would become the dominant scientific force in the world because of its distinctive ability to interpret social laws and to develop reforms aimed at patching up problems within the system.

Comte was in the forefront of the development of positivistic sociology (Halfpenny, 1982; Bryant, 1985), an orientation that in recent years many sociologists and philosophers of science have come to question. Nevertheless, many empirically oriented sociologists and some theorists continue to operate with a positivistic orientation. Jonathan Turner (1985a) is such a theorist. To Turner, Comte's positivism emphasized that "the social universe is amenable to the development of abstract laws that can be tested through the careful collection of data," and "these abstract laws will denote the basic and generic properties of the social universe and they will specify their 'natural relations'" (1985a:24). Turner has made it clear how comfortable he is with Comte's positivism: "I think that we ought to go back to Comte, get comfortable in our armchairs once again, and start theorizing. For only when theorists begin to develop abstract principles and analytic models about invariant and timeless properties of the social universe can sociology hope to cumulate knowledge about human action, interaction, and organization" (1985a:30).

The alternative view, which has attracted many adherents in recent years, is *postpositivism*. It rejects the idea of a rational, objective science in general, as well as specifically within sociology. Schweder and Fiske describe postpositivism in this way:

AUGUSTE COMTE: A Biographical Sketch

Auguste Comte was born in Montpellier, France, on January 19, 1798. Although a precocious student, Comte never received a college-level degree, and this had a negative effect on his teaching career. In 1818 he became secretary (and "adopted son" [Manuel, 1962: 251]) to Claude Henri Saint-Simon, a philosopher forty years Comte's senior. They worked together for several years, but in 1824 they had a falling out because Comte believed that Saint-Simon was not giving him adequate credit for his contributions. Comte later wrote of his relationship with Saint-Simon as "the morbid lesson of his early youth with a depraved juggler" (Durkheim, 1928/1962: 144). Despite his later hostility to Saint-Simon, Comte often acknowledged his great debt to him: "I certainly owe a great deal intellectually to Saint-Simon . . . he contributed powerfully to launching me in the philosophic direction that I clearly created for myself today and which I will follow without hesitation all my life" (Durkheim, 1928/1962:144).

In 1826, Comte concocted a scheme by which he would present a series of seventy-two public lectures on his philosophy of life. The course drew a distinguished audience, but it was halted after only three lectures when Comte suffered a nervous breakdown. He continued to suffer from mental problems and once in 1827 sought to commit suicide by throwing himself into the Seine River.

Although he could not get a regular position at the Ecole Polytechnique, Comte did get a minor position as lecturer there in 1832. In 1837, Comte was given the additional post of admissions examiner, and this, for the first time, gave him an adequate income. During this period, Comte worked on the six-volume work for which he is best known, *Cours de Philosophie Positive,* which was finally published in 1842. In that work, Comte was the first to use the term *sociology.* He also outlined his view that sociology was the ultimate science. He attacked the Ecole Polytechnique in that work, and the result was that in 1844 his lectureship there was not renewed. By 1851 he had completed the four-volume *Système de Politique Positive* which had a more practical intent of offering a grand plan for the reorganization of society.

Comte had a series of bizarre ideas. For example, he believed in "cerebral hygiene," that is, Comte avoided reading the work of other people with the result that he became hopelessly out of touch with intellectual developments. Comte also came to fancy himself as the high priest of a new religion of humanity; he believed in a world that eventually would be led by sociologist-priests. In spite of such outrageous ideas, Comte developed a considerable following in France as well as in other countries.

Auguste Comte died on September 5, 1857.

''The drift in contemporary thinking has been to raise serious doubts about whether there are any standards, canons, or methods definitive of scientific or rational thinking. The idea of objectivity associated with positive science has been under attack from many quarters, and it has been variously defended, clarified, revised and abandoned'' (1986:17). All of the latter efforts can be thought of as postpositivism.

Even though Comte lacked a solid academic base on which to build a school of Comtian sociological theory, he nevertheless laid a basis for the development of a significant stream of sociological theory. But his long-term significance pales in comparison with that of his successor in French sociology and the inheritor of a number of his ideas, Emile Durkheim.

EMILE DURKHEIM (1858–1917) Although for Durkheim, as for Comte, the Enlightenment was a negative influence, it also had a number of positive effects on his work (for example, the emphasis on science and social reformism). However, Durkheim is best seen as the inheritor of the conservative tradition, especially as it was manifested in Comte's work. But whereas Comte had remained outside of academia, Durkheim developed an increasingly solid academic base as his career progressed. Durkheim legitimized sociology in France, and his work ultimately became a dominant force in the development of sociology in general and of sociological theory in particular.

Durkheim was politically liberal, but he took a more conservative position intellectually. Like Comte and the Catholic counterrevolutionaries, Durkheim feared and hated social disorder. His work was informed by the disorders produced by the general social changes discussed earlier in this chapter, as well as by others (such as industrial strikes, disruption of the ruling class, church-state discord, the rise of political anti-Semitism) more specific to the France of Durkheim's time (Karady, 1983). In fact, most of his work was devoted to the study of social order. His view was that social disorders were *not* a necessary part of the modern world and could be reduced by social reforms. Whereas Marx saw the problems of the modern world as inherent in society, Durkheim (along with Comte, Weber, and others) did not. As a result, Marx's ideas on the need for social revolution stood in sharp contrast to the reformism of Durkheim and the others. As sociological theory developed, it was the Durkheimian interest in order and reform that came to dominate, while the Marxian position was eclipsed for many years.

In two books published in the late 1800s, Durkheim developed a distinctive conception of the subject matter of sociology and then tested it in an empirical study. In *The Rules of Sociological Method* (1895/1964) Durkheim argued that it is the special task of sociology to study what he called *social facts*. He conceived of social facts as forces (Takla and Pope, 1985) and structures that are external to, and coercive of, the individual. The study of these large-scale structures and forces—for example, institutionalized law and shared moral beliefs—and their impact on people became the concern of many later sociological theorists. Durkheim was not content simply to define the subject matter of sociology; he sought through sociological research to demonstrate the utility of such a focus. He chose as his subject suicide. In a book entitled *Suicide,* Durkheim (1897/1951) reasoned that if he could link such an individual behavior as suicide to social causes (social facts), he would have made a persuasive case for the importance of the discipline of sociology. But Durkheim did not examine why individual *A* or *B* committed suicide; rather he was interested in the causes of differences in suicide rates among groups, regions, countries, and different categories of people (for example, married and single). His basic argument was that it was the nature of, and changes in, social facts that led to differences in suicide rates. For example, a war or an economic depression would create a collective mood of depression that would in turn lead to increases in suicide rates. As we will see in the chapter on Durkheim, there is much more to be said on this subject, but the key point for our purposes here is that Durkheim developed a distinctive view of sociology and sought to demonstrate its usefulness in a scientific study of suicide.

In *The Rules of Sociological Method,* Durkheim differentiated between two types of social facts—material and nonmaterial. Although he dealt with both in the course of his work, his main focus was on *nonmaterial social facts* (for example, culture, social institutions) rather than *material social facts* (for example, bureaucracy, law). This concern for nonmaterial social facts was already clear in his earliest major work, *The Division of Labor in Society* (1893a/1964). His focus there was a comparative analysis of what held society together in the primitive and modern cases. He concluded that earlier societies were held together primarily by nonmaterial social facts, specifically, a strongly held common morality, or what he called a strong "collective conscience." However, because of the complexities of modern society, there had been a decline in the strength of the collective conscience. The primary bond in the modern world was an intricate division of labor, which tied people to others in dependency relationships. However, Durkheim felt that the modern division of labor brought with it several "pathologies"; it was, in other words, an inadequate method of holding society together. Given his conservative sociology, Durkheim did not feel that revolution was needed to solve these problems. Rather, he suggested a variety of reforms that could "patch up" the modern system and keep it functioning. Although he recognized that there was no going back to the age when a powerful collective conscience predominated, he did feel that the common morality could be strengthened in modern society and that people thereby could cope better with the pathologies that they were experiencing.

In his later work, nonmaterial social facts occupied an even more central position. In fact, he came to focus on perhaps the ultimate form of a nonmaterial social fact—religion—in his last major work, *The Elementary Forms of Religious Life* (1912/1965). In this work, Durkheim examined primitive society in order to find the roots of religion. He believed that he would be better able to find those roots in the comparative simplicity of primitive society than in the complexity of the modern world. What he found, he felt, was that the source of religion was society itself. Society comes to define certain things as religious and others as profane. Specifically, in the case he studied, the clan was the source of a primitive kind of religion, *totemism*, in which things like plants and animals are deified. Totemism, in turn, was seen as a specific type of nonmaterial social fact, a form of the collective conscience. In the end, Durkheim came to argue that society and religion (or, more generally, the collective conscience) were one and the same. Religion was the way society expressed itself in the form of a nonmaterial social fact. In a sense, then, Durkheim came to deify society and its major products. Clearly, in deifying society, Durkheim took a highly conservative stance: one would not want to overturn a deity *or* its societal source. Because he identified society with God, Durkheim was not inclined to urge social revolution. Instead, he was a social reformer seeking ways of improving the functioning of society. In these and other ways, Durkheim was clearly in line with French conservative sociology. The fact that he avoided many of its excesses helped make him the most significant figure in French sociology.

These books and other important works helped carve out a distinctive domain for sociology in the academic world of turn of the century France, and they earned Durkheim the leading position in that growing field. In 1898, Durkheim set up a scholarly journal devoted to sociology, *L'année sociologique* (Besnard, 1983b). It became a powerful force in the development and spread of sociological ideas. Durkheim was intent on fostering the growth of sociology, and he used his journal as a focal point for the development of a group of disciples. They would later extend his ideas and carry them to many other locales and into the study of other aspects of the social world (for example, sociology of law and sociology of the city) (Besnard, 1983a:1). By 1910, Durkheim had established a strong center of sociology in France, and the academic institutionalization of sociology was well under way in that nation. (For an overview of more recent developments in French sociology, see Lemert, 1981.)

Karl Marx and the Development of German Sociology

Whereas the early history of French sociology is a fairly coherent story of the progression from the Enlightenment and the French Revolution to the conservative reaction and to the increasingly important sociological ideas of Saint-Simon, Comte, and Durkheim, German sociology was fragmented from the beginning. A split developed between Marx (and his supporters), who remained on the edge of sociology, and the early giants of mainstream German sociology, Max Weber and Georg Simmel.[4] However, although Marxian theory itself was deemed unacceptable, its ideas found their way in a variety of positive and negative ways into mainstream German sociology. Our discussion here is divided between Marxian and non-Marxian theory in Germany.

THE ROOTS OF MARXIAN THEORY

The dominant intellectual influence on Karl Marx was the German philosopher G. W. F. Hegel (1770–1831). Marx's education at the University of Berlin was shaped by Hegel's ideas as well as by the split that developed among Hegel's followers after his death. The "Old Hegelians" continued to subscribe to the master's ideas, while the "Young Hegelians," although still working in the Hegelian tradition, were critical of many facets of his philosophical system. Among the Young Hegelians was Ludwig Feuerbach (1804–1872), who tried to revise Hegel's ideas. Marx was influenced by both Hegel's ideas and Feuerbach's revisions, but he extended and combined the two philosophies in a novel and insightful way.

Two concepts represent the essence of Hegel's philosophy—the dialectic and idealism (Hegel, 1807/1967; 1821/1967). The very complicated idea of the dialectic will be discussed in the chapter on Marx, but a few introductory words are needed at this point. The *dialectic* is both a way of thinking and an image of the world. On the one hand, it is a way of thinking that stresses the importance of processes, relations, dynamics, conflicts, and contradictions—a dynamic rather than a static way of thinking about the world. On the other hand, it is a view that the *world* is made up not of static structures but of processes, relationships, dynamics, conflicts, and contradictions. Although the dialectic is generally associated with Hegel, it certainly predates him in philosophy. Marx, trained in the Hegelian tradition, accepted the significance of the

---

[4]For an argument against this and for the view of continuity between Marxian and mainstream sociology, see Seidman, 1983.

dialectic. However, he was critical of some aspects of the way Hegel used it. For example, Hegel tended to apply the dialectic only to ideas whereas Marx felt that it applied as well to more material aspects of life, for example, the economy.

Hegel is also associated with the philosophy of *idealism*, which emphasizes the importance of the mind and mental products rather than the material world. It is the social definition of the physical and material worlds that matters most, not those worlds themselves. In its extreme form, idealism asserts that *only* the mind and psychological constructs exist. Some idealists believed that their mental processes would remain the same even if the physical and social worlds no longer existed. Idealists emphasize not only mental processes but also the ideas produced by these processes. Hegel paid a great deal of attention to the development of such ideas, especially to what he referred to as the "spirit" of society.

In fact, Hegel offered a kind of evolutionary theory of the world in idealistic terms. At first, people were endowed only with the ability to acquire a sensory understanding of the world around them. They could understand things like the sight, smell, and feel of the social and physical world. Later, people developed the ability to be conscious of, to understand, themselves. With self-knowledge and self-understanding, people began to understand that they could become more than they were. In terms of Hegel's dialectical approach, a contradiction developed between what people were and what they felt that they could be. The resolution of this contradiction lay in the development of an individual's awareness of his or her place in the larger spirit of society. Individuals come to realize that their ultimate fulfillment lies in the development and the expansion of the spirit of society as a whole. Thus, individuals in Hegel's scheme evolve from an understanding of things, to an understanding of self, to an understanding of their place in the larger scheme of things.

Hegel, then, offered a general theory of the evolution of the world. It is a subjective theory in which change is held to occur at the level of consciousness. However, that change occurs largely beyond the control of actors. Actors are reduced to little more than vessels swept along by the inevitable evolution of consciousness.

Ludwig Feuerbach was an important bridge between Hegel and Marx. As a Young Hegelian, Feuerbach was critical of Hegel for, among other things, his excessive emphasis on consciousness and the spirit of society. Feuerbach's adoption of a materialist philosophy led him to argue that what was needed was to move from Hegel's subjective idealism to a focus not on ideas but on the material reality of real human beings. In his critique of Hegel, Feuerbach focused on religion. To Feuerbach, God is simply a projection by people of their human essence onto an impersonal force. People set God over and above themselves, with the result that they become alienated from God and project a series of positive characteristics onto God (that He is perfect, almighty, and holy) while they reduce themselves to being imperfect, powerless, and sinful. Feuerbach argued that this kind of religion must be overcome and that its defeat could be aided by a materialist philosophy in which people (not religion) became their own highest object, an end in themselves. Real people, not abstract ideas like religion, are deified by a materialist philosophy.

Marx was simultaneously influenced by, and critical of, *both* Hegel and Feuerbach. Marx, following Feuerbach, was critical of Hegel's adherence to an idealist philosophy. Marx took this position not only because of his adoption of a materialist orientation but also because of his interest in practical activities. Social facts like wealth and the state are treated by Hegel as ideas rather than as real, material entities. Even when he examined a seemingly material process like labor, Hegel was looking only at abstract mental labor. This is very different from Marx's interest in the labor of real, sentient people. Thus Hegel was looking at the wrong issues as far as Marx was concerned. In addition, Marx felt that Hegel's idealism led to a very conservative political orientation. To Hegel, the process of evolution was occurring beyond the control of people and their activities. In any case, in that people seemed to be moving toward greater consciousness of the world as it could be, there seemed no need for any revolutionary change; the process was already moving in the "desired" direction. Whatever problems did exist lay in consciousness, and the answer therefore seemed to lie in changing thinking.

Marx took a very different position, arguing that the problems of modern life can be traced to real, material sources (for example, the structures of capitalism), and the solutions, therefore, can be found *only* in the overturning of those structures by the collective action of large numbers of people (Marx and Engels, 1845/1956:254). Whereas Hegel "stood the world on its head" (that is, focused on consciousness, not the real material world), Marx firmly embedded his dialectic in a material base.

Marx applauded Feuerbach's critique of Hegel on a number of counts (for example, its materialism and its rejection of the abstractness of Hegel's theory), but he was far from fully satisfied with Feuerbach's own position. For one thing, Feuerbach focused on the religious world whereas Marx believed that it was the entire social world, and the economy in particular, that had to be analyzed. Although Marx accepted Feuerbach's materialism, he felt that Feuerbach had gone too far in focusing one-sidedly, nondialectically, on the material world. Feuerbach failed to include the most important of Hegel's contributions, the dialectic, in his materialist orientation, particularly the relationship between people and the material world. Finally, Marx argued that Feuerbach, like most philosophers, failed to emphasize praxis—practical activity—in particular, revolutionary activity. As Marx put it, "The philosophers have only *interpreted* the world, in various ways; the point, however, is to *change* it" (Tucker, 1970:109).

Marx extracted what he considered to be the two most important elements from these two thinkers—Hegel's dialectic and Feuerbach's materialism—and fused them into his own distinctive orientation, *dialectical materialism*, which focuses on dialectical relationships within the material world.

Marx's materialism and his consequent focus on the economic sector led him rather naturally to the work of a group of *political economists* (for example, Adam Smith and David Ricardo). Marx was very attracted to a number of their positions. He lauded their basic premise that labor was the source of all wealth. This ultimately led Marx to his *labor theory of value,* in which he argued that the profit of the capitalist was based on the exploitation of the laborer. Capitalists performed the rather simple trick of paying the workers less than they deserved, because they received less pay than the value of what they actually produced in a work period. This *surplus value,* which was retained and reinvested by the capitalist, was the basis of the entire capitalist system. The capitalist system grew by continually increasing the level of exploitation of the workers (and therefore the amount of surplus value) and investing the profits for the expansion of the system.

Marx also was affected by the political economists' depiction of the horrors of the capitalist system and the exploitation of the workers. However, whereas they depicted the evils of capitalism, Marx criticized the political economists for seeing these evils as inevitable components of capitalism. Marx deplored their general acceptance of capitalism and the way they urged people to work for economic success within it. He also was critical of the political economists for failing to see the inherent conflict between capitalists and laborers and for denying the need for a radical change in the economic order. Such conservative economics was hard for Marx to accept, given his commitment to a radical change from capitalism to socialism. With this intellectual background, we can turn briefly to Marx's theories and to the reasons for the negative reaction to them among mainstream sociologists.

KARL MARX (1818-1883)   Marx was not a sociologist and did not consider himself to be one. Although his work is too broad to be encompassed by the term *sociology,* there *is* a sociology to be found in Marx's work. From the beginning, there were those who were heavily influenced by Marx, and there has been a continuous strand of Marxian sociology, primarily in Europe. But for the majority of early sociologists, his work was a negative force, something against which to shape their sociology. Until very recently, sociological theory, especially in America, has been characterized by either hostility to, or ignorance of, Marxian theory. This has, as we will see, changed dramatically in the last two decades, but the negative reaction to Marx's work was a major force in the shaping of much of sociological theory (Gurney, 1981).

The basic reason for this rejection of Marx was ideological. Many of the early sociological theorists were inheritors of the conservative reaction to the disruptions of the Enlightenment and the French Revolution. Marx's radical ideas and the radical social changes he foretold and sought to bring to life were clearly feared and hated by such thinkers. Marx was dismissed as an ideologist. It was argued that he was not a serious sociological theorist. However, ideology per se could not have been the real reason for the rejection of Marx, because the work of Comte, Durkheim, and other conservative thinkers was also heavily ideological. It was the nature of the ideology, not the existence of ideology as such, that put off many sociological theorists. They were ready and eager to buy conservative ideology wrapped in a cloak of sociological theory, but not the radical ideology offered by Marx and his followers.

There were, of course, other reasons why Marx was not accepted by many early theorists. He seemed to be more an economist than a sociologist. Although the early sociologists would certainly admit the importance of the economy, they would also argue that it was only one of a number of components of social life.

Another reason for the early rejection of Marx was the nature of his interests. Whereas the early sociologists were reacting to the disorder created by the Enlightenment, the French Revolution, and later the Industrial Revolution, Marx was not upset by these disorders—or by disorder in general. Rather, what interested and concerned Marx most was the oppressiveness of the capitalist system that was emerging out of the Industrial Revolution. Marx wanted to develop a theory that explained this oppressiveness and that would help overthrow that system. Marx's interest was in revolution, which stood in contrast to the conservative concern for reform and orderly change.

Another difference worth noting is the difference in philosophical roots between Marxian and conservative sociological theory. Most of the conservative theorists were heavily influenced by the philosophy of Immanuel Kant. Among other things, this led them to think in linear, cause-and-effect terms. That is, they tended to argue that a change in *A* (say, the change in ideas during the Enlightenment) leads to a change in *B* (say, the political changes of the French Revolution). In contrast, Marx was most heavily influenced, as we have seen, by Hegel, who thought in dialectical rather than cause-and-effect terms. Among other things, the dialectic attunes us to the ongoing reciprocal effects of social forces. Thus, a dialectician would reconceptualize the example discussed above as a continual, ongoing interplay of ideas and politics. It is admittedly difficult to get a feel for the complicated differences between Kantian and Hegelian philosophy, but the crucial point for our purposes is that these basic philosophical differences were an important source of the negative reaction of early sociological theorists to Marxian theory.

Many volumes have been written about the substance of Marx's theory. Marx published most of his major works in the middle third of the nineteenth century. Not only is there a great deal of his work, but it is a difficult body of work, not easy to summarize.

To oversimplify enormously, Marx offered a theory of capitalist society based on his image of the basic nature of human beings. Marx believed that people are basically productive; that is, in order to survive, people need to work in, and with, nature. In so doing, they produce the food, clothing, tools, shelter, and other necessities that permit them to live. Their productivity is a perfectly natural way by which they express basic creative impulses. Furthermore, these impulses are expressed in concert with other people; in other words, people are inherently social. They need to work together to produce what they need to survive.

Throughout history this natural process has been subverted, at first by the mean conditions of primitive society and later by a variety of structural arrangements erected by societies in the course of history. In various ways, these structures interfered with the natural productive process. However, it is in capitalist society that this breakdown is most acute; the breakdown in the natural productive process reaches its culmination in capitalism.

Basically capitalism is a structure (or, more accurately, a series of structures) that erects barriers between an individual and the production process, the products of that process, and other people; ultimately, it even divides the individual himself or herself. This is the basic meaning of the concept of *alienation*: it is the breakdown of the natural interconnection between people and between people and what they produce. Alienation occurs because capitalism has evolved into a two-class system in which a few capitalists own the production process, the products, and the labor time of those who work for them. Instead of naturally producing for themselves, people produce unnaturally in capitalist society for a small group of capitalists. Intellectually, Marx was very concerned with the structures of capitalism and their oppressive impact on actors. Politically, he was led to an interest in emancipating people from the oppressive structures of capitalism.

Marx actually spent very little time dreaming about what a utopian socialist state would look like. He was more concerned with helping bring about the demise of capitalism. He believed that the contradictions and conflicts within capitalism would lead dialectically to its ultimate collapse, but he did not think that the process was inevitable.

People had to act at the appropriate times and in the appropriate ways for socialism to come into being. The capitalists have great resources at their disposal to forestall the coming of socialism, but they could be overcome by the concerted action of a class-conscious proletariat. What would the proletariat create in the process? What is socialism? Most basically, it is a society in which, for the first time, people could approach Marx's ideal image of productivity. With the aid of modern technology, people could interact harmoniously with nature and other people to create what they needed to survive. To put it another way, in socialist society, people would no longer be alienated.

THE ROOTS OF GERMAN SOCIOLOGY

Although Marx and his followers in the late nineteenth and early twentieth century remained outside of mainstream German sociology, to a considerable extent early German sociology can be seen as developing in opposition to Marxian theory. In the view of some, this explains a large part of the theory of the early giant of German sociology, Max Weber. Albert Salomon, for example, claimed that Weberian theory developed "in a long and intense debate with the ghost of Marx" (1945:596). This is probably an exaggeration, but in many ways Marxian theory did play a negative role in Weberian theory. In other ways, however, Weber was working *within* the Marxian tradition, trying to "round out" Marx's theory. Also, there were many inputs into Weberian theory other than Marxian theory (Burger, 1976). We can clarify a good deal about the sources of German sociology by outlining each of these views of the relationship between Marx and Weber (Antonio and Glassman, 1985; Schroeter, 1985). It should be borne in mind that Weber was not intimately familiar with Marx's work (much of it was not published until after Weber's death) and Weber was reacting more to the Marxists than to Marx's work itself (B. Turner, 1981:19–20; Antonio, 1985:29).

Weber *did* tend to view Marx and the Marxists of his day as economic determinists who offered single-cause theories of social life. That is, Marxian theory was seen as tracing all historical developments to economic bases and viewing all contemporaneous structures as erected on an economic base. Although this is not true of Marx's own theory, it was the position of many later Marxists.

One of the examples of economic determinism that seemed to rankle Weber most was the view that ideas are simply the reflections of material (especially economic) interests, that material interests determine ideology. From this point of view, Weber was supposed to have "turned Marx on his head" (much as Marx had done to Hegel). Instead of focusing on economic factors and their effect on ideas, Weber devoted much of his attention to ideas and their effect on the economy. Rather than seeing ideas as simple reflections of economic factors, Weber saw them as fairly autonomous forces capable of profoundly affecting the economic world. Weber certainly devoted a lot of attention to ideas, particularly systems of religious ideas, and he was especially concerned with the impact of religious ideas on the economy. In *The Protestant Ethic* (1904–1905/1958), he was concerned with Protestantism, mainly as a system of ideas, and its impact on the rise of another system of ideas, the "spirit of capitalism," and ultimately on a capitalist economic system. Weber had a similar interest in other world religions, looking at how their nature might have obstructed the development of capitalism in their respective societies. On the basis of this kind of work, some scholars came to the conclusion that Weber developed his ideas in opposition to those of Marx.

A second view of Weber's relationship to Marx, as mentioned earlier, is that he did not so much oppose Marx as try to round out his theoretical perspective. Here Weber is seen as working more within the Marxian tradition than in opposition to it. His work on religion, interpreted from this point of view, was simply an effort to show that not only do material factors affect ideas, but ideas themselves affect material structures. This interpretation of Weber's work obviously places it much closer to, in fact in line with, Marxian theory.

A good example of the view that Weber was engaged in a process of rounding out Marxian theory is in the area of stratification theory. In his work on stratification, Marx focused on social *class,* the economic dimension of stratification. Although Weber accepted the importance of this factor, he argued that other dimensions of stratification were also important. He argued that the notion of social stratification should be extended to include stratification on the basis of prestige (*status*) and *power.* The inclusion of these other dimensions does not constitute a refutation of Marx but is simply an extension of his ideas.

Both of the views outlined above accept the importance of Marxian theory for Weber. There are elements of truth in both positions; at some points Weber *was* working in opposition to Marx, while at other points he was extending Marx's ideas. However, a third view of this issue may best characterize the relationship between Marx and Weber. In this view, Marx is simply seen as but one of many influences on Weber's thought.

We can identify a number of sources of Weberian theory, including German historians, philosophers, economists, and political theorists. Among those who influenced Weber, the philosopher Immanuel Kant (1724–1804) stands out above all the others. But we must not overlook the impact of Friedrich Nietzsche (1844–1900)—especially his emphasis on the hero—on Weber's work on the need for individuals to stand up to the impact of bureaucracies and other structures of modern society.

The influence of Immanuel Kant on Weber and on German sociology generally shows that German sociology and Marxism grew from different philosophical roots. As we have seen, it was Hegel, not Kant, who was the important philosophical influence on Marxian theory. Whereas Hegel's philosophy led Marx and the Marxists to look for relations, conflict, and contradictions, Kantian philosophy led at least some German sociologists to take a more static perspective. To Kant the world was a buzzing confusion of events that could never be known directly. The world could only be known through thought processes that filter, select, and categorize these events. The content of the real world was differentiated by Kant from the forms through which that content can be comprehended. The emphasis on these forms gave the work of those sociologists within the Kantian tradition a more static quality than that of the Marxists within the Hegelian tradition.

German sociology emerged in a complex interplay with Marxian theory and a variety of other intellectual currents. The foremost exponents of early German sociology were Max Weber and Georg Simmel.

MAX WEBER (1864–1920)   Whereas Karl Marx offered basically a theory of capitalism, Weber's work was fundamentally a theory of the process of rationalization (Kalberg, 1980; Brubaker, 1984). Weber was interested in the general issue of why institutions in the Western world had grown progressively more rational while powerful barriers seemed to prevent a similar development in the rest of the world.

Although rationality is used in many different ways in Weber's work, what interests us here is a process involving one of four types identified by Kalberg (1980; see also Brubaker, 1984; Levine, 1981), *formal rationality*. Formal rationality involves, as was usually the case with Weber, a concern for the actor making choices of means and ends. However, in this case, that choice is made in reference to universally applied rules, regulations, and laws. These, in turn, are derived from various large-scale structures, especially bureaucracies and the economy. Weber developed his theories in the context of a large number of comparative historical studies of the West, China, India, and many other regions of the world. In these studies, he sought to delineate the factors that helped bring about, or impede, the development of rationalization.

Weber saw the bureaucracy (and the historical process of bureaucratization) as the classic example of rationalization, but rationalization is perhaps best illustrated today by the fast-food restaurant (Luxenberg, 1985; Ritzer, 1983). The fast-food restaurant is a formally rational system in which people (both workers and customers) are led to seek the most rational means to ends. The drive-through window, for example, is a rational means by which workers can dispense, and customers can obtain, food quickly and efficiently. Speed and efficiency are dictated by the fast-food restaurants and the rules and regulations by which they operate.

Weber embedded his discussion of the process of bureaucratization in a broader discussion of the political institution. He differentiated among three types of authority systems—traditional, charismatic, and rational-legal. Only in the modern Western world can a rational-legal authority system develop, and only within that system does one find the full-scale development of the modern bureaucracy. The rest of the world remains dominated by traditional or charismatic authority systems, which generally impede the development of a rational-legal authority system and modern bureaucracies. Briefly, *traditional* authority stems from a long-lasting system of beliefs. An example would be a leader who comes to power because his or her family or clan has always provided the group's leadership. A *charismatic* leader derives his or her authority from extraordinary abilities or characteristics, or more likely simply from the *belief* on the part of followers that the leader has such traits. Although these two types of authority are of historical importance, Weber believed that the trend in the West, and ultimately in the rest of the world, is toward systems of *rational-legal* authority. In such systems, authority is derived from rules legally and rationally enacted. Thus, the president of the United States derives his authority ultimately from the laws of society. The evolution of rational-legal authority, with its accompanying bureaucracies, is but one part of Weber's general argument on the rationalization of the Western world.

Weber also did detailed and sophisticated analyses of the rationalization of such phenomena as religion, law, the city, and even music. But we can illustrate Weber's mode of thinking with one other example—the rationalization of the economic institution. This discussion is couched in Weber's broader analysis of the relationship between religion and capitalism. In a wide-ranging historical study, Weber sought to understand why a rational economic system (capitalism) had developed in the West and why it had failed to develop in the rest of the world. Weber accorded a central role to religion in this process. At one level, he was engaged in a dialogue with the Marxists

MAX WEBER: A Biographical Sketch

Max Weber was born in Erfurt, Germany, on April 21, 1864, into a decidedly middle-class family. Important differences between his parents had a profound effect upon both his intellectual orientation and his psychological development. His father was a bureaucrat who rose to a relatively important political position. He was clearly a part of the political establishment and as a result eschewed any activity or idealism that would require personal sacrifice or threaten his position within the system. In addition, the senior Weber was a man who enjoyed earthly pleasures, and in this and many other ways he stood in sharp contrast to his wife. Max Weber's mother was a devout Calvinist, a woman who sought to lead an ascetic life largely devoid of the pleasures craved by her husband. Her concerns were more otherworldly; she was disturbed by the imperfections that were signs that she was not destined for salvation. These deep differences between the parents led to marital tension, and both the differences and the tension had an immense impact on Weber.

Because it was impossible to emulate both parents, Weber was presented with a clear choice as a child (Marianne Weber, 1975:62). He first seemed to opt for his father's orientation to life, but later he drew closer to his mother's approach. Whatever the choice, the tension produced by the need to choose between such polar opposites negatively affected Max Weber's psyche.

At age eighteen, Max Weber left home for a short time to attend the University of Heidelberg. Weber had already demonstrated intellectual precocity, but on a social level he entered Heidelberg shy and underdeveloped. However, that quickly changed after he gravitated toward his father's way of life and joined his father's old dueling fraternity. There he developed socially, at least in part because of the huge quantities of beer he consumed with his peers. In addition, he proudly displayed the dueling scars that were the trademarks of such fraternities. Weber not only manifested his identity with his father's way of life in these ways, but also chose, at least for the time being, the same career—the law.

After three terms, Weber left Heidelberg for military service, and in 1884 he returned to Berlin and to his parents' home to take courses at the University of Berlin. He remained there for most of the next eight years as he completed his studies, earned his Ph.D., became a lawyer, and started teaching at the University of Berlin. In the process, his interests shifted more toward his lifelong concerns—economics, history, and sociology.

in an effort to show that, contrary to what many Marxists of the day believed, religion was not merely an epiphenomenon. Instead, it had played a key role in the rise of capitalism in the West and in its failure to develop elsewhere in the world. Weber argued that it was a distinctively rational religious system (Calvinism) that played the central role in the rise of capitalism in the West. In contrast, in the other parts of the world that he studied, Weber found more irrational religious systems (for example, Confucianism, Taoism, Hinduism), which helped to inhibit the development of a rational economic system. However, in the end, one gets the feeling that these religions provided only temporary barriers, for the economic systems—indeed, the entire social structure—of these societies ultimately would become rationalized.

During his eight years in Berlin, Weber was financially dependent on his father, a circumstance he progressively grew to dislike. At the same time, he moved closer to his mother's values, and his antipathy to his father increased. He adopted an ascetic life and plunged deeply into his work. For example, during one semester as a student, his work habits were described as follows: "He continues the rigid work discipline, regulates his life by the clock, divides the daily routine into exact sections for the various subjects, saves in his way, by feeding himself evenings in his room with a pound of raw chopped beef and four fried eggs" (Mitzman, 1970:48; Marianne Weber, 1975:105). Thus Weber, following his mother, had become ascetic and diligent, a compulsive worker—in contemporary terms a "workaholic."

This compulsion for work led in 1896 to a position as professor of economics at Heidelberg. But in 1897, with Weber's academic career blossoming, his father died following a violent argument between them. Shortly thereafter Weber began to manifest symptoms that were to culminate in a nervous breakdown. Often unable to sleep or to work, Weber spent the next six or seven years in near-total collapse. After a long hiatus, some of his powers began to return in 1903, but it was not until 1904, when he delivered (in the United States) his first lecture in six and one-half years, that Weber was able to begin to return to active academic life. In 1904 and 1905, he published one of his best-known works, *The Protestant Ethic and the Spirit of Capitalism*. In this work, Weber announced the ascendance of his mother's religion on an academic level. Weber devoted much of his time to the study of religion, though he was not personally religious.

Although he continued to be plagued by psychological problems, after 1904 Weber was able to function, indeed to produce some of his most important work. In these years, Weber published his studies of the world's religions in world-historical perspective (for example, China, India, and ancient Judaism). At the time of his death (June 14, 1920), he was working on his most important work, *Economy and Society*. Although this book was published, and subsequently translated into many languages, it was unfinished.

In addition to the voluminous writings produced in this period, Weber undertook a number of other activities. He helped found the German Sociological Society in 1910. His home became a center for a wide range of intellectuals, including sociologists such as Georg Simmel, Robert Michels, and Georg Lukács. In addition, Weber was active politically and wrote essays on the issues of the day.

There was a tension in Weber's life and, more important, in his work, between the bureaucratic mind, as represented by his father, and his mother's religiosity. This unresolved tension permeates Weber's work as it permeated his personal life.

There is a great deal more to Weberian theory than this. For example, his work on rationalization has much more historical detail and innumerable theoretical insights. Beyond that, although rationalization lies at the heart of Weberian theory, it is far from all there is to the theory. But this is not the place to go into that rich body of material. Instead, let us return to the development of sociological theory. A key issue in that development is: Why did Weber's theory prove more attractive to later sociological theorists than Marxian theory?

One reason is that Weber proved to be more acceptable politically. Instead of espousing Marxian radicalism, Weber was more of a liberal on some issues and a conservative on others (for example, the role of the state). Although he was a severe critic of many aspects of modern capitalist society and came to many of the same critical conclusions as did Marx, he was not one to propose radical solutions to problems. In fact, he felt that the radical reforms offered by many Marxists and other socialists would do more harm than good.

Later sociological theorists, especially Americans, saw their society under attack by Marxian theory. Largely conservative in orientation, they cast about for theoretical alternatives to Marxism. One of those who proved attractive was Max Weber. (Durkheim and Vilfredo Pareto were others.) After all, rationalization affected not only capitalist but also socialist societies. Indeed, from Weber's point of view, rationalization constituted an even greater problem in socialist than in capitalist societies.

Also in Weber's favor was the form in which he presented his judgments. He spent most of his life doing detailed historical studies, and his political conclusions were often made within the context of his research. Thus they usually sounded very scientific and academic. Marx, although he did much serious research, also wrote a good deal of explicitly polemical material. Even his more academic work is laced with acid political judgments. For example, in *Capital* (1867/1967), he described capitalists as "vampires" and "werewolves." Weber's more academic style helped make him more acceptable to later sociologists.

Another reason for the greater acceptability of Weber was that he operated in a philosophical tradition that also helped shape the work of later sociologists. That is, Weber operated in the Kantian tradition, which meant, among other things, that he tended to think in cause-and-effect terms. This kind of thinking was more acceptable to later sociologists, who were largely unfamiliar and uncomfortable with the dialectical logic that informed Marx's work.

Finally, Weber appeared to offer a much better rounded approach to the social world than Marx. Whereas Marx appeared to be almost totally preoccupied with the economy, Weber was interested in a wide range of social phenomena. This diversity of focus seemed to give later sociologists more to work with than the apparently more single-minded concerns of Marx.

Weber produced most of his major works in the late 1800s and early 1900s. Although his work was broadly influential in Germany, it was to become even more influential in the United States, especially after Talcott Parsons introduced Weber's ideas (and those of other European theorists) to a large American audience. Although Marx's ideas did not have a significant positive effect on American sociological theorists until the 1960s, Weber was already highly influential by the late 1930s.

GEORG SIMMEL (1858–1918)   Georg Simmel was a somewhat atypical sociological theorist (Frisby, 1981; Levine, Carter, and Gorman, 1976a; 1976b). For one thing, he had an immediate and profound effect on the development of American sociological theory, whereas Marx and Weber were largely ignored for a number of years. Simmel's work helped shape the development of one of the early centers of American sociology—the University of Chicago—and its major theory, symbolic interactionism. The Chicago school and symbolic interactionism came, as we will see, to dominate American sociology in the 1920s and early 1930s (Bulmer, 1984). Simmel's ideas were influential at Chicago mainly because the dominant figures in the early years of Chicago, Albion Small and Robert Park, had been exposed to Simmel in Berlin in the

GEORG SIMMEL: A Biographical Sketch

Georg Simmel was born in the heart of Berlin on March 1, 1858. He studied a wide range of subjects at the University of Berlin. However, his first effort to produce a dissertation was rejected, and one of his professors remarked, "We would do him a great service if we do not encourage him further in this direction" (Frisby, 1984:23). Despite this, Simmel persevered and received his doctorate in philosophy in 1881. He remained at the university in a teaching capacity until 1914, although he occupied a relatively unimportant position as *privatdocent* from 1885 to 1900. In the latter position, Simmel served as an unpaid lecturer whose livelihood was dependent on student fees. Despite his marginality, Simmel did rather well in this position, largely because he was an excellent lecturer and attracted large numbers of (paying) students (Frisby, 1981:17). His style was so popular that even cultured members of Berlin society were drawn to his lectures, which became public events.

Simmel wrote innumerable articles ("The Stranger," "The Metropolis and Mental Life") and books (*The Philosophy of Money*). He was well known in German academic circles and even had an international following, especially in the United States, where his work was of great significance in the birth of sociology. Finally, in 1900, Simmel received official recognition, a purely honorary title at the University of Berlin, which did not give him full academic status. Simmel tried to obtain many academic positions, but he failed in spite of the support of such scholars as Max Weber.

One of the reasons for Simmel's failure was that he was a Jew in a nineteenth-century Germany rife with anti-Semitism (Kasler, 1985). Thus, in a report on Simmel written to a minister of education, Simmel was described as "an Israelite through and through, in his external appearance, in his bearing and in his mode of thought" (Frisby, 1981:25). Another reason was the kind of work that he did. Many of his articles appeared in newspapers and magazines; they were written for a more general audience than simply academic sociologists. In addition, because he did not hold a regular academic appointment, he was forced to earn his living through public lectures. Simmel's audience, both for his writings and his lectures, was more the intellectual public than professional sociologists, and this tended to lead to derisive judgments from fellow professionals. For example, one of his contemporaries damned him because "his influence remained . . . upon the general atmosphere and affected, above all, the higher levels of journalism" (Troeltsch, cited in Frisby, 1981:13).

In 1914 Simmel finally obtained a regular academic appointment at a minor university (Strasbourg), but he once again felt estranged. On the one hand, he regretted leaving his audience of Berlin intellectuals. Thus his wife wrote to Max Weber's wife: "Georg has taken leave of the auditorium very badly. . . . The students were very affectionate and sympathetic. . . . It was a departure at the full height of life" (Frisby, 1981:29). On the other hand, Simmel did not feel part of the life of his new university. Thus, he wrote to Mrs. Weber: "There is hardly anything to report from us. We live . . . a cloistered, closed-off, indifferent, desolate external existence. Academic activity is = 0, the people . . . alien and inwardly hostile" (Frisby, 1981:32).

World War I started soon after Simmel's appointment at Strasbourg; lecture halls were turned into military hospitals, and students went off to war. Thus, Simmel remained a marginal figure in German academia until his death in 1918. He never did have a normal academic career. Nevertheless, Simmel attracted a large academic following in his day, and his fame as a scholar has, if anything, grown over the years.

late 1800s. They were instrumental in bringing Simmel's ideas to students and faculty at Chicago, in translating some of his work, and in bringing it to the attention of a large-scale American audience (Frisby, 1984:29).

Another atypical aspect of Simmel's work is his "level" of analysis, or at least that level for which he became best known in America. Whereas Weber and Marx were preoccupied with large-scale issues like the rationalization of society and a capitalist economy, Simmel was best known for his work on smaller-scale issues, especially individual action and interaction. He became famous early for his thinking, derived from Kantian philosophy, on *forms* of interaction (for example, conflict) and *types* of interactants (for example, the stranger). Basically, Simmel saw that understanding interaction among people was one of the major tasks of sociology. However, it was impossible to study the massive number of interactions in social life without some conceptual tools. This is where forms of interaction and types of interactants came in. Simmel felt that he could isolate a limited number of forms of interaction that could be found in a large number of social settings. Thus equipped, one could analyze and understand these different interaction settings. The development of a limited number of types of interactants could be similarly useful in explaining interaction settings. This work had a profound effect on symbolic interactionism, which, as the name suggests, was focally concerned with interaction. One of the ironies, however, is that Simmel also was concerned with large-scale issues similar to those that obsessed Marx and Weber. However, this work was much less influential than his work on interaction, although there are contemporary signs of a growing interest in the large-scale aspects of Simmel's sociology.

It was partly Simmel's style in his work on interaction that made him accessible to early American sociological theorists. Although he wrote heavy tomes like Weber and Marx, he also wrote a set of deceptively simple essays on such interesting topics as poverty, the prostitute, the miser and the spendthrift, and the stranger. The brevity of such essays and the interest of the material made the dissemination of Simmel's ideas much easier. Unfortunately, the essays had the negative effect of obscuring Simmel's more massive works (for example, *Philosophy of Money,* translated in 1978), which were potentially as significant to sociology. Nevertheless, it was partly through the short and clever essays that Simmel had a much more significant effect on early American sociological theory than either Marx or Weber.

We should not leave Simmel without saying something about *Philosophy of Money,* because its English translation is making Simmel's work attractive to a whole new set of theorists interested in culture and society. Although this macroorientation is clearer in *Philosophy of Money*, it always existed in Simmel's work. For example, it is clear in his famous work on the dyad and the triad. Simmel thought that some crucial sociological developments take place when a two-person group (or *dyad*) is transformed into a *triad* by the addition of a third party. Social possibilities emerge that simply could not exist in a dyad. For example, in a triad, one of the members can become an arbitrator or mediator of the differences between the other two. More important, two of the members can band together and dominate the other member. This represents on a small scale what can happen with the emergence of large-scale structures that become separate from individuals and begin to dominate them.

SIGMUND FREUD: A Biographical Sketch

Sigmund Freud was born in the Austro-Hungarian city of Freiberg on May 6, 1856 (Puner, 1947). In 1859, his family moved to Vienna, and in 1873, Freud entered the medical school at the University of Vienna. Freud was more interested in science than medicine and took a position in a physiology laboratory. He completed his degree in medicine, and after leaving the laboratory in 1882, he worked in a hospital and then set up a private medical practice with a specialty in nervous diseases.

Freud at first used hypnosis in an effort to deal with a type of neurosis known as *hysteria*. He had learned the technique in Paris from Jean Martin Charcot in 1885. Later he adopted a technique, pioneered by a fellow Viennese physician, Joseph Breuer, in which hysterical symptoms disappeared when the patient talked through the circumstances in which the symptoms first arose. By 1895, Freud had published a book with Breuer with a series of revolutionary implications: that the causes of neuroses like hysteria were psychological (not, as had been believed, physiological), and the therapy involved talking through the original causes. Thus was born the practical and theoretical field of *psychoanalysis*. Freud began to part company with Breuer as he came to see sexual factors, or more generally the *libido*, at the root of neuroses. Over the next several years, Freud refined his therapeutic techniques and wrote a great deal about his new ideas.

By 1902, Freud began to gather a number of disciples around him, and they met weekly at his house. By 1903 or 1904, others (like Carl Jung) began to use Freud's ideas in their psychiatric practices. In 1908, the first Psychoanalytic Congress was held, and the next year a periodical for disseminating psychoanalytic knowledge was formed. As quickly as it had formed, the new field of psychoanalysis became splintered as Freud broke with people like Jung and they went off to develop their own ideas and found their own groups. World War I slowed the development of psychoanalysis, but it expanded and developed greatly in the 1920s. With the rise of Nazism, the center of psychoanalysis shifted to the United States, where it remains to this day. But Freud remained in Vienna until the Nazis took over in 1938, despite the fact that he was Jewish and the Nazis had burned his books as early as 1933. On June 4, 1938, only after a ransom had been paid and President Roosevelt had interceded, Sigmund Freud left Vienna. Freud had suffered from cancer of the jaw since 1923, and he died in London on September 23, 1939.

Although he was not a sociologist, Freud influenced the work of many sociologists and continues to be of relevance to sociologists (Carveth, 1982).

This theme lies at the base of *Philosophy of Money*. Simmel was primarily concerned with the emergence in the modern world of a money economy that becomes separate from the individual and predominant. This theme, in turn, is part of an even broader and more pervasive one in Simmel's work, the domination of the culture as a whole over the individual. As Simmel saw it, in the modern world, the larger culture and all of its various components (including the money economy) expand, and as they expand, the importance of the individual decreases. Thus, for example, as the industrial technology associated with a modern economy expands and grows more sophisticated, the skills and abilities of the individual worker grow progressively less important. In the end, the worker is confronted with an industrial machine over which he or she can exert little, if any, control. More generally, Simmel thought that in the modern world, the expansion of the larger culture leads to the growing insignificance of the individual.

Although sociologists have become increasingly attuned to the broader implications of Simmel's work, his early influence was primarily through his studies of small-scale social phenomena, such as the forms of interaction and types of interactants.

The Origins of British Sociology

We have been examining the development of sociology in France (Comte, Durkheim) and Germany (Marx, Weber, and Simmel). We turn now to the parallel development of sociology in England. As we will see, Continental ideas had their impact on early British sociology, but more important were native influences.

POLITICAL ECONOMY, AMELIORISM, AND SOCIAL EVOLUTION

Philip Abrams (1968) contended that British sociology was shaped in the nineteenth century by three often conflicting sources—political economy, ameliorism, and social evolution.[5] Thus when the Sociological Society of London was founded in 1903, there were strong differences over the definition of sociology. However, there were few who doubted the view that sociology could be a science. It was the differences that gave British sociology its distinctive character, and we will look at each of them briefly.

We have already touched on *political economy*, which was a theory of industrial and capitalist society traceable in part to the work of Adam Smith (1723–1790).[6] As we saw, political economy had a profound effect on Karl Marx. Marx studied political economy closely, and he was critical of it. But that was not the direction taken by British economists and sociologists. They tended to accept Smith's idea that there was an "invisible hand" that shaped the market for labor and goods. The market was seen as an independent reality that stood above individuals and controlled their behavior. The British sociologists, like the political economists and unlike Marx, saw the market as a positive force, as a source of order, harmony, and integration in society. Because they saw the market, and more generally society, in a positive light, the task of the sociologists was not to criticize society but simply to gather data on the laws by which it operated. The goal was to provide the government with the facts it needed to understand the way the system worked and to direct its workings wisely.

The emphasis was on facts, but which facts? Whereas Marx, Weber, Durkheim, and Comte looked to the structures of society for their basic facts, the British thinkers tended to focus on the individuals who made up those structures. In dealing with large-scale structures, they tended to collect individual-level data and then combine them to form a collective portrait. In the mid-1800s it was the statisticians who dominated British social science, and this kind of data collection was deemed to be the major task of sociology. The objective was the accumulation of "pure" facts without theorizing

---

[5] For more recent developments in British sociology, see Philip Abrams et al., 1981.
[6] Smith is usually included as a leading member of the Scottish Enlightenment (Chitnis, 1976), one of the Scottish Moralists (Schneider, 1967:xi) who were seeking to establish the basis for sociology.

or philosophizing. As Kent (1981:187) argues, these empirical sociologists were detached from the concerns of social theorists. Instead of general theorizing, the "emphasis settled on the business of producing more exact indicators, better methods of classification and data collection, improved life tables, higher levels of comparability between discrete bodies of data, and the like" (Abrams, 1968:18).

It was almost in spite of themselves that these statistically oriented sociologists came to see some limitations in their approach. A few sociologists began to feel the need for broader theorizing. To them, a problem such as poverty pointed to failings in the market system as well as in the society as a whole. But most, focused as they were on individuals, did not question the larger system; they turned instead to more detailed field studies and to the development of more complicated and more exact statistical techniques. To them, the source of the problem had to lie in inadequate research methods, not in the system as a whole. As Philip Abrams noted, "Focusing persistently on the distribution of individual circumstances, the statisticians found it hard to break through to a perception of poverty as a product of social structure. . . . They did not and probably could not achieve the concept of structural victimization" (1968:27). In addition to their theoretical and methodological commitments to the study of individuals, the statisticians worked too closely with government policy makers to arrive at the conclusion that the larger political and economic system was the problem.

Related to, but separable from, political economy was the second defining characteristic of British sociology—*ameliorism*, or a desire to solve social problems by reforming individuals. Although British scholars began to recognize that there were problems in society (for example, poverty), they still believed in that society and wanted to preserve it. They desired to forestall violence and revolution and to reform the system so that it could continue essentially as it was. Above all, they wanted to prevent the coming of a socialist society. Thus, like French sociology and some branches of German sociology, British sociology was conservatively oriented.

Because the British sociologists could not, or would not, trace the source of problems such as poverty to the society as a whole, the source had to lie within the individuals themselves. This was an early form of what William Ryan (1971) later called "blaming the victim." Much attention was devoted to a long series of individual problems—"ignorance, spiritual destitution, impurity, bad sanitation, pauperism, crime, and intemperance—above all intemperance" (Abrams, 1968:39). Clearly, there was a tendency to look for a simple cause for all social ills, and the one that suggested itself before all others was alcoholism. What made this perfect to the ameliorist was that this was an individual pathology, not a social pathology. The ameliorists lacked a theory of social structure, a theory of the social causes of such individual problems.

But a stronger sense of social structure was lurking below the surface of British sociology, and it burst through in the latter part of the nineteenth century with the growth of interest in *social evolution*. One important influence was the work of Auguste Comte, part of which had been translated into English in the 1850s. Although Comte's work did not inspire immediate interest, by the last quarter of the century, a number of thinkers had been attracted to it and to its concern for the larger structures of society, its scientific (positivistic) orientation, its comparative orientation, and its evolutionary theory. However, a number of British thinkers sharpened their own conception of the world in opposition to some of the excesses of Comtian theory (for example, the tendency to elevate sociology to the status of a religion).

In Abrams's view, the real importance of Comte lay in his providing one of the bases on which opposition could be mounted against the "oppressive genius of Herbert Spencer" (Abrams, 1968:58). In both a positive and a negative sense, Spencer was a dominant figure in British sociological theory, especially evolutionary theory.

HERBERT SPENCER (1820–1903)   In attempting to understand Spencer's ideas, it is useful to compare and contrast them with Comtian theory. Spencer is often categorized with Comte in terms of their influence on the development of sociological theory, but there are some important differences between them. For example, it is less easy to categorize Spencer as a conservative. In fact, in his early years, Spencer is better seen as a political liberal, and he retained elements of liberalism throughout his life. However, it is also true that Spencer grew more conservative during the course of his life and that his basic influence, as was true of Comte, was conservative.

One of his liberal views, which coexisted rather uncomfortably with his conservatism, was his acceptance of a laissez-faire doctrine: he felt that the state should not intervene in individual affairs, except in the rather passive function of protecting people. This meant that Spencer, unlike Comte, was not interested in social reforms; he wanted social life to evolve free of external control.

This difference points to Spencer as a *Social Darwinist* (Jones, 1980). As such, he held the evolutionary view that the world was growing progressively better. Therefore, it should be left alone; outside interference could only worsen the situation. He adopted the view that social institutions, like plants and animals, adapted progressively and positively to their social environment. He also accepted the Darwinian view that a process of natural selection, "survival of the fittest," occurred in the social world. That is, if unimpeded by external intervention, people who were "fit" would survive and proliferate whereas the "unfit" would eventually die out. Another difference was that Spencer emphasized the individual, whereas Comte focused on larger units such as the family.

Although there are important differences between Comte and Spencer, their shared orientations, or at least the similar ways in which they were interpreted, proved to be more important than their differences for the development of sociological theory.

Comte and Spencer shared with Durkheim and others a commitment to a science of sociology, which was a very attractive perspective to early theorists. Another influence of Spencer's work, shared with both Comte and Durkheim, was his tendency to see society as an *organism*. In this, Spencer borrowed his perspective and concepts from biology. He was concerned with the overall structure of society, the interrelationship of the *parts* of society, and the *functions* of the parts for each other as well as for the system as a whole.

Most important, Spencer, like Comte, had an evolutionary conception of historical development. However, Spencer was critical of Comte's evolutionary theory on several grounds. Specifically, he rejected Comte's law of the three stages. He argued that Comte was content to deal with evolution in the realm of ideas, in terms of intellectual development. Spencer, however, sought to develop an evolutionary theory in the real, material world.

Although Spencer is best remembered as an evolutionary theorist, his theory is highly complex, takes varied forms, and is often unclear and ambiguous. Robert Perrin

(1976) has performed a useful service by pointing out that, in fact, Spencer held four different, although sometimes overlapping, theories of social evolution.

In his first theory, Spencer argued that social evolution involved progress toward an ideal social state. As Perrin described it, this future society was to be based upon friendship, altruism, elaborate specialization, recognition for achievements rather than characteristics one is born with, "and, primarily, a voluntary cooperation among highly disciplined individuals" (1976:1343). Such a society would be held together by voluntary contractual relations and, more important, by a strong common morality. Although normative restraint from without would still be necessary, the government's role would be restricted to determining what people ought *not* to do, rather than mandating what they should do. These modern, industrialized societies would be less warlike than the militant types that preceded them.

Spencer's second evolutionary theory is a bit more theoretical and slightly less ideological. It proposes that society is evolving in the direction of the progressive differentiation of a variety of *structures* that fulfill the various *functional* requirements of society. Modern societies develop increasingly differentiated structures to handle such functional problems as procreation, production, exchange, communication, position-role placement, and control over individual behavior. This is in line with what we now call *structural-functional theory*, an approach we will have more to say about later.

In his third theory, Spencer, much as Durkheim was to do later, equated social evolution with the increasing division of labor. Basically, Spencer argued that increasing population growth necessitates increasing social differentiation. Increasing numbers disturb social equilibrium and make necessary a variety of social adjustments. One of those adjustments is an increasing division of labor. The homogeneity of primitive societies is forced to give way to the heterogeneity of more modern societies.

Finally, Spencer adopted a model of social evolution based on the model of biological evolution. In fact, it was Spencer who coined the phrase "survival of the fittest" several years *before* Darwin's work on natural selection. In this theory, Spencer was concerned with why some societies survive and others do not. Basically, his view was that the fittest societies survive, thereby leading to an adaptive upgrading of the world as a whole. A variety of factors are identified as being involved in a society's probability of success: size, fertility levels, efficiency of communication, degree of public control of resources, military organization, and so forth.

Thus Spencer offered a rich and complicated set of ideas on social evolution. As we will see, his ideas first enjoyed great success, then were rejected for many years, and recently have been revived with the rise of neoevolutionary sociological theories. (For a recent appreciation of Spencer's work see J. Turner, 1985b.)

THE REACTION AGAINST SPENCER IN BRITAIN

Despite his emphasis on the individual, Spencer was best known for his large-scale theory of social evolution. In this, he stood in stark contrast to the sociology that preceded him in Britain. However, the reaction against Spencer was based more on the threat that his idea of survival of the fittest posed to the ameliorism so dear to most early British sociologists. Although Spencer later repudiated some of his more outrageous ideas, he *did* argue for a survival of the fittest philosophy and against government intervention and social reform. He did say things like:

Fostering the good-for-nothing at the expense of the good, is an extreme cruelty. It is a deliberate stirring-up of miseries for future generations. There is no greater curse to posterity than that of bequeathing to them an increasing population of imbeciles and idlers and criminals. . . . The whole effort of nature is to get rid of such, to clear the world of them, and make room for better. . . . If they are not sufficiently complete to live, they die, and it is best they should die.

(cited in Abrams, 1968:74)

Such sentiments were clearly at odds with the ameliorative orientation of the British reformer-sociologists.

Italian Sociology: Pareto and Mosca

We can close this sketch of early, primarily conservative, European sociological theory with brief mention of two Italian sociologists, Vilfredo Pareto (1848–1923) and Gaetano Mosca (1858–1941). These two sociologists were influential in their time, but their contemporary relevance is minimal. Few people read Mosca today. There was a brief outburst of interest in Pareto's (1935) work in the 1930s, when the major American theorist, Talcott Parsons, devoted as much attention to him as he gave to Weber and Durkheim. However, in recent years, except for a few of his major concepts, Pareto also has receded in importance and contemporary relevance.

Zeitlin argued that Pareto developed his "major ideas as a refutation of Marx" (1981:171). In fact, Pareto was rejecting not only Marx but also a good portion of Enlightenment philosophy. For example, whereas the Enlightenment philosophers emphasized rationality, Pareto emphasized the role of nonrational factors such as human instincts. This emphasis also was tied to his rejection of Marxian theory. That is, because nonrational, instinctual factors were so important *and* so unchanging, it was unrealistic to hope to achieve dramatic social changes with an economic revolution.

Pareto also developed a theory of social change that stood in stark contrast to Marxian theory. Whereas Marx's theory focused on the role of the masses, Pareto offered an elite theory of social change, which held that society inevitably is dominated by a small elite that operates on the basis of enlightened self-interest. It rules over the masses of people, who are dominated by nonrational forces. Because they lack rational capacities, the masses, in Pareto's system, were unlikely to be a revolutionary force. Social change occurs when the elite begins to degenerate and is replaced by a new elite derived from the nongoverning elite or higher elements of the masses. Once the new elite is in power, the process begins anew. Thus, we have a cyclical theory of social change instead of the directional theories offered by Marx, Comte, Spencer, and others. In addition, Pareto's theory of change largely ignores the plight of the masses. Elites come and go, but the lot of the masses remains the same.

This theory, however, was not Pareto's lasting contribution to sociology. That lay in his scientific conception of sociology and the social world: "My wish is to construct a system of sociology on the model of celestial mechanics [astronomy], physics, chemistry" (Hook, 1965:57). Briefly, Pareto conceived of society as a system in equilibrium, a whole consisting of interdependent parts. A change in one part was seen as leading to changes in other parts of the system. Pareto's systemic conception of society was the most important reason Parsons devoted so much attention to Pareto's work in his 1937 book, *The Structure of Social Action,* and it was Pareto's most important influence on Parsons's thinking. Fused with similar views held by those who had an organic image of society (Comte, Durkheim, and Spencer, for example), Pareto's theory played a central role in the development of Parsons's theory and, more generally, in structural functionalism.

Although few modern sociologists now read Pareto's work (one exception is Powers, 1986), virtually none ever read Mosca's. But his work also can be seen as a rejection of the Enlightenment and of Marxism. The important point is that Mosca, like Pareto, offered an elite theory of social change that stands in opposition to the Marxian perspective.

Turn of the Century Developments in European Marxism

While many nineteenth-century sociologists were developing their theories in opposition to Marx, there was a simultaneous effort by a number of Marxists to clarify and extend Marxian theory. Between roughly 1875 and 1925, there was little overlap between Marxism and sociology. (Weber is an exception to this.) The two schools of thought were developing in parallel fashion with little or no interchange between them.

After the death of Marx, Marxian theory was first dominated by those who saw in his theory scientific and economic determinism. Wallerstein calls this the era of "orthodox Marxism" (1986:1301). Friedrich Engels, Marx's benefactor and collaborator, lived on after Marx's death and can be seen as the first exponent of such a perspective. Basically, this view was that Marx's scientific theory had uncovered the economic laws that ruled the capitalist world. Such laws pointed to the inevitable collapse of the capitalist system. Early Marxian thinkers, like Karl Kautsky, sought to gain a better understanding of the operation of these laws. There were several problems with this perspective. For one thing, it seemed to rule out political action, a cornerstone of Marx's position. That is, there seemed no need for individuals, especially workers, to do anything. In that the system was inevitably crumbling, all they had to do was sit back and wait for its demise. On a theoretical level, deterministic Marxism seemed to rule out the dialectical relationship between individuals and larger social structures.

These problems led to a reaction among Marxian theorists and the development of "Hegelian Marxism" in the early 1900s. The Hegelian Marxists refused to reduce Marxism to a scientific theory that ignored individual thought and action. They are labeled Hegelian Marxists because they sought to combine Hegel's interest in consciousness (which some view Marx as sharing) with the determinists' interest in the economic structures of society. The Hegelian theorists were significant for both theoretical and practical reasons. Theoretically, they reinstated the importance of the individual, consciousness, and the relationship between thought and action. Practically, they emphasized the importance of individual action in bringing about a social revolution.

The major exponent of this point of view was George Lukács (Fischer, 1984). According to Martin Jay, Lukács was "the founding father of Western Marxism" and the author of *Class and Class Consciousness* which is "generally acknowledged as the charter document of Hegelian Marxism" (1984:84). Lukács had begun in the early

1900s to integrate Marxism with sociology (in particular, Weberian and Simmelian theory). This integration was soon to accelerate with the development of critical theory in the 1920s and 1930s.

SUMMARY

This chapter sketches the early history of sociological theory in two parts. The first, and much briefer, section deals with the various social forces involved in the development of sociological theory. Although there were many such influences, we focus on how political revolution, the Industrial Revolution and the rise of capitalism, socialism, urbanization, religious change, and the growth of science affected sociological theory. The second part of the chapter examines the influence of intellectual forces on the rise of sociological theory in various countries. We begin with France and the role played by the Enlightenment, stressing the conservative and romantic reaction to it. It is out of this interplay that French sociological theory developed. In this context, we examine the major figures in the early years of French sociology—Claude Henri Saint-Simon, Auguste Comte, and Emile Durkheim.

Next we turn to Germany and the role played by Karl Marx in the development of sociology in that country. We discuss the parallel development of Marxian theory and sociological theory and the ways in which Marxian theory influenced sociology, both positively and negatively. We begin with the roots of Marxian theory in Hegelianism, materialism, and political economy. Marx's theory itself is touched upon briefly. The discussion then shifts to the roots of German sociology. Max Weber's work is examined in order to show the diverse sources of German sociology. Also discussed are some of the reasons that Weber's theory proved more acceptable to later sociologists than did Marx's ideas. This section closes with a brief discussion of Georg Simmel's work.

The rise of sociological theory in Britain is considered next. The major sources of British sociology were political economy, ameliorism, and social evolution. In this context, we touch on the work of Herbert Spencer as well as on some of the controversy that surrounded it.

This chapter closes with a brief discussion of Italian sociological theory, especially the work of Vilfredo Pareto, and the turn of the century developments in European Marxian theory, primarily economic determinism and Hegelian Marxism.

This concludes our review of the early history of sociological theory. We pick up the discussion of the history of sociological theory in the next chapter where we will deal with more recent developments. The remainder of the book focuses on contemporary theories and theorists.

CHAPTER TWO
A Historical Sketch of Sociological Theory: The Later Years

IN Chapter 1 we discussed the development of sociological theory, largely in nineteenth-century Europe. In this chapter, we turn to late nineteenth- and twentieth-century developments, with particular attention to developments in the United States. Figure 2.1 shows the important intellectual influences on this development as well as the major theories and theorists.

EARLY AMERICAN SOCIOLOGICAL THEORY

It is difficult to give a precise date for the founding of sociology in the United States. There was a course in social problems taught at Oberlin as early as 1858; Comte's term *sociology* was used by George Fitzhugh in 1854; and William Graham Sumner taught

FIGURE 6.1 Sociological Theory: The Later Years

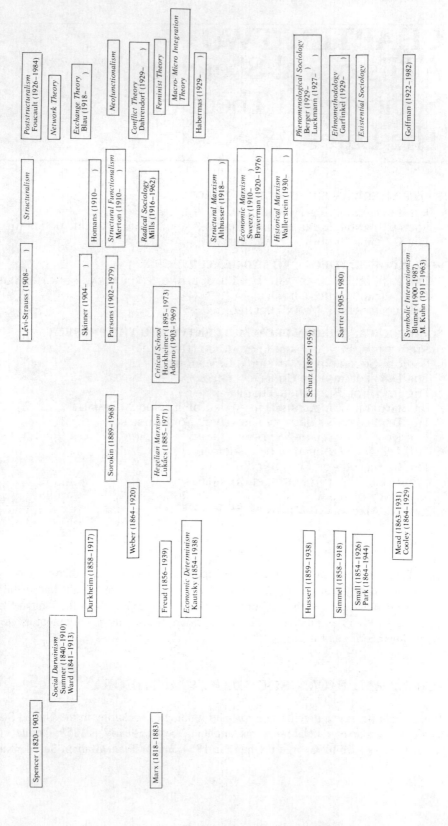

social science courses at Yale beginning in 1873. During the 1880s, courses specifically bearing the title sociology began to appear. The first department with sociology in its title was founded at the University of Kansas in 1889. In 1892, Albion Small moved to the University of Chicago and set up the new department of sociology. The Chicago department became the first important center of American sociology in general and of sociological theory in particular (Matthews, 1977).

The Politics of Early American Sociology

A major study of the politics of early American sociological theory (Schwendinger and Schwendinger, 1974) argued that the early sociologists are best described as political liberals and not, as was true of most early European theorists, as conservatives. The liberalism characteristic of early American sociology had basically two elements. First, it operated with a belief in the freedom and welfare of the individual. In this, it was far more influenced by Spencer's orientation than by Comte's more collective position. Second, many sociologists associated with this orientation adopted an evolutionary view of social progress (W. Fine, 1979). However, they split over how best to bring about this progress. Some argued that steps should be taken by the government to aid social reform, while others pushed a laissez-faire doctrine, arguing that the various components of society should be left to solve their own problems.

Liberalism, taken to its extreme, comes very close to conservatism. The belief in social progress—in reform or a laissez-faire doctrine—and the belief in the importance of the individual both lead to positions supportive of the system as a whole. The overriding belief is that the social system works or can be reformed to work. There is little criticism of the system as a whole; in the American case this means, in particular, that there is little questioning of capitalism. Instead of imminent class struggle, the early sociologists saw a future of class harmony and class cooperation. Ultimately this meant that early American sociological theory helped to rationalize exploitation, domestic and international imperialism, and social inequality (Schwendinger and Schwendinger, 1974). In the end, the political liberalism of the early sociologists had enormously conservative implications.

Social Change, Intellectual Currents, and Early American Sociology

In their analyses of the founding of American sociological theory, Roscoe Hinkle (1980) and Ellsworth Fuhrman (1980) outline several basic contexts from which that body of theory emerged. Of utmost importance are the social changes that occurred in American society after the Civil War (Bramson, 1961). In Chapter 1, we discussed an array of factors involved in the development of European sociological theory; several of these factors (such as industrialization and urbanization) were also intimately involved in the development of theory in America. In Fuhrman's view, the early American sociologists saw the positive possibilities of industrialization, but they were also well aware of its dangers. Although these early sociologists were attracted to the ideas about dealing with the dangers of industrialization generated by the labor movement and socialist groups, they were not in favor of radically overhauling society.

HERBERT SPENCER: A Biographical Sketch

Herbert Spencer was born in Derby, England, on April 27, 1820. He was not schooled in the arts and humanities, but rather in technical and utilitarian matters. In 1837 he began work as a civil engineer for a railway, an occupation he held until 1846. During this period, Spencer continued to study on his own and began to publish scientific and political works.

In 1848 Spencer was appointed an editor of *The Economist,* and his intellectual ideas began to solidify. By 1850, he had completed his first major work, *Social Statics.* During the writing of this work, Spencer first began to experience insomnia, and over the years, his mental and physical problems mounted. He was to suffer a series of nervous breakdowns throughout the rest of his life.

In 1853 Spencer received an inheritance that allowed him to quit his job and live for the rest of his life as a gentleman scholar. He never earned a university degree or held an academic position. As he grew more isolated, and physical and mental illness mounted, Spencer's productivity as a scholar increased. Eventually, Spencer began not only to achieve fame within England, but also an international reputation. As Richard Hofstadter put it: "In the three decades after the Civil War it was impossible to be active in any field of intellectual work without mastering Spencer" (1959:33). Among his supporters was the important industrialist Andrew Carnegie, who wrote the following to Spencer during the latter's fatal illness of 1903:

> Dear Master Teacher . . . you come to me every day in thought, and the everlasting "why" intrudes—Why lies he? Why must he go? . . . The world jogs on unconscious of its greatest mind. . . . But it will wake some day to its teachings and decree Spencer's place is with the greatest.
>
> (Peel, 1971:2)

Arthur Vidich and Stanford Lyman (1985) have recently made a strong case for the influence of Christianity, especially Protestantism, on the founding of American sociology. In their view, American sociologists retained the Protestant interest in saving the world and merely substituted one language (science) for another (religion). They argue: "From 1854, when the first works in sociology appeared in the United States, until the outbreak of World War I, sociology was a moral and intellectual response to the problems of American life and thought, institutions, and creeds" (Vidich and Lyman, 1985:1). Sociologists sought to define, study, and help solve these social problems. While the clergyman worked within religion to help improve it and peoples' lot within it, the sociologist did the same within society. Given their religious roots, and the religious parallels, the vast majority of sociologists did not challenge the basic legitimacy of society.

Another major factor in the founding of American sociology discussed by both Hinkle and Fuhrman is the simultaneous emergence in America, in the late 1800s, of both academic professions (including sociology) and the modern university system. In Europe, in contrast, the university system was already well established *before* the emergence of sociology. Although sociology had a difficult time becoming established in Europe, it

But that was not to be Spencer's fate.

One of Spencer's most interesting characteristics, one that was ultimately to be the cause of his intellectual undoing, was his unwillingness to read the work of other people. In this, he resembled another early giant of sociology, Auguste Comte, who practiced "cerebral hygiene." Of the need to read the works of others, Spencer said: "All my life I have been a thinker and not a reader, being able to say with Hobbes that 'if I had read as much as other men I would have known as little.' A friend asked Spencer's opinion of a book, and "his reply was that on looking into the book he saw that its fundamental assumption was erroneous, and therefore did not care to read it." One author wrote of Spencer's "incomprehensible way of absorbing knowledge through the pores of his skin . . . he never seemed to read books" (Wiltshire, 1978:67).

If he didn't read the work of other scholars, where, then, did Spencer's ideas and insights come from? According to Spencer, they emerged involuntarily and intuitively from his mind. He said that his ideas emerged "little by little, in unobtrusive ways, without conscious intention or appreciable effort." Such intuition was deemed by Spencer to be far more effective than careful study and thought; "a solution reached in the way described is more likely to be true than one reached in the pursuance of a determined effort [which] causes perversion of thought" (Wiltshire, 1978:66).

Spencer suffered because of his unwillingness to seriously read the works of other people. In fact, if he read other work, it was often only to find confirmation for his own, independently created ideas. He ignored those ideas that did not agree with his. Thus, his contemporary, Charles Darwin, said of Spencer: "If he had trained himself to observe more, even at the expense of . . . some loss of thinking power, he would have been a wonderful man" (Wiltshire, 1978:70). Spencer's disregard for the rules of scholarship led him to a series of outrageous ideas and unsubstantiated assertions about the evolution of the world. For these reasons, sociologists in the twentieth century came to reject Spencer's work and to substitute for it careful scholarship and empirical research.

Spencer died on December 8, 1903.

found the going easier in the more fluid setting of the new American university system.

Still another factor was the impact of established European theory on American sociological theory. European theorists largely created sociological theory, and the Americans were able to rely on this groundwork. The Europeans most important to the Americans were Spencer and Comte. Simmel was of some importance in the early years, but the influence of Durkheim, Weber and Marx was not to have a dramatic effect for a number of years. As an illustration of the impact of early European theory on American sociology, the history of the ideas of Herbert Spencer is interesting and informative.

HERBERT SPENCER'S INFLUENCE ON SOCIOLOGY

Why were Spencer's ideas so much more influential in the early years of American sociology than those of Comte, Durkheim, Marx, and Weber? Hofstadter offered several explanations. To take the easiest first, Spencer wrote in English while the others did not. In addition, Spencer did not write very technically, thereby making his work broadly accessible. Indeed, some have argued that the lack of technicality is traceable to Spencer's *not* being a very sophisticated scholar. But there are other, more important reasons for Spencer's broad appeal. He offered a scientific orientation that was attractive to an audience becoming enamored of science and its technological products. He offered a comprehensive theory that seemed to deal with the entire sweep of human history. The breadth of his ideas, as well as the voluminous work he produced, allowed his theory to be many different things to many different people. Finally, and perhaps most important, his theory was soothing and reassuring to a society undergoing the wrenching process of industrialization—society was, according to Spencer, steadily moving in the direction of greater and greater progress.

Spencer's most famous American disciple was William Graham Sumner, who accepted and expanded upon many of Spencer's Social Darwinist ideas. Spencer also influenced other early American sociologists, among them Lester Ward, Charles Horton Cooley, E. A. Ross, and Robert Park.

But by the 1930s, Spencer was in eclipse in the intellectual world in general, as well as in sociology. His Social Darwinist, laissez-faire ideas seemed ridiculous in the light of massive social problems, a world war, and a major economic depression. In 1937 Talcott Parsons announced Spencer's intellectual death for sociology when he echoed historian Crane Brinton's words of a few years earlier, "Who now reads Spencer?" Today Spencer is of little more than historical interest, but his ideas *were* important in shaping early American sociological theory. Let us look briefly at the work of two American theorists who were influenced, at least in part, by Spencer's work.

WILLIAM GRAHAM SUMNER (1840–1910)   It is convenient to start a discussion of early American sociological theorists with William Graham Sumner, because he was the person who taught the first course in the United States that could be called sociology. Sumner contended that he had begun teaching sociology "years before any such attempt was made at any other university in the world" (B. Curtis, 1981:63).

Sumner was the major exponent of Social Darwinism in the United States, although he appeared to change his view late in life (N. Smith, 1979). The following exchange between Sumner and one of his students illustrates his "liberal" views on the need for individual freedom and his position against government interference:

> "Professor, don't you believe in any government aid to industries?"
> "No! It's root, hog, or die."
> "Yet, but hasn't the hog got a right to root?"
> "There are no rights. The world owes nobody a living."
> "You believe then, Professor, in only one system, the contract-competitive system?"
> "That's the only sound economic system. All others are fallacies."
> "Well, suppose some professor of political economy came along and took your job away from you. Wouldn't you be sore?"
> "Any other professor is welcome to try. If he gets my job, it is my fault. My business is to teach the subject so well that no one can take the job away from me."
>
> (Phelps, cited in Hofstadter, 1959:54)

Sumner basically adopted a survival of the fittest approach to the social world. Like Spencer, he saw people struggling against their environment, and the fittest were those who would be successful. Thus Sumner was a supporter of human aggressiveness and competitiveness. Those who succeeded deserved it, and those who did not succeed deserved to fail. Again like Spencer, Sumner was opposed to efforts, especially government efforts, to aid those who had failed. In his view such intervention operated against the natural selection that, among people as among lower animals, allowed the fit to survive and the unfit to perish. As Sumner put it, "If we do not like the survival of the fittest, we have only one possible alternative, and that is survival of the unfittest" (B. Curtis, 1981:84). This theoretical system fit in well with the development of capitalism because it provided theoretical legitimacy for the existence of great differences in wealth and power.

Sumner is of little more than historical interest for two main reasons. First, his orientation and Social Darwinism in general have come to be regarded as little more than a crude legitimation of competitive capitalism and the status quo. Second, he failed to build a solid enough base at Yale to build a school of sociology with many disciples. That kind of success was to occur some years later at the University of Chicago (Heyl and Heyl, 1976). In spite of success in his time, "Sumner is remembered by few today" (B. Curtis, 1981:146).

LESTER F. WARD (1841–1913)   Another sociologist of note in his time but of little lasting significance is Lester Ward. He had an unusual career in that he spent most of it as a paleontologist working for the federal government. During that time, Ward read Spencer and Comte and developed a strong interest in sociology. He published a number of works in the late 1800s and early 1900s in which he expounded his sociological theory. As a result of the notoriety that this work achieved, Ward was elected the first president of the American Sociological Society in 1906. It was only then that he took his first academic position, at Brown University, a position that he held until his death.

Ward, like Sumner, was influenced by the ideas of Herbert Spencer. He accepted the idea that people had evolved from lower forms to their present status. He believed that early society was characterized by its simplicity and its moral poverty, whereas modern society was more complex, happier, and offered greater freedom. One task of sociology, *pure sociology,* was to study the basic laws of social change and social structure. But Ward was not content simply to have sociology study social life. He believed that sociology should have a practical side; there should also be an *applied sociology.* This involved the conscious use of scientific knowledge to attain a better society. Thus, Ward was not an extreme Social Darwinist: he believed in the need for and importance of social reform.

Although of historical significance, Sumner and Ward have not been of long-term significance to sociological theory. We turn now, however, to some theorists and to a school, the Chicago school, that came to dominate sociology in America. The Chicago school was unusual in the history of sociology in that it was one of the few (the Durkheimian school in Paris was another) "collective intellectual enterprises of an integrated kind" in the history of sociology (Bulmer, 1984:1). The tradition begun at the University of Chicago is of continuing importance to sociology and its theoretical (and empirical) status.

The Chicago School[1]

The department of sociology at the University of Chicago was founded in 1892 by Albion Small. Small's intellectual work is of less contemporary significance than the key role he played in the institutionalization of sociology in the United States (Faris, 1970; Matthews, 1977). He was instrumental in creating a department at Chicago that was to become the center of the discipline in the United States for many years. Small collaborated on the first textbook in sociology in 1894. In 1895 he founded the *American Journal of Sociology*, a journal that to this day is a dominant force in the discipline. In 1905, Small cofounded the American Sociological Society, *the* major professional association of American sociologists to this date (Rhoades, 1981). (The embarrassment caused by the initials of the American Sociological Society, A.S.S., led to a name change in 1959 to the American Sociological Association—A.S.A.)

EARLY CHICAGO SOCIOLOGY

The early Chicago department had several distinctive characteristics. For one thing, it had a strong connection with religion (Vidich and Lyman, 1985). Some members were ministers themselves, and others were sons of ministers. Small, for example, believed that "the ultimate goal of sociology must be essentially Christian" (Matthews, 1977:95). This opinion led to a view that sociology must be interested in social reform, and this was combined with a belief that sociology should be scientific.[2] Scientific sociology with an objective of social amelioration was to be practiced in the burgeoning city of Chicago, which was beset by the positive *and* negative effects of urbanization and industrialization.

We might note here the contributions of one of the earliest members of the Chicago sociology department, W. I. Thomas (1863–1947). In 1895, Thomas became a fellow at the Chicago department, where he wrote his dissertation in 1896. Thomas's lasting significance was in his emphasis on the need to do scientific research on sociological issues (Lodge, 1986). Although he championed this position for many years, its major statement came in 1918 with the publication of *The Polish Peasant in Europe and America*, which he coauthored with Florian Znaniecki. Martin Bulmer sees it as a "landmark" study because it moved sociology away from "abstract theory and library research and toward the study of the empirical world utilizing a theoretical framework" (1984:45). Norbert Wiley sees *The Polish Peasant* as crucial to the founding of sociology in the sense of "clarifying the unique intellectual space into which this discipline alone could see and explore" (1986:20). The book was the product of eight years of research in both Europe and the United States and was primarily a study of social disorganization among Polish migrants. The data were of little lasting importance. However, the methodology was significant. It involved a variety of data sources, including

---

[1] See Bulmer (1985) for a discussion of what defines a school and why we can speak of the "Chicago school." Tiryakian (1979; 1986) also deals with schools in general, and the Chicago school in particular, and emphasizes the role played by charismatic leaders as well as methodological innovations. See also Amsterdamska (1985).

[2] As we will see, however, the Chicago school's conception of science was to become too "soft," at least in the eyes of the positivists who later came to dominate sociology.

autobiographical material, paid writings, family letters, newspaper files, public documents, and institutional letters.

Although *The Polish Peasant* was primarily a macrosociological study of social institutions, over the course of his career, Thomas gravitated toward a microscopic, social psychological orientation. He is best known for his social psychological statement: "If men define situations as real, they are real in their consequences" (Thomas and Thomas, 1928:572). The emphasis was on the importance of what people think and how this affects what they do. This microscopic, social psychological focus stood in contrast to the macroscopic, social-structural and -cultural perspectives of such European scholars as Marx, Weber, and Durkheim. It was to become one of the defining characteristics of Chicago's theoretical product—symbolic interactionism (Rock, 1979:5).

Another figure of significance at Chicago was Robert Park (1864–1944). Park had come to Chicago as a part-time instructor in 1913 and quickly worked his way into a central role in the department. As was true of Small, Park's long-term significance was not simply in his intellectual contributions. His importance for the development of sociology lay in several areas. First, he became the dominant figure in the Chicago department, which, in turn, dominated sociology into the 1930s. Second, Park had studied in Europe and was instrumental in bringing Continental thinkers to the attention of Chicago sociologists. Of particular theoretical importance, Park had taken courses with Simmel, and Simmel's ideas, particularly his focus on action and interaction, were instrumental in the development of the Chicago school's theoretical orientation (Rock, 1979:36–48). Third, prior to becoming a sociologist Park had been a reporter, and this experience gave him a sense of the importance of urban problems and of the need to go out into the field to collect data through personal observation. Out of this emerged the Chicago school's substantive interest in urban ecology. Fourth, Park played a key role in guiding graduate students and helping develop "a cumulative program of graduate research" (Bulmer, 1984:13). Finally, in 1921, Park and Ernest W. Burgess published the first truly important sociology textbook, *An Introduction to the Science of Sociology*. It was to be an influential book for many years and was particularly notable for its commitments to science, to research, and to the study of a wide range of social phenomena.

Beginning in the late 1920s and early 1930s, Park began to spend less and less time in Chicago. Finally, his lifelong interest in race relations (he had been secretary to Booker T. Washington before becoming a sociologist) led him to take a position at Fisk University (a black university) in 1934. Although the decline of the Chicago department was not caused solely or even chiefly by Park's departure, its status began to wane in the 1930s. But before we can deal with the decline of Chicago sociology and the rise of other departments and theories, we need to return to the early days of the school and the two figures whose work was to be of the most lasting theoretical significance—Charles Horton Cooley and, most important, George Herbert Mead.

CHARLES HORTON COOLEY (1864–1929)   The association of Cooley with the Chicago school is interesting in that he spent his career at the University of Michigan, not the University of Chicago. But Cooley's theoretical perspective was in line with the theory of symbolic interactionism that was to become Chicago's most important product.

ROBERT PARK: A Biographical Sketch

Robert Park did not follow the typical career route of an academic sociologist—college, graduate school, professorship. Instead, he led a varied career before he became a sociologist late in life. Despite his late start, Park had a profound effect on sociology in general and on theory in particular. Park's varied experiences gave him an unusual orientation to life, and this view helped to shape the Chicago school, symbolic interactionism, and, ultimately, a good portion of sociology.

Park was born in Harveyville, Pennsylvania, on February 14, 1864 (Matthews, 1977). As a student at the University of Michigan, he was exposed to a number of great thinkers, such as John Dewey. Although he was excited by ideas, Park felt a strong need to work in the real world. As Park said: "I made up my mind to go in for experience for its own sake, to gather into my soul . . . 'all the joys and sorrows of the world'" (1927/1973:253). Upon graduation, he began a career as a journalist, which gave him this real-world opportunity. He particularly liked to explore ("hunting down gambling houses and opium dens" [Park, 1927/1973:254]). He wrote about city life in vivid detail. He would go into the field, observe and analyze, and finally write up his observations. In fact, he was already doing essentially the kind of research ("scientific reporting") that came to be one of the hallmarks of Chicago sociology—that is, urban ethnology using participant observation techniques.

Although the accurate description of social life remained one of his passions, Park grew dissatisfied with newspaper work, because it did not fulfill his familial or, more important, his intellectual needs. Furthermore, it did not seem to contribute to the improvement of the world, and Park had a deep interest in social reform. In 1898, at age thirty-four, Park left newspaper work and enrolled in the philosophy department at Harvard. He remained there for a year but then decided to move to Germany, at that time

Cooley received his Ph.D. from the University of Michigan in 1894. He had developed a strong interest in sociology, but there was as yet no department of sociology at Michigan. As a result, the questions for his Ph.D. examination came from Columbia University, where sociology had been taught since 1889 under the leadership of Franklin Giddings. Cooley began his teaching career at Michigan in 1892 before completion of his doctorate, and he remained there throughout his career.

Although Cooley had a wide range of views, he is mainly remembered today for his insights into the social-psychological aspects of social life. His work in this area is in line with that of George Herbert Mead, although Mead was to have a deeper and more lasting effect on sociology than Cooley. Cooley had an interest in consciousness, but he refused (as did Mead) to separate consciousness from the social context. This is best exemplified by a concept of his that survives to this day—the *looking-glass self*. By this concept, Cooley understood that people possess consciousness and that it is shaped in continuing social interaction.

A second basic concept that illustrates Cooley's social-psychological interests, and which is also of continuing interest and importance, is that of the primary group. *Primary groups* are intimate, face-to-face groups that play a key role in linking the actor the heart of the world's intellectual life. In Berlin he encountered Georg Simmel, whose work was to have a profound influence on Park's sociology. In fact, Simmel's lectures were the *only* formal sociological training that Park received. As Park said, "I got most of my knowledge about society and human nature from my own observations" (1927/ 1973:257). In 1904, Park completed his doctoral dissertation at the University of Heidelberg. Characteristically, he was dissatisfied with his dissertation: "All I had to show was that little book and I was ashamed of it" (Matthews, 1977:57). He refused a summer teaching job at the University of Chicago and turned away from academe as he had earlier turned away from newspaper work.

His need to contribute to social betterment led him to become secretary and chief publicity officer for the Congo Reform Association, which was set up to help alleviate the brutality and exploitation then taking place in the Belgian Congo. During this period, he met Booker T. Washington, and he was attracted to the cause of improving the lot of black Americans. He became Washington's secretary and played a key role in the activities of the Tuskegee Institute. In 1912 he met W. I. Thomas, the Chicago sociologist, who was lecturing at Tuskegee. Thomas invited him to give a course on "The Negro in America" to a small group of graduate students at Chicago and Park did so in 1914. It was successful, and he gave it again the next year to an audience twice as large. At this time, he joined the American Sociological Society, and only a decade later he became its president. Park gradually worked his way into a full-time appointment at Chicago, although he did not get a full professorship until 1923, when he was fifty-nine years old. Over the approximately two decades that he was affiliated with the University of Chicago, he played a key role in shaping the intellectual orientation of the sociology department.

Park remained peripatetic even after his retirement from Chicago in the early 1930s. He taught courses and oversaw research at Fisk University until he was nearly eighty years old. He traveled extensively. He died on February 7, 1944, one week before his eightieth birthday.

to the larger society. Especially crucial are the primary groups of the young—mainly the family and the peer group. Within these groups, the individual grows into a social being. It is basically within the primary group that the looking-glass self emerges and that the ego-centered child learns to take others into account and, thereby, to become a contributing member of society.

Both Cooley and Mead rejected a *behavioristic* view of human beings, the view that people blindly and unconsciously respond to external stimuli. On the positive side, they believed that people had consciousness, a self, and that it was the responsibility of the sociologist to study this aspect of social reality. Cooley urged sociologists to try to put themselves in the place of the actors they were studying, to use the method of *sympathetic introspection*, in order to analyze consciousness. By analyzing what they as actors might do in various circumstances, sociologists could understand the meanings and motives that are at the base of social behavior. The method of sympathetic introspection seemed to many to be very unscientific. In this area, among others, Mead's work represents an advance over Cooley's. Nevertheless, there is a great deal of similarity in the interests of the two men, not the least of which is their shared view that sociology should focus on such social-psychological phenomena as consciousness, action, and interaction.

GEORGE HERBERT MEAD (1863–1931) *The* most important thinker associated with the Chicago school and symbolic interactionism was not a sociologist but a philosopher, George Herbert Mead.[3] Mead started teaching philosophy at the University of Chicago in 1894, and he taught there until his death in 1931. He is something of a paradox, given his central importance in the history of sociological theory, both because he taught philosophy, not sociology, and because he published comparatively little during his lifetime. The paradox is, in part, resolved by two facts. First, Mead taught courses in social psychology in the philosophy department, which were taken by many graduate students in sociology. His ideas had a profound effect on a number of them. These students combined Mead's ideas with those they were getting in the sociology department from people like Park and Thomas. Although there was no theory known as symbolic interactionism at the time, it was created by students out of these various inputs. Thus Mead had a deep, personal impact on the people who were later to develop symbolic interactionism. Second, these students put together their notes on Mead's courses and published a posthumous volume under his name. The work, *Mind, Self and Society* (Mead, 1934/1962), moved his ideas from the realm of oral to that of written tradition. Widely read to this day, this volume forms the main intellectual pillar of symbolic interactionism.

We deal with Mead's ideas in Chapter 5, but it is necessary at this point to underscore a few points in order to situate him historically. Mead's ideas need to be seen in the context of psychological behaviorism. Mead was quite impressed with this orientation and accepted many of its tenets. He adopted its focus on the actor and his behavior. He regarded as sensible the behaviorists' concern with the rewards and costs involved in the behaviors of the actors. What troubled Mead was that behaviorism did not seem to go far enough. That is, it excluded consciousness from serious consideration, arguing that it was not amenable to scientific study. Mead vehemently disagreed and sought to extend the principles of behaviorism to an analysis of the "mind." In so doing, Mead enunciated a focus similar to that of Cooley. But whereas Cooley's position seemed unscientific, Mead promised a more scientific conception of consciousness by extending the highly scientific principles and methods of psychological behaviorism.

Mead offered American sociology a social-psychological theory that stood in stark contrast to the primarily societal theories offered by most of the major European theorists—Marx, Weber, Durkheim, Comte, and Spencer. The only exception was Simmel. Thus symbolic interactionism was developed, in large part, out of Simmel's interest in action and interaction and Mead's interest in consciousness. However, such a focus led to a weakness in Mead's work, as well as in symbolic interactionism in general, at the societal and cultural levels.

THE WANING OF CHICAGO SOCIOLOGY

Chicago sociology reached its peak in the 1920s, but by the 1930s, with the death of Mead and the departure of Park, the department began to lose its position of central importance in American sociology. Fred Matthews (1977; see also Bulmer, 1984) pinpoints several reasons for the decline of Chicago sociology, two of which seem of utmost importance.

---

[3]For a dissenting view on this see Lewis and Smith, 1980. We discuss some of their ideas in Chapter 5.

First, the discipline had grown increasingly preoccupied with being scientific—that is, using sophisticated methods and employing statistical analysis. However, the Chicago school was viewed as emphasizing descriptive, ethnographic studies, often focusing on their subjects' personal orientations (in Thomas's terms, their "definitions of the situation"). Park came progressively to despise statistics (he called it "parlor magic") because it seemed to prohibit the analysis of subjectivity, of the idiosyncratic, and of the peculiar. The fact that important work in quantitative methods was done at Chicago (Bulmer, 1984:151–189) tended to be ignored in the face of its overwhelming association with qualitative methods. Second, more and more individuals outside of Chicago grew increasingly resentful of Chicago's dominance of both the American Sociological Society and the *American Journal of Sociology*. The Eastern Sociological Society was founded in 1930, and eastern sociologists became more vocal about the dominance of the Midwest in general and Chicago in particular (Wiley, 1979:63). By 1935, the revolt against Chicago led to a non-Chicago secretary of the association and the establishment of a new official journal, the *American Sociological Review* (Lengermann, 1979). According to Wiley, "The Chicago school had fallen like a mighty oak" (1979:63). This signaled the growth of other power centers, most notably Harvard and the Ivy League in general. Symbolic interactionism was largely an indeterminate, oral tradition and as such eventually lost ground to more explicit and codified theoretical systems like the structural functionalism associated with the Ivy League (Rock, 1979:12).

SOCIOLOGICAL THEORY TO MID-CENTURY

The Rise of Harvard, the Ivy League, and Structural Functionalism

We can trace the rise of sociology at Harvard from the arrival of Pitirim Sorokin in 1930. When Sorokin arrived at Harvard, there was no sociology department, but by the end of his first year one had been organized, and he had been appointed its head. Although Sorokin was a sociological theorist, and he continued to publish into the 1960s, his work is surprisingly little cited today. His theorizing has not stood the test of time very well. Sorokin's long-term significance may well have been in the creation of the Harvard sociology department and the hiring of Talcott Parsons (who had been an instructor of economics at Harvard) for the position of instructor of sociology. Parsons became *the* dominant figure in American sociology for introducing European theorists to an American audience, for his own sociological theories, and for his many students who themselves became major sociological theorists.

PITIRIM SOROKIN (1889–1968)   Sorokin wrote an enormous amount and developed a theory that, if anything, surpassed Parsons's in scope and complexity. The most complete statement of his theory is contained in the four-volume *Social and Cultural Dynamics* published between 1937 and 1941. In it, Sorokin drew on a wide range of empirical data to develop a general theory of social and cultural change. In contrast to those who sought to develop evolutionary theories of social change, Sorokin developed a cyclical theory. He saw societies as oscillating among three different types of mental-

PITIRIM A. SOROKIN: A Biographical Sketch

Pitirim Sorokin was born in a remote village in Russia on January 21, 1889. In his teenage years, and while a seminary student, Sorokin was arrested for revolutionary activities and spent four months in prison. Eventually, Sorokin made his way to St. Petersburg University and interspersed diligent studies, teaching responsibilities, and revolutionary activities that once again landed him in prison briefly. Sorokin's dissertation was scheduled to be defended in March 1917, but before his examination could take place, the Russian Revolution was underway. Sorokin was not able to earn his doctorate until 1922. Active in the revolution, but opposed to the Bolsheviks, Sorokin took a position in Kerensky's provisional government. But when the Bolsheviks emerged victorious, Sorokin once again found himself in prison, this time at the hands of the Bolsheviks. Eventually, under direct orders from Lenin, Sorokin was freed and allowed to return to the university and pick up where he had left off. However, his work was censored, and he was harassed by the secret police. Sorokin finally was allowed to leave Russia, and, after a stay in Czechoslovakia, arrived in the United States in October 1923.

At first, Sorokin gave lectures at various universities but eventually obtained a position at the University of Minnesota. He soon became a full professor. Sorokin already had published several books in Russia, and he continued to turn them out at a prodigious rate in the United States. Of his productivity at Minnesota, Sorokin said: "I knew it exceeded the lifetime productivity of the average sociologist" (1963:224). Books such as *Social Mobility* and *Contemporary Sociological Theories* gave him a national reputation, and by 1929 he was offered (and accepted) the first chair at Harvard University in sociology. The position was placed in the department of economics because there was not yet a sociology department at Harvard.

Soon after his arrival at Harvard, a separate department of sociology was created, and Sorokin was named its first chairman. In that position, Sorokin helped build the most important sociology department in the United States. During this period, Sorokin also completed what would become his best-known work, *Social and Cultural Dynamics* (1937–1941).

Pitirim Sorokin has been described as "the Peck's bad boy and devil's advocate of American sociology" (R. Williams, 1980:100). Blessed with an enormous ego, Sorokin seemed critical of almost everyone and everything. As a result, Sorokin and his work

ities—sensate, ideational, and idealistic. Societies dominated by *sensatism* emphasize the role of the senses in comprehending reality, those dominated by a more transcendental and highly religious way of understanding reality are *ideational*, and *idealistic* societies are transitional types balancing sensatism and religiosity.

The motor of social change is to be found in the internal logic of each of these systems. That is, they are pressed internally to extend their mode of thinking to its logical extreme. Thus a sensate society ultimately becomes so sensual that it provides the groundwork for its own demise. As sensatism reaches its logical end point, people turn to ideational systems as a refuge. But once such a system has gained ascendancy, were the subject of much critical analysis. All of this is clear in an excerpt from a letter he wrote to the editor of the *American Journal of Sociology*:

> The strongly disparaging character of the reviews is a good omen for my books because of a high correlation between the damning of my books . . . and their subsequent career. The more strongly they have been damned (and practically all my books were damned by your reviewers), the more significant and successful were my damned works.
>
> (Sorokin, 1963:229)

One of Sorokin's more interesting and long-running feuds was with Talcott Parsons. Parsons had been appointed at Harvard as an instructor of sociology when Sorokin was chairman of the department. Under Sorokin's leadership, Parsons made very slow career progress at Harvard. Eventually, however, he emerged as the dominant sociologist at Harvard and in the United States. The conflict between Sorokin and Parsons was heightened by the extensive overlap between their theories. Despite the similarities, Parsons's work attracted a far wider and far more enduring audience than did Sorokin's. As the years went by, Sorokin developed a rather interesting attitude toward Parsons's work, which was reflected in several of his books. On the one hand, he was inclined to criticize Parsons for stealing many of his best ideas. On the other hand, he was severely critical of Parsonsian theory. Another tension in their relationship was over graduate students. One of the great achievements of the early Harvard department was its ability to attract talented graduate students like Robert Merton. Although these students were influenced by the ideas of both men, Parsons's influence proved more enduring than Sorokin's. Parsons replaced Sorokin as chairman of the sociology department and transformed it into the Department of Social Relations. Of that, Sorokin said:

> So I am not responsible for whatever has happened to the department since, either for its merging with abnormal and social psychology and cultural anthropology to form a "Department of Social Relations," or for the drowning of sociology in an eclectic mass of the odds and ends of these disciplines. . . . The Department of Social Relations . . . has hardly produced as many distinguished sociologists as the Department of Sociology did . . . under my chairmanship.
>
> (Sorokin, 1963:251)

Sorokin was eventually isolated in the Harvard department, relegated to a "desolate looking" office, and reduced to putting a mimeographed statement under the doors of departmental offices claiming that Parsons had stolen his ideas (Coser, 1977:490). Sorokin died on February 11, 1968.

---

it too is pushed to its end point, with the result that society becomes excessively religious. The stage is then set for the rise of an idealistic culture and, ultimately, for the cycle to repeat itself. Sorokin not only developed an elaborate theory of social change, but he also marshaled detailed evidence from art, philosophy, politics, and so forth to support his theory. It was clearly an impressive accomplishment.

There is much more to Sorokin's theorizing, but this introduction should give the reader a feeling for the breadth of his work. It is difficult to explain why Sorokin has fallen out of favor in sociological theory. Perhaps it is the result of one of the things that Sorokin loved to attack, and in fact wrote a book about, *Fads and Foibles in*

Modern Sociology and Related Sciences (1956). It may be that Sorokin will be rediscovered by a future generation of sociological theorists. At the moment, his work remains outside the mainstream of modern sociological theorizing.

TALCOTT PARSONS (1902–1979)   Although he published some early essays, Parsons's major contribution in the early years was in his influence on graduate students who themselves were to become notable sociological theorists. The most famous was Robert Merton, who received his Ph.D. in 1936 and soon became a major theorist and the heart of Parsonsian-style theorizing at Columbia University. In the same year (1936), Kingsley Davis received his Ph.D. and he, along with Wilbert Moore (who received his Harvard degree in 1940), wrote one of the central works in structural-functional theory, the theory that was to become the major product of Parsons and the Parsonsians. But Parsons's influence was not restricted to the 1930s. Remarkably, he produced graduate students of great influence well into the 1960s.

The pivotal year for Parsons and for American sociological theory was 1937, the year in which he published *The Structure of Social Action*. This book was of significance to sociological theory in America for four main reasons. First, it served to introduce grand European theorizing to a large American audience. The bulk of the book was devoted to Durkheim, Weber, and Pareto. His interpretations of these theorists shaped their images in American sociology for many years.

Second, Parsons devoted almost no attention to Marx, although he emphasized the work of Durkheim and Weber and even Pareto. As a result, Marxian theory was to continue to be largely excluded from legitimate sociology.

Third, *The Structure of Social Action* made the case for sociological theorizing as a legitimate and significant sociological activity. The theorizing that has taken place in the United States since then owes a deep debt to Parsons's work.

Finally, Parsons argued for specific sociological theories that were to have a profound influence on sociology. At first, Parsons was thought of, and thought of himself, as an action theorist (see Chapter 9 for a discussion of action theory in general and Parsons's contributions in particular). He seemed to focus on actors and their thoughts and actions. But by the close of his 1937 work and increasingly in his later work Parsons sounded more like a structural-functional theorist focusing on large-scale social and cultural systems (see Chapter 3 for a discussion of structural functionalism and Parsons's contributions to it). Although Parsons argued that there was no contradiction between these theories, he became best known as a structural functionalist, and he was the primary exponent of this theory, which gained dominance within sociology and maintained that position until recent years. Parsons's theoretical strength, and that of structural functionalism, lay in delineating the relationships among large-scale social structures and institutions.

Parsons's major statements on his structural-functional theory came in the early 1950s in several works, most notably *The Social System* (1951). In that work and others, Parsons tended to concentrate on the structures of society and their relationship to each other. These structures were seen as mutually supportive and tending toward a dynamic equilibrium. The emphasis was on how order was maintained among the various elements of society. Change was seen as an orderly process, and Parsons (1966; 1971) ultimately came to adopt a neoevolutionary view of social change. Parsons was concerned not only with the social system per se but also with its relationship to the other *action systems,* especially the cultural and personality systems. But his basic view on intersystemic relations was essentially the same as his view of intrasystemic relations, that is, that they were defined by cohesion, consensus, and order. In other words, the various *social structures* performed a variety of positive *functions* for each other.

It is clear, then, why Parsons came to be defined primarily as a *structural function-alist.* As his fame grew, so did the strength of structural-functional theory in the United States. His work lay at the core of this theory, but his students and disciples also concentrated on extending both the theory and its dominance in the United States.

Although Parsons played a number of important and positive roles in the history of sociological theory in the United States, his work also had a number of negative consequences. First, he offered interpretations of European theorists that seemed to reflect his own theoretical orientation more than theirs. Many American sociologists were initially exposed to erroneous interpretations of the European masters. Second, as was pointed out above, early in his career Parsons largely ignored Marx, with the result that Marx's ideas continued for many years on the periphery of sociology. Third, his own theory as it developed over the years had a number of serious weaknesses. However, Parsons's preeminence in American sociology served for many years to mute or overwhelm the critics. Not until much later did the weaknesses of Parsons's theory, and more generally of structural functionalism, receive a full airing.

But we are getting too far ahead of the story, and we need to return to the early 1930s and other developments at Harvard. We can gain a good deal of insight into the development of the Harvard department by looking at it through an account of its other major figure—George Homans.

GEORGE HOMANS (born 1910)   A wealthy Bostonian, George Homans received his bachelor's degree from Harvard in 1932 (Homans, 1962; 1984). As a result of the Great Depression, he was unemployed but certainly not penniless. In the fall of 1932, L. J. Henderson, a physiologist, was offering a course in the theories of Vilfredo Pareto, and Homans was invited to attend and accepted. (Parsons also attended the Pareto seminars.) Homans's description of why he was drawn to and taken with Pareto says much about why American sociological theory was so highly conservative, so anti-Marxist:

> I took to Pareto because he made clear to me what I was already prepared to believe. I do not know all the reasons why I was ready for him, but I can give one. Someone has said that much modern sociology is an effort to answer the arguments of the revolutionaries. As a Republican Bostonian who had not rejected his comparatively wealthy family, I felt during the thirties that I was under personal attack, above all from the Marxists. I was ready to believe Pareto because he provided me with a defense.
>
> (Homans, 1962:4)

Homans's exposure to Pareto led to a book, *An Introduction to Pareto* (coauthored with Charles Curtis), published in 1934. The publication of this book made Homans a sociologist even though Pareto's work was virtually the only sociology he had read up to that point.

In 1934 Homans was named a junior fellow at Harvard, a program started to avoid the problems associated with the Ph.D. program. In fact, Homans never did earn a Ph.D. even though he became one of the major sociological figures of his day. Homans was a junior fellow until 1939, and in those years he absorbed more and more sociology. In 1939 Homans was affiliated with the sociology department, but this connection was broken by the war.

By the time Homans had returned from the war, the Department of Social Relations had been founded by Parsons at Harvard, and Homans joined it. Although Homans respected some aspects of Parsons's work, he was highly critical of his style of theorizing. A long-run exchange began between the two men that later manifested itself publicly in the pages of many books and journals. Basically, Homans argued that Parsons's theory was not a theory at all but rather a vast system of intellectual categories into which most aspects of the social world fit. Further, Homans believed that theory should be built from the ground up on the basis of careful observations of the social world. Parsons's theory, however, started on the general theoretical level and worked its way down to the empirical level.

In his own work, Homans amassed a large number of empirical observations over the years, but it was only in the 1950s that he hit upon a satisfactory theoretical approach with which to analyze these data. That theory was psychological behaviorism, as it was best expressed in the ideas of his colleague at Harvard, the psychologist B. F. Skinner. On the basis of this perspective, Homans developed his exchange theory (see Chapter 7). We will pick up the story of this theoretical development later in the chapter. The crucial point here is that Harvard and its major theoretical product, structural functionalism, became preeminent in sociology in the late 1930s, replacing the Chicago school and symbolic interactionism.

The Chicago School in Decline

We left the Chicago department in the mid-1930s on the wane with the death of Mead, the departure of Park, the revolt of eastern sociologists, and the founding of the *American Sociological Review*. But the Chicago school did not disappear. Into the early 1950s it continued to be an important force in sociology. Important Ph.D.s were still produced there, such as Anselm Strauss and Arnold Rose. Major figures remained at Chicago, such as Everett Hughes (Faught, 1980), who was of central importance to the development of the sociology of occupations.

However, the central figure in the Chicago department in this era was Herbert Blumer (1900–1987). He was a major exponent of the theoretical approach developed at Chicago out of the work of Mead, Simmel, Park, Thomas, and others. In fact, it was Blumer who coined the phrase *symbolic interactionism* in 1937. Blumer played a key role in keeping this tradition alive through his teaching at Chicago. He also wrote a number of essays that were instrumental in keeping symbolic interactionism vital into the 1950s. Blumer was also important because of the organizational positions he held in sociology. From 1930 to 1935, he was the secretary-treasurer of the American Sociological Society, and in 1956 he became its president. More important, he held institutional positions that affected the nature of what was published in sociology. Between 1941 and 1952, he was editor of the *American Journal of Sociology* and was instrumental in keeping it one of the major outlets for work in the Chicago tradition in general and symbolic interactionism in particular.

While the East Coast universities were coming under the sway of structural functionalism, the Midwest remained (and to this day remains) a stronghold of symbolic interactionism. In the 1940s, major symbolic interactionists fanned out across the Midwest—Arnold Rose was at Minnesota, Robert Habenstein at Missouri, Gregory Stone at Michigan State, and, most important, Manford Kuhn (1911–1963) at Iowa.

There developed a split between Blumer at Chicago and Kuhn at Iowa; in fact, people began to talk of the differences between the Chicago and the Iowa schools of symbolic interactionism. Basically, the split occurred over the issue of science and methodology. Kuhn accepted the symbolic interactionist focus on actors and their thoughts and actions, but he argued that they should be studied more scientifically—for example, by using questionnaires. Blumer was in favor of "softer" methods such as sympathetic introspection and participant observation.

Despite this flurry of activity, the Chicago school was in decline, especially given the movement of Blumer in 1952 from Chicago to the University of California at Berkeley. The University of Chicago continued to have a strong sociology department, of course, but it had less and less in common with the Chicago tradition. Although the Chicago school was moribund, symbolic interactionism still had some life, with its major exponents being dispersed across the country.

Developments in Marxian Theory

From the early 1900s to the 1930s, Marxian theory had continued to develop largely independently of mainstream sociological theory. At least partially, the exception to this was the emergence of the critical, or Frankfurt, school out of the earlier Hegelian Marxism.

The idea of a Frankfurt school for the development of Marxian theory was the product of Felix J. Weil. The Institute of Social Research was officially founded in Frankfurt, Germany, on February 3, 1923 (Bottomore, 1984; Jay, 1973; 1986). Over the years, a number of the most famous thinkers in Marxian theory were associated with the critical school—Max Horkheimer, Theodor Adorno, Erich Fromm, Herbert Marcuse, and, more recently, Jurgen Habermas.

The institute functioned in Germany until 1934, but by then things were growing increasingly uncomfortable under the Nazi regime. The Nazis had little use for the Marxian ideas that dominated the institute, and their hostility was heightened because many of those associated with the institute were Jewish. In 1934 Horkheimer, as head of the institute, came to New York to discuss its status with the president of Columbia University. Much to Horkheimer's surprise, he was invited to affiliate the institute with the university, and he was even offered a building on campus. And so *a* center of Marxian theory moved to *the* center of the capitalist world. The institute stayed there until after the war, but with the end of the war, pressure mounted to return it to Germany. In 1949, Horkheimer did return to Germany, and he brought the institute with him. Although the institute itself moved to Germany, many of the figures associated with it took independent career directions.

We discuss critical theory in Chapter 4. Here we underscore a few of the most important aspects of this theoretical perspective. In its early years, those associated with the institute tended to be fairly traditional Marxists devoting a good portion of their attention to the economic domain. But around 1930, a major change took place as this group of thinkers began to shift its attention from the economy to the cultural system, which it came to see as the major force in modern capitalist society. This was consistent with, but an extension of, the position taken earlier by Hegelian Marxists like Georg Lukács. To help them understand the cultural domain, the critical theorists were attracted to the work of Max Weber (Greisman and Ritzer, 1981). The effort to combine Marx with Weber gave the critical school some of its distinctive orientation and served to make it more legitimate in later years to sociologists who began to grow interested in Marxian theory.

A second major step taken by at least some members of the critical school was to employ the rigorous social-scientific techniques developed by American sociologists to research issues of interest to Marxists. This, like the adoption of Weberian theory, made the critical school more acceptable to mainstream sociologists.

Third, critical theorists made an effort to integrate individually oriented Freudian theory with the societal- and cultural-level insights of Marx and Weber. This seemed to many sociologists to represent a more inclusive theory than that offered by either Marx or Weber alone. If nothing else, the effort to combine such disparate theories proved stimulating to sociologists and many other intellectuals.

The critical school has done much useful work since the 1920s, and a significant amount of it is of relevance to sociologists. However, the critical school had to await the late 1960s before it was "discovered" by large numbers of American theorists.

SOCIOLOGICAL THEORY FROM MID-CENTURY TO THE PRESENT

Structural Functionalism: Peak and Decline

The 1940s and 1950s were paradoxically the years of greatest dominance and the beginnings of the decline of structural functionalism. In these years, Parsons produced his major statements that clearly reflected his shift from action theory to structural functionalism. Parsons's students had fanned out across the country and occupied dominant positions in many of the major sociology departments (for example, Columbia and Cornell). These students were producing works of their own that were widely recognized contributions to structural-functional theory. For example, in 1945 Kingsley Davis and Wilbert Moore published an essay analyzing social stratification from a structural-functional perspective (see Chapter 3). It was one of the clearest statements ever made of the structural-functional view. In it, they argued that stratification was a structure that was functionally necessary for the existence of society. In other words, in ideological terms they came down on the side of inequality.

In 1949 Merton (1949/1968) published an essay that became *the* program statement of structural functionalism. In it, Merton carefully sought to delineate the essential elements of the theory and to extend it in some new directions. He made it clear that structural functionalism should deal not only with positive functions but also with negative consequences (dysfunctions). Moreover, it should focus on the net balance of functions and dysfunctions or whether a structure is overall more functional or more dysfunctional.

However, just as it was gaining theoretical hegemony, structural functionalism came under attack, and the attacks mounted until they reached a crescendo in the 1960s and 1970s. The Davis-Moore structural-functional theory of stratification was attacked from the start, and the criticisms persist to this day. Beyond that, a series of more general criticisms received even wider recognition in the discipline. There was an attack by C. Wright Mills on Parsons in 1959, and other major criticisms were mounted by David Lockwood (1956), Alvin Gouldner (1959/1967; 1970), and Irving Horowitz (1962/1967). In the 1950s, these attacks were seen as little more than "guerrilla raids," but as sociology moved into the 1960s the dominance of structural functionalism was clearly in jeopardy.[4]

George Huaco (1986) has recently linked the rise and decline of structural functionalism to the position of American society in the world order. As America rose to world dominance after 1945, structural functionalism achieved hegemony within sociology. Structural functionalism supported America's dominant position in the world in two ways. First, the structural-functional view that "every pattern has consequences which contribute to the preservation and survival of the larger system" was "nothing less than a celebration of the United States and its world hegemony" (Huaco, 1986:52). Second, the structural functional emphasis on equilibrium (the best social change is no change) meshed well with the interests of the United States, then "the wealthiest and most powerful empire in the world." The decline of U.S. world dominance in the 1970s coincided with structural functionalism's loss of its preeminent position in sociological theory.

Radical Sociology in America: C. Wright Mills

As we have seen, although Marxian theory was largely ignored or reviled by mainstream American sociologists, there were exceptions, the most notable of which is C. Wright Mills (1916–1962). Although Mills's own lasting theoretical contributions are few, he is notable for his almost single-handed effort to keep a Marxian tradition alive in sociological theory. Modern Marxian sociologists have far outstripped Mills in theoretical sophistication, but they owe him a deep debt nonetheless for the personal and professional activities that helped set the stage for their own work (Alt, 1985–1986). Mills was not a Marxist, and he did not read Marx until the mid-1950s. Even then he was restricted to the few available English translations, because he could not read German. As Mills had published most of his major works by then, his work was not informed by a very sophisticated Marxian theory.

Mills published two major works that reflected his radical politics as well as his weaknesses in Marxian theory. The first was *White Collar* (1951), an acid critique of the status of a growing occupational category, white-collar workers. The second was *The Power Elite* (1956), a book that sought to show how America was dominated by a

---

[4]In spite of this, Patricia Wilner (1985) reports a continuing focus on "consensus" articles in the *American Sociological Review* between 1936 and 1982. However, it should be added that although structural functionalism is sometimes called consensus theory, a focus on consensus does *not* mean that one is necessarily using structural-functional theory.

small group of businessmen, politicians, and military leaders. Sandwiched in between was his most theoretically sophisticated work, *Character and Social Structure* (1953), coauthored with Hans Gerth. Ironically, considering Mills's major role in the history of

C. WRIGHT MILLS: A Biographical Sketch

C. Wright Mills was born on August 28, 1916 in Waco, Texas. He came from a conventional middle-class background; his father was an insurance broker and his mother a housewife. He attended the University of Texas and by 1939 had obtained both a bachelor's and a master's degree. He was quite an unusual student who, by the time he left Texas, already had published articles in the two major sociology journals. Mills did his doctoral work at, and received a Ph.D. from, the University of Wisconsin (Scimecca, 1977). He took his first job at the University of Maryland but spent the bulk of his career, from 1945 until his death, at Columbia University.

Mills was a man in a hurry (Horowitz, 1983). By the time he died at forty-five from his fourth heart attack, Mills had made a number of important contributions to sociology.

One of the most striking things about C. Wright Mills was his combativeness; he seemed to be at war with everyone and everything. He had a tumultuous personal life, characterized by many affairs, three marriages, and a child from each marriage. He had an equally tumultuous professional life. He seemed to have fought with and against everyone and everything. As a graduate student at Wisconsin, he took on a number of his professors. Later, in one of his early essays, he engaged in a thinly disguised critique of the ex-chairman of the Wisconsin department. He called the senior theorist at Wisconsin, Howard Becker, a "real fool" (Horowitz, 1983). He eventually came into conflict with his coauthor, Hans Gerth, who called Mills "an excellent operator, whippersnapper, promising young man on the make, and Texas cowboy à la ride and shoot" (Horowitz, 1983:72). As a professor at Columbia, Mills was isolated and estranged from his colleagues. Said one of his Columbia colleagues:

> There was no estrangement between Wright and me. We began estranged. Indeed, at the memorial services or meeting that was organized at Columbia University at his death, I seemed to be the only person who could not say: 'I used to be his friend, but we became somewhat distant.' It was rather the reverse.
>
> (Horowitz, 1983:83)

Mills was an outsider and he knew it: "I am an outlander, not only regionally, but down deep and for good" (Horowitz, 1983:84). In *The Sociological Imagination* (1959), Mills not only challenged the dominant theorist of his day, Talcott Parsons, but also the dominant methodologist, Paul Lazarsfeld, who also happened to be a colleague at Columbia.

Mills, of course, was not only at odds with people; he was also at odds with American society and challenged it on a variety of fronts. But perhaps most telling is the fact that when Mills visited the Soviet Union and was honored as a major critic of American society, he took the occasion to attack the censorship in the Soviet Union with a toast to an early Soviet leader who had been purged and murdered by the Stalinists: "To the day when the complete works of Leon Trotsky are published in the Soviet Union!" (Tilman, 1984:8).

C. Wright Mills died in Nyack, New York, on March 20, 1962.

Marxian sociological theory, this book was stronger in Weberian and Freudian theory than Marxian theory. Despite this, the book is a major theoretical contribution, though it is not widely read today—possibly because it did not seem to fit well with Mills's best-known radical works. In fact, it was heavily influenced by Hans Gerth, who had a keen interest in Weberian theory.

In the 1950s, Mills's interest moved more in the direction of Marxism and in the problems of the Third World. This interest resulted in a book on the Communist revolution in Cuba, *Listen Yankee: The Revolution in Cuba* (1960) and *The Marxists* (1962). Mills's radicalism put him on the periphery of American sociology. He was the object of much criticism, and he, in turn, became a severe critic of sociology. The critical attitude culminated in *The Sociological Imagination* (1959). Of particular note is Mills's severe criticism of Talcott Parsons and his practice of grand theory. In fact, many sociologists were more familiar with Mills's critique than they were with the details of Parsons's work.

Mills died an outcast in sociology. However, before the decade was out, both radical sociology and Marxian theory were to begin to make important inroads into the discipline.

The Development of Conflict Theory

Another precursor to a true union of Marxism and sociological theory was the development of a conflict-theory alternative to structural functionalism. As we have just seen, structural functionalism had no sooner gained leadership in sociological theory than it came under increasing attack. The attack was multifaceted: structural functionalism was accused of such things as being politically conservative, unable to deal with social change because of its focus on static structures, and incapable of adequately analyzing social conflict.

One of the results of this criticism was an effort on the part of a number of sociologists to overcome the problems of structural functionalism by integrating a concern for structure with an interest in conflict. This work constituted the development of *conflict theory* as an alternative to structural-functional theory. Unfortunately, it often seemed little more than a mirror image of structural functionalism with little intellectual integrity of its own. (This subject will be dealt with in detail in Chapter 3.)

The first effort of note was Lewis Coser's (1956) book on the functions of social conflict. This work clearly tried to deal with social conflict from within the framework of a structural-functional view of the world. Although it is useful to look at the functions of conflict, there is much more to the study of conflict than an analysis of its positive functions.

Other people sought to reconcile the differences between structural functionalism and conflict theory (Coleman, 1971; Himes, 1966; van den Berghe, 1963). Although these efforts had some utility, the authors were generally guilty of papering over the major differences between the two theoretical alternatives (Frank, 1966/1974).

The biggest problem with most of conflict theory was that it lacked what it needed most—a sound basis in Marxian theory. After all, Marxian theory was well developed outside of sociology and should have provided a base on which to develop a sophisticated sociological theory of conflict. The one exception here is the work of Ralf Dahrendorf (born 1929).

Dahrendorf is a European scholar who is well versed in Marxian theory. He sought to embed his conflict theory in the Marxian tradition. However, in the end his conflict theory looked more like a mirror image of structural functionalism than a Marxian theory of conflict. Dahrendorf's major work, *Class and Class Conflict in Industrial Society* (1959), was the most influential piece in conflict theory, but that was largely because it sounded so much like structural functionalism that it was palatable to mainstream sociologists. That is, Dahrendorf operated at the same level of analysis as the structural functionalists (structures and institutions) and looked at many of the same issues. He recognized that although aspects of the social system could fit together rather neatly, there also could be considerable conflict and tension among them.

In the end, conflict theory should be seen as little more than a transitional development in the history of sociological theory. It failed because it did not go far enough in the direction of Marxian theory. It was still too early in the 1950s and 1960s for American sociology to accept a full-fledged Marxian approach. But conflict theory was helpful in setting the stage for the beginning of that acceptance by the late 1960s.

We should note a more recent contribution to conflict theory by Randall Collins (1975). On the one hand, Collins's effort suffers from the same weakness as the other works in the conflict tradition: it is relatively impoverished in terms of Marxian theory. However, Collins did point up another weakness in the conflict tradition, and he attempted to overcome it. The problem is that conflict theory generally focuses on social structures; it has little or nothing to say about actors and their thoughts and actions. Collins, schooled in the phenomenological-ethnomethodological tradition (see below), attempted to move conflict theory in this direction.

The Birth of Exchange Theory

Another important theoretical development begun in the 1950s was the rise of exchange theory. The major figure in this development is George Homans, a sociologist whom we left earlier just as he was being drawn to B. F. Skinner's psychological behaviorism. Skinner's behaviorism is the major source of Homans's, and sociology's, exchange theory (see Chapter 7).

Dissatisfied with Parsons's deductive strategy of developing theory, Homans was casting about for a workable alternative for handling sociological theory inductively. Further, Homans wanted to stay away from the cultural and structural foci of Parsonsian theory and wanted to concentrate instead on people and their behavior. With this in mind, Homans turned to the work of his colleague at Harvard, B. F. Skinner. At first, Homans did not see how Skinner's propositions, developed to help explain the behavior of pigeons, might be useful for understanding human social behavior. But as Homans looked further at data from sociological studies of small groups and anthropological studies of primitive societies, he began to see that Skinner's behaviorism was applicable and that it provided a theoretical alternative to Parsonsian-style structural functionalism. This led to an article entitled "Social Behavior as Exchange" in 1958 and in 1961 to a full-scale, book-length statement of Homans's theoretical position, *Social Behavior: Its Elementary Forms*. These works represented the birth of exchange theory as an important perspective in sociology. Since then exchange theory has attracted a good deal of attention, both positive and negative.

Homans's basic view was that the heart of sociology lies in the study of individual behavior and interaction. He was little interested in consciousness or in the various kinds of large-scale structures and institutions that were of concern to most sociologists. His main interest was rather in the reinforcement patterns, the history of rewards and costs, that lead people to do what they do. Basically, Homans argued that people continue to do what they have found to be rewarding in the past. Conversely, they cease doing what has proved to be costly in the past. In order to understand behavior, we need to understand an individual's history of rewards and costs. Thus, the focus of sociology should not be on consciousness or on social structures and institutions but on patterns of reinforcement.

As its name suggests, exchange theory is concerned not only with individual behavior but also with interaction between people involving an exchange of rewards and costs. The premise is that interactions are likely to continue when there is an exchange of rewards. Conversely, interactions that are costly to one or both parties are much less likely to continue.

Another major statement in exchange theory is Peter Blau's *Exchange and Power in Social Life,* published in 1964. Blau basically adopted Homans's perspective, but there was an important difference. Whereas Homans was content to deal mainly with elementary forms of social behavior, Blau wanted to integrate this with exchange at the structural and cultural levels, beginning with exchanges among actors, but quickly moving on to the larger structures that emerge out of this exchange. He ended by dealing with exchanges among large-scale structures. This is very different from the exchange theory envisioned by Homans. In some senses, it represents a return to the kind of Parsonsian-style theorizing that Homans found so objectionable. Nevertheless, the effort to deal with both small- and large-scale exchange in an integrated way proved a useful theoretical step.

While he was eclipsed for many years by Homans and Blau, Richard Emerson (1981) has recently emerged as a central figure in exchange theory. He is particularly noted for his effort to develop a more integrated macro-micro approach to exchange theory (see Chapter 10), but he is also of significance in exchange theory itself as well as its ties to network theory (see Chapter 9).

In sum, exchange theory has now developed into a significant strand of sociological theory, and it continues to attract new adherents and to take new directions (Cook, forthcoming a).

Dramaturgical Analysis: The Work of Erving Goffman

Erving Goffman (1922–1982) is often thought of as the last major thinker associated with the original Chicago school. He received his Ph.D. from Chicago in 1953, one year after Herbert Blumer (who had been Goffman's teacher) had left Chicago for Berkeley. Soon after, Goffman joined Blumer at Berkeley, where they were able to develop something of a center of symbolic interactionism. However, it never became anything like Chicago had been. Blumer was past his organizational prime, and Goffman did not become a focus of graduate-student work. After 1952 the fortunes of symbolic interactionism declined, although it continues to be a prominent sociological theory.

In spite of the decline of symbolic interactionism in general, Goffman carved out a strong and distinctive place for himself in contemporary sociological theory. Between the 1950s and the 1970s, Goffman published a series of books and essays that gave birth to dramaturgical analysis as a variant of symbolic interactionism. Although Goffman shifted his attention in his later years, he remained best known for his *dramaturgical theory*. (We will discuss Goffman's work in symbolic interactionism in Chapter 5 and his later, more structural work, in Chapter 9.)

Goffman's best-known statement of dramaturgical theory, *Presentation of Self in Everyday Life*, was published in 1959. (Over the next fifteen years Goffman published several books and a number of essays that expanded upon his dramaturgical view of the world.) To put it simply, Goffman saw much in common between theatrical performances and the kinds of "acts" we all put on in our day-to-day actions and interactions. Interaction is seen as very fragile, maintained by social performances. Poor performances or disruptions are seen as great threats to social interaction just as they are to theatrical performances.

Goffman went quite far in his analogy between the stage and social interaction. In all social interaction there is a *front region,* which is the parallel of the stage front in a theatrical performance. Actors on the stage and in social life are both seen as being interested in appearances, wearing costumes, and using props. Furthermore, in both there is a *back region*, a place to which the actors can retire to prepare themselves for their performance. Backstage, or offstage in theater terms, the actors can shed their roles and be themselves.

Dramaturgical analysis is clearly consistent with its symbolic-interactionist roots. It has a focus on actors, action, and interaction. Working in the same arena as traditional symbolic interactionism, Goffman found a brilliant metaphor in the theater to shed new light on small-scale social processes.

Goffman's work is widely read today and acknowledged for its originality and its profusion of insights (Collins, 1986a; Ditton, 1980). Although he is viewed as an important theorist, not everyone accepts that view. There are several reasons for this. First, he is seen as having been interested in rather esoteric topics rather than the truly essential aspects of social life. Second, he was a micro theorist in an era in which the great rewards have gone to macro theorists. As Collins says, "The more we look at this [Goffman's] work . . . the more he emerges as the leading figure in the micro-sociology of our times" (1981b:6). Third, he attracted few students who were able to build upon his insights; indeed, some believe that it is impossible to build upon Goffman's work. It is seen as little more than a series of idiosyncratic bursts of brilliant insight. Finally, little work has been done by others in the dramaturgical tradition (one exception is Lyman and Scott, 1970).

It is difficult to predict the future of dramaturgical analysis, although it has been dimmed because Goffman himself, as we will see later, moved in structural directions in his later work.

The Development of the "Creative" Sociologies

The 1960s and 1970s witnessed a boom (Ritzer, 1985) in several theoretical perspectives that Monica Morris (1977) lumped together under the heading of "creative" sociology. Included under this heading are phenomenological sociology, ethnomethodology, and existential sociology.

PHENOMENOLOGICAL SOCIOLOGY

The philosophy of phenomenology, with its focus on consciousness, has a long history, but the effort to develop a sociological variant of phenomenology can be traced to the publication of Alfred Schutz's *The Phenomenology of the Social World* in Germany in 1932. However, it was not translated into English until 1967, with the result that it has only recently had a dramatic effect on American sociological theory. Schutz arrived in the United States in 1939 after fleeing the Nazis in Austria. Shortly after, he took a position at the New School for Social Research in New York, from which he was able to influence the development of phenomenological, and later ethnomethodological, sociology in the United States.

To orient the reader, we need to say a few words about Schutzian *phenomenological sociology*. As we will see in Chapter 6, Schutzian theory and phenomenology in general are highly abstract, complicated, and sometimes internally inconsistent. Schutz offered both a theory of consciousness and action and a theory that focuses on the cultural constraints (that is, norms and values) on individual thought and action. The problem is that they are, at times, incompatible orientations. Thus at the individual level, Schutz discusses actors' consciousness—the way that people construct social reality—and its relationship to individual thought and action. We are left with the impression, at least at times, that actors are free to construct any reality they like. However, when Schutz focused on the cultural realm, we get a very different impression. That is, we feel that actors are constrained, sometimes even controlled, by the norms and values of society.

The mid-1960s were crucial in the development of phenomenological sociology. Not only was Alfred Schutz's major work translated and his collected essays published, but Peter Berger and Thomas Luckmann collaborated to publish a book, *The Social Construction of Reality* (1967), that became one of the most widely read theory books of the time. It made at least two important contributions. First, it constituted an introduction to Schutz's ideas that was written in such a way as to make it available to a large American audience. Second, it presented an effort to integrate Schutz's ideas with those of mainstream sociology. Since 1967 phenomenology has enjoyed a tremendous boom in interest; it is one of the "hot" theories in contemporary sociology.

ETHNOMETHODOLOGY

Although we will see that there are important differences between them, this theoretical perspective is, in the eyes of many people, hard to distinguish from phenomenology (see Chapter 6). Indeed, the creator of this perspective, Harold Garfinkel, was a student of Alfred Schutz at the New School. Garfinkel had an interesting intellectual background. He was a student of Parsons in the late 1940s and fused his orientation with that of Schutz, whom he was exposed to a few years later. After he received his Ph.D. from Harvard in 1952, Garfinkel arrived in 1954 (Sharrock and Anderson, 1986) at the University of California at Los Angeles (Heritage, 1984), and it was there that ethnomethodology was developed by Garfinkel and his graduate students. Geographically, ethnomethodology was the first distinctive theoretical product of the West Coast, and it has remained centered there to this day (although there is now a large group of British ethnomethodologists). In part, this is a result of the desire of the ethnomethodologists to remain together, but it is at least equally the result of opposition to this perspective by most mainstream sociologists.

Garfinkel became the focal point for a group of students and faculty members at UCLA interested in his approach. A series of seminars was held at UCLA beginning in the early 1950s. A major figure in these seminars, and later in ethnomethodology, was Aaron Cicourel. He received his master's degree from UCLA, went off to Cornell for his Ph.D., and then returned to UCLA as a postdoctoral student. Over the years a number of major ethnomethodologists emerged from this milieu.

Ethnomethodology began to receive a wide national audience with the publication in 1967 of Garfinkel's *Studies in Ethnomethodology*. Although written in a difficult and obscure style, the book elicited a lot of interest. Coming at the same time as the translation of Schutz's *The Phenomenology of the Social World* and the publication of Berger and Luckmann's *The Social Construction of Reality*, it seemed to indicate that "subjective" or "creative" sociology was coming of age.

Basically, *ethnomethodology* is the study of "the body of common-sense knowledge and the range of procedures and considerations [the methods] by means of which the ordinary members of society make sense of, find their way about in, and act on the circumstances in which they find themselves" (Heritage, 1984:4). Writers in this tradition were heavily tilted in the direction of the study of everyday life at the individual level, although they also had a strong interest in large-scale subjective aspects (body of common-sense knowledge and procedures) of social life—norms, values, culture, and so forth. They stood in stark contrast to sociologists in the mainstream, especially to the latter's theoretical focus on such large-scale objective phenomena as bureaucracies, capitalism, the division of labor, and the social system. Ethnomethodologists might be interested in these structures as contexts of everyday life; they are not interested in such structures as phenomena in themselves.

Although the works of ethnomethodologists had links to earlier sociological perspectives such as symbolic interactionism and dramaturgical analysis, there was clearly something threatening here to the mainstream sociologists who were still in control of the discipline. In fact, both phenomenology and, more important, ethnomethodology have been subjected to some brutal attacks by mainstream sociologists. Here are two examples. The first is from a review of Garfinkel's *Studies in Ethnomethodology* by James Coleman:

> Garfinkel simply fails to generate any insights at all from the approach. . . .
> Perhaps the program would be more fertile in the hands of someone more carefully observant but it is strangely sterile here. . . .
> . . . this chapter appears to be not only an ethnomethodological disaster in itself but also

evidence of the more general inadequacies of ethnomethodology. . . .

. . . this chapter is another major disaster, combining the rigidities of the most mathe-
matically enraptured technicians with the technical confusions and errors of the soft clinician
and without the insights or the technical competence of the creative and trained sociologist.

Once again, Garfinkel elaborates very greatly points which are so commonplace that they
would appear banal if stated in straightforward English. As it is, there is an extraordinarily
high ratio of reading time to information transfer, so that the banality is not directly apparent
upon a casual reading.

(Coleman, 1968:126–130)

The second example is Lewis Coser's 1975 presidential address to the American
Sociological Association. Coser saw few redeeming qualities in ethnomethodology and
subjected it to a savage attack, engaging in a great deal of name-calling, labeling
ethnomethodology "trivial," "a massive cop-out," "an orgy of subjectivism," and a
"self-indulgent enterprise." The bitterness of these and other attacks is an indication
of the success of both ethnomethodology and phenomenology and the degree to which
they represent a threat to the establishment in sociology.

EXISTENTIAL SOCIOLOGY

Of the three creative sociologies, existential sociology is the least important, at least at
the moment (see Chapter 9). It shares with the other approaches an interest in actors
and their thoughts and actions. *Existential sociology* focuses on the complexities of individual life and on the ways actors attempt to deal with those complexities. It has a
particular interest in individual feelings, sentiments, and the self. Although it shares a
number of intellectual roots with phenomenology and ethnomethodology, existential
sociology also tries to separate itself from them (see Fontana, 1980; 1984). It sees
itself as more involved in the real world than either of the other creative sociologies. It
also has a number of distinctive sources, such as the work of Jean-Paul Sartre (Craib,
1976). Although existential sociology has made some headway in the discipline (for
example, Douglas and Johnson, 1977; Hayim, 1980; Kotarba and Fontana, 1984;
Manning, 1973; Tiryakian, 1965), it remains on the periphery. But when its influence
is combined with that of ethnomethodology and phenomenology, we can see that the
creative sociologies are making dramatic inroads in sociology despite substantial opposition from many sociologists.

In the last few pages, we have dealt with an array of micro theories—exchange
theory, phenomenological sociology, ethnomethodology, and existential sociology.
Although the last three theories share a sense of a thoughtful and creative actor, such a
view is not held by exchange theorists. Nevertheless, all four theories have a micro
orientation to actors and their actions and behavior. In the 1970s, such theories grew in
strength in sociology and threatened to replace more macro-oriented theories (such as
structural functionalism, conflict theory, neo-Marxian theories) as the dominant
theories in sociology (Knorr-Cetina, 1981; Ritzer, 1985).

The Rise and Fall of Systems Theory

One of the more interesting developments in sociology was the meteoric rise and equally
meteoric fall of systems theory (see Chapter 9). Systems theory more or less burst on

the scene in the 1960s, culminating in the publication of Walter Buckley's *Sociology and Modern Systems Theory* in 1967. Systems theory is derived from the hard sciences, where both organic and mechanical entities are viewed in systems terms. *Systems theory* views society as a huge system composed of a number of interrelated parts. It is necessary to examine the relationship among the parts as well as the relationship between the system and other social systems. Concern is also focused on the inputs into the social system, the way the inputs are processed by society, and the outputs that are produced.

Systems theory seemed quite attractive to sociologists in the 1960s. Structural functionalism was under attack, and systems theory seemed a likely successor. After all, Parsons had entitled his 1951 book *The Social System* and had talked in terms that were close to systems theory. Furthermore, systems theory, with its roots in the hard sciences, was very attractive to sociologists interested in furthering scientific sociology. But systems theory was a bright prospect that never blossomed. Little was done with it either theoretically or empirically. Only eleven years after Buckley's book was published, Robert Lilienfeld (1978) published a blistering attack on systems theory for its failures, its scientific pretensions, and its implicit conservative ideology. It now seems highly unlikely that systems theory will fulfill the promise it held for its supporters in the 1960s.

The Ascendancy of Marxian Sociology

The late 1960s also were the point at which Marxian theory finally began to make significant inroads into American sociological theory (Jay, 1984). There are a number of reasons for this. First, the dominant theory (structural functionalism) was under attack for a number of things, including being too conservative. Second, Mills's radical sociology and conflict theory, although not representing sophisticated Marxian theory, had laid the groundwork for an American theory that was true to the Marxian tradition. Third, the 1960s was the era of black protests, the reawakening of the women's movement, the student movement, and the anti–Vietnam War movement. Many of the young sociologists trained in this atmosphere were attracted to radical ideas. At first, this interest was manifest in what was called in those days "radical sociology" (Colfax and Roach, 1971). This was useful as far as it went, but like Mills's work, it was rather weak on the details of Marxian theory.

It is hard to single out one work as essential to the development of Marxian sociology in America, but one that did play an important role was Henri Lefebvre's *The Sociology of Marx* (1968). It was important for its essential argument, which was that although Marx was not a sociologist, there was a sociology in Marx. Since that time an increasing number of sociologists have turned to Marx's original work, as well as that of many Marxists, for insights that would be useful in the development of a Marxian sociology. At first this simply meant that American theorists were finally reading Marx seriously, but we now see significant pieces of Marxian scholarship by American sociologists.

American theorists have been particularly attracted to the work of the critical school, especially because of its fusion of Marxian and Weberian theory. Many of the works have been translated into English, and a number of American sociologists have made careers for themselves by writing books about the critical school for an American audience (for example, Jay, 1973; 1986).

Along with an increase in interest has come institutional support for such an orientation. Several journals devote considerable attention to Marxian sociological theory, including *Theory and Society, Telos,* and *Marxist Studies.* A section on Marxist sociology was created in the American Sociological Association in 1977. Not only is the first generation of critical theorists now well known in America, but second-generation thinkers, especially Jurgen Habermas, have received wide recognition.

Of greatest importance is the development of significant pieces of American sociology done from a Marxian point of view. One very significant strand is a group of sociologists doing historical sociology from a Marxian perspective (for example, Skocpol, 1979; Wallerstein, 1974). Another is a group analyzing the economic realm from a sociological perspective (for example, Baran and Sweezy, 1966; Braverman, 1974; Burawoy, 1979). Still others are doing fairly traditional empirical sociology, but work that is informed by a strong sense of Marxian theory (Kohn, 1976, for example). There are many other trends and developments in this area, but the key point is that by the 1980s, Marxian sociology had "arrived" in America. Nevertheless, many mainstream sociologists remain hostile to Marxian theory (Bierstedt, 1981:498).

The Challenge of Feminist Theory

In the early 1980s, precisely at the moment that Marxian sociology gained significant acceptance from American sociologists, a new theoretical outsider issued a challenge to established sociological theories—and even to Marxian sociology itself. This latest brand of radical social thought is contemporary feminist theory.

In Western societies, one can trace the record of critical feminist writings back almost 400 years (Rossi, 1974; Spender, 1982), and there has been an organized political movement by and for women for more than 150 years (Banner, 1984; Carden, 1974; Chafetz and Dworkin, 1986; Deckard, 1979; O'Neill, 1971). In America in 1920, that movement finally won the right for women to vote, fifty-five years after that right had been constitutionally extended to black men. Exhausted and to a degree satiated by that victory, the American women's movement over the next thirty years weakened in both size and vigor, only to spring back to life, fully reawakened, in the 1960s. Three factors helped create this new wave of feminist activism: the general climate of critical thinking that characterized the period; the anger of women activists who flocked to the antiwar, civil rights, and student movements only to encounter the sexist attitudes of the liberal and radical men in those movements (Evans, 1980; Snitow et al., 1983); and women's experience of prejudice and discrimination as they moved in ever larger numbers into wage work and higher education (Lengermann and Wallace, 1985). For these reasons, particularly the last, the women's movement in this new second phase continued to expand during the 1970s and into the 1980s, even though the activism of many other 1960s movements faded. Moreover during these years activism by and for women became an international phenomenon.

A major feature of this international women's movement has been an explosively growing new literature on women that makes visible all aspects of women's hitherto unconsidered lives and experiences. This literature, which is popularly referred to as women's studies or the new scholarship on women, is the work of an international and interdisciplinary community of writers, located both within and outside universities, and writing for both the general public and specialized academic audiences. In what must be one of the more impressive examples of sustained intellectual work in recent times, feminist scholars have launched a probing, multifaceted critique that makes visible the complexity of the system that subordinates women.

Feminist theory is the theoretical strand running through this literature: sometimes implicit in writings on such substantive issues as corporate organization (Kanter, 1977) or the training of gynecologists (Scully, 1980); sometimes centrally and explicitly presented, as in the analyses of motherhood by Adrienne Rich (1976) and Nancy Chodorow (1978); and as the new scholarship on women has achieved critical mass, with increasing frequency the sole, systematic effort of a piece of writing. Of this recent spate of wholly theoretical writing, certain statements have been particularly salient to sociology because they are directed to sociologists by people well versed in sociological theory (Chafetz, 1984; Cook and Fonow, 1986; Hartsock, 1983; Smith 1974; 1975; 1978; 1979; Stacey and Thorne, 1986). Journals that bring feminist theory to the attention of sociologists include *Signs, Feminist Studies, Sociological Inquiry,* and *Gender and Society*, as does the professional association, Sociologists for Women in Society (S.W.S).

Feminist theory looks at the world from the vantage point of a hitherto unrecognized and invisible minority, women, with an eye to discovering the significant but unacknowledged ways in which the activities of that minority help to create our world. This viewpoint dramatically reworks our understanding of most subjects, including social life. From this base, feminist theorists have begun to challenge sociological theory.

Those issuing this challenge argue that sociologists have persistently refused to incorporate the insights of the new scholarship on women into their discipline's understanding of the social world. Instead feminist sociologists have been segregated from the mainstream, and feminism's comprehensive theory of social organization has been reduced to a single research variable, sex, and a simple social role pattern, gender (Stacey and Thorne, 1986). To date these charges seem valid. Reasons for sociology's avoidance of feminist theory may include deep antifeminist prejudices, suspicion of the scientific credentials of a theory so closely associated with political activism, and caution born of half recognition of the profoundly radical implications of feminist theory for sociological theory and method. Yet it should also be remembered that it took some time for Marxian theory to "arrive" in sociology and that a significant body of explicitly theoretical feminist writings is a very recent event in academic life. These writings have begun, however, to assume a critical mass. They offer an exciting new and important theory of social life. And those whose experiences and perceptions make them a receptive audience for this theory—women in general and both women and men affected by feminism in particular—are an important constituency in the sociological community. For all these reasons, implications of feminist theory are moving increasingly into the mainstream of the discipline. (One measure of this new trend is the inclusion in this text of Chapter 8, on contemporary feminist theory.)

Structuralism and Poststructuralism

One development that we have said little about up to this point is the increase in interest in *structuralism*. Usually traced to France (and often called *French structuralism* [Clark and Clark, 1982; Kurzweil, 1980]), structuralism has now become an international phenomenon. Although its roots lie outside sociology, structuralism clearly has made its way into sociology. The problem is that structuralism in sociology still is so undeveloped that it is difficult to define it with any precision. The problem is exacerbated by structuralism's more or less simultaneous development in a number of fields; it is difficult to find one single coherent statement of structuralism. Indeed, there are significant differences among the various branches of structuralism.

Although we will deal with it in Chapter 9, we can get a preliminary feeling for structuralism by delineating the basic differences that exist among those who support a structuralist perspective. There are those who focus on what they call the deep structures of the mind. It is their view that these unconscious structures lead people to think and act as they do. The work of the psychoanalyst Sigmund Freud might be seen as an example of this orientation. Then there are structuralists who focus on the invisible larger structures of society and see them as determinants of the actions of people as well as of society in general. Marx is sometimes thought of as someone who practiced such a brand of structuralism, with his focus on the unseen economic structure of capitalist society. Still another group sees structures as the models they construct of the social world. Finally, a number of structuralists are concerned with the dialectical relationship between individuals and social structures. They see a link between the structures of the mind and the structures of society. The anthropologist Claude Lévi-Strauss is most often associated with this view.

The problem with structural sociology at the moment is that it remains largely a melange of ideas derived from various fields, including linguistics (Saussure), anthropology (Lévi-Strauss), psychology (Freud, Lacan), and Marxism (Althusser). Until these ideas are put together in a coherent fashion, structuralism will remain marginal to sociology. However, the developments in related fields have been so significant and so attractive to those in sociology that a structural theory in sociology is likely to attract more attention in coming years.

As structuralism grows within sociology, outside of sociology a movement is developing beyond the early premises of structuralism: *poststructuralism*. We touch on this new development in Chapter 9 and go into some detail on the theories of one of its major practitioners, Michel Foucault.

Neofunctionalism

When we last discussed structural functionalism, it was in a state of decline in the 1960s, a decline that persisted through the 1970s and into the early 1980s. But by the mid-1980s, a determined effort was being made to revive structural functionalism, or *neofunctionalism* as it had come to be called (see Chapter 3). As Paul Colomy proclaimed, "Functionalism is not dead. To the contrary, there are signs that the functionalist tradition is being revitalized" (1986:139). Part of this revival was a renewal of interest in the work of Talcott Parsons. This revival was most notable in German sociology, especially in the work of the critical theorist Jurgen Habermas (Alexander, 1984), but it has its American supporters as well (Sciulli and Gerstein, 1985; Sciulli, 1986). Beyond the revival of interest in Parsonsian theory is a strong political and intellectual effort to overcome some of the weaknesses of structural functionalism and erect in its place a viable neofunctionalism (Alexander, 1985a; Alexander and Colomy, 1985; Colomy, 1986; Faia, 1986).

Linking Macro and Micro Theory

We have seen that in the 1980s, macro theories are either strong (neo-Marxian theories) or showing signs of resurgence (neofunctionalism) *and* that various micro theories (phenomenology, ethnomethodology, exchange theory) appear stronger than ever. At the same time, we have been witnessing throughout the 1980s a wide-scale effort to develop sociological theories that deal with the integration of the macro and micro levels of social reality (Alexander, 1982; Coleman, 1986; Collins, 1981; Giddens, 1984; Ritzer, 1981a). Although both macro and micro theories are likely to remain strong, it is also likely that one of the continuing growth areas in sociology will be in theories that seek in various ways to deal in an integrated fashion with the relationship between the macro and the micro levels of social reality. Chapter 10 of this book is devoted to a discussion of many of these theoretical efforts to integrate macro and micro levels of social reality.

SUMMARY

This chapter picks up where Chapter 1 left off and deals with the history of sociological theory since the beginning of the twentieth century. We begin with the early history of American sociological theory, which was characterized by its liberalism, by its interest in Social Darwinism, and consequently by the influence of Herbert Spencer. In this context, the work of the two early sociological theorists, Sumner and Ward, are discussed. However, they did not leave a lasting imprint on American sociological theory. In contrast, the Chicago school, as embodied in the work of people like Small, Park, Thomas, and, especially, Cooley and Mead, did leave a strong mark on sociological theory, especially on symbolic interactionism.

While the Chicago school was still predominant, a different form of sociological theory began to develop at Harvard. Pitirim Sorokin played a key role in the founding of sociology at Harvard, but it was Talcott Parsons who was to lead Harvard to a position of preeminence in American theory, replacing Chicago's symbolic interactionism. Parsons was important not only for legitimizing "grand theory" in the United States and for introducing European theorists to an American audience, but also for his role in the development of action theory and, more important, structural functionalism. In the 1940s and 1950s, structural functionalism was furthered by the disintegration of the Chicago school that began in the 1930s and was largely complete by the 1950s.

The major development in Marxian theory in the early years of the twentieth century was the creation of the Frankfurt, or critical, school. This Hegelianized form of Marxism also showed the influence of sociologists like Weber and of the psychoanalyst Sigmund Freud. Marxism did not gain a widespread following among sociologists in the early part of the century.

Structural functionalism's dominance within American theory in mid-century was rather short-lived. Although traceable to a much earlier date, phenomenological sociology began to attract significant attention in the 1960s. Marxian theory was still largely excluded from American theory, but C. Wright Mills kept a radical tradition alive in America in the 1940s and 1950s. Mills also was one of the leaders of the attacks on structural functionalism, attacks that mounted in intensity in the 1950s and 1960s. In light of some of these attacks, a conflict theory alternative to structural functionalism emerged in this period. Although influenced by Marxian theory, conflict theory suffered from an inadequate integration of Marxism. Still another alternative born in the 1950s was exchange theory, and it continues to attract a small but steady number of followers. Although symbolic interactionism was in eclipse, the work of Erving Goffman on dramaturgical analysis in this period kept it from being moribund.

Dramatic developments took place in the "creative sociologies" in the 1960s and 1970s. Phenomenological sociology, ethnomethodology, and existential sociology continue to attract a great deal of attention in sociology. At the same time, Marxian sociology came into its own, and its several varieties continue to cause a great deal of excitement in sociological theory. While creative sociology and Marxian theory have been on the rise, systems theory gained popularity in the 1960s only to encounter a dramatic drop in popularity in the 1970s. Some of the most important recent developments in sociological theory are feminist theory, structuralism and poststructuralism, neofunctionalism, and the efforts to link macro and micro theories.

PART TWO
THE MAJOR
THEORIES

CHAPTER THREE
Structural Functionalism, Neofunctionalism, and the Conflict Theory Alternative

THE first part of this chapter focuses on structural functionalism, which was for years the dominant sociological theory. We begin with a discussion of some of its basic principles and historical roots. Then we discuss three major examples of "classic" structural functionalism—the functional theory of stratification, the functional prerequisites of society, and most important, Talcott Parsons's structural-functional theory. Then, we analyze Robert Merton's efforts to deal with some of the problems in classic structural functionalism and to develop a more adequate theoretical perspective. We then turn to the major criticisms of structural functionalism and to the rise of neofunctionalism in the 1980s as an effort to deal with some of these criticisms, which had caused structural functionalism to lose its dominant position in sociological theory.

In the second part of the chapter, we discuss conflict theory as an alternative to structural functionalism, especially in the work of Ralf Dahrendorf. We deal with efforts to integrate conflict and structural-functional theory as well as Collins's attempt to develop a more integrated conflict theory. Finally, we deal with criticisms of conflict theory, the most important of which is that it is not true to its Marxian roots.

CONSENSUS AND CONFLICT

Before turning to the specifics of structural functionalism and conflict theory, we need, following Thomas Bernard (1983), to place these theories in the broader context of the debate between consensus theories (one of which is structural functionalism) and conflict theories (one of which is the sociological conflict theory to be discussed in this chapter). *Consensus theories* see shared norms and values as fundamental to society, focus on social order based on tacit agreements, and view social change as occurring in a slow and orderly fashion. In contrast, *conflict theories* emphasize the dominance of some social groups by others, see social order as based on manipulation and control by dominant groups, and view social change as occurring rapidly and in a disorderly fashion as subordinate groups overthrow dominant groups.

Although these criteria broadly define the essential differences between the sociological theories of structural functionalism and conflict theory, Bernard's view is that the disagreement is far broader and has "been a recurring debate that has taken a variety of different forms throughout the history of Western thought" (1983:6). Bernard traced the debate back to ancient Greece and the differences between Plato (consensus) and Aristotle (conflict). He traced the debate through the history of philosophy, through (the conflict thinker is listed first): Augustine and Aquinas, Machiavelli and Hobbes, and Locke and Rousseau. Later, in sociology the debate was joined by (again, conflict theorist listed first) Marx and Comte, Simmel and Durkheim, and Dahrendorf and Parsons. In this chapter we examine Dahrendorf's conflict theory and Parsons's consensus theory, among others.

Bernard differentiates among four types of consensus and conflict theories, but we focus on only two of them, *sociological consensus* (Parsons, Merton) and *sociological conflict* (Dahrendorf) in this chapter. A third type, *radical conflict theory,* will be discussed in the chapter on neo-Marxian theories. Bernard's final type, *conservative consensus theory,* will not be discussed because it "is not widely held among modern sociologists" (1983:201).

Although we emphasize the differences between structural functionalism and conflict theory, we should not forget that there are important similarities between them. In fact, Bernard argues that "the areas of agreement among them are more extensive than the areas of disagreement" (1983:214). For example, they are both macro-level theories focally concerned with large-scale social structures and social institutions. In George Ritzer's (1980) terms, both theories exist within the same sociological ("social facts") paradigm (see Appendix).

STRUCTURAL FUNCTIONALISM

Many people believed structural functionalism was *the* dominant sociological theory. Robert Nisbet argued that it was "without any doubt, the single most significant body of theory in the social sciences in the present century" (Turner and Maryanski, 1979:xi). Kingsley Davis (1959) took the position that structural functionalism was, for all intents and purposes, synonymous with sociology. Alvin Gouldner (1970) implicitly took a similar position when he attacked Western sociology largely through a critical analysis of the structural-functional theories of Talcott Parsons.

In fact, although it was dominant for some time, structural functionalism has declined in importance as a sociological theory (although, as we will see, there is an ongoing effort to resuscitate it under the heading of "neofunctionalism"). Even Wilbert Moore, a man who is intimately associated with this theory, argued that it had almost "become an embarrassment in contemporary theoretical sociology" (1978:321). Two observers even stated: "Thus, functionalism as an explanatory theory is, we feel, 'dead' and continued efforts to use functionalism as a theoretical explanation should be abandoned in favor of more promising theoretical perspectives" (Turner and Maryanski, 1979:141).[1] Nicholas Demerath and Richard Peterson (1967) took a more positive view, arguing that structural functionalism is not a passing fad. However, they admitted that it is likely to evolve into another sociological theory, just as this theory itself evolved out of the earlier organicism (see following section). The rise of neofunctionalism seems to support Demerath and Peterson's position rather than the more negative perspective of Turner and Maryanski.

In structural functionalism, the terms *structural* and *functional* need not be used in conjunction, although this is typically done by practitioners. We could study the structures of society without being concerned with their functions (or consequences) for other structures.[2] Similarly, we could examine the functions of a variety of social processes that may not take a structural form. Still, the concern for both elements characterizes structural functionalism.

Mark Abrahamson (1978) argued that structural functionalism is not monolithic. He identified three varieties of structural functionalism. The first is *individualistic functionalism*. Here the focus is on the needs of actors and the various large-scale structures (for example, social institutions, cultural values) that emerge as functional responses to these needs. The anthropologist Bronislaw Malinowski was a major proponent of this perspective. The second is *interpersonal functionalism*, and the exemplar was another anthropologist, A. B. Radcliffe-Brown. Here the focus is on social relationships, particularly the mechanisms to accommodate strains that exist in such relationships. The third variety, *societal functionalism*, is the dominant approach among sociological structural functionalists (Sztompka, 1974), and as such will be the focus of this chapter. The primary concern of societal functionalism is with the large-scale social structures and institutions of society, their interrelationships, and their constraining effects on actors.

Historical Roots

Three classic sociologists were the most important influences on contemporary structural functionalism: Auguste Comte, Herbert Spencer, and Emile Durkheim (Turner and Maryanski, 1979).

---

[1] Despite this statement, Jonathan Turner and Alexandra Maryanski (1979) are willing to argue that functionalism can continue to be useful as a method.

[2] This is, in effect, the course taken by structural theory, which will be discussed in Chapter 9.

EMILE DURKHEIM: A Biographical Sketch

Emile Durkheim was born on April 15, 1858, in Epinal, France. He was descended from a long line of rabbis and himself studied to be a rabbi, but by the time he was in his teens, he had rejected his heritage and become an agnostic. From that time on, his lifelong interest in religion was academic rather than theological. He was dissatisfied not only with his religious training but also with his general education and its emphasis on literary and esthetic matters. He longed for schooling in scientific methods and in the moral principles needed to guide social life. He rejected a traditional academic career in philosophy and sought instead to acquire the scientific training needed to contribute to the moral guidance of society. Although he was interested in scientific sociology, there was no field of sociology at that time, so between 1882 and 1887 he taught philosophy in a number of provincial schools in the Paris area.

His appetite for science was whetted further by a trip to Germany, where he was exposed to the scientific psychology being pioneered by Wilhelm Wundt. In the years immediately after his visit to Germany, Durkheim published a good deal, basing his work, in part, on his experiences there. These publications helped him gain a position in the department of philosophy at the University of Bordeaux in 1887. There Durkheim offered the first course in social science in a French university. This was a particularly impressive accomplishment, because only a decade earlier, a furor had erupted in a French university by the mention of Auguste Comte in a student dissertation. Durkheim's main responsibility, however, was the teaching of courses in education to schoolteachers, and his most important course was in the area of moral education. His goal was to communicate a moral system to the educators, who he hoped would then pass it on to young people in an effort to help reverse the moral degeneration he saw around him in French society.

The years that followed were characterized by a series of personal successes for Durkheim. In 1893 he published his French doctoral thesis, *The Division of Labor in Society*, as well as his Latin thesis on Montesquieu. His major methodological statement, *The Rules of Sociological Method,* appeared in 1895, followed (in 1897) by his empirical application of those methods in the study, *Suicide*. By 1896 he had become full professor at Bordeaux. In 1902 he was summoned to the famous French university, the Sorbonne, and in 1906 he was named professor of the science of education, a title that was changed in 1913 to professor of the science of education *and sociology*. The other of his most famous works, *The Elementary Forms of Religious Life*, was published in 1912.

Durkheim is most often thought of today as a political conservative, and his influence within sociology certainly has been a conservative one. But in his time, he was considered a liberal, and this was exemplified by the active public role he played in the defense of Alfred Dreyfus, the Jewish army captain whose court martial for treason was felt by many to be anti-Semitic.

Durkheim was deeply offended by the Dreyfus affair, particularly its anti-Semitism. But Durkheim did not attribute this anti-Semitism to racism among the French people. Characteristically, he saw it as a symptom of the moral sickness confronting French society as a whole. He said:

When society undergoes suffering, it feels the need to find someone whom it can hold responsible for its sickness, on whom it can avenge its misfortunes: and those against whom public opinion already discriminates are naturally designated for this role. These are the pariahs who serve as expiatory victims. What confirms me in this interpretation is the way in which the result of Dreyfus's trial was greeted in 1894. There was a surge of joy in the boulevards. People celebrated as a triumph what should have been a cause for public mourning. At least they knew whom to blame for the economic troubles and moral distress in which they lived. The trouble came from the Jews. The charge had been officially proved. By this very fact alone, things already seemed to be getting better and people felt consoled.

(Lukes, 1972:345)

Thus, Durkheim's interest in the Dreyfus affair stemmed from his deep and lifelong interest in morality and the moral crisis confronting modern society.

To Durkheim, the answer to the Dreyfus affair and crises like it lay in ending the moral disorder in society. Because that could not be done quickly or easily, Durkheim suggested more specific actions such as severe repression of those who incite hatred of others and government efforts to show the public how it is being misled. He urged people to "have the courage to proclaim aloud what they think, and to unite together in order to achieve victory in the struggle against public madness" (Lukes, 1972:347).

Durkheim's (1928/1962) interest in socialism is also taken as evidence against the idea that he was a conservative, but his kind of socialism was very different from the kind that interested Marx and his followers. In fact, Durkheim labeled Marxism as a set of "disputable and out-of-date hypotheses" (Lukes, 1972:323). To Durkheim, socialism represented a movement aimed at the moral regeneration of society through scientific morality, and he was not interested in short-term political methods or the economic aspects of socialism. He did not see the proletariat as the salvation of society, and he was greatly opposed to agitation or violence. Socialism for Durkheim was very different from what we usually think of as socialism; it simply represented a system in which the moral principles discovered by scientific sociology were to be applied.

Durkheim, as we will see throughout this book, had a profound influence on the development of sociology, but his influence was not restricted to it. Much of his impact on other fields came through the journal L'année sociologique, which he founded in 1898. An intellectual circle arose around the journal with Durkheim at its center. Through it, he and his ideas influenced such fields as anthropology, history, linguistics, and—somewhat ironically, considering his early attacks on the field—psychology.

Durkheim died on November 15, 1916, a celebrated figure in French intellectual circles, but it was not until over twenty years later, with the publication of Talcott Parsons's The Structure of Social Action (1937), that he became a significant influence on American sociology.

Comte had a normative conception of the "good" society, which led to an interest in what any given social phenomenon contributes to that society. He also had a sense of equilibrium within societies. However, his theory of *organicism*—the tendency to see analogies between societies and biological organisms—was his most influential concept. He viewed social systems as organic systems that functioned in much the same way as biological organisms. Thus, whereas biology was to study the individual organism, sociology was to study the social organism. Among the specific analogies that Comte saw between biological and social organisms were those of cells on the biological level to families in the social world, of tissues to social classes and castes, and of the organs of the body to cities and communities in the social world.

The English sociologist Herbert Spencer also adopted organicism, but in his sociology it coexisted uncomfortably with a utilitarian philosophy. Thus although his organicism led him to look at social wholes and the contributions of parts to the whole, his utilitarianism led him to focus on self-seeking actors. Despite the intellectual problems this presented, Spencer's organicism was influential in the development of structural functionalism.

Spencer saw various similarities between social and individual organisms. First, both social and individual organisms grow and develop, whereas inorganic matter does not. Second, in both, an increase in size tends to lead to increasing complexity and differentiation. Third, progressive differentiation of structures in both tends to be accompanied by progressive differentiation in function. Fourth, the parts of both organisms are mutually interdependent. Thus a change in one is likely to lead to changes in the other parts. Finally, each of the parts of both social and individual entities can be seen as an organism in itself.

Spencer had a number of other insights that were influential in the development of structural functionalism. His concern with the "needs" of the social organism was picked up by later structural functionalists, who, among other things, translated it into the idea that societies "need" various things in order to survive. Spencer also developed a law of social evolution, which influenced the development of later structural-functional theories of evolution, such as those associated with Durkheim and Parsons. Perhaps of greatest importance was Spencer's use of the terms *structure* and *function* as well as his differentiation between them. He tended to speak of the functions that various structures had for the society as a whole.

Although both Comte and Spencer are important in their own right, their greatest impact on structural functionalism came through their effect on the thinking of Durkheim. Most generally, Durkheim's interest in social facts reflected an interest in the parts of the social organism and their interrelationships as well as their impact on the society as a whole. In terms of structural functionalism, Durkheim had much to say about structures, functions, and their relationship to the needs of society. Perhaps of greatest importance was his separation of the concepts of social cause and social function. The study of social causes is concerned with why a given structure exists as well as why it takes a certain form. In contrast, the study of social functions is concerned with the needs of the larger system met by a given structure.

Modern structural functionalism operates on the basis of several assumptions derived from the ideas of these three classic sociologists. Structural functionalists, especially the societal functionalists, are likely to take a macroscopic approach to the study of social phenomena. They focus on the social system as a whole as well as on the impact of the various parts (especially social structures and social institutions) on it.

They see the components of the system as contributing positively to its continued operation (Abrahamson, 1978). In addition, structural functionalism is concerned with the relationship of one part of the system to another (Davis, 1959). The parts of the system, as well as the system as a whole, are seen as existing in a state of equilibrium, so that changes in one part lead to changes in other parts. Changes in parts may balance each other so that there is no change in the system as a whole; if they do not, the entire system probably changes. Thus although structural functionalism adopts an equilibrium perspective, it is not necessarily a static point of view. In this equilibrium of the social system, those changes that do occur are seen as doing so in an orderly, not a revolutionary, way.

Let us now discuss some more concrete examples of structural functionalism.

The Functional Theory of Stratification and Its Critics

The functional theory of stratification as articulated by Kingsley Davis and Wilbert Moore (1945) is perhaps the best known single piece of work in structural-functional theory. Davis and Moore made it clear that they regarded social stratification as both universal and necessary. They argued that no society is ever unstratified, or totally classless. Stratification is, in their view, a *functional* necessity. All societies need such a system, and this need brings into existence a system of stratification.[3] They also viewed a stratification system as a structure, pointing out that stratification refers not to the individuals in the stratification system but rather to a system of *positions*. They focused on how certain positions come to carry with them different degrees of prestige and not on how individuals come to occupy certain positions.

Given this focus, the major functional issue is how a society motivates and places people in their "proper" positions in the stratification system. This is reducible to two problems. First, how does a society instill in the "proper" individuals the desire to fill certain positions? Second, once people are in the right positions, how does society then instill in them the desire to fulfill the requirements of those positions?

The problem of proper social placement in society arises for three basic reasons. First, some positions are more pleasant to occupy than others. Second, some positions are more important to the survival of society than others. Third, social positions require different abilities and talents.

Although these issues apply to all social positions, Davis and Moore were concerned with the functionally more important positions in society. The positions that rank high within the stratification system are presumed to be those that are *less* pleasant to occupy but *more* important to the survival of society and that require the greatest ability and talent. In addition, society must attach sufficient rewards to these positions so that

---

[3]This is an example of a teleological argument. We will have occasion to discuss this issue later in the chapter, but for now we can define a *teleological argument* as one that sees the social world as having purposes, or goals, which bring needed structures or events into being. In this case society "needs" stratification, so it brings such a system into existence.

the individuals who occupy them will work diligently. The converse was implied by Davis and Moore but not discussed. That is, low-ranking positions in the stratification system are presumed to be *more* pleasant, *less* important, and to require less ability and talent. Also, society has less need to be sure that individuals perform their duties in these positions with diligence.

Davis and Moore did not argue that a society consciously develops a stratification system in order to be sure that the high-level positions are filled, and filled adequately. Rather, they made it clear that stratification is an "unconsciously evolved device." However, it is a device that every society does, and *must*, develop if it is to survive.

In order to be sure that people occupy the higher-ranking positions, society must, in Davis and Moore's view, provide these individuals with various rewards, including great prestige, high salary, and sufficient leisure. For example, to ensure enough doctors for our society, we need to offer them these and other rewards. Davis and Moore implied that we could not expect people to undertake the "burdensome" and "expensive" process of medical education if we did not offer such rewards. The implication seems to be that people at the top must receive the rewards that they do. If they do not, those positions remain unfilled and society would crumble.

The structural-functional theory of stratification has been subject to much criticism since its publication in 1945 (see Tumin, 1953, for the first important criticism; Huaco, 1966, for a good summary of the main criticisms to that date).

One basic criticism is that the functional theory of stratification simply perpetuates the privileged position of those people who already have power, prestige, and money. It does this by arguing that such people deserve their rewards; indeed they need to be offered such rewards for the good of society.

The functional theory also can be criticized for assuming that simply because a stratified social structure has existed in the past, it must continue to exist in the future. It is possible that future societies can be organized in other, nonstratified ways.

In addition, it has been argued that the idea of functional positions varying in their importance to society is difficult to support. Are garbage collectors really any less important to the survival of society than advertising executives? Despite the lower pay and prestige of the garbage collectors, they actually may be *more* important to the survival of the society. Even in cases where it could be said that one position serves a more important function for society, the greater rewards do not necessarily accrue to the more important position. The woman who is a nurse may be much more important to society than the movie actress, but she has far less power, prestige, and income than the actress.

Is there really a scarcity of people capable of filling high-level positions? In fact, many people are prevented from obtaining the training they need to achieve prestigious positions, even though they have the ability. In the medical profession, for example, there is a persistent effort to limit the number of practicing doctors. In general, many able people never get a chance to show that they can handle high-ranking positions even though there is a clear need for them and their contributions. The fact is that those in high-ranking positions have a vested interest in keeping their numbers small and their power and income high.

Finally, it can be argued that we do not have to offer people power, prestige, and income to get them to want to occupy high-level positions. People can be equally motivated by the satisfaction of doing a job well or by the opportunity to be of service to others.

The Functional Prerequisites of a Society

One of the major concerns of structural functionalists is an analysis of the things—the structures, and particularly the functions—that a social system needs in order to survive. We shall examine the major example of this kind of analysis by D. F. Aberle and his associates (1950/1967). Later in this chapter, we will discuss a more general effort by Parsons to define the four functional prerequisites of any action system—adaptation, goal attainment, integration, and pattern maintenance.

Aberle and his colleagues discuss the basic conditions that, were they to cease to exist, would cause the termination of society. The first factor deals with the population characteristics of the society. The extinction, or the dispersion, of its population clearly would threaten the existence of society. This would occur if society lost enough of its population to make its various structures inoperative. Second, an apathetic population would be a threat to society. Although this is a question of degree, because some segments of a society always manifest at least some apathy, at some point the population could become so apathetic that various components of society would cease to operate, and ultimately the entire society would disintegrate. Third, a war of "all against all" within the population would threaten society's existence. A high level of internal conflict within society would require the intervention of various social-control agents who would use force to contain the conflict. Structural functionalists believe that a society cannot operate for any length of time on the basis of force. As Aberle and his colleagues put it, "A society based solely on force is a contradiction in terms" (1950/1967:322). To structural functionalists, society is held together by the consensus of its members; to them, a society held together by force is no society at all. Finally, a society could be terminated by absorption into another society through annexation, conquest, and so forth.

The reverse side of this discussion of functional prerequisites includes the characteristics that a society must have in order to survive. For one thing, a society must have an adequate method of dealing with its environment. Of the two aspects of the environment that can be differentiated, the first is the ecology. A society must be able to extract from the environment what it needs to survive (food, fuel, raw materials, and so forth) without destroying the sources. We are all painfully aware of this problem in an era of environmental pollution, energy shortages, and starvation in many areas of the world. The second aspect of the environment is the other social systems with which a society must be able to cope. This involves, among other things, trade, cultural exchanges, adequate communication, and adequate military defense in the event of intersocietal hostilities.

A society also must have an adequate method for sexual recruitment. Heterosexual relationships have to be patterned in such a way that men and women have adequate opportunities to interact. Beyond that, both sexes must be endowed with the motivation needed for a rate of reproduction sufficient to maintain the society. On the average, a couple must produce something above two children. Furthermore, the society needs to be sure that there is a sufficient number of people and that they have diverse enough interests and skills to allow the society to function.

A society also must have sufficient differentiation of roles, as well as a way of assigning people to those roles. In all societies certain activities must be performed and roles must be constructed so that they can be performed. The most important form of role differentiation is social stratification. As we have seen, one of the basic tenets of structural functionalism is that societies must be stratified to survive. Stratification is seen as performing various functions, such as ensuring that people are willing to take on the responsibilities of high-status positions, assuring the stability of the social system, and so forth.

An adequate communication system is also viewed as a functional requirement of any social system. Its elements include language and channels of communication. Clearly, society itself would be impossible if people were not able to interact and communicate. However, when structural functionalists discuss society's communication system, they also mean the shared symbolic systems that people learn during the socialization process and that make communication possible. Shared symbolic systems make possible a cultural value system. It is the cultural system that is crucial to the structural-functional view of society and how it is held together. The common value pattern is a bulwark against the possibility of continual conflict within society.

Not only must there be a shared cultural system, but structural functionalists also talk of the need for a shared system of values at the individual level. People must look at the world in essentially the same way. This allows them to predict, with a high degree of accuracy, what others will think and do. These mutual cognitive orientations perform various functions. Of perhaps greatest importance, they make social situations stable, meaningful, and predictable. In short, a stable society, which is of enormous importance to structural functionalists, is made possible by the fact that actors operate with shared orientations. Such shared orientations also allow people to account in similar ways for those things that they cannot control or predict; they enable them to sustain their involvement in, and commitment to, social situations.

Structural functionalists also argue that society needs a shared, articulated set of goals. If people were pursuing many unrelated goals, the resulting chaos would make society impossible. Shared goals, such as marital happiness, the success of children, and occupational achievement, help to give a high level of cohesion to society.

Society requires some method of regulating the means to achieve these goals, and the normative system performs this function. Without the normative regulation of means, society would be afflicted by chaos, anomie, and apathy. If occupational success could be obtained by *any* means possible, there would be, according to the structural functionalists, societal disorder.

A society also must regulate affective expression, because unbridled emotions would be another source of chaos. Some emotions are clearly necessary; for example, love and family loyalty are necessary to ensure an adequate population. Although it may be difficult for anyone to define precisely the line between necessary and dangerous levels of emotion, to the structural functionalists it is clear that at some level emotionalism is a threat to the social system.

Implied in many of the preceding points is the idea that society requires the socialization of new members in order to survive. People must learn many things, including their place in the stratification system, the common value system, shared cognitive orientations, acceptable goals, norms defining proper means to these goals, and regulations on affective states. If actors have not learned and internalized such things, society is viewed as impossible by the structural functionalist.

Finally, society requires effective control over disruptive forms of behavior. Ideally, if the socialization process has led actors to internalize all the proper values, then they conform of their own volition. To the structural functionalists, society runs best when there is no need for external control of actors. However, when external control proves necessary, various social-control agents are brought to bear. These range from the raised eyebrow of a friend to the billyclub of the police officer, or in extreme cases, the bayonet of the soldier.

Talcott Parsons's Structural Functionalism

Over the course of his life, Talcott Parsons did a great deal of theoretical work. There are important differences between his early and later work. In this section, we deal with his later, structural-functional, theorizing. In Chapter 9, we discuss his earlier action theory and whether there is continuity between his action theory and his structural-functional theory. We begin this discussion of Parsons's structural functionalism with the four functional imperatives for all "action" systems, his famous AGIL scheme.

AGIL

A function is "a complex of activities directed towards meeting a need or needs of the system" (Rocher, 1975:40). Using this definition, Parsons believes that there are four functional imperatives that are necessary for (characteristic of) all systems—(A) adaptation, (G) goal attainment, (I) integration, and (L) latency, or pattern maintenance (AGIL). In order to survive, a system must perform these four functions:

1. *Adaptation:* A system must cope with external situational exigencies. It must adapt to its environment and adapt the environment to its needs.
2. *Goal attainment:* A system must define and achieve its primary goals.
3. *Integration:* A system must regulate the interrelationship of its component parts. It also must manage the relationship among the other three functional imperatives (A, G, L).
4. *Latency (pattern maintenance):* A system must furnish, maintain, and renew both the motivation of individuals and the cultural patterns that create and sustain the motivation.

At their most general level, the four functional imperatives are linked to the four action systems (discussed in detail shortly). The *biological organism* is the action system that handles the adaptation function by adjusting to and transforming the external world. The *personality system* performs the goal attainment function by defining system goals and mobilizing resources to attain them. The *social system* copes with the integration function by controlling its component parts. Finally, the *cultural system* performs the latency function by providing actors with the norms and values that motivate them for action. Figure 3.1 summarizes the structure of the action system in terms of the AGIL schema:

FIGURE 3.1   Structure of the General Action System

L   I

Cultural System	Social System
Behavioral Organism	Personality System

A   G

Source: Talcott Parsons and Gerald Platt, *The American University* (Cambridge, Mass.: Harvard University Press, 1973:15).

We turn now to a discussion of the four action systems, a discussion which sheds more light on Parsons's structural functionalism.

THE ACTION SYSTEM

The major components of Parsons's action system, especially the four action systems, are outlined in Figure 3.2.

It is obvious that Parsons had a clear notion of "levels" of social reality as well as their interrelationship. The hierarchical arrangement is clear, and the levels are integrated in Parsons's system in two ways. First, each of the lower levels provides the conditions, the energy, needed for the higher levels. Second, the higher levels control those below them in the hierarchy.

In terms of the environments of the action system, the lowest level, the physical and organic environment, involves the nonsymbolic aspects of the human body, its anatomy and physiology. The highest level, ultimate reality, has, as Jackson Toby suggests "a metaphysical flavor," but Toby also argues that Parsons "is not referring to the supernatural so much as to the universal tendency for societies to address symbolically the uncertainties, concerns, and tragedies of human existence that challenge the meaningfulness of social organization" (1977:3).

FIGURE 3.2   Parsons's Action Schema

High information   1. Environment of action: High information
   (controls)   ultimate reality   (controls)
                            2. Cultural system
Hierarchy of   3. Social system   Hierarchy of
conditioning   4. Personality system   conditioning
  factors   5. Behavioral organism   factors
                         6. Environment of action:
                                physical-organic environment
High energy   High energy
(conditions)   (conditions)

Source: Adapted from Talcott Parsons, *Societies* (Englewood Cliffs, N.J.: Prentice Hall, 1966).

In the assumptions that Parsons made regarding his action systems, we encounter the problem of order that was his overwhelming concern from the beginning and that has become a major source of criticism of his work (Schwanenberg, 1971). The Hobbesian problem of order—what prevents a social war of all against all—was not answered to Parsons's (1937) satisfaction by the earlier philosophers. Parsons found his answer to the problem of order in structural functionalism, which operates, in his view, with the following set of assumptions:

1. Systems have the property of order and interdependence of parts.
2. Systems tend toward self-maintaining order, or equilibrium.
3. The systems may be static or involved in an ordered process of change.
4. The nature of one part of the system has an impact on the form that the other parts could take.
5. Systems maintain boundaries with their environments.
6. Allocation and integration are two fundamental processes necessary for a given state of equilibrium of a system.
7. Systems tend toward self-maintenance involving the maintenance of boundaries and of the relationships of parts to the whole, control of environmental variations, and control of tendencies to change the system from within.

These assumptions led Parsons to make the analysis of the *ordered* structure of systems his first priority. In so doing, he virtually ignored the issue of social change, at least until later in his career:

> We feel that it is uneconomical to describe changes in systems of variables before the variables themselves have been isolated and described; therefore, we have chosen to begin by studying particular combinations of variables and to move toward description of how these combinations change only when a firm foundation for such has been laid.
>
> (Parsons and Shils, 1951:6)

Parsons was so heavily criticized for his static orientation that he devoted more and more attention to change; in fact, as we will see, he eventually focused on the evolution of societies. However, in the view of most observers, even his work on social change tended to be highly static and structured.

In reading about the four action systems, the reader should keep in mind that they do not exist in the real world, but are rather conceptual tools for analyzing the real world.

SOCIAL SYSTEM Parsons's conception of the social system begins at the micro level with interaction between ego and alter ego, defined as the most elementary form of the social system. He spent little time analyzing this level, although he did argue that features of this interaction system are present in the more complex forms taken by the social system. Parsons defined a social system thus:

> A social system consists in a plurality of individual actors *interacting* with each other in a situation which has at least a physical or environmental aspect, actors who are motivated in terms of a tendency to the "optimization of gratification" and whose relation to their situations, including each other, is defined and mediated in terms of a system of culturally structured and shared symbols.
>
> (Parsons, 1951:5–6)

This definition seeks to define a social system in terms of many of the key concepts in Parsons's work—actors, interaction, environment, optimization of gratification, and culture.

Despite his commitment to viewing the social system as a system of interaction, Parsons did not take interaction as his fundamental unit in the study of the social system. Rather, he used the *status-role* complex as the basic unit of the system. Interestingly, this is neither an aspect of actors nor an aspect of interaction, but rather a *structural* component of the social system. *Status* refers to a structural position within the social system, and *role* is what the actor does in such a position seen in the context of its functional significance for the larger system. The actor is viewed not in terms of thoughts and actions, but instead (at least in terms of position in the social system) as nothing more than a bundle of statuses and roles.

In his analysis of the social system, Parsons was interested primarily in its structural components. In addition to a concern with the status-role, Parsons was interested in such large-scale components of social systems as collectivities, norms, and values (Parsons, 1966:11). In his analysis of the social system, however, Parsons was not simply a structuralist but also a functionalist. He thus delineated a number of the functional prerequisites of a social system. First, social systems must be structured so that they operate compatibly with other systems. Second, to survive, the social system must have the requisite support from other systems. Third, the system must meet a significant proportion of the needs of its actors. Fourth, the system must elicit adequate participation from its members. Fifth, it must have at least a minimum of control over potentially disruptive behavior. Sixth, if conflict becomes sufficiently disruptive, it must be controlled. Finally, a social system requires a language in order to survive.

It is clear in Parsons's discussion of the functional prerequisites of the social system that his focus was large-scale systems and their relationship to one another. Even when he talked about actors, it was from the point of view of the system. Also, the discussion reflects Parsons's concern with the maintenance of order within the social system.

However, Parsons did not completely ignore the issue of the relationship between actors and social structures in his discussion of the social system. In fact, he called the integration of value patterns and need-dispositions "the fundamental dynamic theorem of sociology" (Parsons, 1951:42). Given his central concern with the social system, of key importance in this integration are the processes of internalization and socialization. That is, Parsons was interested in the ways that the norms and values of a system are transferred to the actors within the system. In a successful socialization process these norms and values are internalized; that is, they become part of the actors' "consciences." As a result, in pursuing their own interests, the actors are in fact serving the interests of the system as a whole. As Parsons put it, "The combination of value-orientation patterns which is acquired [by the actor in socialization] *must in a very important degree be a function of the fundamental role structure and dominant values of the social system*" (1951:227).

In general, Parsons assumed that actors usually are passive recipients in the socialization process.[4] Children learn not only how to act but also the norms and values, the

---

[4]This is a controversial interpretation of Parsons's work with which many disagree. François Bourricaud, for example, talks of "the dialectics of socialization" (1981:108) in Parsons's work and not of passive recipients of socialization.

morality, of society. Socialization is conceptualized as a conservative process in which need-dispositions (which are themselves largely molded by society) bind children to the social system, and it provides the means by which the need-dispositions can be satisfied. There is little or no room for creativity; the need for gratification ties children to the system as it exists. Parsons sees socialization as a lifelong experience. Because the norms and values inculcated in childhood tend to be very general, they do not prepare children for the various specific situations that they encounter in adulthood. Thus socialization must be supplemented throughout the life cycle with a series of more specific socializing experiences. Despite this need later in life, the norms and values learned in childhood tend to be stable and, with a little gentle reinforcement, tend to remain in force throughout life.

Despite the conformity induced by lifelong socialization, there is a wide range of individual variation in the system. The question is, why is this normally not a major problem for the social system, given its need for order? For one thing, a number of social control mechanisms can be employed to induce conformity. However, as far as Parsons was concerned, social control is strictly a second line of defense. A system runs best when social control is used only sparingly. For another thing, the system must be able to tolerate some variation, some deviance. A flexible social system is stronger than a brittle one that accepts no deviation. Finally, the social system should provide a wide range of role opportunities that allow different personalities to express themselves without threatening the integrity of the system.

Socialization and social control are the main mechanisms that allow the social system to maintain its equilibrium. Modest amounts of individuality and deviance are accommodated, but more extreme forms must be met by re-equilibrating mechanisms. Thus social order is built into the structure of Parsons's social system:

> Without deliberate planning on anyone's part there have developed in our type of social system, and correspondingly in others, mechanisms which, within limits, are capable of fore-stalling and reversing the deep-lying tendencies for deviance to get into the vicious circle phase which puts it beyond the control of ordinary approval-disapproval and reward-punishment sanctions.
>
> (Parsons, 1951:319)

Again, Parsons's main interest was the system as a whole rather than the actor in the system—how the system controls the actor, not how the actor creates and maintains the system. This reflects Parsons's commitment on this issue to a structural-functional orientation.

Although the idea of a social system encompasses all types of collectivities, one specific and particularly important social system is *society*, "a relatively self-sufficient collectivity the members of which are able to satisfy all their individual and collective needs and to live entirely within its framework" (Rocher, 1975:60). As a structural functionalist, Parsons distinguished among four structures, or subsystems, in society in terms of the functions (AGIL) they perform (see Figure 3.3). The *economy* is the sub-system that performs the function for society of adapting to the environment through labor, production, allocation. Through such work, the economy adapts the environment to society's needs, and it helps society adapt to these external realities. The

FIGURE 3.3   Society, Its Subsystems, and the Functional Imperatives

L   I

Fiduciary System	Societal Community
Economy	Polity

A   G

Source: Talcott Parsons and Gerald Platt, *The American University* (Cambridge, Mass.: Harvard University Press, 1973:19).

polity (or political system) performs the function of goal attainment by pursuing societal objectives and mobilizing actors and resources to that end. The *fiduciary system* (for example, in the schools, the family) handles the latency function by transmitting culture (norms and values) to actors and allowing it to be internalized by them. Finally, the integration function is performed by the *societal community* (for example, the law), which coordinates the various components of society (Parsons and Platt, 1973).

As important as the structures of the social system were to Parsons, the cultural system was more important. In fact, as we saw earlier, the cultural system stood at the top of his action system, and Parsons (1966) labeled himself a "cultural determinist."

CULTURAL SYSTEM   Parsons conceived of culture as the major force binding the various elements of the social world, or, in his terms, the action system. It mediates interaction among actors and integrates the personality and the social systems. Culture has the peculiar capacity to become, at least in part, a component of the other systems. Thus in the social system culture is embodied in norms and values, and in the personality system it is internalized by the actor. But the cultural system is not simply a part of other systems; it also has a separate existence in the form of the social stock of knowledge, symbols, and ideas. These aspects of the cultural system are available to the social and personality systems, but they do not become part of them (Morse, 1961; Parsons and Shils, 1951).

Parsons defined the cultural system, as he did his other systems, in terms of its relationship to the other action systems. Thus culture is seen as a patterned, ordered system of symbols that are objects of orientation to actors, internalized aspects of the personality system, and institutionalized patterns in the social system. Because it is largely symbolic and subjective, culture is readily transmitted from one system to another. This allows it to move from one social system to another through diffusion and from one personality system to another through learning and socialization. However, the symbolic (subjective) character of culture also gives it another characteristic, the ability to control Parsons's other action systems. Parsons came to the conclusion that moral standards are "the superordinate integrative techniques of a system of action" (Parsons and Shils, 1951:170). This conclusion reflects a crucial idea in Parsons's theory—that the cultural system is preeminent.

PERSONALITY SYSTEM   The personality system is controlled not only by the cultural system, but also by the social system. Parsons seemed to be aware of the charge that the personality system was weak and externally controlled, and he sought to salvage his position by according some independence to the personality system:

> My view will be that, while the main content of the structure of the personality is derived from social systems and culture through socialization, the personality becomes an independent system through its relations to its own organism and through the uniqueness of its own life experience; it is not a mere epiphenomenon.
>
> (Parsons, 1970:82)

One gets the feeling here that Parsons is protesting too much. If the personality system is not an epiphenomenon, it certainly is reduced to secondary or dependent status in his theoretical system.

The *personality* is defined as the organized system of orientation and motivation of action of the individual actor. The basic component of the personality is the need-disposition. Parsons and Edward Shils saw need-dispositions as the "most significant units of motivation of action" (1951:113). They differentiated need-dispositions from *drives,* which are innate tendencies—"physiological energy that makes action possible" (Parsons and Shils, 1951:111). In other words, drives are better seen as part of the biological organism. *Need-dispositions* are then defined as "these same tendencies when they are not innate but acquired through the process of action itself" (Parsons and Shils, 1951:111). Need-dispositions are drives that are shaped by the social setting.

Need-dispositions impel actors to accept or reject objects presented in the environment or to seek new objects if the ones that are available do not satisfy need-dispositions. Parsons differentiated among three basic types of need-dispositions. The first type impels actors to seek love, approval, and so forth, from their social relationships. The second type includes internalized values that lead actors to observe various cultural standards. Finally, role expectations lead actors to give and get appropriate responses.

This gives a very passive image of actors. They seem to be either impelled by drives, dominated by the culture, or, more usually, shaped by a combination of drives and culture (that is, by need-dispositions). A passive personality system is clearly a weak link in Parsons's theory, and Parsons seemed to be aware of it. On various occasions, he tried to endow the personality with some creativity. For example, he said: "We do not mean . . . to imply that a person's values are entirely 'internalized culture' or mere adherence to rules and laws. The person makes creative modifications as he internalizes culture; but the novel aspect is not the cultural aspect" (Parsons and Shils, 1951:72). Despite claims such as these, the dominant impression that emerges from Parsons's work is one of a passive personality system.

Parsons's emphasis on need-dispositions creates other problems. Because it leaves out so many other important aspects of personality, his system becomes a largely impoverished one. Alfred Baldwin, a psychologist, makes precisely this point:

> It seems fair to say that Parsons fails in his theory to provide the personality with a reasonable set of properties or mechanisms aside from need-dispositions, and gets himself into trouble by

not endowing the personality with enough characteristics and enough different kinds of mechanisms for it to be able to function.

(Baldwin, 1961:186)

Baldwin makes another telling point about Parsons's personality system, arguing that even when Parsons analyzed the personality system, he was really not focally interested in it: "Even when he is writing chapters on personality structure, Parsons spends many more pages talking about social systems than he does about personality" (1961:180). This is reflected in the various ways that Parsons linked the personality to the social system. First, actors must learn to see themselves in a way that fits with the place they occupy in society (Parsons and Shils, 1951:147). Second, role expectations are attached to each of the roles occupied by individual actors. Then there is the learning of self-discipline, internalization of value-orientations, identification, and so forth. All these forces point toward the integration of the personality system with the social system, which Parsons emphasized. However, he also pointed out the possible malintegration, which is a problem for the system that needs to be overcome.

Another aspect of Parsons's work reflects the passivity of the personality system. This is his interest in internalization as the personality system's side of the socialization process. Parsons (1970) derived this interest from Durkheim's work on internalization as well as from Freud's work, primarily that on the superego. In emphasizing internalization and the superego, Parsons once again manifested his conception of the personality system as passive and externally controlled.

Although Parsons was willing to talk about the subjective aspects of personality in his early work, he progressively abandoned that perspective (Parsons and Shils, 1951:64). In so doing, he limited the insights into the personality system that he could offer.

BEHAVIORAL ORGANISM   Though he included the behavioral organism as one of the four action systems, Parsons had very little to say about it. It is included because it is the source of energy for the rest of the systems. Although it is based on genetic constitution, its organization is affected by the processes of conditioning and learning that occur during the individual's life. The biological organism is clearly a residual system in Parsons's work, but at the minimum Parsons is to be lauded for including it as a part of his sociology, if for no other reason than that he anticipated the recent revival of interest in sociobiology in sociology.

EVOLUTIONARY THEORY

Parsons's work with such conceptual tools as the functional imperatives and action systems led to the accusation that he offered a static theory that was unable to deal with social change. Parsons had long been sensitive to this charge, arguing that although a study of change was necessary, it must be preceded by a study of structure. But by the 1960s he could resist the charges no longer and made a major shift in his work to the study of social change, particularly the study of social evolution (Parsons, 1977b). Parsons (1966) developed "a paradigm of evolutionary change."

The first component of that paradigm is the process of *differentiation*. Parsons assumed that any society is composed of a series of subsystems that differ in both their *structure* and their *functional* significance for the larger society. As society evolves, new subsystems are differentiated. This is not enough, however; they also must be more specialized and adaptive than earlier subsystems. This led Parsons to the essential aspect of his evolutionary paradigm, the idea of *adaptive upgrading*. Parsons described this process:

> If differentiation is to yield a balanced, more evolved system, each newly differentiated sub-structure . . . must have increased adaptive capacity for performing its *primary* function, as compared to the performance of *that* function in the previous, more diffuse structure. . . . We may call this process the *adaptive upgrading* aspect of the evolutionary change cycle.
>
> (Parsons, 1966:22)

This is a highly positive model of social change. It assumes that as society evolves it grows generally better able to cope with its problems. For this reason, among others, Parsons is often thought of as a very conservative sociological theorist.

Next, Parsons argued that the process of differentiation leads to a new set of problems of *integration* for society. As subsystems proliferate and grow more specialized, the society is confronted with new problems in coordinating the operations of these units.

A society undergoing evolution must move from a system of ascription to one of achievement. A wider array of skills and abilities is needed to handle the more diffuse subsystems. The generalized abilities of people must be freed from their ascriptive bonds so that they can be used by society. Most generally, this means that groups formerly excluded from contributing to the system must be freed for inclusion as full members of the society.

Finally, the *value* system of the society as a whole must undergo change as social structures and functions grow increasingly differentiated. However, because the new system is more diverse, it is harder for the value system to encompass it. Thus a more differentiated society requires a value system that is "couched at a higher level of generality in order to legitimize the wider variety of goals and functions of its sub-units" (Parsons, 1966:23). However, this process of generalization of values often does not proceed smoothly as it meets resistance from groups committed to their own narrow value systems.

Evolution proceeds through a variety of cycles, but no general process affects all societies equally. Some societies may foster evolution, whereas others may "be so beset with internal conflicts or other handicaps" that they impede the process of evolution, or they may even "deteriorate" (Parsons, 1966:23). What most interested Parsons were those societies in which developmental "breakthroughs" occur, because he believed that once they occur, the process of evolution would follow his general evolutionary model.

Although Parsons conceived of evolution as occurring in stages, he was careful to avoid a unilinear evolutionary theory: "We do not conceive societal evolution to be either a continuous or a simple linear process, but we can distinguish between broad levels of advancement without overlooking the considerable variability found in each" (1966:26). Making it clear that he was simplifying matters, Parsons distinguished three broad evolutionary stages—primitive, intermediate, and modern. Characteristically, he differentiated among these stages primarily on the basis of cultural dimensions. The crucial development in the transition from primitive to intermediate is the development of language, primarily written language. The key development in the shift from intermediate to modern is "the institutionalized codes of normative order," or law (Parsons, 1966:26).

Parsons next proceeded to analyze a series of specific societies in the context of the evolution from primitive to modern society. One particular point is worth underscoring here: Parsons turned to evolutionary theory, at least in part, because he was accused of being unable to deal with social change. However, his analysis of evolution is *not* in terms of process; rather, it is an attempt to "order structural types and relate them sequentially" (Parsons, 1966:111). This is comparative *structural* analysis, not really a study of the processes of social change. Thus, even when he was supposed to be looking at change, Parsons remained committed to the study of structures and functions.

Robert Merton's Model of Structural Functionalism

While Talcott Parsons is the most important structural-functional theorist, his student, Robert Merton, authored *the* single most important statement on structural functionalism in sociology, "Toward the Codification of Functional Analysis in Sociology" (1949/1968). In this essay Merton criticized some of the more extreme and indefensible aspects of structural functionalism. But equally important, his new conceptual insights helped to give structural functionalism a continuing usefulness.

Merton criticized what he saw as the three basic postulates of functional analysis. The first is the postulate of the functional unity of society. This postulate holds that all standardized social and cultural beliefs and practices are functional for society as a whole as well as for individuals in society. This view implies that the various parts of a social system must show a high level of integration. However, Merton maintained that although it may be true of small, primitive societies, the generalization cannot be extended to larger, more complex societies.

Universal functionalism is the second postulate. That is, it is argued that *all* standardized social and cultural forms and structures have positive functions. Merton argued that this contradicts what we find in the real world. It is clear that not every structure, custom, idea, belief, and so forth has positive functions. For example, rabid nationalism can be highly dysfunctional in a world of rapidly proliferating nuclear arms.

Third is the postulate of indispensability. The argument here is that all standardized aspects of society not only have positive functions but also represent indispensable parts of the working whole. This postulate leads to the idea that all structures and functions are functionally necessary for society. No other structures and functions could work quite as well as those that are currently found within society. Merton's criticism, following Parsons, was that we must at least be willing to admit that there are various structural and functional alternatives to be found within society.

Merton's position was that all of these functional postulates rely on nonempirical assertions based on abstract, theoretical systems. At a minimum, it is the responsibility of the sociologist to examine each empirically. Merton's belief that empirical tests, not theoretical assertions, are crucial to functional analysis led him to develop his "paradigm" of functional analysis as a guide to the integration of theory and research.

Merton made it clear from the outset that structural-functional analysis focuses on groups, organizations, societies, and cultures. He stated that any object that can be subjected to structural-functional analysis must "represent a standardized (that is, patterned and repetitive) item" (Merton, 1949/1968:104). He had in mind such things as "social roles, institutional patterns, social processes, cultural patterns, culturally patterned emotions, social norms, group organization, social structure, devices for social control, etc." (Merton, 1949/1968:104).

Early structural functionalists tended to focus almost entirely on the *functions* of one social structure or institution for another. However, in Merton's view, early analysts tended to confuse the subjective motives of individuals with the functions of structures or institutions. The focus of the structural functionalist should be on social functions rather than on individual motives. Functions, according to Merton, are defined as "those observed consequences which make for the adaptation or adjustment of a given system" (1949/1968:105). However, there is a clear ideological bias when one focuses only on adaptation or adjustment, for they are always positive consequences. It is important to note that one social fact can have negative consequences for another social fact. To rectify this serious omission in early structural functionalism, Merton developed the idea of a *dysfunction*. Just as structures or institutions could contribute to the maintenance of other parts of the social system, they also could have negative consequences for them. Slavery in the southern United States, for example, clearly had positive consequences for white southerners, such as supplying cheap labor, support for the cotton economy, and social status. It also had dysfunctions, such as making southerners overly dependent on an agrarian economy and therefore unprepared for industrialization. The lingering disparity between the North and the South in industrialization can be traced, at least in part, to the dysfunctions of the institution of slavery in the South.

Merton also posited the idea of *nonfunctions,* which he defined as consequences that are simply irrelevant to the system under consideration. Included here might be social forms that are "survivals" from earlier historical times. Although they may have had positive or negative consequences in the past, they have no significant effect on contemporary society. One example, although a few might disagree, is the Women's Christian Temperance Movement.

To help answer the question of whether positive functions outweigh dysfunctions, or vice versa, Merton developed the concept of *net balance*. However, we never can simply add up positive functions and dysfunctions and objectively determine which outweighs the other, because the issues are so complex and based on so much subjective judgment that they cannot easily be calculated and weighed. The usefulness of Merton's concept comes from the way it orients the sociologist to the question of relative significance. To return to the example of slavery, the question becomes whether, on balance, slavery was more functional or dysfunctional to the South. Still, this question is too broad and obscures a number of issues (for example, that slavery was functional for groups like white slaveholders).

To cope with problems like these, Merton added the idea that there must be *levels of functional analysis*. Functionalists had generally restricted themselves to analysis of the society as a whole, but Merton made it clear that analysis also could be done on an organization, institution, or group. Returning to the issue of the functions of slavery for the South, it would be necessary to differentiate several levels of analysis and ask about the functions and dysfunctions of slavery for black families, white families, black political organizations, white political organizations, and so forth. In terms of net

ROBERT K. MERTON: An Autobiographical Sketch*

It is easy enough to identify the principal teachers, both close at hand and at a distance, who taught me most. During my graduate studies, they were: P. A. Sorokin, who oriented me more widely to European social thought and with whom, unlike some other students of the time, I never broke although I could not follow him in the directions of inquiry he began to pursue in the late 1930s; the then quite young Talcott Parsons, engaged in thinking through the ideas which first culminated in his magisterial *Structure of Social Action*; the biochemist and sometime sociologist L. J. Henderson, who taught me something about the disciplined investigation of what is first entertained as an interesting idea; the economic historian E. F. Gay, who taught me about the workings of economic development as reconstructible from archival sources; and, quite consequentially, the then dean of the history of science, George Sarton, who allowed me to work under his guidance for several years in his famed (not to say, hallowed) workshop in the Widener Library of Harvard. Beyond these teachers with whom I studied directly, I learned most from two sociologists: Emile Durkheim, above all others, and Georg Simmel, who could teach me only through the powerful works they left behind, and from that sociologically sensitive humanist, Gilbert Murray. During the latter period of my life, I learned most from my colleague, Paul F. Lazarsfeld, who probably had no idea of how much he taught me during our uncountable conversations and collaborations during more than a third of a century.

Looking back over my work through the years, I find more of a pattern in it than I had supposed was there. For almost from the beginning of my own work, after those apprenticeship years as a graduate student, I was determined to follow my intellectual interests as they evolved rather than pursue a predetermined lifelong plan. I chose to adopt the practice of my master-at-a-distance, Durkheim, rather than the practice of my master-at-close-range, Sarton. Durkheim repeatedly changed the subjects he chose to investigate. Starting with his study of the social division of labor, he examined methods of sociological inquiry and then turned successively to the seemingly unrelated subjects of suicide, religion, moral education, and socialism, all the while developing a theoretical orientation which, to his mind, could be effectively developed by attending to such varied aspects of life in society. Sarton had proceeded quite the other way: in his earliest years as a scholar, he had worked out a program of research in the history of science that was to culminate in his monumental five-volume *Introduction [sic] to the History of Science* (which carried the story through to the close of the fourteenth century!).

balance, slavery was probably more functional for certain social units and more dysfunctional for other social units. Addressing the issue at these more specific levels helps in analyzing the functionality of slavery for the South as a whole.

The first of these patterns seemed more suitable for me. I wanted and still want to advance sociological theories of social structure and cultural change that will help us understand how social institutions and the character of life in society come to be as they are. That concern with theoretical sociology has led me to avoid the kind of subject specialization that has become (and, in my opinion, has for the most part rightly become) the order of the day in sociology, as in other evolving disciplines. For my purposes, study of a variety of sociological subjects was essential.

In that variety, only one special field — the sociology of science — has persistently engaged my interest. During the 1930s, I devoted myself almost entirely to the social contexts of science and technology, especially in seventeenth-century England, and focused on the unanticipated consequences of purposive social action. As my theoretical interests broadened, I turned, during the 1940s and afterward, to studies of the social sources of nonconforming and deviant behavior, of the workings of bureaucracy, mass persuasion, and communication in modern complex society, and to the role of the intellectual, both within bureaucracies and outside them. In the 1950s, I centered on developing a sociological theory of basic units of social structure: the role-set and status-set and the role models people select not only for emulation but also as a source of values adopted as a basis for self-appraisal (this latter being "the theory of reference groups"). I also undertook, with George Reader and Patricia Kendall, the first large-scale sociological study of medical education, aiming to find out how, all apart from explicit plan, different kinds of physicians are socialized in the same schools of medicine, this being linked with the distinctive character of professions as a type of occupational activity. In the 1960s and 1970s, I returned to an intensive study of the social structure of science and its interaction with cognitive structure, these two decades being the time in which the sociology of science finally came of age, with what's past being only prologue. Throughout these studies, my primary orientation was toward the connections between sociological theory, methods of inquiry, and substantive empirical research.

I group these developing interests by decades only for convenience. Of course, they did not neatly come and go in accord with such conventional divisions of the calendar. Nor did all of them go, after the first period of intensive work on them. I am at work on a volume centered on the unanticipated consequences of purposive social action, thus following up a paper first published almost half a century ago and intermittently developed since. Another volume in the stocks, entitled *The Self-Fulfilling Prophecy*, follows out in a half-dozen spheres of social life the workings of this pattern as first noted in my paper by the same title, a mere third of a century ago. And should time, patience, and capacity allow, there remains the summation of work on the analysis of social structure, with special reference to status-sets, role-sets, and structural contexts on the structural side, and manifest and latent functions, dysfunctions, functional alternatives, and social mechanisms on the functional side.

Mortality being the rule and painfully slow composition being my practice, there seems small point in looking beyond this series of works in progress.

Merton also introduced the concepts of manifest and latent functions. These two terms have also been important additions to functional analysis.[5] In simple terms, *manifest functions* are those that are intended, whereas *latent functions* are unintended. The manifest function of slavery, for example, was to increase the economic productivity of the South, but it had the latent function of providing a vast underclass that served to increase the social status of southern whites, both rich and poor. This idea is related to another of Merton's concepts—*unanticipated consequences*. Actions have both intended and unintended consequences. Although everyone is aware of the intended consequences, it requires sociological analysis to uncover the unintended consequences; indeed, to some this is the very essence of sociology. Peter Berger (1963) has called this "debunking," or looking beyond stated intentions to real effects.

Merton made it clear that unanticipated consequences and latent functions are not the same. A latent function is one type of unanticipated consequence, one that is functional for the designated system. But there are two other types of unanticipated consequences: "those that are dysfunctional for a designated system, and these comprise the latent dysfunctions," and "those which are irrelevant to the system which they affect neither functionally or dysfunctionally . . . non-functional consequences" (Merton, 1949/1968:105).

As further clarification of functional theory, Merton pointed out that a structure may be dysfunctional for the system as a whole and yet may continue to exist. One might make a good case that discrimination against blacks, females, and other minority groups is dysfunctional for American society, yet it continues to exist because it is functional for a part of the social system; for example, discrimination against females is generally functional for males. However, these forms of discrimination are not without some dysfunctions, even for the group for which they are functional. Males do suffer from their discrimination against females; similarly, whites are hurt by their discriminatory behavior toward blacks. One could argue that these forms of discrimination adversely affect those who discriminate by keeping vast numbers of people underproductive and by increasing the likelihood of social conflict.

Merton contended that not all structures are indispensable to the workings of the social system. Some parts of our social system *can* be eliminated. This helps functional theory overcome another of its conservative biases. By recognizing that some structures are expendable, functionalism opens the way for meaningful social change. Our society, for example, could continue to exist (and even be improved) by the elimination of discrimination against various minority groups.

Merton's clarifications are of great utility to modern sociologists (e.g., Gans, 1972) who wish to perform structural-functional analyses.

---

[5]Colin Campbell (1982) has criticized Merton's distinction between manifest and latent functions. Among other things, he points out that Merton is vague about these terms and uses them in various ways (for example, as intended versus actual consequences and as surface meanings versus underlying realities). More important, he feels that Merton (like Parsons) never adequately integrated action theory (see Chapter 9) and structural functionalism. The result is that we have an uncomfortable mixture of the intentionality ("manifest") of action theory and the structural consequences ("functions") of structural functionalism. Due to these and other confusions, Campbell believes, Merton's distinction between manifest and latent function is little used in contemporary sociology.

The Major Criticisms

No single sociological theory in the history of the discipline has been the focus of as much interest as structural functionalism. From the late 1930s to the early 1960s, it was virtually unchallenged as the dominant sociological theory in the United States. In recent years, however, criticism of the theory has increased rapidly and now is far more prevalent than praise. Mark Abrahamson depicts this situation quite vividly: "Thus, metaphorically, functionalism has ambled along like a giant elephant, ignoring the stings of gnats, even as the swarm of attackers takes its toll" (1978:37).

Let us look at some of these major criticisms. First, we will deal with the major *substantive* criticisms of structural functionalism and then focus on the *logical and methodological* problems associated with the theory.

SUBSTANTIVE CRITICISMS

One major criticism is that structural functionalism does not deal adequately with history—that it is inherently ahistorical. In fact, structural functionalism was developed, at least in part, in reaction to the historical evolutionary approach of certain anthropologists. Many of the early anthropologists were seen as describing the various stages in the evolution of a given society or society in general. Frequently, depictions of the early stages were highly speculative. Furthermore, the later stages were often little more than idealizations of the society in which the anthropologist lived. Early structural functionalists were seeking to overcome the speculative character and ethnocentric biases of these works. In its early years in particular, structural functionalism went too far in its criticism of evolutionary theory and came to focus on either contemporary or abstract societies. However, structural functionalism need not be ahistorical (Turner and Maryanski, 1979). Although practitioners have tended to operate as if it were ahistorical, nothing in the theory prevents them from dealing with historical issues. In fact, Parsons's (1966, 1971) work on social change, as we have seen, reflects the ability of structural functionalists to deal with change if they so wish.

Structural functionalists also are attacked for being unable to deal effectively with the *process* of social change (Abrahamson, 1978; P. Cohen, 1968; Mills, 1959; Turner and Maryanski, 1979). Whereas the preceding criticism deals with the seeming inability of structural functionalism to deal with the past, this one is concerned with the parallel incapacity of the approach to deal with the contemporary process of social change. Structural functionalism is far more likely to deal with static structures than with change processes. Percy Cohen (1968) sees the problem as lying in structural functional theory, in which all of the elements of a society are seen as reinforcing one another as well as the system as a whole. This makes it difficult to see how these elements can also contribute to change. While Cohen sees the problem as inherent in the theory, Turner and Maryanski believe, again, that the problem lies with the practitioners and not the theory.

In the view of Turner and Maryanski, structural functionalists frequently do not address the issue of change and, even when they do, it is in developmental rather than revolutionary terms. However, according to them, there is no reason why structural functionalists could not deal with social change. Whether the problem lies in the theory or in the theorists, the fact remains that the main contributions of structural functionalists lie in the study of static, not changing, social structures.

Perhaps the most often voiced criticism of structural functionalism is that it is unable to deal effectively with conflict (Abrahamson, 1978; P. Cohen, 1968; Gouldner, 1970; Horowitz, 1962/1967; Mills, 1959; Turner and Maryanski, 1979). This criticism takes a variety of forms. Alvin Gouldner argues that Parsons, as the main representative of structural functionalism, tended to overemphasize harmonious relationships. Irving Louis Horowitz contends that structural functionalists tend to see conflict as necessarily destructive and as occurring outside the framework of society. Most generally, Abrahamson argues that structural functionalism exaggerates societal consensus, stability, and integration and, conversely, tends to disregard conflict, disorder, and change. The issue once again is whether this is inherent in the theory or in the way that practitioners have interpreted and used it (P. Cohen, 1968; Turner and Maryanski, 1979). Whatever one's position, it is clear that structural functionalism has had little to offer on the issue of social conflict.

The overall criticisms that structural functionalism is unable to deal with history, change, and conflict have led many (for example, P. Cohen, 1968; Gouldner, 1970) to argue that structural functionalism has a conservative bias. As Gouldner vividly puts it in his criticism of Parsons's structural functionalism: "Parsons persistently sees the partly filled glass of water as half *full* rather than half *empty*" (1970:290). One who sees a glass as half full is emphasizing the positive aspects of a situation, whereas one who sees it as half empty is focusing on the negative side. To put this in social terms, a conservative structural functionalist would emphasize the economic advantages of living in our society rather than its disadvantages.

It may indeed be true that there is a conservative bias in structural functionalism that is attributable not only to what it ignores (change, history, conflict) but also to what it chooses to focus on. For one thing, structural functionalists have tended to focus on culture, norms, and values (P. Cohen, 1968; Mills, 1959; Lockwood, 1956). David Lockwood (1956), for example, is critical of Parsons for his preoccupation with the normative order of society. More generally, Cohen (1968) argues that structural functionalists focus on normative elements, although this is not inherent in the theory. Crucial to structural functionalism's focus on cultural and societal factors and what leads to the theory's conservative orientation is a passive sense of the individual actor. People are seen as constrained by cultural and social forces. Structural functionalists (e.g., Parsons) lack a dynamic, creative sense of the actor. As Gouldner says, to emphasize his criticism of structural functionalism, "Human beings are as much engaged in using social systems as in being used by them" (1970:220).

Related to their cultural focus is the tendency of structural functionalists to mistake the legitimizations employed by elites in society for social reality (Gouldner, 1970; Horowitz, 1962/1967; Mills, 1959). The normative system is interpreted as reflective of the society as a whole, when it may in fact be better viewed as an ideological system promulgated by, and existing for, the elite members of society. Horowitz enunciates this position quite explicitly: "Consensus theory . . . tends to become a metaphysical representation of the dominant ideological matrix" (1962/1967:270).

These substantive criticisms point in two basic directions. First, it seems clear that structural functionalism has a rather narrow focus that prevents it from addressing a number of important issues and aspects of the social world. Second, its focus tends to give it a very conservative flavor; as it was often practiced and still is, to some degree, structural functionalism operates in support of the status quo and dominant elites (Huaco, 1986).

METHODOLOGICAL AND LOGICAL CRITICISMS

One of the often expressed criticisms (see, for example, Abrahamson, 1978; Mills, 1959) is that structural functionalism is basically vague, unclear, and ambiguous. For example: What exactly is a structure? A function? A social system? How are parts of social systems related to each other as well as to the larger social system? Part of the ambiguity is traceable to the level on which structural functionalists choose to work. They deal with abstract social systems instead of real societies. In much of Parsons's work, no "real" society is discussed. Similarly, the discussion of functional prerequisites by Aberle and his colleagues (1950/1967) is not concretely tied to a real society but occurs at a very high level of abstraction.

A related criticism is that, although no one grand scheme ever can be used to analyze all societies throughout history (Mills, 1959), structural functionalists have been motivated by the belief that there is a single theory or at least a set of conceptual categories that could be used to do this. The belief in the existence of such a grand theory lies at the base of much of Parsons's work, the functional prerequisites of Aberle and his colleagues (1950/1967), and the Davis-Moore (1945) theory of stratification. Many critics regard this grand theory as an illusion, believing that the best sociology can hope for are more historically specific, "middle-range" (Merton, 1968) theories.

Among the other specific methodological criticisms is the issue of whether there exist adequate methods to study the questions of concern to structural functionalists. Cohen (1968), for instance, wonders what tools can be used to study the contribution of one part of a system to the system as a whole. Another methodological criticism is that structural functionalism makes comparative analysis difficult. If the assumption is that part of a system only makes sense in the context of the social system in which it exists, how can we compare it with a similar part in another system? Cohen asks, for example: If the English family makes sense only in the context of English society, how can we compare it to the French family?

TELEOLOGY AND TAUTOLOGY   Cohen (1968) and Turner and Maryanski (1979) see teleology and tautology as the two most important logical problems confronting structural functionalism. Some tend to see teleology as an inherent problem (Abrahamson, 1978; Cohen, 1968), but the author believes that Turner and Maryanski (1979) are correct when they argue that the problem with structural functionalism is not teleology per se, but *illegitimate* teleology. In this context, *teleology* is defined as the view that society (or other social structures) has purposes or goals. In order to achieve these goals, society creates, or causes to be created, specific social structures and social institutions. Turner and Maryanski do not see this view as necessarily illegitimate; in fact, they argue that social theory *should* take into account the teleological relationship between society and its component parts.

The problem, to Turner and Maryanski, is the extension of teleology to unacceptable lengths. An illegitimate teleology is one that implies "that purpose or end states guide human affairs when such is not the case'' (Turner and Maryanski, 1979:118). For example, it is illegitimate to assume that because society needs procreation and socialization it will create the family institution. A variety of alternative structures could meet these needs; society does not "need" to create the family. The structural functionalist must define and document the various ways in which the goals do, in fact, lead to the creation of specific substructures. It also would be useful to be able to show why other substructures could not meet the same needs. A legitimate teleology would be able to define and demonstrate *empirically* and *theoretically* the links between society's goals and the various substructures that exist within society. An illegitimate teleology would be satisfied with a blind assertion that a link between a societal end and a specific substructure must exist. Turner and Maryanski admit that functionalism is often guilty of presenting illegitimate teleologies: "We can conclude that functional explanations often become illegitimate teleologies—a fact which seriously hampers functionalism's utility for understanding patterns of human organization" (1979:124).

The other major criticism of the logic of structural functionalism is that it is tautological. A tautological argument is one in which the conclusion merely makes explicit what is implicit in the premise or is simply a restatement of the premise. In structural functionalism, this circular reasoning often takes the form of defining the whole in terms of its parts and then defining the parts in terms of the whole. Thus, it would be argued that a social system is defined by the relationship among its component parts, and the component parts of the system are defined by their place in the larger social system. Because each is defined in terms of the other, neither the social system nor its parts are in fact defined at all. We really learn nothing about either the system or its parts. Structural functionalism has been particularly prone to tautologies, although there is some question about whether this propensity is inherent in the theory or simply characteristic of the way most structural functionalists have used, or misused, the theory.

NEOFUNCTIONALISM

Under a barrage of criticisms like those just outlined, structural functionalism declined in significance from the mid-1960s through the early 1980s. However, by the mid-1980s, a major effort was under way to revive the theory under the heading of "neofunctionalism." The term *neofunctionalism* is used to indicate continuity with structural functionalism, but also to demonstrate that an effort is being made to extend structural functionalism and overcome its major difficulties. Jeffrey Alexander and Paul Colomy define *neofunctionalism* as "a self-critical strand of functional theory that seeks to broaden functionalism's intellectual scope while retaining its theoretical core" (1985:11).

Alexander (1985a) has outlined some of the basic orientations of neofunctionalism. First, neofunctionalism operates with a descriptive model of society that sees it as composed of elements which, in interaction with one another, form a pattern. This pattern allows the system to be differentiated from its environment. Parts of the system are "symbiotically connected," and their interaction is not determined by some overarching force. Thus, neofunctionalism rejects any monocausal determinism and is open-ended and pluralistic.

Second, Alexander argues that neofunctionalism devotes roughly equal attention to action and order. It thus avoids the tendency of structural functionalism to focus almost exclusively on the macro-level sources of order in social structures and culture and to give attention to more micro-level action patterns. Neofunctionalism also purports to have a broad sense of action, including not only rational, but also expressive, action.

Third, neofunctionalism retains the structural-functional interest in integration, *not* as an accomplished fact, but rather as a social *possibility*! It recognizes that deviance and social control are realities within social systems. There is concern for equilibrium within neofunctionalism, but it is broader than the structural-functional concern encompassing both moving and partial equilibrium. There is a disinclination to see social systems as characterized by static equilibrium. Equilibrium, broadly defined, is seen as a reference point for functional analysis, but not as descriptive of the lives of individuals in actual social systems.

Fourth, neofunctionalism accepts the traditional Parsonsian emphasis on personality, culture, and social system. In addition to being vital to social structure, the interpenetration of these systems also produces tension that is an ongoing source of both change and control.

Fifth, neofunctionalism focuses on social change in the processes of differentiation within the social, cultural, and personality systems. Thus, change is not productive of conformity and harmony, but rather "individuation and institutional strains" (Alexander, 1985a:10).

Finally, Alexander argues that neofunctionalism "implies the commitment to the independence of conceptualization and theorizing from other levels of sociological analysis" (1985a).

In the end, Alexander is seeking to outline a neofunctionalism that overcomes a variety of problems associated with structural functionalism—"anti-individualism . . . antagonism to change . . . conservatism . . . idealism . . . an anti-empirical bias" (1985a:10). Overcoming these problems and constructing a "new" structural functionalism is an ambitious goal, one which is a long way from attainment as Alexander (1985a:16) readily admits when he says that "neofunctionalism is a tendency rather than a developed theory."

Whereas Alexander has tried to delineate neofunctionalism in general, programmatic terms, Colomy (1986) has dealt more specifically with a revised structural-functional theory of change. He argues that the structural-functional theory of change ("differentiation theory") derived from Parsonsian theory has three basic weaknesses. First, it is highly abstract and lacks empirical and historical specificity. Second, it does not devote enough attention to concrete groups and social processes or to power and conflict. Third, it overemphasizes the integration produced by structural change.

As a result of these criticisms, the structural-functional theory of change has undergone several revisions. First, the original master trend (progressive differentiation) has been supplemented with an analysis of patterned deviations from that trend. For example, in addition to differentiation, societies have experienced *de-differentiation,* or "a type of structural change that rejects societal complexity and moves toward less differentiated levels of social organization" (Colomy, 1986:143). Such de-differentiation is likely to occur as a result of discontent with modernization. Also important is "unequal development" across various institutional spheres as well as "unequal differentiation" within a single institution. "Incomplete differentiation" occurs "where the initial steps toward differentiation are not consummated and, consequently, two or more structures share or compete for the authority to carry out a given function" (Colomy, 1986:44).

Second, revisionists have pushed differentiation theory toward more concern for how concrete groups affect change as well as how change is affected by such factors as power, conflict, and contingency. Various specific groups have been identified as instigators of change in the direction of greater differentiation as have groups that have stood in opposition to such change. This leads to a focus on conflict between groups over the process of differentiation and the forms that a resolution of that conflict might take. Great historical and empirical detail is presented in these studies on the contending groups involved in the process of differentiation. This work also moves away from an overemphasis on integration and toward, in Parsonsian terms, "much more sustained attention to the potential contradictions and strains associated with differentiation between and within cultural, social, and personality systems" (Colomy, 1986: 149). These efforts are, in Colomy's view, leading to a more comprehensive explanatory framework for analyzing differentiation.

Third, early differentiation theory focused on greater efficiency and reintegration as the main effects of the process of differentiation, but more recent work has outlined a much wider array of possible outcomes.

It might be argued that although the theory of differentiation has been widened, it also has lost its distinctive flavor with its new-found focus on conflict and competition. So much has been borrowed from other intellectual traditions that one wonders whether the kind of approach outlined above can, or should, be labelled structural functionalism or even neofunctionalism.

THE CONFLICT THEORY ALTERNATIVE

A premise of this chapter is that conflict theory can be seen as a development that took place, at least in part, in reaction to structural functionalism and as a result of many of the criticisms discussed earlier. However, it should be noted that conflict theory has various other roots, such as Marxian theory and Simmel's work on social conflict. In the 1950s and 1960s, conflict theory provided an alternative to structural functionalism, but it has been superseded in recent years by a variety of neo-Marxian theories (see Chapter 4). Indeed, one of the major contributions of conflict theory was the way it laid the groundwork for theories more faithful to Marx's work, theories that came to attract a wide audience in sociology. The basic problem with conflict theory is that it never succeeded in divorcing itself sufficiently from its structural-functional roots. It was more a kind of structural functionalism turned on its head than a truly critical theory of society.

The Work of Ralf Dahrendorf

Conflict theorists, like functionalists, are oriented toward the study of social structures and institutions. In the main, this theory is little more than a series of contentions that are often the direct opposites of functionalist positions. This is best exemplified by the work of Ralf Dahrendorf (1958; 1959), in which the tenets of conflict and functional theory are juxtaposed. To the functionalists, society is static or, at best, in a state of moving equilibrium, but to Dahrendorf and the conflict theorists every society at every point is subject to processes of change. Where functionalism emphasizes the orderliness of society, conflict theorists see dissension and conflict at every point in the social system. Functionalists (or at least early functionalists) argue that every element in society contributes to stability; the exponents of conflict theory see many societal elements contributing to disintegration and change.

Functionalists tend to see society as being held together informally by norms, values, and a common morality. Conflict theorists see whatever order there is in society as stemming from the coercion of some members by those at the top. Where functionalists focus on the cohesion created by shared societal values, conflict theorists emphasize the role of power in maintaining order in society.

Dahrendorf (1959; 1968) is the major exponent of the position that society has two faces (conflict and consensus) and that sociological theory therefore should be divided into two parts, conflict theory and consensus theory. Consensus theorists should examine value integration in society, and conflict theorists should examine conflicts of interest and the coercion that holds society together in the face of these stresses. He recognized that society could not exist without both conflict and consensus, which are prerequisites for each other. Thus, we cannot have conflict unless there is some prior consensus. For example, French housewives are highly unlikely to conflict with Chilean chess players because there is no contact between them, no prior integration to serve as a basis for a conflict. Conversely, conflict can lead to consensus and integration. An example is the alliance between the United States and Japan that has developed since World War II.

Despite the interrelationship between the processes of consensus and conflict, Dahrendorf was not optimistic about developing a single sociological theory encompassing both processes: "It seems at least conceivable that unification of theory is not feasible at a point which has puzzled thinkers ever since the beginning of Western philosophy" (1959:164). Eschewing a singular theory, Dahrendorf set out to construct a conflict theory of society.[6]

Dahrendorf began with, and was heavily influenced by, structural functionalism. He noted that to the functionalist, the social system is held together by voluntary cooperation or general consensus or both. However, to the conflict (or coercion) theorist, society is held together by "enforced constraint." This means that some positions in society are delegated power and authority over others. This fact of social life led Dahrendorf to his central thesis that the differential distribution of authority "invariably becomes the determining factor of systematic social conflicts" (1959:165).

AUTHORITY

Dahrendorf concentrated on the larger social structures.[7] Central to his thesis is the idea that various positions within society have different amounts of authority. Authority

---

[6]Dahrendorf called conflict and coercion "the ugly face of society" (1959:164). We can ponder whether a person who regards them as "ugly" can develop an adequate theory of conflict and coercion.

[7]In his other work, Dahrendorf (1968) continued to focus on social facts (for example, positions and roles), but he also manifested a concern for the dangers of reification endemic to such an approach.

does not reside in individuals but in positions. Dahrendorf was interested not only in the structure of these positions, but also in the conflict among them: "The *structural* origin of such conflicts must be sought in the arrangement of social roles endowed with expectations of domination or subjection" (1959:165; italics added). The first task of conflict analysis, to Dahrendorf, was to identify various authority roles within society. In addition to making the case for the study of large-scale structures like authority roles, Dahrendorf was opposed to those who focus on the individual level. For example, he was critical of those who focus on the psychological or behavioral characteristics of the individuals who occupy such positions. He went so far as to say that those who adopted such an approach were not sociologists.

The authority attached to positions is the key element in Dahrendorf's analysis. Authority always implies both superordination and subordination. Those who occupy positions of authority are expected to control subordinates; that is, they dominate because of the expectations of those who surround them, not because of their own psychological characteristics. These expectations, like authority, are attached to positions, not people. Authority is not a generalized social phenomenon; those who are subject to control, as well as permissible spheres of control, are specified in society. Finally, because authority is legitimate, sanctions can be brought to bear against those who do not comply.

Authority is not a constant as far as Dahrendorf was concerned. This is traceable to the fact that authority resides in positions and not persons. Thus, a person in authority in one setting does not necessarily hold a position of authority in another setting. Similarly, a person in a subordinate position in one group may be in a superordinate position in another. This follows from Dahrendorf's argument that society is composed of a number of units that he called *imperatively coordinated associations*. These may be seen as associations of people controlled by a hierarchy of authority positions. In that society contains many such associations, an individual can occupy a position of authority in one and a subordinate position in another.

Authority within each association is dichotomous; thus two, and only two, conflict groups can be formed within any association. Those in positions of authority and those in positions of subordination hold certain interests that are "contradictory in substance and direction." Here we encounter another key term in Dahrendorf's theory of conflict —*interests*. Groups on top and at the botton are defined by common interests. Dahrendorf continued to be firm in his thinking that even these interests, which sound so psychological, are basically large-scale phenomena:

> For purposes of the sociological analysis of conflict groups and group conflicts, it is necessary to assume certain *structurally generated* orientations of the actions of incumbents of defined *positions*. By analogy to conscious ("subjective") orientations of action, it appears justifiable to describe these as interests. . . . The assumption of "objective" interests associated with social positions has *no psychological implications* or ramifications; it belongs to the level of sociological analysis proper.
>
> (Dahrendorf, 1959:175; italics added)

Within every association, those in dominant positions seek to maintain the status quo while those in subordinate positions seek change. A conflict of interests within any association is at least latent at all times, which means that the legitimacy of authority is *always* precarious. This conflict of interest need not be conscious in order for super-ordinates or subordinates to act. The interests of superordinates and subordinates are objective in the sense that they are reflected in the expectations (roles) attached to positions. Individuals do not have to internalize these expectations or even be conscious of them in order to act in accord with them. If they occupy given positions, then they will behave in the expected manner. Individuals are "adjusted" or "adapted" to their roles when they contribute to conflict between superordinates and subordinates. Dahrendorf called these unconscious role expectations *latent interests*. *Manifest interests* are latent interests that have become conscious. Dahrendorf saw the analysis of the connection between latent and manifest interests as a major task of conflict theory. Nevertheless, actors need not be conscious of their interests in order to act in accord with them.

Next Dahrendorf distinguished three broad types of groups. The first is the *quasi-group*, or "aggregates of incumbents of positions with identical role interests" (Dahrendorf, 1959:180). These are the recruiting grounds for the second type of group—the *interest group*. Dahrendorf described the two groups:

> Common modes of behavior are characteristic of *interest groups* recruited from larger quasi-groups. Interest groups are groups in the strict sense of the sociological term; and they are the real agents of group conflict. They have a structure, a form of organization, a program or goal, and a personnel of members.
>
> (Dahrendorf, 1959:180)

Out of all of the many interest groups emerge *conflict groups*, or those that actually engage in group conflict.

Dahrendorf felt that the concepts of latent and manifest interests, of quasi-groups, interest groups, and conflict groups, were basic to an explanation of social conflict. Under *ideal* conditions no other variables would be needed. However, because conditions are never ideal, many different factors do intervene in the process. Dahrendorf mentioned technical conditions such as adequate personnel, political conditions such as the overall political climate, and social conditions such as the existence of communication links. The way people are recruited into the quasi-group was another social condition important to Dahrendorf. He felt that if the recruitment is random and determined by chance, then an interest group, and ultimately a conflict group, is unlikely to emerge. In contrast to Marx, Dahrendorf did not feel that the *lumpenproletariat*[8] would ultimately form a conflict group, because people are recruited to it by chance. However, when recruitment to quasi-groups is structurally determined, these groups provide fertile recruiting grounds for interest groups and, in some cases, conflict groups.

The final aspect of Dahrendorf's conflict theory is the relationship of conflict to change. Here Dahrendorf recognized the importance of Lewis Coser's work, which focused on the functions of conflict in maintaining the status quo. Dahrendorf felt, however, that the conservative function of conflict is only one part of social reality; conflict also leads to change and development.

Briefly, Dahrendorf argued that once conflict groups emerge, they engage in actions that lead to changes in social structure. When the conflict is intense, the changes that

---

[8] This is Marx's term for the mass of people at the bottom of the economic system, those who stand below even the proletariat.

occur are radical. When it is accompanied by violence, structural change will be sudden. Whatever the nature of conflict, sociologists must be attuned to the relationship between conflict and change as well as that between conflict and the status quo.

Dahrendorf's conflict theory can be criticized for ignoring order and stability, whereas functionalism has been criticized for ignoring conflict and change. Conflict theory also has been criticized for being ideologically radical, whereas functionalism was criticized for its conservative orientation.

In comparison, conflict theory is far less developed than functional theory. It is not nearly so sophisticated, perhaps because it is not truly an innovative perspective. Furthermore, many of the best sociologists, at least in the United States, until recently, have devoted their attention to functional theory, and relatively few have worked toward developing conflict theory.

Dahrendorf's conflict theory has been subjected to a number of critical analyses (for example, Hazelrigg, 1972; J. Turner, 1973; Weingart, 1969), including some critical reflections by Dahrendorf (1968) himself. First, Dahrendorf's model is not so clear a reflection of Marxian ideas as he claimed. In fact, it constitutes an inadequate translation of Marxian theory into sociology. Second, as has been noted, conflict theory has more in common with structural functionalism than with Marxian theory. Dahrendorf's emphasis on such things as systems (imperatively coordinated associations), positions, and roles links him directly to structural functionalism. As a result, his theory suffers from many of the same inadequacies as structural functionalism. For example, conflict seems to emerge mysteriously from legitimate systems (just as it does in structural functionalism). Further, conflict theory seems to suffer from many of the same conceptual and logical problems (for example, vague concepts, tautologies) as structural functionalism. Finally, like structural functionalism, it is almost wholly a macroscopic theory and as a result has little to offer to our understanding of individual thought and action.

Both functionalism and Dahrendorf's conflict theory are inadequate, because each is itself useful for explaining only a *portion* of social life. Sociology must be able to explain order as well as conflict, structure as well as change. This last fact has motivated several efforts to reconcile conflict and functional theory. Although none has been totally satisfactory, these efforts suggest at least some agreement among sociologists that what is needed is a theory explaining *both* consensus and dissension. Still, not all theorists seek to reconcile these conflicting perspectives. Dahrendorf, for example, saw them as alternative perspectives to be used situationally. According to Dahrendorf, when we are interested in conflict we should use conflict theory; when we wish to examine order, we should take a functional perspective. This seems an unsatisfactory position, because there is a strong need for a theoretical perspective that enables us to deal with conflict and order *simultaneously*.

Jonathan Turner (1975; 1982) has sought to reformulate conflict theory. Turner pointed to three major problems in conflict theories like that of Dahrendorf. First, there is a lack of a clear definition of conflict that delimits both what it is and what it is not. Second, conflict theory remains vague, largely because there is a failure to specify the level of analysis on which one is working: "Typically, just what units are in conflict is left vague—whether they be individuals, groups, organizations, classes, nations, communities, and the like" (J. Turner, 1982:178). Third, there is the implicit functionalism in conflict theory, which leads it away from its Marxian roots.

Turner focused on "conflict as a process of events leading to overt interaction of varying degrees of violence among at least two parties" (1982:183). He developed a nine-stage process leading to overt conflict. Although it appears at first glance to be a one-way causal model, Turner was careful to specify a number of feedback loops, or dialectical relations, among the stages. The nine-stage process looks like this:

1. The social system is composed of a number of interdependent units.
2. There is an unequal distribution of scarce and valued resources among these units.
3. Those units not receiving a proportionate share of the resources begin to question the legitimacy of the system. (Turner noted that this questioning is most likely to take place when people feel their aspirations for upward mobility are blocked, when there are insufficient channels for redressing grievances, and when people are deprived of rewards in a variety of sectors.)
4. Deprived people become aware that it is in their interests to alter the system of resource allocation.
5. Those who are deprived become emotionally aroused.
6. There are periodic, albeit often disorganized, outbursts of frustration.
7. Those involved in the conflict grow increasingly intense about it and more emotionally involved in it.
8. Increased efforts are made to organize the deprived groups involved in the conflict.
9. Finally, open conflict of varying degrees of violence breaks out between the deprived and the privileged. The degree of violence is affected by such things as the ability of the conflict parties to define their true interests and the degree to which the system has mechanisms for handling, regularizing, and controlling conflict.

Turner has done a useful job of filling in conflict theory, especially in beginning to delineate some of the conflict relations between actors and social structures. However, Turner's work, like that of many other conflict theorists, remains embedded within the structural-functional tradition. As a result, he has failed to reflect the many insights into the nature of social conflict found within the various branches of neo-Marxian theory.

Efforts to Reconcile Structural Functionalism and Conflict Theory

To date, Pierre van den Berghe (1963) has made the major effort to reconcile structural functionalism and conflict theory. He noted several points that the two approaches have in common. First, both perspectives are *holistic*; that is, they look at societies as interrelated parts and are concerned with the interrelationship among the parts. Second, the theorists focus on the variables in their own theory while ignoring variables of concern to the other perspective. They should recognize, however, that conflict can contribute to integration and, conversely, that integration can be a cause of conflict. Third, van den Berghe noted that the two theories share an evolutionary view of social change— the view that society is moving forward and upward. A conflict theorist is likely to see society as advancing irrevocably toward a utopian society. A functionalist such as Parsons sees it as becoming increasingly differentiated and ever better able to cope with its environment. Finally, van den Berghe saw both as basically equilibrium theories. Functional theory emphasizes societal equilibrium. In conflict theory, relational processes lead inevitably to a new state of equilibrium in some future stage. Van den Berghe's work demonstrates points in common between the two theories but does not reconcile them; many outstanding differences remain.

The work of Lewis Coser (1956) and Joseph Himes (1966) focused on the functions of social conflict. These basically functional treatments of conflict do move toward integrating conflict and structural-functional theory. Although their concern was the equilibrating effect of conflict, what is needed is parallel work discussing the disequilibrating effects of order. Certain kinds of order or too much order can lead to disequilibrium in the social system; for example, totalitarian rulers, despite their emphasis on order, can destroy the stability of society. However, because little work has been done on the way that order produces change, we focus below on the functions of social conflict.

The early seminal work on the functions of social conflict was done by Georg Simmel, but it has been expanded by Coser, who argued that conflict may serve to solidify a loosely structured group. In a society that seems to be disintegrating, conflict with another society may restore the integrative core. The cohesiveness of Israeli Jews might be attributed, at least in part, to the long-standing conflict with the Arab nations in the Middle East. The end of the conflict might well exacerbate underlying strains in Israeli society. Conflict as an agent for solidifying a society is an idea that has long been recognized by propagandists, who may construct an enemy where none exists or seek to fan antagonisms toward an inactive opponent.

Conflict with one group may serve to produce cohesion by leading to a series of alliances with other groups. For example, conflict with the Arabs has led to an alliance between the United States and Israel. A lessening of the Israeli-Arab conflict might weaken the bonds between Israel and the United States.

Within a society, conflict can bring some ordinarily isolated individuals into an active role. The protests over the Vietnam War motivated many young people to take vigorous roles in American political life for the first time. With the end of that conflict, a more apathetic spirit emerged again among American youth.

Conflict also serves a communication function. Prior to conflict, groups may be unsure of their adversary's position, but as a result of conflict, positions and boundaries between groups often become clarified. Individuals therefore are better able to decide on a proper course of action in relation to their adversary. Conflict also allows the parties to get a better idea of their relative strengths and may well increase the possibility of rapprochement, or peaceful accommodation.

From a theoretical perspective, it is possible to wed functional and conflict theory by looking at the functions of social conflict. Still, it must be recognized that conflict also has dysfunctions.

Himes (1966), like Coser, was interested in the functions of conflict, although he focused specifically on the functions of racial conflict. Himes discussed what he considered to be *rational* group action by American blacks. He was concerned with deliberate collective behavior designed to achieve predetermined social goals. Such behavior involves a conscious attack on overtly defined social abuses. Examples include legal redress (to achieve voting rights, educational opportunities, and public accommodations), political action (such as voting and lobbying), and nonviolent mass action. The kind of conflict with which Himes was concerned involves peaceful work within the system; his analysis excludes acts of violence, such as riots and lynchings.

Although Himes ignored violent collective conflict, we could just as easily perform a functional analysis of these forms as of peaceful conflict. The riots of the late 1960s clearly had functions for American blacks. They demonstrated blacks' power and the weakness of the white power structure, although they certainly had dysfunctions (in the form of white backlash).

As Himes saw it, racial conflict has structural, communications, solidarity, and identity functions. *Structurally*, conflict can change the power balance between blacks and the dominant white majority, increasing the power of blacks so that whites will meet with them to discuss issues of mutual importance. Racial conflict can perform *communications* functions such as increasing attention to racial matters, increasing coverage of racial matters by the mass media, allowing uninformed people to get new information, and changing the content of interracial communication. Racial conflict can put an end to the old "etiquette of race relations," bringing a greater likelihood of open dialogue over substantive issues. Racial conflict may increase *solidarity*, because it may help unify blacks and establish a relationship between the races. Even if this relationship is based only on conflict, ultimately it may form the basis for a more peaceful and long-lasting relationship. The *identity* functions of racial conflict include giving blacks a greater sense of who they are and clarifying group boundaries. Perhaps the most important identity function is the sense black participants can get of their identity as Americans fighting for the basic principle of freedom.

Each of these conflict theories is concerned with integrating, or at least relating, structural functionalism and conflict theory. Virtually all the efforts have remained at the large-scale, societal level. We turn now to a more recent form of conflict theory, one that tries to relate large-scale and small-scale concerns under the heading of conflict theory.

Toward a More Integrated Conflict Theory: The Work of Randall Collins

Randall Collins (1975) made it clear from the beginning that his focus on conflict would not be ideological—that is, he did not begin with a political view that conflict is either good or bad. Rather, he claimed, he chose conflict as a focus on the realistic ground that conflict is a—perhaps *the*—central process in social life.

Unlike the others who started, and stayed, at the societal level, Collins approached conflict from an individual point of view. He made it clear that his theoretical roots lie in phenomenology and ethnomethodology. Despite his preference for individual-level and small-scale theories, Collins was aware that "sociology cannot be successful on the microlevel alone" (1975:11). In his view, sociology cannot do without the societal level of analysis. However, whereas most of the theorists we have encountered in this chapter believed that social structures are external to, and coercive of, the actor, Collins saw social structures as inseparable from the actors who construct them and whose interaction patterns are their essence. Collins was inclined to see social structures as interaction patterns rather than external and coercive entities. In addition, whereas most of the theorists discussed above saw the actor as constrained by external forces, Collins viewed the actor as constantly creating and re-creating social organization.

Collins saw Marxian theory as the "starting point" for conflict theory, but it is, in his view, laden with problems. For one thing, he saw it (like structural functionalism) as heavily ideological, which he wanted to avoid. For another, he tended to see Marx's orientation as reducible to an analysis of the economic domain, although this is an unwarranted criticism of Marx's theory. Actually, although Collins invoked Marx frequently, his conflict theory shows relatively little Marxian influence. It is far more influenced by Weber, Durkheim, and above all phenomenology and ethnomethodology.

Collins chose to focus on social stratification because it is an institution that touches so many features of life, including "wealth, politics, careers, families, clubs, communities, lifestyles" (Collins, 1975:49). In Collins's view, the great theories of stratification are "failures." In this category he placed both the Marxian and the structural-functional theories. He criticized Marxian theory, for example, as "a monocausal explanation for a multicausal world" (Collins, 1975:49). He viewed Weber's theory as little more than an "antisystem" with which to view the features of the two great theories. Weber's work was of some use to Collins, but "the efforts of phenomenological sociology to ground all concepts in the observables of every life" (Collins, 1975:53) were the most important to him because his major focus in the study of social stratification was small-scale, not large-scale. In his view, social stratification, like all other social structures, is reducible to people in everyday life encountering each other in patterned ways.

Despite his ultimate commitment to a microsociology of stratification, Collins began (even though he had some reservations about them) with the large-scale theories of Marx and Weber as underpinnings for his own work. He started with Marxian principles, arguing that they, "with certain modifications, provide the basis for a conflict theory of stratification" (Collins, 1975:58).

First, Collins contended that it was Marx's view that the material conditions involved in earning a living in modern society are the major determinants of a person's life style. The basis of earning a living for Marx is a person's relationship to private property. Those who own or control property are able to earn their livings in a much more satisfactory way than those who do not and who must sell their labor-time to gain access to the means of production.

Second, from a Marxian perspective, material conditions affect not only how individuals earn a living but also the nature of social groups in the different social classes. The dominant social class is better able to develop more coherent social groups, tied together by intricate communication networks, than is the subordinate social class.

Finally, Collins argued that Marx also pointed out the vast differences among the social classes in their access to, and control over, the cultural system. That is, the upper social classes are able to develop highly articulated symbol and ideological systems, systems that they are often able to impose on the lower social classes. The lower social classes have less developed symbol systems, many of which are likely to have been imposed on them by those in power.

Collins viewed Weber as working within and developing further Marx's theory of stratification. For one thing, Weber was said to have recognized the existence of different forms of conflict that lead to a multifaceted stratification system (for example, class, status, and power). For another, Weber developed the theory of organizations to a high degree, which Collins saw as still another arena of conflict of interest. Weber was also important to Collins for his emphasis on the state as the agency that controls the means of violence, which shifted attention from conflict over the economy (means of production) to conflict over the state. Finally, Weber was recognized by Collins for his understanding of the social arena of emotional products, in particular religion. Conflict clearly can occur in this arena, and these emotional products, like other products, can be used as weapons in social conflict.

With this background, Collins turned to his own conflict approach to stratification, which has more in common with phenomenological and ethnomethodological theories than with Marxian or Weberian theory. Collins opened with several assumptions. People are seen as inherently sociable but also as particularly conflict-prone in their social relations. Conflict is likely to occur in social relations because "violent coercion" can always be used by one person or many people in an interaction setting. Collins believed that people seek to maximize their "subjective status," and their ability to do this depends on their resources as well as the resources of those with whom they are dealing. He saw people as self-interested; thus, clashes are possible because sets of interests may be inherently antagonistic.

This conflict approach to stratification can be reduced to three basic principles. First, Collins believed that people live in self-constructed subjective worlds. Second, other people may have the power to affect, or even control, an individual's subjective experience. Third, other people frequently try to control the individual, who opposes them. The result is likely to be interpersonal conflict.

On the basis of this, Collins developed five principles of conflict analysis that he applied to social stratification, although he believed that they could be applied to any area of social life.

First, Collins believed that conflict theory must focus on real life rather than abstract formulations. This seems to reflect a preference for a Marxian-style material analysis over the abstraction of structural functionalism. Collins urged us to think of people as animals whose actions, motivated by self-interest, can be seen as maneuvers to obtain various advantages so that they can achieve satisfaction and avoid dissatisfaction. However, unlike exchange theorists (see Chapter 7), Collins did not see people as wholly rational. He recognized that they are vulnerable to emotional appeals in their efforts to find satisfaction.

Second, Collins believed that a conflict theory of stratification must examine the material arrangements that affect interaction. Although the actors are likely to be affected by such material factors as "the physical places, the modes of communication, the supply of weapons, devices for staging one's public impression, tools, goods" (Collins, 1975: 60), not all actors are affected in the same way. A major variable is the resources that the different actors possess. Actors with considerable material resources can resist or even modify these material constraints, whereas those with fewer resources are more likely to have their thoughts and actions determined by their material setting.

Third, Collins argued that in a situation of inequality, those groups that control resources are likely to try to exploit those that lack resources. He was careful to point out that this need not involve conscious calculation on the part of those who gain from the situation; rather, they are merely pursuing what they perceive to be their best interests. In the process they may be taking advantage of those who lack resources.

Fourth, Collins wanted the conflict theorist to look at such cultural phenomena as beliefs and ideals from the point of view of interests, resources, and power. It is likely that those groups with resources and, therefore, power can impose their idea systems on the entire society; those without resources have an idea system imposed on them.

Finally, Collins made a firm commitment to the scientific study of stratification and every other aspect of the social world. This led him to prescribe several things. Sociologists should not simply theorize about stratification but should study it empirically, if possible in a comparative way. Hypotheses should be formulated and tested empirically through comparative studies. Last, the sociologist should look for the causes of social phenomena, particularly the multiple causes of any form of social behavior.

This kind of scientific commitment led Collins to develop a wide array of propositions about the relationship between conflict and various specific aspects of social life. We can present only a few here, but they should allow readers to get a feel for Collins's type of conflict sociology.

1.0 Experiences of giving and taking orders are the main determinants of individual outlooks and behaviors.
1.1 The more one gives orders, the more he is proud, self-assured, formal, and identifies with organizational ideals in whose name he justifies the orders.
1.2 The more one takes orders, the more he is subservient, fatalistic, alienated from organizational ideals, externally conforming, distrustful of others, concerned with extrinsic rewards, and amoral.

(Collins, 1975:73–74)

Among other things, these propositions all reflect Collins's commitment to the *scientific study* of the small-scale social manifestations of social conflicts.

Collins was not content to deal with conflict within the stratification system but sought to extend it to various other social domains. For example, he extended his analysis of stratification to relationships between the sexes as well as among age groups. He took the view that the family is an arena of sexual conflict, in which males have been the victors, with the result that women are dominated by men and subject to various kinds of unequal treatment. Similarly, he saw the relationship between age groups—in particular, between young and old—as one of conflict. This contrasts with the view of structural functionalists, who saw harmonious socialization and internalization in this relationship. Collins looked at the resources possessed by the various age groups. Adults have a variety of resources, including experience, size, strength, and the ability to satisfy the physical needs of the young. In contrast, one of the few resources young children have is physical attractiveness. This means that young children are likely to be dominated by adults. However, as children mature, they acquire more resources and are better able to resist, with the result of increasing social conflict between the generations.

Collins also looked at formal organizations from a conflict perspective. He saw them as networks of interpersonal influences and also as the arenas in which conflicting interests are played out. In short, "organizations are arenas for struggle" (Collins,

1975:295). Collins again couched his argument in propositional form. For example, he argued that "coercion leads to strong efforts to avoid being coerced" (Collins, 1975: 298). In contrast, he felt that the offering of rewards is a preferable strategy: "Control by material rewards leads to compliance to the extent that rewards are directly linked to the desired behavior" (Collins, 1975:299). These propositions and others all point to Collins's commitment to a scientific, largely micro-oriented study of conflict.

In sum, Collins is, like Dahrendorf, not a true exponent of Marxian conflict theory, although for different reasons. Although he used Marx as a starting point, Weber, Durkheim, and particularly ethnomethodology were much more important influences on his work. Collins's small-scale orientation is helpful; however, despite his stated intentions of integrating large- and small-scale theory, he did not accomplish the task.

Toward a More Marxian Conflict Theory

As a transition to the next chapter on Marxian theories, we now offer Andre Gunder Frank's (1966/1974) criticisms of van den Berghe's efforts to reconcile conflict theory and structural functionalism. Of greatest importance is Frank's contention that conflict theory is an inadequate Marxian theory. Thus, whereas van den Berghe may be able to reconcile conflict theory as it stands with structural functionalism, he would find it much more difficult to reconcile the two if conflict theory were true to Marxian theory.

Frank refuted, point by point, van den Berghe's argument on the reconciliation of conflict and structural-functional theory. Van den Berghe's first point was that both theories take a holistic approach to the social world. Frank admitted that there is at least some correspondence here. He also noted a number of crucial differences. For one thing, Frank argued that true Marxists do tend to focus on the whole, whereas structural functionalists, despite a supposedly similar focus, spend most of their time on parts of social systems. Frank was correct here, but at least some varieties of truer neo-Marxian theory also have tended to focus on one component (for example, the economy, the culture) of the social whole. Frank's second refutation of van den Berghe's first point was more telling. He argued that Marxian thinkers, given their commitment to materialism, look at real social wholes, whereas structural functionalists (and some conflict theorists) tend to look at abstract wholes. Parsons's concept of a social system is an excellent example of the latter point.

Still on the issue of holism, Frank argued that structural functionalists and true Marxian thinkers ask very different questions when they study social totalities. For one thing, the former tend to take the existing social system for granted and do not question its legitimacy. Marxian scholars, however, question existing society (whether it be capitalist, socialist, or communist) and subject it to intense scrutiny and criticism. They are oriented toward the development of some future society, not a deification of the contemporary one. In addition, there is a substantive difference here between the two approaches. True Marxists focus on the social totality and view knowledge of it as helpful in understanding its various parts. But even when structural functionalism focuses on the whole of society, its ultimate goal is to understand the parts, especially specific social institutions.

Finally, because structural functionalists work on abstract systems, they can focus on any totality they wish. In that Marxian thinkers are committed to naturalism, the totality they choose to study is constrained by the real social world. The world, not an abstract theoretical system, determines what they study. Furthermore, the dialectician is oriented to changing the social whole, not just studying it, as is the case with structural functionalists.

Van den Berghe's second point was that each school ignores the variables of concern to the other. Thus structural functionalists are urged by van den Berghe to learn about conflict from conflict theorists and, conversely, conflict theorists can learn about consensus from structural functionalists. Frank criticized this position in several ways. First, he argued that it slights both perspectives, because both Marxian theory and structural functionalism have had things to say about *both* conflict and consensus. Second, Frank contended that when the structural functionalists do try to integrate Marxian ideas, they distort them beyond all recognition. Third, even when structural functionalists are interested in conflict, it is only a very limited concern. For instance, they might be willing to look at the functions of social conflict but not to examine such issues as social disintegration and social revolution.

According to Frank, structural functionalism has a limited ability to integrate the issues of conflict and consensus. However, he felt that these issues could be integrated with Marxian theory. Marxian theory can cover a wide range of kinds and degrees of conflict, including disintegrative conflict. More important, given its commitment to the dialectic, Marxian theory is particularly well suited to deal with the integration of cohesion and conflict.

Van den Berghe's third point was that the two theories share an interest in evolutionary change, but Frank noted three important differences. First, structural functionalists are likely to look solely at change within the system, whereas dialecticians are more likely to be interested in the change of the entire system and its social structure. Second, the two schools have different priorities in their study of change. To structural functionalists, structure is the source of change; to dialecticians, change is the source of structure. Finally, for the functionalist, change is an abstract process, whereas for Marxists it is a dialectical process within real societies.

Finally, van den Berghe argued that both approaches were basically equilibrium theories. This is clearly true of structural functionalism, but it does not adequately describe Marxian theory. It ignores, above all, the Marxian sense of disequilibrium, of negations, within the society. To the Marxist, society contains within it the seeds of its own transformation and revolution. Marxists may have a sense of equilibrium, but they have an even stronger image of disequilibrium and change.

In sum, Frank argued that van den Berghe was not true to Marxian theory in his delineation of conflict theory and its integration with structural functionalism. Although conflict theory has some Marxian elements, it is not a true heir of Marx's original theory. In the next chapter, we turn to those theories that are more legitimate heirs.

SUMMARY

Not too many years ago, structural functionalism was *the* dominant theory in sociology. Conflict theory was its major challenger and was the likely alternative to replace it in that position. However, dramatic changes have taken place in these two theories in recent years. They have both been the subject of intense criticism, whereas a series of alternative theories (to be discussed throughout the rest of this book) have attracted ever greater interest and ever larger followings. Today, structural functionalism and conflict theory certainly are still significant, but they must take their place alongside a number of important theories in sociology.

Although several varieties of structural functionalism exist, our focus here is on societal functionalism and its large-scale focus, its concern with the interrelationships at the societal level and with the constraining effects of social structures and institutions on actors. Societal structural functionalism has its roots in the work of Comte, Spencer, and Durkheim and their interest in organicism, societal needs, and more pointedly, structures and functions. Based on this work, structural functionalists developed a series of large-scale concerns in social systems, subsystems, relationships among subsystems and systems, equilibrium, and orderly change.

We examine four works by structural functionalists (Davis and Moore; Aberle et al.; Parsons; and Merton). Davis and Moore, in one of the best-known and most criticized pieces in the history of sociology, examined social stratification as a social system and the various positive functions it performs. Aberle and his colleagues, in a more general essay, were concerned with the various structures and functions that they believed a society must have in order to survive. Among others, a society must have sufficient population, means to deal with its environment, methods of sexual recruitment, role differentiation and the means to assign people to different roles, communications systems, shared cognitive orientations, shared goals, methods of regulating means to those goals, methods of regulating affectivity, adequate socialization, and effective social control.

We also discuss in some detail Talcott Parsons's structural-functional theory and his ideas on the four functional imperatives of all action systems—adaptation, goal attainment, integration, and latency (AGIL). We also analyze his structural-functional approach to the four action systems—the social system, cultural system, personality system, and behavioral organism. Finally, we deal with his structural-functional approach to social change, his evolutionary theory.

Merton's effort to develop a "paradigm" for functional analysis is the most important single piece in modern structural functionalism. Merton began by criticizing some of the more naive positions of structural functionalism. He then sought to develop a more adequate model of structural-functional analysis. On one point Merton agreed with his predecessors—the need to focus on large-scale social phenomena. But, Merton argued, in addition to focusing on positive functions, structural functionalism should be concerned with dysfunctions and even nonfunctions. Given these additions, Merton urged that analysts concern themselves with the net balance of functions and dysfunctions. Further, he argued, in performing structural-functional analysis, we must move away from global analyses and specify the *levels* on which we are working. Merton also added the idea that structural functionalists should be concerned not only with manifest (intended) but also with latent (unintended) functions.

Next, we discuss the numerous criticisms of structural functionalism that have succeeded in damaging its credibility and popularity. We discuss the criticisms that structural functionalism is ahistorical, unable to deal with conflict and change, highly conservative, preoccupied with societal constraints on actors, accepting of elite legitimations, teleological, and tautological.

Then we discuss the recent emergence of neofunctionalism as an effort to retain the strengths of structural functionalism while overcoming some of its notable weaknesses.

The second part of this chapter is devoted to the major alternative to structural functionalism in the 1950s and 1960s—conflict theory. The best-known work in this tradition is by Ralf Dahrendorf, who, although he consciously tried to follow the Marxian tradition, is best seen as having inverted structural functionalism. Dahrendorf looked at change rather than equilibrium; conflict rather than order; how the parts of society contribute to change rather than stability; and conflict and coercion rather than normative constraint. Dahrendorf offered a large-scale theory of conflict that parallels the structural functionalist's large-scale theory of order. His focus on authority, positions, imperatively coordinated associations, interests, quasi-groups, interest groups, and conflict groups reflects this orientation. Dahrendorf's theory suffers from some of the same problems as structural functionalism; in addition, it represents a rather impoverished effort to incorporate Marxian theory. Dahrendorf also can be criticized for being satisfied with alternative theories of order and conflict rather than seeking a theoretical integration of the two.

This last criticism leads us to several pieces of work aimed at reconciling conflict theory and structural functionalism. Van den Berghe discussed several general points that the two theories have in common, and Coser and Himes analyzed the functions of social conflict. Although all these efforts offer some insights, they have serious weaknesses, especially in the tendency to concentrate almost exclusively on large-scale phenomena. Collins sought to overcome this by integrating the large-scale theories of conflict with an ethnomethodological approach, but he did not do enough with the large-scale phenomena.

We close this chapter with Frank's criticism of van den Berghe's effort to integrate conflict and structural-functional theory. Frank's central point is that conflict theory is an inadequate reflection of insights from Marxian theory. With this in mind, we turn in Chapter 4 to a discussion of a number of the efforts to develop a more adequate Marxian sociological theory.

CHAPTER FOUR
Varieties of Neo-Marxian Sociological Theory

IN Chapter 3 we discussed the emergence of conflict theory as a reaction to some of the problems of structural functionalism. A central point made in that chapter was that although conflict theory purported to be within the Marxian tradition, it was actually a rather poor version of Marxian theory. In this chapter we will deal with a variety of sociological theories that are better reflections of Marx's ideas. As we will note, Marx's influence has been far from uniform. Because Marx's theory is encyclopedic, a variety of different theorists all can claim to be working within the guidelines set down in his original work. In fact, although each claims to be the true inheritor of Marx's theory, there are many irreconcilable differences among them.

It is interesting to note that, in spite of the great attention devoted to neo-Marxian theories in recent years in sociology, textbooks in sociological theory usually devote little or no attention to it. For example, in the third edition of *The Structure of Socio-*

KARL MARX: A Biographical Sketch

Karl Marx was born in Trier, Prussia, on May 5, 1818. His father, a lawyer, provided the family with a fairly typical middle-class existence. Both parents were from rabbinical families, but for business reasons the father had converted to Lutheranism.

In 1841 Marx received his doctorate in philosophy from the University of Berlin, a school heavily influenced by Hegel and the Young Hegelians, supportive, yet critical, of their master. Marx's doctorate was a dry philosophical treatise that bore little resemblance to his later, more radical and more pragmatic work. After graduation he became a writer for a liberal-radical newspaper and within ten months had become its editor-in-chief. However, because of its political positions, the paper was closed shortly thereafter by the government. The early essays published in this period began to reflect a number of the positions that would guide Marx throughout his life. They were liberally sprinkled with democratic principles, humanism, and idealism. He rejected the abstractness of Hegelian philosophy, the naive dreaming of utopian communists, and those activists who were urging what he considered to be premature political action. In rejecting these activists, Marx laid the groundwork for his own life's work:

> Practical attempts, even by the masses, can be answered with a cannon as soon as they become dangerous, but ideas that have overcome our intellect and conquered our conviction, ideas to which reason has riveted our conscience, are chains from which one cannot break loose without breaking one's heart; they are demons that one can only overcome by submitting to them.
>
> (Marx, 1842/1977:20)

Marx married in 1843 and soon thereafter left Germany for the more liberal atmosphere of Paris. There he continued to grapple with the ideas of Hegel and the Young Hegelians, but he also encountered two new sets of ideas—French socialism and English political economy. It was the unique way in which he combined Hegelianism, socialism, and political economy that shaped his intellectual orientation. Also of great importance at this point was meeting the man who was to become his lifelong friend, benefactor, and collaborator—Friedrich Engels (Carver, 1983). The son of a textile manufacturer, Engels had become a socialist critical of the conditions facing the working class. Much of Marx's compassion for the misery of the working class came from his exposure to Engels and his ideas. In 1844 Engels and Marx had a lengthy conversation in a famous café in Paris and laid the groundwork for a lifelong association. Of that conversation Engels said, "Our complete agreement in all theoretical fields became obvious . . . and our joint work dates from that time" (McLellan, 1973:131). During this period Marx produced academic works (many unpublished in his lifetime) that were mainly concerned with sorting out his link to the Hegelian tradition (for example, *The logical Theory*, Jonathan Turner devoted a few pages to critical theory but was forced to add in a footnote: "I am not terribly sympathetic to this school of thought" (1982: 417). It is important that textbooks in the field deal sympathetically with important

---

Holy Family and *The German Ideology*), but he also produced *The Economic and Philosophic Manuscripts of 1844,* which better integrated all of the intellectual traditions in which he was immersed and which foreshadowed his increasing preoccupation with the economic domain.

While Marx and Engels shared a theoretical orientation, there were many differences between the two men. Marx tended to be a highly abstract thinker, a disorderly intellectual, and very oriented to his family. Engels was a practical thinker, a neat and tidy businessman, and a womanizer. In spite of their differences, Marx and Engels forged a close union in which they collaborated on books and articles, worked together in radical organizations, and Engels even helped support Marx throughout the rest of his life so that Marx could devote himself to his intellectual and political endeavors.

In spite of the close association of the names of Marx and Engels, Engels made it clear that he was the junior partner:

> Marx could very well have done without me. What Marx accomplished I would not have achieved. Marx stood higher, saw farther, and took a wider and quicker view than the rest of us. Marx was a genius.

> (McLellan, 1973:131–132)

In fact, many believe that Engels failed to understand many of the subtleties of Marx's work. After Marx's death, Engels became the leading spokesperson for Marxian theory and in various ways distorted and oversimplified it.

Because some of his writings had upset the Prussian government, the French government (at the request of the Prussians) expelled Marx in 1845, and he moved to Brussels. His radicalism was growing, and he had become an active member of the international revolutionary movement. He also associated with the Communist League and was asked to write a document (with Engels) expounding its aims and beliefs. The result was the *Communist Manifesto* of 1848, a work that was characterized by ringing political slogans (for example, "Working men of all countries, unite!").

In 1849 Marx moved to London, and, in light of the failure of the political revolutions of 1848, he began to withdraw from active revolutionary activity and to move into serious and detailed research on the workings of the capitalist system. In 1852, he began his famous studies in the British Museum of the working conditions in capitalism. These studies ultimately resulted in the three volumes of *Capital*, the first of which was published in 1867; the other two were published posthumously. He lived in poverty during these years, barely managing to survive on a small income from his writings and the support of Engels. In 1863 Marx became reinvolved in political activity by joining the *International,* an international movement of workers. He soon gained dominance within the movement and devoted a number of years to it. He began to gain fame both as leader of the *International* and as the author of *Capital*. But the disintegration of the *International* by 1876, the failure of various revolutionary movements, and personal illness took their toll on Marx. His wife died in 1881, a daughter in 1882, and Marx himself on March 14, 1883.

recent developments in sociological theory—in this case, the rise of various branches of neo-Marxian theory.[1]

We have taken care to focus on the sociological elements of the Marxian theories we discuss. To paraphrase Henri Lefebvre's (1968) comment about Marx, there is a sociological theory in neo-Marxism, but not all neo-Marxism is sociological theory.

This chapter generally follows the outline used by Ben Agger (1978; see also Bottomore, 1983) in his book on modern Marxism. Our goal is to survey the wide variety of work being done in neo-Marxian sociological theory. First, we provide a brief statement on the economic determinists. Their work is not directly related to sociology, but it does represent the position that many neo-Marxian sociologists reacted against in developing their own orientation. Second, we deal with some early Hegelian Marxists, in particular Georg Lukács and Antonio Gramsci. Their significance lies in their effort to integrate subjective concerns with traditional Marxian interests in objective, material structures. Third, we discuss the critical, or Frankfurt, school, which turned these early Hegelian criticisms into a full-scale revision of Marxian theory. In connection with this, we comment on those who sought to extend traditional Marxian interests to individual-level phenomena. We devote special attention to the ideas of a contemporary critical theorist, Jurgen Habermas. Fourth, we discuss structural Marxism, which constitutes a reaction against the Hegelian revisionists and a return to what these theorists call Marx's "real" concern with unconscious structures. Fifth, we discuss some of the work in institutional neo-Marxian economics that is relevant to sociology (for example, Baran and Sweezy, 1966; Braverman, 1974; Burawoy, 1979). Sixth, we touch on some of the work being done in historically oriented Marxism (for example, Wallerstein, 1974; 1980). Finally, we touch on one of the most recent developments in neo-Marxian theory. As we proceed we offer a variety of critiques of these Marxian theories.

ECONOMIC DETERMINISM

In a number of places in his work, Marx sounded like an economic determinist; that is, he seemed to consider the economic system of paramount importance and to argue that it determined all other sectors of society—politics, religion, idea systems, and so forth. Although Marx did see the economic sector as preeminent, at least in capitalist society, as a dialectician he could not have taken a deterministic position because the dialectic is characterized by the notion that there is continual feedback and mutual interaction among the various sectors of society. Politics, religion, and so on cannot be reduced to epiphenomena determined by the economy, because they affect the economy just as they are affected by it. Despite the nature of the dialectic, Marx still is being interpreted as an economic determinist. Although some aspects of Marx's work would lead to this conclusion, adopting it means ignoring the overall dialectical thrust of his theory.

Agger (1978) argued that economic determinism reached its peak as an interpretation of Marxian theory during the period of the Second Communist International, between 1889 and 1914. This historical period is often seen as the apex of early market

---

[1] It is interesting to note that in the most recent edition of his book, J. Turner (1986) has been forced to devote more attention to neo-Marxian theory.

capitalism, and its booms and busts led to many predictions about its imminent demise. Those Marxists who believed in economic determinism saw the breakdown of capitalism as inevitable. In their view, Marxism was capable of producing a scientific theory of this breakdown (as well as other aspects of capitalist society) with the predictive reliability of the physical and natural sciences. All an analyst had to do was examine the structures of capitalism, especially the economic structures. Built into these structures was a series of processes that would inevitably bring down capitalism, so it was up to the economic determinist to discover how these processes worked.

Friedrich Engels, Marx's collaborator and benefactor, led the way in this interpretation of Marxian theory, as did such people as Karl Kautsky and Eduard Bernstein. Kautsky, for example, discussed the inevitable decline of capitalism as:

> unavoidable in the sense that the inventors improve technic and the capitalists in their desire for profit revolutionize the whole economic life, as it is also inevitable that the workers aim for shorter hours of labor and higher wages, that they organize themselves, that they fight the capitalist class and its state, as it is inevitable that they aim for the conquest of political power and the overthrow of capitalist rule. Socialism is inevitable because the class struggle and the victory of the proletariat is inevitable.
>
> (Kautsky, cited in Agger, 1979:94)

The imagery here is of actors impelled by the structures of capitalism into a series of actions.

It was this imagery that led to the major criticism of scientifically oriented economic determinism—that it was untrue to the dialectical thrust of Marx's theory. Specifically, the theory seemed to short-circuit the dialectic by making individual thought and action insignificant. The economic structures of capitalism that determined individual thought and action were the crucial element. This interpretation also led to political quietism and therefore was inconsistent with Marx's thinking. Why should individuals act if the capitalist system was going to crumble under its own structural contradictions? Clearly, given Marx's desire to integrate theory and practice, a perspective that omits action and even reduces it to insignificance would not be in the tradition of his thinking.

HEGELIAN MARXISM

As a result of the criticisms just discussed, economic determinism began to fade in importance, and a number of theorists developed other varieties of Marxian theory. One group of Marxists returned to the Hegelian roots of Marx's theory in search of a subjective orientation to complement the strength of the early Marxists at the objective, material level. The early Hegelian Marxists sought to restore the dialectic between the subjective and the objective aspects of social life. Their interest in subjective factors laid the basis for the later development of critical theory, which came to focus almost exclusively on subjective factors. A number of thinkers could be taken as illustrative of Hegelian Marxism (for example, Karl Korsch), but we will focus on the work of one who has gained great prominence: Georg Lukács, especially his book *History and Class Consciousness* (1922/1968). We also give brief attention to the ideas of Antonio Gramsci.

Georg Lukács

The attention of Marxian scholars of the early twentieth century was limited mainly to Marx's later, largely economic works, such as *Capital* (1867/1967). The early work, especially *The Economic and Philosophic Manuscripts of 1844* (1932/1964), which was more heavily influenced by Hegelian subjectivism, was largely unknown to Marxian thinkers. The rediscovery of the *Manuscripts* and their publication in 1932 was a major turning point. However, by the 1920s, Lukács already had written his major work, in which he emphasized the subjective side of Marxian theory. As Martin Jay puts it, "*History and Class Consciousness* anticipated in several fundamental ways the philosophical implications of Marx's *1844 Manuscripts,* whose publication it antedated by almost a decade" (1984:102).

Lukács's major contribution to Marxian theory lies in his work on two major ideas—reification and class consciousness. Lukács made it clear from the beginning that he was not totally rejecting the work of the economic Marxists on reification, but simply seeking to broaden and extend their ideas. Lukács commenced with the Marxian concept of commodities, which he characterized as "the central, structural problem of capitalist society" (1922/1968:83). A *commodity* is at base a relation among people that, they come to believe, takes on the character of a thing and develops an objective form. People in their interaction with nature in capitalist society produce various products, or commodities (for example, bread, automobiles, motion pictures). However, people tend to lose sight of the fact that they produce these commodities and give them their value. Value comes to be seen as produced by a market that is independent of the actors. The *fetishism of commodities* is the process by which commodities and the market for them are granted independent objective existence by the actors in capitalist society. Marx's concept of the fetishism of commodities was the basis for Lukács's concept of reification.

The crucial difference between the fetishism of commodities and reification is in the extensiveness of the two concepts. Whereas the former is restricted to the economic institution, the latter is applied by Lukács to all of society—the state, the law, *and* the economic sector. The same dynamic applies in all sectors of capitalist society: people come to believe that social structures have a life of their own, and as a result they do come to have an objective character. Lukács delineated this process:

> Man in capitalist society confronts a reality "made" by himself (as a class) which appears to him to be a natural phenomenon alien to himself; he is wholly at the mercy of its "laws"; his activity is confined to the exploitation of the inexorable fulfillment of certain individual laws for his own (egoistic) interests. But even while "acting" he remains, in the nature of the case, the object and not the subject of events.
>
> (Lukács, 1922/1968:135)

In developing his ideas on reification, Lukács integrated insights from Weber and Simmel. However, because reification was embedded in Marxian theory, it was seen as a problem limited to capitalism and not, as it was to Weber and Simmel, the inevitable fate of humankind.

The second major contribution of Lukács was his work on *class consciousness,* which refers to the belief systems shared by those who occupy the same class position within society. Lukács made it clear that class consciousness is neither the sum nor the average of individual consciousnesses; rather, it is a property of a group of people who share a similar place in the productive system. This view leads to a focus on the class consciousness of the bourgeoisie and especially of the proletariat. In Lukács's work, there is a clear link between objective economic position, class consciousness, and the "real, psychological thoughts of men about their lives" (Lukács, 1922/1968:51).

The concept of class consciousness necessarily implies, at least in capitalism, the prior state of *false consciousness*. That is, classes in capitalism generally do not have a clear sense of their true class interests. For example, until the revolutionary stage, members of the proletariat do not fully realize the nature and extent of their exploitation in capitalism. The falsity of class consciousness is derived from the class's position within the economic structure of society: "Class consciousness implies a class-conditioned *unconsciousness* of one's own socio-historical and economic condition. . . . The 'falseness,' the illusion implicit in this situation, is in no sense arbitrary" (Lukács, 1922/1968:52). Most social classes throughout history have been unable to overcome false consciousness and thereby achieve class consciousness. The structural position of the proletariat within capitalism, however, gives it the peculiar ability to achieve class consciousness.

The ability to achieve class consciousness is peculiar to capitalist societies. In precapitalist societies, a variety of factors prevented the development of class consciousness. For one thing, the state, independent of the economy, affected social strata; for another, status (prestige) consciousness tended to mask class (economic) consciousness. As a result, Lukács concluded, "There is therefore no possible position within such a society from which the economic basis of all social relations could be made conscious" (1922/1968:57). In contrast, the economic base of capitalism is clearer and simpler. People may not be conscious of its effects, but they are at least unconsciously aware of them. As a result, "class consciousness arrived at the point where *it could become conscious*" (Lukács, 1922/1968:59). At this stage, society turns into an ideological battleground in which those who seek to conceal the class character of society are pitted against those who seek to expose it.

Lukács compared the various classes in capitalism on the issue of class consciousness. He argued that the petty bourgeoisie and the peasants cannot develop class consciousness because of the ambiguity of their structural position within capitalism. Because these two classes represent vestiges of society in the feudal era, they are not able to develop a clear sense of the nature of capitalism. The bourgeoisie can develop class consciousness, but at best it understands the development of capitalism as something external, subject to objective laws, that it can experience only passively.

The proletariat has the capacity to develop true class consciousness, and as it does, the bourgeoisie is thrown on the defensive. Lukács refused to see the proletariat as simply driven by external forces but viewed it instead as an active creator of its own fate. In the confrontation between the bourgeoisie and the proletariat, the former class has all the intellectual and organizational weapons, whereas all the latter has, at least at first, is the ability to see society for what it is. As the battle proceeds, the proletariat moves from being a "class in itself," that is, a structurally created entity, to a "class for itself," a class conscious of its position and its mission. In other words, "the class struggle must be raised from the level of economic necessity to the level of conscious aim and effective class consciousness'' (Lukács, 1922/1968:76). When the struggle reaches this point, the proletariat is capable of the action that can overthrow the capitalist system.

Lukács had a rich sociological theory, although it is embedded in Marxian terms. He was concerned with the dialectical relationship among the structures (primarily economic) of capitalism, the idea systems (especially class consciousness), individual thought, and, ultimately, individual action. His theoretical perspective provides an important bridge between the economic determinists and more modern Marxists.

Antonio Gramsci

The Italian Marxist Antonio Gramsci, although offering a less rich theoretical perspective than Lukács, also played a key role in the transition from economic determinism to more modern Marxian positions (Salamini, 1981). Gramsci was critical of Marxists who are ''deterministic, fatalistic and mechanistic'' (1971:336). In fact, he wrote an essay entitled ''The Revolution against *Capital*'' (Gramsci, 1917/1977) in which he celebrated ''the resurrection of political will against the economic determinism of those who reduced Marxism to the historical laws of Marx's best-known work [*Capital*]''(Jay, 1984:155). Although he recognized that there were historical regularities, he rejected the idea of automatic or inevitable historical developments. Thus, the masses had to act in order to bring about a social revolution. But to act, the masses had to become conscious of their situation and the nature of the system in which they lived. Thus, although Gramsci recognized the importance of structural factors, especially the economy, he did not believe that these structural factors led the masses to revolt. The masses needed to develop a revolutionary ideology, but they could not do so on their own. Gramsci operated with a rather elitist conception in which ideas were generated by intellectuals and then extended to the masses and put into practice by them. The masses could not generate such ideas, and they could only experience them, once in existence, on faith. The masses could not become self-conscious on their own; they needed the help of social elites. However, once the masses had been influenced by these ideas, they would take the actions that lead to social revolution. Gramsci, like Lukács, focused on collective ideas rather than on social structures like the economy, and both operated within traditional Marxian theory.

Gramsci's central concept, and one that reflects his Hegelianism, is hegemony. According to Gramsci, ''the essential ingredient of the most modern philosophy of praxis [the linking of thought and action] is the historical-philosophical concept of 'hegemony''' (1932/1975:235). *Hegemony* is defined by Gramsci as cultural leadership exercised by the ruling class. He contrasts hegemony to coercion that is ''exercised by legislative or executive powers, or expressed through police intervention'' (Gramsci, 1932/1975:235). Economic Marxists tended to emphasize the economy and the coercive aspects of state domination. In contrast, Gramsci emphasized '''hegemony' and cultural leadership'' (1932/1975:235). In an analysis of capitalism, Gramsci wanted to know how some intellectuals, working on behalf of the capitalists, achieved cultural leadership and the assent of the masses.

Not only does the concept of hegemony help us to understand domination within capitalism, but it also serves to orient Gramsci's thoughts on revolution. That is, through revolution, it is not enough to gain control of the economy and the state apparatus; it is also necessary to gain cultural leadership over the rest of society. It is here that Gramsci sees a key role for communist intellectuals and the communist party.

We turn now to critical theory, which grew out of the work of Hegelian Marxists like Lukács and Gramsci, and which has moved even further from the traditional Marxian roots of economic determinism.

CRITICAL THEORY

Critical theory is the product of a group of German neo-Marxists who were dissatisfied with the state of Marxian theory, particularly its tendency toward economic determinism. The school was officially founded in Frankfurt, Germany, on February 23, 1923, although a number of its members had been active prior to that time. With the coming to power of the Nazis in the 1930s, many of the major figures emigrated to the United States and continued their work at an institute affiliated with Columbia University in New York City. Following World War II, some of the critical theorists returned to Germany; others remained in the United States (Bottomore, 1984; G. Friedman, 1981; Held, 1980; Jay, 1973; 1986; Slater, 1977). Today critical theory has spread beyond the confines of the Frankfurt school, but the most important work is being done by a group of second-generation critical thinkers based in Germany. Critical theory was and is today largely a European orientation, although its influence in American sociology is growing (van den Berg, 1980).

The Major Critiques

Critical theory is composed largely of criticisms of various aspects of social and intellectual life. It takes its inspiration from Marx's work, which was first shaped by a critical analysis of philosophical ideas and later by critiques of the nature of the capitalist system. The critical school constitutes a critique both of society and of various systems of knowledge (Farganis, 1975). Much of the work is in the form of critiques, but its ultimate goal is to reveal more accurately the nature of society (Bleich, 1977). First we focus on the major criticisms offered by the school, all of which manifest a preference for oppositional thinking and for unveiling and debunking various aspects of social reality (Connerton, 1976).

CRITICISMS OF MARXIAN THEORY

Critical theory is a variant of Marxian theory that takes as its starting point a critique of Marxian theories. The critical theorists are most disturbed by the economic determinists, the mechanistic, or mechanical, Marxists (Antonio, 1981; Schroyer, 1973; Sewart, 1978). Some (for example, Habermas, 1971) criticize the determinism implicit in parts of Marx's original work, but most focus their criticisms on the neo-Marxists, primarily because they had interpreted Marx's work too mechanistically. The critical theorists do not say that economic determinists were wrong in focusing on the economic realm but that they should have been concerned with other aspects of social life as well. As we will see, the critical school seeks to rectify this imbalance by focusing its attention on the cultural realm (Schroyer, 1973:33).

CRITICISMS OF POSITIVISM

Critical theorists also focus on the philosophical underpinnings of scientific inquiry, especially positivism (Bottomore, 1984). The criticism of positivism is related, at least in part, to the criticism of economic determinism, because some of those who were determinists accepted part or all of the positivistic theory of knowledge. Positivism is depicted as standing for various things (Schroyer, 1970; Sewart, 1978). Positivism accepts the idea that a single scientific method is applicable to all fields of study. It takes the physical sciences as the standard of certainty and exactness for all disciplines. Positivists believe that knowledge is inherently neutral. They feel that they can keep human values out of their work. This, in turn, leads to the view that science is not in the position of advocating any specific form of social action. (See Chapter 1 for a further discussion of positivism.)

Positivism is opposed by the critical school on various grounds (Sewart, 1978). For one thing, positivism tends to reify the social world and see it as a natural process. The critical theorists prefer to focus on human activity as well as on the ways in which such activity affects larger social structures. In short, positivism loses sight of the actors (Habermas, 1971), reducing them to passive entities determined by "natural forces." Given their belief in the distinctiveness of the actor, the critical theorists would not accept the idea that the general laws of science can be applied without question to human action. Positivism is assailed for being content to judge the adequacy of means toward given ends and for not making a similar judgment about ends. This leads to the view that positivism is inherently conservative, incapable of challenging the existing system. As Martin Jay says of it, "The result was the absolutizing of 'facts' and the reification of the existing order" (1973:62). Positivism leads the actor and the social scientist to passivity. Few Marxists of any type would support a perspective that does not relate theory and practice. Despite these criticisms of positivism, some Marxists (for example, some structuralists) espouse positivism, and Marx himself was often guilty of being overly positivistic (Habermas, 1971).

CRITICISMS OF SOCIOLOGY

The critical school also has taken on sociology as a target (Frankfurt Institute for Social Research, 1973). It is attacked for its "scientism," that is, for making the scientific method an end in itself. In addition, sociology is accused of accepting the status quo. The critical school maintains that sociology does not seriously criticize society, nor does it seek to transcend the contemporary social structure. Sociology, the critical school contends, has surrendered its obligation to help people oppressed by contemporary society.

In addition to such political criticisms, the critical school also has a related substantive criticism. That is, it is critical of sociologists' tendency to reduce everything human to social variables. When sociologists focus on society as a whole rather than on individuals in society, they ignore the interaction of the individual and society. Although most sociological perspectives are *not* guilty of ignoring this interaction, this view is a cornerstone of the critical school's attacks on sociologists. Because they ignore the individual, sociologists are seen as being unable to say anything meaningful about political changes that could lead to a "just and humane society" (Frankfurt Institute for Social Research, 1973:46). As Zoltan Tar put it, sociology becomes "an integral part of the existing society instead of being a means of critique and a ferment of renewal" (1977:x).

CRITIQUE OF MODERN SOCIETY

Most of the critical school's work is aimed at a critique of modern society and a variety of its components. Whereas much of early Marxian theory aimed specifically at the economy, the critical school has shifted its orientation to the cultural level in light of what it considers the realities of modern capitalist society. That is, the locus of domination in the modern world had shifted from the economy to the cultural realm. Still, the critical school retains its interest in domination,[2] although in the modern world it is likely to be domination by cultural rather than economic elements. The critical school thus seeks to focus on the cultural repression of the individual in modern society.

The critical thinkers have been shaped not only by Marxian theory but also by Weberian theory, as reflected in their focus on rationality as the dominant development within the modern world. As Trent Schroyer (1970) made clear, the view of the critical school is that in modern society the repression produced by rationality has replaced economic exploitation as the dominant social problem. The critical school clearly has adopted Weber's differentiation between *formal rationality* and *substantive rationality,* or what the critical theorists think of as *reason.* To the critical theorists, formal rationality is concerned unreflectively with the question of the most effective means for achieving any given purpose (Tar, 1977). This is viewed as "technocratic thinking," in which the objective is to serve the forces of domination, not to emancipate people from domination. The goal is simply to find the most efficient means to whatever ends are defined as important by those in power. Technocratic thinking is contrasted to reason, which is, in the minds of critical theorists, the hope for society. Reason involves the assessment of means in terms of the ultimate human values of justice, peace, and happiness. Critical theorists identified Nazism in general, and its concentration camps more specifically, as examples of formal rationality in mortal combat with reason. Thus, as George Friedman puts it, "Auschwitz was a rational place, but it was not a reasonable one" (1981:15).

Despite the seeming rationality of modern life, the critical school views the modern world as rife with irrationality. This can be labeled the "irrationality of rationality," or more specifically the irrationality of formal rationality. As Herbert Marcuse saw it, although it appears to be the embodiment of rationality, "this society is irrational as a whole" (1964:ix; see also Farganis, 1975). It is irrational that the rational world is destructive of individuals and their needs and abilities; that peace is maintained through a constant threat of war; and that despite the existence of sufficient means, people remain impoverished, repressed, exploited, and unable to fulfill themselves.

The critical school focuses primarily on one form of formal rationality—modern technology. Marcuse (1964), for example, was a severe critic of modern technology. He saw technology in modern society as leading to totalitarianism. In fact, he viewed it as

---

[2]This is made abundantly clear by Trent Schroyer (1973), who entitles his book on the critical school *The Critique of Domination.*

leading to new, more effective, and even more "pleasant" methods of external control over individuals. The prime example is the use of television to socialize and pacify the population (other examples are mass sports and sex). He rejected the idea that technology is neutral in the modern world and saw it instead as a means to dominate people. It is effective because it is made to seem neutral when it is in fact enslaving. It serves to suppress individuality. The actor's inner freedom has been "invaded and whittled down" by modern technology. The result is what Marcuse called "one-dimensional society" in which individuals lose the ability to think critically and negatively about society. Marcuse did not see technology per se as the enemy, but rather technology as it is employed in modern capitalist society: "Technology, no matter how 'pure,' sustains and streamlines the continuum of domination. This fatal link can be cut only by a revolution which makes technology and technique subservient to the needs and goals of free men" (Marcuse, 1969:56). Marcuse retained Marx's original view that technology is not inherently a problem and that it can be used to develop a "better" society.

CRITIQUE OF CULTURE

According to Friedman, "the Frankfurt School focused its most intense attention on the cultural realm" (1981:136). The critical theorists level significant criticisms at what they called the "culture industry," the rationalized, bureaucratized structures (for example, the television networks) that control modern culture. Interest in the culture industry reflects their concern with the Marxian concept of "superstructure" rather than with the economic base. The culture industry, producing what is conventionally called "mass culture," is defined as the "administered . . . nonspontaneous, reified, phony culture rather than the real thing" (Jay, 1973:216). Two things worry the critical thinkers most about this industry. First, they are concerned about its falseness. They think of it as a prepackaged set of ideas mass-produced and disseminated to the masses by the media. Second, the critical theorists are disturbed by its pacifying, repressive, and stupefying effect on people (Friedman, 1981; Tar, 1977:83).

The critical school is also interested in and critical of what they call the "knowledge industry," which refers to entities concerned with knowledge production (for example, universities and research institutes) that have become autonomous structures in our society. Their autonomy has allowed them to extend themselves beyond their original mandate (Schroyer, 1970). They have become oppressive structures interested in expanding their influence throughout society.

Marx's critical analysis of capitalism led him to have hope for the future, but many critical theorists have come to a position of despair and hopelessness. They see the problems of the modern world not as specific to capitalism, but as endemic to a rationalized world, including socialist societies. They see the future, in Weberian terms, as an "iron cage" of increasingly rational structures from which hope for escape lessens all the time.

Much of critical theory (like the bulk of Marx's original formulation) is in the form of critical analyses. Even though the critical theorists also have a number of positive interests, one of the basic criticisms made of critical theory is that it offers more criticisms than it does positive contributions. This incessant negativity galls many, and for this reason they feel that critical theory has little to offer sociological theory.

The Major Contributions

SUBJECTIVITY

The great contribution of the critical school has been its effort to reorient Marxian theory in a subjective direction. Although this constitutes a critique of Marx's materialism and his dogged focus on economic structures, it also represents a strong contribution to our understanding of the subjective elements of social life. The subjective contributions of the critical school are at both the individual and the cultural levels.

The Hegelian roots of Marxian theory are the major source of interest in subjectivity. Many of the critical thinkers see themselves as returning to those roots, as expressed in Marx's early works, especially *The Economic and Philosophic Manuscripts of 1844* (1932/1964). In this, they are following up on the work of the early twentieth-century Marxian revisionists, such as Karl Korsch and Georg Lukács, who sought not to focus on subjectivity but simply to integrate such an interest with the traditional Marxian concern with objective structures (Agger, 1978). Korsch and Lukács did not seek a fundamental restructuring of Marxian theory, although the later critical theorists do have this broader and more ambitious objective.

We begin with the critical school's interest in culture. Reversing the traditional Marxian focus, the critical school has shifted to a concern with the "superstructure" rather than with the economic "base." One factor motivating this shift is that the critical school feels that Marxists have overemphasized economic structures and that this has served to overwhelm their interest in the other aspects of social reality, especially the culture. In addition to this factor, a series of external changes in the society point to such a shift (Agger, 1978). In particular, the prosperity of the post–World War II period *seems* to have led to a disappearance of internal economic contradictions in general and class conflict in particular. False consciousness *seems* to be nearly universal as all social classes, including the working class, appear to be beneficiaries and ardent supporters of the capitalist system. To this might be added the growing realization that the Soviet Union, despite its socialist economy, is at least as oppressive as capitalist society. Because the two societies have different economies, the critical thinkers have had to look elsewhere for the major source of oppression. What they looked toward initially was the culture.

To the previously discussed aspects of the Frankfurt school's concerns—rationality, the culture industry, and the knowledge industry—can be added an additional set of concerns, the most notable of which is an interest in ideology. By ideology they mean the idea systems, often false and obfuscating, produced by societal elites. All of these specific aspects of the superstructure and the critical school's orientation to them can be subsumed under the heading of a "critique of domination" (Agger, 1978; Schroyer, 1973). This interest in domination was at first stimulated by fascism in the 1930s and 1940s, but it has shifted to a concern with domination in capitalist society. The modern world has reached a stage of unsurpassed domination of individuals. In fact, the control is so complete that it no longer requires deliberate actions on the part of the leaders. The control pervades all aspects of the cultural world and, more important, is internalized in the actor. In effect, actors have come to dominate themselves in the name of the larger social structure. Domination has reached such a complete stage that it no longer appears to be domination at all. Because domination is no longer perceived as personally damaging and alienating, it often seems as if the world is the way it is supposed to be. It is no longer clear to actors what the world *ought* to be like. This buttresses the pessimism of the critical thinkers, who no longer can see how rational analysis can help alter the situation.

One of the critical school's concerns at the cultural level is with what Habermas (1975) called *legitimations*. These can be defined as systems of ideas generated by the political system, and theoretically by any other system, to support the existence of the system. They are designed to "mystify" the political system, to make it unclear exactly what is happening. Above all, these systems of ideas legitimate the status quo. However, people are having increasing difficulty in accepting these legitimations, with the result that modern political systems, like the one in the United States, are undergoing a "legitimation crisis." Ralph Miliband (1974), for example, wondered how long people can be expected to believe in democracy in the light of increasingly centralized state capitalism. Habermas (1975) asked whether people would continue to believe in the idea of a better life in the future in view of problems such as inflation and recession.

In addition to such cultural interests, the critical school is also concerned with actors and their consciousness and what happens to them in the modern world. The consciousness of the masses came to be controlled by external forces (such as the culture industry). As a result, the masses failed to develop a revolutionary consciousness. Unfortunately, the critical theorists, like most Marxists and most sociologists, often fail to differentiate clearly between individual consciousness and culture, nor do they specify the many links between them. In much of their work, they move freely back and forth between consciousness and culture with little or no sense that they are changing levels.

Of great importance here is the effort by critical theorists, most notably Marcuse (1969), to integrate Freud's insights at the level of consciousness (and unconsciousness) into the critical theorists' interpretation of the culture. Friedman (1981) argues that critical theorists derive three things from Freud's work: (1) a psychological structure to work with in their theories; (2) a sense of psychopathology that allowed them to understand both the negative impact of modern society and the failure to develop revolutionary consciousness; and (3) the possibilities of psychic liberation. One of the benefits of this interest in individual consciousness is that it offers a useful corrective to the pessimism of the critical school and its focus on cultural constraints. Although people are controlled, imbued with false needs, and anesthetized, in Freudian terms they are also endowed with a libido (broadly conceived as sexual energy), which provides the basic source of energy for creative action oriented toward the overthrow of the major forms of domination.

DIALECTICS

The second main positive focus of critical theory is an interest in dialectics in general, as well as in a variety of its specific manifestations. At the most general level, a dialectical approach means a focus on the social *totality*.[3] Paul Connerton gave a good sense of the critical approach to the social totality: "No partial aspect of social life and no isolated phenomenon may be comprehended unless it is related to the historical whole,

---

[3] Jay (1984) sees "totality" as the heart of Marxian theory in general, not just of critical theory.

to the social structure conceived as a global entity'' (1976:12). This involves a rejection of a focus on any *specific* aspect of social life, especially the economic system, outside of its broader context. This approach also means a concern with the interrelation of the various levels of social reality—most important, individual consciousness, the cultural superstructure, and the economic structure. Dialectics also carries with it a methodological prescription: one component of social life cannot be studied in isolation from the rest.

This idea has both diachronic and synchronic components. A *synchronic* view leads us to be concerned with the interrelationship of components of society within a contemporary totality. A *diachronic* view carries with it a concern for the historical roots of today's society as well as for where it might be going in the future (Bauman, 1976). The domination of people by social and cultural structures—the "one-dimensional" society, to use Marcuse's phrase—is the result of a specific historical development and is not a universal characteristic of humankind. This historical perspective counteracts the common-sense view that emerges in capitalism that the system is a natural and inevitable phenomenon. In the view of the critical theorists (and other Marxists), people have come to see society as "second nature"; it is "perceived by common-sensical wisdom as an alien, uncompromising, demanding and high-handed power—exactly like non-human nature. To abide by the rules of reason, to behave rationally, to achieve success, to be free, man now had to accommodate himself to the 'second nature'" (Bauman, 1976:6).

The critical theorists also are oriented to thinking about the future, but following Marx's original lead, they refuse to be utopian; rather, they focus on criticizing and changing contemporary society. However, instead of directing their attention to society's economic structure as Marx had done, they concentrate on its cultural superstructure. Their dialectical approach commits them to work in the real world. On one level, this means that they are not satisfied with seeking truth in scientific laboratories. The ultimate test of their ideas is the degree to which they are accepted and used in practice. This process they call *authentication*, which occurs when the people who have been the victims of distorted communication take up the ideas of critical theory and use them to free themselves from that system (Bauman, 1976:104). This leads to another aspect of the concerns of the critical thinkers—the *liberation* of humankind (Marcuse, 1964:222).

In more abstract terms, critical thinkers can be said to be preoccupied with the interplay and relationship between theory and practice. The view of the Frankfurt school was that the two have been severed in capitalist society (Schroyer, 1973:28). That is, theorizing is done by one group, which is delegated, or more likely takes, that right, whereas practice is relegated to another, less powerful group. In many cases, the theorist's work is uninformed by what went on in the real world, leading to an impoverished and largely irrelevant body of Marxian and sociological theory. The point is to unify theory and practice so as to restore the relationship between them. Theory thus would be informed by practice whereas practice would be shaped by theory. In the process, both theory and practice would be enriched.

Despite this avowed goal, most of critical theory has failed abysmally to integrate theory and practice. In fact, one of the most often voiced criticisms of critical theory is that it is written in such a way as to be totally inaccessible to the mass of people. Furthermore, in its commitment to study culture and superstructure, it addresses a number of very esoteric topics and has little to say about the pragmatic, day-to-day concerns of most people.

One of the best known dialectical concerns of the critical school is that of Jurgen Habermas (1970; 1971). His interest in the relationship between knowledge and human interests is an example of a broader dialectical concern with the relationship between subjective and objective factors. But he has been careful to point out that subjective and objective factors cannot be dealt with in isolation from one another. To Habermas, knowledge exists at the objective level whereas human interests are a more subjective phenomena.

Habermas differentiated among three knowledge systems and their corresponding interests. The interests that lie behind and guide each system of knowledge are generally unknown to laypeople, and it is the task of the critical theorists to uncover them. The first type of knowledge is *analytic science*, or *classical positivistic scientific systems*. In Habermas's view, the underlying interest of such a knowledge system is technical control, which can be applied to the environment, other societies, or people within society. In Habermas's view, analytic science lends itself quite easily to enhancing oppressive control. The second type of knowledge system is *humanistic knowledge*, and its interest is in *understanding* the world. It operates from the general view that understanding our past generally helps us to understand what is transpiring today. It has a practical interest in mutual and self-understanding. It is neither oppressive nor liberating. The third type is *critical knowledge*, which Habermas, and the Frankfurt school in general, espoused. The interest attached to this type of knowledge is *human emancipation*. It was hoped that the critical knowledge generated by Habermas and others would raise the self-consciousness of the masses (through mechanisms articulated by the Freudians) and lead to a social movement that would result in the hoped-for emancipation.

Criticisms of Critical Theory

A number of criticisms have been leveled at critical theory (Bottomore, 1984). First, critical theory has been accused of being largely ahistorical, of examining a variety of events (for example, Nazism in the 1930s; anti-Semitism in the 1940s; student revolts in the 1960s) without paying much attention to their historical and comparative contexts. This is a damning criticism of any Marxian theory, which should be inherently historical and comparative. Second, the critical school, as we have seen already, generally has ignored the economy. Finally, and relatedly, critical theorists have tended to argue that the working class has disappeared as a revolutionary force, a position decidedly in opposition to traditional Marxian analysis.

Criticisms such as these have led such traditional Marxists as Bottomore to conclude, "The Frankfurt School, in its original form, and as a school of Marxism or sociology, is dead" (1984:76). Similar sentiments have been expressed by Greisman who labels critical theory "the paradigm that failed" (1986:273). If it is dead as a distinctive school, it is because many of its basic ideas have found their way into Marxism, neo-Marxian sociology, and even mainstream sociology. Thus, as Bottomore himself concludes in the case of Habermas, the critical school has undergone a rapprochement

with Marxism and sociology and "at the same time some of the distinctive id
Frankfurt School are conserved and developed" (1984:76).

Although critical theory *may* be on the decline, Jurgen Habermas and his theories
are very much alive. Although we have touched on a few of his thoughts earlier in this
chapter, we close this section on critical theory with a more detailed look at his ideas.

The Ideas of Jurgen Habermas

A good place to begin a discussion of Habermas's ideas is with his views on Karl
Marx's theories. As Habermas makes clear, his goal over the years has been "to
develop a theoretical program that I understand as a reconstruction of historical materialism" (1979:95). Habermas takes Marx's starting point (human potential, species-
being, "sensuous human activity") as his own. However, Habermas (1971) argues
that Marx failed to distinguish between two analytically distinct components of
species-being—work (or labor, purposive-rational action) and social (or symbolic) interaction (or communicative action). In Habermas's view, Marx tended to ignore the
latter and to reduce it to work. As Habermas put it, the problem in Marx's work is the
"*reduction of the self-generative act of the human species* to labor" (1971:42). Thus,
Habermas says: "I take as my starting point the fundamental distinction between *work*
and *interaction*" (1970:91). Throughout his writings, Habermas looks at this distinction, although he is most prone to use the terms "purposive-rational action" (work)
and "communicative action" (interaction).

Under the heading of purposive-rational action, Habermas distinguishes between
instrumental action and strategic action. Both involve the calculated pursuit of self-
interest. *Instrumental action* is concerned with a single actor rationally calculating the
best means to a given goal. *Strategic action* involves two or more individuals coordinating purposive-rational action in the pursuit of a goal. The objective of *both* instrumental and strategic action is instrumental mastery.

Habermas is most interested in *communicative action,* or where

> the actions of the agents involved are coordinated not through egocentric calculations of suc-
> cess but through acts of *reaching understanding.* In communicative action participants are not
> primarily oriented to their own successes; they pursue their individual goals under the condi-
> tion that they can *harmonize* their plans of action on the basis of *common situation definitions.*
> (Habermas, 1984:286; italics added)

Whereas the end of purposive rational action is to achieve a goal, the objective of communicative action is to achieve communicative understanding.

Clearly, there is an important speech component in communicative action. However, such action is broader than that encompassing "speech acts or equivalent non-
verbal expressions" (Habermas, 1984:278).

Habermas's key point of departure from Marx is to argue that communicative action, *not* purposive-rational action (work), is the most distinctive and most pervasive
human phenomenon. It (not work) is the foundation of all socio-cultural life as well as
all of the human sciences. Whereas Marx was led to focus on work, Habermas is led to
focus on communication.

Not only did Marx focus on work, but he took free and creative work (species-being) as his baseline for critically analyzing work in various historical epochs, especially capitalism. Habermas, too, adopts a baseline, but in the realm of communicative rather than purposive-rational action. Habermas's baseline is undistorted communication, communication without compulsion. With this baseline, Habermas is able to critically analyze distorted communication. Habermas is concerned with those social structures that distort communication, just as Marx examined the structural sources of the distortion of work. Although they have different baselines, both Habermas and Marx *have* baselines, and these permit them to escape relativism and render judgments about various historical phenomena. Habermas is critical of those theorists, especially Weber and previous critical theorists, for their lack of such a baseline and their lapse into relativism.

There is still another parallel between Marx and Habermas and their baselines. For both, these baselines represent not only their analytical starting points, but also their political objectives. That is, whereas for Marx the goal was a communist society in which undistorted work (species-being) would exist for the first time, for Habermas the political goal is a society of undistorted communication (communicative action). In terms of immediate goals, Marx seeks the elimination of (capitalist) barriers to undistorted work, and Habermas is interested in the elimination of barriers to free communication.

Here Habermas (1973), like other critical theorists, draws on Freud and sees many parallels between what psychoanalysts do at the individual level and what he thinks needs to be done at the societal level. Habermas sees psychoanalysis as a theory of distorted communication and as preoccupied with allowing individuals to communicate in an undistorted way. The psychoanalyst seeks to find the sources of distortions in individual communication, that is, repressed blocks to communication. Through reflection, the psychoanalyst attempts to help the individual overcome these blocks. Similarly, through *therapeutic critique,* "a form of argumentation that serves to clarify systematic self-deception" (Habermas, 1984:21), the critical theorist (and the communist party [Habermas, 1973]) attempts to aid people in general to overcome social barriers to undistorted communication. There is, then, an analogy (many critics think an illegitimate analogy) between psychoanalysis and critical theory. The psychoanalyst aids the patient in much the same way that the social critic helps oppressed groups in society.

As for Marx, the basis of Habermas's ideal future society exists in the contemporary world. That is, for Marx elements of species-being are found in work in capitalist society. For Habermas, elements of undistorted communication are to be found in every act of contemporary communication.

This brings us to the central issue of rationalization in Habermas's work. Here Habermas is influenced not only by Marx's work, but by Weber's as well. In his work on rationalization, Habermas's distinction between purposive-rational and communicative action remains centrally important. Most prior work, in Habermas's view, has focused on the rationalization of purposive-rational action, which has led to a growth of productive forces and an increase in technological control over life (Habermas, 1970). This form of rationalization, as it was to Weber and Marx, is a major, perhaps, *the* major, problem in the modern world. However, the problem is rationalization of purposive-rational action, *not* rationalization in general. In fact, for Habermas, the solution to the problem of the rationalization of purposive-rational action lies in the rationalization of communicative action. The rationalization of communicative action leads to communication free from domination, free and open communication. Rationalization here involves emancipation, *"removing restrictions on communication"* (Habermas, 1970:118; see also Habermas, 1979). This is where Habermas's previously mentioned work on *legitimations* and, more generally, *ideology* fits in. That is, these are two of the main causes of distorted communication, causes that must be eliminated if we are to have free and open communication.

At the level of social norms, such rationalization would involve decreases in normative repressiveness and rigidity leading to increases in individual flexibility and reflectivity. The development of this new, less restrictive or nonrestrictive normative system lies at the heart of Habermas's theory of social evolution. Instead of a new productive system, rationalization for Habermas (1979) leads to a new, less distorting normative system. Although he regards it as a misunderstanding of his position, many have accused Habermas of cutting his Marxian roots in this shift from the material to the normative level.

The end point of this evolution for Habermas is a rational society. *Rationality* here means removal of the barriers that distort communication, but more generally it means a communication system in which ideas are openly presented and defended against criticism; unconstrained agreement develops during argumentation. To understand this better, we need more details of Habermas's communications theory.

Habermas distinguishes between the previously discussed communicative action and discourse. Whereas communicative action occurs in everyday life, *discourse* is:

> that form of communication that is removed from contexts of experience and action and whose structure assures us: that the bracketed validity claims of assertions, recommendations, or warnings are the exclusive object of discussion; that participants, themes, and contributions are not restricted except with reference to the goal of testing the validity claims in questions; that no force except that of the better argument is exercised; and that all motives except that of the cooperative search for truth are excluded.
>
> (Habermas, 1975:107–8)

In the theoretical world of discourse, but also hidden and underlying the world of communicative actions, is the "ideal speech situation," in which force or power does not determine which arguments win out; instead the better argument emerges victorious. The weight of evidence and argumentation determine what is considered to be valid or true. The arguments that emerge from such a discourse (and that the participants agree on) are true. Thus Habermas adopts a consensus theory of truth (rather than a copy [or "reality"] theory of truth). This truth is part of all communication, and its full expression is the goal of Habermas's evolution theory. As Thomas McCarthy says, "The idea of truth points ultimately to a form of interaction that is free from all distorting influences. The 'good and true life' that is the goal of critical theory is inherent in the notion of truth; it is anticipated in every act of speech" (1982:308).

Consensus arises theoretically in discourse (and pretheoretically in communicative action) when four types of validity claims are raised and recognized by interactants. First, the speaker's utterances are seen as understandable, comprehensible. Second, the propositions offered by the speaker are true; that is, the speaker is offering reliable knowledge. Three, the speaker is being truthful (veracious) in offering the propositions;

the speaker is reliable. Fourth, it is right and proper for the speaker to utter such propositions; he or she has the right to do so. Consensus arises when all of these validity claims are raised and accepted; it breaks down when one or more are questioned (for example, questioning the right of the speaker to utter certain propositions). Returning to an earlier point, there are forces in the modern world that distort this process, prevent the emergence of a consensus, and that would have to be overcome for Habermas's ideal society to come about.

Thus, within the tradition of critical theory, Habermas has developed a powerful variant of his own. Although it remains broadly within the critical theory and, more generally, Marxian traditions, it has a number of quite distinctive elements. Furthermore, the theory continues to develop, and in his recent work Habermas (1984) has moved in some interesting new directions, directions that take his theory even futher from critical and Marxian theory. We discuss these recent developments in Habermas's theory in the final chapter of this book.

STRUCTURAL MARXISM

Structural Marxism is usually associated with a group of French thinkers (for example, Louis Althusser, Nicos Poulantzas, and Maurice Godelier) and thus is sometimes called French structuralism. However, because this approach has many followers outside of France, we refer to this school as structural Marxism.

As the name suggests, *structural Marxism* represents the fusion of two schools—Marxism and structuralism. Structuralism is devoted to the analysis of the hidden, underlying structures of social life. Later we will see that structuralism encompasses a wide array of complicated ideas. In Chapter 9, in addition to a detailed discussion of structuralism, we will include a discussion of the relationship between structuralism in general and structural Marxism in particular. We will see that although the two orientations have a number of things in common, there are important differences between them. Our concern here is with the kind of Marxism that structural Marxism represents; later we will deal with it as a kind of structuralism.

Criticisms of Other Marxian Theories

A good way to approach structural Marxism is to discuss its criticisms of other Marxian theories. In general, structural Marxists see themselves as being truest to Marx's work, especially his later work. In addition to questioning the purity of other Marxian theorists, structural Marxists make a number of more specific attacks (Burris, 1979).

First, structural Marxists criticize the tendency of many Marxists to emphasize empirical data in their analyses. In the view of such structural Marxists as Godelier (1972a), the truly important realities of capitalist life are to be found in its underlying structure and not in the observable facts that often obscure the true nature of that structure.

Second, structural Marxists reject the tendency of many Marxists toward historical research, because historicism is also seen as focusing on empirical data and neglecting the underlying structure. In addition, they reject historicism because of their belief that the primary task of Marxism is the study of contemporary structure. Only after we

understand the basic structure of the contemporary world can we begin to grasp historical processes. Interestingly, this is reminiscent of the position taken by a major critic of
Marxian theory, Talcott Parsons, who also argued that a study of structure was a prerequisite to a theory of history and social change.

Third, structural Marxists sharply criticize the reductionistic economic determinism
that is characteristic of some Marxian theories. Although the structural Marxists see
the importance of the economy and even see it as determinant "in the last instance,"
they also accord significance to other sectors of the social world, especially the
political and ideological structures. Poulantzas, for example, rejected the idea that the
state merely reflects the economy; it can be seen as possessing "relative autonomy."
More specifically, he took issue with those determinists who argue that economic
development would follow whatever type of state exists. In other words, he criticized
those who argued that it makes no difference whether we have fascism or democracy.
Poulantzas concluded, "Here, as elsewhere, the forms that bourgeois domination
assumes are far from a matter of indifference" (1976:21).

Poulantzas singled out for criticism the passive position of those Marxian theorists
who argued that fascism somehow would crumble as a result of its own internal
economic contradictions and that thus there was no need to take any action against
fascist societies. Poulantzas also criticized those who argued that imperialism is simply
an economic phenomenon. To him, it is a much more complex process, involving
political, ideological, and economic aspects. Although Poulantzas (and other structural
Marxists) recognized the importance of the economy, they also contended that at any
given moment other social structures may come to occupy a dominant position.

Finally, the structural Marxists criticize the tendency of a large number of other Marxists (especially critical theorists) to subjectivize and humanize the field. As Jay puts it,
structural Marxists "disdainfully rejected the humanist, subjectivist concept of
Marxism" (1984:388). To the structuralists, the focus should be on the objective structures of society—economy, polity, ideology—and not the human actors within those
structures. Thus the structuralists reject a humanistic interpretation of Marx's theory; the
effort to resurrect Marx's historical concerns; a focus on Marx's more humanistic works
(for example, the *1844 Manuscripts*); the emphasis on the Hegelian roots of Marxian
theory; and a focus on voluntaristic actors, feelings, interpersonal relations, or even conscious efforts at self-organization (Appelbaum, 1979). For example, instead of seeing
social classes as composed of voluntaristic actors, structuralists see them as "objectively
antagonistic relations" (Burris, 1979:14). Althusser depicted the emphasis on structures
and the fact that actors are determined by those structures:

> The structure of the relations of production determines the *places* and *functions* occupied and
> adopted by the agents of production, who are never anything more than the occupants of these
> places, insofar as they are the "supports" . . . of the functions. The true "subjects" (in the
> sense of constitutive subjects of the process) are therefore not these occupants or functionar-
> ies . . . but the *relations* of *production* (and political and ideological social relations).
>
> (Althusser, cited in Burris, 1979:8)

In sum, in rejecting humanistic Marxism, the structuralists clearly have enunciated an
interest in the structures of capitalist society. Let us now state the premises of structural
Marxism in more positive terms.

Tenets of Structural Marxism

Structural Marxists are oriented to the study of the hidden underlying structures of capitalist society. Although their basic concern is not "real" structures, they do believe that there are real structures in the world that constrain or determine what actors think and do. Structural Marxists accept the importance of the economy but also look at various other structures, especially political and ideological structures. Furthermore, although they accept the idea of the economy as determinant in the last instance, they do not simply reduce other structures to reflections of it. In fact, not only do structural Marxists accept the importance of the polity and ideology, but they also see them as possessing "relative autonomy." These structures may follow rather independent paths of development and may at any given time come to be the dominant forces in society.

Whatever structures they focus on, to structural Marxists actors simply fill positions in those structures; that is, they are seen as largely constrained by those structures. Despite the passive implications of such a viewpoint, as practicing Marxists the structuralists are disinclined to conclude that people should simply sit and wait for the ultimate breakdown of the structural system. As Poulantzas said, "If we confine ourselves to waiting, we will not get the 'great day' at all, but rather the tanks in the small hours of the morning" (1976:133).

The idea of a breakdown of the structures of society implies another major concern of structural Marxists—the contradictions within the system. Their tendency is to focus on contradictions among structures rather than on the contradictions that confront the actor.

Structural Marxists emphasize the importance of theoretical rather than empirical research. Clearly, because the structures are invisible, the presumption is that they can only be ascertained theoretically; thus no amount of empirical research can uncover them.

In part for the same reason, structural Marxists focus on *contemporary* society. They put little credence in historical data or research. They believe that the priority should be the study of static structures rather than historical processes; history only can be known when we have a good grasp of contemporary structure.

Reanalyzing Marx:
The Work of Louis Althusser

The work of Louis Althusser is defined largely by the nature of his focus on Marx's work. Althusser's view was that most Marxists had not interpreted Marx's work properly; indeed, he felt that they had done great violence to it. He sought to deal with this problem by developing what he believed to be a "correct" reading of Marx's work. Althusser's work is best examined in the context of the debate surrounding Marx's work.

One issue in the debate is whether Marx took a consistent intellectual position throughout his life (Veltmeyer, 1978). This is related to the issue of whether Marx is a structural and deterministic, or a humanistic and dialectical, thinker. Those Marxists who see Marx as a structuralist focus on his later works, particularly *Capital* (1867/ 1967). Others point to what they see as a more humanistic perspective in the essential continuity between *Capital* and *The Economic and Philosophic Manuscripts of 1844* (1932/ 1964). In fact, there is ample evidence in Marx's work to support either interpretation.[4]

One of the most convincing pieces of evidence for those who see Marx as a structural or economic determinist, or both, is the preface to the *Critique of Political Economy:*

> In the social production of their existence, men inevitably enter into definite relations, which are independent of their will, namely relations of production appropriate to a given stage in the development of their material forces of production. The totality of these relations of production constitutes the economic structure of society, the real foundation, on which arises a legal and political superstructure and to which correspond definite forms of social consciousness. The mode of production of material life conditions the general process of social, political, and intellectual life. It is not the consciousness of men that determines their existence, but their social existence that determines their consciousness. At a certain stage of development, the material productive forces of society come into conflict with the existing relations of production or—this merely expresses the same thing in legal terms—with the property relations within the framework of which they have operated hitherto. From forms of development of the productive forces these relations turn into their fetters. Then begins an era of social revolution. The changes in the economic foundation lead sooner or later to the whole immense superstructure.
>
> (Marx, 1859/1970:21)

The earliest and most general response to this theme, as we have seen, was to consider Marx an *economic* determinist, a view that persists in many quarters to this day. However, the most recent interpretations by critical theorists and others deny that Marx was, or even could have been, an economic determinist. First, it can be argued that even though Marx devoted the bulk of his attention to the economic dimension in capitalism, that does not mean that the same factor would predominate in other types of social systems. That is, it can be argued that Marx's focus on economics is peculiar to capitalism because of the exaggerated significance that sector acquires in that particular social system.

Second, it is doubtful that Marx devoted as much attention to the economic dimension as many think. When Marx wrote about productive activity, he was not restricting himself to work or economic production (Mészáros, 1970:115). Rather, productive activity can include not only the production of cars but also the production of religious ideas, the development of the Constitution, and the composition of music.

Third, the whole notion of economic determinism contradicts the dialectical method that stands at the base of Marx's thinking. As István Mészáros argued, "The Marxian system . . . is organized in terms of an inherently historical—'open'—teleology which cannot admit 'fixity' at any stage whatsoever" (1970:118).

---

[4] Among those who see continuity in Marx's work are Meszaros (1970), Ollman (1976), and Wallimann (1981), and those who support the discontinuity thesis include McMurty (1978) and Gandy (1979). An interesting middle-ground position is developed by Barbalet, who argues that although there is continuity in Marx's use of essential concepts, and although the early works do provide the foundation for the later ones, the same concepts "are understood through different theoretical frameworks at different stages of his development" (1983:2).

Fourth, Bertell Ollman (1976) argued that because Marx wrote in dialectical fashion, we cannot always assume that he meant the same thing by his words as we do by ours. It is virtually impossible to write dialectically. Thus Marx's deterministic statements must be reinterpreted as simply partial statements of causality that exist within a broader dialectical system. Vernon Venable summed up the now dominant interpretation of Marx on this issue: "No, no monism, technological or other, can be made out of the Marxian theory of production" (1945:95). Specifically addressing himself to the quotation above from the *Critique of Political Economy*, Ollman stated that when Marx says, "The mode of production of material life conditions the general process of social, political, and intellectual life," we must understand this claim "in a way that allows the latter group of factors to vitally affect the mode of production, and in a way that removes

---

LOUIS ALTHUSSER: A Biographical Sketch

On November 16, 1980, Louis Althusser, a renowned French structural Marxist, ran clad in his pajamas into the courtyard of the school where he had taught for many years, shouting that he had just killed his wife. Those who went to his quarters found that his wife Hélène, a noted scholar-sociologist in her own right, had been strangled. Althusser, who had suffered from increasingly serious bouts of depression (Benton, 1984), had been hospitalized for four months not long before the murder. Instead of being taken to jail, Althusser was whisked off to a hospital. A judge who went to the hospital to tell him that he was to be charged with the murder found him too seriously depressed to understand the information or to be questioned about the event.

Althusser is not only a well-known scholar but a renowned public figure in France. He is best known as an active member and severe critic of the French Communist party. He believed that Marx had developed a new and highly rigorous science in his later economic works and that the members and leaders of the French Communist party had strayed too far from these basic ideas.

Althusser was born in Algeria on October 16, 1918, and spent five years as a prisoner of war during World War II. He completed his studies after World War II at the École Normale Supérieure. Later he came to occupy the position of professor of philosophy there.

Prior to the war Althusser had been politically conservative and active in Catholicism, but after the war he turned to the ideas and the practice of communism. He formally joined the French Communist party in 1948. Since that time, Althusser has made his mark as both a political figure and as a major interpreter of the ideas of Karl Marx. In his best-known works, *For Marx* and *Reading Capital,* he established the view that there is a major discontinuity in Marx's work. Whereas the early Marx was humanistic and philosophical, the later Marx was much more rigorously scientific and important, Althusser maintained. Althusser made his reputation as a writer and was relatively inactive in French political affairs. For example, he played little, if any, role in the 1968 student rebellion in France, a highly significant event in recent French history. This absence from political activity was very unusual for a Marxist committed to the integration of theory and practice.

the automatic dependence of the social superstructure on the economic base. We must do this, because this is how Marx used his theories in practice'' (1976:8-9).

It is ironic that the belief in Marx as an economic determinist persists even though Engels confronted the issue directly and gave an eminently reasonable explanation for Marx's focus on economics as well as his simultaneous rejection of a one-sided determinism:

> Marx and I are ourselves partly to blame for the fact that younger writers sometimes lay more stress on the economic side than is due it. We had to emphasize this main principle in opposition to our adversaries, who denied it, and we had not always the time, the place or the opportunity to allow the other elements involved in the interaction to come into their rights.
>
> (Engels, 1890/1972:642)

Althusser represents a somewhat different but equally deterministic perspective on Marx's work. This is clear from his position in the debate about the "two Marxes," or "What distinguishes the object of *Capital* . . . from the object . . . of the *1844 Manuscripts*" (Althusser and Balibar, 1970:14). To Althusser, the *1844 Manuscripts* were written while Marx was still heavily influenced by Hegel, philosophy, humanism, and a concern for the devastating effect of the alienating conditions of capitalism on the individual. As far as Althusser was concerned, such concerns were unscientific and needed to be overcome in order to develop scientific materialism (Anderson, 1976). The philosophical, humanistic, and historical bases of Marx's early work led him to center on an active, creative, and free actor. Such imagery was, in Perry Anderson's view, anathema to Althusser: "The archetypical delusion was men's belief that they were in any way free in their volition, when in fact they were permanently governed by *laws* of which they were *unconscious*" (Anderson, 1976:65; italics added). Althusser believed that the heart of Marxian theory lies in the structure of society and the laws that govern the operation of these structures rather than with free actors. In his view, in *Capital* this focus emerges most clearly. As Althusser said, "If we take seriously what Marx tells us about the real dialectic of history, it is not 'men' who make history, although its dialectic is realized in them and in their practice, but the masses in the relations of class struggle" (1977:168).

Althusser argued that there is a clear "epistemological break" in the history of Marx's work and that Marx shifted, rather dramatically, from philosophical subjectivity (an ideological position) to abstract theory (a scientific position) (Benton, 1984:53). Although he detailed a number of substages, Althusser basically divided Marx's work into the pre- and the post-1845 works. Prior to 1845, Marx was largely a philosophical humanist. This was his ideological period. After 1845 he moved toward a more scientific orientation, his scientific period. Althusser argued that in 1845 Marx made "a scientific discovery without historical precedent, in its nature and effects. . . . Marx established a new *science*: the science of the history of 'social formations'" (1969:13).

In Althusser's view, in 1845 "Marx broke radically with every theory that based history and politics on an essence of man" (1969:227). He saw three main elements to this dramatic change. First, Marx developed a whole new set of concepts, replacing ideas like alienation, species-being, and other humanistic concepts with a new set of scientific structural concepts such as social formations, superstructure, relations of production, and forces of production. Second, Marx engaged in a theoretical critique of all varieties of philosophical humanism. Third, Marx defined humanism as a form of ideology—an elitist and distorted idea system. Althusser concluded: "This rupture with every *philosophical* . . . humanism is no secondary detail; it is Marx's scientific discovery" (1969:227).

Althusser's position constitutes something of a throwback to the economistic and mechanistic thinking that dominated communist theorists prior to the 1917 Russian Revolution. This position was dominant earlier in part because *Capital*, which was easily interpreted mechanistically, was available to Marxian scholars, whereas the *1844 Manuscripts* were lost and not published until 1932. As we saw earlier in this chapter, however, even before these more humanistic works were available, there were critics (for example, Gramsci) of mechanical Marxism. Gramsci's humanistic image of Marxism was anathema to Althusser and was seen by him as characteristic of the early Marx.

This debate has been radically affected by the belated publication of seven notebooks drafted by Marx in the winter of 1857–1858 and now known as the *Grundrisse* (Marx, 1857–1858/1974). Although published in two parts in 1939 and 1941 in the Soviet Union, the German original was not published until 1953, and the English version did not appear until 1974. Many observers (for example, McLellan, 1971; Mészáros, 1970; Nicolaus, 1974; Ollman, 1976; Struik, 1964) believe that the *Grundrisse* tends to support Gramsci's interpretation of Marx rather than Althusser's. Ollman was quite clear on this point: "The *Grundrisse* . . . which served as Marx's first draft for *Capital*, contains many pages which could have been lifted bodily from the *1844 Manuscripts*. Even in the published version of *Capital*, there is much more of Marx's 'earlier' ideas and concepts than is generally recognized" (1976:xv). Ollman was arguing not that Marx's ideas were always the same, but rather that there was an evolution of ideas already present in the early works. This view has been accepted by a significant number of Marxian scholars, but some, like Althusser, still see Marx as a structural determinist.

In addition to trying to develop a structural interpretation of Marx's work, Althusser tried to derive a structural analysis of capitalist society from it. To begin with, Althusser adopted the position that the economy is the determinant "in the last instance." This is certainly a weaker position than that taken by the economic determinists. But despite the basic importance of the economy, other structural components of capitalist society are of great, if not paramount, importance.

As mentioned above, Althusser conceived of capitalist society as a *social formation*, a concrete, complex totality at a specific point in historical development. This is a static, ahistorical conception of capitalist society.

Althusser also examined the major components of the social formation. In this, he rejected the simple dichotomization of base and superstructure. To Althusser, the superstructures of capitalist society do not merely reflect the economic base; rather, they have *relative autonomy* and may even come to predominate at any given time. In the end, of course, the economy will be dominant. In Althusser's view, a social formation is composed of three basic elements—the economy, polity, and ideology. The interaction of these structural components makes up the social whole at any given time.

As a Marxist, Althusser was attuned to the contradictions among these structural entities. This concern for contradictions led Althusser to develop the concept of overdetermination, derived from the work of Lenin and Mao. *Overdetermination* means that any given contradiction within a social formation cannot work itself out simply on its own, because other contradictions within society affect it. This interpenetration of contradictions led Althusser to the idea that societies cannot evolve uniformly; there is always *uneven development*. The idea of uneven development within the different components of the social formation allowed Althusser to go beyond a totally deterministic position. Actors are determined by structures, but because of uneven development, social formations are not totally determined. Contradictions within the social formation give Althusser's formations their dynamic quality. The result is that the development of societies cannot be explained by a single determinant. This allowed Althusser to be critical of the economic determinists.

> It is "*economism*" (mechanism) and not the true Marxist tradition that sets up the hierarchy of instances once and for all, assigns each its essence and role and defines the universal meaning of their relations; it is economism that identifies roles and actors eternally, not realizing that the necessity of the process lies in an exchange of roles "according to circumstances."
>
> (Althusser, 1969:213)

Althusser went on to criticize economic determinists for defining economic factors as always occupying the principal position and other factors, such as politics and ideology, as always occupying the role of secondary factors. In Althusser's view, it is possible for social institutions other than the economy (for example, the polity) to occupy a position of preeminence, at least for a time. Furthermore, we must be attuned to the relationships among various social institutions. Thus, although Althusser had a deterministic view of actors, he did not have a similar view of structures; there is a dialectic among structures.

Nicos Poulantzas: Economics, Politics, and Ideology

Nicos Poulantzas is another major contemporary structural Marxist, and he has much in common with Althusser and other French structural Marxists. However, whereas Althusser is best known for his critique of Marx's texts, Poulantzas concentrated more on an analysis of the real world and such issues as social class, fascism, and dictatorship. In the process, Poulantzas developed a critique not only of economism (economic determinism) but also of the structuralism of Althusser and his colleagues. He thus saw himself as set apart, at least in some ways, from others in the school of French structural Marxism. For instance, Poulantzas (1975) tried resolutely to make his theorizing concrete. Second, he was much more engaged in ongoing revolutionary activities than other structural Marxists. In fact, over the course of his life, Poulantzas gradually moved away from a structuralist mode of analysis (Jessop, 1985). Also, Poulantzas (1975) did not try to develop a general theory, because he saw himself and other theorists as incapable of this.

Nevertheless Poulantzas does share with other structural Marxists a number of orientations. For example, he too rejected the economism of earlier Marxists:

How . . . is the neglect of theoretical study of the State . . . to be explained? . . . The absence of a study of the State derived from the fact that the dominant conception . . . was a deviation, *economism*, which is generally accompanied by an absence of revolutionary strategy. . . . In effect, economism considers the other levels of social reality, including the State, as epiphenomena reducible to the economic "base." . . . Economism considers that every change in the social system happens first of all in the economy and that political action should have the economy as its principal objective.

(Poulantzas, 1972:239)

Poulantzas (1973; 1975) rejected not only economistic Marxism but also Hegelian Marxism (for example, the work of Lukács) and the critical school, both of which emphasize subjective factors. Poulantzas especially opposed a focus on individual actors:

This is a problematic of *social actors*, of individuals as the origin of *social action*: sociological research thus leads finally, not to the study of objective co-ordinates that determine the distribution of agents into social classes and the contradictions between these classes, but to the search for *finalist* explanations founded on the *motivations of conduct* of the individual actors. This is notoriously one of the aspects of the problematic both of Weber and of contemporary functionalism. To transpose this problematic of the subject into Marxism is in the end to admit the epistemological principles of the adversary and to risk vitiating one's own analyses.

(Poulantzas, 1972:242–243)

Poulantzas also rejected a focus on the motivations of actors:

Thus the characterization of the existing social system as capitalist in no way depends on the motivations of the conduct of managers. Furthermore: to characterize the class position of managers, one need not refer to the motivations of their conduct, but only to their place in production and their relationship to the ownership of the means of production.

(Poulantzas, 1972:243–244)

The heart of Poulantzas's work and that of structural Marxism in general is the view that modern capitalism is composed of three major components—the state, ideology, and the economy. Poulantzas adopted a realist view of these structures and, unlike other structural Marxists, analyzed them in great empirical detail in his works. However, his major contribution goes beyond empirical detail and is found in the theoretical analysis that is needed to uncover the hidden structures of capitalist society. One of his key theoretical ideas (Jessop, 1985), again shared with other structural Marxists, is *relative autonomy,* or the idea that the various structures of capitalist society are relatively independent of each other. Poulantzas applied this idea more broadly than most other thinkers. He argued that the capitalist state is characterized by "the relative separation of the economic from the political, and the relative autonomy of the state from the dominant classes" (Poulantzas, 1974:313). The same point can be made about the economy and ideology. Poulantzas's extension of the idea of relative autonomy to other areas of society is distinctive. He discussed, for example, the relative autonomy of various components of a social class, such as "various cliques, factions, and clans" (Poulantzas, 1976:112). Poulantzas saw all the structural com-

NICOS POULANTZAS: A Biographical Sketch

Born in Athens, Greece, on September 21, 1936, Nicos Poulantzas became "the single most important and influential Marxist theorist of the state and politics in the postwar period" (Jessop, 1985:5). His father was a professor and a leading figure in Greek society. A precocious student, Poulantzas became fluent in French at an early age and received his baccalaureate in 1953 at age seventeen. He then entered the school of law at Athens University and completed his law degree by 1957. Although he took a law degree, it was not so much because he was interested in law as it allowed him to study philosophy and the social sciences. Although somewhat active in left-wing politics during this period, Poulantzas had not yet become a Marxist. After three years in the Greek navy, Poulantzas was admitted to the bar, but he never actually practiced law. Instead, he went abroad to do graduate work and soon found his way to Paris.

Poulantzas arrived at the Sorbonne in 1960, obtained a coveted teaching assistantship, and taught law there until 1964. He completed his doctoral dissertation in that year, and in the interim had become active in French intellectual life, developing close ties with people like Jean-Paul Sartre and Simone de Beauvoir. He married a young novelist, Annie Leclerc, in 1966, and they had a daughter in 1970.

In the 1960s and 1970s, Poulantzas grew more involved in Marxist thought and political activity. He remained in France, and his ideas were shaped by French intellectual life, but he also retained ties with Greece. He wrote about issues relevant to ongoing events in Greece and became a card-carrying member of the Greek Communist party. But as Jessop says, "He tended to react to Greek events with French eyes" (1985:13).

In the late 1960s, Poulantzas's writings began to attract international attention. He also began teaching sociology at an experimental French university. He published actively in the 1960s and 1970s and was involved in both French and Greek political life. Poulantzas committed suicide on October 3, 1979. Since that time his work has attracted world attention and is regarded as one of the most significant neo-Marxist perspectives.

ponents of capitalist society as interrelated, although he also emphasized that each is relatively autonomous.

This leads to another distinctive aspect of Poulantzas's work—his discussion of the various components of many of the structures that he analyzed. He was disinclined to think of structures as unified totalities but saw them rather as composed of a number of substructures. His best-known idea here is that of *fractions* of social classes (Poulantzas, 1975:23). In other words, a social class is not a unified totality, but is rather composed of various subunits (Poulantzas, 1976:92). Similarly, within political and ideological structures he spoke of subunits, this time called *categories* and "defined principally by their place in the political and ideological relations. Examples of categories include the state bureaucracy, defined by its relation to the state apparatuses, and the intellectuals, defined by their role in elaborating and deploying ideology" (Poulantzas, 1975:23). He also differentiated among the various subunits within the state (*apparatuses*), whose main function is maintaining social cohesion politically and ideologically. These apparatuses include

> on the one hand, the repressive state apparatus in the strict sense and its branches: army, police, prisons, judiciary, civil service; on the other hand, the ideological state apparatuses: the educational apparatus, the religious apparatus (the churches), the information apparatus (radio, television, press), the cultural apparatus (cinema, theatre, publishing), the trade-union apparatus of class collaboration and the bourgeois and petty-bourgeois political parties, etc., as well as in a certain respect, at least in the capitalist mode of production, the family.
> (Poulantzas, 1975:24–25)

Thus Poulantzas had a much more complicated image of the structures of capitalism and its numerous substructures than did many of his peers.

Poulantzas took great care in these structural differentiations, because he saw each of the substructures as having relatively autonomous social consequences. Furthermore, each has at least the potential to play a central role in society (Poulantzas, 1975; 1973).

Poulantzas's thinking on contradictions was shaped by his pluralistic image of the structures of capitalist society. Like other structural Marxists, Poulantzas did not restrict himself to the analysis of economic contradictions but was interested in, among other things, the contradictions among the economy, the polity, and ideology. Poulantzas, however, went much further and examined the contradictions among the various fractions, categories, and apparatuses within each of the three basic structural units. For example, Poulantzas argued "that every bourgeois state is riven by contradictions between its various apparatuses and branches (and not just between political parties), as the organizational bases of one or other fraction and component of the power bloc" (1976:103–104).

Poulantzas's main theoretical focus, and that of most structural Marxists, was on the interrelationship of the three major components of capitalist society. For example, he linked the state and ideology by arguing that the *state* can never exercise its function of domination, in the long run, by repression alone; this must always be accompanied by *ideological* domination (Poulantzas, 1976).

Poulantzas also linked ideology to the economy. The most important role of ideology, expressed through the socialization process, is training people to occupy various positions and occupations within the economic sector. Although he saw socialization as important, he was careful to point out that a capitalist society must not only produce (socialize) people to fill positions, but it also must continually produce the positions for these people to fill. To underscore his structuralist orientation, Poulantzas stated clearly that the primary significance lies with structural positions and not with actors and their socialization:

> While it is true that the agents themselves must be reproduced—"trained" and "subjected"—in order to occupy certain places, it is equally true that the distribution of agents does not depend on their own choices or aspirations but on the reproduction of these places themselves. This is because the principal aspect of class determination is that of their places, and not that of the agents that occupy these places.
> (Poulantzas, 1975:29)

Although he recognized the importance of socialization, Poulantzas carefully differentiated his position from that taken by many sociologists, in which ideological factors are given much greater significance than he thought due them:

However, in order to break with the misunderstandings of the "functionalist-institutionalist" tradition, which has always spoken of . . . the "socialization process," it is necessary to go further. On the one hand, . . . it is because there is extended reproduction of places, and to the extent that this is so, that there is this or that reproduction and distribution of agents between places. On the other hand, we should not forget that the determining role, as far as the distribution of agents in the social formation as a whole is concerned, falls to the labour market, as the expression of the extended reproduction of the relations of production.

(Poulantzas, 1975:34)

In terms of links between the state and the economy, Poulantzas argued that in the stage of monopoly capitalism the state acquires decisive importance. This follows logically from his more general position that "there was *never* a stage in capitalism in which the state did not play an important economic role" (Poulantzas, 1974:220; italics added).

At the most general level, Poulantzas was likely to look at the interrelationship of *all three* of the basic structures of capitalism. For example, he noted that imperialism "is not a phenomenon which can be reduced to economic developments alone. . . . Imperialism is a phenomenon with economic, political, and ideological implications" (Poulantzas, 1974:22). This is another way of saying that Poulantzas rejected the simplistic economic determinism of many Marxists. To Poulantzas the superstructure that is made of "juridico-political and ideological forms . . . intervenes decisively in the production process" (1974:41). Such a pluralistic notion led Poulantzas, like Althusser, to the notion of the uneven development of the capitalist system. This, in turn, gave Poulantzas's work a dialectic at the structural level that kept it, like the work of Althusser, from being totally deterministic.

We conclude this discussion of Poulantzas's orientation with mention of his work on social classes. As a structuralist, Poulantzas argued, according to Andor Skotnes, that "social classes are *structurally determined*; they exist objectively, independent of the will and 'consciousness' of class members" (1979:35). However, classes are not determined totally by economic structures (Poulantzas, 1974) but also by political and ideological factors. Poulantzas made a great effort to avoid that perpetual problem of structuralists, a static view of social classes. He argued that social classes are determined only in the continuing process of class struggle, which is itself broken down into economic, political, and ideological struggles. Classes are formed out of the confluence of these ongoing struggles.

Poulantzas was careful to differentiate between such a general analysis of social classes and class positions at any given historical juncture. At any particular point in history, classes or fractions of classes may take up positions not in accord with their general structural position. A labor aristocracy, for example, may identify with the bourgeoisie, or members of the middle class may take positions aligned with those of the proletariat. But these are temporary historical developments not in line with the general structure of class struggle. Thus deviations are possible within the broad sweep of history. This is another area of flexibility and dialectical process within Poulantzas's structural Marxism.

Critical Reactions to Structural Marxism

Structural Marxism has come under attack by other Marxists. First, it has been attacked for being ahistorical. The famous Marxist historian E. P. Thompson (1978) correctly viewed Althusser (whom he singled out for discussion) as unleashing an attack on precisely what Thompson is best known for—empirically oriented, historical Marxian research. Thompson argued that Althusser's position is that history is scientifically and politically valueless:

> Not only does it turn out that men have never "made their own history" at all (being only . . . vectors of ulterior structural determinations) but it is also revealed that the enterprise has been misbegotten from the start, since "real" history is unknowable and cannot be said to exist.
>
> (E. P. Thompson, 1978:194)

Thompson regarded Althusser's position as ludicrous. He argued that structuralists do not understand historical categories and therefore are unable to deal with contradiction, class struggle, and social change. Thompson argued that the structuralists have not even accomplished their goal of being true to Marx: "Althusser's structuralism is a structuralism of *stasis*, departing from Marx's own historical method" (1978:197). In the end, Thompson regarded Althusser as a dangerous intellectual who had become the darling of bourgeois intellectuals who do not really understand what he is saying. They are attracted to his work because of its pseudosophistication and because it does not require them to sully themselves in the real world of class struggle.

Similarly, Val Burris argued that structural Marxists have lost sight of the fact that to Marx the analysis of structures is specific to a given historical epoch. Thus they misrepresented historically specific structures as "universal principles of social organization" (1979:16).

Second, structural Marxists have been attacked for their blind support of scientism. "At a time when science is one of the principal legitimating props of the social order, an uncritical belief in science is urged upon us . . . [and] dogmatic authority is reasserted on all fronts" (Appelbaum, 1979:26).

Third, there is the view that structuralism leads to an elitist orientation:

> Structuralism is dogmatism—a "learned and sophisticated variety," to be sure—but dogmatism nonetheless. The Party scientists and bureaucrats alone possess truth—they alone have symptomatically read the works of Marx, Engels, Lenin, and Gramsci—and they alone understand history: they reveal the hidden facts and the underlying laws, the masses submit.
>
> (Appelbaum, 1979:25)

Fourth, structuralism has been attacked for losing sight of the actor and consciousness. As Appelbaum put it, "Here structuralism has at last arrived at its ultimate objective: it has achieved 'scientificity' by obliterating the conscious individual" (1979:25).

Fifth, structuralists have been criticized for giving inadequate attention to empirical research. This position was taken by Ralph Miliband in a response to Poulantzas's attack on his work:

> After all, it was none other than Marx who stressed the importance of empirical validation (or invalidation) and who spent many years of his life in precisely such an undertaking: and while

I do not suggest for a moment that Poulantzas is unaware of this fact, I do think that he, and the point also goes for Louis Althusser and his collaborators, may tend to give it rather less attention than it deserves.

(Miliband, 1972:256)

Sixth, structuralism has been attacked for its determinism. Miliband stated:

But his [Poulantzas's] own analysis seems to me to lead straight towards a kind of structural determinism, or rather a structural super-determinism, which makes impossible a truly realistic consideration of the dialectical relationship between the state and "the system." . . . The political danger of structural super-determinism would seem to me to be obvious. For if the state elite is as totally imprisoned in objective structures as is suggested, it follows that there is *really* no difference between a state ruled, say, by bourgeois constitutionalists, whether conservative or social-democrat and one ruled by, say, fascists.

(Miliband, 1972:259)

Interestingly, structuralism has come to be associated in the minds of some critics with sociological theories that most Marxists find anathema—structural functionalism and conflict theory:

What remains when Hegel has been excised appears to be little more than a pluralist functionalism recast in Marxian categories. . . . Thus stated, Althusser's formulation is itself a formal inversion of structural-functionalism, perhaps not so distant from what is sometimes termed "conflict theory."

(Appelbaum, 1979:27–28)

Even as sympathetic a critic as Jessop critiques the "implicit functionalism" (1985: 111) of some aspects of Poulantzas's work. Along these same lines, Nancy DiTomaso (1982) has seen strong similarities in the work of Althusser and Parsons.

Structural Marxism is one of the most controversial developments in neo-Marxian theory. It involves pointed criticism of other varieties of Marxian theory and is itself subject to much criticism by Marxists of other theoretical persuasions.

NEO-MARXIAN ECONOMIC SOCIOLOGY

As we have seen throughout this chapter, many neo-Marxists (for example, critical theorists, structural Marxists) have made relatively few comments on the economic institution, at least in part as a reaction against the excesses of the economic determinists. However, these reactions have themselves set in motion a series of counterreactions. In this section we will deal with the work of those Marxists who have returned to a focus on the economic realm. Their work does not simply repeat early Marxian theory; it constitutes an effort to adapt Marxian theory to the realities of modern capitalist society.

There is, of course, a vast literature dealing with economic issues from a Marxian point of view. Much of this is relevant only to the field of economics, but some of it also has been influential in sociology. We focus on two works that have been particularly influential in sociology—Paul Baran and Paul M. Sweezy's *Monopoly Capital*

(1966) and Harry Braverman's *Labor and Monopoly Capital* (1974). At the end of this section, we will discuss some more recent works of this genre.

Monopoly Capital

Marx's original insights into economic structures and processes were based on his analysis of the capitalism of his time—what we can think of as competitive capitalism. Capitalist industries were comparatively small, with the result that no one industry, or small group of industries, could gain complete and uncontested control over a market. Much of Marx's economic work was based on the premise, accurate for his time, that capitalism was a competitive system. To be sure, Marx foresaw the possibility of future monopolies, but he commented only briefly on them. Many later Marxian theorists continued to operate as if capitalism remained much as it had been in Marx's time.

It is in this context that we must examine the work of Baran and Sweezy (1966). They began with a criticism of Marxian social science for repeating familiar formulations and for failing to explain important recent developments in capitalistic society. They accused Marxian theory of stagnating because it continued to rest on the assumption of a competitive economy. A modern Marxian theory must, in their view, recognize that competitive capitalism has been largely replaced by monopoly capitalism.

A central issue for Baran and Sweezy was a delineation of the nature of monopoly capitalism. Monopoly capitalism means that one, or a few, capitalists control a given sector of the economy. Clearly, there is far less competition in monopoly capitalism than in competitive capitalism. In competitive capitalism, organizations competed on a price basis; that is, capitalists tried to sell more goods by offering lower prices. In monopolistic capitalism, firms no longer have to compete in this way because one or a few firms control a market; competition shifts to the sales domain. Advertising, packaging, and other methods of appealing to potential consumers are the main areas of competition.

The movement from price to sales competition is part of another process characteristic of monopoly capitalism—*progressive rationalization*. Price competition comes to be seen as highly irrational. That is, from the monopoly capitalist's point of view, offering lower and lower prices can lead only to chaos in the marketplace, to say nothing of lower profits and perhaps even bankruptcy. Sales competition, in contrast, is not a cutthroat system; in fact, it even provides work for the advertising industry. Furthermore, prices can be kept high, with the costs of the sales and promotion simply added to the price. Thus sales competition is also far less risky than price competition.

Another crucial aspect of monopoly capitalism is the rise of the giant corporation, with a few large corporations controlling most sectors of the economy. In competitive capitalism, the organization was controlled almost singlehandedly by an entrepreneur. The modern corporation is owned by a large number of stockholders, but a few large stockholders own most of the stock. Although stockholders "own" the corporation, managers exercise the actual day-to-day control. The managers are crucial in monopoly capitalism, whereas the entrepreneurs were central in competitive capitalism. Managers have considerable power, which they seek to maintain. They even seek financial independence for their firms by trying, as much as possible, to generate whatever funds they need internally rather than relying on external sources of funding.

Baran and Sweezy commented extensively on the central position of the corporate manager in modern capitalist society. Managers are viewed as a highly rational group oriented to maximizing the profits of the organization. Therefore they are not inclined to take the risks that were characteristic of the early entrepreneurs. They have a longer time perspective than the entrepreneur. Whereas the early capitalist was interested in maximizing profits in the short run, modern managers are aware that such efforts may well lead to chaotic price competition that might adversely affect the long-term profitability of the firm. The manager will thus forgo *some* profits in the short run to maximize long-term profitability.

The central issue in monopoly capitalism is the ability of the system to generate and use economic surplus. *Economic surplus* is defined as the difference between the value of what a society produces and the costs of producing it. Because of their concern with the surplus issue, Baran and Sweezy moved away from Marx's interest in the exploitation of labor and stressed instead the links between the economy and other social institutions, in particular in the absorption of economic surplus by these other institutions.

Modern capitalistic managers are victims of their own success. On the one hand, they are able to set prices arbitrarily because of their monopolistic position in the economy. On the other hand, they seek to cut costs within the organization, particularly the costs associated with blue-collar work. The ability to set high prices and to cut costs leads to the rising level of economic surplus.

The issue that then confronts the capitalist is what to do with the surplus. One possibility is to consume it—to pay managers huge salaries and stockholders huge dividends that are turned into yachts, Rolls-Royces, jewelry, and caviar. This *is* done to some extent, but the surplus is so huge that elites could never consume even a small part of it. In any case, conspicuous consumption was more characteristic of the early entrepreneurs than of the modern manager and stockholder.

A second alternative is to invest the surplus in such things as improved technology and foreign ventures. This seemingly reasonable action, which is taken by managers to some extent, has the major drawback that such investments, if made wisely, generate even more surplus. This only exacerbates the problem of using economic surplus.

Increasing sales effort also may absorb some of the surplus. Modern capitalists can stimulate the demand for their products by advertising; by creating and expanding the markets for their products; and by such devices as model changes, planned obsolescence, and readily available consumer credit. However, this alternative also has problems. First, it cannot absorb enough surplus. Second, it is likely to stimulate even further expansion of the corporation, which, in turn, leads to still greater levels of surplus.

According to Baran and Sweezy, the only choice remaining is *waste*. The surplus needs to be squandered, and there are two ways of so doing. The first is nonmilitary government spending through keeping millions of workers in government jobs and supporting myriad government programs. The second is military spending, including the military's vast payroll and its budget of billions of dollars for expensive hardware that rapidly becomes obsolete.

Baran and Sweezy's position has several weaknesses. For one thing, it seems as if there is really *no good way* of getting rid of surplus, and perhaps that is the view Baran and Sweezy wish communicated. It leaves us with the clear impression that this is an irresolvable contradiction within capitalism. Virtually all of the capitalists' expenditures lead to greater demand and ultimately to greater surpluses. Government and military employees spend their money on more goods; as some military equipment is consumed, there is a demand for new and better equipment.

Another criticism that can be leveled at Baran and Sweezy is that they overemphasize the rationality of managers. Herbert Simon (1957), for example, would argue that managers are more interested in finding (and are only able to find) minimally satisfactory solutions than they are in finding the most rational and most profitable solutions. Another issue is whether managers are, in fact, the pivotal figures in modern capitalism. Many would argue that the large stockholders really control the capitalistic system.

In sum, Baran and Sweezy accepted the traditional economic focus of Marxian theory, then moved it in a new and important direction. In particular, they shifted the focus from the labor process to economic structures of modern capitalistic society. We turn now to Braverman, who was influenced by the work of Baran and Sweezy but sought to return to the traditional Marxian interest in the labor process.

Labor and Monopoly Capital

Harry Braverman (1974) considered the labor process and the exploitation of the worker to be the heart of Marxian theory. Although his emphasis is different from that of Baran and Sweezy, he saw his work as tied closely to theirs (Braverman, 1974). The title of his book, *Labor and Monopoly Capital*, reflects his main focus, and its subtitle, *The Degradation of Work in the Twentieth Century*, shows his interest in adapting Marx's perspective to the realities of work in the twentieth century.

Braverman intended not only to update Marx's interest in manual workers but also to examine what has happened to white-collar and service workers. Marx paid little attention to these two groups, but since his time they have become major occupational categories that need to be subjected to serious scrutiny. In relation to Baran and Sweezy's work, it could be said that one of the major developments in monopoly capitalism has been the relative decline in blue-collar workers and the simultaneous increase in white-collar and service workers to staff the large organizations characteristic of monopoly capitalism.

Braverman's analysis begins with a point reminiscent of Marx's orientation. Braverman made it quite clear that his criticisms of the contemporary work world do not reflect a yearning for an era now past. He said that he was not romanticizing the old-time crafts and "the outworn conditions of now archaic modes of labor" (Braverman, 1974:6). Also like Marx, Braverman was a critic not of science and technology per se but simply of the way that they are used in capitalism "as weapons of domination in the creation, perpetuation and deepening of a gulf between classes in society" (Braverman, 1974:6). In the employ of the capitalist, science and technology have been used systematically to rob work of its craft heritage without providing anything to take its place. Braverman believed that in different (that is, socialist) hands, science and technology could be used differently to produce

> an age that has not yet come into being, in which, for the worker, the craft satisfaction that arises from conscious and purposeful mastery of the labor process will be combined with the

marvel of science and the ingenuity of engineering, an age in which everyone will be able to benefit, in some degree, from this combination.

(Braverman, 1974:7)

Toward the goal of extending Marx's analysis of blue-collar workers to white-collar and service workers, Braverman argued that the concept "working class" does not describe a specific group of people or occupations but is rather an expression of a process of buying and selling labor power. In terms of that process, Braverman argued that in modern capitalism virtually no one owns the means of production; therefore the many, including most white-collar and service workers, are forced to sell their labor power to the few who do. In his view, capitalist control and exploitation, as well as the derivative processes of mechanization and rationalization, are being extended to white-collar and service occupations, although their impact is not yet as great as it has been on blue-collar occupations.

Braverman based his analysis on Marx's anthropology, specifically his concept of human potential (species-being). Braverman argued that all forms of life need to sustain themselves in their natural environment; that is, they need to appropriate nature for their own use. Work is the process by which nature is altered in order to enhance its usefulness. In that sense, animals work, too, but what is distinctive about humans is their consciousness. People have a set of mental capacities that other animals lack. Human work is thus characterized by a unity of conception (thought) and execution (action). This unity can be dissolved, and capitalism is a crucial stage in the destruction of the unity of thought and execution in the working world.

A key ingredient in this breakdown in capitalism is the sale and purchase of labor power. Capitalists can purchase certain kinds of labor power and not others. For instance, they can purchase manual labor and insist that mental labor be kept out of the process. Although the opposite can also occur, it is less likely. As a result, capitalism is characterized by an increasing number of manual workers and fewer and fewer mental workers. This seems to contradict the statistics, which reflect a massive growth in white-collar, presumably mental, occupations. However, as we will see, Braverman believed that many white-collar occupations are being *proletarianized*, made indistinguishable in many ways from manual work.

MANAGERIAL CONTROL

Braverman recognized economic exploitation, which was Marx's focus, but concentrated on the issue of *control*. He asked the question: How do the capitalists control the labor power that they employ? One answer is that they exercise such control through managers. In fact, Braverman defined management as *"a labor process conducted for the purpose of control within the corporation"* (1974:267).

Braverman concentrated on the more impersonal means employed by managers to control workers. One of his central concerns was the utilization of specialization to control workers. Here he carefully differentiated between the division of labor in society as a whole and specialization of work within the organization. All known societies have had a division of labor (for example, between men and women, farmers and artisans, and so forth), but the specialization of work within the organization is a special development of capitalism, although it appears in existing socialist societies as well.

Braverman believed that the division of labor at the societal level may enhance the individual, whereas specialization in the workplace has the disastrous effect of subdividing human capabilities: "The subdivision of the individual, when carried on without regard to human capabilities and needs, is a crime against the person and against humanity" (1974:73).

Specialization in the workplace involves the continual division and subdivision of tasks or operations into minute and highly specialized activities, each of which is then likely to be assigned to a *different* worker. This constitutes the creation of what Braverman calls "detail workers." Out of the range of abilities any individual possesses, capitalists select a small number that the worker is to use on the job. As Braverman put it, the capitalist first breaks down the work process and then "dismembers the worker as well" (1974:78) by requiring the worker to use only a small proportion of his or her skills and abilities. In Braverman's terms, the worker "never voluntarily converts himself into a lifelong detail worker. This is the contribution of the capitalist" (1974:78).

Why does the capitalist do this? First, it increases the control of management. It is easier to control a worker doing a specified task than it is one employing a wide range of skills. Second, it increases productivity. That is, a group of workers performing highly specialized tasks can produce more than the same number of craftspeople, each of whom has all the skills and performs all the production activities. For instance, workers on an automobile assembly line produce more cars than would a corresponding number of skilled craftspeople, each of whom produces his or her own car. Third, specialization allows the capitalist to pay the least for the labor power needed. Instead of highly paid, skilled craftspeople, the capitalist can employ lower paid, unskilled workers. Following the logic of capitalism, employers seek progressively to cheapen the labor of workers, which results in a virtually undifferentiated mass of what Braverman called "simple labor."

Specialization is not a sufficient means of control for capitalists and the managers in their employ. Another important means is scientific technique, including such efforts as scientific management, which is an attempt to apply science to the control of labor on the behalf of management. To Braverman, scientific management is the science of "how best to control alienated labor" (1974:90). Scientific management is found in a series of stages aimed at the control of labor—gathering many workers in one workshop, dictating the length of the workday, supervising workers directly to ensure diligence, enforcing rules against distractions (for example, talking), and setting minimum acceptable production levels. Overall scientific management contributed to control by *"the dictation to the worker of the precise manner in which work is to be performed"* (Braverman, 1974:90). For example, Braverman discussed F. W. Taylor's early work on the shoveling of coal, which led him to develop rules about the kind of shovel to use, the way to stand, the angle at which the shovel should enter the coal pile, and how much coal to pick up in each motion. In other words, Taylor developed methods that assured almost total control over the labor process. Workers were to be left with as few independent decisions as possible; thus, a separation of the mental and manual was accomplished. Management used its monopoly over work-related knowledge to control each step of the labor process. In the end, the work itself was left without any meaningful skill, content, or knowledge. Craftsmanship was utterly destroyed.

Braverman also saw machinery as a means of control over workers. Modern machinery comes into existence "when the tool and/or the work are given a fixed motion path by the structure of the machine itself" (Braverman, 1974:188). The skill is built into the machine rather than left for the worker to acquire. Instead of controlling the work process, workers come to be controlled by the machine. Furthermore, it is far easier for management to control machines than workers.

Braverman argued that through such mechanisms as the specialization of work, scientific management, and machines, management has been able to extend its control over its manual workers. Although this is a useful insight, especially the emphasis on control, Braverman's distinctive contribution has been his effort to extend this kind of analysis to sectors of the labor force that were not analyzed in Marx's original analysis of the labor process. Braverman argued that white-collar and service workers are now being subjected to the same processes of control that were used on manual workers in the last century.

One of Braverman's examples is white-collar clerical workers. At one time such workers were considered to be a group distinguished from manual workers by such things as their dress, skills, training, and career prospects (Lockwood, 1956). However, today both groups are being subjected to the same means of control. Thus it has become more difficult to differentiate between the factory and the modern factorylike office, as the workers in the latter are progressively proletarianized. For one thing, the work of the clerical worker has grown more and more specialized. This means, among other things, that the mental and manual aspects of office work have been separated. Office managers, engineers, and technicans now perform the mental work whereas the "line" clerical workers do little more than manual tasks such as typing, filing, and keypunching. As a result, the level of skills needed for these jobs has been lowered, and the jobs require little or no special training.

Scientific management also is now seen as invading the office. Clerical tasks have been scientifically studied, and as a result of that research, they have been simplified, routinized, and standardized. Finally, mechanization is beginning to make significant inroads into the office, primarily through the computer and computer-related equipment.

By applying these mechanisms to clerical work, managers find it much easier to control such workers. It is unlikely that such control mechanisms are as strong and effective in the office as in the factory; still, the trend is toward the development of the white-collar "factory."[5]

Several obvious criticisms can be leveled at Braverman. For one thing, he has probably overestimated the degree of similarity between manual and clerical work. For another, his preoccupation with control has led him to devote relatively little attention to the dynamics of economic exploitation in capitalism. Nonetheless, he has enriched our understanding of the labor process in modern capitalist society.

---

[5]It is important to note that Braverman's book was written before the boom in computer technology in the office, especially the now-widespread use of the word processor. It may be that such technology, requiring greater skill and training than older office technologies, will serve to increase worker autonomy.

More Recent Examples of Marxian Economic Sociology

Sociological work on the economy, influenced in whole or in part by Marxian theory, continues to develop (*Theory and Society*, 1986; Zukin and DiMaggio, 1986). Before closing this section, we briefly examine a few of the major recent works of this genre.

Although Braverman recognized economic exploitation, which was Marx's focus, he concentrated, as we have seen, on the issue of managerial *control* over workers. The issue of control is even more central to Richard Edwards in his book, *Contested Terrain: The Transformation of the Workplace in the Twentieth Century* (1979). To Edwards control lies at the heart of the twentieth-century transformation of the workplace. Following Marx, Edwards sees the workplace, both past and present, as an arena of class conflict, in his terms a "contested terrain." Within this arena, dramatic changes have taken place in the way in which those at the top control those at the bottom. During nineteenth-century competitive capitalism, "simple" control was used in which "bosses exercised power personally, intervening in the labor process often to exhort workers, bully and threaten them, reward good performance, hire and fire on the spot, favor loyal employees, and generally act as despots, benevolent or otherwise" (Edwards, 1979:19). Although this system of control continues in many small businesses, it has proven too crude for modern, large-scale organizations. In such organizations, simple control has tended to be replaced by impersonal and more sophisticated technical and bureaucratic control. Modern workers can be controlled by the technologies with which they work. The classic example of this is the automobile assembly line in which the workers' actions are determined by the incessant demands of the line. Another example is the modern computer, which can keep careful track of how much work an employee does and how many mistakes he or she makes. Modern workers also are controlled by the impersonal rules of bureaucracies rather than the personal control of supervisors. Capitalism is constantly changing and with it the means by which workers are controlled.

Also of note is Michael Burawoy's *Manufacturing Consent: Changes in the Labor Process under Monopoly Capital* (1979). Burawoy is interested in the question of why workers in a capitalist system work so hard. He rejects Marx's explanation that such hard work is a result of coercion. The advent of labor unions and other changes have largely eliminated the arbitrary power of management. "Coercion alone could no longer explain what workers did once they arrived on the shop floor" (Burawoy, 1979:xii). To Burawoy, workers, at least in part, consent to work hard in the capitalist system, and at least part of that consent is produced in the workplace.

We can illustrate Burawoy's approach with one aspect of his research, the games that workers play on the job and, more generally, the informal practices that they develop. Most analysts see these as workers' efforts to reduce alienation and other job-related discontent. In addition, they usually have been seen as social mechanisms that workers develop to oppose management. In contrast, Burawoy concludes that these games "are usually neither independent nor in opposition to management" (1979:80). In fact, "Management, at least at the lower levels, actually participates not only in the organization of the game, but in the enforcement of its rules." Rather than challenging management, the organization or, ultimately, the capitalist system, these games actually support them. For one thing, playing the game creates consent among the workers about the rules on which the game is based and, more generally, about the system of social relations (owner-manager-worker) that defines the rules of the game. Second, because managers and workers both are involved in the game, the system of antagonistic social relations to which the game was supposed to respond is obscured.

Burawoy argues that such methods of generating active cooperation and consent are far more effective in getting workers to cooperate in the pursuit of profit than coercion (such as firing those who do not cooperate). In the end, Burawoy believes that games and other informal practices all are methods of getting workers to accept the system and of eliciting their contributions to ever higher profits.

One other work worth noting is Dan Clawson's *Bureaucracy and the Labor Process* (1980), in which he examines the bureaucratization and technological advance of American industry between 1860 and 1920. His main thesis is that the degradation of work during this period was (and is) *not* inevitable. That is, this problem was not inherent in bureaucracy and technology, but in the way that they were employed in capitalist society. In Clawson's view, therefore, we can have efficiency, abundance, *and* satisfying human work. Work was degraded because capitalists used bureaucracies and technologies to control laborers and the labor process. Clawson takes as his objective and the objective of socialism the "reorganization of the labor process, so that it becomes the most important arena for people to freely develop their human capacities rather than an area where people are mutilated and degraded" (1980:260).

In sum, the works of Baran and Sweezy, Braverman, Edwards, Burawoy, and Clawson represent a return to the traditional Marxian focus on the economic sector. At a theoretical level, they are valuable for reinstilling interest in the economic factor as well as refining and making more contemporary our understanding of this dimension. In addition, they have been important sources of sociological thinking and research into various aspects of work and industry.

HISTORICALLY ORIENTED MARXISM

Structural Marxism makes the case *for* ahistorical and *against* historical analyses, but many Marxists are oriented toward historical research. In adopting this orientation, they argue that they are being true to the Marxian concern for historicity. The most notable of Marx's historical researches was his study of precapitalist economic formations (Marx, 1857–1858/1964). There is a good deal of subsequent historical work from a Marxian perspective (for example, Amin, 1977; Dobb, 1964; Hobsbawm, 1965). In this section, we deal with two pieces of work that reflect a historical orientation—Immanuel Wallerstein's *The Modern World-System* (1974) and Theda Skocpol's *States and Social Revolutions* (1979). Although these are not typical of Marxian historical research in all respects, they are among the most influential in contemporary sociology.

The Modern World-System

Wallerstein chose a unit of analysis unlike those used by most Marxian thinkers. He did not look at workers, classes, or even states, because he found most of these too narrow for his purposes. Instead, he looked at a broad economic entity with a division of labor that is not circumscribed by political or cultural boundaries. He found that unit in his concept of the *world-system*, which is a largely self-contained social system with a set of boundaries and a definable life span; that is, it does not last forever. It is composed internally of a variety of social structures and member groups. However, Wallerstein was not inclined to define the system in terms of a consensus that holds it together. Rather, he saw the system as held together by a variety of forces that are in inherent tension. These forces always have the potential for tearing the system apart.

The world-system is a very abstract concept, and in fact Wallerstein offered it only at the end of his book, after he had discussed all the historical detail needed for its formulation. Wallerstein argued that thus far we have had only two types of world-systems. One was the world empire, of which ancient Rome is an example. The other is the modern capitalist world-economy. A world empire is based on political (and military) domination, whereas a capitalist world-economy relies on economic domination. A capitalist world-economy is seen as more stable than a world empire for several reasons. For one thing, it has a broader base, because it encompasses many states. For another, it has a built-in process of economic stabilization. The separate political entities within the capitalist world-economy absorb whatever losses occur, while economic gain is distributed to private hands. Wallerstein foresaw the *possibility* of still a third world-system, a *socialist world government*. Whereas the capitalist world-economy separates the political from the economic sector, a socialist world-economy would reintegrate them.

To orient the reader for the historical discussion to follow, we now introduce the concepts developed by Wallerstein that describe the geographical division of labor in the world-system of greatest concern to him—the capitalist world-economy—the core, the periphery, and the semiperiphery. In general, the *core* geographical area dominates the world economy and exploits the rest of the system. The *periphery* consists of those areas that provide raw materials to the core and are heavily exploited by it. The *semiperiphery* is a residual category that encompasses a set of regions somewhere between the exploiting and the exploited. The key point here is that to Wallerstein the international division of exploitation is defined not by state borders but by the economic division of labor in the world.

Although Wallerstein had a broader, long-term interest, in *The Modern World-System* (1974) he dealt with the origin of the world system roughly between the years 1450 and 1640. The significance of this development was the shift from political (and thus military) to economic dominance. Wallerstein saw economics as a far more efficient and less primitive means of domination than politics. Political structures are very cumbersome, whereas economic exploitation "makes it possible to increase the flow of the surplus from the lower strata to the upper strata, from the periphery to the center, from the majority to the minority" (Wallerstein, 1974:15). In the modern era, capitalism had provided a basis for the growth and development of a world-economy; this has been accomplished without the aid of a unified political structure. Capitalism can be seen as an economic alternative to political domination. It is better able to produce economic surpluses than the more primitive techniques employed in political exploitation.

Wallerstein argued that three things were necessary for the rise of the capitalist world-economy out of the "ruins" of feudalism: geographical expansion through exploration and colonization; development of different methods of labor control for zones (for example, core, periphery) of the world-economy; and development of strong states that were to become the core states of the emerging capitalist world-economy. Let us look at each of these in turn.

GEOGRAPHICAL EXPANSION

Wallerstein argued that geographical expansion by nations is a prerequisite for the other two stages. Portugal took the lead in overseas exploration, and other European nations followed. Wallerstein was wary of talking about specific countries or about Europe in

---

IMMANUEL WALLERSTEIN: A Biographical Sketch

Although he achieved recognition in the 1960s as an expert on Africa, Immanuel Wallerstein's most important contribution to sociology is his 1974 book, *The Modern World-System*. That book was an instant success. It has received world wide recognition and has been translated into nine languages and Braille.

Born on September 28, 1930, Wallerstein received all of his degrees from Columbia University, including a doctorate in 1959. He next assumed a position on the faculty at Columbia; after many years there, and a five-year stint at McGill University in Montreal, Wallerstein became, in 1976, Distinguished Professor of Sociology at the State University of New York at Binghamton.

Wallerstein was awarded the prestigious Sorokin Award for *The Modern World-System* in 1975. Since that time, he has continued to work on the topic and has produced a number of articles as well as a second volume, in which he takes his analysis of the world-system up to the year 1750. We can anticipate more work from Wallerstein on this issue in the coming years. He is in the process of producing a body of work that will attract attention for years to come.

In fact, in many ways the attention it has already attracted and will continue to attract is more important than the body of work itself. The concept of world-system has become the focus of thought and research in sociology, an accomplishment few scholars can lay claim to. Many of the sociologists now doing research and theorizing about the world-system are critical of Wallerstein in one way or another, but they all clearly recognize the important role he played in the genesis of their ideas.

Although the concept of the world-system is an important contribution, at least as significant has been the role Wallerstein played in the revival of theoretically informed historical research. The most important work in the early years of sociology, by people like Marx, Weber, and Durkheim, was largely of this variety. However, in more recent years, most sociologists have turned away from this kind of research and toward using such ahistorical methods as questionnaires and interviews. These methods are quicker and easier to use than historical methods, and the data produced are easier to analyze with a computer. Use of such methods tends to require a narrow range of technical knowledge rather than a wide range of historically oriented knowledge. Furthermore, theory plays a comparatively minor role in research utilizing questionnaires and interviews. Wallerstein has been in the forefront of those involved in a revival of interest in historical research with a strong theoretical base.

general terms. He preferred to see overseas expansion as caused by a group of people acting in their immediate interests. Elite groups, such as nobles, needed overseas expansion for various reasons. For one thing, they were confronted with a nascent class war brought on by the crumbling of the feudal economy. The slave trade provided them with a tractable labor force on which to build the capitalist economy. The expansion also provided them with various commodities needed to develop it—gold bullion, food, and raw materials of various types.

A WORLDWIDE DIVISION OF LABOR

Once the world had undergone geographical expansion, it was prepared for the next stage, the development of a worldwide division of labor. In the sixteenth century, capitalism replaced statism as the major mode of dominating the world, but capitalism did not develop uniformly around the world. In fact, Wallerstein argued, the solidarity of the capitalist system was ultimately based on its unequal development. Given his Marxian orientation, Wallerstein did not think of this as a consensual equilibrium, but rather as one that was laden with conflict from the beginning. Different parts of the capitalist world-system came to specialize in specific functions—breeding labor power, growing food, providing raw materials, and organizing industry. Furthermore, different areas came to specialize in producing particular types of workers. For example, Africa produced slaves; western and southern Europe had many peasant tenant-farmers; western Europe was also the center of wage workers, the ruling classes, and other skilled and supervisory personnel.

More generally, each of the three parts of the international division of labor tended to differ in terms of mode of labor control. The core had free labor; the periphery was characterized by forced labor; and the semiperiphery was the heart of sharecropping. In fact, Wallerstein argued that the key to capitalism lies in a core dominated by a free labor market for skilled workers and a coercive labor market for less skilled workers in peripheral areas. Such a combination is the essence of capitalism. If a free labor market should develop throughout the world, we would have socialism.

Some regions of the world begin with small initial advantages, which are used as the basis for developing greater advantages later on. The core area in the sixteenth century, primarily western Europe, rapidly extended its advantages as towns flourished, industries developed, and merchants became important. It also moved to extend its domain by developing a wider variety of activities. At the same time, each of its activities became more specialized in order to produce more efficiently. In contrast, the periphery stagnated and moved more toward what Wallerstein called a "monoculture," or an undifferentiated, single-focus society.

DEVELOPMENT OF CORE STATES

The third stage of the development of the world-system involved the political sector and how various economic groups used state structures to protect and advance their interests. Absolute monarchies arose in western Europe at about the same time as capitalism developed. From the sixteenth to the eighteenth centuries, the states were the central economic actors in Europe, although the center later shifted to economic enterprises. The strong states in the core areas played a key role in the development of capitalism and ultimately provided the economic base for their own demise. The European states strengthened themselves in the sixteenth century by, among other things, developing and enlarging bureaucratic systems and creating a monopoly of force in society, primarily by developing armies and legitimizing their activities so that they were assured of internal stability. Whereas the states of the core zone developed strong political systems, the periphery developed correspondingly weak states.

In addition to this general perspective, Wallerstein offered considerable historical detail on the various European states and their roles in the development of the world economy. In fact, Wallerstein would probably say that his theoretical system emerged from his historical data, because this would be in line with the orientation of historical Marxian sociologists, who do not want to separate empirical historical research from theory. Thus Wallerstein described the rise and fall of Spain and the Netherlands as centers of the world economy and then described the more pervasive influence of England. This historical detail was important to the development of Wallerstein's conceptual system.

In a later work, Wallerstein (1980) picked up the story of the consolidation of the world economy between 1600 and 1750. This was not a period of a significant expansion of the European world economy, but there were a number of significant changes within that system. For example, Wallerstein discussed the rise and subsequent decline in the core of the Netherlands. Later, he analyzed the conflict between two core states, England and France, as well as the ultimate victory of England. In the periphery, Wallerstein detailed, among other things, the cyclical fortunes of Hispanic America. In the semiperiphery we witness, among other things, the decline of Spain and the rise of Sweden. Wallerstein continued his historical analysis from a Marxian viewpoint of the various roles played by different societies within the division of labor of the world economy. Although Wallerstein paid close attention to political and social factors, his main focus remained the role of economic factors in world history.

Marxists have criticized the world-system perspective for its failure to adequately emphasize relations between social classes (Bergesen, 1984). From their point of view, Wallerstein focuses on the wrong issue. To them the key is not the core-periphery international division of labor, but rather class relationships *within* given societies. Bergesen seeks to reconcile these positions by arguing that there are strengths and weaknesses on both sides. His middle-ground position is that core-periphery relations are not only unequal exchange relations, but also global *class* relations. His key point is that core-periphery relations *are* important, not only as exchange relations, as Wallerstein argues, but also, and more important, as power-dependence relationships, that is, class relationships.

States and Social Revolutions

Another example of Marxian-influenced historical research is Theda Skocpol's *States and Social Revolutions* (1979). Although she shared some intellectual roots with Wallerstein, she had a much different orientation. Skocpol recognized the importance of Wallerstein's work and of the world-system, but she argued that it is not necessary to "accept arguments that national economic developments are actually determined by the overall structure and market dynamics of a 'world capitalist system'" (1979:70).

In fact, she accused Wallerstein of being "economically reductionistic." Similarly, Skocpol accorded Marx the central position in her theoretical roots, even though she was also critical of him: "Marxism failed to foresee or adequately explain the autonomous power, for good or ill, of states as administrative and coercive machineries embedded in a militarized international states system" (1979:292). Skocpol thus made it clear that although she was working within the Marxian tradition, she intended to stress political rather than economic factors.

In a historical-comparative study that focused on social revolutions in France (1787–1800), Russia (1917–1921), and China (1911–1949), Skocpol concentrated on the similarities among these revolutions. However, she was also attuned to crucial differences. Her objective was to develop explanations of social revolutions that were both historically grounded and generalizable. For comparative purposes, Skocpol also looked at nations (Japan, Prussia, England) where revolutions did not take place.

The focus of Skocpol's research was social revolutions, which she defined as "rapid, basic transformations of a society's state and class structures; and they are accompanied and in part carried through by class-based revolts from above" (Skocpol, 1979:4). Despite this objective, she returned over and over again to economic (class-based) considerations.

In that our focus is on theory, the general principles that stand behind her work are our concern here. First, she intended to adopt what she called a "structural, nonvoluntaristic perspective." Second, she considered it important to single out the international and world-historical contexts for particular examination. Third, her objective was to focus on the *state* as at least a potentially autonomous unit. We shall consider each of these principles separately.

Skocpol began by setting her approach apart from what she called "voluntaristic images" (1979:14) of how revolutions occur. Most observers, in her view, see revolutions as deliberate efforts by leaders, followers, or both. She saw this tendency in Marx's work itself, but it was exaggerated by those who followed in his tradition. This is manifest in the Marxian focus on such factors as class consciousness and the party organization. However, Skocpol rejected this position outright: "No successful social revolution has ever been 'made' by a mass-mobilizing, avowedly revolutionary movement" (1979:17).

In rejecting a voluntaristic image of social revolutions, Skocpol rejected a focus on both the thoughts and motives of actors and the large-scale idea systems, such as ideology and class consciousness. Skocpol's focus on the structural level *may* be right, but that does not mean that the other levels are insignificant.

In Skocpol's view revolutions are not made; they happen. This includes both causes and outcomes of revolutions. We need to focus on the structural factors that cause revolutions. As she pointedly put it: "A structural perspective . . . is essential for the analysis of social revolutions" (Skocpol, 1979:18).

Skocpol recognized the importance of intranational factors, but she underscored the importance of transnational, or international, factors: "Transnational relations have contributed to the emergence of all social revolutionary crises and have invariably helped to shape revolutionary struggles and outcomes" (1979:18). However, she set herself apart from Wallerstein, who had adopted a similar perspective. He focused on international *economic* relations, whereas her intention was to focus on international *political* factors. Although not denying the importance of international economic variables, Skocpol looked to what she called the "international system of competing states." However, she did recognize the interplay between the two factors: "Throughout modern history, it [the international states system] represents an analytically autonomous level of transnational realism—interdependent in its structure and dynamics with world capitalism, but not reducible to it" (Skocpol, 1979:2).

Skocpol differentiated between two aspects of transnational relations in time—the structural relationships between states in the contemporary period, and relationships between states over time. For example, actors in a later revolution are affected by the successes and failures of actors in an earlier revolution. Breakthroughs such as the Industrial Revolution create a series of new opportunities and necessities between one social revolution and the other.

Within the structural realm, Skocpol singled out the state for special attention. She said that the state is "a structure with a logic and interests of its own not necessarily equivalent to, or fused with, the interests of the dominant class in society or the full set of member groups in the polity" (Skocpol, 1979:27). She argued that there is a need for an explanation of social revolutions that is more state-centered than economic-centered. Political factors are not epiphenomena but rather have direct effects on social revolutions. Skocpol here adopted the structural Marxian position on the potential autonomy of the state. However, she was careful to point out that the degree to which the state is autonomous, free from class control, varies from one setting to another.

Skocpol closed her theoretical introduction with a clear statement of her perspective:

> We shall analyze the causes and processes of social revolutions from a nonvoluntarist, structural perspective, attending to international and world-historical, as well as intranational structures and processes. And an important theoretical concomitant will be to move states—understood as potentially autonomous organizations located at the interface of class structures and international situations—to the very center of attention.
>
> (Skocpol, 1979:33)

Skocpol found the roots of the French, Russian, and Chinese revolutions in the political crises that existed in what she termed their "old-regime states." Crises developed when those states were unable to meet the challenges of evolving international relations. The states faced not only international problems but intranational conflicts among social classes, especially between the landed aristocracy and the peasantry. Unable to cope with these pressures, the old-regime autocratic states broke down.

These crises made the situation ripe for revolution, but a revolution would not have occurred unless the sociopolitical structures were conducive to it. Because these were primarily agrarian societies, the peasantry rather than the urban workers were crucial to the revolution. Skocpol said, "Peasant revolts have been the crucial insurrectionary ingredient in virtually all (that is, successful) social revolutions to date" (1979: 112–113).

In this explanation of peasant revolts, Skocpol rejected extant theories that focus on ideology as well as theories focusing on relative deprivation of actors. Instead, her view was that the key factors in peasant rebellions are structural and situational. One such factor is the degree of solidarity of the peasant communities. Another is the degree of freedom of the peasants from the direct day-to-day supervision and control of land-lords and their agents. Finally, the relaxation of the state's coercive sanctions against peasants is likely to be conducive to revolutionary activity. The susceptibility of the old-regime states to international pressures and the existence of such structures in the agrarian sector were, in Skocpol's view, the "sufficient" causes of the revolutions in France in 1789, Russia in 1917, and China in 1911.

Such structural factors were significant not only in the genesis of social revolutions but also in their outcomes. That is, the outcomes of these revolutions were "funda-mental and enduring structural transformations" in the societies in question (Skocpol, 1979:161). There are important variations in the cases she studied, but there are also these important similarities. First, the agrarian class relationships were dramatically transformed. Second, the autocratic and proto-bureaucratic regimes of the old states were replaced by bureaucratic, professionalized states able to manage masses of peo-ple. Third, the prerevolutionary landed upper classes lost exclusive privileges.

In her discussion of structural outcomes of revolutions, Skocpol attacked those who emphasize ideological factors. She refused to see the leaders of social revolutions as merely the representatives of social classes and their actions as simple reflections of the ideologies of those classes. Rather, she wanted to focus on what revolutionary leaders *do*—struggle for state power. She took their activities more seriously than the ideo-logical pressures on them. Furthermore, the results of their activities are determined not by ideologies but by structural exigencies: "Revolutionary crises are *not* total breakpoints in history that suddenly make anything at all possible if only it is envisaged by willful revolutionaries" (Skocpol, 1979:171). We need to look at real structural forces and constraints and not people's ideas about them.

RECENT DEVELOPMENTS:
GAME-THEORETIC MARXISM

Neo-Marxian theory today is lively. There are changes in the schools discussed earlier and the development of new theoretical perspectives. One such development is what Scott Lash and John Urry (1984) have called "game-theoretic" Marxism. It has ap-peared most notably in the work of John Roemer (1982) and Jon Elster (1982). As the name suggests, this variety of Marxian theory has its origins in game theory, prominent in economics. This theory begins with the assumption that actors are rational and seek to maximize their gains. Although it recognizes structural constraints, it does not sug-gest that they completely determine actors' choices. Game-theoretic Marxism thus continues the effort so prominent in critical theory to give Marxian theory a micro-foundation, although game theory's rational actor is very different from critical theory's actor, who is derived largely from a Freudian base.

Game theory allows the analyst to go beyond the rational choices of a single actor and to deal with the interdependence of the decisions and actions of a number of actors. The analysis of "games" (intellectual games such as "prisoner's dilemma," in which actors end up worse off if they follow their self-interests than if they sacrifice those in-terests) helps explain the strategies of the various actors and the emergence of such col-lectivities as social classes.

We can illustrate this approach by Elster's recent *Making Sense of Marx* (1985), in which he argues that Marx's basic method for explaining social phenomena was a concern for the unintended consequences of human action. To Elster, Marx practiced "methodological individualism," or "the doctrine that all social phenomena—their structure and their change—are in principle explicable in ways that only involve individuals—their properties, their goals, their beliefs and their actions" (1985:5). To Elster, Marx was concerned with actors, their intentions, and their rational choices. He fully recognizes that this view stands in stark contrast to the macro-structural positions that have dominated Marxian theory (and this chapter). He contrasts his position to theirs in the case of the capitalist: "Capitalist entrepreneurs are *agents* in the genuinely active sense. They cannot be reduced to mere place-holders in the capitalist system of production" (Elster, 1985:13). Game-theoretic Marxism focuses on these rational agents (capitalist and proletarian) and their interrelationships.

SUMMARY

In this chapter we examine a wide range of approaches that can be categorized as neo-Marxian sociological theories. All of them take Marx's work as their point of departure, but they often go in very different directions. Although these diverse developments give neo-Marxian theory considerable vitality, they also create at least some unnecessary and largely dysfunctional differentiation and controversy. Thus one task for the modern Marxian sociological theorist is to integrate this broad array of theories while recognizing the value of various specific pieces of work.

The first neo-Marxian theory historically, but the least important at present, especially to the sociologically oriented thinker, is economic determinism. It was against this limited view of Marxian theory that other varieties developed. Hegelian Marxism, especially in the work of Georg Lukács, was one such reaction. This approach sought to overcome the limitations in economic determinism by returning to the subjective, Hegelian roots of Marxian theory. Hegelian Marxism is also of little contemporary relevance; its significance lies largely in its impact on later neo-Marxian theories.

The critical school, which was the inheritor of the tradition of Hegelian Marxism, *is* of contemporary importance to sociology. The great contributions of the critical theorists (Marcuse, Habermas, and so forth) are the insights offered into culture, consciousness, and their interrelationships. These theorists have enhanced our understanding of such cultural phenomena as instrumental rationality, the "culture industry," the "knowledge industry," communicative action, domination, and legitimations. To this they add a concern with consciousness, primarily in the form of an integration of Freudian theory in their work. However, critical theory has gone too far in its efforts to compensate for the limitations of economic determinism; it needs to reintegrate a concern for economics, indeed, for large-scale social forces in general.

Another vibrant neo-Marxian approach is structural Marxism. Whereas the critical school emphasizes subjective factors, the structural Marxists focus primarily on structural factors. Structural Marxists like Althusser and Poulantzas also take economic determinism as their starting point. This leads them toward such structures as the state and ideology, which are seen as having "relative autonomy" vis-á-vis the economy.

Nevertheless, the economy is still seen as *the* most important structural factor. The structural Marxists not only reject the limitations of economic determinism at the structural level but are also highly critical of the subjectivity of the critical school and Hegelian Marxism. They regard these developments as dangerous, antiscientific trends in Marxian theory. Although the structural Marxists are highly critical of other branches of Marxian theory, they themselves have been the subject of a series of strong attacks from both within and without Marxian theory.

The chapter continues with two other major examples of neo-Marxian theory. The first, represented especially by the work of Baran and Sweezy and of Braverman, is an effort to return to the traditional economic focus of Marxian theory. This work is significant for its effort to update Marxian economics by taking into account the realities of modern capitalist society. Second, there are two examples of Marxian historical scholarship: Wallerstein, who analyzed economics and world-systems; and Skocpol, who focused on politics and social revolution.

Of course, Marxian theory continues to develop and change. We have touched on some very recent developments in this chapter (game-theoretic Marxism) and in Chapter 9, under the heading of structuralism, we discuss the ideas of Michel Foucault, whose work comes in part out of a Marxian tradition and has come to represent a challenge to that tradition (Jay, 1984).

In sum, modern Marxian sociological theory is lively, controversial, sometimes confused, and likely to continue to attract the attention of large numbers of sociologists.

CHAPTER FIVE
Symbolic Interactionism

LIKE other major sociological theories, symbolic interactionism presents an extremely broad perspective. The theories of George Herbert Mead and, to a lesser extent, Charles Horton Cooley and W. I. Thomas provided its initial cohesive core, but it has become a group of clearly differentiated perspectives in recent years. Traditional symbolic interactionism is represented by the ideas of Herbert Blumer; other varieties include Manford Kuhn's more "scientific" approach, Erving Goffman's dramaturgical approach, and perhaps even ethnomethodology and phenomenology.[1] The last two theories are conceived of as separate orientations[2] and will be dealt with in Chapter 6. Here we discuss the core of symbolic interaction theory, as represented primarily in the works of Mead and Blumer, although some of the other approaches also receive attention.

---

[1] This was manifest in the plenary session of the 1979 meetings at the Society of Symbolic Interaction, at which the theme was varieties of symbolic interaction. Two of the speakers were George Psathas (a phenomenologist) and Don Zimmerman (an ethnomethodologist).

[2] For a debate between symbolic interactionists and an ethnomethodologist that points out the the deep differences between these two schools, see Gallant and Kleinman (1983; 1985); Rawls (1985).

THE MAJOR HISTORICAL ROOTS

We begin our discussion of symbolic interactionism with Mead,[3] who actually taught philosophy, not sociology, at the University of Chicago from 1894 to 1931 (Faris, 1970). However, many graduate students in sociology took his courses. Those students were later instrumental in Mead's "oral tradition" of symbolic interactionism (M. Kuhn, 1964) being turned into a written one, since their notes from Mead's classes were used as the basis for his seminal work, *Mind, Self and Society: From the Standpoint of a Social Behaviorist* (Mead, 1934/1962). The two most significant intellectual roots of Mead's work in particular, and of symbolic interactionism in general, are the philosophy of pragmatism and psychological behaviorism (Rock, 1979).

Pragmatism

Pragmatism is a wide-ranging philosophical position, from which we can identify several aspects that influenced Mead's developing sociological orientation (Charon, 1985). First, to pragmatists truth, or reality, does not exist "out there" in the real world; it "is actively created as we act in and toward the world" (Hewitt, 1984:8; see also Shalin, 1986). Second, people remember and base their knowledge of the world on what has proven useful to them. They are likely to alter what no longer "works." Third, people define the social and physical "objects" that they encounter in the world according to their use for them. Finally, if we want to understand actors, we must base that understanding on what they actually do in the world. Three points are critical for symbolic interactionism: (1) a focus on the interaction between the actor and the world; (2) a view of both the actor and the world as dynamic processes and not static structures; and (3) the great importance attributed to the actor's ability to interpret the social world.

The last point is most pronounced in the work of the philosophical pragmatist John Dewey. Dewey did not conceive of the mind as a thing or a structure, but rather as a thinking process that involves a series of stages. These stages include defining objects in the social world, outlining possible modes of conduct, imagining the consequences of alternative courses of action, eliminating unlikely possibilities, and finally selecting the optimal mode of action (Stryker, 1980). This focus on the thinking process was enormously influential in the development of symbolic interactionism.

In fact, David Lewis and Richard Smith argue that Dewey (along with William James) was more influential in the development of symbolic interactionism than Mead. They go so far as to say that "Mead's work was peripheral to the mainstream of early Chicago sociology" (Lewis and Smith, 1980:xix).[4] In making this argument, they distinguish between two branches of pragmatism—"philosophical realism" (associated with Mead) and "nominalist pragmatism" (associated with Dewey and James). In their view, symbolic interactionism was more influenced by the nominalist approach and even inconsistent with philosophical realism. The nominalist position is that although macro-level phenomena exist, they do not have "independent and determining

---

[3]The entire Fall, 1981 issue of *Symbolic Interaction* was devoted to Mead; see also Fisher and Strauss (1979).

[4]For a review symposium on this work, see *Symbolic Interaction* 6 (1983): 127–174.

effects upon the consciousness of and behavior of individuals'' (Lewis and Smith, 1980:24). More positively, this view ''conceives of the individuals themselves as existentially free agents who accept, reject, modify, or otherwise 'define' the community's norms, roles, beliefs, and so forth, according to their own personal interests and plans of the moment'' (Lewis and Smith, 1980:24). In contrast, to social realists the emphasis is on society and how it constitutes and controls individual mental processes. Rather than being free agents, actors and their cognitions and behaviors are controlled by the larger community.[5]

Given this distinction, Mead fits better into the realist camp and therefore did not mesh well with the nominalist direction taken by symbolic interactionism. The key figure in the latter development is Herbert Blumer who, while claiming to operate with a Meadian approach, was in fact himself better thought of as a nominalist. The issue of the differences between Mead and Blumer is important; we encounter it later in this chapter in a discussion of methodology. Theoretically, Lewis and Smith catch the essence of their differences:

> Blumer . . . moved completely toward psychical interactionism. . . . Unlike the Meadian social behaviorist, the psychical interactionist holds that the meanings of symbols are not universal and objective; rather meanings are individual and subjective in that they are ''attached'' to the symbols by the receiver according to however he or she chooses to ''interpret'' them.
>
> (Lewis and Smith, 1980:172)

Behaviorism

Buttressing the Lewis and Smith interpretation of Mead is the fact that he was also influenced by psychological behaviorism, a perspective which also led him in a realist and empirical direction. In fact, Mead called his basic concern *social behaviorism* to differentiate it from the *radical behaviorism* of John B. Watson.

Radical behaviorists of Watson's persuasion were concerned with the *observable* behaviors of individuals. Their focus was on the stimuli that elicited the responses, or behaviors, in question. They either denied or were disinclined to attribute much importance to the covert mental process that occurred between the time that a stimulus was applied and a response emitted. Mead recognized the importance of observable behavior, but he also felt that there were *covert* aspects of behavior that the radical behaviorists had ignored. But because he accepted the empiricism that was basic to behaviorism, Mead did not simply want to philosophize about these covert phenomena. Rather, he sought to extend the empirical science of behaviorism to them—that is, to what goes on between stimulus and response. Bernard Meltzer summarized Mead's position:

> For Mead, the unit of study is ''the act,'' which comprises both overt and covert aspects of human action. Within the act, all the separated categories of the traditional, orthodox psychologies find a place. Attention, perception, imagination, reasoning, emotion, and so forth, are seen as parts of the act . . . the act, then encompasses the total process involved in human activity.
>
> (Meltzer, 1964/1978:23)

---

[5]For a criticism of the distinctions made here, see D. Miller (1982; 1985).

Mead and the radical behaviorists also differed in their views on the relationship between human and animal behavior. Whereas radical behaviorists tended to see no difference between humans and animals, Mead argued that there was a significant, qualitative difference. The key to this difference was seen as the human possession of mental capacities that allowed people to use language between stimulus and response in order to decide how to respond.

Mead simultaneously demonstrated his debt to Watsonian behaviorism and dissociated himself from it. Mead made this clear when he said that on the one hand, "we shall approach this latter field [social psychology] from a behavioristic point of view." On the other hand, Mead criticized Watson's position when he said: "The behaviorism which we shall make use of is *more adequate* than that of which Watson makes use" (1934/1962:2; italics added).

Charles Morris, in his introduction to *Mind, Self and Society*, enumerated three basic differences between Mead and Watson. First, Mead considered Watson's exclusive focus on behavior too simplistic. In effect, he accused Watson of wrenching behavior out of its broader social context. Mead wanted to deal with behavior as a small part of the broader social world.

Second, Mead accused Watson of an unwillingness to extend behaviorism into mental processes. Watson had no sense of the actor's consciousness and mental processes, as Mead made vividly clear: "John B. Watson's attitude was that of the Queen in *Alice in Wonderland*—'Off with their heads!'—there were no such things. There was no . . . consciousness" (1934/1962:2-3). Mead contrasted his perspective with Watson's: "It is behavioristic, but unlike Watsonian behaviorism it recognizes the parts of the act which do not come to external observation" (1934/1962:8). More concretely, Mead saw his mission as extending the principles of Watsonian behaviorism to include mental processes.

Finally, because Watson rejected the mind, Mead saw him as having a passive image of the actor as puppet. Mead, on the other hand, subscribed to a much more dynamic and creative image of the actor, and it was this that made him attractive to later symbolic interactionists.

Pragmatism and behaviorism, especially in the theories of Dewey and Mead, were transmitted to many graduate students at the University of Chicago, primarily in the 1920s. These students, among them Herbert Blumer, established symbolic interactionism. Of course, other important theorists influenced these students, the most important of whom was Georg Simmel. Simmel's interest in forms of action and interaction was both compatible with, and an extension of, Meadian theory. There were, of course, many other influences on the development of symbolic interaction, but pragmatism, radical behaviorism, and Simmelian theory are far and away the most important.

Between Reductionism and Sociologism

Blumer coined the term *symbolic interactionism* in 1937 and wrote several essays that were instrumental in its development. Whereas Mead sought to differentiate the nascent symbolic interactionism from behaviorism, Blumer saw symbolic interactionism as embattled on two fronts. First was the reductionist behaviorism that had worried Mead. To this was added the serious threat from larger-scale sociologistic theories, especially structural functionalism. To Blumer, behaviorism and structural function-alism both tended to focus on factors (for example, external stimuli and norms) that cause human behavior. As far as Blumer was concerned, both ignored the crucial proc-ess by which actors endow the forces acting upon them and their own behaviors with meaning.

To Blumer, behaviorists, with their emphasis on the impact of external stimuli on individual behavior, were clearly psychological reductionists. In addition to behavior-ism, several other types of psychological reductionism troubled Blumer. For example, he criticized those who seek to explain human action by relying on conventional no-tions of the concept of ''attitude'' (Blumer, 1955/1969:94). In his view, most of those who use the concept think of an attitude as an ''already organized tendency'' within the actor; they tend to think of actions as being impelled by attitudes. In Blumer's view, this is very mechanistic thinking; what is important is not the attitude as an internalized tendency, ''but the defining process through which the actor comes to forge his act'' (Blumer, 1955/1969:97). Blumer also singled out for criticism those who focus on conscious and unconscious motives. He was particularly irked by their view that actors are impelled by independent, mentalistic impulses over which they are supposed to have no control. Freudian theory, which sees actors as impelled by such forces as the id or libido, is an example of the kind of psychological theory to which Blumer was op-posed. In short, Blumer was opposed to any psychological theory that ignores the proc-ess by which actors construct meaning—the fact that actors have selves and relate to themselves. Blumer's general criticisms were similar to Mead's, but he extended them beyond behaviorism to include other forms of psychological reductionism as well.

Blumer also was opposed to sociologistic theories that view individual behavior as determined by large-scale external forces. In this category Blumer included theories that focus on such social structural and cultural factors as '''social system,' 'social structure,' 'culture,' 'status position,' 'social role,' 'custom,' 'institution,' 'collective representation,' 'social situation,' 'social norm,' and 'values''' (Blumer, 1962/1969:83). Both sociologistic theories and psychological theories ignore the importance of meaning and the social construction of reality. Blumer summarized his criticisms of both psychological and sociologistic theories in this way:

> In both such typical psychological and sociological explanations the meanings of things for the human beings who are acting are either bypassed or swallowed up in the factors used to ac-count for their behavior. If one declares that the given kinds of behavior are the result of the particular factors regarded as producing them, there is no need to concern oneself with the meaning of the things towards which human beings act.
>
> (Blumer, 1969b:3)

With this background of symbolic interactionism, we are ready to discuss the basic principles of its contemporary manifestations. First, however, we examine the ideas of George H. Mead, the most important thinker in the founding of symbolic inter-actionism, and his most important work, *Mind, Self and Society.* Lest we think Mead's work is merely of historical interest, in a major recent work in symbolic interactionism, Robert Perinbanayagam sees him ''as a genius of the first rank'' and says that his own book, *Signifying Acts,* ''proves after all a study of Mead's views'' (1985:xiii).

GEORGE HERBERT MEAD: A Biographical Sketch

Most of the important theorists discussed throughout this book achieved their greatest recognition in their lifetimes for their published work. George Herbert Mead, however, was at least as important, at least during his lifetime, for his teaching as for his writing. His words had a powerful impact on many people who were to become important sociologists in the twentieth century. As one of his students said, "Conversation was his best medium; writing was a poor second" (T. V. Smith, 1931:369). Let us have another of his students, himself a well-known sociologist — Leonard Cottrell — describe what Mead was like as a teacher:

For me, the course with Professor Mead was a unique and unforgettable experience. . . . Professor Mead was a large, amiable-looking man who wore a magnificent mustache and a Vandyke beard. He characteristically had a benign, rather shy smile matched with a twinkle in his eyes as if he were enjoying a secret joke he was playing on the audience. . . .

As he lectured — always without notes — Professor Mead would manipulate the piece of chalk and watch it intently. . . . When he made a particularly subtle point in his lecture he would glance up and throw a shy, almost apologetic smile over our heads — never looking directly at anyone. His lecture flowed and we soon learned that questions or comments from the class were not welcome. Indeed, when someone was bold enough to raise a question there was a murmur of disapproval from the students. They objected to any interruption of the golden flow. . . .

His expectations of students were modest. He never gave exams. The main task for each of us students was to write as learned a paper as one could. These Professor Mead read with great care, and what he thought of your paper was your grade in the course. One might suppose that students would read materials for the paper rather than attend his lectures but that was not the case. Students always came. They couldn't get enough of Mead.

(Cottrell, 1980:49–50)

Over the years, many of Mead's sociological ideas came to be published, especially in *Mind, Self and Society.* This book and others of Mead's works have had a powerful influence on contemporary sociology.

Born in South Hadley, Massachusetts, on February 27, 1863, Mead was trained mainly in philosophy and its application to social psychology. He received a bachelor's degree from Harvard University in 1888, and after three years of study and travel abroad, he took a position as instructor at the University of Michigan. It is interesting to note that Mead *never* received any graduate degrees. In 1894, at the invitation of John Dewey, he moved to the University of Chicago and remained there for the rest of his life.

George Herbert Mead died on April 26, 1931.

MEAD: <u>MIND, SELF AND SOCIETY</u>

In *Mind, Self and Society*, Mead started with the radical Watsonian behaviorist assumption that social psychology begins with observable activity—that is, social action and interaction. However, unlike Watson and more traditional behaviorists, Mead extended behaviorism in two directions, into the mind and into society. Thus, we are dealing with two types of behaviorism here. The first, associated with Watson, is traditional, psychological, reductionistic or "radical" behaviorism. The second is the *social* behaviorism that Mead sought to develop to overcome the problems of the Watsonian perspective. Mead argued that psychological behaviorism, with its roots in animal psychology, ignored both the internal (mental) and the external (societal) dimensions. Animal psychologists cannot really "understand" the mind of a rat, but sociologists can understand human mental processes. Similarly, Mead doubted that animals are capable of creating a society in the same sense that people are. Mead was not content simply to postulate a society; he was also eager to accord it causal primacy in his system: "We attempt, that is, to explain the conduct of the individual in terms of the organized conduct of the social group, rather than to account for the organized conduct of the social group in terms of the conduct of the separate individuals belonging to it" (Mead, 1934/1962:7). Given Mead's association with symbolic interactionism, this statement seems startling. However, as we will soon see, Mead promised more on large-scale social structures than he actually delivered.

Mead's argument progressed through three main components—mind, self, and society. Although he did not discuss behavior at length in *Mind, Self and Society*, it is clear that he had a strong conception of it. He felt that he was building his own theory on the well-known basis of behaviorism.

Mind

Mead did not conceive of the human mind as a thing, an entity. Rather, he viewed it as a social process. In Mead's view, the human mind is qualitatively different from the minds of lower animals. To illustrate the latter, he described a dog fight as merely a *conversation of gestures*. That is, one dog's actions elicit another dog's reactions. No mental deliberation intervenes between the two. Although some human behavior occurs in this way, most action involves the intervention of deliberative mental processes between stimulus and response. In a human fight, the raised fist of an opponent becomes not simply a gesture, but a *significant symbol*. It has for all of us a set of meanings. Because the same symbol can have a multitude of meanings, depending on the context, we need our mental capacities to interpret the meaning. In a dark alley, a raised fist may well mean an impending struggle, but on a busy street corner it may simply mean an effort to flag a cab. Significant symbols may take the form of such physical symbols or a linguistic form. This capability of creating, storing, and using language ultimately sets humans apart from other animals. Language enables us to respond not only to physical symbols but also to words. The words *ice cream* then can stimulate much the same reaction in people as the actual physical presence of the dessert. The human possession of language accounts for the enormous qualitative difference between the human mind and those of lower animals.

In fact, the existence of language, which is a *social* product, ultimately allows the mind to exist. The mind can be defined as an internal conversation with one's self through the use of significant symbols. Pivotal for Mead in this deliberative process was the ability to take the role of the other in the interaction process. By putting ourselves in the place of the other, we can better understand the meaning of what that person says or does. In the example of the fight, we are able to understand the meaning of the raised fist by placing ourselves in the position of the actor in a dark alley or busy street. The conversation we have with ourselves over the meaning of that gesture is, in Mead's view, the essence of the mind.

It is important for the existence of social life that actors share significant symbols. The processes of thinking and, ultimately, of acting and interacting are facilitated by the fact that significant symbols have basically the same meaning for all and arouse the same reaction in the people using them as in the people reacting to them. Mead also placed great importance on the flexibility of the mind. Beyond a base of shared meanings of symbols, this flexibility allows interaction to occur even in situations where a given stimulus does not have an identical meaning for all involved. People do have the mental ability to adapt constantly to each other and to the situation and thus figure out the meaning of a particular symbol.

The verbal significant symbol was particularly important to Mead, because we can almost always hear ourselves, although we may not always be able to see our physical gestures. What we say affects us as well as those with whom we are communicating. Thus, as we are speaking, and before the other person has a chance to react, we can decide whether what we are saying is likely to elicit the desired reaction. If we decide that it is not going to elicit the response we want, we can quickly clarify our meaning.

The concept of meaning was important to Mead. Conduct is meaningful when we can use our minds to put ourselves in the place of others in order to interpret their thoughts and actions. Yet here, as elsewhere, Mead argued that meaning comes originally not from the mind but from the social situation. It is present in the social act before the emergence of consciousness of it. An act is meaningful if a gesture indicates to one actor the resultant behavior of another actor. Meaning need not be conscious. Before people created significant symbols, meaning was not conscious. However, now that we have such symbols, meaning has the potential of becoming a conscious phenomenon. Still, not all of our actions are consciously meaningful to us. Unconsciously motivated actions—that is, stimulus-response reflexes involving nonsignificant symbols—fall into this category.

Mead's ideas on the thinking process are deeply embedded in his behavioristic orientation. From this point of view, what is critical about the thinking process is the ability to inhibit action temporarily. That is, when a stimulus is presented, people do not inevitably emit the desired response. They decide what they want to do by trying out mentally a set of alternatives before acting in that situation. This set of alternatives "makes possible the exercise of intelligent or reflective choice in the acceptance of that one among these possible alternative responses" (Mead, 1934/1962:98). This gives the human being unparalleled ability to organize and control action. Lower animals are capable only of trial and error. It is far more costly to try and to fail than to mentally reject courses of action that one feels have a high probability of failure. Lower animals can only react immediately, but humans can delay their reactions, and "delayed reaction is necessary to intelligent conduct" (Mead, 1934/1962:99). Intelligence, for Mead, includes a number of abilities, including remembering, foreseeing, delaying, organizing, and selecting.

Although Mead placed great importance on the mind, he rejected as "hopeless" the use of introspection as a methodological tool to study it (Mead, 1934/1962:105). For

Mead, "consciousness is functional, not substantive" (Mead, 1934/1962:112). In other words, the process of thinking is part of the social world, not something occurring solely in the head. Mead believed, for that reason, that mental processes should be studied in the social world and not as things that are simply in the actor's head. In this way, the mind can be seen as a relationship between actor and situation, mediated by a set of symbols.

In rejecting the ideas of introspection and of a separable consciousness, Mead fell into a dangerous trap (the same trap that Alfred Schutz fell into; see Chapter 6). That is, Mead, schooled as a behaviorist, did not see introspection as a scientific method, nor did he see the mind as an entity that can be studied scientifically. This orientation leaves much to be desired, because it eliminates an important part of social life from serious scientific consideration.

Self

To Mead, reflexiveness, or the ability to respond to one's self as one does to others, "is the essential condition, within the social process, for the development of mind" (Mead, 1934/1962:134). In this sense, the self, like the mind, is not an object but a conscious process that involves several dimensions:

1. The ability to respond to one's self as others respond to it
2. The ability to respond to one's self as the collectivity, the *generalized other*, responds to it
3. The ability to take part in one's own conversation with others
4. The ability to be aware of what one is saying and to use that awareness to determine what one is going to do next

This process is not purely mental, and the abilities needed to engage in it are socially acquired. Of central importance is language, by means of which we use and interpret verbal significant symbols.

Mead's general theory of the stages of socialization is important here, for people need to learn more than simply language to acquire a self. In the *play stage,* the child learns to take the roles of specific significant people, such as father, mother, sister, or brother. This important stage in the life cycle gives children a discrete sense of social reality. Because children take a series of discrete roles, they develop a very discrete sense of their selves. They can see themselves in different ways, as a number of different people might see them. However, they lack a coherent or integrated sense of the self.

To acquire a more coherent sense of the self, children must move on to the *game stage*, in which they develop the ability to take a more generalized view of the situation and of the self. In Mead's terms, they learn to take the role of the "generalized other." To illustrate this idea, Mead used the example of a baseball game. In the play stage the child was able to take the role, alternately, of manager, fan, catcher, pitcher, batter, and so on. However, these discrete images did not give the child a coherent sense of what the game of baseball was all about. In the game stage, the child begins to acquire such an overall perspective, not only as it relates to baseball but to the social world in general. This perspective leads to a more coherent sense of the self. Once again, Mead gave priority to social causes. For the self to arise, the group must already exist.

Mead's two basic components of the self are the *I* and the *me*. Once again, remember that these are not things, but processes within the self. The *me* is that part of the self of which the actor is aware, the internalization of the organized attitude of others, of the generalized other. It represents the forces of conformity and of social control. The *I* is that part of the self of which the actor is unaware; we are only aware of it after an act is completed. It is the immediate response of the actor that both calls out and responds to the *me*. The self is the product of the relationship between the *I* and the *me*. "The 'I' is the response of the individual to the organized attitude of the community as this appears in his own experience. Its response to that organized attitude in turn changes it" (Mead, 1934/1962:196).

The existence of the *I* gives Mead's social psychology much dynamism. Mead does have, at least to some degree, a creative dynamic sense of consciousness. Mead said, for example, "the 'I' gives the sense of freedom, of initiative" (1934/1962:177). He also maintained that "the 'I' is something that is never entirely calculable" (Mead, 1934/1962:178). Later, "the attitudes involved are gathered from the group, but the individual in whom they are organized has the opportunity of giving them an expression which perhaps has never taken place before" (Mead, 1934/1962:198). Although Mead was willing to discuss what takes place internally, he saw it as simply the internal phase of a broader, naturalistic social process. This applies to both the self and the mind.

Society

In the discussions of mind and self, we have seen the outlines of Mead's very sophisticated treatment of consciousness, at least from the naturalistic perspective of a behaviorist. However, the rest of Mead's sociology is weak, especially his conception of society. When Mead discussed society, he had little or no sense of the kind of large-scale structures that so interested Marx, Weber, or Durkheim. To Mead, society was little more than the social organization in which mind and self arise, a residual category. Also, he conceived of society largely as patterns of interaction: "The society in which we belong represents an organized set of responses to certain situations in which the individual is involved" (Mead, 1934/1962:270). Similarly, he viewed an institution as nothing more than a set of common responses. Thus, despite the title of his main work, Mead did not offer a large-scale sociology to complement his very strong insights into individual action and consciousness. What is important about Mead's conception of society is that for him society is prior to the individual, and mental processes emerge from society.

CONTEMPORARY SYMBOLIC INTERACTIONISM

The heart of this chapter is our discussion of the basic principles of contemporary symbolic interaction theory. Although we try to characterize the theory in general terms, this is not easy to do for, as Paul Rock says, it has a "deliberately constructed vagueness" and a "resistance to systematisation" (1979:18–19). There are significant differences within symbolic interactionism, some of which are discussed as we proceed. We also address a number of the criticisms of symbolic interactionism. Finally, we discuss the work of Sheldon Stryker (1980), which can be seen as an effort to cope with at least some of the most important of these criticisms.

A number of symbolic interactionists (Blumer, 1969a; Manis and Meltzer, 1978; Rose, 1962) have tried to enumerate the basic principles of the theory. These principles include the following:

1. Human beings, unlike lower animals, are endowed with the capacity for thought.
2. The capacity for thought is shaped by social interaction.
3. In social interaction people learn the meanings and the symbols that allow them to exercise their distinctively human capacity for thought.
4. Meanings and symbols allow people to carry on distinctively human action and interaction.
5. People are able to modify or alter the meanings and symbols that they use in action and interaction on the basis of their interpretation of the situation.
6. People are able to make these modifications and alterations because, in part, of their ability to interact with themselves, which allows them to examine possible courses of action, assess their relative advantages and disadvantages, and then choose one.
7. The intertwined patterns of action and interaction make up groups and societies.

Capacity for Thought

The crucial assumption that human beings possess the ability to think differentiates symbolic interactionism from its behaviorist roots. This assumption also provides the basis for the entire theoretical orientation of symbolic interactionism. Bernard Meltzer, James Petras, and Larry Reynolds stated that the assumption of the human capacity for thought is one of the major contributions of early symbolic interactionists, such as James, Dewey, Thomas, Cooley, and of course Mead: "Individuals in human society were not seen as units that are motivated by external or internal forces beyond their control, or within the confines of a more or less fixed structure. Rather, they were viewed as reflective or interacting units which comprise the societal entity" (1975:42). The ability to think enables people to act reflectively rather than just behave unreflectively. People must often construct and guide what they do, rather than just release it.

The ability to think is embedded in the mind, but the symbolic interactionists have a somewhat unusual conception of the mind. They distinguish it from the physiological brain. People must have brains in order to develop minds, but a brain does not inevitably produce a mind, as is clear in the case of lower animals (Troyer, 1946). Also, symbolic interactionists do not conceive of the mind as a thing, a physical structure, but rather as a continuing process. It is a process that is itself part of the larger process of stimulus and response. The mind is related to virtually every other aspect of symbolic interactionism, including socialization, meanings, symbols, the self, interaction, and even society.

Thinking and Interaction

People possess only a general capacity for thought. This capacity must be shaped and refined in the process of social interaction. Such a view leads the symbolic interactionist to focus on a specific form of social interaction—*socialization*. The human ability to think is developed early in childhood socialization and is refined during adult socialization. Symbolic interactionists have a view of the socialization process that is different from that of most other sociologists. To symbolic interactionists, conventional sociologists are likely to see socialization as simply a process by which people learn the things that they need to survive in society (for instance, culture, role expectations). To the symbolic interactionists, socialization is a more dynamic process that allows people to develop the ability to think, to develop in distinctively human ways. Furthermore, socialization is not simply a one-way process in which the actor receives information, but is a dynamic process in which the actor shapes and adapts the information to his or her own needs (Manis and Meltzer, 1978:6).

Symbolic interactionists are, of course, interested not simply in socialization but in interaction in general, which is of "vital importance in its own right" (Blumer, 1969b:8). Interaction is the process in which the ability to think is both developed and expressed. All types of interaction, not just interaction during socialization, refine our ability to think. Beyond that, thinking shapes the interaction process. In most interaction, actors must take account of others and decide if and how to fit their activities to others. However, not all interaction involves thinking. The differentiation made by Blumer (following Mead) between two basic forms of social interaction is relevant here. The first, nonsymbolic interaction—Mead's conversation of gestures—does not involve thinking. The second, symbolic interaction, does require mental processes.

The importance of thinking to symbolic interactionists is reflected in their views on *objects*. Blumer differentiates among three types of objects: *physical objects*, such as a chair or a tree; *social objects*, such as a student or a mother; and *abstract objects*, such as an idea or a moral principle. Objects are seen simply as things "out there" in the real world; what is of greatest significance is the way that they are defined by actors. This leads to the relativistic view that different objects have different meanings for different individuals: "A tree will be a different object to a botanist, a lumberman, a poet, and a home gardener" (Blumer, 1969b:11).

Individuals learn the meanings of objects during the socialization process. Most of us learn a common set of meanings, but in many cases, as with the tree mentioned above, we have different definitions of the same objects. Although this can be taken to an extreme, symbolic interactionists need not deny the existence of objects in the real world. All they need do is point out the crucial nature of the definition of those objects as well as the possibility that actors may have different definitions of the same object. As Herbert Blumer said: "The nature of an object . . . consists of the meaning that it has for the person for whom it is an object" (1969b:11).

Learning Meanings and Symbols

Symbolic interactionists, following Mead, tend to accord causal significance to social interaction. Thus, meaning does not stem from mental processes but from the process of interaction. This focus derives from Mead's pragmatism: he focused on human action and interaction, not isolated mental processes. Symbolic interactionists have in general continued in this direction. Among other things, the central concern is not how people mentally create meanings and symbols but how they learn them during interaction in general and socialization in particular.

People learn symbols as well as meanings in social interaction. Whereas people respond to signs unthinkingly, they respond to symbols in a thoughtful manner. Signs stand for themselves (for example, the gestures of angry dogs or water to a person dying of thirst). "*Symbols are social objects used to represent* (or 'stand in for,' 'take the place of') whatever people agree they shall represent" (Charon, 1985:39). Not all social objects stand for other things, but those that do are symbols. Words, physical artifacts, and physical actions (for example, the world *boat,* a cross or a Star of David, and a clenched fist) all can be symbols. People often use symbols to communicate something about themselves: they drive Rolls-Royces, for instance, to communicate a certain style of life.

Symbolic interactionists conceive of language as a vast system of symbols. Words are symbols, because they are used to stand for things. Words make all other symbols possible. Acts, objects, and other words exist and have meaning only because they have been and can be described through the use of words.

Symbols are crucial in allowing people to act in distinctively human ways. Because of the symbol, the human being "does not respond passively to a reality that imposes itself but actively creates and re-creates the world acted in" (Charon, 1985:62). In addition to this general utility, symbols in general and language in particular have a number of specific functions for the actor (Charon, 1985).

First, symbols allow people to deal with the material and social world by allowing them to name, categorize, and remember the objects that they encounter there. In this way, people are able to order a world that otherwise would be confusing. Language allows people to name, categorize, and especially remember much more efficiently than they could with other kinds of symbols, such as pictorial images.

Second, symbols improve people's ability to perceive the environment. Instead of being flooded by a mass of indistinguishable stimuli, the actor can be alerted to some parts of the environment rather than others.

Third, symbols improve the ability to think. Although a set of pictorial symbols would allow a limited ability to think, language greatly expands this ability. Thinking, in these terms, can be conceived of as symbolic interaction with one's self.

Fourth, symbols greatly increase the ability to solve various problems. Lower animals must use trial and error, but human beings can think through symbolically a variety of alternative actions before actually taking one. This reduces the chance of making costly mistakes.

Fifth, the use of symbols allows actors to transcend time, space, and even their own persons. Through the use of symbols, actors can imagine what it was like to live in the past or might be like to live in the future. In addition, actors can transcend their own persons symbolically and imagine what the world is like from another person's point of view. This is the well-known symbolic interactionist concept of *taking the role of the other* (Miller, 1981).

Sixth, symbols allow us to imagine a metaphysical reality, such as heaven or hell. Seventh, and most generally, symbols allow people to avoid being enslaved by their environment. They can be active rather than passive—that is, self-directed in what they do.

Action and Interaction

Symbolic interactionists' primary concern is with the impact of meanings and symbols on human action and interaction. Here it is useful to employ Mead's differentiation between covert and overt behavior. *Covert behavior* is the thinking process, involving symbols and meanings. *Overt behavior* is the actual behavior performed by an actor. Some overt behavior does not involve covert behavior (habitual behavior or mindless responses to external stimuli). However, most human action involves both kinds. Covert behavior is of greatest concern to symbolic interactionists, whereas overt behavior is of greater concern to exchange theorists or to traditional behaviorists in general.

Meanings and symbols give human social action (which involves a single actor) and social interaction (which involves two or more actors engaged in mutual social action) distinctive characteristics. Social action is that in which the individuals are "acting with others in mind" (Charon, 1985:130). In other words, in undertaking an action, people simultaneously try to gauge its impact on the other actors involved. Although they often engage in mindless, habitual behavior, people have the capacity to engage in social action.

In the process of social interaction, people symbolically communicate meanings to the others involved. The others interpret those symbols and orient their responding action on the basis of their interpretation. In other words, in social interaction, actors engage in a process of mutual influence.

Making Choices

Partly because of the ability to handle meanings and symbols, people, unlike lower animals, can make choices in the actions in which they engage. People need not accept the meanings and symbols that are imposed on them from without. On the basis of their own interpretation of the situation, "humans are capable of forming new meanings and new lines of meaning" (Manis and Meltzer, 1978:7).

W. I. Thomas was instrumental in underscoring this creative capacity in his concept of *definition of the situation*: "If men define situations as real, they are real in their consequences" (Thomas and Thomas, 1928:572). Thomas knew that most of our definitions of situations have been provided for us by society. In fact, he emphasized this, pointing especially to the family and the community as sources of our social definitions. However, Thomas's position is distinctive for his emphasis on the possibility of "spontaneous" individual definitions of situations, which allow people to alter and modify meanings and symbols.

We also can say that to the symbolic interactionist, actors have at least some autonomy. They are not simply constrained or determined; they are capable of making unique and independent choices. Furthermore, they are able to develop a life that has a uniqueness and a style of its own (Perinbanayagam, 1985:53).

This ability of actors to make a difference is reflected in a recent essay by Gary Fine and Sherryl Kleinman (1983) in which they look at the phenomenon of a "social network" (see Chapter 9). Instead of viewing a social network as an unconscious and/or constraining social structure, Fine and Kleinman see a network as a set of social relationships that people endow with meaning and which are used by people for personal and/or collective purposes.

The Self

The self is a concept of enormous importance to symbolic interactionists. In fact, Rock argues that the self "constitutes the very hub of the interactionists' intellectual scheme. All other sociological processes and events revolve around that hub, taking from it their analytic meaning and organization" (1979:102). In attempting to understand this concept beyond its initial Meadian formulation, we must first understand the idea of the *looking-glass self* developed by Charles Horton Cooley. Cooley defined this concept as:

> a somewhat definite imagination of how one's self—that is, any idea he appropriates—appears in a particular mind, and the kind of self-feeling one has is determined by the attitude toward this attributed to that other mind. . . . So in imagination we perceive in another's mind some thought of our appearance, manners, aims, deeds, character, friends, and so on, and are variously affected by it.
>
> (Cooley, 1902/1964:169)

By the looking-glass self Cooley meant the capacity to see ourselves as we see any other social object. The idea of a looking-glass self can be broken down into three components. First, we imagine how we appear to others. Second, we imagine what their judgment of that appearance must be. Third, we develop some self-feeling, such as pride or mortification, as a result of our imagining others' judgments.

Cooley's concept of the looking-glass self and Mead's concept of the self were important in the development of the modern symbolic interactionist conception of the self. Blumer defined the self in extremely simple terms: "Nothing esoteric is meant by this expression [self]. It means merely that a human being can be an object of his own action . . . he acts toward himself and guides himself in his actions toward others on the basis of the kind of object he is to himself" (1969b:12). The self is a process, not a thing (Perinbanayagam, 1985). As Blumer made clear, the self helps allow human beings to act rather than simply respond to external stimuli:

> The process [interpretation] has two distinct steps. First, the actor indicates to himself the things toward which he is acting; he has to point out in himself the things that have meaning. . . . This interaction with himself is something other than an interplay of psychological elements; it is an instance of the person engaging in a process of communicating with himself. . . . Second, by virtue of this process of communicating with himself, interpretation becomes a matter of handling meanings. The actor selects, checks, suspends, regroups, and transforms the meanings in the light of the situation in which he is placed and the direction of his action.
>
> (Blumer, 1969b:5)

Although this underscores the part played by the self in the process of choosing how to act, Blumer has really not gone much beyond the early formulations of Cooley and Mead. However, other modern thinkers and researchers have refined the concept of the self.

THE WORK OF MORRIS ROSENBERG

Although mainstream symbolic interactionists have made important contributions to our understanding of the self (for example, Ralph Turner, 1968), the best-known recent work on this topic has been done by a sociologist not usually associated with this theory,

Morris Rosenberg (1979). Although not a symbolic interactionist, Rosenberg has been heavily influenced by people like Mead and Cooley. His thoughts on the self generally are compatible with and extend the symbolic interactionist orientation to this concept.

Rosenberg began by making it clear that his main interest was in the self-concept and not the self. The self is a more general concept, being both a subject and an object. The self-concept is the self as an object. Rosenberg defines the self-concept as: *"the totality of the individual's thoughts and feelings having reference to himself as an object"* (1979:7). Thus the self-concept is only a part of the self and an even smaller part of the total personality, but it is endowed with unusual significance, because it "is an important object to everyone, usually the most important object in the world" (Rosenberg, 1979:24). In addition to their importance, beliefs about the self are distinctive in a number of other ways. For example, they are the only attitudes that are reflexive—that is, the individual is both subject and object. The self-concept is the result of certain incommunicable information; it reflects the individual's unique body of information and point of view about himself. Although attitudes toward the self have much in common with other attitudes, there are unique attitudes toward the self, especially pride and shame. Accuracy and verifiability are much more important in attitudes toward the self than in attitudes toward bowling or tuna fish. In spite of its importance, the accuracy of self-attitudes "is difficult to ascertain because of low verifiability" (Rosenberg, 1979:33).

Rosenberg differentiated among the content, the structure, the dimensions, and the boundaries of the self-concept. In terms of *content*, Rosenberg distinguished social identities from dispositions. *Social identities* are the "groups, statuses or categories" to which an individual "is socially recognized as belonging" (Rosenberg, 1979:10). Examples include being recognized as a Democrat, middle-aged, black, or male. An individual not only sees himself or herself in terms of such categories, but also as possessing certain tendencies to respond, certain *dispositions*. A person who sees himself or herself as brave or introverted or liberal is likely to have his or her actions affected by such dispositions. In addition to the content of the self-concept, Rosenberg also discussed its structure. The *structure* of the self is the relationship among an individual's various social identities and dispositions. *Dimensions* refers to the attitudes and feelings one has about one's self. Self-attitudes, like all other attitudes, vary on a variety of dimensions, including "content, direction, intensity, salience, consistency, stability, clarity, accuracy and verifiability" (Rosenberg, 1979:23). Finally, Rosenberg discussed the *boundaries* of the self-concept, especially the ego-extensions to which it is applied. These are objects outside the actor that lead him or her to feel pride and shame: "pride in my shiny new automobile, shame at my unfashionable clothes, pride in an honor bestowed, shame or embarrassment at the defeat of my school team" (Rosenberg, 1979:35).

Rosenberg also distinguished among the extant self, the desired self, and the presenting self. The *extant self* is our picture of what we are like; the *desired self* is a picture of what we would like to be like; and the *presenting self* is the way we present ourselves in a given situation.

Rosenberg underscored the point that the self-concept involves a set of motivations, a set of desired goals for the actors. Two motives stand out above all others. First is *self-esteem*, or "the wish to think well of one's self" (Rosenberg, 1979:53). Second is *self-consistency*, or "the wish to protect the self-concept against change or to maintain one's self-picture" (Rosenberg, 1979:53). Rosenberg has done extensive empirical research on self-esteem and is widely recognized for this research. However, his conceptual analysis of the self-concept is an important contribution to the key idea of symbolic interactionism.

THE WORK OF ERVING GOFFMAN

Another important work on the self is *Presentation of Self in Everyday Life* (1959) by Erving Goffman, one of the most exciting modern symbolic interactionists. Goffman's conception of the self is deeply indebted to Mead's ideas, in particular his discussion of the tension between *I*, the spontaneous self, and *me*, social constraints within the self. This is mirrored in Goffman's work on what he called the "crucial discrepancy between our all-too-human selves and our socialized selves" (1959:56). The tension is due to the difference between what people expect us to do and what we may want to do spontaneously. We are confronted with the demand to do what is expected of us; moreover, we are not supposed to waver. As Goffman put it, "We must not be subject to ups and downs" (1959:56). In order to maintain a stable self-image, people perform for their social audiences. As a result of this interest in performance, Goffman focused on *dramaturgy*, or a view of social life as a series of dramatic performances akin to those performed on the stage.

DRAMATURGY   Goffman's sense of the self was shaped by his dramaturgical approach. To Goffman (as to Mead and most other symbolic interactionists), the self is:

> not an organic thing that has a specific location. . . . In analyzing the self then we are drawn from its possessor, from the person who will profit or lose most by it, for he and his body merely provide the peg on which something of collaborative manufacture will be hung for a time. . . . The means for producing and maintaining selves do not reside inside the peg.
>
> (Goffman, 1959:252–253)

He perceived the self not as a possession of the actor but rather as the product of the dramatic interaction between actor and audience. The self "is a dramatic effect arising . . . from a scene that is presented" (Goffman, 1959:253). Because the self is a product of dramatic interaction, it is vulnerable to disruption during the performance. Goffman's dramaturgy is concerned with the processes by which such disturbances are prevented or dealt with. Although the bulk of his discussion focuses on these dramaturgical contingencies, Goffman pointed out that most performances are successful. The result is that in ordinary circumstances a firm self is accorded to performers, and it "appears" to emanate from the performer.

Goffman assumed that when individuals interact, they want to present a certain sense of self that will be accepted by others. However, even as they present that self, actors are aware that members of the audience can disturb their performance. For that reason actors are attuned to the need to control the audience, especially those elements of it that might be disruptive. The actors hope that the sense of self that they present to the audience will be strong enough for the audience to define the actors as the actors want. The actors also hope that this will cause the audience to act voluntarily as the actors want them to. Goffman characterized this central interest as "impression management." It involves techniques actors use to maintain certain impressions, problems they are likely to encounter, and methods they use to cope with these problems.

Following his theatrical analogy, Goffman spoke of a front stage. The *front* is that part of the performance that generally functions in rather fixed and general ways to define the situation for those who observe the performance. Within the front stage, Goffman further differentiated between the setting and the personal front. The *setting* refers to the physical scene that ordinarily must be there if the actors are to perform. Without it, the actors usually cannot perform. For example, a surgeon generally requires an operating room, a taxi driver a cab, and an ice skater ice. The *personal front* consists of those items of expressive equipment that the audience identifies with the performers and expects them to carry with them into the setting. A surgeon, for instance, is expected to dress in a medical gown, have certain instruments, and so on.

Goffman then subdivided the personal front into appearance and manner. *Appearance* includes those items that tell us the performer's social status (for instance, the surgeon's medical gown). *Manner* tells the audience what sort of role the performer expects to play in the situation (for example, the use of physical mannerisms, demeanor). A brusque manner and a meek manner indicate quite different kinds of performances. In general, we expect appearance and manner to be consistent.

Although Goffman approached the front and other aspects of his system as a symbolic interactionist, he did discuss their structural character. For example, he argued that fronts tend to become institutionalized so that "collective representations" arise about what is to go on in a certain front. Very often when actors take on established roles they find particular fronts already established for such performances. The result, Goffman argued, is that fronts tend to be selected, not created. This conveys a much more structural image than we would receive from most symbolic interactionists.

Despite such a structural view, Goffman's most interesting insights lie in the domain of interaction. He argued that because people generally[6] try to present an idealized picture of themselves in their front stage performances, inevitably they feel that they must hide things in their performances. First, actors may want to conceal secret pleasures (for instance, drinking alcohol) engaged in prior to the performance or in past lives (for instance, as drug addicts) that are incompatible with their performance. Second, actors may want to conceal errors that have been made in the preparation of the performance as well as steps that have been taken to correct these errors. For example, a taxi driver may seek to hide the fact that he started in the wrong direction. Third, actors may find it necessary to show only end products and to conceal the process involved in producing them. For example, professors may spend several hours preparing a lecture, but they may want to act as if they have always known the material. Fourth, it may be necessary for actors to conceal from the audience that "dirty work" was involved in the making of the end products. Dirty work may include tasks that "were physically unclean, semi-legal, cruel, and degrading in other ways" (Goffman, 1959:44). Fifth, in giving a certain performance, actors may have to let other standards slide. Finally, actors probably find it necessary to hide any insults, humiliations, or deals made so that the performance could go on. Generally, actors have a vested interest in hiding all such facts from their audience.

---

[6]But not always—see Ungar (1984) on self-mockery as a way of presenting the self.

Another aspect of dramaturgy in the front stage is that actors often try to convey the impression that they are closer to the audience than they actually are. For example, actors may try to foster the impression that the performance in which they are engaged at

ERVING GOFFMAN: A Biographical Sketch

Erving Goffman died in 1982 at the peak of his fame. He had been long regarded as a peripheral, even underground figure in sociological theory (Collins, 1986b), but by the 1980s he had emerged as a centrally important theorist. In fact, he had been elected president of the American Sociological Association in the year he died but was unable to give his presidential address because of advanced illness. Given Goffman's maverick status, Randall Collins says of this address: "Everyone wondered what he would do for his Presidential address: a straight, traditional presentation seemed unthinkable for Goffman with his reputation as an iconoclast . . . we got a far more dramatic message: Presidential address cancelled, Goffman dying. It was an appropriately Goffmanian way to go out" (1986b:112).

Goffman was born in Alberta, Canada, on June 11, 1922 (Williams, 1986). He did his graduate work at the University of Chicago and is usually thought of as a member of the Chicago school and a symbolic interactionist. (But it is hard to squeeze his work into a single category, and so we also deal with his later, more structural work in Chapter 9.) In creating his theoretical perspective, Goffman drew on many sources and created a distinctive orientation.

Collins (1986b; Williams, 1986) links Goffman more to social anthropology than to symbolic interactionism. As an undergraduate at the University of Toronto, Goffman had studied with an anthropologist, and at Chicago "his main contacts were not with Symbolic Interactionists, but with W. Lloyd Warner [an anthropologist]" (Collins, 1986b:109). In Collins's view, an examination of the citations in Goffman's early work indicates that he was influenced by social anthropologists, rarely cited symbolic interactionists, and when he did, it was to be critical of them. However, Goffman was influenced by the descriptive studies produced at Chicago and integrated their outlook with that of social anthropology to produce his distinctive perspective. Thus whereas a symbolic interactionist would look at how people create or negotiate their self-image, Goffman was concerned with how "society . . . forces people to present a certain image of themselves . . . because it forces us to switch back and forth between many complicated roles, is also making us always somewhat untruthful, inconsistent, and dishonorable" (Collins, 1986a:107).

Despite the distinctiveness of his perspective, Goffman had a powerful influence on symbolic interactionism. In addition, it could be argued that he had a hand in shaping another "creative sociology," ethnomethodology. In fact, Collins sees Goffman not only as the "father" of ethnomethodology, but of conversation analysis as well: "It was Goffman who pioneered the close empirical study of everyday life, although he had done it with his bare eyes, before the days of tape recorders and video recorders." (1986b: 111). (See Chapter 6 for a discussion of the relationship between ethnomethodology and conversation analysis.) In fact, a number of important ethnomethodologists (Sacks, Schegloff) studied with Goffman at Berkeley and not with the founder of ethnomethodology, Harold Garfinkel.

Given their influence on symbolic interactionism, structuralism, and ethnomethodology, Goffman's theories are likely to be influential for a long time.

the moment is their only performance or at least their most important one. To do this, actors have to be sure that their audiences are segregated so that the falsity of the performance is not discovered. Even if it is discovered, Goffman argued, the audiences themselves may try to cope with the falsity, so as not to shatter their idealized image of the actor. This reveals the interactional character of performances. A successful performance depends on the involvement of all of the parties. Another example of this kind of impression management is an actor's attempt to convey the idea that there is something unique about this performance as well as his or her relationship to the audience. The audience, too, wants to feel that it is the recipient of a unique performance.

Actors try to make sure that all the parts of any performance blend together. In some cases, a single discordant aspect can disrupt a performance. However, performances vary in the amount of consistency required. A slip by a priest on a sacred occasion would be terribly disruptive, but if a taxi driver made one wrong turn it would not be likely to damage the overall performance greatly.

Another technique employed by performers is *mystification*. Actors often tend to mystify their performance by restricting the contact between themselves and the audience. By generating "social distance" between themselves and the audience, they try to create a sense of awe in the audience. This, in turn, keeps the audience from questioning the performance. Again Goffman pointed out that the audience is involved in this process and often itself seeks to maintain the credibility of the performance by keeping its distance from the performer.

This leads us to Goffman's interest in teams. To Goffman, as a symbolic interactionist, a focus on individual actors obscured important facts about interaction. Goffman's basic unit of analysis was thus not the individual but the team. A *team* is any set of individuals who cooperate in staging a single routine. Thus the preceding discussion of the relationship between the performer and audience is really about teams.[7] Each member is reliant on the others, because all can disrupt the performance and all are aware that they are putting on an act. Goffman concluded that a team is a kind of "secret society."

Goffman also discussed a *back stage* where facts suppressed in the front or various kinds of informal actions may appear. A back stage is usually adjacent to the front stage, but it is also cut off from it. Performers can reliably expect no members of their front audience to appear in the back. Furthermore, they engage in various types of impression management to make sure of this. A performance is likely to become difficult when actors are unable to prevent the audience from entering the back stage. There is also a third, residual domain, the *outside*, which is neither front nor back.

No area is *always* one of these three domains. Also, a given area can occupy all three domains at different times. A professor's office is front stage when a student visits, back stage when the student leaves, and outside when the professor is at a university basketball game.

IMPRESSION MANAGEMENT   Goffman closed *Presentation of Self in Everyday Life* with some additional thoughts on the art of impression management. In general, impres-

---

[7]A performer and the audience are one kind of team, but Goffman also talked of a group of performers as one team and the audience as another. Interestingly, Goffman argued that a team can also be a single individual. His logic, following classic symbolic interactionism, was that an individual can be his or her own audience—can *imagine* an audience to be present.

sion management is oriented to guarding against a series of unexpected actions, such as unintended gestures, inopportune intrusions, and faux pas, as well as intended actions, such as making a scene. Goffman was interested in the various methods of dealing with such problems. First, there is a set of methods involving actions aimed at producing dramaturgical loyalty by, for example, fostering high ingroup loyalty, preventing team members from identifying with the audience, and changing audiences periodically so that they do not become too knowledgeable about the performers. Second, Goffman suggested various forms of dramaturgical discipline, such as having the presence of mind to avoid slips, maintaining self-control, and managing the facial expressions and verbal tone of one's performance. Third, he identified various types of dramaturgical circumspection, such as determining in advance how a performance should go, planning for emergencies, selecting loyal teammates, selecting good audiences, being involved in small teams where dissension is less likely, making only brief appearances, preventing audience access to private information, and settling on a complete agenda to prevent unforeseen occurrences.

The audience also has a stake in successful impression management by the actor or team of actors. The audience often acts to save the show through such devices as giving great interest and attention to it, avoiding emotional outbursts, not noticing slips, and giving special consideration to a neophyte performer.

Goffman followed up on his work in *Presentation of Self in Everyday Life* with a series of fascinating and important books and essays (for instance, Goffman, 1961; 1963a; 1963b; 1967; 1971; 1972; 1974; 1976). We close this discussion with just a few illustrations of his distinctive mode of thought.

In "Role Distance" (1961) Goffman was interested in the degree to which an individual embraces a given role. In his view, because of the large number of roles, few people get completely involved in any given role. Role distance deals with the degree to which individuals separate themselves from the roles that they are in. For example, if older children ride on a merry-go-round, they are likely to be aware that they are really too old to enjoy such an experience. One way of coping with this is to demonstrate distance from the role by doing it in a careless, lackadaisical way or performing seemingly dangerous acts while on the merry-go-round. In performing such acts the older children are really explaining to the audience that they are not as immersed in the activity as small children might be, or if they are, it is because of the special things they are doing.

One of Goffman's key insights is that role distance is a function of one's social status. High-status people often manifest role distance for reasons other than do those in low-status positions. For example, a high-status surgeon may manifest role distance in the operating room to relieve the tension of the operating team. People in low-status positions usually manifest more defensiveness in exhibiting role distance. For instance, people who clean toilets may do so in a lackadaisical and uninterested manner. They may be trying to tell their audience that they are too good for such work.

One of Goffman's most interesting books is *Stigma* (1963b). Goffman was interested in the gap between what a person ought to be, "*virtual social identity*," and what a person actually is, "*actual social identity*." Anyone who has a gap between these two identities is stigmatized. The book focuses on the dramaturgical interaction between stigmatized people and normals. The nature of that interaction depends on which of the two types of stigma an individual is troubled by. In the case of *discredited* stigma, the actor assumes that the differences are known by the audience members or are evident to them (for example, a paraplegic or someone who has lost a limb). A *discreditable* stigma is one in which the differences are neither known by audience members nor perceivable by them (for example, a person who has had a colostomy or a homosexual passing as straight). For someone with a discredited stigma, the basic dramaturgical problem is managing the tension produced by the fact that people know of the problem. For someone with a discreditable stigma, the dramaturgical problem is managing information so that the problem remains unknown to the audience.

Most of the text of *Stigma* is devoted to people with obvious, often grotesque stigmas (for instance, the loss of a nose). However, as the book unfolds, the reader realizes that Goffman is really saying that we are all stigmatized at some time or other, or in one setting or other. His examples include the Jew "passing" in a predominantly Christian community, the fat person in a group of people of normal weight, and the individual who has lied about his past and must be constantly sure that the audience does not learn of this.

At this point mention of the more recent directions and changes in Goffman's mode of thinking is called for. In *Frame Analysis* (1974), Goffman moved away from his classic symbolic interactionist roots and toward the study of the small-scale structures of social life. Although he still felt that people define situations in the sense meant by W. I. Thomas, he now thought that such definitions were less important: "Defining situations as real certainly has consequences, but these may contribute very marginally to the events in progress" (Goffman, 1974:1). Furthermore, even when people define situations, they do not ordinarily create those definitions. Action is defined more by mechanical adherence to rules than through an active, creative, and negotiated process. Goffman enunciated his goal: "to try to isolate some of the basic frameworks of understanding available in our society for making sense out of events and to analyze the special vulnerabilities to which these frames of reference are subject" (1974:10).

Goffman's primary interest became the small-scale structures that govern the thoughts and actions of actors. In the view of some, this was a shift in emphasis and a movement away from classic symbolic interactionism. In fact, George Gonos said that "Goffman's work stands opposed to the central tenets and most basic assumptions of symbolic interactionism" (1977:855). Gonos argued that Goffman's work, especially *Frame Analysis*, is better seen as structuralism than symbolic interactionism.

However, a number of observers have made the point that there may not have been much of a shift after all (Collins, 1986b; Perinbanayagam, 1985). For example, Perinbanayagam describes Goffman's dramaturgy as "an examination of the *instruments* and *techniques* of communication that actors use" (1985:66). It can be argued that Goffman always had a dual concern with structuring *and* structures. (As Perinbanayagam says, "Structure is both noun and verb" [1985:75].) Thus, in contrast to Gonos, Perinbanayagam concludes that frame analysis and symbolic interactionism are "interdependent" perspectives in Goffman's work (1985:75). (We will discuss this issue further in Chapter 9.)

Although Goffman may or may not have changed his perspective, his earlier work on dramaturgy has been most influential. For example, David Snow, Louis Zurcher, and Robert Peters (1984) have recently looked at the victory celebrations of crowds at a football game as dramaturgical performances; Jack Haas and William Shaffir (1982) have looked at the medical profession from a dramaturgical viewpoint; Zurcher (1985) has examined the dramaturgy of war games; and Michio Kitahara (1986) looked back at the dramaturgical devices (showing rank, deploying ships, brandishing weapons) used by Commodore Perry to open Japan to the West between 1853 and 1854.

Groups and Societies

Symbolic interactionism was concerned with the interrelationships of individual thought and action and this gave it a distinctive perspective on society's large-scale structures.

BLUMER ON LARGE-SCALE SOCIAL STRUCTURES

Symbolic interactionists are generally highly critical of the tendency of other sociologists to focus on macro structures. As Rock says, "Interactionism discards most macrosociological thought as an unsure and overambitious metaphysics . . . not accessible to intelligent examination" (1979:238). Dmitri Shalin points to "interactionist criticism aimed at the classical view of social order as external, atemporal, determinate at any given moment and resistant to change" (1986:14). Rock also says, "Whilst it [symbolic interactionism] does not wholly shun the idea of social structure, its stress upon activity and process relegates structural metaphors to a most minor place" (1979:50).

Blumer is in the forefront of those who are critical of this "sociological determinism [in which] the social action of people is treated as an outward flow or expression of forces playing on them rather than as acts which are built up by people through their interpretation of the situations in which they are placed" (1962/1969:84). This focus on the constraining effects of large-scale social structures leads traditional sociologists to a set of assumptions about the actor and action different from those held by symbolic interactionists. Instead of seeing actors as those who actively define their situations, traditional sociologists tend to reduce actors to "mindless robots on the societal or aggregate level" (Manis and Meltzer, 1978:7). In an effort to stay away from determinism and a robotlike view of actors, symbolic interactionists take a very different view of large-scale social structures, a view that is ably presented by Blumer.[8]

To Blumer, society is not made up of macro structures. The essence of society is to be found in actors and action: "Human society is to be seen as consisting of acting people, and the life of the society is to be seen as consisting of their actions" (Blumer, 1961/1969:85). Human society is action; group life is a "complex of ongoing activity." However, society is not made up of an array of isolated acts. There is collective action as well, which involves "individuals fitting their lines of action to one another . . . participants making indications to one another, not merely each to himself" (Blumer, 1969b:16). This gives rise to what Mead called the *social act* and Blumer, *joint action*.

Blumer accepted the idea of emergence, that large-scale structures emerge from micro processes. For Blumer, joint action is the largest-scale concern. A joint action is not simply the sum total of its individual acts—it comes to have a character of its own.

---

[8] Although they recognize that Blumer does take this view, Wood and Wardell (1983) argue that Mead did *not* have an "astructural bias." See also Joas (1981).

A joint action thus is not external to nor coercive of actors and their actions; rather, it is created by actors and their actions. The study of joint action is, in Blumer's view, the domain of the sociologist.

From this discussion one gets the sense that the joint act is almost totally flexibile— that is, that society can become almost anything that the actors want it to be. However, Blumer was not prepared to go as far as that. He argued that each instance of joint action must be formed anew, but he did recognize that joint action is likely to have a "well-established and repetitive form" (Blumer, 1969b:17). Not only does most joint action recur in patterns, but Blumer was also willing to admit that such action is guided by systems of pre-established meanings, such as culture and social order.

It would appear that Blumer admitted that there are large-scale structures and that they are important. Here Blumer followed Mead (1934/1962), who admitted that such structures are very important. Despite this, such structures have an extremely limited role in symbolic interactionism. For one thing, Blumer most often argued that large-scale structures are little more than "frameworks" within which the really important aspects of social life, action and interaction, take place (Blumer, 1962/1969:87). Large-scale structures do set the conditions and set limitations on human action, but they do not determine it. In his view, people do not act within the context of such structures as society; rather, they act in situations. Large-scale structures are important in that they shape the situations in which individuals act and supply to actors the fixed set of symbols that enable them to act.

Even when Blumer discussed such pre-established patterns, he hastened to make it clear that "areas of unprescribed conduct are just as natural, indigenous, and recurrent in human group life as those areas covered by pre-established and faithfully followed prescriptions of joint action" (Blumer, 1969b:18). Not only are there many unprescribed areas, but even in prescribed areas joint action has to be consistently created and re-created. Actors are guided by generally accepted meanings in this creation and re-creation, but they are not determined by them. They may accept them as is, but they also can make minor and even major alterations in them. In Blumer's words, "It is the social process in group life that creates and upholds the rules, not the rules that create and uphold group life" (1969b:19).

Clearly, Blumer was not inclined to accord culture independent and coercive status in his theoretical system. Nor was he about to accord this status to the extended connections of group life, or what is generally called "social structure," for example the division of labor. "A network or an institution does not function automatically because of some inner dynamics or system requirements; it functions because people at different points do something, and what they do is a result of how they define the situation in which they are called on to act" (Blumer, 1969b:19).

METHODOLOGICAL PRINCIPLES

In addition to its theoretical principles, symbolic interactionism also encompasses a set of methodological postulates.

Blumer on Methods

Blumer had great respect for the difficulties involved in studying the action and interaction that take place in the real world. He often spoke of the "obdurate character" of the real world. Sociologists must engage in constant efforts to develop ways of studying it. Scientific models are to be developed and tested in and against the real world and are only useful if they help us understand that world.

Blumer was a severe critic of what he considered the tendency toward mindless scientism in sociology. He did not reject the use of quantitative methods, though he clearly saw them as far less valuable than most conventional sociologists consider them. Many methods may prove useful in understanding the real world. Similarly, Blumer (1956/1969) was critical of the tendency to reduce the complexity of social life to scientific variables. The simplistic correlation of variables tends to ignore the interpretive process that is so central to social life. Blumer criticized abstract theoretical schema for much the same reason: "primarily an interpretation which orders the world into its mold, not a studious cultivation of empirical facts to see if the theory fits" (1954/1969:141).

Blumer also was critical of most sociological concepts that serve as prescriptions for what sociologists should see in the real world. Such concepts do enormous violence to the reality of that world. Instead of traditional concepts, Blumer supported the use of "sensitizing concepts" (1954/1969:148), which simply suggest what to look for and where to look and which do less violence to the real world. Finally, Blumer urged the use of *sympathetic introspection* to study social life. In other words, in their research, symbolic interactionists must put themselves in the places of the actors whom they are studying in order to understand the situation from their point of view. This leads to a preference for "soft" rather than "hard" methods in symbolic interactionism. However, Blumer did not believe that this preference reflects the scientific immaturity of sociology; rather, it indicates the distinctive subject matter of the field.

Blumer was not the only spokesperson for symbolic interactionism on methodological issues (or any other issue, for that matter). We can get a sense of at least one of the schisms in symbolic interactionism by discussing the methodological differences between Blumer, a leading spokesperson for the Chicago school, and Manford Kuhn, the major representative of the Iowa school of symbolic interactionism.

BLUMER VERSUS KUHN ON METHODS

The most basic differences between Blumer and Kuhn are methodological (Meltzer, Petras, and Reynolds, 1975). Blumer, as we have seen, argued for a distinctive methodology for studying human behavior, a methodology that is nongeneralizing. Manford Kuhn (1964), in contrast, stressed the unity of the scientific method; all scientific fields, including sociology, should aim toward generalization and laws. Although Blumer and Kuhn agreed on at least one essential subject matter of symbolic interactionism—"what goes on 'inside the heads' of humans" (Meltzer, Petras, and Reynolds, 1975:57)—they disagreed on how it should be studied.

Blumer was inclined to use sympathetic introspection in order to get inside the actors' world and view it as they do. Sociologists should use their intuition in order to take the point of view of the actors whom they are studying, even going so far as using the same categories as they do. Kuhn was interested in the same empirical phenomena, but he urged sociologists to reject nonscientific techniques and instead use overt behavioral indices of what goes on in actors' heads. For instance, the answers of respondents to a series of questions should be the data for the symbolic interactionist to work with, not the "unreliable" and "unscientific" intuition of the sociologist.

In addition, Blumer accepted less formal sensitizing concepts and rejected the use of more scientific operational concepts to define the real world. Kuhn preferred the traditional scientific methods of using researchable variables and operational definitions. For example, Kuhn operationalized the concept of the self, which can be so elusive in traditional symbolic interactionism, as the answer to the question "Who am I?" The responses that people gave to this simple question were viewed as the empirical manifestations of the self. Also, Blumer was inclined to attack sociological variables as mechanistic tools, but Kuhn accepted and used them. Whereas Blumer saw large elements of unpredictability in human action, Kuhn held that action was socially determined and hence could be studied scientifically in the search for antecedent causes of action. Finally, Blumer was inclined to think in terms of continuing processes, whereas Kuhn was inclined to think in more static terms, which are also more amenable to scientific study.

BLUMER'S INTERPRETATION OF MEAD

The debate between supporters of Blumer and supporters of Kuhn continues, but Blumer's orientation is still the dominant position within symbolic interactionism. However, questions recently have been raised about whether Blumer was being as true to his Meadian roots as he claimed (Lewis and Smith, 1980; Warshay and Warshay, 1986).[9] Clark McPhail and Cynthia Rexroat (1979) argued that there are marked differences between the methodological orientations of Mead and Blumer. Because of the influence of behaviorism, Mead was much more oriented to "hard" science than was Blumer and may, in fact, have been closer to Kuhn than Blumer. As McPhail and Rexroat expressed their position, "Mead's emphasis on systematic observation and experimental investigation is quite different from Blumer's naturalistic methodology. . . . Naturalistic inquiry neither complements nor extends Mead's methodological perspective, nor is Blumer's framework suited to the investigation and development of Mead's theoretical ideas" (1979:449).

Blumer (1980) responded heatedly to the charges made by McPhail and Rexroat. He argued that they "seriously misrepresented" his views on social reality and naturalistic study, as well as Mead's views on social behavior and scientific method. McPhail and Rexroat (1980) responded that Blumer in his reply failed to specify his criteria for arguing that they misinterpreted him and that he failed to use systematic evidence in support of his position. Blumer was accused of often failing to cite the relevant passages in Mead's work in his counterargument. McPhail and Rexroat argued that in many cases Blumer "simply asserts that *his* interpretation of Mead is *the* correct one" (1980:420). In the end, we have Blumer proclaiming his interpretation of Mead to be the correct one and McPhail and Rexroat taking the opposite position. Although this

---

[9]On the ambiguities in Mead's work, especially *Mind, Self and Society,* and the impossibility of arriving at a single interpretation, see Fine and Kleinman (1986).

debate is of current interest, the historical fact is that it was Blumer's interpretation of Mead's position, not Mead's methodological position itself, that became the dominant orientation in symbolic interactionism.

The key issue in the debate between Blumer and McPhail and Rexroat is the "hard" versus "soft" science issue. In Blumer's view, McPhail and Rexroat are interested in fostering a "hard" science image of Meadian theory:

> I discern underneath the McPhail-Rexroat discussion what they really have in mind in alleging ontological and methodological differences between Mead and me. Their fundamental intention is to justify and promote a special mode of scientific inquiry that relies on controlled experiments. But they also regard themselves as followers of George Herbert Mead. They are, thus, forced to interpret Mead in such a way as to support their methodological orientation. They seek to do this in two ways. First, they try to interpret Mead's thought on "scientific method" in such a way as to uphold their methodological preference. Second, they endeavor to depict Mead's "social behaviorism" in such a manner as to fit their experimental or near-experimental commitment.
>
> (Blumer, 1980:414–415)

In McPhail and Rexroat's response to Blumer, they argued that Mead favored *both* experimental and nonexperimental methods. Whether or not Mead did, McPhail and Rexroat clearly favored more of a "hard" science, experimental approach to symbolic interaction than did Blumer. The issue is whether complex forms of social behavior are amenable to experimental study. Blumer felt that they are not, whereas McPhail and Rexroat felt that they are. Here, at least in part, is a more recent version of the debate between Blumer and Kuhn.

CRITICISMS

Having analyzed the ideas of symbolic interactionism, particularly those of the Chicago school of Mead, Blumer, and Goffman, we will now enumerate some of the major criticisms of this perspective.

The first criticism is that the mainstream of symbolic interactionism has too readily given up on conventional scientific techniques. Eugene Weinstein and Judith Tanur expressed this point well: "Just because the contents of consciousness are qualitative, does not mean that their exterior expression cannot be coded, classified even counted" (1976:105). Science and subjectivism are *not* mutually exclusive.

Second, Manford Kuhn (1964), William Kolb (1944), Bernard Meltzer, James Petras, and Larry Reynolds (1975), and many others have criticized the vagueness of essential Meadian concepts such as mind, self, I, and me. Most generally, Kuhn (1964) spoke of the ambiguities and contradictions in Mead's theory. Beyond Meadian theory, they have criticized many of the basic symbolic interactionist concepts for being confused and imprecise and therefore incapable of providing a firm basis for theory and research. Because these concepts are imprecise, it is difficult, if not impossible, to operationalize them; the result is that testable propositions cannot be generated (Stryker, 1980).

The third criticism of symbolic interactionism is that larger structures are ignored. Somewhat less predictable is the fourth criticism, that symbolic interactionism is not sufficiently microscopic, that it ignores the importance of such factors as the unconscious and emotions (Meltzer, Petras, and Reynolds, 1975; Stryker, 1980). Similarly, symbolic interactionism has been criticized for ignoring such psychological factors as needs, motives, intentions, and aspirations. In their effort to deny that there are immutable forces impelling the actor to act, symbolic interactionists have focused instead on meanings, symbols, action, and interaction. They ignore psychological factors that might impel the actor, which parallels their neglect of the larger societal constraints on the actor. In both cases, symbolic interactionists are accused of making a "fetish" out of everyday life (Meltzer, Petras, and Reynolds, 1975:85). This, in turn, leads to a marked overemphasis on the immediate situation and an "obsessive concern with the transient, episodic, and fleeting" (Meltzer, Petras, and Reynolds, 1975:85).

The major criticism of symbolic interactionism has been of its tendency to ignore large-scale social structures. This has been expressed in various ways. For example, Weinstein and Tanur (1976:106) argued that symbolic interactionism ignores the connectedness of outcomes to each other: *"It is the aggregated outcomes that form the linkages among episodes of interaction that are the concern of sociology qua sociology. . . .* The concept of social structure is necessary to deal with the incredible density and complexity of relations through which episodes of interaction are interconnected." Sheldon Stryker argued that the micro focus of symbolic interactionism serves "to minimize or deny the facts of social structure and the impact of the macro-organizational features of society on behavior" (1980:146). Meltzer, Petras, and Reynolds were inclined to see this weakness at the structural level as one of the two main problems with symbolic interactionism:

Of all the presumed difficulties of the symbolic interactionist paradigm, then, two stand forth as the most crucial: (1) limited consideration of human emotions, and (2) unconcern with social structure. In effect, the first of these shortcomings implies that symbolic interaction is not psychological enough, while the second implies that symbolic interaction is not sociological enough.

(Meltzer, Petras, and Reynolds, 1975:120)

TOWARD A MORE ADEQUATE SYMBOLIC INTERACTIONISM

To become a more adequate sociological theory, symbolic interactionism must focus on both smaller-scale and larger-scale phenomena. The latter seems to be the more important task. We close this chapter with a discussion of the work of Sheldon Stryker (1980) and his effort to develop a more macroscopically oriented symbolic interactionism. (For an argument against such a development, see Rock, 1979.) We agree with David R. Maines (1977), who argued that symbolic interactionism has not competely ignored large-scale social structures, although it has not paid as much attention to them as structural functionalism and conflict theory. However, Maines is also right in arguing that "there is nothing inherent in the perspective that precludes the analysis of social organizations and social structure" (1977:235)—and this is what Stryker's work demonstrates.

Stryker enunciated an integrative goal for symbolic interactionism: "A satisfactory theoretical framework must bridge social structure and person, must be able to move from the level of the person to that of large-scale social structure and back again. . . . There must exist a conceptual framework facilitating movement across the levels of organization and person" (1980:53). Recently, Perinbanayagam articulated a similar goal for symbolic interactionism: "the existence of structure *and* meaning, self *and* others, the dialectic of being and emergence, leading to a dialectical interactionism" (1985:xv). Stryker embedded his orientation in Meadian symbolic interactionism but sought to extend it to the societal level, primarily through the use of role theory:

> This version begins with Mead, but goes beyond Mead to introduce role theoretic concepts and principles, in order to adequately deal with the reciprocal impact of social person and social structure. The nexus in this reciprocal impact is interaction. It is in the context of the social process—the ongoing patterns of interaction joining individual actors—that social structure operates to constrain the conceptions of self, the definitions of the situation, and the behavioral opportunities and repertoires that bound and guide the interaction that takes place.
>
> (Stryker, 1980:52)

Stryker developed his orientation in terms of eight general principles:

1. Human action is dependent on a named and classified world in which the names and classifications have meaning for actors. People learn through interaction with others how to classify the world as well as how they are expected to behave toward it.
2. Among the most important things that people learn are the symbols used to designate social *positions*. A critical point here is that Stryker conceived of positions in structural terms: "the relatively stable, morphological components of social structure" (Stryker, 1980:54). Stryker also accorded *roles* central importance, conceiving of them as the shared behavioral expectations attached to social positions.
3. Stryker also recognized the importance of larger social structures, although he was inclined, like other symbolic interactionists, to conceive of them in terms of organized patterns of behavior. In addition, his discussion treated social structure as simply the "framework" within which people act. Within these structures, people name one another, that is, recognize one another as occupants of positions. In so doing people evoke reciprocal expectations of what each is expected to do.
4. Furthermore, in acting in this context people not only name each other, but they name themselves; that is, they apply positional designations to themselves. These self-designations become part of the self, internalized expectations with regard to their own behavior.
5. When interacting, people define the situation by applying names to it, to other participants, to themselves, and to particular features of the situation. These definitions are then used by the actors to organize their behavior.
6. Social behavior is not determined by social meanings, although it is constrained by them. Stryker is a strong believer in the idea of *role making*. People do not simply take roles; rather, they take an active, creative orientation to their roles.
7. Social structures also serve to limit the degree to which roles are "made" rather than just "taken." Some structures permit more creativity than others.
8. The possibilities of role making make various social changes possible. Changes can occur in social definitions—in names, symbols, and classifications, and in

the possibilities for interaction. The cumulative effect of these changes can be alterations in the larger social structures.

Although Stryker offered a useful beginning toward a more adequate symbolic interactionism, his work has a number of limitations. The most notable is that he said little about larger social structures per se. Stryker saw the need to integrate these larger structures in his work, but he recognized that a "full-fledged development of how such incorporation could proceed is beyond the scope of the present work" (Stryker, 1980:69). Stryker saw only a limited future role for large-scale structural variables in symbolic interactionism. He hoped ultimately to incorporate such structural factors as class, status, and power as variables constraining interaction, but he was disinclined to see symbolic interactionism deal with the interrelationships among these structural variables (Stryker, 1980). Presumably, this kind of issue is to be left to other theories that focus more on large-scale social phenomena.

A similar link to larger structure is found in Robert Perinbanayagam's recent work, especially in his ideas on *programs*, or "plans to be realized in time and moves to be initiated for consummation at a later moment" (1985:104). Programs are not mental fantasies but are "essentially *social* and systematically involve other human participants as well as investments of time, resources (money, etc.), and institutional structures like families, schools, banks, and bureaucracies" (Perinbanayagam, 1985: 104). Programs have a temporal aspect and can take the form of *proximate programs*, dealing with the immediate future ("I'm going to school tomorrow"), *intermediate programs*, dealing with one's life plans ("I'm going to be a sociologist"), and *ultimate programs* that deal with the hereafter ("I'm going to heaven"). More important for our purposes is the social structure of programs, especially the number of actors involved. A program can involve only a single actor, but it is more likely to involve other people and range all the way from a dyad (husband and wife) to the nation or even humankind. Programs not only are linked to the larger society by the number of people involved, but the social structure of society affects the availability of certain programs to various groups. Thus, for example, race, ethnic status, and social class allow some groups access to certain programs and closes them to other groups.

SUMMARY

Symbolic interactionism, like structural functionalism, was for many years a dominant force in American sociological theory. Recently, however, it too has receded somewhat in importance. Nevertheless, it has historical and contemporary significance.

This chapter begins with a brief discussion of the roots of symbolic interactionism in philosophical pragmatism (the work of John Dewey) and psychological behaviorism (the work of John B. Watson). Out of the confluence of pragmatism, behaviorism, and other influences, such as Simmelian sociology, symbolic interactionism developed at the University of Chicago in the 1920s.

The symbolic interactionism that developed stood in contrast to the psychological reductionism of behaviorism and the structural determinism of more macro-oriented sociological theories, such as structural functionalism. Its distinctive orientation was toward the mental capacities of actors and their relationship to action and interaction. All of this was conceived in terms of process; there was a disinclination to see the actor impelled by either internal psychological states or large-scale structural forces.

The single most important work in symbolic interactionism is Mead's *Mind, Self and Society.* Basically, Mead sought to extend the principles of psychological behaviorism to one of the basic concerns of pragmatists—mental processes. Mead's great concern was the relationship among mental processes, action, and interaction. In analyzing this relationship, he defined many of the basic interests of symbolic interactionists: gestures, symbols, language, meanings, self, *I* and *me,* and socialization. Although Mead told us much about mind and self, his work was relatively impoverished in its analysis of society, of large-scale structures, and of institutions in general.

The current state of symbolic interactionism may be summarized by the following basic principles:

1. Human beings, unlike lower animals, are endowed with a capacity for thought.
2. The capacity for thought is shaped by social interaction.
3. In social interaction, people learn the meanings and the symbols that allow them to exercise their distinctively human capacity for thought.
4. Meanings and symbols allow people to carry on distinctively human action and interaction.
5. People are able to modify or alter the meanings and symbols that they use in action and interaction on the basis of their interpretation of the situation.
6. People are able to make these modifications and alterations because, in part, of their ability to interact with themselves, which allows them to examine possible courses of action, assess their relative advantages and disadvantages, and then choose one.
7. The intertwined patterns of action and interaction make up groups and societies.

In the context of these general principles, we seek to clarify the nature of the work of several important thinkers in the symbolic interactionist tradition, including Charles Horton Cooley, Herbert Blumer, Morris Rosenberg, and most important, Erving Goffman. We present in detail Goffman's dramaturgical analysis of the self and his related works on ''role distance'' and stigma. However, we also note that Goffman's recent work has exaggerated a tendency in his earlier work and moved further in the direction of a structuralist analysis.

Although we are not interested in methodology per se in this book, several of the methodological principles of symbolic interactionism are discussed, because they help us gain a greater understanding of this theoretical orientation. Especially important here is the debate between Blumer, representing the ''soft,'' intuition-guided Chicago school orientation to symbolic interactionism, and Manford Kuhn, representing the more ''hard science'' approach characteristic of the Iowa school. Although this debate continues, the Chicago approach has predominated within symbolic interactionism.

We close with a discussion of a number of the criticisms of symbolic interactionism, in particular its weakness at the level of large-scale phenomena. In this context, we discuss Stryker's recent effort to move symbolic interactionism toward a structural level.

CHAPTER SIX
Phenomenological Sociology and Ethnomethodology

SIMILARITIES AND DIFFERENCES

PHENOMENOLOGICAL SOCIOLOGY
  The Ideas of Edmund Husserl
  The Theories of Alfred Schutz
  Examples of Phenomenological Sociology

ETHNOMETHODOLOGY
  Examples of Ethnomethodology
  Criticisms of Traditional Sociology
  Ethnomethodology: A Basic Program
  The Strain toward Structural Constraint

$\mathbf{T}$WO of the most frequently discussed and debated theories in contemporary sociological theory are phenomenological sociology and ethnomethodology. The two theories often are discussed together. George Ritzer (1975a) sees them as two theoretical components of the social-definition paradigm; Monica Morris (1977) sees them as two varieties of what she calls "creative sociology"; Jack Douglas (1980) and Andrew Weigert (1981) include them under the heading of the "sociologies of everyday life"; and Richard Hilbert (1986) sees them as varieties of "social constructionism."[1] However, there are persuasive reasons why the two theories should not be discussed together. Thus, after a brief analysis of their similarities and differences, we will analyze the two theories separately. We first deal with phenomenological sociology because it is the older of the two theories and provided some of the roots for the development of ethnomethodology. Later we discuss some of the main aspects of ethnomethodology as a sociological theory.

SIMILARITIES AND DIFFERENCES

Contemporary practitioners of both phenomenological sociology and ethnomethodology trace their intellectual roots to the philosophical work of Edmund Husserl (1859–1938). Many of his ideas are the inspiration for a number of contemporary aspects of

---

[1] These are not the only theories discussed under these headings. Symbolic interactionism, which we have already discussed at length in Chapter 5, and existential sociology, to be discussed in Chapter 9, also are often included under these rubrics. However, phenomenological sociology and ethnomethodology are the two theories of this kind that are receiving the most attention.

phenomenological sociology. More important, they were the major inspiration for the work of Alfred Schutz. Schutz took Husserl's philosophy and transformed it into a sociology, and it is that orientation that lies at the base of both phenomenological sociology and ethnomethodology. Contemporary phenomenological sociology is traceable directly to the work of Schutz. In ethnomethodology, Husserl's influence is less direct. Harold Garfinkel, the founder of ethnomethodology, studied with Schutz, and it is Garfinkel's (and his supporters') adaptation of Schutz's ideas that is a major basis of ethnomethodology.

The two theories have a similar set of interests in the social world. Both theories focus on social definitions—how actors come to define social situations and to act on the basis of those definitions (Ritzer, 1975a). Both are creative sociologies, that is, actors are not seen as passive receptacles but as active creators of the social scene (Morris, 1977). In addition, phenomenology and ethnomethodology both have a micro focus on the sociology of everyday life, that is, on highly commonplace thoughts and actions (Douglas, 1980). Social definitions, creativity, and a micro focus are not the only substantive elements the two theories have in common, but they illustrate their overlapping concerns.

In spite of these and other similarities, many adherents of both theories seem to agree that there are differences between the two and that it is best to keep them separate. For example, James Heap and Phillip Roth (1973) argued that ethnomethodology involves a combination of phenomenology and elements of sociology that has produced a unique and independent domain of study. Similarly, Don Zimmerman contended that despite their common intellectual heritage, the two theories are not equivalent: "Strictly speaking, the term 'phenomenological' is inappropriate as a blanket characterization of the working tools, methods and problems of ethnomethodology, if for no other reason than that it blurs the distinction between heritage and intellectual content" (1978:8). Although phenomenology, both philosophical and sociological, has influenced ethnomethodology, ethnomethodology also has been shaped by linguistics, anthropology, and even mainstream sociology. Ethnomethodology has blended phenomenology with these other sources to produce a theoretical orientation that is not reducible to phenomenology (Sharrock and Anderson, 1986).

One key area of difference between the two theories is methodology. In general, those who practice phenomenological sociology tend to remain true to their philosophical roots and to write conceptual pieces and do thought experiments (Freeman, 1980). Phenomenological sociology has spawned comparatively little empirical research—that is, few experiments, surveys, or observational studies. Some see this as inherent in phenomenological sociology, but others see it as a stage in the development of the theory. Psathas, for example, said that because of the "current stage" of the development of phenomenological sociology practitioners focus on their "theoretical and philosophical underpinnings" (1973a:1). Psathas believed that in the future phenomenological sociologists would be doing much more empirical research.

Ethnomethodology, however, has been highly empirical and has produced many more empirical works than theoretical or philosophical treatises. Examples include studies of telephone conversations, maps, newspaper reports, courtroom procedures, political speeches, and even walking. In these studies, ethnomethodologists have generally used methods not too different from those used in mainstream sociological research. They also have developed some distinctive methodologies. One of the best known is the so-called *breaching experiments* developed by Garfinkel as a way of demonstrating basic ethnomethodological principles. The basic procedure is for the researcher to enter a social setting, violate (or breach) the rules that govern it, and then study how people deal with the breach. Among other things, the ethnomethodologist hopes to study the way people construct, or reconstruct, social reality. Another rather distinctive methodology is detailed analysis of audio and videotapes. Ethnomethodologists are very interested in conversational analysis, and they have used audiotapes to good advantage. Videotapes have proven useful in the analysis of such behaviors as walking, face-to-face communication, and interaction in various settings.

Robert Freeman (1980) saw these methodological differences as derived from more fundamental differences in the substantive focuses of the two theories. Phenomenological sociologists have a great concern for consciousness. Ethnomethodologists, following in the phenomenological tradition, accept the fundamental importance of consciousness in social life. However, given their roots in traditional sociology, they tend to focus on more empirically observable social activities.

One of the most difficult problems in the history of all of sociology has been how to study consciousness empirically. Like other theorists, phenomenologists have not been able to solve this problem adequately. As a result, their best work lies in their efforts to philosophize, theorize, or reflect on the operation of consciousness and meaning construction. However, because ethnomethodologists focus on more observable activities stemming from conscious processes, they can rely more on traditional sociological research methods.

Finally, Freeman (1980) offered another useful contrast between the two theories by pointing out that they tend to pick up two different, and in some ways conflicting, strands in the work of Alfred Schutz. As we will see, Schutz offered a highly complicated and in some ways self-contradictory phenomenological theory. Hence it is entirely possible for two theoretical schools, both claiming Schutz as their inspiration, to go in different directions.

Schutz was interested in consciousness but as it is constrained by the larger culture with its language, typifications, and recipes. This orientation most influenced those phenomenological sociologists who tend to emphasize the constraining effects of cultural phenomena on consciousness. Although they recognize that actors are creative, they emphasize the forces that shape and constrain that creativity. Ethnomethodology tends to focus less on cultural constraints, which means that many of its practitioners have an image of the actor as more creative. The actors are thus seen as sustaining society, not vice versa. Freeman's point was that this image of the actor as more creative is also found in Schutz's work: "Society is regarded as originating in the *sense of social structure* members sustain through their interpretive procedures" (1980:134; italics added). The emphasis is on the "sense of structure" and how it is constructed and maintained, not on the structure per se.

Accentuating the differences, Mary Rogers argues "that ethnomethodology is *not* significantly phenomenological in its conceptualizations and methods" (1983:117). She argues that ethnomethodology makes little use of phenomenological terminology, generally ignores post-Schutzian phenomenologists, and, most important, "ethnomethodologists make rare reference to and adopt no clear position on human consciousness" (p. 117).

Ethnomethodologists focus on overt actions like conversation and interaction but largely ignore the foundations of these actions in consciousness. Here, Rogers paraphrases one of Garfinkel's well-known statements: "nothing in actor heads concerns ethnomethodology; there are only brains" (p. 119). Furthermore, Rogers argues that ethnomethodology is not as macroscopic as phenomenology because ethnomethodology "excludes explicit attention to institutions, collectivities, the social stock of knowledge, and other macro-level social realities" (p. 130). In other words, in Rogers's view, ethnomethodology is neither as microscopic (not dealing with consciousness) nor as macroscopic (not dealing with social institutions and structures) as phenomenology.

PHENOMENOLOGICAL SOCIOLOGY

At the broadest level, phenomenological sociology is that sociology which operates on the basis of philosophical phenomenology. It tries, without doing too much damage to its original sources, to apply the principles of philosophical phenomenology to sociological questions. In this, the work of philosophers such as Husserl, as well as Henri Bergson, Franz Brentano, and Maurice Merleau-Ponty, provide its ultimate source, and the work of Schutz, its closest source.

Can we find a clear statement that gives us a good idea about what phenomenology in general, and phenomenological sociology in particular, do? Rogers orients us generally by arguing that "virtually all phenomenologists assign primacy to human consciousness . . . concern themselves . . . with meaning, experience, constitution, the self" (1983:ix). As a result of its phenomenological orientation, this sociology takes as its objective the *description* of the universal structure of *subjective* orientations (Psathas, 1973a). Derived from this approach is the view held by phenomenological sociology that the objective features of society rest on this universal subjective base (Psathas, 1973a). Like phenomenological philosophy, phenomenological sociology is a science because of its rigorous, systematic, and critical attempt to uncover the basic realities of social life.

We will begin with a brief discussion of the ideas of Edmund Husserl, who was a major influence on the thinking of Alfred Schutz but is also important for his more direct influence on post-Schutzian phenomenological sociologists.

The Ideas of Edmund Husserl

Husserl's highly complicated philosophy is not easily translated into sociological concepts and, indeed, a good portion of it is not directly relevant to sociology (Srubar, 1984). We discuss here a few of his main ideas that have proven useful to sociological phenomenologists.

Joseph Kockelmans noted the essence of the problem in dealing with Husserl's phenomenology, indeed with philosophical phenomenology in general: "Anyone familiar with the situation knows that as soon as he uses the term 'phenomenology' he enters a sphere of ambiguity" (1967b:24). This ambiguity is one of the main reasons that Husserl's phenomenology is so difficult to translate into usable sociological concepts.

Husserl's general orientation to the social world can be used as a starting point (Freeman, 1980). In general, people view the world in a highly ordered way. Actors are always engaged in the active and highly complex process of ordering the world. However, they are most often unaware that they are ordering the social world; hence they do not question it. To Husserl, this is the general thesis of the "natural standpoint." To actors, the social world is naturally ordered, not ordered by them. However, phenomenologists are acutely aware that ordering is being done, and it becomes for them an important subject of phenomenological investigation.

The natural standpoint, or "natural attitude," was conceived by Husserl as an obstacle to the discovery of phenomenological processes. These basic components are hidden to actors and remain hidden to phenomenologists if they are unable to overcome their own natural attitude to the world. Philosophers must be able to set aside ("bracket") the natural attitude so that they will be able to get to the most basic aspects of consciousness. The natural attitude is, to Husserl, a source of bias and distortion for the phenomenologist.

One of the key orientations of Husserl's work was the *scientific* study of the basic structures of consciousness. As Husserl put it, he wanted to develop "philosophy as a rigorous science" (Kockelmans, 1967b:26). However, to Husserl science did not mean empiricism and statistics. In fact, he feared that such a science would reject consciousness as an object of scientific scrutiny and that it would either be found too metaphysical or be turned into something physical.[2]

What Husserl did mean by science was a philosophy that was rigorous, systematic, and critical. In using science in this way, phenomenologists ultimately could arrive at absolutely valid knowledge of the basic structures of consciousness. This orientation to science has had two effects on contemporary phenomenologists. First, most modern phenomenological sociologists continue to eschew the tools of modern social science research—elaborate methods, high-powered statistics, and computerized results. They prefer, as did Husserl, a serious and systematic reflection on the nature and constitution of consciousness. Second, modern phenomenologists do not favor vague, "soft" intuitionism. Philosophizing about consciousness is a rigorous and systematic enterprise.

Husserl's phenomenology involves a commitment to penetrate the various layers constructed by actors in the real world in order to get to the essential structure of consciousness. To do this, the phenomenologist must "disconnect" the natural attitude, a very difficult task (Freeman, 1980). Once the natural attitude is set aside or is "bracketed," the phenomenologist can begin to examine the invariant properties of consciousness that govern all people. The phenomenologist also must set aside the incidental experiences of life that tend to dominate consciousness. Husserl's ultimate objective was to look beyond all the layers in order to see the basic properties of the "transcendental ego" in all its purity. Another way to put this is that Husserl was interested in the pure form of consciousness stripped of all empirical content.

The idea of the transcendental ego reflects Husserl's interest in the basic and invariant properties of human consciousness. Although he is often misinterpreted on this

---

[2]These same fears animated the work of the father of symbolic interactionism, George Herbert Mead. Behaviorism, as it was practiced in Mead's day, and even today, either rejects the idea of consciousness or turns it into physical phenomena.

point, he did not have a mentalistic, metaphysical conception of consciousness. For him, it was not a thing or a place but a process. Consciousness was found not in the head of the actor but in the relationship between the actor and the objects in the world. Husserl expressed this in his notion of *intentionality*. For him, consciousness is always consciousness of something, some object. Consciousness is found in this relationship: consciousness is not interior to the actor; as we saw in the preceding chapter, it is relational. Furthermore, meaning does not inhere in the objects but in the relationship of actors to those objects. This conception of consciousness as a process that gives meaning to objects is at the heart of contemporary phenomenological sociology.

INTERPRETING HUSSERL'S IDEAS

Heap and Roth (1973) pointed out that many contemporary phenomenological sociologists who operate within the Husserlian tradition have done grave damage to his original orientation. An overriding problem from their point of view is that sociologists have used Husserl's terminology as it is understood in everyday conversation rather than as it was meant by Husserl or used by rigorous phenomenologists. Let us look at a few examples.

Heap and Roth argued that Husserl's concept of *intention* is "greatly misunderstood and misinterpreted" (1973:355). For example, sociologists have interpreted intention as relaxed when things are running smoothly for the actors but called into play when problems arise in the social world. However, for Husserl, intentionality is not operant at some times and inoperant at others. Rather, consciousness always involves intentionality and an object. What some sociologists are thinking of here is the ability of actors to attend to objects, which actors may or may not do. However, whether or not actors pay attention to the world, take note of it, and try to manipulate it, their consciousness involves intentionality, for, according to Heap and Roth, "intention is an essential feature of consciousness *prior to* the operation of attention" (1973:355; italics added). To put it another way, "Consciousness is not 'intentionally' directed—consciousness *is* intentional" (Heap and Roth, 1973:355).

Another Husserlian concept that has been misinterpreted by some sociologists is the idea of *reduction*, or *bracketing*. To some sociologists, this often means reducing one aspect of the real world to another aspect of that world. In this sense of the word, Marx might be said to be reducing ideological manifestations to their material or economic roots. However, this is not what phenomenologists mean by reduction. Instead of reduction within the empirical world, the phenomenologist brackets all of the empirical world in order to get at the essence of consciousness. (Again, to bracket is to set aside the idea that the real world is naturally ordered.) Thus, the phenomenologist, unlike Marx, would bracket not only ideological factors but material factors as well. No sociologists, not even ethnomethodologists, bracket the real world, because their primary concerns lie in that realm.

Heap and Roth offered a further example of a sociological distortion of a phenomenological concept. That is the idea of *phenomenon*, clearly implied as a basic concern of phenomenology. Husserl urged that phenomenologists return to things in themselves, phenomena devoid of reality attributed to them by actors in the real world. Thus those sociologists are wrong who argue that Durkheim's dictum that social facts are to be studied as things is the equivalent of Husserl's idea that we should return to the things themselves. Durkheim's social facts are still theoretical constructs, whereas Husserl's phenomena are devoid of *all* theorizing.

Finally, we come to the Husserlian concept of *essence*. To Husserl, essences are the invariant properties of consciousness that do not exist in the real world (Heap and Roth, 1973). When sociologists invoke Husserl's concept of essence, they are most often referring to what they consider to be the essential aspect of the world. It is probably important to look for such essential structures, but it is important to recognize that one is not looking for essences in the sense used by Husserl.

The basic problem, in Heap and Roth's view, is that sociologists interested in phenomenology have used the terminology of phenomenology but have fundamentally misunderstood the original meanings. In fact, to be absolutely faithful to phenomenology, sociology would have to be fundamentally reconstituted, a dramatic alteration not envisioned by many sociologists attracted to Husserlian theory: "Any attempt to graft phenomenological concepts onto a sociology that has not been fundamentally reconstituted can only lead to a distortion, if not perversion, of both phenomenology and sociology" (Heap and Roth, 1973:359). In sum, "the possibility of a phenomenological sociology in the sense envisioned by Husserl is highly questionable" (Heap and Roth, 1973:361).

Ilja Srubar (1984) argues that not only did Husserl do a rigorous philosophy of consciousness, but he also laid the groundwork for a phenomenological sociology. That is, Husserl found it necessary to extend his concerns to the world of interpersonal relations, the "life world," in which the meaning of all human knowledge is generated. Thus Husserl's work leads to the position that "phenomenology must become a science of the life world" (Srubar, 1984:70) and that, according to Srubar, is the direction taken in Schutz's work. This brings us to a discussion of Schutz's work, although as we will soon see, Srubar's position is only one of several on the true nature of Schutz's perspective.

The Theories of Alfred Schutz

Schutz's theories are complex and hard to unravel. We begin this section with a discussion of some of the very different interpretations of his work. We then turn to a discussion of his ideas with the objective of clearing up at least some of the confusion.

INTERPRETATIONS OF SCHUTZ'S WORK

We can divide traditional interpretations of Schutz's work into several camps. First, ethnomethodologists and phenomenologists saw in Schutz the source of their interest in the way actors create or construct social reality. Among the ethnomethodologists, for example, Hugh Mehan and Houston Wood argued that the focus of their approach was on the way actors "create situations and rules, and so at once create themselves and their social realities" (1975:115). They went on to say that "ethnomethodologists adopted this research program from Schutz" (p. 115). Monica Morris, in her book on creative sociology, came to a similar conclusion: "For Schutz, the subject matter of sociology is the manner in which human beings constitute, or create, the world of everyday life" (1977:15). These commentators as well as many others generally have seen Schutz as focusing on the way actors create social reality, and they have lauded him for this micro orientation.

Other commentators have taken a similar view of the substance of his work but have come to very different conclusions about it. A good example is Robert Bierstedt, who criticized Schutz for his focus on the way actors construct social reality and his corresponding lack of concern with the reality of the larger structures of society:

> The phenomenological reduction . . . has consequences of a . . . rather serious kind for sociology. . . . Society itself, as an objective phenomenon, tends to disappear in the realm of the intersubjective. That is, society itself . . . comes to be a creation of the mind in intersubjectivity and something that is wholly exhausted in the common-place affairs of daily living.
>
> (Bierstedt, 1963:91)

Thus Bierstedt criticized Schutz for precisely the same thing for which Mehan and Wood, Morris, and others praised him.

Although these two camps came to very different conclusions about Schutz's work, they did at least agree on its focus. A third school of thought, however, views Schutz in an almost diametrically opposite way, as a cultural determinist. For example, Robert Gorman (1975a, 1975b, 1977) suggested that, contrary to the interpretations of the ethnomethodological and sociological establishments, Schutz emphasized the constraints imposed on the actor by society. Actors do not freely choose beliefs or courses of action, nor do they freely construct a sense of social reality. Rather, as members of society, they are free only to obey.

> Socially determined action patterns are adhered to by free actors. Each actor bases his action on his stock of knowledge at hand, and this knowledge consists of these socially determined action patterns. Each of us chooses, for himself, to act as these patterns prescribe, even though they have been imposed from outside.
>
> (Gorman, 1975a:11)

Gorman concluded that for Schutz ''social behavior is apparently caused by factors independent of the subject [actor]'' (1977:71).

In a more complex argument, Burke Thomason (1982) argues that although Schutz methodologically focused on the way people construct social reality, ontologically he did not believe that such conscious construction processes were all there was to the social world:

> He never claimed that the social world *was* more than what it was defined to be or that the *only* reality relevant to social science was the reality within the minds of individuals. His advocacy of constructionist social theory, in short, was persistently *methodological* in that it was limited implicitly to asserting the usefulness of constructionist *assumptions*, constructionist ways of *seeing* the world and constructionist ways of *doing* sociology.
>
> (Thomason, 1982:162)

According to Thomason, ontologically, for Schutz, people do construct social reality but within the confines of a constraining social world.

As we discuss Schutz's ideas in some detail and clarify them, we hope also to shed some light on the debate implied by these contrasting views of his work.

SCIENCE AND THE SOCIAL WORLD

Schutz differentiated between and tried to interrelate those aspects of the social world that were to be analyzed philosophically and those that were amenable to scientific sociological inquiry. Schutz tried to provide both a philosophical base for sociology and the basic premises of a science of sociology. Despite these laudable goals, his efforts, as we will see, were not always successful.

Schutz philosophized a great deal about what we may term "consciousness" as well as the actions that emanate from conscious processes. He recognized that people have minds, that they engage in the social construction of reality, and that their constructions set the limits for their activity. It is social actors who construct the social world through their conscious activity. The constructions, in turn, constrain further creative activity. Schutz provided us with a dialectical image of social reality in which, on the one hand, people are constrained by social forces and, on the other, people are able and are sometimes forced to overcome these constraints.

Although the social world is in actuality peopled by social actors who have minds and who engage in creative activity, and although Schutz discussed this world at length

ALFRED SCHUTZ: A Biographical Sketch

Alfred Schutz was not widely known during his lifetime, and only in recent years has his work attracted the attention of large numbers of sociologists. Although his obscurity was in part a result of his intellectual orientation —his then highly unusual interest in phenomenology— a more important cause was his very unusual career as a sociologist.

Born in Vienna, Austria, in 1899, Schutz received his academic training at the University of Vienna (Wagner, 1983). Soon after completing his law examination, he embarked on a lifelong career in banking. Although rewarding economically, banking did not satisfy his need for deeper meaning in his life. Schutz found that meaning in his work on phenomenological sociology. He was not an academician in the 1920s, but many of his friends were, and he participated in a number of informal lecture and discussion circles (Prendergast, 1986). Schutz was drawn to Weberian theory, especially Weber's work on action and the ideal type. Although impressed with Weber's work, Schutz sought to overcome its weaknesses by integrating ideas from the philosophers Edmund Husserl and Henri Bergson. According to Christopher Prendergast (1986), Schutz was motivated to provide the Austrian School of Economics with a scientific, subjective theory of action. These influences led to the publication by Schutz in 1932 of what was to become a very important book in sociology, *The Phenomenology of the Social World*. It was not translated into English until 1967, so that a wide appreciation of Schutz's work in the United States was delayed thirty-five years.

As World War II approached, Schutz emigrated to the United States, where for many years he divided his time between serving as legal counsel to a number of banks and writing about and teaching phenomenological sociology. Simultaneously with his work in banking, Schutz began teaching courses in 1933 at the New School for Social Research in New York City. As Richard Grathoff points out, the result was that "the and offered rich insights into it, he concluded that it is not amenable to scientific analysis. As we shall see, what Schutz called "we relations" and the world of directly experienced reality (*umwelt*) are difficult if not impossible to analyze scientifically. Consciousness and the social construction of reality are far too ephemeral and idiosyncratic to be subject to the rigorous demands of an objective science. Schutz argued that a science of sociology must focus on social forces in abstraction. These forces have been constructed, negotiated, and modified in social interaction, but as ongoing processes, they cannot be studied scientifically.

Schutz found himself in the paradoxical position of attempting to develop a subjective sociology in the tradition of Max Weber while also meeting the demands of a rigorous conception of science. As Schutz put it, "How is it, then, possible to grasp by a system of objective knowledge subjective meaning structures?" (1962:35). As we will see in the rest of this section, the bulk of Schutz's work was devoted to answering this question.

REALMS OF THE SOCIAL WORLD   Schutz identified four distinct realms of social reality. Each is an abstraction of the social world and is distinguished by its degree of

---

social theorist for whom scientific thought and everyday life defined two rather distinct and separate realms of experience upheld a similar division in his personal life" (1978: 112). Not until 1956 did Schutz give up his dual career and concentrate entirely on teaching and writing phenomenological sociology. Because of his interest in phenomenology, his dual career, and his teaching at the then avant-garde New School, Schutz remained on the periphery of sociology during his lifetime. Nevertheless, Schutz's work and his influence on students (for example, Peter Berger, Thomas Luckmann, Harold Garfinkel) moved him to the center of sociological theory.

Another factor in Schutz's marginal position in sociological theory was that his theory seemed highly abstract and irrelevant to the mundane social world. Although Schutz did separate theory from reality, he did not feel that his work was irrelevant to the world in which he lived. To put it in terms of his phenomenology, he saw a relationship between the everyday construction of reality and the pre-given historical and cultural world. To think otherwise is to think that the man who fled National Socialism (Nazism) regarded his academic work as irrelevant. The following quotation from one of his letters indicates that although Schutz was not optimistic, he was not prepared to accept the irrelevance of his theorizing and, more generally, the social construction of reality to the world as a whole:

> You are still optimist enough to believe that phenomenology may save itself among the ruins of this world—as the *philosophica aera perennis*? I do not believe so. More likely the African natives must prepare themselves for the ideas of national socialism. This shall not prevent us from dying the way we have lived; and we must try, therefore, to build . . . order into *our* world, which we must find lacking in—our *world*. The whole conflict is hidden in this shift of emphasis.
>
> (Grathoff, 1978:130)

In short, although the ability of people to affect the larger society is restricted by such phenomena as Nazism, they must continue to strive to build a social and cultural reality that is *not* beyond their reach and control.

immediacy (the degree to which situations are within reach of the actor) and determinability (the degree to which they can be controlled by the actor). The four realms are: *umwelt*, the realm of directly experienced social reality; *mitwelt*, the realm of indirectly experienced social reality; *folgewelt*, the realm of successors; and *vorwelt*, the realm of predecessors. The realms of successors and predecessors (*folgewelt* and *vorwelt*) were of peripheral interest to Schutz. However, we shall deal with them briefly because the contrast between them illustrates some of the characteristics of Schutz's major focus—the *umwelt* and the *mitwelt*.

Folgewelt and Vorwelt   The future (*folgewelt*) is a purely residual category in Schutz's work (in contrast to Marx's, where it plays a crucial role in his dialectic). It is a totally free and completely indeterminate world that is not dominated by any scientific laws. It can only be anticipated by the social scientist in a very general way and cannot be pictured in any detail. Given its indeterminate quality, it falls outside the bounds of Schutz's scientific work.

The past (*vorwelt*), on the other hand, is partially amenable to scientific analysis. The action of those who lived in the past is totally determined; there is no element of freedom, because the causes of their actions, the actions themselves, and their outcomes have already occurred. Despite its determinacy, the study of predecessors presents difficulties for a subjective sociology. It is difficult to interpret the actions of people who lived in an earlier time because we would probably have to use contemporary categories of thought in the historical glance back rather than the categories that prevailed at the time. The interpretation of contemporaries is likely to be more accurate because sociologists share interpretive categories with those whose action they seek to understand. Thus, although a subjective sociology of the past is possible, the probability of misinterpretation is great.

The essential point here is that the objective for Schutz was to develop a sociology based on the interpretations of the social world made by the actors being studied. It is difficult to know the interpretations of predecessors and impossible to understand those of successors. However, it is possible to understand contemporaries (*mitwelt*) and even more possible to understand the interpretations of those with whom we are in immediate face-to-face contact (*umwelt*).

Umwelt   The realms of directly experienced social reality (*umwelt*) and indirectly experienced social reality (*mitwelt*) are more central to Schutz's work. Within the realm of immediate experience, the social construction of reality takes place, and the scientist has a good chance of understanding it. An analysis of the actor's experience within immediate social reality necessarily would deal with both the actor's consciousness and face-to-face interaction. Within this realm the actor, in Schutz's view, has a considerable amount of freedom and creativity. But Schutz asserted that the free, conscious, and therefore unpredictable actor is outside the realm of scientific sociology. Although Schutz recognized the creative potential of mental processes and offered many philosophical insights into their operation, he eliminated them from scientific consideration. Schutz went so far as to say that we can ignore "the ultimate roots of the action in the person's consciousness" (1932/1967:190).

Schutz was disinclined to deal with face-to-face interaction in the *umwelt* for much the same reason. All people have minds and therefore are unpredictable, especially in their face-to-face interaction with other people. After all, in the process of relating to other people individuals can, and very often do, change their actions based on what other people do or even on what they think other people have in mind. As with mental processes, Schutz was inclined to eliminate face-to-face interaction from scientific sociology. In Schutz's terms, the *umwelt*, the world composed of directly experienced fellow interactants, cannot be part of a science of sociology.

In recently published correspondence between Schutz and Parsons, Schutz stated his position in no uncertain terms:

I fully agree with you that cultural systems may be considered as products of action. But these systems of culture furnish the best example of a field open to element analysis where the action categories are not analytically significant. . . . There is an analytical level where the action element drops out. . . . All action sciences, that is my thesis, may reach an analytical level, where they deal exclusively with the objects constituted by and through acts of an actor without considering the actor and his acts or, in other words, by dropping the action categories themselves.

(Grathoff, 1978:100)

Because of his commitment to science, Schutz's definition of sociology excluded real actors and their minds as well as the *umwelt*. What, then, is the appropriate subject matter of scientific sociology? Instead of looking at the *umwelt*, Schutz focused on the *mitwelt*, or the realm of contemporaries whom sociologists do not encounter as actual individuals but merely as types.

Mitwelt   The *mitwelt* is that aspect of the social world in which people ordinarily deal with types of people or with larger social structures, rather than with actual actors. People do fill these types and these structures, but in the world of contemporaries, these people are rarely experienced directly. Because actors are dealing with types rather than with actual people, their knowledge of people is not subject to constant revision on the basis of face-to-face interaction. This relatively constant knowledge of general types of subjective experience can be studied scientifically and can shed light on the general process by which people deal with the social world. A number of specific examples of the *mitwelt* will be discussed below.

The *mitwelt* is a stratified world with levels arranged by degree of anonymity. The more anonymous the level, the more people's relationships are amenable to scientific study. Some of the major levels within the *mitwelt*, beginning with the least anonymous, are:

1. Those whom actors encountered face to face in the past and could meet again. Actors are likely to have fairly current knowledge of them because they have been met before and could be met again. Although there is a relatively low level of anonymity here, such a relationship does not involve ongoing face-to-face interaction. If these people were to be met personally at a later date, this relationship would become part of the *umwelt* and no longer be part of the *mitwelt*.

2. Those once encountered not by us but by people with whom we deal. Because this level is based on second-hand knowledge of others, it involves more anonymity than the level of relationships with people we have encountered in the past. If we were ever to meet people at this level, the relationship would become part of the *umwelt*.
3. Those whom we are on the way to meet. As long as we have not yet met them, we relate to them as types, but once we actually meet them, the situation again becomes part of the *umwelt*.
4. Those whom we know not as concrete individuals but simply as positions and roles. For example, we know that there are people who sort our mail or process our checks, but, although we have attitudes about them as types, we never encounter them personally.
5. Collectivities whose function we may know without knowing any of the individuals who exist within them. For example, we know about the Senate, but few people actually know any of the individuals in it, although we do have the possibility of meeting those people.
6. Collectivities that are so anonymous that we have little chance of ever encountering people in them. For most people, the Mafia would be an example of such a collectivity.
7. Objective structures of meaning that have been created by contemporaries with whom actors do not have and have not had face-to-face interaction. The rules of English grammar would be an example of such a structure of meaning.
8. Physical artifacts that have been produced by a person we have not met and whom we are not likely to meet. For example, people would have a highly anonymous relationship with a museum painting.

As we move further into the *mitwelt* relationships, they become more impersonal and anonymous. People do not have face-to-face interaction with others and thus cannot know what goes on in others' minds. Their knowledge is therefore restricted to "general types of subjective experience" (Schutz, 1932/1967:181).

Typifications can be defined as *recipes* for action that exist in the culture as a whole. As people are socialized, they learn these recipes, these typical actions for typical situations, and use them in situations that they have learned are appropriate for them. In any given situation, an action is determined "by means of a type constituted in earlier experiences" (Schutz and Luckmann, 1973:229). These typifications are part of the social stock of knowledge, but we also carry many of them around in our heads as a result of socialization. Knowledge of contemporaries is not of a specific person, but of a *type* of person. For example, it is not necessary to know the particular person who sorts and distributes the mail; it is enough to have knowledge of the type of person who does that and the type of actions that person undertakes. Within the realm of indirect experience, knowledge is "homogeneous and repeatable" and shared by people, with the result that it is amenable to scientific study.

Although cultural typifications of contemporaries are constant, we often encounter unusual situations, or we may find that a tried and true recipe does not work in a given situation. We could conceivably meet an actual contemporary (for example, the person who sorts our mail) and revise our typifications of such a person on the basis of the encounter. We could be forced to revise our typifications if the actual person *did not behave as we expected.* We may, for example, expect a post-office employee to sort our mail accurately, but we may be forced to revise that typification if we constantly receive the wrong mail. Remember, however, that although we may revise our own typifications, the cultural typifications remain untouched.

Schutz was well aware of the ability of actors to revise typifications in the real world, but he constructed a scientific world in which actors lack this kind of freedom. All that the scientifically constructed social actors, the *homunculi*, can do in a given situation is use the scientifically imposed recipe. Homunculi lack the ability to improvise, because they are not endowed with creative mental abilities. To build a scientific sociology, Schutz felt that he must not include creativity in his definition of ideal-typical human action, so he created mindless automata, homunculi, that he could use in a series of thought experiments. Schutz realized that this was an unrealistic way of studying social behavior; however, because of his commitment to a *science* of subjective meaning, he based his investigations on typifications.

SCIENTIFIC PROCEDURES   Now we can return to Schutz's problematic question: How is a science of subjective meaning possible? Schutz resolved the paradox by using the common-sense constructs (typifications) characterizing the realm of indirectly experienced social reality (*mitwelt*) as the base upon which to build scientific concepts. In so doing, he tried to capture the meaning of the social world from the actor's perspective. In Schutz's words, "The thought objects constructed by the social scientist, in order to grasp . . . reality, have to be founded upon the thought objects constructed by the commonsense thinking of men, living their daily life within their social world" (1962:59). However, to meet the demands of "science," the meaning of the world from the actor's perspective must be captured in abstraction from its unique and unpredictable expression within immediate reality. In other words, Schutz was concerned with "typical," *not* "real," actors. That is, scientific constructs must be derived in an objective (read "value-free") manner.

How does the social scientist proceed? The investigator first must establish a scientific attitude, then construct ideal types of social conduct. There are three crucial differences between the common-sense and scientific attitudes toward the social world. First, the common-sense actor is pragmatically oriented to the social world. The scientist, in contrast, is disinterested; the theorizing of the scientist serves no pragmatic purpose in the actor's everyday world. Second, the stock of knowledge of the common-sense actor is derived from the everyday world, whereas that of the scientist is scientifically derived. Third, the scientist must become detached from his or her personal situation during the investigative process. Typifications within the common-sense world, in contrast, receive a unique *biographical* expression. Once the social scientist has established detachment, the first step, attaining a scientific attitude, has been reached.

The second step is the scientific construction of ideal types of social action. This technique involves replacing the actual human beings with puppets (homunculi) created by the social scientist (Schutz, 1962). The content of the puppets' consciousness is restricted to what is necessary to perform the typical course of action relevant to the scientific problem. The puppets are not embedded in biographical situations. They do not selectively perceive objects in their environment that are relevant for the solution of problems at hand. The puppets do not choose, nor do they have knowledge outside of the typical knowledge imputed to them by the social scientist. In short, the homunculi are completely determined by typifications; they are animated and constrained entirely by social forces. Thus through the construction of ideal types of social action, the social scientist is able to focus attention on the typical aspects of social life.

The construction of ideal types is not an arbitrary process. To reflect subjective meaning adequately, ideal types must meet the following criteria:

1. *Postulate of relevance*: Following Weber, Schutz asserted that the social problem to be investigated should determine what is to be studied and how it is to be approached (Schutz, 1962).
2. *Postulate of adequacy*: According to this principle, ideal types should be constructed so that actors' behavior in the life world that corresponds to the ideal type constructed by the scientist would make sense to the actors and to their contemporaries.
3. *Postulate of logical consistency*: Types must be constructed with a high degree of clarity and distinctness and must be compatible with the principles of formal logic. Fulfillment of this postulate "warrants the objective validity of the thought objects constructed by the social scientist" (Schutz, 1962:43).
4. *Postulate of compatibility*: The constructed types either must be compatible with a scientific stock of knowledge or demonstrate why this stock of knowledge is inadequate.
5. *Postulate of subjective interpretation*: The model of the social world must have reference to the subjective meaning that behavior has for real actors.

Schutz posited four different social worlds and a methodological scheme that eliminates two of them from social scientific consideration. He eliminated the worlds of directly experienced associates (*umwelt*) and of successors (*folgewelt*) from scientific sociological study because of the freedom of the actors in them. Predecessors (*vorwelt*) lack freedom and are therefore a proper subject for a subjective sociology. However, this science will probably be a weak one, because our knowledge of those who came before us is likely to be vague and tentative. *Thus the world of contemporaries* (mitwelt) *is the one most amenable to social scientific study.* This is true for two reasons. First, it is dominated by types rather than free and unpredictable actual actors. Second, because the social scientist lives in that world, he or she is better able to understand the types that exist in it.

In his discussion of the *mitwelt*, Schutz's focus was on the coercive effect of cultural phenomena (for example, typifications) on actors. This theme was also prominent in his thoughts on the life world.

THE LIFE WORLD

To Schutz the concept *life world* encompasses the cultural, taken-for-granted framework of social life and its impact on the thoughts and actions of actors. Although he was interested in the impact of cultural forces on actors, Schutz accorded greatest significance to the cultural level itself. He was most interested in culturally prescribed and socially transmitted patterns of belief and conduct. The cultural components of the life world both precede and succeed us in time. This framework, imposed on us from outside, is not a continuing individual construction of reality. It serves to constrain actors, to set limits on their everyday conduct. Actors are provided with ready-made courses of action, solutions to problems, interpretations of the social world, and so forth. As a result, in nonproblematic situations, actors tend to be reduced to habitual response patterns. In the *mitwelt,* actors are likely to experience few problematic situations and therefore have little need to question the taken-for-granted cultural framework. However, in the *umwelt* more problematic situations are likely to arise in face-to-face relations, with the result that typifications are more likely to be called into question. For example, meeting a semiliterate college professor would lead us to question our typifications of professors.

The life world includes the totality of typifications upon which all experience, knowledge, and conduct are based. It is a world taken for granted by the typical actor; it is simply there. Although particular typifications may be questioned, the larger structure of typifications ordinarily is not. That the social world is, to a large extent, predefined by cultural impositions leads, paradoxically, to more freedom for actors. Because actors do *not* have to negotiate every aspect of every situation and can rely on definition by type and conduct by recipe, they are free to modify knowledge and conduct in particular problematic parts of their lives.

The unquestioning attitude of actors toward the cultural aspects of the life world is what, as we have seen, is called the "natural attitude":

> I find continually present and standing over against me the one spatio-temporal fact-world to which I myself belong. . . . This "fact-world" . . . I find to *be out there*, and also *take it just as it gives itself to me as something that exists out there.* All doubting and rejecting of the data of the natural world leaves standing the *general thesis of the natural standpoint.* "The" world is as fact-world always there; at the most it is at odd points "other" than I supposed . . . but the "it" remains ever, in the sense of the general thesis, a world that has its being out there.
>
> (Husserl, 1931:106)

Schutz's interest in the totality of typifications in the life world and the actors' natural attitude toward them lends support to Gorman's (1975a, 1975b, 1977) view that Schutz's main concern is with the coercive effect of cultural structures.

COMPONENTS OF THE LIFE WORLD   Schutz was interested in specific components of the life world, for example, the three routine elements of knowledge that are part of the taken-for-granted reality of everyday life—knowledge of skills, useful knowledge, and knowledge of recipes. Each is part of the social stock of knowledge and leads to more or less habitual action.

Knowledge of skills is the most basic form of knowledge in that it rarely becomes problematic and thus is accorded a high degree of certainty. An example is the skill of walking. (A rare exception would occur in the case of a temporary paralysis.)

Useful knowledge is a definite solution to a problem that was once problematic. Although this type of knowledge is not absolutely trustworthy, it has achieved a high level of certainty. Examples include courses of action, such as driving a car or playing a piano, as well as intellectual perspectives, such as philosophy.

Knowledge of recipes, the third form of habitual knowledge, is the most variable but still is standardized. In certain situations, recipes are called forth as standard ways to cope. Whenever possible an actor employs a recipe. For example, in dealing with most customers, a salesperson can use time-tested techniques, but should the situation become problematic and the customer behave in unusual ways, the salesperson can employ an alternative recipe or even come up with an innovative response.

Private Components of Knowledge   Schutz also was aware that all the elements of the cultural realm can and often do vary from individual to individual because personal experience differs. In Schutz's terms, the stock of knowledge is "biographically articulated":

> That means that I "know" more or less adequately that it is the "result" of prior situations. And further, I "know" that this, my situation, is in that respect absolutely "unique." Indeed, the stock of knowledge, through which I determine the present situation, has its "unique" biographical articulation. This refers not only to the content, the "meaning" of all the prior experiences sedimented in it, in situations. It refers also to the intensity, . . . duration, and sequence of these experiences. This circumstance is of singular importance, since it really constitutes the individual stock of knowledge.
>
> (Schutz and Luckmann, 1973:111–112)

Thus, according to Schutz, the stock of knowledge always has a private component. However, even this unique and private component of the stock of knowledge is not solely of the actor's own making: "It must be stressed . . . that sequence, experiential depth and nearness, and even the duration of experiences and the acquisition of knowledge, are socially objectivated and determined. In other words, there are social categories of biographical articulation" (Schutz and Luckmann, 1973:113).

Because of their source in individual biography, private stocks of knowledge are not part of the life world. Because they are biographical in nature, Schutz did not feel that the unique and private components of knowledge are amenable to scientific study. They are, in Schutz's view, nonetheless important components of the everyday life of actual actors.

WE AND THEY RELATIONS   Within the life world are both we and they relations. Schutz's interest in scientific sociology led him to focus on the latter. They relations are dominated by cultural forces that can be studied scientifically, whereas we relations are dominated by individual conscious processes that cannot be studied in this way.

We Relations   *We relations* are defined by a relatively high degree of intimacy, which is determined by the extent to which the actors are acquainted with one another's personal biographies. The pure we relation is a face-to-face relationship "in which the partners are aware of each other and sympathetically participate in each other's lives for however short a time" (Schutz, 1932/1967:164). The we relation encompasses the consciousness of the participants as well as the patterns of action and interaction that characterize face-to-face interaction. To put it another way, the we relation is characteristic of the *umwelt*, a domain that, as we have seen, Schutz defined as not capable of study by scientific sociology, although he saw it as crucially important in the everyday world. Relations at this level are far too problematic, far too subject to idiosyncratic negotiation by actors, to be treated by scientific sociology. Finally, the we relation is distinguished from the they relation by the particular orientation to the other person in the interaction. Specifically, the we relation is characterized by a "thou orientation," which "is the universal form in which the other is experienced 'in person'" (Schutz and Luckmann, 1973:62). In other words, we relations are highly personal and immediate.

The immediacy of interaction has two implications for social relations. First, in a we relation, unlike in a they relation, there are abundant indicators of the other's subjective experience. Immediacy allows each actor to enter into the consciousness of the other. Second, when entering any social relation, we or they, an individual has only typical knowledge of the other. However, in the continuing process of a face to face interaction, typifications of the other are tested, revised, re-enacted, and modified. That is, interaction with others necessarily modifies typologies.

Schutz not only offered a number of insights into we relations per se, but also linked these relationships to cultural phenomena in the real world. For example, in we relations actors learn the typifications that allow them to survive socially. Without recipes, actors would have to invent a proper response in every new situation. Clearly, people need typifications to live socially. They are learned within the everyday life world through socialization by parents, teachers, and peers, generally in we relations. This socialization takes place throughout the life cycle as people acquire the recipes that they need to survive in different settings.

People not only learn recipes in we relations but use them there as well—trying them out, altering them when they prove ineffective or inappropriate. In general, people use recipes as long as they work; they "try to determine new situations as familiar" (Schutz and Luckmann, 1973:141). However, because the everyday world often proves unreceptive to typical courses of action, a recipe that has worked many times in the past may prove ineffective. In these circumstances actors, using their creative minds, abandon a typical strategy and invent a new one appropriate to this particular circumstance or person. Although Schutz recognized that this happens in the everyday world, he did not regard it as an appropriate subject matter for a scientific sociology, because it is so unpredictable. Schutz could philosophize about such matters, but he did not believe that they could be studied scientifically.

Schutz was aware that there is considerable give and take among actors in we relations. People try out different courses of action on other people. They may quickly abandon those that elicit hostile reactions and continue to use those that are accepted. People also may find themselves in situations where recipes do not work at all, and they must create appropriate and workable sets of actions. In other words, in we relations people constantly adjust their actions to those with whom they interact.

People also adjust their conceptions of others. They enter a given relationship with certain assumptions about what the other actors are thinking. In general, people assume that the thinking of others is of the same order as their own. Sometimes this is confirmed by what they find, but in other circumstances the facial expressions, the movements, the words, and the actions of others are inconsistent with people's sense of what others are thinking. People then must revise their view of others' thought processes and then adjust their responses on the basis of this new image of what others are thinking. This is an indirect process, because people cannot actually know what others are thinking. Thus they may tentatively change their actions in the hope that this will elicit responses consistent with what they now think is going on in others' minds. People may be forced to revise their conception of others' thought processes and their actions a number of times before they are able to understand why others are acting in a particular way. It is even conceivable that in some instances people cannot make an adequate number of adjustments, with the result that they are likely to flee the particular interaction, completely confused. In such a case, they may seek more comfortable situations where familiar recipes can be applied.

Even within we relations in everyday life most action is guided by recipes. People do not *usually* reflect on what they do or on what others do. However, when they encounter problems, inappropriate thoughts and actions, they must abandon their recipes and reflect on what is going on to create an appropriate response. This is psychologically costly, because people prefer to act and interact in accord with recipes.

They Relations   In Schutz's view, they relations, in contrast to we relations, can be studied scientifically. What interested Schutz as a scientist are routine aspects of social reality, those that are dominated by cultural forces. They relations—which are found within the realm of Schutz's interest, the *mitwelt*—fall into this category. *They relations* are characterized by interaction with impersonal contemporaries (for example, the unseen postal employee who sorts our mail) rather than associates (for example, a personal friend). In they relations, the thoughts and actions of people are dominated by anonymous typifications.

In the "pure" they relation, the typical schemes of knowledge used to define other actors are not available for modification. Because we do not interact with actual people but with impersonal contemporaries, information that varies from our typifications is not provided to us. In other words, new experiences are not constituted in they relations. Cultural typifications determine action, and they cannot be altered by the thoughts and actions of actors in a they relationship. Thus, whereas we relations are subject to negotiation, they relations are not. A science of typifications is possible in they relations. Although Schutz held this view, he was aware that these typifications have their historical roots in a group of people's thoughts and actions: "The first and originally objective solution of a problem was still largely dependent on the subjective relevance awareness of the individual" (Schutz and Luckmann, 1973:225). However, these solutions ultimately become more typified and anonymous—in short, more and more a part of the cultural realm.

CONSCIOUSNESS

If the action and interaction patterns of we relations are not amenable to scientific study, then it is far less likely that one can study scientifically what goes on in individual consciousness. Schutz believed that in the everyday life world, as long as things are proceeding smoothly in accord with recipes, actors pay little attention to what is going on in the minds of others. Similarly, he believed that in a science of sociology, one can also ignore individual consciousness (Schutz, 1932/1967:190). In fact, because Schutz found the mind impervious to scientific study, and because he wanted to focus instead on cultural typifications, he admitted that in his own work he was going to "abandon the strictly phenomenological method," which has historically focused on mental processes (Schutz, 1932/1967:97). We thus have the paradoxical situation of a sociologist who is the field's best-known phenomenologist saying that he is abandoning the subject matter he is best known for.

Despite Schutz's avowed position on science, he offered many philosophical insights into consciousness. In fact, Schutz argued that the base of all of his sociological concerns lay in the "processes of meaning establishment and understanding occurring within individuals, processes of interpretation of the behavior of other people and processes of self-interpretation" (1932/1967:11).

The philosophical basis of Schutz's image of the social world, albeit a basis that is, for him, not amenable to scientific study, is deep consciousness (durée), in which is found the processes of meaning establishment, understanding, interpretation, and self-interpretation. A phenomenological sociology must be based on "the way meaning is constituted in the individual experience of the solitary Ego. In so doing we shall track meaning to its very point of origin in the inner time consciousness in the duration of the ego as it lives through its experience" (Schutz, 1932/1967:13). This is the domain that was of central concern to Schutz's philosophical predecessors, Henri Bergson and Edmund Husserl. They were interested in philosophizing about what went on in the mind, but a central question to Schutz was how to turn this interest into a scientific sociological concern.

Schutz was drawn to the work of Max Weber, particularly that part of Weber's work concerned with social action, because it reflected, he thought, both an interest in consciousness and a concern for a scientific sociology. However, the interest in individual action was only a minor and secondary concern for Weber, who was more concerned with the impact of social structures on action than with the bases of action in consciousness. According to Prendergast, Schutz had "no apparent interest in Weber's theory of bureaucracy, sociology of religion, political sociology, or general economic history" (1986:15). Schutz, therefore, was only concerned with a small and peripheral portion of Weber's sociology. But even in that, Weber was a less than satisfying model for Schutz but not for the reasons implied above. To Schutz, the problem with Weber's work was that there were inadequacies in his conception of consciousness. Weber failed to distinguish among types of meanings, and he failed to distinguish meanings from motives. In clarifying what Weber failed to do, Schutz told us much about his own conception of consciousness.

MEANINGS AND MOTIVES Schutz argued that we must distinguish meanings from motives. In the process, he differentiated between two subtypes of both meanings and motives. Although he did not always succeed in keeping them neatly separated, for Schutz *meanings* concern how actors determine what aspects of the social world are important to them, whereas *motives* involve the reasons that actors do what they do. One type of meaning is the *subjective* meaning context. That is, through our own independent mental construction of reality, we define certain components of reality as meaningful. However, although this process is important in the everyday life world,

Schutz did not see it as amenable to scientific study because it is too idiosyncratic.

Of concern to scientific sociology is the second type of meaning, the *objective* meaning context, the sets of meanings that exist in the culture as a whole and that are the shared possession of the collectivity of actors. In that these sets of meanings are shared rather than idiosyncratic, they are as accessible to sociologists as to anyone else. In that they have an objective existence, they can be studied scientifically by the sociologist, and they were one of Schutz's main concerns. Schutz was critical of Weber for failing to differentiate between subjective and objective meaning and for failing to make it clear that only objective meaning contexts can be scrutinized in scientific sociology.

Schutz also differentiated between two types of motives—"in order to" and "because." Both involve the meaningful reasons for an individual's actions, but only because motives are accessible to the sociologist. *In-order-to motives* are the reasons an actor undertakes certain actions in an effort to bring about some future occurrence. They are apparent only when the action is taking place. They are part of deep consciousness, the continuing stream of consciousness, and as such are inaccessible to the scientific sociologist. Sociology cannot concern itself with in-order-to motives because they cannot be studied scientifically. But sociology can study *because motives*, or retrospective glances at the factors that have caused individuals to behave as they did. In that the actions have already occurred, the motives for them are accessible to both the social scientist and the actor. In fact, however, Schutz was as little inclined to study because motives as in-order-to motives. Both are much too subjective, much too individualistic, for his orientation to the study of shared meaning systems.

SOCIAL ACTION AND PROBLEMATIC SITUATIONS

Action is conduct based on a preconceived plan. The plan makes action meaningful from the point of view of the social actor. Without it, behavior becomes mere unconscious doing. If the plan or project takes into account another actor, then it becomes social action. Further, all action necessarily involves choice among projects. If there were no alternatives to choose among, conduct would require no project and, once again, behavior would be reduced to mere unconscious doing. Action, involving the process of ascertaining and choosing between alternative projects, becomes necessary only when the application of recipes to typically defined situations is no longer adequate to accomplish practical purposes, that is, when situations become problematic.

The conditions under which a situation becomes problematic can be any of the following: first, "an actual experience does not readily 'fit' into a type on hand in the stock of knowledge"; second, "the determinateness of the type does not suffice for mastery of the situation"; third, "one becomes cognizant of the incompatibility ('contradictions') between two elements of knowledge which until now coexisted in a taken-for-granted way in the stock of knowledge" (Schutz and Luckmann, 1973:202). In providing a solution to the problem, the actor has constituted a new type; an addition has been made to the existing stock of knowledge. "In other words, a type arises from a situationally adequate solution to a problematic situation through the new determination of an experience which could not be mastered with the aid of the stock of knowledge already on hand" (Schutz and Luckmann, 1973:231).

When situations become problematic, typical knowledge and routine patterns of conduct are no longer sufficient for the mastery of situations. At this point, the actor must consciously choose a behavioral response to the problematic situation. Action necessarily involves choosing among plans, projects, or alternative lines of conduct. In the enactment of the chosen project of action, new experiences are constituted; an addition has been made to the existing stock of knowledge.

When problematic situations are social, then the solution, the choosing and enactment of a plan, is "social" action, action that is oriented toward another actor. The dynamics of consciousness that underlie social action (the coming to be of a "problem," the positing of alternative courses of conduct, and the ultimate choice and enactment of a project) are the foundations upon which we relations are based. A we relation is a relation in which the subjective consciousness of one actor is oriented toward the consciousness of another actor. We relations presume social action. The implication is that in every immediate, intense, and vivid interaction in which there is a reciprocal thou orientation (each actor is oriented to the consciousness of the other), perceptions of the social world are available for modification, new types are formed, and the social stock of knowledge is enlarged.

Action, according to Schutz's formulation of the concept, represents the manifestation of voluntarism at the individual level. The actor is a "free agent" in choosing among projects of action, although choosing is limited by one's stock of knowledge. The stock of knowledge, the set of types that underlies the actor's conception of and behavior within the social world, is the base. The conscious choice of conduct in response to a problematic situation is the dynamic that modifies or enlarges the stock of knowledge.

INTERPRETING SCHUTZIAN THEORY

In many ways, Schutzian theory is more difficult to interpret than the work of most other major theorists. First, Schutz is probably the most single-mindedly abstract theorist whom we have encountered. Others have been much more deeply involved in the empirical world. Weber, for example, offered a theory embedded in a great deal of historical detail. Marx moved back and forth between theoretical abstraction and the real-world evils of capitalism. Even Parsons, who was a highly abstract thinker, touched base now and again with the real world.

Second, Schutz's theory is embedded in a philosophical tradition that is foreign to sociology and translates only with great difficulty into sociological terms. James Heap and Phillip Roth (1973) argue that it is highly questionable whether Husserl's phenomenology, which is one of the main roots of Schutzian theory, can be translated into sociology. We can characterize Schutz's work as an effort to do just that. The success of Schutz's efforts is illustrated by the popularity of theories derived from his work—particularly phenomenological sociology and ethnomethodology. Nevertheless, his roots in phenomenological philosophy make it difficult for us to adequately grasp his sociology.

Third, and perhaps most important, is the major discontinuity in his thinking. Although he offered philosophical insights into a wide range of issues, he viewed only some of them as amenable to scientific sociology. Thus in thinking about his work, we need to differentiate between what was amenable to scientific sociological study and what was not.

This differentiation brings us back to the debate with which we began this section. First, some commentators praise Schutz for his micro focus on how actors create the social world. Others criticize him for this. Still others see Schutz as having a large-scale, cultural focus. All these positions are defensible, at least to some degree. The first two rely on Schutz's philosophical ideas; the third focuses on his thoughts about scientific sociology. Followers of the first position applaud Schutz for creating a philosophical sociology of consciousness. Those who take the second position criticize Schutz for this orientation and for his failure to deal adequately with social structures. Supporters of the third position see Schutz as creating a scientific sociology of the cultural constraints on actors. That such diverse interpretations are all defensible tells us much about the richness of and the confusions in Schutzian theory.

Examples of Phenomenological Sociology

We will now deal with two examples of phenomenological sociology. The first, by George Psathas and Frances C. Waksler (1973), on face-to-face interaction, illustrates the micro-level focus of much of phenomenology. Although such an orientation is the norm, it is not inevitable. Psathas recognized the micro concerns of phenomenological sociologists, their interest in "the understanding of ordinary activities in the everyday world," but he also argued that such an orientation is unintentional and as a result "phenomenological sociology may come to be identified with the study of interaction, or small gatherings, and of events that are not societal in magnitude and scope" (1973a: 12). Psathas clearly believed that with phenomenological sociology, larger-scale phenomena, such as organizations, groups, cultures, and societies, can be studied.

The second example is the work of Peter Berger and Thomas Luckmann (1967) and their effort to integrate small-scale phenomenological insights with more traditional large-scale sociological work.

FACE-TO-FACE INTERACTION

Psathas and Waksler (1973) started with the assumption that face-to-face interaction is the basis of the more complex, larger-scale social phenomena; however, they opted to concentrate on the individual levels of analysis, especially consciousness.

By outlining their argument we can follow the structure the authors used. They divide the elements of face-to-face interaction into three basic components: features of the actors, features of the relations between actors, and features of action.

1. Features of the Actors
    a. Both Ego and Other are conscious and they are aware of that consciousness. It is significant for phenomenological sociology that Psathas and Waksler began their analysis of face-to-face interaction with consciousness. True to their intellectual roots, they did not focus on action but turned directly to consciousness. Also, they conceived of consciousness as intentional; consciousness may be of something that "is real or ideal, existent or imaginary" (Psathas and Waksler, 1973:168).
        In this phase of the analysis of face-to-face interaction, the observer must ascertain whether Ego and Other are both conscious and see themselves as

conscious. Face-to-face interaction cannot be said to occur unless the parties are conscious and aware that they are conscious.

b. Both Ego and Other have constituted a self. For interaction to occur, both parties must have a sense of themselves; that is, they must "see themselves as unitary beings, acted upon and acting on the world." Having a self also involves the actors' seeing themselves "as having a past, present and future" and being "capable of reacting to the other and eliciting reactions in him." Finally, for sociologists to be assured that the parties have selves, they "must judge that each is at least potenially effective in his world" (p. 169).

c. Both Ego and Other have acquired and are able to use a stock of knowledge and a system of relevance. For interaction to occur and to be comprehensible to both actors, during their socialization they must have acquired bodies of knowledge as well as schemes for interpreting knowledge and information. However, if the two parties have entirely different, nonoverlapping bodies of knowledge and systems of relevance, then they cannot interact. They must share at least some knowledge and systems of relevance for them to be able to interact.

d. Both Ego and Other are able to communicate and to use a symbolic system of meaning. In order to interact, the parties must be able to communicate with each other using both *signs* and *symbols* in the sense that Mead meant. That is, signs are such things as physical gestures that stand for themselves, whereas symbols involve both a physical and verbal phenomena that can stand for something else. Actors do not have to use symbols every time they communicate, but the symbols must be at least potentially available to them. Symbolic systems of meaning serve two very important functions. First, they make the ensuing steps in the interaction process possible. Second, they make "possible that internal conversation by means of which the person interprets the meaning of his experiences" (p. 170).

e. Both Ego and Other are motivated to act. Both parties are ready to act and interested in acting.

f. Both Ego and Other view their bodies as fields of experience. This means that, in lay terms, "body language" is important to interaction. To deal with each other, actors must be able to "read" the meaning of such things as facial expressions, body tension, and body movements. And in fact, we all do pay a great deal of attention to such phenomena during the interaction process.

2. Features of the Relations Between Actors

a. Both Ego and Other are present. Physical presence of the actors is necessary but not sufficient condition for interaction to occur. Each party may be within reach of the other without interaction occurring. However, being close enough to use one's senses in order to interact is a precondition of face-to-face interaction.

b. Ego and Other are each aware of the other's bodily presence. For interaction to occur, mere physical presence must be supplemented by a mutual awareness that the potential actors are in each other's presence.

c. Ego and Other constitute each other as actors with the features of actors. Another prerequisite for interaction is that Ego and Other attribute to each other all the characteristics discussed above; in other words, each must think of the other as an actor. In Schutz's terms, a we relationship can be said to exist when each party is conscious of the other. That awareness is involved in the next two aspects of the process delineated by Psathas and Waksler.

d.   Both Ego and Other are aware that each is conscious of the other person's presence.

e.   Both Ego and Other are aware that each constitutes the other as an actor. Each party must be aware not only of the other's bodily presence, but also of the other's consciousness of him as being present and being accepted as an actor. As a result of this mutual awareness, both parties are in a position to receive and interpret information about the other's subjective experiences as they are occurring.

3.   Features of Action

a.   Both Ego and Other project action of affecting-the-other type. Even at this stage in the process, action has not yet occurred. We are still at the stage of the psychological formulation of a plan of action. To use Schutz's terms again, Ego's "in-order-to" motive is to cause some kind of conscious experience for the Other.

b.   Both Ego and Other develop an act on the basis of their plan of action. On the basis of the plan developed mentally, each party develops a plan of action.

c-1.   Ego acts. At this point we move from the psychological presuppositions of action to the arena of action. One party has now acted, but interaction cannot be said to have occurred yet. The following stages are needed:

d-1.   Other is aware of Ego's act as arising from his plan of action. We return here to consciousness, because in order for interaction to occur, Other must interpret Ego's act as meaningful and as arising out of Ego's plan for action.

c-2.   Other acts.

d-2.   Ego is aware of Other's act as arising from his or her project of action. Thus, for interaction to occur, we must have not only mutual action but also mutual awareness of each party's consciousness.

With this return to consciousness, Psathas and Waksler complete the analysis at the same level as that on which they began. Of course, in the real world, one set of actions and reactions rarely closes an interactional episode; rather, the process is likely to continue.

A few generalizations can be derived from Psathas and Waksler's analysis and applied to phenomenological sociology. First, the analysis illustrates the preoccupation of phenomenologists with the individual level of analysis. Second, at this level, consciousness is more interesting to phenomenologically oriented sociologists than is action or interaction; they are more concerned with the psychological prerequisites for action than with action itself. Although Psathas and Waksler set out to deal with interaction, they devoted most of their analysis to consciousness. Third, Psathas and Waksler used no data, in the conventional sense of the term; that is, their analysis was not empirical. This reflects the fact that phenomenological sociology remains highly descriptive, theoretical, and philosophical.

THE SOCIAL CONSTRUCTION OF REALITY

The preoccupation with individual thought and action was undoubtedly one of the reasons for Berger and Luckmann's book *The Social Construction of Reality* (1967), which tried to extend the concerns of phenomenological sociology to social structures and institutions. Furthermore, the authors sought to integrate the individual and societal levels. We will be concerned not only with what they have done but with how successful they have been in achieving their ambitious objectives.

Berger and Luckmann's work is one of the most widely read and influential books in contemporary sociology. One of its main attractions is that it translated Alfred Schutz's sometimes arcane phenomenology into the terms of mainstream sociological theory. Berger and Luckmann also attempted to go beyond Schutz's work, to buttress it with Mead's social psychology and to complement both Schutz's and Mead's work with the work of Marx and Durkheim on society and culture. They attempted to integrate Weber's work on social action with Durkheim's thoughts on social facts as external realities. In relating these thinkers to one another, Berger and Luckmann made it quite clear that they wanted to deal in an integrated fashion with "the dual character of society in terms of objective facticity *and* subjective meaning" (1967:18). Even more explicit is this statement, which seems to give the essence of an approach to social reality that integrates a concern with large- and small-scale phenomena: "*Society is a human product. Society is an objective reality. Man is a social product*" (p. 61). In other words, people are the products of the very society that they create.

The book's subtitle, *A Treatise in the Sociology of Knowledge*, provides the key to their analysis. Their view of the sociology of knowledge is unusual. To them, it is concerned with the social construction of reality. In articulating this view, their goal was to move the sociology of knowledge away from the study of intellectual history and to the everyday construction of reality, the process of everyday knowledge production in which we all engage. However, despite their intent to deal with both large- and small-scale phenomena, and their commitment to deal with the work of people such as Marx and Durkheim, they said little about objectivity, especially large-scale social structures, even though the longest chapter in their book is titled "Society as Objective Reality."

EVERYDAY LIFE   Berger and Luckmann began their analysis at the individual level with the reality of everyday life, the common-sense world. Here Berger and Luckmann relied almost exclusively on the work of Alfred Schutz.

Berger and Luckmann were particularly interested in people's phenomenological tendency to view subjective processes as objective realities. In their view, people tend to apprehend everyday life as an ordered reality; that is, social reality seems to the actor to be independent of the actor's apprehension of it. It appears already objectified, and it seems to impose itself on the actor. Crucial to this tendency toward objectification is language, which "continuously provides [people] with the necessary objectifications and posits the order within which these make sense and within which everyday life has meaning for [people]" (Berger and Luckmann, 1967:23). We take the reality of everyday life for granted; although we could question it, we suspend that ability in order to live comfortably within it. The thrust of Berger and Luckmann's discussion was a view of the social world as the cultural product of conscious processes.

Berger and Luckmann's discussion of face-to-face interaction is welcome, although it adds little to Schutz's work and lacks the detail of Psathas and Waksler's (1973) work. What is significant about their micro-level analysis is that Berger and Luckmann, unlike Schutz, were willing to include the individual level in their sociology. In their description of face-to-face interactions, which, following Schutz, they called *we relationships,* Berger and Luckmann emphasized that such relationships involve an immediate interchange of meanings. In we relationships, there is much less typification than in they relationships (which involve anonymous others). In other words, instead of relating to people on the basis of culturally defined recipes, in we relationships people relate to each other in more personalized ways. Because we relationships are less dominated by typifications, there is more latitude for negotiations among the actors. As we move away from immediate, face-to-face relationships to relationships with people with whom we are less intimate or even strangers, there is more likelihood of typification and less of interpersonal negotiation. In other words, our relationships with others in the they relationship grow progressively more impersonal and stereotypic. The importance of typifications to Berger and Luckmann is illustrated by their definition of social structures, a definition clearly not in line with an objective view of such structures. They define *social structures* as "the sum total of these typifications and of the recurrent patterns of interaction established by means of them" (p. 33).

As with many phenomenologists, language is very important to Berger and Luckmann, especially as it relates to the typification process. Berger and Luckmann viewed language as a specific form of the process of "signification," a subtype of objectification distinguished by its explicit purpose of standing for a wide range of subjective meanings. Language is a system of vocal symbols, the most important symbol system in society. The reason for its importance is that language can be detached from the here and now, from face-to-face interaction, and can communicate meanings that are not immediate expressions of subjectivity. Language also allows us to deal with things that we never have experienced and perhaps never will experience ourselves. It also can help us accumulate meanings and knowledge that can then be passed on to future generations. In these and other ways, language is, in Berger and Luckmann's system, the most important social structure: "I encounter language as a facticity external to myself and it is coercive on me" (p. 38). Here they self-consciously took a Durkheimian position on language as an external and coercive social fact. However, this is an exception to their general tendency to pay little attention to social structures, or the objective components of society.

OBJECTIVE COMPONENTS OF SOCIETY Despite their perspective on language, Berger and Luckmann are weakest on the objective components of society. For example, they defined social structure as nothing more than recurrent patterns of action. In their chapter, "Society as an Objective Reality," they were interested primarily in the process by which that world, such as it is, is produced and how a *sense* of its objectivity is created. They carefully reminded readers that this sense as well as whatever objective reality there "really" is out there, is produced by people.

INSTITUTIONALIZATION Beneath this process by which a sense of social reality is constructed lies the fact that people must externalize; that is, they must do such things as produce what they need to survive and interact with others. In the process of externalizing, people are prone to develop habitualized patterns of acting and interacting in recurrent situations. Life would be impossible without habits. It would be very difficult to decide the proper action in every new situation.

Habitualized actions set the stage for the development of institutionalization. This occurs when people develop typifications of what others are likely to do in a given situation. Berger and Luckmann defined an *institution* as a kind of reciprocal process of typification. This microscopic conception of an institution is quite different from most sociological conceptions of institutions. Although to Berger and Luckmann institutions are not large-scale phenomena, they are nonetheless external and coercive. They argued that institutions "*control* human conduct by setting up predefined patterns of conduct" (Berger and Luckmann, 1967:55).

The stream of history allows these institutions to acquire objectivity. However, when Berger and Luckmann considered these institutions, they were inclined to think of them subjectively also:

> This means that the institutions that now have been crystallized . . . are *experienced* as existing over and beyond the individuals who "happen to" embody them at the moment. In other words, the institutions are now *experienced* as possessing a reality of their own, a reality that confronts the individual as an external and coercive fact.
> (Berger and Luckmann, 1967:58; italics added)

By emphasizing the *experience* of institutions, rather than their external reality, Berger and Luckmann made their subjective biases quite clear, even when they were supposedly dealing with external realities.

Children perceive the institutional world as an objective reality; that is, it was there before they were born and it will be there after they die. As individuals mature they apprehend their biographies as episodes within the objective history of society.

The various institutions within society tend to "hang together," but in Berger and Luckmann's view this is due not to their objective qualities but to the tendency of people to perceive them in that way. In other words, what is crucial is the knowledge that people have of society. Thus sociology should focus on how people reconstruct their knowledge of social reality, not only in the historical production of the world but also in the continuing creation of that world on a day to day basis.

ROLES   Berger and Luckmann's definition of roles is typical of their sense of objective social reality. To them, roles are typifications of what can be expected of actors in given social situations. Roles are not to be confused with objective positions, as they tend to be in the work of many others. The role was particularly important to Berger and Luckmann because it constitutes a mediation or link between the large- and small-scale worlds. In Berger and Luckmann's hands, it served to mediate *only* between culture and consciousness: "The analysis of role is of particular importance to the sociology of knowledge because it reveals the mediations between the macroscopic *universe of meaning* objectivated in a society and the ways in which these universes are *subjectively* real to individuals" (p. 79; italics added).

REIFICATION   Reification is a particularly important tool for dealing in an integrated way with the social world, but Berger and Luckmann limited its utility by the way they used it. They defined *reification* solely as a subjective phenomenon: "the apprehension of human phenomena as if they were things, that is, in nonhuman or possibly suprahuman terms'' (p. 89). Reification is the tendency to *perceive* human products as if they were something else, "such as facts of nature, results of cosmic laws, or manifestations of divine will'' (p. 89). In other words, people simply lose sight of the dialectical relationship between them and their products. People can objectify social phenomena without reifying them; that is, they can produce objects and view the world in objective terms without forgetting that people produce them. However, Berger and Luckmann gave absolutely no sense of the other aspect of reification—that is, the degree to which society, as a result of the subjective processes they describe, objectively comes to acquire a life of its own.

LEGITIMATIONS   Also telling, in terms of their tendency to ignore objective structures, was Berger and Luckmann's extensive treatment of *legitimations*, or the explanations and justifications of the institutional system. Again, instead of dealing with the structures themselves, Berger and Luckmann focused on the knowledge that is used to support their existence: "Legitimation 'explains' the institutional order by ascribing cognitive validity to its objectivated meaning. Legitimation justifies the institutional order by giving a normative dignity to its practical imperatives'' (p. 83). The focus is not on the structures being legitimated but on the means by which they are legitimated.

CRITICISMS   Berger and Luckmann's chapter on society as objective reality really dealt with subjective phenomena. In their next chapter, on society as a subjective reality, Berger and Luckmann discussed the socialization process, the process by which cultural phenomena are communicated to and internalized in consciousness. This chapter added little beyond elementary knowledge about socialization.

Berger and Luckmann provided an almost purely subjective characterization of the social world. However, this may not be a fair criticism, because their stated intention was to present a sociology of knowledge. Furthermore, near the end of their work they admitted the need for a structural sociology to complement their subjective orientation (p. 186). Still, they are vulnerable to criticism because they promised more than simply a subjective sociology, including integrating Freud, Mead, and Weber on social action with Marx and Durkheim on social structures—and they did not deliver. More important was what they promised in their pivotal statement: "*Society is a human product. Society is an objective reality. Man is a social product*" (p. 61). They failed to produce any sense of society as an objective reality; as a result, their entire dialectic loses much of its significance. In Marx's hands a similar discussion is much more powerful, because of his strong sense of the obdurate structures of the social world and the difficulties involved in overcoming these structures. Berger and Luckmann were right to state that they needed Marx's sociology, but unfortunately they did not follow through on this.

In spite of the harsh criticism aimed at Berger and Luckmann in this section, they are to be praised for the effort to extend phenomenology beyond its traditional focus on consciousness. Their failure to deal satisfactorily with social structures, despite their avowed desire to do so, does not mean that phenomenological sociology *cannot* integrate a concern with social structure into its approach, but it does mean that it will be difficult. Phenomenological sociology *may* be able to deal with larger-scale social structures, but that remains to be demonstrated. Its strengths continue to lie in the understanding of consciousness and its relationship to action and interaction, and in the study of culture and its constraining effects on actors.

ETHNOMETHODOLOGY

Given its Greek roots, the term *ethnomethodology* literally means the methods people use on a daily basis. The central concern of ethnomethodology "is to demonstrate how society is the ongoing practical accomplishment of rational individuals" (Weigert, 1981:38). Ethnomethodology was "invented" by Harold Garfinkel in the 1940s. Since that time it has expanded enormously and moved in a number of different directions. This has led Don Zimmerman to conclude that there is no longer one ethnomethodology, but several. As Zimmerman put it, ethnomethodology now "encompasses a number of more or less distinct and sometimes incompatible lines of inquiry" (1978:6). We will start with this diversity and describe a number of different studies done from an ethnomethodological perspective. The heart of ethnomethodology lies in these specific studies and not in general theoretical or programmatic statements (Sharrock and Anderson, 1986). To ethnomethodologists "research and theorizing are to be done in conjunction, such that the theorizing is tied to the materials generated by the research" (Sharrock and Anderson, 1986:40). Nevertheless, ethnomethodology does have a core of shared ideas which we discuss after the analysis of the specific studies. In order to give the reader a general orientation to reading about these studies, we repeat the definition of ethnomethodology offered in Chapter 2: the study of "the body of commonsense knowledge and the range of procedures and considerations by means of which the ordinary members of society make sense of, find their way about in, and act on the circumstances in which they find themselves" (Heritage, 1984:4).

A major branch of ethnomethodology is *conversation analysis,* or the "description and explication of the competences that ordinary speakers use and rely on in participating in intelligible, socially organized interaction," or "the procedures by which conversationalists produce their own behavior and understand and deal with the behavior of others" (Heritage and Atkinson, 1984:1). Conversation analysts look for the order, the regularities produced by and found in peoples' conversations. Ethnomethodologists in general deal with behavior; conversational analysts focus on a specific type of behavior, conversation.

Methodologically, conversational analysts are led to study conversations in naturally occurring situations, often using audio and videotape. This method allows information to flow from the real world rather than being imposed on it by the researcher. The researcher can examine and re-examine the actual conversation rather than his or her notes on it. This technique also allows the researcher to do highly detailed analyses of conversations.

Conversational analysis is based on the assumption that conversations are the bedrock of other forms of interpersonal behavior. They are the most pervasive form of interaction, and a conversation "consists of the fullest matrix of socially organized communicative practices and procedures" (Heritage and Atkinson, 1984:13). Describing conversational analysis, but perhaps speaking of all of ethnomethodology, Harvey Sacks says, "It is possible that detailed study of small phenomena may give an enormous understanding of the way humans do things" (1984:24).

Examples of Ethnomethodology

"DOING" WALKING

Few of us ever give more than a passing thought to the common-sense knowledge and procedures involved in the act of walking, let alone subject it to serious sociological analysis, but that is precisely what A. Lincoln Ryave and James N. Schenkein (1974) did. Their concern was not simply with walking but with "doing" walking. Although we all possess routine, methodical practices for walking, we must actually use those routines to "do" walking. Furthermore, we must do it in concert with the other people who walk with, by, or toward us; in other words, walking is the concerted accomplishment of members of the community. Ryave and Schenkein examined walking not just to understand this specific act but to understand a wide range of such phenomena: "In treating this commonplace phenomenon as the problematic achievement of members, we hope to build towards a greater understanding of social phenomena as on-going situated accomplishments" (1974:265).

Their basic resource in this study was a series of videotapes of people walking. Their central concern was the ways in which people navigate and avoid collisions. For successful walking to occur, the parties must not only *recognize* what they are doing but also *produce* the appropriate walking strategy. This is a striking example of how, using ethnomethodology, sociologists can take a mundane situation and demonstrate its problematic character.

Let us take the issue of how walking together is accomplished. To walk together, people have to produce a collective pattern. For example, they must maintain a certain proximity to each other. If one participant gets too far ahead or behind, that person engages in "repair work" in order to restore walking together. The individual may hurry up, slow down, or explain (at the time or later on) why he or she was out of step. If the participant refuses to engage in repair work and continues out of step, it becomes a serious threat to the reality of walking together.

The act of walking together also makes possible a set of walking together activities: "For example, such activities as conversing, being available for conversation, touching, laughing, offering of offerables such as cigarettes or sweets, parting, and so on, are made relevant, and expectable, by the sheer fact of walking together" (p. 272).

Ryave and Schenkein also viewed the phenomenon of walking alone as a social accomplishment. For example, how does the lone walker avoid the appearance of walking together when he or she passes another walker on the street? Ryave and Schenkein's videotapes indicate that the individual manipulates direction, pace, and body attitude so that the moment of co-presence is only fleeting. Similarly, it takes work to avoid engaging in violations while walking. For example, an individual could easily seem to be "following" someone in the street. The manner of one's approach could appear to be a threat to others. To avoid such violations or appearances of violations, walkers not only must be conscious that these acts are possible but also must be ready and able to take actions that would prevent their occurrence.

TELEPHONE CONVERSATIONS: IDENTIFICATION AND RECOGNITION

In this example and the four that follow, we turn to conversational analysis. The goal is to look at the taken-for-granted ways in which conversation is organized. Conversational analysts are concerned with the relationship among utterances rather than the relationship between speakers and hearers (Sharrock and Anderson, 1986:68).

Emanuel A. Schegloff (1979) viewed his examination of the way in which telephone conversations are opened as part of a larger effort to understand the orderly character of social interaction:

> The work in which my colleagues and I have been engaged is concerned with the *organization of social interaction*. We bring to the materials with which we work—audio and videotapes of *naturally occurring* interaction, and transcripts of those tapes—an interest in *detecting* and *describing* the *orderly* phenomena of which conversation and interaction are composed, and an interest in depicting the *systematic organizations* by reference to which those phenomena are produced.
>
> (Schegloff, 1979:24; italics added)

The interest of Schegloff and his colleagues extended to various orderly phenomena within interaction, such as the organization of turn taking in conversations and the ways in which people seek to repair breaches in normal conversational procedure. Beyond this, they were interested in the overall structure of a conversation, including openings, closings, and regularly recurring internal sequences.

In this context Schegloff looked at the opening of a phone conversation, which he defined as "a place where the type of conversation being opened can be proffered, displayed, accepted, rejected, modified—in short, incipiently constituted by the parties to it" (p. 25). Although the talk one hears on the phone is no different from that in face-to-face conversations, the participants lack visual contact. Schegloff focused on one element of phone conversations not found in face-to-face conversations, the sequence by which the parties who have no visual contact identify and recognize each other.

In his research, Schegloff drew on data from 450 telephone openings. He found that telephone openings are often quite straightforward and standardized:

A. Hello?
B. Shar'n?
A. Hi!

Or:

A. Hello.
B. Hello, Charlie?
A. Oh, hi.

(Schegloff, 1979:52)

But some openings "look and sound idiosyncratic—almost virtuoso performances" (p. 68).

A. Hello.
B. Hello Margie?
A. Yes.
B. hhh We do painting, antiquing,
A. is that right.
B. eh, hh—hhh

A. hnh, hnh, hnh
B. nhh, hnh, hnh! hh
A. hh
B. keep people's pa'r tools
A. y(hhh)! hnh, hnh
B. I'm sorry about that—that—I din' see that.

(Adapted from Schegloff, 1979:68)

Although these may be different from the usual openings, they are not without their organization. They are "engendered by a systematic sequential organization adapted and fitted by the parties to some particular circumstances" (p. 68). For example, the preceding conversation is almost incomprehensible until we understand that *B* is calling to apologize for keeping some borrowed power tools too long. *B* makes a joke out of it by building it into a list (painting, antiquing), and it is only at the end when both are laughing that the apology comes.

Schegloff's conclusion was that even where cases are very idiosyncratic, they are to be examined for their organizational pattern:

> Particular cases can, therefore, be examined for their local, interactional, biographical, ethnographic, or other idiosyncratic interest. The same materials can be inspected so as to extract from their local particularities the formal organization into which their particularities are infused. For students of interaction, the organizations through which the work of social life gets accomplished occupy the center of attention.
>
> (Schegloff, 1979:71)

INVITING LAUGHTER

Gail Jefferson (1979; see also Jefferson, 1984) looked at the question of how one knows when to laugh in the course of a conversation. The lay view is that laughter is a totally free event in the course of a conversation or interaction. However, Jefferson found that several basic structural characteristics of an utterance are designed to induce the other party to laugh. The first is the placement, by the speaker, of a laugh at the end of his utterance:

Dan.   I thought that was pretty out of sight. Did you hear me say you're a junkie . . .
       heh, heh
Dolly. heh, heh, heh.

(Adapted from Jefferson, 1979:80)

The second device reported by Jefferson is within-speech laughter—for example, in mid-sentence:

A. You know I didn't . . . you know
B. Hell, *you* know I'm on ret (haha);
A. ehh, yeh, ha ha.

(Adapted from Jefferson, 1979:83)

Jefferson concluded from these examples that the occurrence of laughter is more organized than we realize:

It appears, then, that the order of alternative responses to a candidate laughable is not organized as freely as one might suppose; i.e., the issue is not that *something* should occur, laughter *or* whatever else, but that *laughter* should occur, on a volunteer basis *or* by invitation.

(Jefferson, 1979:83)

But Jefferson was interested not only in the decision to laugh but also in the declining of an invitation to laugh. She found that silence after an invitation is not enough, that a clear signal is required indicating refusal of the invitation. If, for example, someone refuses to laugh, a strategy would be to commence, just after the onset of the speaker's laugh, a serious pursuit of the topic.

GENERATING APPLAUSE

Derived from a body of work developed by J. Maxwell Atkinson (1984a; 1984b), John Heritage and David Greatbatch (1986) recently have studied the rhetoric of British political speeches and uncovered basic devices by which speakers generate applause from their audiences. They argue that applause is generated by "statements that are verbally constructed (a) to *emphasize* and thus highlight their contents against a surrounding background of speech materials and (b) to *project a clear completion point* for the message in question" (Heritage and Greatbatch, 1986:116). Emphasis tells the audience that applause is appropriate, and advance notice of a clear completion point allows the audience to begin applauding more or less in unison. In their analysis of British political speeches, Heritage and Greatbatch uncovered seven basic rhetorical devices:

1. *Contrast.* For example, a politician might argue; "Too much is spent on war . . . too little is spent on peace." Such a statement generates applause because, for emphasis, the same point is made first in negative and then in positive terms. The audience is also able to anticipate when to applaud by matching the unfolding of the second half of the statement with the already completed first half.
2. *List.* A list of political issues, especially the often used three-part list, provides emphasis as well as a completion point that can be anticipated by the audience.
3. *Puzzle solution.* Here the politician first poses a puzzle for the audience and then offers a solution. This double presentation of the issue provides emphasis, and the audience can anticipate the completion of the statement at the end of the solution.
4. *Headline—punch line.* Here the politician proposes to make a statement and then makes it.
5. *Combination.* This involves use of two or more of the devices just listed.
6. *Position-taking.* This involves an initial description of a state of affairs that the speaker would be expected to feel strongly about. However, at first it is presented nonevaluatively. Only at the end does the speaker offer his or her own position.
7. *Pursuit.* This occurs when an audience fails to respond to a particular message. The speaker may actively pursue applause by, for example, restating the central point.

In the political party conferences studied by Heritage and Greatbatch, these seven devices accounted for slightly more than two-thirds of the total applause. Of the seven, the *contrast* (accounting for almost a quarter of applause events) was by far the most commonly applauded format. In addition to these devices, the speaker's manner of delivering the message ("intonation, timing, and gesture") also is important (Heritage and Greatbatch, 1986:143). Finally, the authors note that the seven devices are not restricted to political speech making, but also are found in advertising slogans, newspaper editorials, scientific texts, and so forth. In fact, they conclude that these devices have their roots and are found in everyday, natural, conversational interaction. The implication is that we all use these devices daily to generate positive reactions from those with whom we interact.

THE INTERACTIVE EMERGENCE OF SENTENCES

Charles Goodwin (1979) challenged the traditional linguistic assumption that sentences can be examined in isolation from the process of interaction in which they occur. His view was that "sentences emerge with conversation" (Goodwin, 1979:97). The fact is that the "speaker can reconstruct the meaning of his sentence *as he is producing it* in order to maintain its appropriateness to its recipient of the moment" (p. 98; italics added).

Goodwin's essential point was that speakers pay acute attention to listeners as they are speaking. As the listeners react verbally, facially, or with body language, the speaker adjusts the sentence as it is emerging on the basis of these reactions. The reactions allow the speaker to decide whether his or her point is being made, and if not, to alter the structure of the sentence. In a rather complicated conversation that he analyzed, Goodwin described some of the alterations that took place in a particular sentence sequence:

> In the course of its production the unfolding meaning of John's sentence is reconstructed twice, a new segment is added to it, and another is deleted prior to its production but replaced with a different segment. The sentence eventually produced emerges as the product of a dynamic process of interaction between speaker and hearer as they mutually construct the turn of talk.
>
> (Goodwin, 1979:112)

In other words, sentences are the products of collaborative processes.

FORMULATIONS

Heritage and Watson (1979) were interested in the general issue of orderliness within conversations. They placed this issue within the general context of ethnomethodological concerns:

> A central focus of ethnomethodological work is the analysis of the practical sociological reasoning through which social activity is rendered accountable and orderly. Assumed by this concern is the notion that all scenic features of social interaction [for example, biographies, events, personalities, locations] are occasioned and established as a concerted practical accomplishment, in and through which the parties display for one another their competence in the practical management of social order. As analysts, our interest is to explicate, in respect of naturally occurring occasions of use, the methods by which such orderliness can be displayed, managed, and recognized by members.
>
> (Heritage and Watson, 1979:123–124)

Their specific concern was the issue of when conversational order itself becomes a topic of conversation for the participants. Specifically, they looked at *formulations*, which they defined as a part of a conversation used to describe that conversation. In particular, their concern was a specific type of formulation, one in which an actor seeks to "characterize states of affairs already described or negotiated (in whole or in part) in the preceding talk" (p. 126).

The conversations that Heritage and Watson used are too lengthy to include here, but the following gives a sense of what they meant by formulations:

A. I was so depressed that . . .
B. Yes
A. . . . that I climbed on the railing of the bridge
B. *You were prepared to commit suicide because* . . .
A. Yes, I am so overweight.

In this example, in saying that *A* was prepared to commit suicide, *B* is formulating what *A* was trying to say in his previous two statements.

Such formulations illustrate the practical management of conversations. A formulation is a part of a conversation in which the objective "is manifestly and specifically to exhibit participants' understanding" (p. 129). A formulation is one example of how members demonstrate their understanding of what is occurring.

INTEGRATION OF TALK AND NONVOCAL ACTIVITIES

Conversational analysts have focused on talk and other ethnomethodologists on nonvocal activities. Some researchers are using videotapes and films to analyze the integration of vocal and nonvocal activities. Goodwin (1984), for example, examined a videotape of a dinner party involving two couples. One issue in the relationship between vocal and nonvocal activities is the body posture of a person (Ann) who tells a story at the party:

Ann clasps her hands together, places both elbows on the table, and leans forward while gazing toward her addressed recipient, Beth. With this posture the speaker displays full orientation toward her addressed recipient, complete engagement in telling her story, and lack of involvement in any activities other than conversation. The posture appears to . . . constitute a visual display that a telling is in progress.

(Goodwin, 1984:228)

More generally, Goodwin concludes, "Ann's telling is thus made visible not only in her talk but also in the way in which she organizes her body and activities during the telling" (p. 229).

Another nonvocal activity examined by Goodwin is the gaze, which he relates to talk:

When a speaker gazes at a recipient that recipient should be gazing at him. When speakers gaze at nongazing recipients, and thus locate violations of the rule, they frequently produce phrasal breaks such as restarts and pauses, in their talk. These phrasal breaks both orient to the event as a violation by locating the talk in progress at that point as impaired in some fashion and provide a remedy by functioning as requests for the gaze of the hearer. Thus just after phrasal breaks nongazing recipients frequently begin to move their gaze to the speaker.

(Goodwin, 1984:230)

Body posture and gaze are only two of many nonvocal activities that are intimately related to vocal activities.

DIRECTIONAL MAPS

As we have seen, many ethnomethodologists have focused on oral communication; however, that need not always be the case, as George Psathas has shown:

> Just as spoken materials can be examined to discover the methods of practical reasoning which their users depend upon to make what they say understandable, so written materials can be studied with the same purpose . . . letters, diaries, notes, reports, essays, and the like can, on close examination, be found to contain methods of practical reasoning.
>
> (Psathas, 1979a:203)

To illustrate his point, Psathas focused on the maps that we occasionally draw to give people directions on how to get places. Despite his choice of materials, Psathas shared the traditional ethnomethodological concern with the ordered properties of practical reasoning.[3] He contended that the goal of his analysis is ''to discover the methods of practical reasoning which members must and do use to make and read the map. These methods have their ordered properties discernible in and through the careful examination of the maps'' (p. 224).

Three basic conclusions emerge from Psathas's analysis of map making and map reading. First, ''methodical and orderly'' aspects of a map make it ''recognizable, readable, and interpretable'' as a map to the potential reader. The lines, the names of streets, the words, and other elements make it clear that the object is a map drawn for a certain specific use, namely, getting to an ultimate destination. Second, the map maker only does part of the work involved; map readers accomplish the work of the map through their reading of it. Finally, the map provides readers with methods (arrows, words) that allow them to find the ultimate destination.

As Psathas concluded: ''It is remarkable that a number of lines on paper can be interpreted by members as being about a world'' (p. 224). Map makers, through a few lines and words, and readers, through their common-sense interpretive procedures, are able to ''make'' a map that allows one to get to a destination. Map making and map reading are practical accomplishments.

ACCOMPLISHING GENDER

It seems incontrovertible that one's gender—male or female—is biologically based. People are seen as simply manifesting the behaviors that are an outgrowth of their biological makeup. People are not usually thought of as *accomplishing* their gender. In contrast, sexiness is clearly an accomplishment; people need to speak and act in certain

---

[3]By *practical reasoning*, ethnomethodologists mean the logic used by people in everyday life rather than formal logic.

ways in order to be seen as sexy. However, it is generally assumed that one does not have to do or say *anything* to be seen as a man or a woman. Ethnomethodology has investigated the issue of sexuality, with some very unusual results.

The ethnomethodological view is traceable to one of Harold Garfinkel's (1967) now classic demonstrations of the utility of this orientation. In the 1950s, Garfinkel met a person named Agnes, who seemed unquestionably a woman. Not only did she have the figure of a woman, but it was virtually a "perfect" figure with an ideal set of measurements. She also had a pretty face, a good complexion, no facial hair, and plucked eyebrows—and she wore lipstick. This was clearly a woman, or was it? Garfinkel discovered that Agnes had not always appeared to be a woman. In fact, at the time he met her, Agnes was trying to convince officials that she needed an operation to remove her male genitalia and create a vagina.

Agnes was defined as a male at birth. In fact, she was by all accounts a boy until she was sixteen years of age. At that age, sensing something was awry, Agnes ran away from home and started to dress like a girl. She soon discovered that dressing like a woman was not enough; she had to *learn to act* like a woman if she was to be accepted as one. She did learn the accepted practices and as a result came to be defined, and to define herself, as a woman. The more general point here is that we are not simply born men or women; we all also learn and routinely use the common-place practices that define us as men or women. It is only in doing this that we come to be, in a sociological sense, a man or a woman.

BREACHING EXPERIMENTS

In its early years, ethnomethodology gained much notoriety for its use of the *breaching experiment*. Despite the name, even Garfinkel (1967) recognized that these are not really experiments in the formal sense of the term and might better be called "breaching demonstrations." In these demonstrations, social reality is "breached" in order to demonstrate the basic principles of ceaseless reality construction. The assumption behind this research is not only that the social construction of reality occurs all the time, but also that the participants are generally unaware that it is occurring. The objective of the breaching experiment is to disrupt normal procedures so that the process by which reality is constructed or reconstructed can be observed. In his work, Garfinkel discussed a number of examples of breaching experiments, most of which were undertaken by his students to illustrate the basic principles of ethnomethodology. Let us give one example to illustrate the procedure.

Garfinkel asked his students to spend between fifteen minutes and an hour in their homes imagining that they were boarders and then acting on the basis of that assumption. "They were instructed to conduct themselves in a circumspect and polite fashion. They were to avoid getting personal, to use formal address, to speak only when spoken to" (Garfinkel, 1967:47). In the vast majority of cases, family members were dumbfounded by such behavior: "Reports were filled with accounts of astonishment, bewilderment, shock, anxiety, embarrassment, and anger, and with charges by various family members that the student was mean, inconsiderate, selfish, nasty, or impolite" (p. 47). These reactions indicate how important it is that people act in accord with the common-sense assumptions about how they are supposed to behave.

What most interested Garfinkel were the ways in which the family members sought in common-sense ways to cope with such a breach. They demanded explanations from the students for their behavior. In their questions, they often implied an explanation of the aberrant behavior:

"Did you get fired?"
"Are you sick?"
"Are you out of your mind or are you just stupid?"

(Garfinkel, 1967:47)

Family members also sought to explain the behaviors to themselves in terms of previously understood motives. For example, a student was thought to be behaving oddly because she was working too hard or had had a fight with her fiancé. Such explanations are important to participants—the other family members, in this case—because the explanations help them feel that under normal circumstances interaction would occur as it always had.

If the student did not acknowledge the validity of such explanations, family members were likely to withdraw and to seek to isolate, denounce, or retaliate against the culprit. Deep emotions were aroused because the effort to restore order through explanation was rejected by the student. The other family members felt that more intense statements and actions were necessary to restore the equilibrium:

"Don't bother with him, he's in one of his moods again."
"Why must you always create friction in our family harmony?"
"I don't want any more of *that* out of *you* and if you can't treat your mother decently you'd better move out!"

(Garfinkel, 1967:48)

In the end, the students explained the experiment to their families, and in most situations harmony was restored. However, in some instances hard feelings lingered.

Breaching experiments are undertaken to illustrate the way people make sense out of their everyday lives. These experiments also reveal the fragility of social reality and the common-sense ways in which people seek to understand and to heal breaches. It is assumed that the way people handle these breaches tells us much about how they handle their everyday lives (Handel, 1982). Although these experiments seem innocent enough, they often lead to highly emotional reactions. These extreme reactions reflect how important it is to people to engage in routine, common-sense activities. The reactions to breaches are sometimes so extreme that Hugh Mehan and Houston Wood have cautioned about their use: "*Interested persons are strongly advised not to undertake any new breaching studies*" (1975:113).

Criticisms of Traditional Sociology

As we have seen, the idea of reflexivity is basic to ethnomethodology. This means, on the one hand, that actors are seen as self-conscious about their activities. On the other, and more germane at this point, it means that ethnomethodologists believe that sociologists should be self-conscious and self-critical about their own activities. Sociology and its common-sense knowledge and procedures must be studied with the same basic strategies used to study any social phenomenon. In fact, one of the ethnomethodologist's basic criticisms of sociology is that it has not been sufficiently self-critical.

Ethnomethodologists criticize traditional sociologists for imposing *their* sense of social reality on the social world (Mehan and Wood, 1975). They believe that sociology has not been attentive enough or true enough to the everyday world that should be its ultimate source of knowledge (Sharrock and Anderson, 1986). Enamored of their own view of the social world, sociologists have tended not to share the same social reality as those they study. As Mehan and Wood put it, "in attempting to do a social *science*, sociology has become alienated from the social" (1975:63).

Within this general orientation, Mehan and Wood (see also Sharrock and Anderson, 1986) leveled a number of specific criticisms at sociology. The concepts used by sociologists are said to distort the social world, to destroy its ebb and flow. Further distortion is caused by sociology's reliance on scientific techniques and statistical analyses of data. Statistics simply do not usually do justice to the elegance and sophistication of the real world. The coding techniques used by sociologists, when they translate human behavior into their preconceived categories, distort the social world. Furthermore, the seeming simplicity of the codes conceals the complicated and distorting work involved in turning aspects of the social world into the sociologist's preconceived categories. Sociologists are also seen as tending to accept unquestioningly a respondent's description of a phenomenon rather than looking at the phenomenon itself. Thus, a description of a social setting is taken to *be* that setting rather than one conception of that setting. Finally, Mehan and Wood argued that sociologists are prone to offer abstractions of the social world that are increasingly removed from the reality of everyday life.

Taking a slightly different approach, Don Zimmerman and Melvin Pollner (1970) argued that conventional sociology has suffered from a confusion of *topic* and *resource*. That is, the everyday social world is a resource for the favorite topics of sociology, but it is rarely a topic in its own right. This can be illustrated in a variety of ways. For example, Roy Turner (1970; see also Sharrock and Anderson, 1986) argued that sociologists usually look at everyday speech not as a topic in itself, but as a resource with which to study hidden realities such as norms, values, attitudes, and so on. However, instead of being a resource, everyday speech can be seen as one of the ways in which the business of social life is carried on—a topic in itself. Matthew Speier (1970) argued that when sociologists look at childhood socialization, they look not at the processes themselves but at a series of abstract "stages" generalized from those processes. Speier argued that "*socialization is the acquisition of interactional competencies*" (1970:189). Thus, the ethnomethodologist must look at the way these competencies are acquired and used in the everyday reality of the real world.

Another analysis of childhood socialization, by Robert W. Mackay (1974), is even more useful as a critique of traditional sociology and the confusion of topic and resource. Mackay contrasted the "normative" approach of traditional sociology with the interpretive approach of ethnomethodology. The normative approach is seen as arguing that socialization is merely a series of stages in which "complete" adults teach "incomplete" children the ways of society. Mackay viewed this as a "gloss" that ignores the reality that socialization involves an interaction between children and adults.

Children are not passive, incomplete receptacles; rather, they are active participants in the socialization process, because they have the ability to reason, invent, and acquire knowledge. Socialization is a two-sided process. Mackay believed that the ethno-methodological orientation "restores the interaction between adults and children based on interpretive competencies as the phenomenon of study" (1974:183).

Don Zimmerman and Melvin Pollner (1970) cited other examples of the confusion of topic and resource. For example, they argued that sociologists normally explain action in bureaucracies by the rules, norms, and values of the organization. However, had they looked at organizations as topics, they would have seen that actors often simply make it *appear* through their actions that those actions can be explained by the rules. It is not the rules, but the actors' *use* of the rules, that should be the topic of sociological research. Zimmerman and Pollner then cited the example of a code of behavior among prison convicts. Whereas traditional sociology would look at the ways in which actors are constrained by a convict code, ethnomethodologists would examine how the convicts use the code as an explanatory and persuasive device. Don Zimmerman and Lawrence Wieder offered the following generalization on the confusion of topic and resource:

> The ethnomethodologist is *not* concerned with providing causal explanations of observably regular, patterned, repetitive actions by some kind of analysis of the actor's point of view. He *is* concerned with how members of society go about the task of *seeing, describing,* and *explaining* order in the world in which they live.
>
> (Zimmerman and Wieder, 1970:289)

Social order is not a reality in itself to the ethnomethodologist but an accomplishment of social actors.

Another way of putting this argument is in terms of Garfinkel's (1967) view that sociology treats its actors as "judgmental dopes." Sociology sees actors as constrained by external forces, unable to make independent judgments or take independent action. Ethnomethodology, however, accepts the idea that actors make crucially important judgments and, in fact, makes this fact a centerpiece of the orientation.

These criticisms of traditional sociology give us an overview of ethnomethodology, but in negative terms. We turn now to a more positive characterization of this theory, starting with Mehan and Wood's program statement.

Ethnomethodology: A Basic Program

Mehan and Wood (1975) have offered ethnomethodology's most basic program statement. Their approach is similar to that of Berger and Luckmann: "The person begins with certain materials that set limits, and then acts and in acting alters those limits. These new limits form the material of another creative act, ad infinitum" (Mehan and Wood, 1975:203). This is a very strong statement of the relationship between people and the structures they create. However, Mehan and Wood tended to discuss this only in contemporary terms and paid insufficient attention to the historically created social structures that constrain activity.

In developing their approach, Mehan and Wood attempted to set themselves apart from those ethnomethodologists who go too far and regard the "objective reality of social facts'' as nonexistent except for the practices by which they are constituted by actors. They accepted the importance of meaning constructions but refused to fall into the trap of arguing that there are no objective realities: ''People create meanings, but the world comes to them independently of their interpretive activities'' (p. 194). They concluded that ''the facticity of an objective world is now an explicit feature of the theory'' (p. 197).

Mehan and Wood also rejected the idea that ethnomethodology should focus on mental activities. Instead, they focused on the action and interaction that flow from mental activities. In this, they viewed themselves as following in the tradition of Garfinkel, who stated:

> I shall exercise a theorist's preference and say that meaningful events are entirely and exclusively events in a person's behavioral environment. . . . Hence there is no reason to look under the skulls since nothing of interest is to be found there but brains. The skin of the person will be left intact.
>
> (Garfinkel, 1963:190)

Once again, we are confronted with the reluctance of sociologists to focus on mental activities, even among ethnomethodologists, who, one would presume, would be concerned with them.

The heart of Mehan and Wood's program statement lies in the view that ethnomethodology sees social reality as:

> dependent upon ceaseless (1) reflexive use of (2) bodies of social knowledge in (3) interaction. As this reflexive interactional work assembles the reality, without it, the reality could not be sustained. Hence, each reality (4) is fragile. Insofar as people may experience more than one reality, realities are said to be (5) permeable.
>
> (Mehan and Wood, 1975:6)

This position involves five basic views of the nature of social reality:

1. *Reality as reflexive activity.*   To ethnomethodologists, we are all engaged in the process of creating social reality through our thoughts and actions. However, we are rarely aware of this process, usually because we conceal it from ourselves. (This is why ethnomethodologists use breaching experiments.) When we say hello to someone and the person responds similarly, we are not conscious of the reflexive work both parties are doing. But when the other person scowls and walks away in response to our hello, we become aware that we were trying to create a certain social reality and that we failed. We may then often try to reaffirm the world of greetings as we know it by trying to explain away the individual's inappropriate response (''He didn't hear me'' or ''He wasn't feeling well'').

2. *Reality as a coherent body of knowledge.*   People in their everyday lives as well as sociologists studying them organize the world into coherent realities. Problems arise when the social scientist imposes an order that is not the same as the one used by the participants. Ethnomethodologists, with their basic commitment to the study of reflexivity, would generally be more aware of this problem and strive to limit the distortions.

3. *Reality as interactional activity.* Social reality is not simply "out there." Instead, its existence depends on the ceaseless reciprocal interaction and social construction of reality of the participants.
4. *The fragility of realities.* Social realities are not hardened structures but highly fragile creations that can be disrupted in various ways. This view is another of the bases of the ethnomethodologist's interest in breaching experiments. Because of their fragility, social realities can be breached by both the ethnomethodologist and the layperson. The ethnomethodologist can do this consciously in order to study the process of reality construction.
5. *The permeability of realities.* People live within a variety of social worlds and can move from one reality to another. For instance, on a day to day basis we move easily from classroom to athletic field, two very different areas of social life. A more extreme case occurs when people pass from being "straight" to dope addiction or from atheism to religious fundamentalism. Behaviors (for instance, cannibalism) that we find objectionable in one context might be acceptable in another (for instance, survival techniques for those involved in a plane crash on a desolate mountain).

SOME BASIC CONCEPTS

As Mehan and Wood made clear, ethnomethodologists have developed some interesting and unusual concepts. We now examine several of these concepts to gain an idea of the essential nature of ethnomethodology.

ACCOUNTS   *Accounting* is the process by which people make sense out of the world (Handel, 1982:24). *Accounts* are the ways in which actors do such things as describe, analyze, criticize, and idealize specific situations (Bittner, 1973:115). Ethnomethodologists devote a lot of attention to analyzing people's accounts as well as to the ways in which accounts are offered and accepted (or rejected) by others. This is one of the reasons that ethnomethodologists are preoccupied with conversational analysis. To take an example, when a student explains to her professor why she failed to take an examination, she is offering an account. The student is trying to make sense out of an event for her professor. Ethnomethodologists are interested in the nature of that account, as well as the *accounting practices* (Sharrock and Anderson, 1986) by which the student offers the account and whether it is accepted by the professor. At a very different level, the work of ethnomethodologists—indeed, of all sociologists—should be seen as a series of accounts that are analyzable in the same way as all other accounts.

INDEXICALITY   The term *indexicality* is drawn from linguistics, where it describes the property of sentences to have different meanings in different contexts. "'It's raining' has different meanings: on the day of a long awaited picnic, at the end of a drought, when the rivers are already overflowing their banks, or when one is driving and the temperature is near freezing" (Handel, 1982:41). Ethnomethodologists adopt the view that all accounts—in fact, all expressions and all practical actions—must be interpreted within their particular context. This means that the ethnomethodologists must not impose their view of reality on the actors. Instead, they must try to put themselves in the actors' place in order to understand what is transpiring.

ET CETERA PRINCIPLE   All situations involve incomplete aspects that must be filled in by the participants. Despite being confronted with ambiguities, we carry on our social life. In a given situation, we allow unclear information to pass on the assumption that it will be clarified later on. As the action proceeds, we seek information within the context that allows us to clarify and grasp what happened. If we stopped to question every ambiguity, little social life would take place. We must all practice the et cetera principle if social life is to be possible.

DOCUMENTARY METHOD   Both laypeople and sociologists use the documentary method, which involves an effort to identify "an *underlying pattern* behind a series of appearances such that each appearance is seen as referring to, an expression of, or a document of, the underlying pattern" (T. Wilson, 1970:68; italics added). Neither the layperson nor the sociologist is content with the analysis of isolated events; both need to uncover the underlying pattern.

NATURAL LANGUAGE   This system of practices allows people to speak, hear, and witness the objective production and display of social life. Natural language is not the same as linguistic categories; it is a concern with the basic structure of speaker-hearer interaction. This is the concern, as we have seen, of the conversation analysts. Examples of this include the way in which people take turns in conversations or seek to cope with disruptions in a conversation (Zimmerman, 1978).

The Strain Toward Structural Constraint

Ethnomethodology always has encompassed an impossible dichotomy. On the one hand, its adherents have talked of the actor as a constructor of social reality, and they have excoriated mainstream sociology for seeing the actor as overly constrained by large-scale structures. On the other hand, many ethnomethodologists have adopted the view that the field should focus on the more micro-level constraints on actors, the constraints that exist within "natural language," for example. Zimmerman came to be a strong supporter of this latter position, as witnessed by his view that natural language is both "(1) prior to and independent of any particular speaker, that is, external, and (2) less preferential than obligatory, that is, constraining" (1978:10). This sounds remarkably like Durkheim's treatment of social facts, which the ethnomethodologists have been so critical of, but at the individual rather than the social-cultural level. Zimmerman often has sounded like a structuralist as he examined the "invariant" properties of natural language. However, he also spoke of natural language as a resource used by actors in the accomplishment of social life. It is unclear whether actors are "judgmental dopes" or active creators of their social lives. There is an unresolved strain in Zimmerman's work as well as in ethnomethodology in general.

This strain toward structuralism is even clearer in the work of another important ethnomethodologist, Aaron Cicourel (1974). Cicourel criticized traditional sociology for seeing the actor as overly constrained by large-scale structures. He viewed the actor as a creator of social reality. Simultaneously, however, he adopted a structuralist view of cognitive processes and viewed the interpretive procedures actors use as similar to deep-structure grammatical rules. These deep structures allow actors to cope with their social setting, yet they are not enslaving. They enable "the actor to generate appropriate (*usually innovative*) responses to changing situated settings" (Cicourel, 1974:27). He viewed interpretive procedures that have *invariant* properties as allowing the actor to behave *innovatively*. One of the ways that Cicourel sought to handle this paradox was to argue that interpretive procedures emerge developmentally through the life cycle. Thus the actor is constantly developing new procedures to handle new situations.

Cicourel developed a complicated theory that sought to integrate ethnomethodology with linguistics (deep structures) and traditional sociology (normative or surface rules). Social life emerges from the interaction of creative actors, deep structures, and normative constraint.

More recently, Heritage and Atkinson have taken the following position on this issue:

> The perspective focuses on the underlying structures informing the interpretation and treatment of a speaker's action by a recipient and maintains, except in specific cases, a relatively *agnostic* stance on the question of how far the speaker consciously aimed at some particular interpretation . . . the objects of study are institutionalized structures of talk that are oriented to by speakers with varying degrees of reflexive awareness.
> (Heritage and Atkinson, 1984:7; italics added)

The crucial issue for all ethnomethodologists who study the deep structures of linguistics is how such structures allow for creativity. On the surface, it would appear that they constrain, if not determine, what actors think and do. Ethnomethodologists with this orientation need to demonstrate better how such determinism is consistent with their view of actors as creators.

Given the historical concern of ethnomethodology with small-scale phenomena, a number of observers (for instance, Zimmerman, 1978) have started to think about how ethnomethodology can be integrated with a concern for social structures. Zimmerman viewed cross-fertilization with macro sociology as "an open question, and an intriguing possibility" (1978:12). Indeed, Zimmerman and others (for instance, Chua, 1977) have discussed the relationship between ethnomethodology and Marxian theory. Little work has been done in this area up to the present, but it is an area of ethnomethodology that probably will continue to develop in the future.

SUMMARY

In this chapter, we discuss two separate but related theories—phenomenological sociology and ethnomethodology. We begin with a treatment of the general similarities of the two theories. For instance, they have a common intellectual base in the work of Edmund Husserl and Alfred Schutz, and they both focus on individual thought and action.

Next we discuss the important differences between the two theories. Most generally, ethnomethodology seems to have taken phenomenology and fused it with traditional sociology to produce a unique perspective. Ethnomethodologists tend to emphasize empirical research, whereas phenomenologists concentrate on "think pieces"; ethnomethodologists tend to focus more on action and interaction, whereas phenomenologists are more concerned with consciousness and culture; and ethnomethodologists tend to emphasize the freedom of actors, whereas phenomenologists see them as rather constrained. Thus, in spite of the similarities, there are enough differences between them to make it necessary to deal with the two approaches separately.

The discussion of phenomenology begins with a few of the most relevant ideas of Edmund Husserl, including his notions of the natural attitude, bracketing, a science of consciousness, and intentionality. Although contemporary phenomenologists often trace their roots to Husserl's philosophy, they often distort his orientation. In fact, there is very little pure phenomenology in phenomenological sociology.

The discussion of Husserl is followed by a lengthy analysis of the work of Alfred Schutz, the most important sociological phenomenologist. Schutz offered a complex, often confusing theory that is difficult to summarize and has been subject to conflicting analyses.

Schutz's work becomes clearer when we discuss his differentiation between the everyday world and science. In the everyday world, the thoughts and actions of individuals are very important. However, these micro phenomena, especially consciousness, are not amenable to scientific sociological analysis. Amenable to scientific study are the cultural aspects of the social world. We see this illustrated in various ways in Schutz's work.

At one level, Schutz differentiated among four basic realms of the social world. The realms of successors, the future (*folgewelt*), and predecessors, the past (*vorwelt*), are of marginal importance from a scientific point of view. The *umwelt*, the world of directly experienced social reality, is important, but it cannot be analyzed scientifically. What can be studied scientifically is the *mitwelt*, or the world of indirectly experienced social reality. In this realm people deal with abstract types rather than with actual people in face-to-face interaction. Because people do not deal with actual others in this realm, their thoughts and actions are determined by various cultural phenomena such as "typifications." People learn "recipes" and then simply employ them at the appropriate moment. They do not deal with actors but simply with types.

In this effort to demarcate a realm of scientific sociology, Schutz sometimes went even further and substituted homunculi, or puppets, for real actors. Such homunculi are incapable of thought and action; they are totally determined by cultural phenomena like typifications.

We also discuss Schutz's analysis of cultural forces in the life world, which involves the general, taken-for-granted framework of social life and its impact on actors' thoughts and actions. The life world is a framework imposed on actors from without; it is the totality of typifications upon which all experience, knowledge, and conduct is based. The actor takes an unquestioning attitude to the life world and adopts what Schutz called the "natural attitude." We discuss as well several of Schutz's specific components of the life world such as skills, useful knowledge, and knowledge of recipes. Schutz recognized that in the everyday world these elements receive specific biographical articulations, or personal expressions

The distinction between we and they relationships is taken up next. Although the personal, face-to-face interaction of we relationships is important in the everyday world, it is not amenable to scientific analysis in Schutz's view. However, they relationships, which involve indirect interaction with impersonal contemporaries rather than personal associates, can be the subject of scientific study. In they relationships, thoughts and actions of people are dominated by anonymous typifications.

Although his definition of scientific sociology excludes consciousness, Schutz offered many insights into the concept. In this area, we analyze his work on meanings and motives. Schutz also offered useful ideas on how people act in the face of problematic situations. Despite a rich set of insights here, Schutz's great strength lies in the analysis of cultural constraints on people.

We then discuss two examples of phenomenological sociology. First we look at how George Psathas and Frances Waksler examined face-to-face interaction from the point of view of micro-level phenomenology. Although such small-scale analyses predominate within phenomenology, there are also broader efforts, such as Peter Berger and Thomas Luckmann's important but aborted attempt to integrate the traditional small-scale concerns of phenomenology with larger-scale issues.

Because ethnomethodology is dominated by empirical studies, the bulk of the second part of this chapter is devoted to a series of examples of the kinds of research undertaken by ethnomethodologists. We look at studies devoted to how people "do" walking, open telephone calls, invite laughter, generate applause, produce sentences in the course of interaction, formulate summaries during a conversation, integrate talk and nonvocal activities, read directional maps, accomplish their gender, and repair breaches in interactional encounters.

We also discuss a number of the ethnomethodologists' criticisms of traditional sociology, especially its tendency to impose *its* sense of reality on the social world rather than letting the sense emerge from the setting itself. To the ethnomethodologists, the sociologist's concepts, techniques, and statistics distort the true nature of social reality. Furthermore, ethnomethodologists have argued that although the real social world has been a resource for the analyses of traditional sociologists, it rarely has been a topic in its own right for them. Finally, they attack traditional sociologists for treating actors as "judgmental dopes" rather than as active creators of their social worlds.

The work of Hugh Mehan and Houston Wood is offered as a basic program statement of ethnomethodology. It involves five basic propositions:

1. Reality involves reflexive activity.
2. Reality is organized into coherent bodies of knowledge.
3. Reality is the product of ceaseless interaction.
4. Reality is fragile.
5. Reality is permeable.

We also discuss several of the basic concepts of ethnomethodology, including accounts, indexicality, the et cetera principle, documentary method, and natural language. We note that some ethnomethodologists have tended to move away from an image of the actor as creator and toward a more structural interpretation. We close with a discussion of the possibility of integrating the micro orientation of ethnomethodology with larger-scale theories.

In sum, despite some similarities, there are important differences between phenomenological sociology and ethnomethodology. Still, in the future there may well be an increased effort to integrate the two.

CHAPTER SEVEN
Exchange Theory and
Behavioral Sociology

SKINNER AND BEHAVIORISM

BEHAVIORAL SOCIOLOGY
BASIC CONCEPTS
BEHAVIOR MODIFICATION

EXCHANGE THEORY
HOMANS AND DURKHEIM
HOMANS AND LEVI-STRAUSS
HOMANS AND STRUCTURAL FUNCTIONALISM
HOMANS'S BASIC PROPOSITIONS
CRITICISMS OF HOMANS'S THEORY OF SOCIETY AND CULTURE
BLAU'S INTEGRATED EXCHANGE THEORY
CRITICISMS OF HOMANS'S THEORY OF CONSCIOUSNESS

THE CURRENT STATUS OF BEHAVIORAL THEORIES

EXCHANGE theory and behavioral sociology are unique sociological theories. First, they take their inspiration primarily from psychology, specifically from the behaviorism of B. F. Skinner (Tarter, 1973). Second, another influence, especially in exchange theory, is economics, also outside the domain of sociology. Third, in their most extreme forms they constitute an outright rejection of all the other sociological theories discussed in this book.

Given the preeminent place of B. F. Skinner and his behaviorism in exchange theory, we begin this chapter with his general orientation. Next, we discuss behavioral sociology, because it represents the most pristine translation of Skinner's ideas into sociological principles. Finally, we turn to exchange theory per se, particularly as it is presented in the work of its two foremost sociological practitioners—George Homans and Peter Blau.[1]

Omitted from this chapter is an explicit discussion of the work of an increasingly important exchange theorist—Richard Emerson (1972a; 1972b; 1976; 1981; forthcoming). The reason is that his most important contribution to exchange theory lies in linking macro and micro theory (Cook, forthcoming b). Hence, we will defer discussing his work until Chapter 10, which is devoted entirely to the issue of macro-micro links.

---

[1] Homans and Blau are not the only exchange theorists of note. Also of importance is the work of John Thibaut and Harold H. Kelley (1959), B. F. Meeker (1971), and Robert L. Hamblin and John K. Kunkel (1977).

A number of sociologists focus on behavior and exchange without accepting much, if any, of Skinner's behavioral sociology or Homans's and Blau's versions of exchange theory. Alvin Gouldner's (1960) classic essay on reciprocity and William Goode's (1960) work on role strain illustrate this long-standing tradition of nonbehavioristic exchange theory. This version of exchange theory emphasizes the reciprocal nature of social relationships and how power and prestige grow out of imbalances in reciprocity (Goode, 1978). Although these thinkers are likely to think of themselves as exchange theorists, they are not likely to think of themselves as either sociological or psychological behaviorists. In this chapter, we focus on the sociological work on behavior and exchange that is heavily influenced by psychological behaviorism. We are not concerned with work of this genre done from nonbehavioristic perspectives.

Although all of the chapters in this book are shaped, at least in part, by the author's sense of sociology's multiple paradigms (see Appendix) as well as the place of various theorists and theories within them, this perspective plays a far greater role in this chapter. Therefore, we discuss that schema briefly, and in the process we can consider the theories discussed thus far as components of sociology's multiple paradigms.

In the author's view (Ritzer, 1975a; 1975b), sociology is composed of three major paradigms—the social-facts, social-definition, and social-behavior paradigms. Each paradigm has four major components, but of importance to us at the moment are only the paradigms' images of the subject matter of sociology and the theories each encompasses. The social-facts paradigm takes as the subject matter of sociology large-scale social structures and institutions and their coercive effect on actors and their thoughts and actions. Structural functionalism, conflict theory, and several varieties of neo-Marxian theory are associated with the social-facts paradigm. The social-definition paradigm accepts as the primary concern of sociology actors, the ways in which they construct social reality, and the action that results from such construction. Thus actors, to the social definitionist, are relatively free and creative, whereas to the social factist they are largely determined by large-scale structures and institutions. Symbolic interactionists, phenomenologists, ethnomethodologists, and at least some neo-Marxists operate within this paradigm. Finally, there is the social-behavior paradigm, in which the subject matter of sociology is individual behavior and the reinforcers and punishers that affect it. The theories we are about to discuss, behavioral sociology and exchange theory, are encompassed by this paradigm.

This multiple paradigm schema plays a key role in this chapter. First, it attunes us to the main concerns of the two theories—behavior, reinforcement, and punishment. Second, it alerts us to the fact that the theorists associated with this paradigm are not primarily concerned with, and some even reject an interest in, large-scale structures and institutions as well as the social construction of reality and social action. Third, although many associated with this paradigm have adopted a dogmatic position on what it should and should not concern itself with, some others have sought to integrate the traditional concerns of social behaviorism with those of social factism and social definitionism. Throughout this chapter we try to sort out the complex interrelationship between social behaviorism and the other sociological paradigms.

SKINNER AND BEHAVIORISM

Behaviorism has a long history in the social sciences and in particular in psychology. However, modern behaviorism in all the social sciences and in particular in sociology can be traced to the work of B. F. Skinner. Skinner's work, although steadfastly devoted to the principles of behaviorism, has covered a broad spectrum, including scientific tracts (Skinner, 1938), a utopian novel (Skinner, 1948), polemical and political essays (Skinner, 1971), practical applications of behaviorism (Skinner, 1968), and autobiographical works (Skinner, 1983). His scientific, utopian, political, and practical works all have played a role in the development of a sociological version of behaviorism.

First, let us examine Skinner's attitudes toward other sociological theories. He regarded them as rather mystical enterprises. He felt this way about the macro theories associated with the social-facts paradigm, such as structural functionalism and conflict theory, as well as the micro theories associated with the social-definition paradigm, such as symbolic interactionism, ethnomethodology, and phenomenology. He saw these theories as constructing mystical entities that distract the sociologist from the only concrete entities of study—behavior and the consequences that make that behavior more or less likely to occur (Molm, 1981). Take, for example, Skinner's criticism of the concept of culture, often defined by a typical social factist as "traditional (i.e., historically derived and selected) ideas and especially their attached values" (Skinner, 1971:121). He argued that this definition has created unnecessarily mystical elements such as "ideas" and "values." Scientists do not see ideas and values when they look at society. Instead, they see "how people live, how they raise their children, how they gather or cultivate food, what kinds of dwellings they live in, what they wear, what games they play, how they treat each other, how they govern themselves, and so on" (Skinner, 1971:121). The culture of a community is composed of behaviors. To understand behaviors we do not need concepts such as *ideas* and *values*; instead, we need to understand such things as rewards and costs.

Skinner leveled his strongest criticisms at the theories of social definitionism. One of Skinner's major goals in *Beyond Freedom and Dignity* (1971) was to eliminate the idea that he labels "autonomous man" from the social sciences—indeed, from the world. The idea of an autonomous man is an integral part of the social-definition paradigm (for example, Mead's *I* is close to Skinner's hated autonomous man), and an attack on it thus means an attack on the social definitionists. Skinner, speaking for social behaviorism, did not want to reconcile his differences with the social definitionists. In fact, he was interested in eliminating the theories associated with the social-definition paradigm.

What is this notion of an autonomous man that Skinner sought to eliminate? We imply that people are autonomous when we attribute to them such things as feeling, thinking, freedom, and dignity. People, in this view, have an inner core from which their actions emanate. This inner core enables them to initiate, originate, and create. This active, creative, voluntaristic view of people is clearly in line with the social definitionist position, and Skinner's effort to destroy this idea is, indirectly, an effort to destroy the theories of social definitionism.

To Skinner, the idea that people have an inner, autonomous core is a mystical, metaphysical position of the kind that must be eliminated from the social sciences: "Autonomous man serves to explain only the things we are not yet able to explain in other ways. His existence depends on our ignorance, and he naturally loses status as we come to know more about behavior" (1971:12). Behavior, as well as the conditions that produce behavior, primarily other behaviors, are the primary subject matter to Skinner. He believed we should not focus on such concepts as "feelings"; we should mainly focus on the examination (and control) of behavior and the contingencies that affect it.[2] Linda Molm amplified this point by arguing that Skinner was concerned with what he called "private events," or "events that take place inside an individual and that are not directly observable by others" (1981:161). In this category, he included thoughts, feelings, and perceptions. However, Skinner was only willing to accept a concern with such internal states under two conditions. First, they cannot be independent, or mediating, variables but can only occupy the role of dependent variables in a behaviorist's schema. In other words, they cannot be explanatory variables, only variables to be explained by other factors. Second, they must be observable in some way. The self-reports of actors (as well as their behaviors) count as observable phenomena. Such a limited, scientific view of mental states is not likely to be acceptable to those who adopt the social-definition paradigm.

Skinner and social behaviorists in general are interested in the relationship between individuals and their environment (Molm, 1981), which is composed of a variety of social and nonsocial objects. The social behaviorist argues that the principles that govern the relationship between an individual and a social object are the same as those that govern the relationship between an individual and a nonsocial object.[3] Don Bushell and Robert Burgess defined the subject matter of behaviorists as "the behavior of individuals that operates on the environment in such a way as to produce some consequence or change in it which, in turn, modifies subsequent performances of that behavior" (1969:27). Thus they focus on the "functional relationship" between behavior and changes in the environment of the actor. This means that a child tossing a stone into a river is an object of study to the behaviorist in exactly the same way as are a mother scolding a child, a teacher instructing a class, or a business executive meeting a board of directors.

Social behaviorists claim they are interested in an interaction process, but the process is conceptualized very differently from the way it is in the theories of the social definitionists. Actors, to the social definitionist, are dynamic, creative forces in the interaction process (Perinbanayagam, 1981). They do not simply respond to stimuli but interpret them and act on the basis of their definitions of them. The social behaviorist, in contrast, allows the individual far less freedom. To the behaviorist, "Thinking is the behavior of the brain. Most brain activity is not conscious" (Baldwin and Baldwin, 1986:264). Thus, whereas to the social definitionist the actor is busily consciously constructing social reality, to the social behaviorist, he or she is unconsciously responding to stimuli. The individual's response is determined by the nature of the external stimuli. The image is of a much more mechanical person than that conceived by the social definitionists.[4]

---

[2] A number of behaviorists are willing to include such things as cognition, emotion, the "mind" in their domain. For example, Arthur Staats (1976) made the case for including the mind in behaviorism. John Baldwin and Janice Baldwin (1978) argued that behaviorists, indeed all sociologists, should use both traditional scientific techniques and the *verstehen* methodology to understand a variety of social phenomena, including subjectivity and meaning.

[3] This is one of the places in which Molm disagreed with more traditional social behaviorists, such as Homans. She took pains to differentiate between the orientations of behavioral psychologists and behavioral sociologists.

[4] As we will see, this is still another point on which Molm disagreed.

   The image of actors in social-factist theories (for example, structural functionalism) is almost as mechanistic as in the social-behaviorist paradigm. The social factist sees the individual as determined by external norms, values, structures, and the like. The difference between social factism and social behaviorism lies in the source of control over the individual. To the social factist, large-scale structures and institutions control the individual. Social behaviorists are concerned with the relationship between individuals and the consequences that make a behavior more or less likely to occur.

BEHAVIORAL SOCIOLOGY

Behavioral sociology (or as Baldwin and Baldwin [1986] call it, "behavior science") represents an effort to apply the principles of psychological behaviorism to sociological questions. The behavioral sociologist is concerned with the relationship between the effects of an actor's behavior on the environment and their impact on the actor's later behavior. This is basic to *operant conditioning*, or the learning process by which "behavior is modified by its consequences" (Baldwin and Baldwin, 1986:6). To put this in another way, an actor emits some behavior. One might almost think of this, at least initially, as a random behavior. The environment in which the behavior exists, be it social or physical, is affected by the behavior and in turn "acts" back in various ways. That reaction, positive, negative, or neutral, affects the actor's later behavior. If the reaction has been rewarding to the actor, the same behavior is likely to be emitted in the future in similar situations. If the reaction has been painful or punishing, the behavior is less likely to occur in the future. The behavioral sociologist is interested in the relationship between the *history* of environmental reactions or consequences and the nature of present behavior. The behavioral sociologist is saying that the past consequences of a given behavior govern its present state. By knowing what elicited a certain behavior in the past, we can predict whether an actor will produce the same behavior in the present situation.

Basic Concepts

A key concept in behavioral sociology is *reinforcement*, which may be defined as a reward. Nothing inherent in an object makes it a reward. Reinforcers cannot be defined on a priori grounds apart from their effects on behavior. Thus a "reward" that does not affect the actor is not a reinforcer. Food might generally be considered a reward in our society, but if a given individual is not hungry, food will not serve as a reinforcer. One crucial determinant of whether a given reward will, in fact, serve as a reinforcer is the actors' level of deprivation. If actors have been deprived of food, for example, they will be hungry and food will act as a reinforcer. But if they have just eaten, their level of deprivation will be minimal and food will not be an effective reinforcer. This is an example of physiological deprivation. If we deny people food, sex, water, or air, these things serve as potent reinforcers. If, however, the people's physiological needs are well met, these things will not be useful reinforcers. Reinforcers also can be learned. Once we learn to need things, they serve as reinforcers when we are deprived of them.

Reinforcers may be either positive or negative (Baldwin and Baldwin, 1986). Positive reinforcement occurs when environmental changes take the form of rewards, "which thereby increase the probability of behavior occurring in the future" (Bushell and Burgess, 1969:28–29). In this situation the actor is rewarded; for example, the salesperson knocks on a door and makes a sale. Behavioral theorists would view the sale as a positive reinforcement, *if* the salesperson then knocks on more doors in the hopes of repeating the success. Baldwin and Baldwin conclude: *"People usually enjoy learning via positive reinforcement because it increases the good effects and pleasurable experiences in their lives"* (1986:15). Negative reinforcement also increases the likelihood of a behavior occurring in the future, but it takes the form of removing something aversive from the environment. Turning off a noisy radio, for example, may improve a person's ability to write or read. In the future, a person's ability to write or read may improve when the radio is turned off.

In considering reinforcers, *punishment* must also be taken into account: "A consequence which decreases the frequency of the response that precedes it is a *punisher*" (Bushell and Burgess, 1969:29; see also Baldwin and Baldwin, 1986:25). For example, a whip or even the mere threat of a whip may prevent someone from repeating a given act. However, a punishment to one person may be a reward to another. A masochist, for instance, may find the whip rewarding and would be more likely to repeat a given act. Thus in order to determine whether something will be a reward or a punishment, we must know the personal history as well as the physiological properties of the individual.

Punishments, like reinforcers, can be either positive or negative. But remember, punishers are aimed at reducing the frequency of a response. A positive punishment occurs with the use of an aversive stimulus that suppresses behavior. Striking a child every time he or she cries is an example of a positive form of punishment. Punishment takes a negative form when behavior is suppressed because we remove or threaten to remove a reward. This is labeled *response cost*, or loss of reinforcers. If we remove or threaten to remove privileges enjoyed by a child because he or she is crying, we are employing a negative form of punishment. Don Bushell and Robert Burgess argued that response cost "is the mainstay of control procedures in social organizations" (1969:30). Rather than reward or positively punish, most social organizations prefer to remove, or threaten to remove, rewards already being enjoyed.

As pointed out earlier, the behavioral sociologist is concerned primarily with the relationship between actors and their environment. The reinforcement-punishment relationship between actors and their environment occurs in patterns, some of which are naturally determined (for example, by food deprivation) and some of which are socially determined. In the simplest pattern, reinforcement follows each and every act. This pattern of continuously reinforced behavior is most likely to be found in childhood when, for example, a child's cry is immediately followed by attention from parents. This pattern is less likely to occur in adulthood. Adult reinforcement is much more likely to be intermittent, with reinforcement occurring at an uneven pace. Traveling salespeople do not expect every knock on a door to produce a sale; but knocks on doors do lead to some sales, which keep salespeople on the job. If they were never rewarded with a sale, their sales behavior would be *extinguished*, and they would cease functioning as salespeople. Interestingly, continuously reinforced behavior is more easily extinguished than intermittently rewarded behavior. Salespeople become accustomed to intermittent reward, and a good deal of time passes after the last sale before they realize that they may not be rewarded again. Thus extinguishing their sales behavior takes a long time. If they had been rewarded continuously and the rewards suddenly stopped, they might continue working for only a short time. They would cease their activities far more quickly than they would had they been rewarded intermittently.

Reinforcement is far more complex than simply doing something and receiving the desired (or undesired) reaction. Many conditions in the environment determine the probability for reinforcement of a given act. Some conditions make the response likely, whereas others make it less likely. These conditions are things that have in the past been associated with a reinforcement or a punishment. If, for example, the person doing the reinforcing has always worn some sort of uniform, that uniform may elicit a given response even when it is worn by someone else. Similarly, if a classroom has always been associated with punishment, a response to punishment will be elicited even if the student is transferred to a rewarding classroom situation. This is the process by which originally neutral stimuli—for example, the uniform—become *secondary,* or *conditioned, reinforcers.* Once transformed, a neutral stimulus can become a positive reinforcer. Because reinforcement rarely occurs in a vacuum, a number of secondary reinforcers inevitably become associated with the original one. By this process the number of reinforcers mushrooms.

Although many reinforcers are specific to a given situation, some are *generalized reinforcers.* These are defined by Bushell and Burgess as reinforcers that:

> have great power and importance in social analyses because they retain their effectiveness in the absence of any specific deprivation. The term "generalized" refers to the fact that these stimuli stand for, represent, or provide access to a wide range of other reinforcers, both unconditioned and conditioned, which may differ from time to time and from person to person.
> (Bushell and Burgess, 1969:38)

Money and status are two good examples of generalized reinforcers. They can be used to acquire many other desirable things. Because generalized reinforcers represent a number of other different things, they become more and more reinforcing in themselves. The behavioral sociologist sees the individual as difficult to satiate in terms of such generalized reinforcers. Large amounts of money or status are not likely to dull the desire for more.

Behavior Modification

When a given response is reinforced, a whole series of other responses similar to the one being rewarded are almost inevitably reinforced at the same time. This fact allows the behavioral sociologist to speak of *systematic shaping behavior,* or *behavior modification.* Here is the way that John Baldwin and Janice Baldwin define this phenomenon: *"Systematic shaping involves changing behavior in steps of successive approximation toward a preestablished final performance. At each step, reinforcement is given for behavior that best approximates the final performance"* (1986:159). Figure 7.1 illustrates this process.

FIGURE 7.1   Behavior Modification: Existing and Desired Behaviors

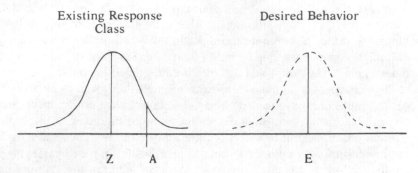

Source: Adapted from Don Bushell and Robert Burgess, "Some Basic Principles of Behavior." In Robert Burgess and Don Bushell (eds.), *Behavioral Sociology* (New York: Columbia University Press, 1969:40).

Because we possess a given reward, we are able to elicit behavior Z from an individual. In eliciting this behavior, we also elicit a number of similar behaviors, including A. Suppose that the behavior we really want to elicit is E. How do we get our subject to respond with behavior E? We begin by rewarding A, which is already in our range of elicited responses. By repeatedly eliciting A, we move the center of the curve beyond A and bring behaviors closer to E, the desired behavior, within our range. Ultimately, we elicit behavior E. The process is illustrated in Figure 7.2.

The process of *behavior modification* has been adapted to therapeutic situations. Behavior modification is seen as a six-step process:

1. Therapists must identify the specific final behaviors that they want to elicit.
2. They must determine the nature of the existing response class of the subject, that is, the range of behaviors currently being elicited and how close this is to the desired behavior.

FIGURE 7.2   Behavior Modification: Eliciting the Desired Behavior

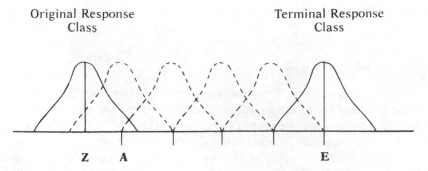

Source: Adapted from Don Bushell and Robert Burgess, "Some Basic Principles of Behavior." In Robert Burgess and Don Bushell (eds.), *Behavioral Sociology* (New York: Columbia University Press, 1969:41).

3. Therapists must construct a favorable training site. "This means eliminating distracting stimuli, the possibility of conflicting or incompatible behavior, and providing stimuli which are discriminative for the desired response" (Bushell and Burgess, 1969:43).
4. Therapists must establish motivation in the subject by acquiring an effective reinforcer. Although specific reinforcers can be used, general reinforcers such as money, social attention, and social status are most often used.
5. Therapists must begin the shaping process by "differential reinforcement of responses that are successively closer to the terminal state" (pp. 43–44).
6. Finally, when the modification has "taken," therapists should apply the reinforcers more intermittently. The reinforcement should eventually come less from an artificial device and more from the natural world.

The applications of behavioral sociology—for example, to behavior modification—set it apart from other sociological theories, including exchange theory. Although there are instances such as the human relations school of industrial sociology, which seeks to manipulate group processes in order to increase the productivity of workers, behavioral sociology has far more of an applied, practical character than any other sociological theory (Baldwin and Baldwin, 1986).

EXCHANGE THEORY

Exchange theory constitutes an effort to take the principles of behaviorism, fuse them with other ideas, and apply them to the concerns of sociologists. Although exchange theory can be traced back many years (Knox, 1963), it underwent a boom in the 1950s and 1960s in the work of George Homans (Beniger and Savory, 1981). Much of Homans's exchange theory can be viewed as a reaction to the social-facts paradigm and its sociological theories, especially structural functionalism.

Homans and Durkheim

Homans (1969) confronted the structural functionalists by directly attacking the work of Emile Durkheim on three points: the issue of emergence, his view of psychology, and his method of explanation. Homans recognized Durkheim's view that during interaction new phenomena emerge. He felt that such a view is acceptable to social behaviorists. However, how do we explain what emerges from interaction? Homans took the position that no new propositions, beyond those already applying to simple individual behavior, are needed. He said, "All the usual examples of emergent social phenomena can readily be shown to follow from psychological propositions" (Homans, 1969:14). Thus, Durkheim thought that emergent forms could only be explained by sociology, whereas Homans felt they could be explained by psychological principles.

Homans pointed out correctly that because Durkheim wrote in the late nineteenth century, the psychology that he knew was primitive. Psychology in his day focused primarily on instinctive forms of behavior and assumed that human nature was the same in all individuals. Thus Durkheim was right to disentangle sociology from the psychology of his day. "Sociology is surely not a corollary of the kind of psychology

Durkheim had in mind'' (Homans, 1969:18). However, contemporary psychology is far more sophisticated and complex than the psychology of Durkheim's time; that Durkheim was able to separate psychology from sociology does not mean that the same feat can be accomplished today.

Finally, Homans attacked Durkheim for his method of explanation. Homans argued that Durkheim considered something explained if we were able to find its cause or causes. Specifically, a social fact is explained when we can find the social facts that cause it. Homans admitted that social facts are often the cause of other social facts, but such a finding does not in his view constitute an explanation. To Homans, what needs to be explained is the *relationship* between cause and effect, why one social fact causes another social fact. Homans thought that explanation was inevitably psychological. (It should be noted that when Homans used the term *psychological* he meant *behavioral*, ''the behavior of men as men,'' as he put it.) Homans's explanation of a particular historical cause and effect is instructive:

> The price rise of the sixteenth century, which I take to be a social fact, was certainly a determining cause of the enclosure movement among English landlords. But were we to construct an explanation why this particular cause has this particular effect, we should have to say that the price rise presented English landlords both with great opportunities for monetary gain and great risks of monetary loss, that enclosure tended to increase the gain and avoid the loss, that the landlords found monetary gain rewarding (which is a state of individual consciousness, if you like), and finally, that men are likely to take actions whose results they find rewarding— which, as I cannot repeat too often, is a general psychological proposition.
>
> (Homans, 1969:19)

Thus individual responses (behavior) always intervene between social facts. Homans argued that social facts lead to individual responses, which in turn lead to new social facts. However, the essential factor is the behavior, not the social fact.

Homans and Lévi-Strauss

Homans reacted not only against Durkheim but also against those who followed in the Durkheimian tradition. Peter P. Ekeh (1974) has argued that Homans's orientation was shaped directly as a reaction against the work of neo-Durkheimian anthropologist Claude Lévi-Strauss (Homans and Schneider, 1955). In fact, what Homans reacted against was Lévi-Strauss's neo-Durkheimian version of exchange theory. (We encounter a very different aspect of Lévi-Strauss's theory in Chapter 9.) We learn a good deal about Homans's exchange theory by examining his reaction to Lévi-Strauss's orientation to the same theoretical perspective.

Ekeh's basic position was that exchange theory emerged out of two ''nonmarriageable'' traditions. On the one hand, Lévi-Strauss (1949) developed his view of exchange theory, at least in part, in the French collectivist tradition, of which Durkheim was the major exponent. On the other, Homans was the inheritor of the British individualistic tradition, of which Herbert Spencer was a major spokesman. With such different orientations, it is not surprising that Lévi-Strauss and Homans came to have such different images of exchange theory. In Ekeh's view, Lévi-Strauss developed his orientation first, and Homans shaped his own ideas in reaction to the collectivist thrust of Lévi-Strauss's work.

In his dispute with Lévi-Strauss, Homans believed that he was doing battle with a newer version of Durkheimian theory, with its focus on collectivities and its tendency to view the individual as nonessential. Homans saw Durkheim's work (and therefore Lévi-Strauss's) as an assault on "one of the unstated assumptions of the western intellectual tradition, the notion that the nature of individuals determined finally the nature of society" (1962:8). Homans said of Durkheimian functionalism, with its focus on the functions of social facts for society as a whole: "I was suspicious of it from the beginning without learning why. It had been a splinter under my skin that has taken me a long time to get out" (1962:23). And Homans did get the "splinter" of functionalism out, in large part in his critique of Lévi-Strauss's neo-Durkheimian exchange theory: "His reading of Lévi-Strauss . . . was the last straw that broke his patience with functionalism of the Durkheimian type" (Ekeh, 1974:88).

Durkheim saw the actor as constrained by social facts, especially the collective conscience, but Lévi-Strauss went further, because he believed in a collective *unconscious*, which is buried deep in humanity and is unknown to the actors themselves. This was, from Homans's point of view, even more constraining, pernicious, and mystifying than Durkheim's ideas of collective conscience and social facts. As Ekeh put it, "In Lévi-Strauss' work the individual is accorded less of a place in social processes than in Durkheim's sociology" (p. 42). With this general background, we now turn to a brief outline of Lévi-Strauss's exchange theory and, more important, Homans's critical reaction to it.

According to Ekeh, Lévi-Strauss erected his exchange theory on two basic assumptions. First, he believed that social exchange is a distinctively human process of which lower animals are incapable. By implication, one cannot learn about human exchange from the behavior of nonhuman animals. Humans are capable of culturally directed action, whereas lower animals can only respond naturally. Similarly, Lévi-Strauss saw actors as capable of creative, dynamic action, whereas animals behave in a static way. Homans's reaction to this was that there is no distinctive difference between humans and lower animals. Thus he rejected all of Lévi-Strauss's ideas about the distinctiveness of human behavior.

Second, Lévi-Strauss rejected the idea that human exchange can be explained in terms of individual self-interest. He did not deny that such self-interest may be involved, but he argued that it is not sufficient to sustain social relationships based on exchange. Lévi-Strauss argued that social exchange is sustained by supraindividual forces, by collective forces, by cultural forces. Thus human exchange is seen by Lévi-Strauss as symbolic rather than self-interested.

Society plays a variety of roles in the exchange process. Where there is scarcity, society must intervene to provide rules of appropriate conduct in order to forestall destructive human conduct. In some situations a social exchange is justified in terms of social expectations rather than the benefits the exchange brings those involved. This is done in order to inhibit the development of disruptive negative feelings. For example, people hold a wedding reception because it is the custom rather than because they want to benefit from the gifts received. Finally, customs may develop in which one feels obliged to reciprocate another's action not by repaying him or her but by rewarding a

GEORGE CASPAR HOMANS: An Autobiographical Sketch

How I became a sociologist, which was largely a matter of accident, I have described in other publications. [For a full autobiography, see Homans, 1984.] My sustained work in sociology began with my association, beginning in 1933, with Professors Lawrence Henderson and Elton Mayo at the Harvard Business School. Henderson, a biochemist, was studying the physiological characteristics of industrial work, Mayo, a psychologist, the human factors. Mayo was then and later the director of the famous researches at the Hawthorne Plant of the Western Electric Company in Chicago.

I took part in a course of readings and discussions under Mayo's direction. Among other books, Mayo asked his students to read several books by prominent social anthropologists, particularly Malinowski, Radcliffe-Brown, and Firth. Mayo wanted us to read these books so that we should understand how in aboriginal, in contrast to modern, societies social rituals supported productive work.

I became interested in them for a wholly different reason. In those days the cultural anthropologists were intellectually dominant, and friends of mine in this group, such as Clyde Kluckhohn, insisted that every culture was unique. Instead I began to perceive from my reading that certain institutions of aboriginal societies repeated themselves in places so far separated in time and space that the societies could not have borrowed them from one another. Cultures were not unique and, what was more, their similarities could only be explained on the assumption that human nature was the same the world over. Members of the human species working in similar circumstances had independently created the similar institutions. This was not a popular view at the time. I am not sure it is now.

By this time I had also been exposed to a number of concrete or "field" studies of small human groups both modern and aboriginal. When I was called to active duty in the Navy in World War II, I reflected on this material during long watches at sea. Quite suddenly, I conceived that a number of these studies might be described in concepts common to them all. In a few days I had sketched out such a conceptual scheme.

Back at Harvard with a tenured position after the war, I began working on a book, later entitled *The Human Group*, which was intended to apply my conceptual scheme to the studies in question. In the course of this work it occurred to me that a conceptual

third party. For example, instead of repaying parents for all they have done, children may instead pass similar benefits on to their own children. In general, Lévi-Strauss saw a *moral system of exchange* rather than the operation of individual self-interest.

Homans, of course, rejected all of this. He focused on two-party exchanges rather than on the more extended societal forms of exchange implied in the last example of parent and child. Homans also rejected the emphasis on a moral system, arguing instead that the basis of human exchange lies in self-interest based on a combination of economic and psychological needs.

scheme was useful only as the starting point of a science. What was next required were propositions relating the concepts to one another. In *The Human Group,* I stated a number of such propositions, which seemed to hold good for the groups I had chosen.

I had long known Professor Talcott Parsons and was now closely associated with him in the Department of Social Relations. The sociological profession looked upon him as its leading theorist. I decided that what he called theories were only conceptual schemes, and that a theory was not a theory unless it contained at least a few propositions. I became confident that this view was correct by reading several books on the philosophy of science.

Nor was it enough that a theory should contain propositions. A theory of a phenomenon was an explanation of it. Explanation consisted in showing that one or more propositions of a low order of generality followed in logic from more general propositions applied to what were variously called given or boundary conditions or parameters. I stated my position on this issue in my little book *The Nature of Social Science* (1967).

I then asked myself what general propositions I could use in this way to explain the empirical propositions I had stated in *The Human Group* and other propositions brought to my attention by later reading of field and experimental studies in social psychology. The general propositions would have to meet only one condition: in accordance with my original insight, they should apply to individual human beings as members of a species.

Such propositions were already at hand—luckily, for I could not have invented them for myself. They were the propositions of behavioral psychology as stated by my old friend B. F. Skinner and others. They held good of persons both when acting alone in the physical environment and when in interaction with other persons. In the two editions of my book *Social Behavior* (1961 and revised in 1974), I used these propositions to try to explain how, under appropriate given conditions, relatively enduring social structures could arise from, and be maintained by, the actions of individuals, who need not have intended to create the structures. This I conceive to be the central intellectual problem of sociology.

Once the structures have been created, they have further effects on the behavior of persons who take part in them or come into contact with them. But these further effects are explained by the same propositions as those used to explain the creation and maintenance of the structures in the first place. The structures only provide new given conditions to which the propositions are to be applied. My sociology remains fundamentally individualistic and not collectivistic.

Homans and Structural Functionalism

In addition to these specific attacks on Durkheim and Lévi-Strauss, Homans attacked the structural-functionalist explanation of *institutions*, which he defined as "relatively persistent patterns of social behavior to whose maintenance the actions of many men contribute" (Homans, 1969:6). He argued that four types of explanation have been used in analyzing institutions; the two he rejected are associated with structural functionalism.

The first type of explanation is *structural*; it argues that a "particular institution exists because of its relation to other institutions in a social system" (Homans, 1969:6). For Homans, the assertion that certain institutions are correlated with others does not explain them. The second type of explanation, which is *functional*, contends that "the institution exists because the society could not survive or remain in equilibrium without it" (Homans, 1969:6). This is a vulgarized form of functional explanation that ignores the modern work on the subject, such as that of Robert Merton (1949/1968). Having set up the functional explanation as a straw man, Homans then attacked it:

> The trouble with functional explanations in sociology is not a matter of principle but of practice. From the characteristic general proposition of functionalism we can draw the conclusion in logic that a society failing to survive did *not* possess institutions of type x—whatever x may be. Now there are societies—a very few—that have not survived in any sense of the word. For some of these societies we have accounts of the social organization before their disappearance, and it turns out that they did not possess institutions of type x. If these societies failed to survive, it was not for lack of social institutions, unless resistance to measles and alcohol be a social institution. That is, there is inadequate evidence so far for the truth of the general propositions of functionalism—and after all truth does make a difference. It is conceivable that the difficulties will be overcome, that better statements of the conditions for the survival or equilibrium of any society may be devised, from which nothing but true conclusions will be drawn. But in spite of endless efforts nothing of the sort is in sight. Whatever its status in principle, functional explanation in sociology is in practice a failure.
>
> (Homans, 1969:9)

Had Homans taken on Merton's functional paradigm, rather than a vulgarized form of functionalism that no contemporary functionalist would support, we could take Homans more seriously. Having taken on only easy targets, Homans could cavalierly conclude that structural explanation is no explanation at all and functional explanation is unsatisfactory, since it leads to both true and false conclusions.

Homans (1969) used the label *historical* for the third type of explanation of institutions. Here the institution is seen as the end-product of a historical process. Interestingly, he saw historical explanation as basically a *psychological* explanation, his fourth type of explanation. He saw institutional change as ubiquitous and its study as central to sociology. When we perform a historical analysis correctly we must conclude that the explanation of this change lies at the psychological level:

> All human institutions are products of processes of historical change. In fact, most institutions are continually changing. When we have enough factual information, which we often do not, even to begin explaining historical change, and when we try to supply the major premises of our unstated deductive systems, we find that there are certain premises we absolutely cannot avoid using, and that these premises are not propositions about the interrelations of institutions, as in structural explanation, or propositions about the conditions for the survival of societies, as in functional explanation, but . . . propositions about the behavior of men as men. . . . That is, they are psychological propositions: in their major premises history and psychology are one.
>
> (Homans, 1969:11)

In sum, Homans argued that institutional change must be explained by sociologists and that any explanation of change will be psychological at its base. Homans illustrated this with the example of the introduction of power-driven machinery into the English textile industry in the eighteenth century. He argued that this event was of great sociological importance, because it was one of the first steps in the Industrial Revolution that led to many of our present-day institutions. His starting point was the growth in English cotton exports in the eighteenth century:

> [This] led to an increased demand on the part of the industrial entrepreneurs for supplies of cotton thread, a demand that was not fully met by the existing labor force, spinning thread by hand on spinning wheels, so that the wages of spinners began to rise, threatening to raise the price of cloth and thus check the expansion of trade.
>
> (Homans, 1969:10)

To prevent this rise in wages, costs, and prices, and reduction in trade, entrepreneurs in the textile industry, who already knew of power-driven machines in other industries, developed machines driven by water power or steam that could spin several threads at a time. Driven by the thought of higher profits, many tried to develop such machines, and some succeeded.

Homans argued that this process can be reduced to a deductive system that would explain why entrepreneurs took the actions they did. This deductive system, based upon psychological principles, takes the following form:

1. Men are likely to take actions that they perceive are, in the circumstances, likely to achieve rewarding results.
2. The entrepreneurs were men.
3. As entrepreneurs, they were likely to find results in the form of increasing profits rewarding (Homans, 1969).

Starting with his basic assumption about the psychological nature of human beings, Homans argued that he had explained the coming of power-driven machines to the eighteenth-century English textile industry. By using this example, Homans concluded that historical change can be explained only by psychological principles. Homans drummed structural functionalism out of sociology and argued that the only true sociology is based on psychological principles. However, Homans was more than simply polemical; he tried to develop a theory based on psychological principles.

Homans's Basic Propositions

Although some of Homans's propositions deal with at least two interacting individuals, he was careful to point out that his propositions are based on psychological principles. According to Homans, they are psychological for two reasons. First, "they are usually stated and empirically tested by persons who call themselves psychologists" (Homans, 1967:39–40). Second, and more important, they are psychological because of the level at which they deal with the individual in society: "They are propositions about the behavior of individual human beings, rather than propositions about groups or societies as such; and *the behavior of men, as men*, is generally considered the province of psychology" (Homans, 1967:40; italics added). As a result of this position, Homans admitted to being "what has been called—and it is a horrid phrase—a psychological reductionist" (1974:12). Reductionism, to Homans is "The process of showing how the propositions of one named science [in this case, sociology] follow in logic from the more general propositions of another named science [in this case, psychology]" (1984:338).

Although Homans made the case for psychological principles, he did not think of individuals as isolated. He recognized that people are social and spend a considerable portion of their time interacting with other people. He attempted to explain social behavior with psychological principles: "What the position [Homans's] does assume is that the general propositions of psychology, which are propositions about the effects on human behavior of the results thereof, do not change when the results come from other men rather than from the physical environment" (Homans, 1967:59). Homans did not deny the Durkheimian position that something new emerges from interaction. Instead, he argued that those emergent properties can be explained by psychological principles; there is no need for new sociological propositions to explain social facts. He used the basic sociological concept of a norm to illustrate this:

> The great example of a social fact is a social norm, and the norms of the groups to which they belong certainly constrain towards conformity the behavior of many individuals. The question is not that of the existence of constraint, but of its explanation. . . . The norm does not constrain automatically: individuals conform, when they do so, because they perceive it is to their net advantage to conform, and it is psychology that deals with the effect on behavior of perceived advantage.
>
> (Homans, 1967:60)

In numerous publications Homans detailed a program to, in his words, "bring men back in[to]" sociology, but he also tried to develop a theory that focuses on psychology, people, and the "elementary forms of social life." That theory has come to be called *exchange theory*. According to Homans, it "envisages social *behavior* as an exchange of activity, tangible or intangible, and more or less rewarding or costly, between at least two persons" (Homans, 1961:13; italics added).

In the example discussed above, Homans sought to explain the development of power-driven machinery in the textile industry and thereby the Industrial Revolution through the psychological principle that people are likely to act in such a way as to increase their rewards. More generally, in his version of exchange theory, he sought to explain elementary social behavior in terms of rewards and costs. He was motivated in part by the work of the social factists, in particular the structural-functional theories of his acknowledged "colleague and friend," Talcott Parsons. He argued that such theories "possess every virtue except that of explaining anything" (Homans, 1961:10). To Homans, the structural functionalists did little more than create conceptual categories and schemes. Homans admitted that a scientific sociology needs such categories, but sociology "also needs a set of general propositions about the relations among the categories, for without such propositions explanation is impossible. No explanation without propositions!" (Homans, 1974:10). Homans, therefore, set for himself the task of developing those propositions that focus on the psychological level; these form the groundwork of exchange theory.

In *Social Behavior: Its Elementary Forms* (1961/1974),[5] Homans acknowledged that his exchange theory is derived from both behavioral psychology and elementary economics. In fact, Homans (1984) regrets that his theory was labeled "exchange theory" because he sees it as a behavioral psychology applied to specific situations. Homans began with a discussion of the exemplar of the behaviorist paradigm, B. F. Skinner, in particular of Skinner's study of pigeons.

> Suppose, then, that a fresh or naive pigeon is in its cage in the laboratory. One of the items in its inborn repertory of behavior which it uses to explore its environment is the peck. As the pigeon wanders around the cage pecking away, it happens to hit a round red target, at which point the waiting psychologists or, it may be, an automatic machine feeds it grain. The evidence is that the probability of the pigeon's emitting the behavior again—the probability, that is, of its not just pecking but pecking on the target—has increased. In Skinner's language the pigeon's behavior in pecking the target is an *operant*; the operant has been *reinforced*; grain is the *reinforcer*; and the pigeon has undergone *operant conditioning*. Should we prefer our language to be ordinary English, we may say that the pigeon has learned to peck the target by being rewarded for doing so.
>
> (Homans, 1961:18)

Skinner was interested in this instance in pigeons; Homans's concern was humans. According to Homans, Skinner's pigeons are not engaged in a true exchange relationship with the psychologist. The pigeon is engaged in a one-sided exchange relationship, whereas human exchanges are always two-sided. The pigeon is being reinforced by the grain, but the psychologist is not truly being reinforced by the pecks of the pigeon. The pigeon is carrying on the same sort of relationship with the psychologist as it would with the physical environment. Because there is no reciprocity, Homans defined this as *individual behavior*. Homans seemed to relegate the study of this sort of behavior to the psychologist, whereas he urged the sociologist to study social behavior "where the activity of each of at least two animals reinforces (or punishes) the activity of the other, and where accordingly each influences the other" (Homans, 1961:30). However, it is significant that, according to Homans, *no new propositions* are needed to explain social behavior as opposed to individual behavior. The laws of individual behavior as developed by Skinner in his study of pigeons explain social behavior as long as we take into account the complications of mutual reinforcement. Homans admitted that he might ultimately have to go beyond the principles derived by Skinner, but only reluctantly.

In his theoretical work, Homans restricted himself to everyday social interaction. It is clear, however, that he believed that a sociology built on his principles would ultimately be able to explain all social behavior. Here is the case Homans used to exemplify the kind of exchange relationship he was interested in:

> Suppose that two men are doing paperwork jobs in an office. According to the office rules, each should do his job by himself, or, if he needs help, he should consult the supervisor. One

---

[5]In the following discussion we move back and forth between the two editions of Homans's book. We do not restrict ourselves to the revised edition because many aspects of the first edition more clearly reflect Homans's position. In the preface to the revised edition, he said that although it is a thorough revision, he had not "altered the substance of the underlying argument" (Homans, 1974:v). Thus we feel safe in dealing simultaneously with both volumes.

Suppose that two men are doing paperwork jobs in an office. According to the office rules, each should do his job by himself, or, if he needs help, he should consult the supervisor. One of the men, whom we shall call Person, is not skillful at the work and would get it done better and faster if he got help from time to time. In spite of the rules he is reluctant to go to the supervisor, for to confess his incompetence might hurt his chances for promotion. Instead he seeks out the other man, whom we shall call Other for short, and asks him for help. Other is more experienced at the work than is Person; he can do his work well and quickly and be left with time to spare, and he has reason to suppose that the supervisor will not go out of his way to look for a breach of rules. Other gives Person help and in return Person gives Other thanks and expressions of approval. The two men have exchanged help and approval.

(Homans, 1961:31–32)

Although Homans would ultimately deal with more complex social behavior, initially he aimed his exchange theory at this level. Focusing on this sort of situation, and basing his ideas on Skinner's findings on pigeons, Homans developed several propositions. These are the basis of his exchange theory of social behavior.

THE SUCCESS PROPOSITION

For all actions taken by persons, the more often a particular action of a person is rewarded, the more likely the person is to perform that action.

(Homans, 1974:16)

In terms of Homans's Person-Other example in an office situation, this proposition means that a person is more likely to ask others for advice if he or she has been rewarded in the past with useful advice. Furthermore, the more often a person received useful advice in the past, the more often he or she will request more advice. Similarly, the other person will be more willing to give advice and give it more frequently, if he or she often has been rewarded with approval in the past. Generally, behavior in accord with the success proposition involves three stages: first, a person's action; next, a rewarded result; and finally, a repetition of the original action or at minimum one similar in at least some respects.

Homans specified a number of things about the success proposition. First, although it is generally true that increasingly frequent rewards lead to increasingly frequent actions, this cannot go on indefinitely. At some point individuals simply cannot act that way as frequently. Second, the shorter the interval between behavior and reward, the more likely a person is to repeat the behavior. Conversely, long intervals between behavior and reward lower the likelihood of repeat behavior. Finally, it was Homans's view that intermittent rewards are more likely to elicit repeat behavior than regular rewards. Regular rewards lead to boredom and satiation, whereas rewards at irregular intervals (as in gambling) are very likely to elicit repeat behaviors.

THE STIMULUS PROPOSITION

If in the past the occurrence of a particular stimulus, or set of stimuli, has been the occasion on which a person's action has been rewarded, then the more similar the present stimuli are to the past ones, the more likely the person is to perform the action, or some similar action.

(Homans, 1974:23)

Again looking at Homans's office example: if, in the past, Person and Other found the giving and getting of advice rewarding, then they are likely to engage in similar actions in similar situations in the future. Homans offered an even more down to earth example: "A fisherman who has cast his line into a dark pool and has caught a fish becomes more apt to fish in dark pools again" (1974:23).

Homans was interested in the process of *generalization*; that is, the tendency to extend behavior to similar circumstances. In the fishing example, one aspect of generalization would be to move from fishing in dark pools to fishing in any pool with any degree of shadiness. Similarly, success in catching fish is likely to lead from one kind of fishing to another (for instance, fresh water to salt water) or even from fishing to hunting. However, the process of *discrimination* is also operant. That is, the actor may fish only under the specific circumstances that proved successful in the past. For one thing, if the conditions under which success occurred were too complicated, then similar conditions may not stimulate behavior. If the crucial stimulus occurs too long before behavior is required, then it may not actually stimulate that behavior. An actor can become oversensitized to stimuli, especially if they are very valuable to the actor. In fact, the actor could respond to irrelevant stimuli, at least until the situation is corrected by repeated failures. All of this is affected by the individual's alertness or attentiveness to stimuli.

THE VALUE PROPOSITION

The more valuable to a person is the result of his action, the more likely he is to perform the action.

(Homans, 1974:25)

In the office example, if the rewards each offers to the other are considered valuable, then the actors are more likely to perform the desired behaviors than if the rewards are not valuable. At this point, Homans introduced the concepts of rewards and punishments. Rewards are actions with positive values; an increase in rewards is more likely to elicit the desired behavior. Punishments are actions with negative values; an increase in punishment means that the actor is less likely to manifest undesired behaviors. Homans found punishments to be an ineffective means of getting people to change their behavior. It is preferable simply not to reward undesirable behavior; then it eventually becomes extinguished. Punishments are even less likely to work as a means of getting someone to do something. Rewards are clearly to be preferred, but they may be in short supply. Homans did make it clear that his is not simply a hedonistic theory; rewards can be either materialistic (for example, money) or altruistic (helping others).

THE DEPRIVATION-SATIATION PROPOSITION

The more often in the recent past a person has received a particular reward, the less valuable any further unit of that reward becomes for him.

(Homans, 1974:29)

In the office, Person and Other may reward each other so often for giving and getting advice that the rewards cease to be valuable to either. Time is crucial here; people are less likely to become satiated if particular rewards are stretched over a long period of time.

At this point, Homans defined two other critical concepts: cost and profit. The *cost* of any behavior is defined as the rewards an actor has lost in forgoing alternative lines of action. *Profit* in social exchange is seen as the greater number of rewards gained over costs incurred. These concepts led Homans to recast the deprivation-satiation proposition as "the greater the profit a person receives as a result of his action, the more likely he is to perform the action" (1974:31).

THE AGGRESSION-APPROVAL PROPOSITIONS

Proposition A: When a person's action does not receive the reward he expected, or receives punishment he did not expect, he will be angry; he becomes more likely to perform aggressive behavior, and the results of such behavior become more valuable to him.

(Homans, 1974:37)

In the office case, if Person did not get the advice he or she expected and Other did not receive the praise he or she anticipated, then both were likely to be angry.[6] We are surprised to find the concepts of frustration and anger in Homans's work, because they would seem to refer to mental states. In fact, Homans admitted as much: "When a person does not get what he expected, he is said to be frustrated. A purist in behaviorism would not refer to the expectation at all, because the word seems to refer . . . to a state of mind" (1974:31). Homans went on to argue that frustration of such expectations need *not* refer "only" to an internal state. It can also refer to "wholly external events," observable not just by Person but also by outsiders.

Proposition A on aggression-approval refers only to negative emotions, whereas Proposition B deals with more positive emotions:

Proposition B: When a person's action receives the reward he expected, especially a greater reward than he expected, or does not receive punishment he expected, he will be pleased; he becomes more likely to perform approving behavior, and the results of such behavior become more valuable to him.

(Homans, 1974:39)

For example, in the office, when Person gets the advice that he or she expects and Other gets the praise that he or she expects, both are pleased and more likely to get or give advice. Advice and praise become more valuable to each.

In the end, Homans's theory can be condensed to a view of the actor as a rational profit seeker. However, Homans was unable to completely eradicate mental states or large-scale structures from his system. For example, Homans was forced to admit that institutional history makes a difference in individual behavior. On consciousness Homans admitted the need for a "more fully developed psychology" (1974:45).

Despite such admissions, Homans remained a behaviorist who worked resolutely at the behavioral level and who argued that large-scale structures can be understood if we

---

[6] Although Homans still called this the "law of distributive justice" in the revised later edition, he developed the concept more extensively in the first edition. *Distributive justice* refers to whether the rewards and costs are distributed fairly among the individuals involved. In fact, Homans originally stated it as a proposition: "The more to a man's disadvantage the rule of distributive justice fails of realization, the more likely he is to display the emotional behavior we call anger" (1961:75).

adequately understand elementary social behavior. He contended that exchange processes are "identical" at the individual and societal levels, although he admitted that at the societal level, "the way the fundamental processes are combined is more complex" (Homans, 1974:358).

Criticisms of Homans's Theory of Society and Culture

Homans's exchange theory called forth strong criticism in sociology (see, for example, Abrahamsson, 1970; Ekeh, 1974; Mitchell, 1978; Molm, 1981). We focus on the two crucial weaknesses in Homans's theory as well as criticisms of them by other sociologists. The key problems are Homans's failure to deal adequately with the cultural and societal levels and his failure to deal with internal mental processes.

Ekeh (1974), for example, criticized Homans for focusing solely on two-person, or dyadic, exchange and for ignoring more large-scale patterns of exchange. Ekeh was also critical of Homans for ignoring the norms and values that symbolically shape exchange relations. However, the criticism of Talcott Parsons, from a social-factist point of view, best illustrates the problems in Homans's work at the societal level.

PARSONS VERSUS HOMANS

Parsons pinpointed two basic differences between himself and Homans. First, he contended that Homans tended to "slur" the difference between the behavior of people and that of lower animals. Parsons, however, saw a very clear dividing line. To Parsons, the principles used to explain human behavior are qualitatively different from those used to explain animal behavior. Parsons objected to Homans's derivation of human exchange principles from Skinner's study of pigeons.

Parsons's second objection is even more crucial: "The most general formulations applicable to men as men (which *I* would call principles of *action*, rather than psychological) do *not* suffice to explain . . . the complex subsystems of action" (Parsons, 1964:216). In other words, psychological principles do not, indeed cannot, explain social facts. Homans had been unable to show how psychological principles apply at the societal level. As Parsons said, "Homans is under obligation to show how his principles can account for the principal structural features of large scale social systems" (1964:216). He concluded that even if Homans were to try to do this, he would inevitably fail, because social facts are variables capable of explaining, and being explained, without reference to Homans's psychological principles:

> The alternative to this [Homans's] emphasis is to see acting units as part of organized systems, which have properties other than those attributable to . . . the . . . interaction between "men as men." They have languages, cultural values, legal systems, various kinds of institutional norms and generalized media. Concrete behavior is not a function simply of elementary properties, but of the kinds of systems, their various structures and the processes taking place within them. From this point of view it is quite legitimate to be concerned with the organization of complex systems . . . long before their properties can be derived from elementary principles.
>
> (Parsons, 1964:219)

In reply to Parsons, Homans maintained that the key issue concerns explanations of the structures and institutions of complex societies: "Here is the nub of the matter. Parsons thinks psychological propositions do not suffice to explain them; I think they do" (Homans, 1971:375). Homans recognized that social facts emerge out of interaction, but he thought that they could be explained by psychological principles. Conversely, Parsons thought that only social facts could explain social facts.

Homans replied to the attack by Parsons and others with a counterattack aimed at social factists:

> Let them therefore specify what properties of social behavior they consider to be emergent and show, by constructing the appropriate deductive systems, how they propose to explain them without making use of psychological propositions. I guarantee to show either that the explanations fail to explain or that they in fact use psychological propositions, in however disguised a form.
>
> (Homans, 1971:376)

What has occurred between Homans and Parsons is a series of charges and counter charges, with each party claiming that the other's theory has little explanatory power. Replying to Parsons's statements that he is under an obligation to show how his principles can explain the structural features of large-scale societies, Homans said: "I am under no more obligation than Parsons is under himself, who has not shown how his principles can explain the existence of these principal structural features. Indeed, it is not at all clear what his principles *are*" (1971:376). We are left with an unresolved argument in which Parsons says that Homans has not explained structure and Homans says that Parsons has not explained structure. However, the dialogue does clarify once again the battle lines between the social-facts and social-behaviorist paradigms in general and between structural functionalism and exchange theory in particular.

Blau's Integrated Exchange Theory

Whereas Homans and Parsons can manage nothing better than a simple declaration of the boundaries that separate them, Peter Blau (1964) went a good deal further in his effort to develop an exchange theory that combines social behaviorism and social factism. (We encounter a very different form of Blau's theorizing in Chapter 9.) Blau's goal was "an understanding of social structure on the basis of an analysis of the social processes that govern the relations between individuals and groups. The basic question . . . is how social life becomes organized into increasingly complex structures of associations among men" (1964:2). Blau's intention, as stated here, was to go beyond Homans's concern with elementary forms of social life and into an analysis of complex structures. Homans was content to work at the behavioral level, but Blau viewed such work only as a means to a larger end: "The main sociological purpose of studying processes of face-to-face interaction is to lay the foundation for an understanding of the social structures that evolve and the emergent social forces that characterize their development" (1964:13).[7]

---

[7]It is interesting to note that Blau (forthcoming) no longer accepts the idea of building macro theory on a micro base.

Blau focused on the process of exchange, which, in his view, directs much of human behavior and underlies relationships among individuals as well as among groups. In effect, Blau envisioned a four-stage sequence leading from interpersonal exchange to social structure to social change:

Step 1: Personal exchange transactions between people give rise to . . .
Step 2: Differentiation of status and power, which leads to . . .
Step 3: Legitimation and organization, which sow the seeds of . . .
Step 4: Opposition and change.

On the individual level, Blau and Homans were interested in similar processes. However, Blau's concept of social exchange is limited to actions that are contingent, that depend on rewarding reactions from others—actions that cease when expected reactions are not forthcoming. People are attracted to each other for a variety of reasons that induce them to establish social associations. Once initial ties are forged, the rewards that they provide to each other serve to maintain and enhance the bonds. The opposite situation is also possible: with insufficient rewards, an association will weaken or break. Rewards that are exchanged can be either intrinsic (for instance, love, affection, respect) or extrinsic (for instance, money, physical labor). The parties cannot always reward each other equally; when there is inequality in the exchange, a difference of power will emerge within an association.

When one party needs something from another but has nothing comparable to offer in return, four alternatives are available. First, people can force other people to help them. Second, they can find another source to obtain what they need. Third, they can attempt to get along without what they need from the others. Finally, and most important, they can subordinate themselves to the others, thereby giving the others "generalized credit" in their relationship; the others then can draw on this credit when they want them to do something. (This latter alternative is, of course, the essential characteristic of power.)

Up to this point, Blau's position is similar to Homans's position, but Blau extended his theory to the level of social facts. He noted, for example, that we cannot analyze processes of social interaction apart from the social structure that surrounds them. Social structure emerges from social interaction, but once this occurs social structures have a separate existence that affects the process of interaction.

Social interaction exists first within social groups. People are attracted to a group when they feel that the relationships offer more rewards than those in other groups. Because they are attracted to the group, they want to be accepted. To be accepted, they must offer group members rewards. This involves impressing the group members by showing the members that associating with the new people will be rewarding. The relationship with the group members will be solidified when they have impressed the group —when members have received the rewards they expected. Newcomers' efforts to impress group members generally lead to group cohesion, but competition and, ultimately, social differentiation can occur when too many people actively seek to impress each other with their abilities to reward.

The paradox here is that although group members with the ability to impress can be attractive associates, their impressive characteristics also can arouse fears of dependence in other group members and cause them to acknowledge their attraction only reluctantly. In the early stages of group formation, competition for social recognition among group members actually acts as a screening test for potential leaders of the group. Those best able to reward are most likely to end up in leadership positions. Those group members with less ability to reward want to continue to receive the rewards offered by the potential leaders, and this usually more than compensates for their fears of becoming dependent on them. Ultimately, those individuals with the greater ability to reward emerge as leaders, and the group is differentiated.

The inevitable differentiation of the group into leaders and followers creates a renewed need for integration. Once they have acknowledged the leader's status, followers have an even greater need for integration. Earlier, followers flaunted their most impressive qualities. Now, to achieve integration among fellow followers, they display their weaknesses. This is, in effect, a public declaration that they no longer want to be leaders. This self-deprecation leads to sympathy and social acceptance from the other also-rans. The leader (or leaders) also engages in some self-deprecation at this point, in order to improve overall group integration. By admitting that subordinates are superior in some areas, the leader reduces the pain associated with subordination and demonstrates that he or she does not seek control over every area of group life. These types of forces serve to reintegrate the group despite its new, differentiated status.

All of this is reminiscent of Homans's discussion of exchange theory. Blau, however, moved to the societal level and differentiated between two types of social organization. Exchange theorists and behavioral sociologists also recognize this emergence, but there is, as we will see, a basic difference between Blau and "purer" social behaviorists on this issue. The first type, in which Blau recognized the emergent properties of social groups, emerges from the processes of exchange and competition discussed above. The second type of social organization is not emergent but is explicitly established to achieve specified objectives—for example, manufacturing goods that can be sold for a profit, participating in bowling tournaments, engaging in collective bargaining, and winning political victories (Blau, 1964). In discussing these two types of organization, Blau clearly moved beyond the "elementary forms of social behavior" that are typically of interest to social behaviorists.

In addition to a concern with these organizations, Blau was interested in the subgroups within them. For example, he argued that leadership and opposition groups are found in both types of organization. In the first type, these two groups emerge out of the process of interaction. In the second, leadership and opposition groups are built into the structure of the organization. In either case, differentiation between the groups is inevitable and this lays the groundwork for opposition and conflict within the organization between leaders and followers.

Having moved beyond Homans's elementary forms of behavior and into complex social structures, Blau knew that he must adapt exchange theory to the societal level. Blau (1964) recognized the essential difference between small groups and large collectivities, whereas Homans minimized this difference in his effort to explain all social behavior in terms of basic psychological principles.

The complex social structures that characterize large collectives differ fundamentally from the simpler structures of small groups. A structure of social relations develops in a small group in the course of social interaction among its members. Since there is no direct social interaction among most members of a large community or entire society, some other mechanism must mediate the structure of social relations among them.

(Blau, 1964:253)

This statement requires scrutiny. On the one hand, Blau clearly ruled out social behaviorism as an adequate paradigm for dealing with complex social structures. On the other, he ruled out the social-definitionist paradigm, because he argued that social interaction and the social definitions that accompany it do not occur directly in a large-scale organization. Thus, starting from the social-behavior paradigm, Blau aligned himself with the social-facts paradigm in dealing with more complex social structures.

For Blau, the mechanisms that mediate among the complex social structures are the norms and values (the value consensus) that exist within society:

Commonly agreed upon values and norms serve as media of social life and as mediating links for social transactions. They make indirect social exchange possible, and they govern the processes of social integration and differentiation in complex social structures as well as the development of social organization and reorganization in them.

(Blau, 1964:255)

Other mechanisms mediate among social structures, but Blau focused upon value consensus. Looking first at social norms, Blau argued that they substitute indirect exchange for direct exchange. One member conforms to the group norm and receives approval for that conformity and implicit approval for the fact that conformity contributes to the group's maintenance and stability. In other words, the group or collectivity engages in an exchange relationship with the individual. This is in contrast to Homans's simpler notion, which focused on interpersonal exchange. Blau offered a number of examples of collectivity-individual exchanges replacing individual-individual exchanges:

Staff officials do not assist line officials in their work in exchange for rewards received from them, but furnishing this assistance is the official obligation of staff members, and in return for discharging these obligations they receive financial rewards from the company.

Organized philanthropy provides another example of indirect social exchange. In contrast to the old-fashioned lady bountiful who brought her baskets to the poor and received their gratitude and appreciation, there is no direct contact and no exchange between individual donors and recipients in contemporary organized charity. Wealthy businessmen and members of the upper class make philanthropic contributions to conform with the normative expectations that prevail in their social class and to earn the social approval of their peers, not in order to earn the gratitude of the individuals who benefit from their charity.

(Blau, 1964:260)

The concept of norm in Blau's formulation moves Blau to the level of exchange between individual and collectivity, but the concept of values moves him to the largest-scale societal level and to the analysis of the relationship *among collectivities*. Blau said:

Common values of various types can be conceived of as media of social transactions that expand the compass of social interaction and the structure of social relations through social space and time. Consensus on social values serves as the basis for extending the range of social transactions beyond the limits of direct social contacts and for perpetuating social structures beyond the life span of human beings. Value standards can be considered media of social life in two senses of the term; the value context is the medium that molds the form of social relationships; and common values are the mediating links for social associations and transactions on a broad scale.

(Blau, 1964:263–264)

In Blau's view, there are four basic types of values, each of which performs different functions. First are *particularistic* values, which are the media of integration and solidarity. These values serve to unite the members of a group around such things as patriotism, or the good of the school, or the company. These are seen as similar at the collective level to sentiments of personal attraction that unite individuals on a face-to-face basis. However, they extend integrative bonds beyond mere personal attraction. Particularistic values also differentiate the ingroup from the outgroup, thereby enhancing their unifying function.

The second type of values is *universalistic* values. These are standards by which the relative worth of the various things that can be exchanged is assessed. The existence of these standards allows for the possibility of indirect exchange. An individual may make a contribution to a segment of a community, and universalistic values allow the community to assess the value of the contribution and to reward the individual in an appropriate manner (for example, by higher social status).

The values that *legitimate authority* are the third type. The value system that accords some people (for example, bosses, presidents) more power than others extends the scope of organized social control. This is related to the fourth type of value—values of *opposition*. Opposition (or revolutionary) values allow for the spread of a feeling for a need for change far beyond that possible merely by personal contact among those who oppose the established order. These values (for example, socialism and anarchism in a capitalist society) legitimate opposition to those whose power is legitimated by authority values.

Blau's four types of values have carried us far from Homans's version of exchange theory. The individual and individual behavior, paramount for Homans, almost have disappeared in Blau's conception. Taking the place of the individual are a wide variety of *social facts*. For example, Blau discussed groups, organizations, collectivities, societies, norms, and values. Blau's analysis is concerned with what holds large-scale social units together and tears them apart, clearly traditional concerns of the social factist.

Although Blau argued that he was simply extending exchange theory to the societal level, in so doing he twisted exchange theory beyond recognition. He was even forced to admit that processes at the societal level are fundamentally different from those at the individual level. In his effort to extend exchange theory, Blau managed only to transform it into another theory congruent with the social-facts paradigm. Blau seemed to recognize that exchange theory is primarily concerned with face-to-face relations. As a result, it needs to be complemented by other theoretical orientations that focus mainly on macro structures. Blau (forthcoming) has now come to recognize this and his most recent work (see Chapter 9) focuses on macro-level, structural phenomena.

Criticisms of Homans's Theory of Consciousness

The other major criticism of Homans's theory was aimed at its failure to do an adequate analysis of consciousness. Bengt Abrahamsson, for example, argued that Homans tends to focus on overt behaviors and ignore the inner experiences of the actors: "Knowing the *experience* of individuals and their perceptions of rewards of certain acts is often of great importance for understanding and predicting their behavior" (1970:283). Jack N. Mitchell also was critical of Homans's reductionism and his failure to deal with the dynamics of consciousness: "Any theory that purports to explain or 'get to' the nature of man's social behavior cannot assume explicitly or tacitly that interaction is merely the working out of the rationality of needs, biological or psychological—or of economic processes. What is lacking . . . is a sense of . . . uncertainty, problematics and negotiation" (1978:81). To overcome the limitations of exchange theory in the analysis of consciousness, Mitchell argued for the incorporation into exchange theory of insights from the work of social definitionists such as Goffman and Garfinkel.

INTEGRATING EXCHANGE THEORY AND SYMBOLIC INTERACTIONISM

Peter Singelmann (1972) has made an explicit effort to integrate the main concepts of symbolic interaction and exchange theory. Singelmann began with Mead's categories of mind, self, and society in his effort to establish convergences between these two theories.

MIND   Singelmann stated that to the symbolic interactionist, the concept of mind "reflects the human capacity to *conceive* what the organism *perceives*, define situations, evaluate phenomena, convert gestures into symbols, and exhibit pragmatic and goal-directed behavior" (1972:416). According to Singelmann, the actor is an active agent to both the symbolic interactionist and the exchange theorist. He argued that the symbolic interactionist concept of the mind has been "explicitly recognized" by exchange theorists. As evidence that such a concept of mind exists among exchange theorists, he cited discussions by exchange theorists of such things as individuals' awareness of alternatives, aspirations, and expectations. He also detected evidence of mental processes in Homans's concept of distributive justice. One must subjectively evaluate different rewards in order to determine whether the law of distributive justice has been violated.

On the basis of this kind of analysis, Singelmann concluded, "Current exchange theory has thus gone beyond the purely 'behavioristic' approach of many reinforcement theories by recognizing, more or less explicitly, that the human mind mediates the relationships between stimuli and behavioral responses" (1972:417). Thus, a reward is not a reward in itself but must be *defined* as a reward to operate as a reinforcer. In Singelmann's view, this process of definition brings exchange theory in line with the symbolic interactionist position.

Most behaviorists would agree with Singelmann that there is nothing inherent in an object that makes it a reward. A reward may be defined as a reinforcer if it in fact affects behavior. However, Singelmann aside, behaviorists, though aware of the process of social definition, are not concerned with it. They are concerned only with the behavioral manifestations of the definition process, not the process itself.

Singelmann's efforts at reconciliation, as well as Blau's similar effort to extend exchange theory to the level of social facts, show that all of these levels *can be integrated*. However, many exchange theorists are likely to reject this aspect of both Singelmann's and Blau's work. Singelmann, in fact, transformed exchange theory into a social-definitionist perspective. It is no longer exchange theory, nor does it fall within the behaviorist paradigm. Similarly, Blau's extension of exchange theory to the societal level is no longer within the behaviorist paradigm.

SELF Singelmann pointed out that symbolic interactionists are concerned with the idea of self both in the sense used by Mead, "as process in which actors reflect on themselves as objects" (1972:417), and in the sense of the self-concept held by actors. Singelmann suggested that at some level exchange theorists understand that an individual has a self and a self-concept and that these ideas are perfectly appropriate to exchange theory. For exchange relationships to develop and persist, each party must be able to take the role of the other as well as the generalized other, in order to determine what rewards they should offer and what rewards they are likely to receive. Although this is a useful insight, many exchange theorists are not likely to find it relevant to their concerns. They are not concerned with the process by which individuals decide what rewards they will offer, but only in the exchange relationship itself. Pure exchange theorists would want to know about behavior and not about such concepts as self, generalized other, and taking the role of the other. These are for a philosopher to dabble in, not something of concern to the "scientist" who identifies with the behaviorist paradigm. Thus, for example, Skinner defined the self as simply "a repertoire of behavior" (1971:189), a definition very different from that of symbolic interactionists.

SOCIETY Singelmann argued that both symbolic interactionists and exchange theorists focus on the micro social level in analyzing social structure. In addition, he saw two other points of convergence. First, he argued that symbolic interactionists focus on how people fit their interaction patterns together, whereas Homans is concerned with the stabilization of relationships on the basis of the most profitable exchanges. Both imply a constant construction and reconstruction of interaction patterns. Second, Singelmann argued that "exchange may be conceptualized as symbolic interaction" (1972:419), meaning that exchange entails a communication of symbols. This is a clue to Singelmann's implicit argument that exchange theory can be subsumed under symbolic interactionism. Exchange theory is transformed into something very different by Singelmann, but symbolic interactionism remains unscathed.

Interestingly, Singelmann is weakest on the societal level of integration, which reflects his orientation toward symbolic interactionism. To him society seems to be little more than patterned interaction and symbols. The real strength of Singelmann's analysis is in his discussion of mind and self and how the insights of symbolic interactionism and exchange theory are mutually reinforcing on those issues. In his conclusion, Singelmann attempted a theoretical synthesis involving four basic points:

1. In exchange, actors construct normative and existential definitions of themselves, others, actions, goals, and assessments of "fairness."
2. These definitions are not only subjectively constructed but to a large extent socially shared and thus constitute a constraint external to the individual actors.

3. In exchange, the hedonistic strivings of actors are limited and qualified by the nature of the subjective and socially shared definitions of the objective world which includes the self and others.
4. In exchange, actors will change their behaviors or definitions when:
   a. changes in the objective world render existing behaviors and definitions problematic,
   b. changes in some of their subjective definitions render other definitions or existing objective conditions and behaviors problematic.

(Singelmann, 1972:422)

The word *definition* appears over and over in Singelmann's four propositions. He has transformed exchange theory beyond recognition and placed it within social definitionism.[8] In so doing, he actually does the same thing that Blau did in trying to move exchange theory into the social facts camp. Nevertheless, both Blau and Singelmann did try to reconcile the disparate theories. It is questionable, however, whether transforming one theory into another really contributes to the reconciliation of theoretical differences.

THE CURRENT STATUS OF BEHAVIORAL THEORIES

It is appropriate at this point to offer some thoughts on the current status and future prospects of behavioral sociology and exchange theory as well as on the social behavior paradigm in general.

First, it is clear that this is one of the genuine growth areas in contemporary sociology in general and in theory in particular (Beniger and Savory, 1981; Cook, forthcoming b). Much of importance has been published in recent years (for example, Chadwick-Jones, 1976; Cook, forthcoming a; Hamblin and Kunkel, 1977; Michaels and Green, 1978; Molm and Wiggins, 1979), and one can safely predict considerable work on the theories and in the empirical work derived from them in the coming years. Within sociological theory, one can anticipate greater links with network theory (Willer and Anderson, 1981).

Second, although some remain tied to a dogmatic view of psychological behaviorism as the basis of sociological work in this area, others seem willing and eager to move it beyond its traditional bounds to encompass consciousness as well as large-scale structures and institutions (for example, Bredemeier, 1978; Emerson, 1981). As Cook (forthcoming b) puts it: "The focus of substantive work is shifting clearly away from dyadic analysis to the investigation of larger networks of exchange." Among those who have moved in this direction are Marsden (forthcoming) and Yamagishi (forthcoming).

Third, one can anticipate an acceleration of the criticism of sociological behaviorism as the paradigm gains momentum. Sentiments expressed by Kurt Back are likely to be repeated even more stridently in the future:

---

[8]Social behaviorists published a bitter reply to Singelmann in the *American Sociological Review*. In effect, they accused Singelmann of distorting behaviorism by integrating it with social definitionism. They were resisting Singelmann's effort to destroy "pure" behaviorism with this political attack on him (see Abbott, Brown, and Crosbie, 1973).

Many scientists exhibit a tremendous talent, even a joy, in finding some human behavior which can be explained in a nonhuman way by reference either to an animal model or to a completely mechanical model. . . . When the history of current social science is written, it will be largely a story of treating social science as if it were something else, or trying to get away from the human properties of human beings, and of the strange faith of scientists who can measure exactly stimulus and response to reinforcement.

(Back, 1970:1100)

In this context it is instructive to look in detail at a useful work by Linda Molm (1981), in which the major criticisms of social behaviorism were reviewed and responses to them offered.

Molm's basic position is that social behaviorism is a legitimate form of sociology, one that is not as different from other sociological approaches as many believe. Molm blamed both behaviorists and their opponents for a distorted view of this perspective: "In attempting to establish the behavioral perspective as a distinctive approach, behavioral sociologists tended to emphasize their differences from other sociologists and these differences were sometimes distorted, in the course of debate, into wide gulfs" (1981:153). She concluded that the differences from other sociological theories "are based more on misunderstanding than on fact" (p. 154). It is in the context of this view of the misunderstandings surrounding sociological behaviorism that Molm looked at the three basic criticisms of it.

The first criticism is that social behaviorism is reductionistic, because it focuses on individual behavior. This, in her view, is certainly not true of macro behaviorists (such as Blau), but further she felt that it is not even true of micro-behavioral sociologists. Although she agreed that behavioral psychologists are reductionistic, she argued that behavioral sociologists are not. Behavioral psychologists "study how a single subject's behavior is affected by *individual* or independent contingencies: relationships in which the individual's reinforcers are contingent solely on his own behavior" (p. 154). Behavioral sociologists, in contrast, "study how two or more subjects' behaviors are jointly affected by mutual *social* contingencies: relationships in which each person's reinforcers are at least partially contingent on the behaviors of one or more other persons" (p. 154).

Whereas Homans and other purists focus on how one individual's behavior is affected by another person's behavior, many behavioral sociologists "are asking how the *relationship* between persons' *behaviors* is affected by the *relationship* between their *behaviors and rewards*" (p. 155). Social behaviorists are not reductionistic because they look at the "*structural relationships* between persons, and thus they are clearly within the domain of sociology. They are not characteristics of individuals or aggregations of individual characteristics; they are truly *relational* variables" (p. 155).

In fact, Molm went further and argued that social behaviorism is actually less reductionistic than other sociological theories:

The behavioral sociologists' study of dyadic or group behavior stands in sharp contrast to most of contemporary social psychology and much of structural sociology, in which the individual is the unit of analysis, and aggregated, nonrelational variables are studied. At the same time, it should be evident that behavioral sociologists who study social contingencies *are* studying structural variables, albeit micro structures.

(Molm, 1981:156)

Molm certainly is correct in saying that much of the rest of sociology is reductionistic when it conducts empirical research (Akers, 1981; McPhail, 1981), but this does not constitute a solid defense against behaviorism's reductionism. Robert Perinbanayagam made this point when he argued that Molm's position "hardly meets the criticism: the charge of reductionism is applied when the key explanatory variables do not take into account the emergent properties of interactions, exchanges, groups, and even situations" (1981:168). Even in Cook's (forthcoming a) volume on exchange theory, which is self-consciously aimed at moving to the macro levels, Turner (forthcoming) concludes: "The chapters in this volume are decidedly micro in tone."

The second criticism of behavioral sociology is that it leaves many things unexplained, especially norms and values. On the one hand, Molm argued that behaviorists (Stolte, forthcoming) have done no worse on this score than other sociologists. On the other hand, she argued that they do have a theory of the formation of norms and values, albeit in this author's view a very questionable theory, extending individual behavioristic principles to large-scale units: "To understand the formation of norms, we must examine the learning history of the group, institution, or culture under consideration, just as we would examine the learning history of an individual to understand individual behavior" (p. 158).

The third criticism of social behaviorism is that it operates with a mechanical and unfeeling conception of the actor. Molm countered this claim by arguing that operant behaviors "are not automatically elicited by any prior stimulus; they simply occur—they are emitted by the organism, not *elicited* by a stimulus" (1981:160). But this is hardly an active, creative image of the actor, as Perinbanayagam pointed out: "Such claims, far from meeting the criticism of mechanism, merely confirm it. They neatly capture the behaviorist image of a human as a passive, machinelike entity, incapable of volition and originality, that 'emits' behaviors" (1981:166). In other words, Molm's image of the actor has nothing to say about "*constructing a social act*" (Perinbanayagam, 1981:166).

In more positive terms, the latest developments in exchange theory are linked to theoretical developments to be discussed later in this book. First, exchange theory is increasingly influenced by the work of Richard Emerson (see Chapter 10) and his focus on the macro-micro linkage from an exchange perspective. The second is the ties between exchange theory and network theory (Chapter 9). As Cook (forthcoming b) puts it: "The significance of this development [Emerson's notion of exchange networks] is that the entire recent body of work on social networks . . . becomes relevant to exchange theory." Thus, we will have more to say of relevance to recent developments in exchange theory later in this book.

SUMMARY

In this chapter we discuss behavioral sociology and exchange theory as well as their roots in psychological behaviorism. We trace exchange theory back to its source in the work of behavioral psychologist B. F. Skinner. Skinner is a virtually pure behaviorist, and as such he rejected the tenets of theories associated with social definitionism (for instance, symbolic interactionism, phenomenology, ethnomethodology) *and* social factism (for instance, structural functionalism and conflict theory).

The focus of behavioral sociologists is almost single-mindedly microscopic. Their concern is with the relationship between the history of environmental consequences and the nature of present behavior. In short, individuals are seen as likely to repeat behaviors that in the past have been rewarding, but not those that proved costly. In this context, we discuss a number of the concepts of central importance to the behavioral sociologist—positive and negative reinforcers, positive and negative punishments, response cost, generalized reinforcers, and behavior modification.

Next we examine exchange theory, the major representative of behaviorism in sociology. The most important spokesperson for exchange theory is George Homans, who was heavily and directly influenced by the work of B. F. Skinner. Homans criticized the macro-level explanations of social behavior of such people as Durkheim, Parsons, and Lévi-Strauss. Instead, he sought to explain social behavior in terms of psychological principles—that is, behaviorism. He believed that psychological principles can be used to explain not only individual behavior but also social structures *and* social change. The heart of Homans's theory lies in the following basic propositions:

1. *The success proposition*:   "For all actions taken by persons, the more often a particular action of a person is rewarded, the more likely the person is to perform that action."
2. *The stimulus proposition*:   "If in the past the occurrence of a particular stimulus, or set of stimuli, has been the occasion on which a person's action has been rewarded, then the more similar the present stimuli are to the past ones, the more likely the person is to perform the action, or some similar action, now."
3. *The value proposition*:   "The more valuable to a person is the result of his action, the more likely he is to perform the action."
4. *The deprivation-satiation proposition*:   "The more often in the recent past a person has received a particular reward, the less valuable any further unit of that reward becomes for him."
5. *The aggression-approval propositions*:   *A.* "When a person's action does not receive the reward he expected, or receives punishment he did not expect, he will be angry; he becomes more likely to perform aggressive behavior, and the results of such behavior become more valuable to him." *B.* "When a person's action receives the reward he expected, especially a greater reward than he expected, or does not receive punishment he expected, he will be pleased; he becomes more likely to perform approving behavior, and the results of such behavior become more valuable to him."

Given its orientation to individual behavior, Homans's theory has been criticized by social factists for ignoring large-scale structures and by social definitionists for ignoring mental processes. The debate between Parsons and Homans can be seen in terms of the differences between the social-factist and the social-behaviorist orientations. Although such a dialogue is important, even more significant was the effort by Peter Blau to extend exchange theory from the individual to the societal level. Blau outlined a four-stage sequence leading from interpersonal exchange to social structure to social change:

1. Personal exchange transactions between people give rise to . . .
2. Differentiation of status and power, which leads to . . .
3. Legitimation and organization, which sow the seeds of . . .
4. Opposition and change.

Blau's work, although commendable, transforms exchange theory at the societal level so that it is no longer identifiable as a behavioristic orientation.

In addition to being criticized for its weaknesses at the societal level, exchange theory has been criticized for its inattention to mental processes. In this context, we look at Singelmann's work as an effort to integrate symbolic interactionism and exchange theory. Although also commendable, Singelmann's work seems to be vulnerable to the same criticism as Blau's; that is, it transforms exchange theory so that its behaviorism is no longer recognizable. The chapter closes with an assessment of the current status and future prospects of sociological behaviorism, in light of Molm's effort to respond to the major criticism of this orientation.

CHAPTER EIGHT
Contemporary Feminist Theory

PATRICIA MADOO LENGERMANN
The George Washington University
JILL NIEBRUGGE-BRANTLEY
Northern Virginia Community College

FEMINIST theory is that part of the new scholarship on women that implicitly or formally presents a generalized, wide-ranging system of ideas about the basic features of social life and of human experience as these can be understood from a woman-centered perspective. Feminist theory is woman centered in three ways. First, its major "object" for investigation, the starting point of all its investigation, is the situation (or the situations) and experiences of women in society. Second, it treats women as the central "subjects" in the investigative process; that is, it seeks to see the world from the distinctive vantage point (or vantage points) of women in the social world. Third, feminist theory is critical and activist on behalf of women, seeking to produce a better world for women—and thus, they argue, for humankind.

Feminist theory, however, differs from most sociological theories in a number of ways. First, it is the work of an interdisciplinary community, which includes not only sociologists but also scholars from other disciplines, such as anthropology, biology, economics, history, law, literature, philosophy, political science, psychology, and theology;

The authors thank Carole Tuchrello of The George Washington University Sociology Department for her patient aid in manuscript preparation; Rhonda Schrieber of The George Washington University Women's Studies Program for her aid in compiling the bibliography; and Gail Short Hanson, Dean of Students of The George Washington University for biographical materials on Dorothy Smith.

people best recognized as creative writers; people who see themselves primarily as political activists; spokespersons for women of color; and writers from various European or Third World intellectual communities.[1] Second, feminist sociologists, like other feminist theorists, orient their efforts only in part to extending their discipline of origin. Much more central to all feminist scholarship is the development of a critical understanding of society intended to change the social world in directions deemed more just and humane. Third, most sociologists have been particularly hesitant to incorporate feminist theory into their sociological work, in part because that theory seems so new and radical, in part because so many of its creators are not sociologists, and in part because of suspicions about the scientific credentials of a scholarly undertaking so closely linked to political activism. Fourth, feminist theory is not anchored in any one of the three paradigms that have long patterned sociology's orientation to its subject matter—the social-facts paradigm, the social-definition paradigm, and the social-behavior paradigm (see Appendix). One of the most exciting implications of feminist theory for sociology is that it presents a perspective that seems to dissolve the hitherto watertight boundaries between the three paradigms, showing us how social life is an intricate interweaving of nonreflective behavioristic processes, determining social institutions and structures, and ongoing definitional processes by individuals and collectivities. More than juxtaposing these various orientations to social life, feminist theory effectively synthesizes them into a social theory that appears to transcend these classic paradigms and to fit with the integrated paradigm outlined in the Appendix.

In the remainder of this chapter we describe the basic theoretical questions addressed by feminist theorists; look briefly at the history of feminist thought, particularly within sociology; and then examine in more detail the varieties of feminist theory that have become visible over the course of this history. In the chapter's main section, we discuss major themes in contemporary feminist sociological theory.

THE BASIC THEORETICAL QUESTIONS

The impetus for contemporary feminist theory is a deceptively simple question: *"And what about the women?"* In other words, where are the women in any situation being investigated? If they are not present, why? If they are present, what exactly are they doing? How do they experience the situation? What do they contribute to it? What does it mean to them?

The consequences of trying to answer feminism's basic question—and what about the women—have been revolutionary. Dramatically, the contemporary scholarly community discovered that what it had assumed to be the universe of experience was really a particularistic account of male actors and male experience. The recognition of a whole new set of actors called for a reworking of our understanding and patterning of every social situation. Women, feminists exulted, could lay claim to "half the firmament." And indeed, the effect was rather like discovering, through the lens of a new telescope, a multitude of hitherto undetected stars in the universe, a fundamentally new configuration for each constellation.

---

[1] This chapter, however, draws primarily on the English language contribution to this international effort.

Twenty years of posing this question have produced some generalizable conclusions. Women are present in most social situations. Where they are not, it is not for lack of ability or interest but because there have been deliberate efforts to exclude them. Where they are present, women have played roles very different from the popular conception of them (as, for example, passive wives and mothers). Indeed, both as wives and mothers and in a series of other roles, women have, along with men, actively created the situations being studied. Yet though women are actively present in most social situations, scholars and social actors themselves have been blind to their presence. Moreover, women's roles in most social situations, although essential, have not been identical to those of the men in those situations. Overall, their roles have been different from, less privileged than, and subordinate to those of men. Their invisibility is only one indicator of this inequality.

All of this leads us to feminism's second basic question: *"Why then is all this as it is?"* As the first question calls for a description of the social world, this second question requires that one develop an explanation of that world. Description and explanation of the social world are two faces of any sociological theory. Feminism's attempts to answer its two central questions have therefore produced a theory of universal importance for sociology.[2]

How general is this theory? Some might argue that because the questions are particular to the situation of a "minority group," women, the theory that is produced will also be particular and restricted in scope, equivalent to sociology's theories of deviance, or small group processes. But in fact feminism's two basic questions have produced a theory of social life universal in its applicability. The appropriate parallels to feminist theory are not theories of small groups or deviance, each of which is created when sociologists turn their attention away from the "whole picture" to the details of a feature of that picture. Rather, the appropriate parallel is to one of Marx's epistemological accomplishments. Marx helped social scientists discover that the knowledge people had of society, what they assumed to be an absolute and universal statement about reality, in fact reflected the experience of those who economically and politically ruled the social world. Marxian theory effectively demonstrated that one could also view the world from the vantage point of the world's workers, those who, though economically and politically subordinate, were nevertheless indispensable producers of our world. This new vantage point relativized ruling class knowledge and, in allowing us to juxtapose that knowledge with knowledge gained from taking the workers' perspective, vastly expanded our ability to analyze social reality. A century after Marx's death we are still assimilating the implications of this discovery.

Feminism's two theoretical questions similarly produce a revolutionary switch in our understanding of the world. These questions too lead us to discover that what we have taken as universal and absolute knowledge of the world is, in fact, knowledge derived from the experiences of a powerful section of society, men as "masters." That knowledge is relativized if we rediscover the world from the vantage point of a hitherto invisible, unacknowledged "underside": women, who in subordinated but indispensable "serving" roles have worked to sustain and re-create the society that we live in.

---

[2]The third question for all feminists is *"How can we change and improve the world?"* Within sociology only the theories of Marx and neo-Marxism share this intense interest in change. We include descriptions of feminist programs for change in later sections of this chapter.

This discovery raises questions about everything that we have thought we knew about society. This discovery and its implications constitute the essence of contemporary feminist theory's significance for sociological theory.

THE MAJOR HISTORICAL ROOTS

To understand the significance of the present convergence between feminist theory and sociology, we need to look at two past strands of intellectual work. First is the tradition of feminist writings, which has formed part of the Western record of social protest for over 300 years, a tradition that lays the foundation for contemporary feminist theory and that formed part of the environment within which sociology itself took shape. Second is the deeply ambivalent position, from the 1840s to the 1960s, taken by sociologists on the issue of gender inequality.

Feminism: 1600–1960

In one sense, there always has been a feminist perspective. Wherever women are subordinated, and they have been subordinated almost always and everywhere, they seem to have recognized and protested that situation in some form (Chafetz and Dworkin, 1986). In the Western world, the formal dating of feminism begins with the *published* works of protest. With one or two exceptions, these first appeared in the 1630s and continued for about another 150 years as a thin but persistent trickle. Then, in the two centuries from 1780 to the present, feminist writing increasingly becomes a significant collective effort, growing both in the number of its participants and the scope of its critique. (Fuller descriptions of the ideas of these earlier feminists are to be found in Cott, 1977; Lougee, 1976; Martin, 1972; Rossi, 1974; Showalter, 1971; Spender, 1982; 1983.)

The record of feminism, however, is not one of steady, uninterrupted development. Women are after all a relatively powerless and subordinated group in Western societies —a "minority."[3] Feminist protest of this minority status always threatens and therefore is opposed by the more powerful and dominant "majority"—men. The opportunities for public feminist protest expand and contract as societies swing between moments of liberationist change and receptivity on the one hand and periods of greater conservatism and repression on the other. The high points in the record of feminist activity and writing occur in the liberationist "moments" of modern Western history: a first flurry of productivity in the 1780s and 1790s; a far more organized, focused effort in the 1850s; massive mobilization for suffrage in the early twentieth century; and in the 1960s and 1970s, the modern, broad-based, multi-faceted movement discussed in Chapter 2. In the intervals between those periods, feminism becomes far less visible, essentially because dominant groups deliberately try to repress it (Spender, 1982).

Yet throughout all this, women created feminist theories (Figure 8.1 lists a few of the most significant of these works). Each is a distinctive product, a particular patterning of critical ideas shaped by the writer's historical context, milieu, personality, and biography. Yet amidst all this diversity three broad types of theory are discernible: one orientation that focuses on gender differences, another that focuses on gender inequality,

---

[3]The terms *minority* and *majority* describe the relative power of groups rather than their relative size.

FIGURE 8.1 Selected Influences in the Feminist Intellectual Tradition in the English-Speaking World Prior to 1960[1]

DATE	EVENT	HISTORICAL CONTEXT—LIBERATIONIST MOVEMENT	DEVELOPMENT IN SOCIOLOGY
1650	**Anne Bradstreet** (1612–1672), *The Tenth Muse Lately Sprung Up in America*	Puritan revolution in England and America	
1670	**Aphra Behn** (1640–1680), *The Forced Marriage*	Restoration England (period of loosening social norms)	
1694	**Mary Astell** (1668–1731), *A Serious Proposal for the Ladies*	The Glorious Revolution in England	
1770s–1780s	**Abigail Adams** (1744–1818) and **Mercy Otis Warren** (1728–1814), letters to each other and Abigail to husband John (American statesman who will be second President)	American Revolution	
1790	**Judith Sargent Murray** (1751–1820), "On the Equality of the Sexes"	American Revolution and subsequent debates on Constitution and Bill of Rights	
1792	**Mary Wollstonecraft** (1759–1797), *A Vindication of the Rights of Women*	Effects of American and French Revolutions in Britain	
1837	**Harriet Martineau** (1802–1876), "The Political Non-existence of Women" in *Society in America*	Rise of middle-class reformism	1830–1842 Comte (1798–1857), *The Positive Philosophy*
1838	**Sarah Grimké** (1792–1873), *Letters on the Equality of the Sexes*	Worldwide anti-slavery movement	
1845	**Margaret Fuller** (1810–1850), *Women in the Nineteenth Century*	Romanticism, abolitionism, nationalism	

Year		Social context	Year	
1848	**Lucretia Mott** (1793–1880), **Elizabeth Cady Stanton** (1815–1902), **Lucy Stone** (1818–1893), **Susan B. Anthony** (1820–1906), Seneca Falls Convention (first women's rights meeting in America)	Anti-slavery movement	1848	Marx (1818–1883) and Engels (1820–1895), *The Communist Manifesto*
1860	**Elizabeth Blackwell** (1821–1910) and **Emily Blackwell** (1826–1911), *Medicine as a Profession for Women*	Anti-slavery movement	1851	Spencer (1820–1903), *Social Statics*
1869	**John Stuart Mill** (1806–1873) with **Harriet Taylor** (1807–1858), *The Subjection of Women*	Middle-class reformism	1867	Marx, *Capital*
1881	**E. C. Stanton, S. B. Anthony, and Matilda Joslyn Gage** (1826–1898), *History of Woman Suffrage*	Stirrings of Progressivism and revisionist Social Darwinism	1880–1918	Simmel (1858–1918), essays
1883	**Olive Schreiner** (1855–1920), *The Story of an African Farm*	Working class political movements		
1884	**Friedrich Engels** (1820–1895), *Origins of the Family*	Working class political movements	1893–1897	Durkheim (1858–1917), *Suicide, The Rules of Sociological Method, The Division of Labor*
1896	**Ida Wells Barnett** (1862–1931) and **Mary Church Terrell** (1863–1954), National Association of Colored Women	Populism		
1898	**Ida H. Harper** (1851–1931), *The Life and Work of Susan B. Anthony*	Progressivism		
1898	**E. C. Stanton**, *The Woman's Bible*	Populism Progressivism		

[1]Major sources for this study of the tradition are Rossi (1974) and Spender (1983).

FIGURE 8.1 (continued)

DATE	EVENT	HISTORICAL CONTEXT—LIBERATIONIST MOVEMENT	DEVELOPMENT IN SOCIOLOGY
1899	**Charlotte Perkins Gilman** (1860–1935), *Women and Economics*	Socialism	1904–1905 Weber (1864–1920), *The Protestant Ethic*
1910	**Jane Addams** (1860–1935), *Twenty Years at Hull House*	Progressivism	
1911	**Sylvia Pankhurst** (1882–1960), *The Suffragette*	Nationalism and socialism in Europe	
1913	**Christabel Pankhurst** (1880–1956), *The Great Scourge and How to End It*	Nationalism and socialism in Europe	
1917	**Margaret Sanger** (1879–1966), *Family Limitation*	Progressivism	
1918	British women over 30 granted suffrage	Suffrage movement and working class political struggles	1918 Thomas (1863–1947) and Znaniecki (1882–1958), *The Polish Peasant*
1920	American women win suffrage	Suffrage movement and last gasp of Progressivism	1920 Weber, *Economy and Society* (incomplete at death)
			1921 Park (1864–1944) and Burgess (1886–1966), *Introduction to the Science of Sociology*

Year			Year	
1926	Suzanne LaFollette (1882–1941), *Concerning Women*	Progressivism, suffrage movement	1893–1931	Mead (1863–1931), lectures that will become *Mind, Self and Society*
1931	Virginia Woolf (1882–1941), *A Room of One's Own*	Socialism, cultural post-Victorianism		
1933	Eleanor Roosevelt (1884–1963), *It's Up to the Women*	New Deal		
1935	Margaret Mead (1901–1978), *Sex and Temperament in Three Primitive Societies*	Pacifism (from World War I) Cultural relativism of social science training	1937	Parsons (1902–1979), *The Structure of Social Action*
1938	V. Woolf, *Three Guineas*	Socialism, cultural post-Victorianism		
1946	Mary Ritter Beard (1876–1958), *Women as a Force in History*	Reaction against totalitarianism, fascism		
1957	Simone de Beauvoir (1908–1985), *The Second Sex*	Existentialism	1951	Parsons, *The Social System*
1959	Betty Friedan (b. 1921), *The Feminine Mystique*	Civil rights movement	1959	Mills (1916–1962), *The Sociological Imagination*

and a third that focuses on gender oppression. These orientations are more fully described in the next section of this chapter, at least in their contemporary articulation. With all its diversity, this body of theory was consistently critical of existing social arrangements and focused on such essential sociological variables as social inequality, social change, power, interests and beliefs, and the social institutions of family, law, politics, work, religion, and education.

Sociology and Feminism: 1840-1960

Sociology took shape first as a perspective between 1840 and 1860, during one high point in feminist protest, and then as an organized professional undertaking between 1890 and 1920, during another expansionary feminist phase. How did the early sociologists respond to this intellectual tradition?

Three broad tentative answers are advanced here. First, between 1840 and 1960, as sociology emerged as a perspective and then as an organized and professionalized academic discipline, the people who were central to creating that discipline were all men. Second, feminist concerns filtered into sociology only on the margins of the field, in the work of marginal male theorists or of women who were over the period always restricted to the fringes of the profession. Third, the men who created sociology, particularly those most securely situated in the profession, from Spencer, through Weber and Durkheim, to Parsons, were essentially untouched by feminist ideas.

The data supporting our first generalization are easy to come by. As a quick glance back over the earlier chapters of this text will show, sociology has a well-known list of "founding fathers" both from the classic period between 1840 and 1935 and from the period of the major modern theorists that extends from 1935 to about 1965. But no text on the history of this period identifies a single "founding mother." Moreover, over almost the whole period no woman held significant office in any of the national associations of sociologists nor, except in "women's colleges," senior academic positions in a sociology department.

Our second generalization is that until 1960, feminist ideas were introduced into sociology only on the margins of the discipline. For example, such ideas came from various male theorists who were marginal to professional sociology, even though their ideas were subsequently influential on sociology. Thinkers like Simmel (Oakes, 1984), W. I. Thomas (Rosenberg, 1982), and Marx and Engels can be included in this group. This generalization also holds for the earliest formally trained women social scientists, who tried to deal with the issue of gender relations only to find that their research and arguments were relegated to the margins of the field because they were women (Rosenberg, 1982).

Finally, the more centrally situated men in the profession essentially were untouched by feminism. The major works of these theorists, the statements that have fundamentally shaped the sociological perspective, give almost no attention to gender as a social arrangement, and on those rare occasions when women's lives are discussed, as in Durkheim's analysis of suicide, the approach is wholly conventional and uncritical.

The best example of this conventionality perhaps is to be found in the theories of Talcott Parsons (see Chapter 3). Central to all of Parsons's theory[4] is the assertion that

---

[4]The description of Parsons's gender theories in this and the next paragraph is a restatement of an argument presented in Lengermann and Wallace (1985:11-12).

the institution of the family is an indispensable prerequisite for social stability. As the primary socializing agent for children, the family is essential to that internalization of social control on which any society's stability ultimately depends. Moreover, as the primary focus in the emotional life of adults, the family is a formidable agent of external social control and a vital outlet for those adult tensions that might otherwise erupt into public life.

Parsons argues that for the family to function effectively, there must be a sexual division of labor in which adult males and females play very different roles. Men who tie the family unit into the wider social system must be "instrumental" in orientation, manifesting qualities of drive, ambition, and self-control. Women, whose task is the internal functioning of the family, supportive of both children and adult males, must be "expressive," that is, gentle, nurturant, loving, and emotionally open. If men and women become too similar in family function and orientation, competition between them will disrupt family life, weakening the family's vital role in upholding social stability (Parsons, 1954:79). As is self-evident, this sociology of sex roles is essentially, if perhaps unintentionally, antifeminist in orientation, perhaps the most dramatic instance of mainstream sociology's lack of involvement, down to the 1960s, with feminism.

VARIETIES OF CONTEMPORARY FEMINIST THEORY

Contemporary feminist theory forms the literature base for the development of any feminist sociological theory, such as the one presented in the next major section of this chapter. Thus we present here an overview of feminist theory, that system of general ideas designed to describe and explain social life and human experience from a woman-centered vantage point. Our goal in this review is to present the themes that feminist theory offers for the construction of a feminist sociological theory.

Contemporary feminist scholars have produced a rapidly growing, extraordinarily rich, and highly diverse collection of theoretical writings, a demonstration of effective intellectualism that Jessie Bernard (1987) labeled "the feminist enlightenment." The range and continuous expansion of this literature makes trying to map it challenging, rewarding, and sometimes a little confusing. The "map" of feminist theory presented here is *one* construct, or ideal type, for patterning this complex body of intellectual work.[5]

Our typology of feminist theory is based on the two basic questions (discussed above) that unite all these theories: the descriptive question, *What about the women?* and the explanatory question, *Why is this situation as it is?* The pattern of response to the descriptive question generates the main categories for our classification. Essentially we see three answers to the question, "What about the women?" The first answer is

---

[5]Several other classificatory systems already exist: for example those developed by Glennon, 1979; Jaggar, 1983; Jaggar and Rothenberg, 1986; Lengermann and Wallace, 1985; Snitow et al., 1983; and Sokoloff, 1980. Readers might turn to these for balance or amplification of the ideal type presented here. In combination these efforts have generated a long list of types of feminist theory, including black feminism, conservatism, expressionism, instrumentalism, lesbian feminism, liberalism, Marxism, polarism, psychoanalytic feminism, radicalism, separatism, socialism, and synthesism. Our own typology attempts to include most of these theories, though not always as identified by these specific labels.

that women's location in, and experience of, most situations is *different* from that of the men in that situation. Investigation then focuses on the details of that difference. A second answer is that women's location in most situations is not only different from but less privileged than or *unequal* to that of men. The focus of the ensuing description then is on the nature of that inequality. A third answer is that women's situation also has to be understood in terms of a direct power relationship between men and women. Women are *oppressed*, that is, restrained, subordinated, molded, and used and abused by men. Descriptions then focus on the quality of the oppression. Each of the various types of feminist theory can be classified as a theory of *difference*, or of *inequality*, or of *oppression*.

In our discussion we make distinctions within these basic categories—difference, inequality, and oppression—in terms of their differing answers to the second or explanatory question, "Why is this as it is?"

This classificatory method has an important function: it allows us to pattern not only the general body of contemporary feminist theory, but also the expanding literature, particularly the theoretical literature on gender that has developed within sociology since the 1960s. The burgeoning of this literature reflects not only the reactivation of visible feminist protest in the society, but also the unparalleled movement of women into higher education, as undergraduates, graduates, and faculty between 1960 and the present (Lengermann and Wallace, 1985; Vetter et al., 1982). Feminist questions have

FIGURE 8.2 Overview of Varieties of Feminist Theory

The left column categorizes varieties of feminist theory by their answer to the basic question, "What about the women?" The right column presents distinctions within these categories in terms of the basic explanatory question, "Why is women's situation as it is?"

BASIC VARIETIES OF FEMINIST THEORY—ANSWERS TO THE DESCRIPTIVE QUESTION: "WHAT ABOUT THE WOMEN?"	DISTINCTIONS WITHIN THEORIES— ANSWERS TO THE EXPLANATORY QUESTION: "WHY IS WOMEN'S SITUATION AS IT IS?"
Theories of Difference	
Women's location in and experience of most situations is different from that of men in the situation.	Bio-social explanations of difference Institutional explanations of difference Social-psychological explanations of difference
Theories of Inequality	

Women's locations in most situations are not only different from but less privileged than or *unequal* to that of men.	Liberal feminist explanations of inequality
	Marxian explanations of inequality
	  Marx and Engels's explanation
	  Contemporary Marxian explanations

Theories of Oppression	
Women are *oppressed*, not just different from or equal to, but actively restrained, subordinated, molded, and used and abused by men.	Psychoanalytic explanations of oppression Radical feminist explanations of oppression Socialist feminist explanations of oppression

by this latter means been injected directly into the university-based, academic discourse of professional sociology. But as sociologists have turned their efforts to an exploration of gender issues, they have typically used some portion of the existing body of sociological theory as a point of departure for what is called in the discipline the *sociology of gender*. Although the term *gender* is often used euphemistically in sociology for "women," the sociology of gender is, more precisely, the study of socially constructed male and female roles, relations, and identities—a somewhat different subject from feminism's focus on women. This focus on the interrelationship of men and women is not equivalent to a feminist theory. As we have said before, feminist theory seeks to present a woman-centered patterning of human experience. As we shall show later, a feminist sociology can describe the social world from a woman-centered standpoint. Overall the sociology of gender simply treats gender as one variable among many within social relations and structures. Nevertheless, some sociologists who begin from a sociology of gender standpoint have produced works of significance for feminist theory (and many sociologists are directly involved in producing feminist theory).

The remainder of this section explores the feminist theories of difference, of inequality, and of oppression, describing in each case the general features of the approach, some key lines of variation within it, and its recommendations for change. Two notes of caution are, however, important. First, many theorists' work resists neat categorization. One must either talk about their main theoretical emphasis or distinguish among various of their theoretical statements. Second, this is a selective review. Given the volume of recent feminist and sociological writings on women's situation, comprehensiveness is beyond the scope of this chapter.

Theories of Gender Differences

Although a focus on gender differences is a minority position in contemporary feminism, some influential contributions to modern feminist theory do take this approach (Baker Miller, 1976; Bernikow, 1980; Gilligan, 1982; Kessler and McKenna, 1978; Ruddick, 1980; Snitow, 1979). There also have been research documents (Masters and Johnson, 1966; Hite 1976) with findings on male/female differences that have deeply affected contemporary feminist thinking. In addition, a great deal of the recent sociological literature on gender has gender difference as its topic. Included here are theoretical works anchored in an essentially institutional, quasi-functionalist view of society (Bernard, 1982), bio-social writings (Rossi, 1977; 1983), symbolic interactionist statements (Best, 1983; Lever, 1978), phenomenological works (Berger and Kellner, 1964) and ethnomethodological statements (Garfinkel, 1967). Indeed if we add to this basic core of theoretical statements the vast empirical literature by sociologists that now factors in "sex" or "gender" as a key independent variable, the focus on gender differences may be the dominant one in sociology (Huber 1976; Stacey and Thorne, 1986).

The central theme in the contemporary literature on gender differences is that women's inner psychic life is, in its overall configuration, different from that of men. In their basic values and interests (Ruddick, 1980), their mode of making value judgments (Gilligan, 1982), their construction of achievement motives (Kaufman and Richardson, 1982), their literary creativity (Gilbert and Gubar, 1979), their sexual fantasies

(Hite, 1976; Radway, 1984; Snitow, 1983), their sense of identity (Laws and Schwartz, 1977), and in their general processes of consciousness and selfhood (Baker Miller, 1976; Kasper, 1986), women bring a different vision and a different voice to the construction of social reality. A second theme is that the overall configuration of women's relationships and life experiences is distinctive. Women relate differently from men to their biological offspring (Rossi, 1977; 1983); boys and girls have distinctively different styles of play (Best, 1983; Lever, 1978); adult women relate to each other (Bernikow, 1980) and to the women subjects they study as scholars (Ascher et al., 1984) in unique ways. Indeed the overall life experience of females from infancy to old age is fundamentally different from that of men (Bernard, 1981). In combination this literature on differences in consciousness and life experience presents one unique answer to the question, "What about the women?"

Raising the second question, "Why?," identifies the key lines of variation within this overall focus on gender differences. Explanations of the psychological and relational differences between women and men are essentially of three types: biological, institutional, and, broadly construed, social psychological.

BIOLOGICAL EXPLANATIONS
OF GENDER DIFFERENCES

Biological explanations have been the standby of conservative thinking on gender differences. Freud traced the different personality structures of men and women to their different genitals and to cognitive and emotional processes that begin when children discover these physiological differences. Contemporary sociobiologists Lionel Tiger and Robin Fox (1971) write of variable "biogrammars" laid down in early hominid evolution that lead women to bond emotionally with their infants and men to bond practically with other men. But the biological argument also has been used in writings much more sympathetic to feminism. Masters and Johnson's exploration of the anatomy of female sexuality has given feminist theorists basic facts for rethinking the whole question of the social patterning of sexuality, and Alice Rossi (1979; 1983) has given serious attention to the biological foundations of gender-specific behavior. Rossi has linked the different biological functions of males and females to different patterns of hormonally determined development over the life cycle and this, in turn, to sex-specific variation in such traits as sensitivity to light and sound and to differences in left and right brain connections. These differences, she feels, feed into the different play patterns in childhood noted by Carol Gilligan (1982), Janet Lever (1978), and Raphaela Best (1983); to the well-known female "math anxiety"; and also to the apparent fact that women are more predisposed to care for infants in a nurturing way than are men. Rossi's feminism leads her to argue for sociocultural arrangements that make it possible for each gender to compensate, through social learning, for biologically "given" disadvantages, but as a biosociologist she also argues for rational acknowledgment of the implications of biological research.

INSTITUTIONAL EXPLANATIONS
OF GENDER DIFFERENCES

Institutional explanations of gender differences often also lay great stress on women's distinctive functions in bearing and caring for infants. This responsibility for mothering is seen as a major determinant of the broader sexual division of labor that links women in general to the functions of wife, mother, and household worker, to the private sphere of the home and family, and thus to a lifelong series of events and experiences very different from those of men. In this setting, women develop distinctive interpretations of achievement, distinctive interests and values, characteristic but necessary skills for openness in relationships, "caring attention to others," and particular networks of support with the other women (mothers, daughters, sisters, co-wives, friends) who inhabit their separate sphere. Although some of the institutional theorists of difference accept the sexual division of labor as socially necessary (Berger and Berger, 1983), others are aware that the separate spheres for women and men may be embedded within broader patterns of gender inequality (Bernard, 1981; Kelly-Godol, 1983) or even of oppression (Ruddick, 1980). The writings cited in this section, however, focus primarily on gender difference and its institutional roots.

SOCIAL PSYCHOLOGICAL THEORIES OF GENDER

Social psychological explanations of gender difference are of two types: broadly phenomenological theories and socialization theories. Phenomenological theories (Garfinkel, 1967; Kessler and McKenna, 1978; Laws and Schwartz, 1977) focus on the pervasive patterning of our taken-for-granted knowledge of everyday reality by the simple dichotomous categories, or "typifications," of maleness and femaleness, on the interactional and conceptual "work" we all do to maintain these typifications, and on the ways in which this collective work determines, through definition, the distinctive spheres and psychological profiles of women and men. Socialization theory (see Stockard and Johnson, 1980; Walum-Richardson, 1981 for selected bibliographies) complements institutional analyses by exploring the social learning experiences that mold people in general but particularly young children for the separate roles and institutional spheres of maleness and femaleness.

Except for conservative, nonfeminist theorists who argue simply for the inevitability of difference and therefore for the need to yield to its demands, the recommendations about women's situation that flow from these theories of gender difference center on the need for *respect*. Theorists of difference typically demand that women's distinctive ways of being be recognized not as departures from the normal but as viable alternatives to male modes and that public knowledge, academic scholarship, and the very patterning of social life adjust to take serious account of female ways of being. Indeed at the most militantly feminist end of the continuum of this theoretical approach, we find a centuries old claim of feminism: that when a major infusion of women's ways becomes part of public life the world will be a safer, more humane place for all of us.

Theories of Gender Inequality

Four themes characterize the theories of gender inequality. First, men and women are not only differently situated in society, they are unequally situated. Specifically, women get less of the material resources, social status, power, and opportunities for self-actualization than the men who share their social location—be it a location based on class, race, occupation, ethnicity, religion, education, nationality, or any other socially significant factor. Second, this inequality results from the organization of society, not from any significant biological or personality differences between women and men. For the third theme of all inequality theory is that although individual human beings may vary somewhat from each other in their profile of potentials and traits, no significant pattern of natural variation distinguishes the sexes. Instead, all human beings are characterized by a deep need for freedom to seek self-actualization and by a fundamental malleability that leads them to adapt to the constraints or opportunities of the situations in which they find themselves. To say that there is gender inequality, then, is to claim that women are situationally less empowered than men to realize the need they share with men for self-actualization. Fourth, inequality theories all assume that both women and men will respond fairly easily and naturally to more egalitarian social structures and situations. They affirm, in other words, that it is possible to change the situation. In this these theorists contrast with the theorists of gender difference who present a picture of social life in which gender differences are, whatever their cause, durable, deeply penetrative of personality, and only partially reversible.

Explanations of gender inequality vary around this common core of interpretation. Two major variants of contemporary feminist theory that focus on and try to explain gender inequality are reviewed here: liberal feminism and Marxian feminism.

LIBERAL FEMINISM

Within contemporary feminist theory, liberal feminism is a minority position (Bird, 1979; Friedan, 1963; 1981; Janeway, 1981; Lipman-Blumen, 1985; Trebilcot, 1973). Yet at the same time, liberal feminism is the most widely diffused approach within the contemporary women's movement in America: it undergirds much popular writing on careers for women, equal parenting, and the need for gender-free schooling for young children; it guides many of the policies initiated by the movement (Gelb and Paley, 1982; Tinker, 1983) and is embodied in the programmatic statement of the most powerful of women's organizations, the National Organization for Women (NOW). An easy complementarity between liberal feminism and the mainstream of American political beliefs helps to make understandable the popularity of this variant on feminist theory.

Liberal feminism's explanation of gender inequality begins where theories of gender differences leave off: with an identification of the sexual division of labor, the existence of separate public and private spheres of social activity, men's primary location in the former and women's in the latter, and the systematic socialization of children so that they can move into the adult roles and spheres appropriate to their gender. In contrast to theorists of difference, however, liberal feminists see nothing of particular value about the private sphere, except perhaps that it permits emotional openness. Instead, the private sphere consists of the endless round of demanding, mindless, unpaid, and undervalued tasks associated with housework, child care, and the emotional, practical, and sexual servicing of adult men. The true rewards of social life—money, power, status, freedom, opportunities for growth and self-worth—are to be found in the public sphere. The system that restricts women's access to that sphere, burdens them with private-sphere responsibilities, isolates them in individual households, and excuses their mates from any sharing of private-sphere drudgeries is the system that produces gender inequality.

When asked to identify the key forces in this system, liberal feminists point to *sexism,* an ideology similar to racism, which consists partly of prejudices and discriminatory practices against women, partly of taken-for-granted beliefs about the "natural" differences between women and men that suit them to their different social destinies. Because of sexism, females are, from childhood on, limited and maimed, so that they can move into their adult roles and in those roles "dwindle" from full humanness into the mindless, dependent, subconsciously depressed beings created by the constraints and requirements of their gender-specified roles.

The description of women dwindling from full humanness is taken from Jessie Bernard's *The Future of Marriage* (1982). Bernard is a sociologist who has been writing about the issue of gender since the 1940s, long before it was perceived as a significant topic by sociologists. *The Future of Marriage* is perhaps her best-known book on this topic. In the dispassionate voice of mainstream, institutionally oriented, empirically anchored sociology, Bernard presents sociologists with a novel and devastating portrait of the institution of marriage. Marriage is at one and the same time a cultural system of beliefs and ideals, an institutional arrangement of roles and norms, and a complex of interactional experiences for individual women and men. Culturally, marriage is idealized as the destiny and source of fulfillment for women; a mixed blessing of domesticity, responsibility, and constraint for men; and for American society as a whole an essentially egalitarian association between husband and wife. Institutionally, marriage empowers the role of husband with authority and with the freedom, indeed, the obligation, to move beyond the domestic setting; it meshes the idea of male authority with sexual prowess and male power; and it mandates that wives be compliant, dependent, self-emptying, and essentially centered on the activities and chores of the isolated domestic household. Experientially then there are two marriages in any institutional marriage: the man's marriage, in which he holds to the belief of being constrained and burdened, while experiencing what the norms dictate—authority, independence, and a right to domestic, emotional, and sexual service by the wife; and the wife's marriage, in which she affirms the cultural belief of fulfillment while experiencing normatively mandated powerlessness and dependence, an obligation to provide domestic, emotional, and sexual services, and a gradual "dwindling away" of the independent young person she was before marriage. The results of all this are to be found in the data that measure human stress: *married* women, whatever their claims to fulfillment, and *unmarried* men, whatever their claims to freedom, rank high on all stress indicators, including heart palpitations, dizziness, headaches, fainting, nightmares, insomnia, and fear of nervous breakdown; *unmarried* women, whatever their sense of social stigma, and *married* men rank low on all the stress indicators. Marriage then is good for men and bad for women and will only cease to be so unequal in its impact when couples feel free enough from the prevailing institutional constraints to negotiate the kind of marriage that best suits their individual needs and personalities.

To liberal feminists, American society, anchored in its constitutionally given institutions and rights, permits more individual freedom and equality than most other societies. Even here, however, equal opportunity is limited by both racism and sexism. These belief systems are functionless carry-overs from earlier times, supported by little more than tradition, convention, and unsubstantiated prejudice. Sexism, like racism, forces men and women into rigid characterological molds, denies the community the full range of talents available in the population, diminishes women, and poses a constant denial of our most cherished cultural values of individual worth and freedom. Because of

JESSIE BERNARD: A Biographical Sketch

Jessie Bernard's life and work have been characterized by an extraordinary capacity for growth and outgrowth: she has constantly moved beyond herself into new intellectual territory.* She has described this process in "My Four Revolutions: An Autobiographical History of the ASA" (1974). In this article and in her current work, Bernard treats her last revolution as a movement toward contemporary feminism or toward what she will eventually name as "the feminist enlightenment" (Bernard, forthcoming). By tracing Bernard's movement to participation in the feminist enlightenment, we can see much of the history of women's participation in twentieth-century American sociology.

Bernard was born Jessie Ravitch on June 8, 1903, in Minneapolis. Her first significant outgrowth was to move from her Jewish immigrant family to the University of Minnesota at the age of 17. At the university not only did she go outside that first immigrant milieu, more significantly, she herself became connected with the attempts to establish sociology as a fully recognized profession within American academia. She studied with Sorokin, who would go on to establish the sociology department at Harvard, and with L. L. Bernard, who would be instrumental in founding the *American Sociological Review*. Jessie Ravitch served as Bernard's research assistant for four years and married him in 1925. Her study with Bernard gave her a grounding in a positivistic approach to sociology as science that left its mark on all her later work in her ability to draw successfully on quantitative research to do what would increasingly become qualitative and critical analysis.

Bernard moved with her husband as he held a variety of academic appointments. She earned her Ph.D. in sociology at Washington University in St. Louis in 1935. By the mid-1940s, the Bernards were at Pennsylvania State University and Jessie was in the midst of her outgrowth of positivism.

Jessie Bernard's movement away from positivism came in response to the events of World War II. The Nazi holocaust destroyed her faith in the capacity of science to know and produce a just world—it also made her re-examine her own Jewish immigrant roots. These experiences increased Bernard's sensitivity to the social contextuality of all knowledge, although she would move slowly toward this feminist position.

Coinciding with the beginnings of this break with positivism, in the mid-1940s, Bernard began to establish her own independent academic position at Penn State. Her husband died in 1951 but Jessie remained at Penn State until about 1960, teaching, writing, and raising her three children. During the early sixties she commuted between Washington, D.C., and Penn State and finally moved out of academic life to devote her-

*This biographical sketch is heavily indebted to Lipman-Blumen (1978) and Bernard (1974).

all this, liberal feminists maintain, contemporary American society must be changed to eliminate sexism, and they believe that most people can be educated to see the reasonableness of the feminist critique.

Liberal feminists propose the following strategies for eliminating gender inequality: mobilization to use existing political and legal channels for change; equal economic opportunities; changes in family, school, and mass media messages so that people no self full-time to writing and research. Her home base since the mid-sixties has been Washington, D.C., although she remains Professor Emeritus at Penn State. Thus, the two decades following World War II constituted yet another period of growth and out-growth for Bernard, one in which she established a professional identity independent at first of her husband and then of the conventional trappings of the university and began an increasingly public rejection of sociology as positivistic science.

But the most dramatic period of growth and outgrowth has been from 1964 to the present. This fact is significant both in terms of the quality and quantity of Bernard's productivity and also for what it says in itself about the career patterns of women's lives. During this period, Bernard has published twelve books and offered innumerable arti-cles and presentations, establishing herself as one of the leading interpreters of the sociology of gender. Her movement to leadership has been marked by this same pat-tern of growth and outgrowth. Thus, she has declined traditional leadership roles, such as the presidency of the ASA, in favor of time for research, writing, and increasing in-volvement with the women's movement. She has also rethought her own early writings on family and gender, moving increasingly toward a feminist interpretation.

Bernard's interest in women's lives illustrates her ability to rethink core concerns within new intellectual contexts. She has been studying and writing about women's lives since the late 1930s. Her major works include: *American Family Behavior* (1942), *Mar-riage and Family Among Negroes* (1956), *Remarriage: A Study of Marriage* (1957), *Academic Women* (1964), *The Sex Game: Communication Between the Sexes* (1968), *Women and the Public Interest: An Essay on Policy and Protest* (1971), *The Future of Motherhood* (1974), *Women, Wives, Mothers: Values and Options* (1975), *The Female World* (1980), *The Future of Marriage* (1982), *The Female World in a Global Perspective* (1987), and *The Feminist Enlightenment* (forthcoming).

These works are characterized by four essential qualities. One, Bernard is consist-ently able to bring macro-level data to bear in reaching conclusions about micro-interaction and subjective experience. Two, she increasingly recognizes the impor-tance of subjective experience in the establishment of macro-social structures. Three, an obvious outgrowth of two, she increasingly emphasizes the social contextuality of knowledge and the methodological necessity of studying the lives of invisible groups in and of themselves, not merely in comparison to the dominant patriarchally determined type. Four, she has moved from a framing of her curiosity about women's lives within the traditional context of the sociology of the family through a framing that focuses on women within the sociology of gender to a framing that is critical and feminist.

Bernard has garnered numerous honors in her career and has had perhaps the highest honor of having several awards named after her—awards designed, as Lipman-Blumen says, to mark "those who, like Jessie Bernard herself, have contributed intellectually, professionally, and humanely to the world of scholarship and feminism" (Lipman-Blumen, 1978:55).

longer are socialized into rigidly compartmentalized sex roles; and attempts by all in-dividuals to challenge sexism where they encounter it in daily life. For liberal femin-ists, the ideal gender arrangement is one in which each individual chooses the life style most suitable to her or him and has that choice accepted and respected, be it for house-wife or househusband, unmarried careerist or part of a dual income family, childless or with children, heterosexual or homosexual. Liberal feminists see this ideal as one that enhances the practice of freedom and equality, central cultural ideals in America. Liberal feminism then is consistent with the dominant American ethos in its basic acceptance of America's institutions and culture, its reformist orientation, and its appeal to the values of individualism, choice, freedom, and equality of opportunity.

MARXIAN FEMINISM

Marxism presents one of the best-known and intellectually most elaborate theories of social oppression. Beginning with Marx and Engels and continuing through the whole body of neo-Marxian literature this perspective develops the theory of social class oppression, focusing on the domination of workers in the interests of the ruling class and on the pervasiveness of class domination, oppression, and conflict in patterning both intranational and international social relations. Marxian feminism brings together Marxian class analysis and feminist social protest. Yet this amalgam produces not an intensified theory of oppression but rather a more muted statement of inequality; that is, of gender inequality.[6] The foundation of this theory was laid by Marx and Engels.

MARX AND ENGELS   The major concern of Marx and Engels was social class oppression, but they frequently turned their attention to gender oppression. Their most famous exploration of this issue is presented in *The Origins of the Family, Private Property and the State*, written and published by Engels in 1884 from extensive notes made by Marx in the years immediately preceding Marx's death in 1883 (Barrett, 1984). The major arguments of this book are:

1. Woman's subordination results not from her biology, which is presumably immutable, but from social arrangements that have a clear and traceable history, arrangements that presumably may be changed. (This claim alone, taken in the context of nineteenth-century beliefs about women, makes *The Origins* a feminist text.)
2. The relational basis for women's subordination lies in the family, an institution aptly named from the Latin word for servant, because the family as it exists in complex societies is overwhelmingly a system of dominant and subordinate roles. Key features of the family in Western societies are that it centers on a mating pair and their offspring typically located within a single household; it is patrilineal, with descent and property passing through the male line, patriarchal, with authority invested in the male household head, and monogamous at least in the enforcement of the rule that the wife have sexual relations only with her husband. The double standard allows men far greater sexual freedom. Within such an institution, particularly when, as in the middle-class family, the woman has no job outside the house and no economic independence, women are in fact the chattels or possessions of their husbands.
3. Society legitimizes this family system by claiming that such a structure is the fundamental institution in all societies. This is in fact a false claim, as much anthropological and archeological evidence shows. For much of human prehistory there were no family structures of this type. Instead, people were linked in extensive kin networks—the *gens,* large-scale associations among people sharing blood ties. Moreover these ties were traced through the female line because one's direct link

---

[6]This theory has been elaborated in recent times by Benston, 1970; James and Dalla Costa, 1973; Kuhn and Wolpe, 1978; Mitchell, 1975; Reed, 1970; Rowbotham, 1973; Vogel, 1984; Zaretsky, 1976.

to one's mother was far more easily demonstrable than one's ties to one's father—the *gens* was in other words matrilineal. It was also matriarchal, with significant power resting in the hands of women who in those primitive hunting and gathering economies had an independent and crucial economic function as the gatherers, crafters, storers, and distributors of essential materials. This power was exercised in collective and cooperative communal living arrangements, commodity use, child rearing and decision making, and through the free and unencumbered choice of love and sexual partners by both women and men. This type of society, which Marx and Engels describe elsewhere as primitive communism, is associated in *The Origins* with a free and empowered social status for women.

4. The factors that destroyed this type of social system, producing what Engels calls "the world historic defeat of the female sex" (Engels and Marx, 1884:87) are economic, specifically the replacement of hunting-gathering by herding, horticulture, and farming economies. With this change emerged *property,* the idea and reality of some group members claiming as their own the essential resources for economic production. It was men who asserted this claim, as their mobility, strength, and monopoly over certain tools gave them economic ascendency. With these changes men also, as property owners, developed both enforceable needs for a compliant labor force, be they slaves, captives, women-wives, or children, and for heirs who would serve as a means of preserving and passing on property. Thus emerged the first *familia,* a master and his slave-servants, wife-servants, children-servants, a unit in which the master fiercely defended his claim to sole sexual access to his wives and thus to certainty about his heirs. And the sons too would support this system of sexual control, because on it would rest their property claims.

5. Since then, the exploitation of labor has developed into increasingly complex structures of domination, most particularly class relations; the political order was created to safeguard all these systems of domination; and the family itself has evolved along with the historic transformations of economic and property systems into an embedded and dependent institution, reflecting all the more massive injustices of the political economy and consistently enforcing the subordination of women. Only with the destruction of property rights in the coming communist revolution will women attain freedom of social, political, economic, and personal action.

The Origins has been challenged by anthropologists and archeologists on questions of evidence and by feminists for failing in various ways to grasp the full complexity of women's oppression. But in making the claim at all that women are oppressed, in analyzing how this oppression is sustained by the family, an institution regarded as almost sacred by powerful sectors of society, and in tracing the ramifications of this subordination for women's economic and sexual status, *The Origins* presents a powerful sociological theory of gender inequality, one that contrasts dramatically with Parsons's mainstream sociological theory.

CONTEMPORARY MARXIAN FEMINISM   Contemporary Marxian feminists embed gender relations within what they consider to be the more fundamental structure of the class system and particularly within the structure of the contemporary capitalist class system. From this theoretical vantage point, the quality of each individual's life experiences is a reflection first of his or her class position and only second of his or her gender. Women of markedly different class backgrounds have fewer life experiences in common than women of any particular class have with the men of their class. For example, in both their class-determined experiences and interests, upper-class, wealthy women are antagonistic to blue-collar or poor, welfare women, but share many experiences and interests with upper-class, wealthy men. Given this starting point, Marxian feminists acknowledge that *within* any class, women are less advantaged than men in their access to material goods, power, status, and possibilities for self-actualization. The causes of this inequality lie in the organization of capitalism itself.

The embeddedness of gender inequality within the class system is most simply and starkly visible within the dominant class of contemporary capitalism, the bourgeoisie. Bourgeois men own the productive and organizational resources of industrial production, commercialized agriculture, and of national and international trade. Women of the bourgeois class are not propertied, but are themselves property, the wives and possessions of bourgeois men, men who understand at the deepest level the art of possession. Bourgeois women are attractive and distinctive commodities in an ongoing process of exchange between men (Rubin, 1975) and often are a means of sealing property alliances among men. Bourgeois women produce and train sons who will inherit their fathers' socio-economic resources. Bourgeois women also provide emotional, social, and sexual services for the men in their class. For all of this, they are rewarded with an appropriately luxurious life style. Bourgeois women are, to use Rosa Luxemburg's phrase, "the parasite of a parasite" (Luxemburg, 1971:220; quoted in MacKinnon, 1982:7).

Gender inequality in the wage-earning classes also is functional for capitalism, and therefore perpetuated by capitalists. Women as wage earners are, because of their lower social status, more poorly paid and because of their sense of wage-sector marginality, difficult to unionize. Thus they serve as an unresisting source of profit for the ruling classes. Moreover, women's marginality to the wage sector makes them an important part of the reserve labor force that, as a pool of alternative workers, acts as a threat to and a brake on unionized male wage demands. As housewives, wives, and mothers, women unwittingly further support the process of bourgeois profit making as consumers of goods and services for the household and as unpaid caregivers who subsidize and disguise the real costs of reproducing and maintaining the work force (Gardiner, 1975). Finally, but for Marxians least significantly, the wage earner's wife provides her spouse with a minuscule experience of personal power, compensation for his actual powerlessness in society. She is, in other words, "the slave of a slave" (MacKinnon, 1982:8).

Women, then, are unequal to men not because of any basic and direct conflict of interest between the genders, but because of the working out of class oppression, with its attendant factors of property inequality, exploited labor, and alienation. The fact that within any class women are less advantaged than men, rather than vice versa, seems in Marxian feminism to have no immediate structural cause. Rather, as in liberal feminism, this fact results from a historic carry-over from the collapse of primitive communism that Engels described. Consequently, the solution for gender inequality is the destruction of class oppression. This destruction will come through revolutionary action by a united wage-earning class, including both women and men. Any direct mobilization of women against men is counterrevolutionary, because it divides the potentially revolutionary working class. A working class revolution that destroys the class system by making all economic assets the assets of the entire community also will free society from the by-product of class exploitation, gender inequality.

Theories of Gender Oppression

All theories of gender oppression describe women's situation as the consequence of a direct power relationship between men and women in which men, who have fundamental and concrete interests in controlling, using, subjugating, and oppressing women, effectively implement those interests. Women's situation, then, for these theorists, is centrally that of being used, controlled, subjugated, and oppressed by men. This pattern of oppression is incorporated in the deepest and most pervasive ways into society's organization, a basic structure of domination most commonly called *patriarchy*. Patriarchy is not the unintended and secondary consequence of some other set of factors—be it biology or socialization or sex roles or the class system. It is a primary power structure sustained by strong and deliberate intention. Indeed, to most theorists of oppression, gender differences and gender inequality are by-products of patriarchy.

Whereas most earlier feminist theorists focused on issues of gender inequality, a hallmark of contemporary feminist theory is the breadth and intensity of its concern with oppression (Jaggar, 1983). It is probably fair to say that a majority of contemporary feminist theorists are oppression theorists and certainly that the richest and most innovative theoretical developments within contemporary feminism have been the work of this cluster of theorists. Theoretical works on gender oppression constitute the cutting edge, the dynamic and expanding frontier of contemporary feminist theory. In contrast, although, as we shall see, a few sociologists have made important contributions to this literature, sociologists who deal with gender issues are not, as a community, strongly attracted to theories of oppression. It is probably this divergence of theoretical orientation to women's situation, with sociologists favoring theories of difference and inequality and feminist theorists favoring theories of oppression that explains the ongoing disagreement between the two communities about whether sociological theory has taken any serious account of the implications of issues raised by feminist scholarship.

We turn now to three major variants of feminist theory, all of which focus on oppression but each of which is distinctive in its explanation of oppression. These theories are psychoanalytic feminism, radical feminism, and socialist feminism.

PSYCHOANALYTIC FEMINIST THEORY

Contemporary psychoanalytical feminists attempt to explain patriarchy by using the theories of Freud and his intellectual heirs (al-Hibri, 1981; Chodorow, 1978; Dinnerstein, 1976; Kittay, 1983). These theories, broadly speaking, map and emphasize the emotional dynamics of personality, emotions often deeply buried in the subconscious or unconscious areas of the psyche; they also highlight the importance of infancy and early childhood in the patterning of these emotions. In attempting to use Freud's theories, however, feminists have to undertake a fundamental reworking of his conclusions. For Freud himself was notoriously patriarchal. He acknowledged gender differences and gender inequality but not gender oppression. Women to him were second-class human beings whose basic psychic nature fit them only for a lesser life than that experienced by men. Feminist theorists therefore, have had to follow through on directions implicit in Freud's theories while rejecting his gender-specific conclusions.

Psychoanalytic feminists operate with a particular model of patriarchy. Like all oppression theorists, they see patriarchy as a system in which men subjugate women, a universal system, pervasive in its social organization, durable over time and space, and triumphantly maintained in the face of occasional challenge. Distinctive to psychoanalytic feminism, however, is the view that this system is one that all men, in their individual daily actions, work continuously and energetically to create and sustain. Women resist only occasionally but are to be discovered far more often either acquiescing in or actively working for their own subordination. The puzzle that psychoanalytical feminists set out to solve is why men bring everywhere enormous, unremitting energy to the task of sustaining patriarchy and why there is an absence of countervailing energy on the part of women.

In searching for an explanation to this puzzle, these theorists give short shrift to the argument that a cognitive calculus of practical benefits is sufficient for male support for patriarchy. Cognitive mobilization does not seem a sufficient source for the intense energy that men invest in patriarchy, especially because, in light of the human capacity to debate and second guess, men may not always and everywhere be certain that patriarchy is of unqualified value to them. Moreover, an argument anchored in the cognitive pursuit of self-interest would suggest that women would as energetically mobilize against patriarchy. Instead, these theorists look to those aspects of the psyche so effectively mapped by the Freudians: the zone of human emotions, of half recognized or unrecognized desires and fears, and of neurosis and pathology. Here one finds a clinically proven source of extraordinary energy and debilitation, one springing from psychic structures so deep that they cannot be recognized or monitored by individual consciousness. In searching for the energic underpinnings of patriarchy, psychoanalytical feminists have identified two possible explanations for male domination of women: the fear of death and the socio-emotional environment in which the personality of the young child takes form.

Fear of death, of the ceasing of one's individuality, is viewed in psychoanalytic theory as one of those existential issues that everyone, everywhere, must on occasion confront and, in that confrontation, experience terror. Feminist theorists who develop this theme argue that women, because of their intimate and protracted involvement with bearing and rearing new life, are typically far less oppressed than men by the realization of their own mortality (al-Hibri, 1982; Dinnerstein, 1976). Men, however, respond with deep dread to the prospect of their individual extinction and adopt a series of defenses, all of which lead to their domination of women. Men are driven to produce things that will outlast them—art and architecture, wealth and weapons, science and religion. All of these then become resources by which men can dominate women (and each other). Men also are driven partly by envy of women's reproductive role, partly by their own passionate desire for immortality through offspring to seek to control the reproductive process itself. They claim ownership of women, seek to control women's bodies, and lay claim through norms of legitimacy and paternity to the products of those bodies, children. Finally, driven by fear, men seek to separate themselves from everything that reminds them of their own mortal bodies: birth, nature, sexuality, their human bodies and natural functions, and women, whose association with so many of these makes them the symbol of them all. All these aspects of existence must be denied, repressed, and controlled as men seek constantly to separate from, deny, and repress their own mortality. And women, who symbolize all these forbidden topics, also must be treated as Other: feared, avoided, controlled.

The second theme in psychoanalytical feminism centers on early childhood development and the fact that in all societies infants and children experience their earliest and most crucial development in a close, uninterrupted, intimate relationship to a woman, their mother or mother substitute (Chodorow, 1978; Dinnerstein, 1976). As infants and young children, for considerable periods lacking even language as a tool for understanding experience, individuals experience their earliest phases of personality development as an ongoing turbulence of primitive emotions: fear, love, hate, pleasure, rage, loss, desire. The emotional consequences of these early experiences stay with people always as potent but often unconscious "feeling memories." Central to that experiential residue is a cluster of deeply ambivalent feelings for woman/mother/caregiver: need, dependence, love, possessiveness, but also fear and rage over her ability to thwart one's will. Children's relationship to the father/man is much more occasional, secondary, and emotionally uncluttered. From this beginning, the male child, growing up in a culture that positively values maleness and devalues femaleness and increasingly aware of his own male identity, achieves a fairly rapid and complete separation of identity from the woman/mother. In adulthood the emotional carry-over from early childhood toward women—need, love, hate, possessiveness—energizes the man's quest for a woman of his own who meets his emotional needs and yet is dependent on and controlled by him. The female child, bearing the same feelings toward woman/mother, discovers her own female identity in a culture that devalues women. She grows up deeply ambivalent toward herself as well as toward the woman/mother and in that ambivalence dissipates much of her potential for mobilized resistance to her social subordination. Instead, she seeks to resolve her emotional carry-over in adulthood by sexual attraction and bonding with a male, emotional need of and dependence on females (sisters, mother, friends), and in re-creating but reversing through her own mothering the early infant-woman relationship.

Psychoanalytical feminists, then, explain women's oppression in terms of men's deep emotional need to control women, a drive arising from near-universal male neuroses centering on the fear of death and on ambivalence toward the mothers who reared them. Women either lack these neuroses or are subject to complementary neuroses, but in either case they are left psychically without an equivalent source of energy to resist domination. Much clinical psychiatric evidence supports the argument that these neuroses are in fact widespread, at least in Western societies. But these theories, in drawing a straight line from universal human emotions to universal female oppression, fail to explore the intermediate social arrangements that link emotion to oppression and fail to suggest possible lines of variation in either emotions, social arrangements, or oppression. Moreover, and partly because of these omissions, psychoanalytical feminist theory suggests very few strategies for change, except perhaps that we restructure our childbearing practices and begin some massive psychocultural reworking of our orientation toward death. These theories thus give us some provocative insights into and deepened understanding of the roots of gender oppression, but require a great deal more elaboration of both sociological factors and change strategies. Both of these tasks are taken up more fully by the other two variants of oppression theory: radical feminism and socialist feminism.

RADICAL FEMINISM

Central to radical feminism is an intense positive valuation of women and, as part of this, deep grief and rage over their oppression.[7] Radical feminists affirm woman's special worth in defiance of a universal system that devalues her; they rage at woman's oppression by presenting a detailed and shocking catalogue of the offenses committed against her worldwide. In this passionate mixture of love and rage, radical feminists resemble the more militant mode of racial and ethnic groups, the "black is beautiful" claims of black Americans or the detailed "witnessing" of oppression by Jews. As we explore radical feminists' appeal for and on behalf of women, we also can see quite clearly their position on social organization, gender oppression, and strategies for change.

Radical feminists see all of society as characterized by oppression. Every institution is a system by which some people dominate others, and in society's most basic structures, in the associational patterns between broad groups or categories of people, one perceives a continuous pattern of domination and submission—between classes, castes, racial, ethnic, and religious groups, age and gender categories. Of all these systems of domination and subordination, the most fundamental structure of oppression is gender, the system of patriarchy. Patriarchy was not only, as Engels described, historically the first structure of domination and submission, it continues as the most pervasive and enduring system of inequality, the basic societal model of domination. Through participation in patriarchy men learn how to hold other human beings in contempt, to see them as nonhuman and to control them. Within patriarchy men see and women learn what subordination looks like. Patriarchy creates guilt and repression, sadism and masochism, manipulation and deception, all of which drive men and women to other forms of tyranny. Patriarchy, to radical feminists, is the least noticed and yet the most significant structure of social inequality.

Central to this analysis is the image of patriarchy as violence practiced by men and by male-dominated organizations against women. Violence may not take the form of overt physical cruelty. It can be hidden in more complex practices of exploitation and control: in standards of fashion and beauty; in tyrannical ideals of motherhood, monogamy, chastity, and heterosexuality; in sexual harassment in the workplace; in the practices of gynecology, obstetrics, and psychotherapy; in unpaid household drudgery and underpaid wage work. Violence exists whenever one group controls in its own interests the life chances, environments, actions, and perceptions of another group, as men do women.

But the theme of violence as overt physical cruelty lies at the heart of radical feminism's linking of patriarchy to violence; rape, sexual abuse, sexual slavery in enforced prostitution, spouse abuse, incest, sexual molestation of children, hysterectomies and other excessively radical forms of surgery, and the explicit sadism in pornography are all linked to historic and cross-cultural practices of witch burning, the stoning deaths of adultresses, the persecution of lesbians, female infanticide, Chinese footbinding, the forced suicides of Hindu widows, and the savage practice of clitorectomy. Through the radical lens, we are given an image of women mutilated and bleeding as the visual representation of what patriarchy does.

Patriarchy exists as a near-universal social form ultimately because men can muster the most basic power resource, physical force, to establish control. Once patriarchy is

[7] This section is adapted from Lengermann and Wallace, 1985:141–144.

in place, the other power resources—economic, ideological, legal, and emotional—also can be marshaled to sustain it. But physical violence always remains its last line of defense, and in both interpersonal and intergroup relations, that violence repeatedly is used to protect patriarchy from women's individual and collective resistance.

Men create and maintain patriarchy not only because they have the resources to do so, but because they have real interests in making women serve as compliant tools. Women are, for one thing, a uniquely effective means of satisfying male sexual desire. Their bodies are, further, essential to the production of children, who satisfy both practical and, as psychoanalysts have shown, neurotic needs for men. Women are a useful labor force, as the Marxians have noted. They also can be ornamental signs of male status and power. As carefully controlled companions to both the child and the adult male, they are pleasant partners, sources of emotional support, and useful foils who reinforce, over and over again, the males' sense of their own central social significance. These useful functions mean that men everywhere seek to keep women compliant. But differing social circumstances give different rank orders to these functions and therefore lead to cross-cultural variations in the patterning of patriarchy. Radical feminists, unlike psychoanalytic feminists, give us both an explanation of universal gender oppression *and* a model for understanding cross-cultural variations in this oppression.

How is patriarchy to be defeated? Radicals hold that this defeat must begin with a basic reworking of women's consciousness, so that each woman recognizes her own value and strength; rejects patriarchal pressures to see herself as weak, dependent, and second class; and works in unity with other women, regardless of differences among them, to establish a broad-based sisterhood of trust, support, appreciation, and mutual defense. With this sisterhood in place, two strategies suggest themselves: a critical confrontation with any facet of patriarchal domination whenever it is encountered; and a degree of separatism as women withdraw into women-run businesses, households, communities, centers of artistic creativity, and love relationships.

How does one evaluate radical feminism? Emotionally each of us will respond to it in light of our own degree of personal radicalism, some seeing it as excessively critical and others as entirely convincing. But in attempting a theoretical evaluation, one should note that radical feminism incorporates arguments made by both Marxian and psychoanalytical feminists about the reasons for women's subordination and yet moves beyond those theories. It is the broadest of the variants of feminism that we have thus far encountered. Radical feminists, moreover, have done significant research to support their thesis that patriarchy ultimately rests on the practice of violence against women (Barry, 1979; Dworkin, 1976; 1978; Griffin, 1978; 1981; Millet, 1970; Rich, 1976). They have a reasonable though perhaps incomplete program for change. They have been faulted in their exclusive focus on patriarchy. This focus seems to simplify the realities of social organization and social inequality and thus to approach the issues of ameliorative change somewhat unrealistically. The third group of gender oppression theories, socialist feminism, sets out explicitly to address this criticism of radical feminism's unidimensional concern with patriarchy.

SOCIALIST FEMINISM

Socialist feminism is a highly diverse cluster of theoretical writings unified more by a theoretical agenda and less by substantive theoretical conclusions (Eisenstein, 1979;

Frye, 1983; Hartman, 1979; Hartsock, 1983; Lorde, 1984; MacKinnon, 1982; Ruddick, 1982; Smith, 1974; 1975; 1978; 1979). Three goals guide all socialist feminism: theoretical synthesis, a combination of theoretical breadth and precision, and an explicit and adequate method for social analysis and social change.

Socialist feminists have set themselves the formal project of achieving both a synthesis of and a theoretical step beyond extant feminist theories. More specifically, socialist feminists seek to bring together what they perceive as the two broadest and most valuable feminist traditions: Marxian and radical feminist thought.

Out of this project of synthesis have flowed two distinctive sub-varieties of socialist feminism. The first focuses exclusively on women's oppression and on understanding it in a way that brings together knowledge (from Marxism) of class oppression and (from radical feminism) of gender oppression. Through this theoretical intersection, these theorists seek to map the commonalities and variations in women's experiences of subordination. The term most frequently used by these theorists for the system they describe is *capitalist patriarchy* (Eisenstein, 1979; Hartman, 1979).

The second variant of socialist feminism sets out to describe and explain all forms of social oppression, using knowledge of class and gender hierarchies as a base from which

DOROTHY E. SMITH: A Biographical Sketch

Dorothy E. Smith presents a fascinating study for the biographer: a sociologist who insists on the social locatedness of knowledge, she is remarkably indirect in reference to her own personal life. Smith's personal life seems to have been framed by what she herself sees as "not so much a career as a series of contingencies, of accidents" (Smith, 1979:151). Whether they occurred by accident or design, the following events appear to the outsider as significant stages in Smith's development. She was born in 1926 in Great Britain; she earned her bachelor's degree in sociology from the University of London in 1955 and her Ph.D. in sociology from the University of California at Berkeley in 1963. During this same period, she had "the experience of marriage, of immigration [to Canada] closely following marriage, of the arrival of children, of the departure of a husband rather early one morning, of the jobs that became available" (Smith, 1979:151). Of these events, Smith stresses, they "were moments in which I had in fact little choice and certainly little foreknowledge." The jobs that became available included research sociologist at Berkeley; lecturer in sociology at Berkeley; lecturer in sociology at the University of Essex, Colchester, England; associate professor and then professor in the department of sociology at the University of British Columbia; and since 1977, professor of sociology in education at The Ontario Institute for Studies in Education, Toronto.

Smith has written on a fairly wide variety of topics, all connected by a concern with "bifurcation," sometimes as a central theme and sometimes as a motif. Smith sees the experience of bifurcation manifesting itself in the separation between social scientific description and people's lived experience, between women's lived experience and the patriarchal ideal types they are given for describing that experience, between the micro world and the macro world structures that dictate micro experience, and, especially, to explore systems of oppression centering not only on class and gender, but also on race, ethnicity, age, sexual preference, and location within the global hierarchy of nations. The term most frequently used by these theorists for the system they describe is *domination* (Frye, 1983; Lorde, 1984; Smith, 1979). Women remain central to this theoretical approach in two ways. First, as with all feminism, the oppression of women remains a primary topic for analysis. The theorists of domination can map even more elaborately than those of capitalist patriarchy the variations and permutations in that oppression. Second, women's location and experience of the world serve as the essential vantage point on domination in all its forms. Ultimately, though, these theorists are concerned with all experiences of oppression, either by women or by men. They even explore how some women, themselves oppressed, may yet actively participate in the oppression of other women, as for example white women in American society oppressing black women. Indeed, one strategy of all socialist feminists is to confront the prejudices and oppressive practices *within* the community of women itself (Frye, 1983; Lorde, 1984).

Both the focus on capitalist patriarchy and on domination are linked to a commitment, either explicit or implicit, to historical materialism as an analytical strategy (Jaggar, 1984). *Historical materialism*, a basic principle in Marxian social theory, refers to

between the micro world of the oppressed and the micro world of the dominants whose actions create the macro structures of oppression. The concretization of these themes can be seen in a selective review of the titles of some of Smith's works: "The Statistics on Women and Mental Illness: How Not to Read Them" (1975), "What It Might Mean to Do a Canadian Sociology: The Everyday World as Problematic" (1976), "K Is Mentally Ill: The Anatomy of a Factual Account" (1978), "Where There Is Oppression, There Is Resistance" (1979), "Women, Class and Family" (1981)—and above all, her most important contribution to feminist sociology, "A Sociology for Women" (1979).

What Smith is producing for feminist sociologists, and indeed for all sociologists interested in the theoretical frontiers of the profession, is a sociology that integrates neo-Marxian concerns with the structures of domination and phenomenological insights into the variety of subjective and micro-interactional worlds. Smith sees these various everyday life worlds as being commonly shaped by macro structures which are themselves shaped by the historical specifics of economic demand. What Smith wishes to avoid, in developing this line of reasoning, is a vision of the world in which the oppressors are consistently interpreted as individual actors making rational decisions on the basis of self-interest. What Smith sees is that self-interest itself is structurally situated and what she calls for sociologists to focus on is always the ultimate structure producing the outcome at hand. But she believes that this structure can only become known by beginning with the outcome at hand, that is, by exploring the everyday worlds of situated individuals. Smith is concerned that much social science serves to obfuscate rather than clarify the structures that produce these worlds because much social science begins with an assumption that the structures are already known and can be known separately from the everyday life worlds.

Sociologists working out of a feminist perspective are currently turning increasingly to Smith for a systematic framing of their major concerns. The implications of Smith's work for sociological theory form the basis for much of this chapter.

the position that the material conditions of human life, inclusive of the activities and relationships that produce those conditions, are the key factors that pattern human experience, personality, ideas, and social arrangements; that those conditions change over time because of dynamics immanent within them; and that history is a record of the changes in the material conditions of a group's life and of the correlative changes in experiences, personality, ideas, and social arrangements. Historical materialists hold that any effort at social analysis must trace in historically concrete detail the specifics of the group's material conditions and the links between those conditions and the experiences, personalities, events, ideas, and social arrangements characteristic of that group. In linking historical materialism to their focus on domination,[8] socialist feminists attempt to realize their goal of a theory that probes the broadest of human social arrangements, domination, and yet remains firmly committed to precise, historically concrete analyses of the material and social arrangements that frame particular situations of domination.

The historical materialism that is a hallmark of socialist feminism shows clearly that school's indebtedness to Marxian thought. But in their use of this principle, socialist feminists move beyond the Marxians in three crucial ways: in their focus on domination, their redefinition of material conditions, and their re-evaluation of the significance of ideology. First, the object of analysis is for them not primarily class inequality as it is for most Marxians, but a wider range of social inequalities. Second, they broaden the meaning of the material conditions of human life. Marxians typically mean by this idea the economic dynamics of society, particularly the ways in which goods of a variety of types are created for and exchanged in the market. In the various exploitative arrangements here, which make some wealthy and others poor, they locate the roots of class inequality and class conflict. Socialist feminists, however, go beyond economic dynamics and speak more broadly of the conditions that create and sustain human life: the human body, its sexuality and involvement in procreation and child rearing; home maintenance with its unpaid, invisible round of domestic tasks; emotional sustenance. In all these life-sustaining activities, exploitative arrangements profit some and impoverish others. Full comprehension of all these basic arrangements of life production and exploitation is the essential foundation for a theory of domination.

This redefinition of the concept of material conditions transforms the Marxian assumption that human beings are producers of goods into a theme of human beings as creators and sustainers of other human beings. The focus thus shifts from the value of goods to the constitution of human personality. This shift brings us to the third point of difference between Marxian historical materialism and historical materialism as it is developed in socialist feminism, namely the latter perspective's emphasis on what some Marxians might call, dismissively, mental or ideational phenomena: consciousness, motivation, ideas, social definitions of the situation, knowledge, ideology, the will to act in one's interests or acquiesce to the interests of others.[9] To socialist feminists

---

[8] From here on, we use the term *domination* to refer to the central concerns of both variants of socialist feminism. Both groups are in fact concerned with hierarchy, broadly conceived, rather than with any particular system of hierarchy.

[9] Admittedly some neo-Marxians, notably the critical theorists, have also re-evaluated the explanatory significance of ideology (see Chapter 4).

all these factors deeply affect human personality, human action, and the structures of domination that are realized through that action. Moreover, these aspects of human subjectivity are produced by social structures as elaborate and powerful as those that produce economic goods. Within these structures, too, exploitative arrangements enrich and empower some while impoverishing and immobilizing others. Analysis of the processes that pattern human subjectivity are vital to a theory of domination, and that analysis also can be honed to precision by applying the principles of historical materialism (Frye, 1983; MacKinnon, 1982; Smith, 1979).

Socialist feminism thus develops a portrait of social organization in which the macro-social structures of economy, polity, and ideology interact with the intimate, private, micro-social processes of human reproduction, domesticity, sexuality, and subjectivity to sustain a multi-faceted system of domination, the workings of which are discernible both as massive social patterns and in the subtleties and details of interpersonal relationships. To analyze this system, socialist feminists shuttle between a mapping of large-scale systems of domination and a situationally specific, detailed exploration of the mundane daily experiences of oppressed people. Their strategy for change rests in this process of discovery, in which they attempt to involve the oppressed groups that they study and through which they hope that both individuals and groups, in large and small ways, will learn to act in pursuit of their collective emancipation. Many other insights and discoveries from this theoretical enterprise will be discussed in the section that follows.

In concluding this overview of major conceptual themes in feminist theory, we review the two major general criticisms of that theory. First, because of its many varieties, feminist theory sometimes is perceived as no theory at all but as a seemingly endless wrangling among insiders to the women's movement. Counter answers are, first, that most feminist theorists take as a given the location of knowledge in the social situation and believe that the just resolution of a social situation lies in an equal hearing of the viewpoints of all interested parties; and, second, that all feminist theorists offer a woman-centered vision of social life and that this permits thinking about feminist theory as a unity.

A second, more serious criticism, raised by women of color (Hooks, 1984; Moraga and Anzaldua, 1981; Rollins, 1985), is that despite claims to be seeking a just resolution, most feminist theory reflects white, middle-class experience. There is a growing concern within feminist theory over the exploitation of women of one class, race, ethnic group, or global position by women of another. In other words, a new question is emerging for feminist theorists: *"And what about differences among women?"*

Despite the many varieties of contemporary feminist theory, there is a consistent concern with the basic sociological question of how and why social organization takes the form it does in any particular society at any particular time. We will see the significance of feminist theory for a sociological theory of social organization in the next section.

A FEMINIST SOCIOLOGICAL THEORY

One of the principles of intellectual practice raised by feminism and which we take as a starting point for a feminist *sociological* theory is that there can be no disinterested observers. For example, even sociologists observe social organization from a social position of relative social advantage. Therefore, we should identify our position as feminists. According to the descriptions we have set forth, we are oppression theorists who fall somewhere between radical and socialist theory.[10] From that perspective, we identify four distinctive features of a feminist sociology:

1. A distinctive style of dialectical thinking
2. A distinctive model of the organization of society at the macro-social level
3. An exploration of the relational situation of women that alters the traditional sociological understanding of micro-interaction
4. A revision of sociology's model of subjectivity.

The Feminist Dialectic

The logic of feminist sociological theory is best understood as a distinctive and radical form of dialectical thinking. This mode of thinking is rooted in assumptions that lie at the core of feminism as a world view and, in part, in women's fundamental life experiences.

At the core of a feminist dialectic is a sociology of knowledge, a conception that the world is known from the varied vantage points of actors differently situated in the social structure. Actors construct their knowledge on the foundations of their situated experiences and interests. Feminists, starting where Marx left off, have identified three crucial groups—owners, workers, *and* women—whose life circumstances and relations with each other are only in part patterned by economic factors. Then, as feminists have explored differences among women, they have discovered a multiplicity of differently situated groups of women and, extending this view, a multiplicity of differently situated groups of people. In tracing the relationships among all these groups, feminists have moved beyond a class model of domination to a vision of a complex system of unequally empowered groups relating through shifting arrangements of coalition and opposition. Within such a system the view that knowledge is anchored in and patterned by the knower's structurally situated vantage point leads one to the position that knowledge is itself the key *problematic*. In describing knowledge as "the key problematic," we mean that for a feminist sociology the central issue is understanding how any knowledge of social reality is possible, given the fact that people's (including sociologists') perceptions of social reality are always partial and interest-based. Thus a feminist sociology seeks to understand how people come to their views of social reality, how they justify those views in the face of seemingly contradictory opinions and evidence, act on those views, condone their own behavior according to those views, or reconcile themselves to their social situation according to those views. Because feminist

---

[10]The fullest sense of our intellectual position may be suggested by acknowledging our intellectual debt at both the theoretical and empirical levels to Dorothy Smith's pioneering woman-centered sociology (Smith, 1974; 1975; 1978; 1979; 1985). Other major feminist sources of this effort are Bernard (1976); Chodorow (1978); Gilligan (1982); Harding (1986); Hartsock, (1985); Kasper (1986); Lever (1978); Lorde (1984); MacKinnon (1986); Rich (1976; 1979); Rubin (1976; 1983); Ruddick (1980); and Stacey and Thorne (1985).

sociologists ultimately are concerned with providing a theoretical foundation for practical action, they are concerned with bringing people together to try to achieve something similar to Jurgen Habermas's call for a "rational discourse" (see Chapter 4)—save that feminist sociologists seek above all an "egalitarian discourse" that they believe will lead to a just and open society.

It is important to emphasize here that the feminist dialectic does not necessarily lead to the view that we can never discover the truth about anything. Feminism does not doubt that there is a reality to be known and described by a knower. But feminists seek that knowledge in the descriptions of reality presented from a multiplicity of vantage points and systems of knowing, none of which has any final and determinative authenticity. Indeed, some of these viewpoints may be deliberately manipulative and thus inauthentic. Many sociological theorists who have arrived at a similar awareness have backed away from it because of what seems to be its logical conclusion: a paralyzing and total relativism. In contrast, feminist theorists have moved to solve the problem of relativism by locating their point of creative tension directly within the processes of knowledge. They argue that the truth of any situation is to be discovered in the point of intersection that exists among the competing viewpoints and knowledge systems of the unequally empowered groups involved in that situation. But the authenticity of a situation can only be determined when a system of discourse can be achieved that allows for an egalitarian exchange of views in which all parties openly acknowledge both the partialness and the interest-based character of their views. And it logically follows from feminist theory that the people who will have the most difficulty entering into this egalitarian discourse are those who are most empowered and thus have the most to lose from any change in the social structure.

This particular version of the sociology of knowledge provides the philosophic basis for feminists' insistent valuation of the viewpoints of less privileged groups. For a major factor in privilege is that the viewpoints of favorably situated actors become "the viewpoints of the society," or in Marx's famous aphorism, "The ruling ideas of any age are the ideas of its ruling class." This awareness presses feminists constantly to call attention not only to the "women's" view of a situation, but to the views among differing groups of women. Thus the feminist agenda seeks to explore the situated perceptions of reality held by upper-, middle-, working- and lower-class women, by women of various racial and ethnic backgrounds, and by women of various political, religious, and sexual orientations.

This feminist dialectic not only stems from a feminist sociology of knowledge, but equally from women's daily experiences. Women's social situation traditionally has made them central maintainers and balancers of a variety of views. Repeatedly in their roles as wives, mothers, and daughters and in the larger, slightly less gender-prescribed world of economic, educational, religious, and political production, women are expected and expect themselves to serve as moderators who ensure that all positions receive a fair hearing. Women thus find knowledge not in unilateral claims to the truth, but in balancing and weighing the accounts of reality presented to them by a variety of others.

The feminist dialectic also demands a restructuring of sociological practice to allow sociologists fully to capture the processes by which people, including sociologists, create social knowledge. From this perspective, sociologists must relocate themselves, must look again at their most treasured concepts, must see that the attempt to build static concepts denies them access to the fluid nature of social reality, and must see that too often they have simply mirrored the distortions they sought to study. In the end, as the feminist dialectic makes clear, the social world is a construct created by the exchanges of people from all vantage points. Not all these people have an equal say in the final form that that construction takes, but they are all involved, even when invisible, in that construction.

People understand and act toward reality from the vantage point of their structurally patterned situations. Because this fact extends even to the sociologist, certainty about the truth becomes a suspect and elusive condition. That certainty can only be achieved if sociologists: (1) seek their facts at the point of intersection between the understandings of the world held by differently situated and often oppositionally related groups; (2) stay focused not only on these different accounts but on the situated vantage points from which they arise; (3) remain sensitive to the situationality of their own professional efforts to know the world; (4) remain sensitive to the differences in perception that people may have about the requirements of their structural locations; (5) stay modest about their "certainty" and recognize its processual basis, its precarious state, and the permeability of all their concepts; and (6) stay constantly aware of and attempt to compensate for the ways that structural inequalities weight different groups' accounts of social reality.

The Macro Social Order

Feminist sociology's view of the macro social order emphasizes the impact of both social structure (or macro-objective productions) and ideology (or macro subjectivity) on actors' perceptions of social reality.

Feminist sociology begins by expanding the Marxian concept of economic production into a much more general concept of social production, that is, the production of all human social life. Along with the production of commodities for the market, social production for feminists also includes arrangements like family and health care, which reproduce and sustain human life; arrangements like the organization of housework, which produce outside of the market or money economy the essential commodities and services of the household; arrangements like the social organization of sexuality, which pattern and satisfy human desire and human emotional needs for acceptance, approval, love, and self-esteem; arrangements such as the state and religion, which create the rules and laws of a community; and arrangements like politics, mass media, and academic discourse, which establish institutionalized, public definitions of the situation.

Thus framed and expanded, the Marxian model of intergroup relations remains visible in feminist theory's model of social organization. Each of the various types of social production is based on an arrangement by which some actors, controlling the resources crucial to that activity, act as dominants or "masters" who dictate and profit from the circumstances of production. Within each productive sector, productivity rests on the work of subordinates, or "servants," whose energies create the world ordered into being by their masters and whose exploitation denies them the rewards and satisfactions produced by their work. Through feminist theory, we see, more vividly than through Marxian theory, the intimate association between masters and servants that lies at the heart of *all* production and the indispensability of the servant's work in creating and sustaining everything necessary to human social life. Social production occurs through a multi-dimensional structure of domination and exploitation that organizes class, gender, race, sex, power, and knowledge into overlapping hierarchies of intimately associated masters and workers.

Turning to another aspect of the macro order, feminist research shows that women do not experience social life as a movement among compartmentalized roles, as structural functionalists assert. Instead, they are involved in a balancing of roles, a merging of role-associated interests and orientations, and, through this merging, in a weaving together of social institutions. This is true of the working mother as well as working women in "typically female" job categories like secretary or nurse. It is also true when women link the activities of housewife and economic consumer or of mother of school-age children and spouse of wage-sector participant. Moreover, in the classic double bind or "no-win situation" which marks women's experience of subordination, this blending and balancing is expected of women while used as a basis of invidious comparison between women's role behavior and "typical" or compartmentalized role performance. Thus it is said disparagingly that women "bring outside concerns into the office," "let their emotions affect their performance," and "cannot keep the fact that they are women out of the situation."

The feminist model of stratification in social production offers a direct critique of the structural-functionalist vision of a society composed of a system of separate institutions and distinct through interrelated roles. Feminist theory claims that this image is not generalizable, but that instead it depicts the experiences and vantage points of a particularly situated group—white, male, upper class, and adult. Indeed, one indicator of this group's control over the situations of production may be that they can achieve this kind of purposive compartmentalization in *their* role behavior, a condition that serves to reproduce their control over situations. But feminist sociology stresses that this condition depends on the subordinate services of actors who cannot compartmentalize their lives and actions. Indeed, were these subordinate actors to similarly compartmentalize, the whole system of production in complex industrialized societies would collapse. In contrast to the structural-functionalist model, the feminist model emphasizes that the role-merging experience of women may be generalizable to the experience of many other subordinate "servant" groups whose work produces the fine-grained texture of daily life. The understandings that such subordinated groups have of the organization of social life may be very different from the understanding depicted in structural-functionalist theory; even their identification of key institutional spheres may differ. Yet their vantage point springs from situations necessary to society as it is presently organized and from work that makes possible the masters' secure sense of an institutionally compartmentalized world.

Further, feminism emphasizes the centrality of ideological domination to the structure of social domination. Ideology is an intricate web of beliefs about reality and social life that is institutionalized as public knowledge and disseminated throughout society so effectively that it becomes taken-for-granted knowledge for all social groups. Thus what feminists see as "public knowledge of social reality" is not an overarching culture, a consensually created social product, but a reflection of the interests and experiences of society's dominants and one crucial index of their power in society. What distinguishes this view from most Marxian views is that for feminists ideological control is *the* basic process in domination, and the hierarchical control of discourse and knowledge is the key element in societal domination.

Central to feminist concerns about the macro social order, of course, is the macro-structural patterning of gender inequality. Ideology plays a crucial role in the maintenance of this societal vector of dominance and subordination. Gender inequality is reproduced by a system of institutionalized knowledge that reflects the interests and experiences of men. Among other things, this gender ideology identifies men as the bearers of sociocultural authority and allocates to the male role the right to dominate and to the female role the obligation to serve in all dimensions of social production. Gender ideology also systematically flattens and distorts women's productive activities by: (1) trivializing some of them, e.g., housework; (2) idealizing to the point of unrecognizability other activities, e.g., mothering, and (3) making invisible yet other crucial work, e.g., women's multiple and vital contributions to the production of marketplace commodities. These ideological processes may be generalizable to the macro-structural production of all social subordination.

The Micro Social Order

At the micro-interactional level, feminist sociology (like some micro-sociological perspectives) focuses on how individuals take account of each other as they pursue objective projects or subjectively shared meanings. Feminist sociology differs in five important ways from social definitionism and social behaviorism, both of which focus on the micro-interactional order. A review of these five differences reveals important aspects of the feminist model of the micro order.

RESPONSIVE ACTION VERSUS PURPOSEFUL ACTION

Most mainstream micro sociology presents a model of purposive human beings setting their own goals and pursuing these in linear courses of action in which they (individually or collectively) strive to link means to ends. In contrast, feminist research shows, first, that women's lives have a quality of incidentalness, as women find themselves caught up in agendas that shift and change with the vagaries of marriage, husbands' courses of action, children's unpredictable impact on life plans, divorce, widowhood, and the precariousness of most women's wage-sector occupations. Second, in their daily activities, women find themselves not so much pursuing goals in linear sequences but responding continuously to the needs and demands of others. This theme has been developed from Chodorow's (1978) analysis of the emotional and relational symbiosis between mothers and daughters, through Lever's (1978) and Gilligan's (1982) descriptions of intensely relational female play groups, to analyses of women in their typical occupations as teachers, nurses, secretaries, receptionists, and office helpers, and in accounts of women in their roles as wives, mothers, and community and kin coordinators. In calling women's activities ''responsive,'' we are not describing them as passively reactive. Instead, we are drawing a picture of beings who are oriented not so much to their own goals but to the tasks of monitoring, coordinating, facilitating, and moderating the wishes, actions, and demands of others. In place of micro sociology's conventional model of purposeful actors, then, feminist research presents a model of actors who are in their daily lives responsively located at the center of a web of others' actions and who in the long term find themselves located in one or another of these situations by forces that they can neither predict nor control.

INTERMITTENT INTERACTION VERSUS CONTINUOUS INTERACTION

Micro sociology's typical picture of social life shows purposive actors who are almost continuously in face-to-face interactions in which they orient to each other and in which they assume that all the other actors in the situation are fundamentally like them. Feminist theory describes a world in which women experience highly variable interactions that seldom assume all the interactive qualities of that model. For long periods of each day, adult women located in households work in isolation from face-to-face interactions and orient to others only subjectively and responsively rather than purposively. In other settings, particularly in low-status office, factory, or service jobs, women find themselves working at structurally patterned routines in proximity to but not in interaction with each other. In many of their most significant interactive situations, they find themselves relating to other beings whom they do not assume to be fundamentally like themselves: children so young that they must be treated as less than self and adult men whom they know to be fundamentally different from them in personality, experience of life, and social situation—their existential "other" (de Beauvoir, 1957). Only when they come together in spontaneous and open association with other adult women does their interactive experience meet assumptions built into the conventional micro-sociological model of typical interaction. Feminist theory then raises these questions: Whose experiences of interaction provide sociology with its model of prototypical interaction? What, from the standpoint of women, constitutes prototypical interaction? Feminists answer these questions by claiming, first, that the experience of dominant men is mirrored in sociology's basic model of interaction, and, second, that women's relationship to these men is, at least in its frequency and practical consequences, women's crucial and prototypical interaction. Feminists' exploration of male-female interactions takes us further into the feminist model of micro-interaction.

THE ASSUMPTION OF INEQUALITY VERSUS THE ASSUMPTION OF EQUALITY

Conventional micro-social theory assumes that the pressures in interactive situations toward collaboration and meaning construction are so great that actors, bracketing considerations of the macro structure, orient toward each other on an assumption of equality. Feminist research on interactions between women and men flatly contradicts this, showing that these social interactions are pervasively patterned by influences from their macro-structural context. In their daily activities, women are affected by the fact that they are structurally subordinate to the men with whom they interact in casual associations, courtship, marriage, family, and wage work. Any interpersonal equality or dominance that women as individuals may achieve is effectively offset, within the interactive process itself, by these structural patterns—of which the most pervasive is the institution of gender. The macro-structural patterning of gender inequality is intricately woven through the interactions between women and men and affect not only its broad division of labor in who sets and who implements projects, but also its processual details, which repeatedly show the enactment of authority and deference in seating and seating/standing arrangements, forms of address and conversation, eye contact, and the control of space and time.

STRATIFIED MEANINGS VERSUS COMMON MEANINGS

Conventional micro sociology either brackets the issue of meaning (the social behaviorists) or assumes that the activities and relationships that occur in situated interactions become the basis and focus of collaborative meaning construction (the social definitionists). Actors, seeing each other in activity and interaction, form shared understandings through communication and ultimately a common vantage point on their experiences. Feminists argue that this assumption must be drastically qualified by the fact that micro-interactions are embedded in and permeated by the macro structure. Women's everyday actions and relationships occur against a backdrop of public or institutionalized understanding of everyday experience, that is, as we have said, a macro-structural layer of ideology that flattens and distorts the reality by trivializing, idealizing, or making invisible women's activity and experience. This ideology patterns the meanings assigned to activities in interaction. Men (dominants) in interaction with women are more likely to assign to women's activity meanings drawn from the macro structure of gender ideology than either to enter the situation with an attitude of open inquiry or to draw on any other macro-level typing for interpreting women's activity. Women, immersed in the same ideological interpretation of their experiences, stand at a point of dialectical tension, balancing this ideology against the actuality of their lives. A great diversity of meanings develop out of this tension.

As everything that has been said so far indicates, social definitionists assume that actors, relating and communicating intimately and over long periods of time, create a common vantage point or system of shared understanding. Feminists research on what may be the most intimate, long-term, male-female association, marriage, shows that, for all the reasons reported above, marriage partners remain strangers to each other and inhabit separate worlds of meaning. Moreover, Dorothy Smith (1979) argues convincingly that this ''stranger-ness'' may be a variable in which the dominant man, in the interests of effective control, is more a stranger to women's meanings than women as subordinates can afford to be to the dominant's meanings.

CONSTRAINT VERSUS CHOICE IN MEANING-CREATING LOCATIONS

A profoundly democratic ethos shapes both social definitionist and social behaviorist descriptions of interaction. Conventional models consistently imply that people have considerable equality of opportunity and freedom of choice in moving in and out of interactional settings. Feminist research shows that the interactions in which women are most free to create with others meanings that depict their life experiences are those which occur when they are in relationship and communication with similarly situated women. Moreover, these associations can be deeply attractive to women because of the practical, emotional, and the meaning-affirming support that they provide. Women, however, are not freely empowered to locate in these settings. Law, interactional domination, and ideology restrict and demean this associational choice, so that, insidiously, even women become suspicious of its attractions. Under these circumstances, the association becomes not a free and open choice, but a subterranean, circumscribed, and publicly invisible arena for relationship and meaning.

What does all this add up to in a feminist sociology of the micro order? First, it suggests not that the conventional models are wholly inaccurate, but that they are only partial models. But if we return to our starting point, that truth lies at the intersection of vantage points, then a partial model must have elements of distortion—especially when that partial model is allowed to stand unchallenged. The conventional model of interaction may depict how equals in the macro-structural, power-conferring categories create a vantage point. It may also depict how, from the vantage point of structural dominance, one experiences interaction with both equals and subordinates. And it may well suggest a strain or tendency in all interactional arrangements. But, and second, when structural unequals interact, there are many other qualities to their association than these suggested by the conventional models. Indeed, these other features suggest another model that better captures the realities of the subordinate's experience: incidentalness of project, responsiveness of action, movement in and out of very different interaction experiences, continuous enactment of power differentials, activities whose meanings are invisible or obscured, estrangement from the meanings of others involved in the interaction, and restricted access to those settings where meaningfulness is most likely to be a genuinely shared experience. Third, we need to ask whether this latter model is not generalizable to the experience of all subordinates and whether sociologists must not plot the reality of the micro-interactional order at the dialectical intersection of all these models of interpersonal association.

Subjectivity

One of the most striking features of feminist sociology is its insistence on a third level of social activity—the subjective. Most sociological theories subsume this level under micro-social action (micro subjectivity) or as "culture" or "ideology" at the macro level (macro subjectivity). Feminist sociology, however, insists that the actor's individual interpretation of goals and relationships must be looked at as a distinct level. This insistence, like so much of feminist sociology, grows out of the study of women's lives and seems applicable to the lives of subordinates in general. Women (and perhaps other subordinates) are particularly aware of the distinctiveness of their subjective experience precisely because, as we have indicated, their own experience so often runs counter to prevailing cultural and micro-interactionally established definitions.

When sociologists do look at the subjective level of experience, usually as part of the micro-social order, they focus on four major issues: role-taking and knowledge of the other; the process of the internalization of community norms; the nature of the self as social actor; and the nature of the consciousness of everyday life. This section explores the feminist thesis on each of these issues.

THE ISSUE OF ROLE-TAKING AND THE SENSE OF OTHER

The conventional sociological model of subjectivity (as presented to us in the theories of Mead [see Chapter 5] and Schutz [see Chapter 6] assumes that in the course of role-taking, the social actor learns to see the self through the eyes of others deemed more or less the same as the actor. But feminist sociology shows that women are socialized to see themselves through the eyes of men. Even when significant others are women, they have been so socialized that they too take the male view of self and of other women. Women's experience of learning to role-take is shaped by the fact that they must, in a way men need not, learn to take the role of the genuine *other*, not just a social other who is taken to be much like oneself. The other for women is the male and is alien. The other for men is, first and foremost, men who are to some degree like them in a quality that the culture considers of transcendent importance: gender.

THE INTERNALIZATION OF
COMMUNITY NORMS

Role-taking usually is seen as culminating in the internalization of community norms via the social actor's learning to take the role of "the generalized other," a construct that the actor mentally creates out of the amalgam of macro- and micro-level experiences that form her or his social life. The use of the singular *other* indicates that micro sociologists usually envision this imagined generalized other as a cohesive, coherent, singular expression of expectations. But feminists argue, first, that in a male-dominated patriarchal culture, the generalized other represents a set of male-dominated community norms that force the woman to picture herself as "less than" or "unequal to" men. To the degree that a woman succeeds in formulating a sense of a generalized other that accurately reflects the dominant perceptions of the community, she may have in a sense damaged her own possibilities for self-esteem and self-exploration.

Second, the insights of feminism call into question the very existence of a unified generalized other for the majority of people—indeed, perhaps for all people. The central point with which we began this section is that the truth of a given social situation lies in the intersection of vantage points. Presumably any of these vantage points could constitute a generalized other by which a person might view herself or himself as an object and judge her or his performance. Only with the awareness of how a multiplicity of others affect an individual's sense of self can we begin to capture the potential complexity of having or being a self. The subordinate, in particular, does not have the luxury or the illusion of the existence of a single standardized other (unless the subordinate has been so oppressed as to have surrendered all powers of separate reflection).

THE NATURE OF THE SELF
AS A SOCIAL ACTOR

Micro sociologists describe the social actor as picturing the everyday world as something to be mastered according to one's particular interests. Feminist sociologists argue that women may find themselves so overwhelmingly limited by their status as women that the idea of projecting their own plans onto the world becomes meaningless in all but theory. Further, women may not experience the life-world as something to be mastered according to their own particular interests. They may be socialized to experience that life-world as a place in which one balances a variety of actors' interests. Indeed, Gilligan (1982) has been at pains to assure women that one mark of maturity is an ability to have and protect one's own interests as a way of protecting oneself for others.

Women may not have the same experience of control of particular spheres of space, free from outside interference. They find themselves still in search of "a room of one's own." Similarly, their sense of time rarely can follow the simple pattern of first things first because they have as a life project the balancing of the interests and projects of others. Thus women may experience planning and actions as acts of concern for a variety of interests, their own and others, and as acts above all of cooperation and not mastery.

This idea ties in with the idea discussed earlier of women's role experience as one of "role merging." In combination, these ideas suggest the need for renaming role *conflict* as role *balancing* (to stay within the confines of the present language). Then the ability to role balance, one of women's and other subordinates' primary abilities and experiences of space and time, would come to be explored as a positive social value. Compartmentalization then might be seen as a sign of the "less than" functional personality.

CONSCIOUSNESS OF EVERYDAY LIFE

Feminist sociologists have critically evaluated the thesis of a unified consciousness of everyday life that traditional micro sociologists usually assume. Feminist sociologists stress that for women the most pervasive feature of the cognitive style of everyday life is that of a bifurcated consciousness. Women experience what Smith (1979) has called "a line of fault" between their own personal, lived, and reflected-on experience and the established types available in the social stock of knowledge to describe that experience. Everyday life itself thus divides into two realities for subordinates: the reality of actual, lived, reflected-on experience and the reality of social types. Often aware of the way that their own experience differs from that of the culturally dominant males with whom they interact, women are less trusting of the case of shared subjectivity. And as biological and social beings whose activities are not perfectly regulated by patriarchal standard time, they are more aware of the demarcation between time as lived experience and time as a social mandate. A feminist sociology of subjectivity perhaps would begin here: how do people survive when their own experience does not fit the established social typifications of that experience? We know already that some do so by avoiding acts of sustained reflection; some do so by cultivating their own series of personal types to make sense of their experience; some do so by seeking community with others who share this bifurcated reality; some do so by denying the validity of their own experience. But survive they do.

What we have generalized here for women's subjectivity may be true for the subjectivity of all subordinates. One, their experience of role-taking is complicated by their intense awareness that they must learn the expectations of an other who by virtue of differences in power is alien. Two, they must relate not to a generalized other but to many generalized others, many subcultures, both the subculture of the powerful and the various subcultures of the less empowered and the disempowered. Three, they do not experience themselves as purposive social actors who can chart their own course through life—although they may be constantly told that they can do so, especially within the American ethos. And finally, and most pervasively, they live daily with a bifurcated consciousness, a sense of the line of fault between their own lived experiences and what the dominant culture tells them is the social reality.

Ties to Sociological Paradigms

We end this section by returning to a claim that we made in our introduction, that a feminist sociological theory effectively synthesizes the three paradigms—the social-facts, the social-definition, and the social-behavior paradigms—that traditionally have separated sociologists. We also argue that within feminist sociological theory, traditional divisions between macro-social organization (social facts) and micro-social organization (social definitions and social behaviors) are successfully transcended.

A feminist sociological theory has strong elements of the social-facts paradigm, particularly in the latter's conflict theory formulations. A central thesis of feminist sociological theory is to see a macro-structural pattern of social production encompassing a pattern of hierarchical organization or inequality. In society as it is presently organized, production and inequality are closely interrelated. Production turns on the commands of dominants acting in their own interests and is realized through the labor of subordinates who reap far less from the productive process than they contribute. In societies like ours, there is a complex system of inequality in which the division into dominants and subordinates itself is based on the possession or lack of such traits as maleness, whiteness, professional/managerial/capitalist class position, and "middle-aged maturity." This complex system of inequality is sustained by ideology—that is, macro-social definitions of reality that embody dominants' interests but shape all groups' perceptions.

Feminist sociological theory builds an important bridge to social definitionism by emphasizing a broad construction of "production" that stresses the importance of micro-interactions in the creation of the social world. What is produced, what counts as work for feminist sociological theory, includes the production of ideas, emotional well-being, and sufficiently shared definitions of the situation to allow social life to continue. This production usually is accomplished at the micro-interactional level in intricate networks of intimate face-to-face associations that involve coordinated activity and mutual orientation, albeit between unequally empowered actors. The dynamics of domination and control that sustain the macro order are enacted and thus made real in these associations by interactive sequences of power, authority, deference, and submission and by the fundamentally different understandings of the situation held by dominants and subordinates who remain intimate strangers to each other. Much of the work of producing sufficient intimacy and understanding to allow social life to continue among people who are by virtue of differences in power also strangers to each other is done by subordinates, particularly by women. This awareness permeates feminist sociology and lets it bridge the traditional boundary between the social-definition and the social-facts paradigms.

Feminist sociological theory also partly explains this quality of people co-existing in social life as intimate strangers by acknowledging the insight of the social-behavior paradigm: that much human action is the result of unthinking behavior motivated by some unreflected-upon sense of the society's system of rewards and punishments. Thus many of the continuities of inequality, the unquestioned enactments of dominance and subordination, are the results of actors responding nonreflectively to the social scripts that they acquire in socialization. But in the exchange model of the behaviorist paradigm, actors are also capable of a rational calculus for achieving rewards and avoiding punishments within the established social system. Feminist sociological theory sees that this exchange model may be a valid representation of the experience of dominants and that within this model women, for instance, may learn how to make themselves valued objects to dominant males. Feminist sociological theory, however, does not accept this exchange model as a general theory but instead sees it as an example of one of feminist sociological theory's basic points: that knowledge is a construction based on social situatedness. Exchange theory may indeed explain some actions by some actors within a particular historical setting characterized by domination, but it is not a general, ahistorical explanation of human social behavior.

Within feminist sociological theory, those themes usually associated with these distinct paradigms are so intimately interwoven as to constitute a unified theory. Similarly, within feminist sociological theory, the divisions in sociology between macro and micro (see Chapter 10) are effectively transcended. Drawing on women's experience as subordinates, feminist sociological theory traces the ways in which the subordinate group maintains the macro world through micro-interactions as well as the ways in which these maintenance activities are shaped by the demands of the macro structure of domination. Thus feminist sociological theory analyzes the interface between macro structure and micro-interaction whether it begins at the macro level or the micro level. This sense of interface is captured in the feminist principle: ''The personal is political.'' The social world for feminist sociological theory is dialectically constituted out of the tension among macro structures of domination, micro interactions of maintenance and resistance, and subjective acts of interpretation leading to acquiesence or critique.

SUMMARY

Feminist sociological theory grows out of feminist theory in general, that branch of the new scholarship on women that seeks to provide a system of ideas about human life that features woman as object and subject, doer and knower.

Feminism has a history as long as women's subordination—and women have been subordinated almost always and everywhere. From 1630 to about 1780 feminist writing survives as a thin but persistent trickle of protest. From the 1780s to the present, feminist writing becomes a growing tide of critical work involving increasing participants and areas of critique. But this growth has not been steady, precisely because women as minority or oppressed members of society always have found their protests subject to suppression by male interests and patriarchal power. Generally, feminist theory, at least from the 1780s, has paralleled the swings between reform and retrenchment in Western social movements.

Feminist theory also has paralleled the growth of sociology itself. But feminist theory has remained on the margin of sociology, ignored by the central male formulators of the discipline until 1960. Feminist concerns have been addressed by female and male sociologists who were on the margins of the profession when they wrote (for instance, Marx and Engels). The central figures in the discipline have largely ignored feminist concerns and knowledge, and when they have looked at gender issues they have been conventional and uncritical in their treatment (as for instance, in the work of Talcott Parsons).

The feminist questions so rich in possibility for sociological theory today have been kept alive in the body of feminist theory formulated between 1960 and the present. This body of ideas can be classified according to the two basic questions of feminist scholarship, *And what about the women?* and *Why is women's situation as it is?* The answers to the first question provide our major categories of varieties of feminist theory. In our system, there have been three main descriptions of women's social situation: (1) it is different from men's; (2) it is unequal to men's; (3) it is that of an oppressed group and the oppressors are men or the male-constructed patriarchal social system.

Within each of these broad categories—difference, inequality, and oppression—there are further variations based on the answers to the question of why women's situation is as it is. Theorists who see women's situation as essentially different from men's explain that difference in three basic ways: bio-social conditioning, institutional socialization, and social-psychological interfacing. Theorists who emphasize inequality explanations account for women's positions in terms of *liberal feminism's* view of unequal opportunity structures and *Marxian* accounts of women's position as part of a complex class-system of exploitation in which women exploit and are exploited partly in terms of gender and partly in terms of class position. Theorists who emphasize oppression explain that oppression in terms of *psychoanalytic* theories that see males as having an innate need to subjugate women in order to achieve deep psychological goals. Others offer a *radical feminist* answer that sees the root of patriarchal oppression in males' greater ability and willingness to use brute force to subjugate others. Still others offer a *socialist feminist* analysis that attempts to synthesize various forms and theories of oppression, using terms such as capitalist patriarachy and domination to describe the multi-faceted system of oppression based on arrangements of production, class, age, ethnicity, sexual preference, and global position, as well as gender—a system oppressing all women and most men.

Feminist theory offers a basis for a revision of standard sociological theories of social organization. The feminist sociological theory that we present as an exemplar of what feminist theory can offer to general sociological theory may be summarized in terms of six main propositions, which draw on and synthesize the varieties of feminist theory. First, the practice of sociological theory must be based on a dialectical analysis of the knowledge process. There is a constant tension between subject and object in which each acts on and changes the other. This tension informs both the formal practice of sociology and the construction of knowledge in everyday life. Thus knowledge of the social world is always created from a social location. The knower or subject must acknowledge the interaction with the object of knowledge.

Second, macro social structures are based in processes controlled by dominants acting in their own interests and executed by subordinates whose work is made largely invisible and undervalued even to themselves by the social ideology. Thus even the understanding of what constitutes production is distorted. Focusing on women's position can give particular insights into these macro structures of subordination because women, whatever their class position, are primary doers of invisible work: housework, childbearing and rearing, emotional and sexual service, and coordinating activities (such as waiting, adjusting, being interrupted) in wage-sector work.

Third, micro-interactional processes in society make real these dominant-subordinate power arrangements and the nonacknowledgment or distortion of the subordinates' contribution. Thus, women find their contributions to social production either disregarded, as in housework or wage-sector coordinating activities, or idealized beyond any recognition of actual experience, as in mothering.

Fourth, these conditions create in women's subjectivity a constant "line of fault" that they must navigate. This line of fault separates the patriarchal ideology and women's reflected-on experience of the actuality of their roles in producing social life at the macro and micro levels. Women navigate this line of fault in various ways—by repression, by acquiesence, by rebellion, and by attempts at micro and macro organization for reform.

Fifth, what has been said for women may be applicable to all subordinate people in some parallel although not identical form.

Sixth, one must question the use of any categories developed by an essentially male-dominated discipline. The closing question of feminist sociological theory raises for everyone this issue: can we stay within the established disciplinary categories for describing and explaining the world, or must we create new concepts if we are to describe and explain the world as viewed by its subordinate, disadvantaged, and often invisible members?

CHAPTER NINE
Recent Developments in Sociological Theory

THIS chapter is devoted to a discussion of a number of theories not yet examined in detail in the text—action theory, systems theory, structuralism and post structuralism, structural theory, network theory, and existential sociology. Some are rising stars in sociological theory, others are fading, at least at the moment. Sociological theories tend not to disappear, but rather to ebb and flow in popularity. David Wagner and Joseph Berger agree, arguing that theories, or what they call "orienting strategies," are "seldom, if ever, replaced by another" (1985:701; see also Wagner, 1984). Their overall perspective is close to the one that informs this chapter: "Of course, changes within and among orienting strategies do occur. There is revision and rethinking of ideas. There is certainly extensive discussion and challenge among ideas. However, in the sense of one strategy leading to, generating, or being replaced by a 'better' strategy, theoretical growth simply does not occur frequently" (p. 702). Although Wagner and Berger do not see growth in the kinds of theories discussed in this book, they do believe that in other, narrower, senses sociological theories do grow.

ACTION THEORY

Not too many years ago, a book on sociological theory would have devoted a great deal of attention to action theory (MacIver, 1931; 1942; Parsons, 1937; Znaniecki, 1934). Today, however, interest in action theory has faded, although at the end of this section we will deal with some recent work (Coleman, 1986; Sciulli, 1986) that has helped resuscitate it to some degree.

Action theory had its origin in Max Weber's work on social action. Although Weber embedded his work in assumptions on actors and action, his real interest was in the cultural and structural constraints on them. Instead of focusing on this aspect of Weber's work, action theory operated at the level of individual thought and action. This is clear from Roscoe Hinkle's summary of the tenets of action theory:

1. Men's social activities arise from their consciousnesses of themselves (as subjects) and of others and the external situations (as objects).
2. As subjects, men act to achieve their (subjective) intentions, purposes, aims, ends, objectives, or goals.
3. They use appropriate means, techniques, procedures, methods, and instruments.
4. Their courses of action are limited by unmodifiable conditions or circumstances.
5. Exercising will or judgment, they choose, assess, and evaluate what they will do, are doing, and have done.
6. Standards, rules, or moral principles are invoked in arriving at decisions.
7. Any study of social relationships requires the researcher to use subjective investigative techniques such as *"verstehen,"* imaginative or sympathetic reconstruction, or vicarious experience. (Hinkle, 1963:706–707)

There is some evidence that such a micro-level action approach was anticipated by pre–World War I sociologists such as Lester Ward, E. A. Ross, Franklin Giddings, Albion Small, and Charles H. Cooley, although their link to modern action theory is tenuous. Most of these early sociologists were preoccupied with the large-scale question of societal evolution. They discussed an active, creative view of the individual, but tended to give society coercive power over the individual.

The exception to this tendency was Cooley. Although he accepted some of the tenets of his contemporaries, and their interest in evolution, "what became ultimately significant in social life [were] subjective consciousness and personal feelings, sentiments, ideas, or ideals in terms of which men initiate and terminate their actions toward one another" (Hinkle, 1963:709).

Sociologists who worked between the end of World War I and the Depression exhibited far more connection with later action theory. Among the more important of these sociologists were Robert Park, Ellsworth Faris, W. I. Thomas, George Herbert Mead, and Talcott Parsons. Parsons was the major inheritor of the Weberian orientation, and his use of action theory in his early work gave that approach its widest audience.

Parsons's Action Theory

Parsons was eager to differentiate action theory from behaviorism. In fact, he chose the term *action* because it had a different connotation from that of *behavior.* Behavior implied mechanical response to stimuli, whereas action implied an active, creative, "mental" process. Parsons was careful to differentiate action theory from behaviorism: "A theory which, like behaviorism, insists on treating human beings in terms which exclude his subjective aspect, is not a theory of action" (1937:77–78).

From the beginning Parsons (1937) made it clear that action theory could not adequately explain social structures and institutions, although it could deal with the most elementary forms of social life.[1] This foreshadowed Parsons's later work, in which, many people feel, he almost totally abandoned action theory for a structural-functional orientation (see Chapter 3) more appropriate to the study of social structures and culture.

UNIT ACT

The basic phenomenon in Parsons's action theory is what he called the *unit act*, which he defined in terms of four components. First, it implies the existence of an *actor*. Second, the unit act involves an *end*, or a future state toward which action is oriented. Third, the action takes place in a *situation* that involves two elements: things the actor cannot control (*conditions*) and those over which the actor can exert control (*means*). Finally, *norms* and *values* serve to shape the actor's choice of means to ends (Parsons, 1937). Parsons said that there is "no such thing as action except as effort to conform to norms" (1937:76–77). Already in the unit act we see the integrative concerns that were to dominate Parsons throughout his life. Although he began with an interest in actors and their actions, he implied an interest in consciousness in terms of the voluntary choice of means to ends. But that choice is not free, which implies an interest on Parsons's part in the social structures that constrain action. Cultural entities such as norms and values play a key role here, as they do throughout Parsons's work.

Parsons's initial interest in the unit act has been the source of considerable confusion in interpreting his work, because he claimed that he never abandoned the unit act even in his later focus on larger-scale issues. Because in his early work Parsons sounds very much like a symbolic interactionist, it is difficult to reconcile this with his later structural-functional analysis of structures and institutions. Some (Toby, 1977; J. Turner, 1974) saw a considerable amount of symbolic interactionism in Parsonsian theory. For example, Jackson Toby said:

> By action, Parsons means the attempt to realize their symbolically defined intentions in symbolically defined environments. . . . It sounds as though Parsons is a symbolic interactionist in the Cooley-Mead-Blumer tradition. It ought to; there is no important intellectual distinction between the action frame of reference and that provided by symbolic interaction. Both perspectives insist that the meaning of behavior to the participants, a meaning provided by their common interpretation of shared symbols, is essential for sociological understanding.
>
> (Toby, 1977:2)

In a comment on Jonathan Turner's essay analyzing the similarities between his action approach and symbolic interactionism, Parsons indicated general agreement with this view of his work:

---

[1] As we saw in Chapter 7, Parsons's conception of the most elementary forms of social analysis does not coincide with that of such social behaviorists as George Homans.

In general I am entirely sympathetic with this position. . . . I think, at the very least, there is a very substantial area of overlap between social interaction theory, notably in the version presented by George Herbert Mead himself, and the theory of action. . . . They are, of course, by no means identical.

(Parsons, 1974:62)

The position taken in this book is similar to that taken by Herbert Blumer (1974), who argued that although Parsons's initial action orientation may have been similar in a number of ways to symbolic interactionism, the bulk of his theory, beginning with the last chapter of *The Structure of Social Action* in 1937, is devoted to the structural-functional analysis of large-scale structures—particularly what Parsons calls the social and cultural systems.

VOLUNTARISM

Intimately related to the unit act and the issue of the degree to which Parsons is a symbolic interactionist is Parsons's concept of voluntarism, which has been the subject of a hot debate. *Voluntarism*, a concept prominent in *The Structure of Social Action* (1937), pertains to actors who are seen as making choices in social situations (Procter, 1978). This is not to say that the actors are totally free in those choices; voluntarism is not equivalent to free will. Nevertheless, the concept of voluntarism clearly implies a mind, consciousness, and individuals making decisions. Parsons's focus on voluntarism in 1937 and the meaning of the concept are clear; the question is whether he abandoned voluntarism after 1937 and in the process moved from a small-scale to a large-scale sociology. John F. Scott (1963) is the strongest proponent of the idea that Parsons abandoned voluntarism after 1937 as part of a general abandonment of small-scale sociology. Jonathan Turner and Leonard Beeghley (1973; see also Münch, 1982) argue for continuity in Parsons's thinking, contending that he never abandoned the voluntaristic thesis. Scott's error, they say, was to equate voluntarism with free will. Parsons never argued for a free will position; instead, he always believed that individual choice is circumscribed by norms, values, ideas, situations, and so forth.

Problems in Parsons's Action Theory

The goal of integrating action and structure runs through a large portion of Parsons's work. This work has been applauded by some; however, others see it as "muddled" and "confused" (for example, Alexander, 1978; Menzies, 1977). These critics argue that Parsons began *The Structure of Social Action* as a micro-oriented action theorist, but that even before he finished that work, and progressively as the years passed, he moved more and more in the direction of a macro-oriented structural-functional theory. Some confusion is seen in Parsons's work as a result of his inability to give up older theoretical positions or to integrate them adequately with newer ones. As early as the preface to the second edition of *The Structure of Social Action*, Parsons spoke of his shift

from the analysis of the structure of social action as such to the structural-functional analysis of social systems. They are, of course, in the last analysis, systems of social action. But the structure of such systems is, in the newer version, treated not directly in action terms, but as "institutionalized patterns."

(Parsons, 1949:D)

TALCOTT PARSONS: A Biographical Sketch

Talcott Parsons was born in 1902 in Colorado Springs, Colorado. He came from a religious and intellectual background; his father was a Congregational minister, a professor, and ultimately president of a small college. Parsons got an undergraduate degree from Amherst College in 1924 and set out to do graduate work at the London School of Economics. In the next year, he moved on to Heidelberg, Germany. Max Weber had spent a large portion of his career at Heidelberg, and although he had died five years before Parsons arrived, Weber's influence survived and his widow continued to hold meetings in her home, meetings that Parsons attended. Parsons was greatly affected by Weber's work and ultimately wrote his doctoral thesis at Heidelberg dealing, in part, with Weber's work.

Parsons became an instructor at Harvard in 1927, and although he switched departments several times, Parsons remained at Harvard until his death in 1979. His career progress was not rapid; he did not obtain a tenured position until 1939. Two years previously, he had published *The Structure of Social Action*, a book that not only introduced major sociological theorists like Weber to large numbers of sociologists, but also laid the groundwork for Parsons's own developing theory.

After that, Parsons made rapid academic progress. He was made chairman of the Harvard sociology department in 1944 and two years later set up and chaired the innovative Department of Social Relations, which included not only sociologists, but a variety of other social scientists. By 1949 he had been elected president of the American Sociological Association. In the 1950s and into the 1960s, with the publication of such books as *The Social System* (1951), Parsons became the dominant figure in American sociology.

However, by the late 1960s, Parsons came under attack from the emerging radical wing of American sociology. Parsons was seen as being a political conservative, and his theory was seen as highly conservative and little more than an elaborate categorization scheme. But in the 1980s, we have begun to witness a resurgence in interest in Parsonsian theory not only in the United States, but around the world (Sciulli and Gerstein, 1985). Furthermore, Parsons's ideas are not only influencing conservative thinkers, but neo-Marxian theorists as well.

One view (Menzies, 1977), shared by this author, is that a basic problem of Parsons's work stems from his never having completed the shift from action theory to structural functionalism, with the result that the two theories are interrelated in a muddled fashion throughout his work. It is not that the integration of action theory and structural functionalism is impossible or undesirable; rather, it is that Parsons never did reconcile them adequately. They often stand side by side in his work rather than being intertwined.

Parsons's frequent use of two different definitions of many key concepts reflects the continuing duality of his theoretical orientation. For example, Ken Menzies (1977) said that in defining *deviance*, Parsons used both a structural-functional approach, emphasizing the larger system's failure to socialize the actor adequately, and an action theory approach, defining it as a "motivated tendency for an actor to behave in contravention of one or more institutionalized normative patterns" (Parsons, 1951:250).

Upon his death, a number of his former students, themselves sociologists of considerable note, reflected on Parsonsian theory as well as on the man behind the theory. In their musings, these sociologists offered some interesting insights into Parsons and his work. The few glimpses of Parsons reproduced here do not add up to a coherent picture, but they do offer some provocative glimpses of the man and his work.

Robert Merton was one of his students when Parsons was just beginning his teaching career at Harvard. Merton, who became a noted theorist in his own right, makes it clear that graduate students did not come to Harvard in those years to study with Parsons, but rather with Pitirim Sorokin, the senior member of the department, who was to become Parsons's archenemy:

> Of the very first generation of graduate students coming to Harvard . . . precisely none came to study with Talcott. They could scarcely have done so for the simplest of reasons: in 1931, he had no public identity whatever as a sociologist.

> Although we students came to study with the renowned Sorokin, a subset of us stayed to work with the unknown Parsons.
>
> (Merton, 1980:69)

Merton's reflections on Parsons's first course in theory are interesting too, especially because the material provided the basis for one of the most influential theory books in history:

> Long before Talcott Parsons became one of the Grand Old Men of world sociology, he was for an early few of us its Grand Young Man. This began with his first course in theory. . . . [It] would provide him with the core of his masterwork, *The Structure of Social Action* which . . . did not appear in print until five years after its first oral publication.
>
> (Merton, 1980:69–70)

Although all would not share Merton's positive evaluation of Parsons, they would acknowledge the following:

> The death of Talcott Parsons marks the end of an era in sociology. When [a new era] does begin . . . it will surely be fortified by the great tradition of sociological thought which he has left to us.
>
> (Merton, 1980:71)

In part, Parsons's integrative work is muddled because he never reconciled his Weberian action theory (as he interpreted Weber) with his Durkheimian structural functionalism.

This is the crucial ambiguity and problem in action theory. The approach was long perceived as oriented toward individual thought and action, but its two major exponents, Weber and Parsons, devoted most of their attention to the constraints imposed by cultural phenomena. This ambiguity is clarified when we realize that although Weber and Parsons assumed that actors were dynamic and creative, the bulk of their sociology was devoted to analyses of cultural constraints. Action theory was most influential in the development of such theories as symbolic interactionism and phenomenology, but because its major focus is on the societal level, it really should have had at least as large a role in the development of larger-scale theories. To give one example, the methodology of *verstehen* is usually interpreted as a tool for under-standing the relationship between consciousness and action, when it was in fact more useful and was in the past more likely to be used as a tool for understanding the nor-mative constraints on actors. The idea was for sociologists to put themselves in the place of the actors they were studying in order to understand the constraints on them.

Thus one of the main reasons for the decline of action theory was that certain confu-sions were built into it from the beginning. Also, most of its basic assumptions about consciousness, action, and interaction have been taken over and dealt with much more consistently by other micro-oriented theories—for example, symbolic interactionism, phenomenology, and ethnomethodology. These assumptions are quite compatible with other aspects of these theories, indeed they are probably more compatible with them than they ever were with the other components of action theory. Still it is unfortunate that the large-scale orientation of action theory seems to have largely been lost on these other theories. Even though action theory never really adequately integrated its large-scale and small-scale concerns, that does not mean that it could not be done. In Chapter 10 we will deal with a number of more successful efforts at macro-micro integration.

Recent Work in Action Theory

Recently, James Coleman (1986) has sought to revive action theory by returning to its roots in Parsons's 1937 work, *The Structure of Social Action*. He feels that Parsons made a mistake in abandoning his action theory developed in that work for structural functionalism. Coleman's basic argument is that we must not "discard notions of pur-pose, goal-directedness, and homeostasis (as is true in causal analyses that remain at the social system level), but to limit their employment to the level of *actors* in the social system—not positing them for the system itself" (1986:1312). Thus, Coleman seeks to move action theory back to its micro roots, although the actor for Coleman, as it was to Parsons, can be "either persons or corporate actors"[2] (1986:1312).

Also included in this genre is Sciulli's (1986) effort to clarify the meaning of volun-taristic action and to link it to work in legal theory. Without getting into the details of Sciulli's effort, we can say that its attempt to extend action theory in new directions as well as Coleman's effort to return to its original roots may ultimately help to resuscitate it.

SYSTEMS THEORY

Whereas action theory has declined since peaking in the 1930s and early 1940s, systems theory in less than two decades experienced a meteoric rise and a precipitous fall. Systems theory, which rose and fell in the 1960s and 1970s, has not yet fulfilled and may never fulfill the promise that its early supporters thought it had. As a result, in recent years it has lost some ground in sociology and today merits little more than a brief discussion.

Systems theory is the product of a variety of scientific ideas imported into sociology from other fields, including cybernetics, information theory, operations research, and

---

[2] We deal with some of the details of Coleman's analysis in the next chapter.

economic systems theory (Lilienfeld, 1978). These ideas were then remolded to apply to social life. In *Sociology and Modern Systems Theory* (1967), Walter Buckley answered the question of what sociology has to gain from systems theory.

First, because systems theory is derived from the hard sciences and because it is, at least in the eyes of its proponents, applicable to *all* behavioral and social sciences, it promises a common vocabulary to unify them. Second, systems theory is multileveled and can be applied equally well to the largest-scale and the smallest-scale, to the most objective and the most subjective, aspects of the social world. Third, systems theory is interested in the varied relationships of the many aspects of the social world and thus operates against piecemeal analyses of the social world. The argument of systems theory is that the intricate relationship of parts cannot be treated out of the context of the whole. Systems theorists reject the idea that society or other large-scale components of society should be treated as unified social facts. Instead, the focus is on relationships or processes at various levels within the social system. Buckley described the focus:

> The kind of system we are interested in may be described generally as a complex of elements or components directly or indirectly related in a causal network, such that each component is related to at least some others in a more or less stable way within any particular period of time.
>
> (Buckley, 1967:41)

Richard A. Ball offers a clear conception of the relational orientation of systems theory, or what he calls General Systems Theory (GST):

> GST begins with a processual conception of reality as consisting fundamentally of relationships among relationships, as illustrated in the concept of "gravity" as used in modern physics. The term "gravity" does not describe an entity at all. There is no such "thing" as gravity. It is *a set of relationships*. To think of these relationships as entities is to fall into reification. . . . The GST approach demands that sociologists develop the logic of relationships and conceptualize social reality in relational terms.
>
> (Ball, 1978:66)

Fourth, the systems approach tends to see all aspects of the sociocultural system in process terms, especially as networks of information and communication. Fifth, and perhaps most important, systems theory is inherently integrative. Buckley, in his definition of the perspective, saw it involving the integration of large-scale objective structures, symbol systems, action and interaction, and "consciousness and self-awareness." Ball also accepted the idea of integration of levels: "The individual and society are treated equally, not as separate entities but as mutually constitutive fields, related through various 'feedback' processes" (1978:68). In fact, systems theory is so attuned to integration that Buckley criticized the tendency of other sociologists to make analytical distinctions among levels:

> We note the tendency in much of sociology to insist on what is called an "analytical distinction" between "personality" (presumably intracranial), symbol systems (culture), and matrices of social relations (social systems), though the actual work of the proponents of the distinctions shows it to be misleading or often untenable in practice.
>
> (Buckley, 1967:101)

(Buckley was somewhat unfair here, because he did much the same thing throughout his own work. Making analytical distinctions is apparently acceptable to systems theorists as long as one is making such distinctions in order to make better sense out of the interrelationships among the various aspects of social life.) Finally, systems theory tends to see the social world in dynamic terms, with an overriding concern for "sociocultural emergence and dynamics in general" (Buckley, 1967:39).

Buckley discussed the relationship among sociocultural systems, mechanical systems, and organic systems. Buckley focused on delineating the essential differences among these systems. On a number of dimensions a continuum runs from mechanical systems to organic systems to sociocultural systems—going from least to most complexity of the parts, from least to most instability of the parts, and from lowest to highest degree to which the parts are attributable to the system as a whole.

On other dimensions, the systems differ qualitatively rather than simply quantitatively. In mechanical systems, the interrelationships of the parts are based on transfers of energy. In organic systems, the interrelationships of the parts are based more on exchange of information than on energy. In sociocultural systems, the interrelationships are based even more on information exchange.

The three types of systems also differ in the degree to which they are open or closed—that is, in the degree of interchange with aspects of the larger environment. A more open system is better able to respond selectively to a greater range and detail of the endless variety of the environment. In these terms, mechanical systems tend to be closed; organic systems more open; and sociocultural systems the most open of the three. The degree of openness of a system is related to two crucial concepts in systems theory: *entropy*, or the tendency of systems to run down; and *negentropy*, or the tendency of systems to elaborate structures. Closed systems tend to be entropic, whereas open systems tend to be negentropic. Sociocultural systems also tend to have more tension built into them than the other two. Finally, sociocultural systems can be purposive and goal-seeking because they receive feedback from the environment that allows them to keep moving toward their goals.

Feedback is an essential aspect of the cybernetic approach that systems theorists take to the social system. This is in contrast to the equilibrium approach, which is characteristic of many sociologists (for instance, Parsons) who purportedly operate from a systems approach. Using feedback enables cybernetic systems theorists to deal with friction, growth, evolution, and sudden changes. The openness of a social system to its environment and the impact of environmental factors on the system are important concerns to these systems theorists.

A variety of internal processes also affect social systems. Two other concepts are critical here. *Morphostasis* refers to those processes that help the system maintain itself, whereas *morphogenesis* refers to those processes that help the system change, grow more elaborate. Social systems develop more and more complex "mediating systems" that intervene between external forces and the action of the system. Some of these mediating systems help the system to maintain itself, and others help it to change. These mediating systems grow more and more independent, autonomous, and determinative of the actions of the system. In other words, these mediating systems permit the social system to grow less dependent on the environment.

These complex mediating systems perform a variety of functions in the social system. For example, they allow the system to adjust itself temporarily to external conditions. They can direct the system from harsh to more congenial environments. They can also allow the system to reorganize its parts in order to deal with the environment more effectively.

Buckley (1967) moved from a discussion of general principles to the specifics of the social world to show the applicability of systems theory. He began at the individual level, where he was very impressed by Mead's work, in which consciousness and action are interrelated. In fact, Buckley recast the Meadian problematic in systems theory terms. Action begins with a *signal* from the environment, which is transmitted to the actor. However, the transmission may be complicated by *noise* in the environment. When it gets through, the signal provides the actor with *information*. On the basis of this information, the actor is allowed to *select* a response. The key here is the actor's possession of a mediating mechanism—self-consciousness. Buckley discussed self-consciousness in the terminology of systems theory:

> In the language of cybernetics, such self-consciousness is a mechanism of internal feedback of the system's own states which may be mapped or compared with other information from the situation and from memory, permitting a selection from a repertoire of actions in a goal-directed manner that takes one's own self and behavior explicitly into account.
>
> (Buckley, 1967:100)

To Mead and the symbolic interactionists and systems theorists, consciousness is not separated from action and interaction, but rather is an integral part of both.

Despite his views that consciousness and interaction are interrelated and that levels should not be separated, Buckley did move from consciousness to the interactional domain. Patterns of interaction—namely, imitation and response—clearly fit into a systemic view of the world. More important, Buckley tied the interpersonal realm directly to the personality system; indeed, he saw the two as mutually determinative. Finally, Buckley turned to the large-scale organization of society, especially roles and institutions, which he saw in systemic terms and as related to, if not indistinguishable from, the other levels of social reality.

Buckley concluded by discussing some of the general principles of systems theory as they apply to the sociocultural domain. First, the systems theorist accepts the idea that tension is a normal, ever-present, and necessary reality of the social system. Second, there is a focus on the nature and sources of variety in the social system. The emphasis on both tension and variety makes the systems perspective a dynamic one. Third, there is a concern for the selection process at both the individual and the interpersonal levels, whereby the various alternatives open to the system are sorted and shifted. This lends further dynamism. Fourth, the interpersonal level is seen as the basis of the development of larger structures. The transactional processes of exchange, negotiation, and bargaining are the processes out of which emerge relatively stable social and cultural structures. Finally, despite the inherent dynamism of the systems approach, there is a recognition of the processes of perpetuation and transmission. As Buckley put it, "Out of the continuous transactions emerge some relatively stable accommodations and adjustments" (1967:160).

An interesting note: there are a number of rather striking similarities between systems theory and the dialectical approach, even though they are derived from extremely different sources (one scientific, the other philosophical) and have very different vocabularies (Ball, 1978). Similarities between them include a focus on relations, process, creativity, and tension.

Criticisms of Systems Theory

Despite the initial excitement about systems theory, it has failed to become the major sociological theory that most of its adherents had hoped. Robert Lilienfeld (1978) criticized systems theory on several grounds. He argued that when it has been employed in sociology, as well as in other fields, systems theory has been a failure. To exemplify this, Lilienfeld (citing Hoos) noted the case of the San Francisco Bay Area Rapid Transit system, which is based on a systems approach:

> The Bay Area Rapid Transit system . . . built lines through and to many places [which were] so laid waste by the protracted and inept construction stages that it may be years before former use patterns will be restored, if ever. Terminals are out in the fields and way stations stand as sole occupants of once prosperous and now desolate business sections.
>
> (Lilienfeld, 1978:123)

Lilienfeld found analogous, if not so enormous, failures in the products of sociological systems theorists.

Lilienfeld criticized the scientific pretensions of sociological systems theorists. He maintained that they tended to pick up details from the sciences that supported their view and to disregard those that did not. Lilienfeld also assailed the systems theorists' love of analogies (or "isomorphisms") between one field and another. Although these may be esthetically appealing, they are not necessarily accurate. Then Lilienfeld criticized the generality of systems theory, arguing that it "achieves its all-encompassing 'universality' only by its very abstractness," by ignoring "the specific, the concrete, the substantive" (1978:192).

Lilienfeld found systems theory to be highly speculative, a general problem that is exacerbated as systems theory "migrates" from the "hard" sciences to other fields, where it "becomes ever more loosely defined and impressionistic in usage" (1978: 277). He viewed it as a mixture of speculation and empirical data that is satisfying as neither. When systems theorists venture into the social world, their work suffers because of their ignorance of the way it works. Lilienfeld argued that no new findings based on systems theory can be found in any science. Finally, he contended that systems theory cannot be tested and thus cannot be proven right or wrong.

Lilienfeld concluded that systems theory should be seen more as an ideological system than as a scientific approach. He saw it as a form of consciousness and a way of interpreting and understanding the world that justifies and maintains specific relations of power. To Lilienfeld, systems theory not only supports the status quo but also tends to have authoritarian implications.

The future of systems theory is uncertain. Its openness to a multileveled, integrative approach to the social world is attractive, but it needs to overcome a number of its weaknesses before it will gain the broad sociological audience that it once promised to attract.

STRUCTURALISM

Although we have already looked at it several times in this book, it is now time to discuss structuralism systematically. What, exactly, is structuralism? We can define *structuralism* as the search for the "universal and invariant laws of humanity that are operative at all levels of human life—at the most primitive and at the most advanced" (Ekeh, 1982:128).

Although structuralism is a relatively recent development in the intellectual world in general and sociology in particular, in the view of some it is already in the process of being revised or even superseded. Writing about French structuralism (still the heart of structuralism in general), Edith Kurzweil said, "In Paris, the structuralist age is nearly over" (1980:2). Kurzweil (and others) have written about the development of "post-structuralism," while others are discussing "neostructuralism" (Wuthnow et al., 1984). Although structuralism may be in the process of change or even of being changed radically, it remains of relevance to contemporary sociological theory, which is just now being dramatically affected by it (Rossi, 1982; 1983).

Roots in Linguistics

Structuralism is emerging from diverse developments in various fields. The source of modern structuralism and its strongest bastion to this day is linguistics. The work of Ferdinand de Saussure (1857–1913) stands out in the development of structural linguistics and, ultimately, structuralism in various other fields (Culler, 1976). Of particular interest to us is Saussure's differentiation between *langue* and *parole*, which was to have enormous significance. *Langue* is the formal, grammatical system of language. It is a system of phonic elements whose relationships are governed, Saussure and his followers believed, by determinate laws. Much of linguistics since Saussure's time has been oriented to the discovery of those laws. The existence of *langue* makes *parole* possible. *Parole* is actual speech, the way that speakers use language to express themselves. Although Saussure recognized the significance of people's use of language in subjective and often idiosyncratic ways, he believed that that cannot be the concern of the scientifically oriented linguist. Such a linguist must look at *langue*, the formal system of language, not at the subjective ways in which it is used by actors.

The concern for structure has been extended beyond language to the study of all sign systems. This focus on the structure of sign systems has been labeled *semiotics* and has attracted many followers (Hawkes, 1977). Semiotics is broader than structural linguistics, because it encompasses not only language but also other sign and symbol systems, such as facial expressions, body language, literary texts, indeed all forms of communication.

Many of the fields to which structuralism has been extended are concerned in one way or another with communication. These include Marxism, psychiatry, the plastic arts, musical theater, literary criticism, philosophy, and—most important for the development of a structural sociology—anthropology, especially in the work of Claude Lévi-Strauss (Ehrmann, 1970; Rossi, 1982). Although there are a number of similarities in the use of structuralism in these various fields, there are also a number of important differences. Structuralism is far from a unified perspective at the present time.

Anthropological Structuralism: Claude Lévi-Strauss

The most important work in structuralism (Kurzweil calls Lévi-Strauss "the father of structuralism" [1980:13]) as far as sociology is concerned, has been done in anthropology by Claude Lévi-Strauss. Over the years he has produced an enormous body of complex work that has dramatically altered the field of anthropology—and other fields as well. Structuralists in sociology have been influenced strongly by Lévi-Strauss's work.

One of the reasons for the complexity of Lévi-Strauss's work is that various types of structures are to be found in it. The first type, the large-scale structures and institutions of the social world, is the kind that he took pains to deny are structures. Although these are structural realities to most anthropologists and sociologists, to Lévi-Strauss they serve to conceal the real underlying structures of society. This leads to the second, and more important, type of structure in Lévi-Strauss's work, the model that the social scientist constructs to get at the underlying structure of society. But there is a third, and most important, type of structure to Lévi-Strauss, and that is the structure of the human mind (Leach, 1974). The models of the social world that social scientists construct take similar forms in diverse societies because human products around the world have the same basic source, the human mind. *It is the structure of the mind that is the ultimate structure in Lévi-Strauss's work.*

At one level, Lévi-Strauss can be seen as simply extending Saussure's work on language to anthropological issues—for example, to myths in primitive societies. However, Lévi-Strauss went further and applied structuralism more broadly to all forms of communication. His major innovation was to reconceptualize a wide array of social phenomena (for instance, kinship systems) as systems of communication and thereby make them amenable to structural analysis (Burris, 1979). The exchange of spouses, for example, can be analyzed in the same way as the exchange of words. Both are social exchanges that can be studied through the use of structural anthropology.

We can illustrate Lévi-Strauss's (1967) thinking with the example of the similarities between linguistic systems and kinship systems. First, terms used to describe kinship, like phonemes in language, are basic units of analysis to the structuralist. Second, neither the kinship terms nor phonemes have meaning in themselves. Instead, both acquire meaning only when they are integral parts of a larger system. The overall structure of the system gives each of the component parts meaning. Third, Lévi-Strauss admitted that there is empirical variation from setting to setting in both phonemic and kinship systems, but even these variations can be traced to the operation of general, although implicit, laws. Finally, and ultimately in terms of Lévi-Strauss's sense of structure, both phonemic systems and kinship systems are the products of the structures of the mind. However, they are not the products of a conscious process. Instead, they are the products of the unconscious, logical structure of the mind. These systems, as well as the logical structure of the mind from which they are derived, operate on the basis of general laws.

Lévi-Strauss subjected anthropological data to structural analysis in much the same way that Saussure analyzed linguistic data. In contrast, most anthropologists and sociologists, for that matter, are likely to accept the subjective reports of respondents. To Lévi-Strauss, such reports are simply the basic resources out of which to construct the underlying structures. In his analyses of primitive societies, Lévi-Strauss was interested in uncovering the underlying structure of myths and kinship systems, indeed of the entire society.

Although Lévi-Strauss devoted his attention to primitive societies, he believed that all societies, including modern ones, have a similar underlying structure. He focused on primitive societies because there is less distortion and it is easier to discover the structure. In modern societies, a series of conscious models, or normative systems, have been developed to conceal the structural reality. Lévi-Strauss did not totally denigrate the importance of such models. These normative systems, including their biases and distortions, are important products of people in a society. However, these systems are not of primary importance, because "cultural norms are not of themselves structures" (Lévi-Strauss, 1967:274).

Most anthropologists study what people say and do, but Lévi-Strauss was more concerned with their human products (Rossi, 1974b). He was concerned with the objective structure of these products, not their subjective meanings or their origins in subjective processes. In looking at various human products—myths, kinship systems, and others—Lévi-Strauss was interested in their interrelationships. The charting of such interrelationships is *the* structure or at least a structure. Because a structure is created by the observer, different observers can construct different structures. Two important points need to be underscored here. First, structures are the creations of observers. Second, the structures that are created do not exist in the real world. As Lévi-Strauss put it, "The term 'social structure' has nothing to do with empirical reality but with models which are built up after it" (1967:271).

Lévi-Strauss was not interested in simply charting the structure of a simple primitive society. Rather, his concern was in comparing a wide array of available data on a number of such societies. He hoped that such comparative analyses would yield an underlying structure common to all societies. Although he searched for such structure, Lévi-Strauss did not adopt the dogmatic point of view that structures are the same for all places and for all times. Contrary to the view of most observers, he saw flexibility in his system.

Lévi-Strauss rejected the traditional orientations of anthropologists. For example, he rejected the idea that myths can be explained either by their narrative content or by their functions for society. Instead, the meaning of myths must be sought at the unconscious structural level. Lévi-Strauss's methodology for analysis of myths can be broken down into a series of steps. First, he would examine a number of variants of a particular myth. Second, he would isolate in these variants the basic thematic elements. Third, he would chart the complex patterns in which thematic elements within each variant are interwoven. Fourth, he would construct "a table of possible permutations between these terms" (Lévi-Strauss, 1963:16). Fifth, the table itself would become the structure, "the general object of analysis which, at this level only, can yield necessary connections, the empirical phenomenon considered at the beginning being only one possible combination among others'' (Lévi-Strauss, 1963:16). Finally, such a table, or structure, would allow the analyst not only to understand the myth in general but also to hypothesize about the meaning of a particular myth within a particular society.

On the surface, it would appear that Lévi-Strauss's structures are the same as Durkheim's social facts; both seem to have a life of their own that is external to, and coercive of, the actor. However, Lévi-Strauss did not operate at the societal level, at the level of social facts. Lévi-Strauss was influenced by Durkheim's later work on primitive classification rather than his earlier work on social facts. Lévi-Strauss's actors are constrained, but not by social facts. People, in his view, are constrained by the structures of the mind.

Perhaps, then, it was Sigmund Freud, not Durkheim, who was closest to Lévi-Strauss in orientation and a major influence on his work. It would appear that Lévi-Strauss accepted the view of Freudian psychiatry that actors are determined by unconscious forces. Although Lévi-Strauss was interested in the unconscious, there is a crucial difference between Lévi-Strauss and Freud on this issue (Rossi, 1974a). Freud conceived of the unconscious largely in terms of its hidden emotional content; actors are seen as impelled by emotions that are unknown to them at a conscious level. However, Lévi-Strauss was clearly not interested in the emotional aspects of the unconscious; his focus in the unconscious was "the permanent and logical structures of the mind" (Rossi, 1974a:19). Lévi-Strauss's actors are constrained not by unconscious emotions, but by the unconscious, logical structures of their minds. Here is one way in which Lévi-Strauss expressed his interest in the unconscious:

> If, as we believe to be the case, the unconscious activity of the mind consists in imposing forms upon content, and, if these forms are fundamentally the same for all minds—ancient or modern, primitive or civilized . . . then it is necessary and sufficient to grasp the unconscious structure underlying each institution and each custom in order to obtain a principle of interpretation valid for other institutions and other customs, provided, of course, that the analysis is carried far enough.
>
> (Lévi-Strauss, 1967:21–22)

Lévi-Strauss's view, of course, led to a problem common in the social sciences: that the mind is not accessible to immediate observation (Scheffler, 1970). This caused Lévi-Strauss to focus on the human products discussed above and their interrelationships. Here his interest was not in those products in themselves, but in what they can tell us about the logical structure of the mind. Thus his studies of the structure of the primitive world in general and kinship and mythical systems in particular are not ends in themselves but rather means to help him understand basic mental structures.

In his search for the basic structures of the mind, it would seem that Lévi-Strauss undertook a project resembling those of at least some phenomenologists. However, Lévi-Strauss, like most structuralists, had a deep distaste for phenomenology (Petit, 1975). In his view, phenomenologists seek to place human, subjective consciousness at the center of the social sciences. To structuralists, consciousness is not amenable to scientific analysis. Whereas phenomenologists (and others associated with this approach, such as ethnomethodologists and existentialists) are seen as engaged in an effort to humanize the social sciences, structuralists almost self-consciously seek to *dehumanize* those fields. They want to remove people from the center of the social sciences and substitute various structures, such as the logical structure of the mind, language, various components of society, or society in general. Charles Lemert (1979), for example, was pleased to see that the social sciences are witnessing the approach of the demise of people as the heart of their fields. In the view of most structuralists, a focus on people, especially on their subjective processes, retards, if not prevents, the development of social *science*. To engage in a science, the focus must shift from people to some sort of objective structure.

Lévi-Strauss's orientation and interest in mental structures would suggest that he was engaged in an enterprise similar to that undertaken by the philosopher Immanuel Kant. Although there are some similarities, there is also a crucial difference between them. As a philosopher, Kant sought to uncover the basic mental categories through introspection or philosophizing or both. As a social *scientist*, Lévi-Strauss rejected such methods and sought instead to examine empirically the structures of the social world, in order to shed light on mental structures.

Thus, although it seems that Lévi-Strauss was doing work resembling that of a number of other thinkers, a closer examination indicates important differences between Lévi-Strauss and all of them. Indeed, this is a measure of Lévi-Strauss's distinctive and important contribution to the social sciences.

Somewhat harshly, Kurzweil concludes, "Structuralism as originally conceived by Lévi-Strauss is dead. The universal mental structures have not emerged, albeit no one any longer searches for them" (1980:10). Nevertheless, she recognizes that Lévi-Strauss laid the groundwork for other types of structuralism as well as poststructuralism.

Structural Marxism

In addition to the anthropological structuralism of Lévi-Strauss, another important variant of structuralism is the French structural Marxism which we discussed in Chapter 8.

In this section, we focus on what is distinctive about French structural Marxism, differentiating it from other varieties of structuralism, particularly that of Lévi-Strauss. First, however, we will look at the similarities between structuralism in general and structural Marxism (Glucksmann, 1974)—in other words, the reasons that the work of Althusser, Poulantzas, and others *is* structuralism.

Although we have presented the case that modern structuralism began with Saussure's work in linguistics, there are those who argue that it started with the work of Karl Marx: "When Marx assumes that structure is not to be confused with visible relations and explains their hidden logic, he inaugurates the modern structuralist tradition" (Godelier, 1972b:336). Although structural Marxism and structuralism in general are both interested in "structures," each field conceptualizes structure differently.

At least some structural Marxists share with structuralists an interest in the study of structure as a prerequisite to the study of history. As Maurice Godelier said: "The study of the internal functioning of a structure must precede and illuminate the study of its genesis and evolution" (1972b:343). In another work, Godelier said, "The inner *logic* of these systems must be analyzed *before* their *origin* is analyzed'' (1972a:xxi). Another view shared by structuralists and structural Marxists is that structuralism should be concerned with the structures, or systems, that are formed out of the interplay of social relations. Both schools see structures as real (albeit invisible), although they differ markedly on the nature of the structure that they consider real. For Lévi-Strauss, the real structure is the model, whereas for structural Marxists it is the underlying structure of society.

Perhaps most important, both structuralism and structural Marxism reject empiricism and accept a concern for underlying invisible structures. Godelier argued: ''What both structuralists and Marxists reject are the empiricist definitions of what constitutes a social structure'' (1972a:xviii). Godelier also made this statement:

> For Marx as for Lévi-Strauss a structure is *not* a reality that is *directly* visible, and so directly observable, but a *level of reality* that exists *beyond* the visible relations between men, and the functioning of which constitutes the underlying logic of the system, the subjacent order by which the apparent order is to be explained.
>
> (Godelier, 1972a:xix)

Godelier went even further and argued that such a pursuit defines all science: ''What is visible is a *reality* concealing *another*, deeper reality, which is hidden and the discovery of which is the very purpose of scientific cognition'' (1972a:xxiv).

Despite the similarities between structural Marxism and structuralism, in general there are major differences between structuralism (Marxian and non-Marxian) and at least the main thrust of Marxian theory. First, the two schools use different modes of logic. Marxists generally adopt dialectical reasoning, whereas structuralists are more inclined to employ analytic reason. Structuralists expound on the need to do synchronic studies; Marxists are more likely to see the need for diachronic analyses. Humanistic Marxists are likely to focus on the human subject, but structuralists (Marxian and non-Marxian) see such a concern as nonscientific (Burris, 1979). Marxists believe that theory can help in social change. The argument of the structuralists is that, given the universality of certain structures and that people, especially in modern society, are inclined to mystify the social world, the chance of meaningful political change is small (Glucksmann, 1974).

Perhaps the ultimate difference between structuralism in general and Marxism in general lies in their levels of analysis. In Val Burris's (1979) terms, the difference is between materialism and psychological reductionism. Marxists tend to focus on the structures of society (economic, political, ideological), whereas structuralists are concerned with the ''deep structures'' of the mind. Thus Marx and most Marxists are concerned with the underlying logic of the large-scale structures of capitalist society. Although structuralists may deal with large-scale structures, it is usually not as an end in itself, but only a means to understand the ultimate subject, the structure of the mind. Some structuralists are interested in the societal level and some Marxists in structures of the mind, but there is a basic difference in focus.

In this light, it is interesting to underscore a point made by Godelier. As a French structural Marxist trained in Lévi-Strauss's structuralism, Godelier was in a good position to analyze the relationship between French structural Marxism and structuralism.

Although he recognized some overlap and some differences, Godelier argued for an integration of the two, so that their strengths would be fused and their weaknesses overcome. For example, in discussing the weaknesses in Lévi-Strauss's work, Godelier stated that:

> What is lacking is analysis of the precise functions of these forms of thought, of the circulation of these forms of ideology with other levels of social reality, and of the conditions of their transformation. . . . To go further than a structural morphology means, therefore, trying to account for the forms, functions, modes of articulation and conditions of transformation of the social structures within the concrete societies studied by the historian and the anthropologist. It is precisely in order to accomplish this complex task, which presupposes a combination of several theoretical methods, that Marx's hypothesis of the determination, in the last analysis, of the forms and the evolution of societies by the conditions of production and reproduction of their material life is needed as the central hypothesis.
>
> (Godelier, 1972a:xli)

Godelier's main sympathies seem to lie with Marxism. However, true integration would require serious attention to the strengths and weaknesses of both orientations.

Sociological Variants

Structuralism holds a number of attractions for sociologists, especially those oriented to the development of a science of sociology (Goddard, 1976). For example, it has a highly abstract system of thought that allows a good deal of analytical rigor. It promises the possibility of formal modeling as well as the use of sophisticated statistical and mathematical techniques. It also seems to offer a transhistorical perspective on social life. Above all, it offers a perspective with great scope capable of dealing with everything from the structure of the mind to the structure of society to the structure of the natural world.

For these reasons and others, at least some sociologists have gravitated toward a structuralist orientation in recent years. For example, some ethnomethodologists, most notably Aaron Cicourel, have sought to employ a structuralist orientation. Cicourel argued that ethnomethodologists should be interested in actors' basic interpretive procedures, which he sees as being "like deep structure grammatical rules" (1974:27). Interestingly, Cicourel, with his roots in ethnomethodology, a "creative sociology," saw these deep structures in a nondeterministic way, that is, as generating *innovative* responses to social situations.

GOFFMAN'S STRUCTURALISM

The work of Erving Goffman, especially his later works, including *Frame Analysis* (1974), also illustrates the drift toward structuralism. George Gonos argued that Goffman's work constitutes "an American variant of contemporary structuralism" (1977: 854). Goffman looked beyond and behind everyday situations in a search for the structures that invisibly govern them. These are "'schemata of interpretation' that enable individuals 'to locate, perceive, identify, and label' occurrences within their life space and the world at large. By rendering events or occurrences meaningful, frames function to organize experience and guide action, whether individual or collective" (Snow et al.,

1986:464). Goffman labeled these invisible structures *frames*. Although situations may vary in their particularities, the frames retain stable rules of operation. Gonos provided other structural characteristics of frames:

> From Goffman's analyses of particular framed activities, we can derive certain principal characteristics of frames. A frame is not conceived as a loose, somewhat accidental amalgamation of elements put together over a short time-span. Rather, it is constituted of a set number of essential components, having a definite arrangement and stable relations. These components are not gathered from here and there, as are the elements of a situation, but are always found together as a system. The standard components cohere and are complete. . . . Other less essential elements are present in any empirical instance and lend some of their character to the whole. . . . In all this, frames are very close in conception to "structures."
>
> (Gonos, 1977:860)

To George Gonos (1980), frames are largely rules or laws that fix interaction. The rules are usually unconscious and ordinarily nonnegotiable. Among the rules identified by Gonos are those that define "how signs are to be 'interpreted,' how outward indications are to be related to 'selves,' and what 'experience' will accompany activity" (1980:160). Gonos concludes, "Goffman's problematic thus promotes the study not of observable interaction of 'everyday life' as such, but its eternal structure and ideology; not of situations, but of their frames" (p. 160). Goffman seems to be offering a conception of structures of interaction that promises the possibility of integration with Lévi-Strauss's mental structures and the French structural Marxists' large-scale structures.

BARRIERS TO ACCEPTANCE

Despite these trends, structuralism has far to go to achieve widespread acceptance in sociology. There are some almost insurmountable barriers it must overcome. As David Goddard (1976) so well understood, structuralism not only has little to offer to traditional sociological concerns, but also constitutes a deep threat to those interests. For example, structuralists are generally little interested in such traditional small-scale sociological topics as creative consciousness, actors, action, behavior, and interaction. The actor and various individual-level processes are difficult to find in structuralism. Moreover, structuralism, except for French structural Marxism, seems almost totally inapplicable to the traditional large-scale concerns of sociologists:

> To put it bluntly, if there were laws of structural organization in large-scale, heterogeneous societies—laws relating to significant phenomena such as class, bureaucracy, power, change, development, solidarity, and the varied interrelations between these phenomena—structural analysis could not provide the requisite assumptions, methods or theories which would lead to the discovery of such laws.
>
> (Goddard, 1976:126)

To Goddard and many others, structuralism represents a frontal assault on many of the basic premises of sociology. In fact, Goddard saw dire consequences should sociology adopt a structural paradigm because such an approach would "compromise absolutely what is perhaps its own fundamental premise . . . that ideas and symbols are formed in their material context of given social milieux . . . the idea of a sociological materialism which inaugurated sociology as a special discipline would have to be completely abandoned'' (1976:132). Given such harsh attacks, it will be difficult for structuralism to achieve general acceptance in sociology.

Poststructuralism: The Ideas of Michel Foucault

We turn now to the ideas of a contemporary French theorist, Michel Foucault (1926–1984), whose work is associated with both structuralism and poststructuralism. Although Foucault's work spreads far beyond the borders of sociology, there is clearly a sociology or maybe several sociologies in it (Smart, 1985). It is a wide-ranging body of work encompassing methodological concerns (Foucault, 1966; 1969) as well as specific empirical studies of madness and the asylum (Foucault, 1965), medicine and the birth of clinical practice (Foucault, 1975), crime and the carceral system (Foucault, 1979), and sex and social control over sexuality (Foucault, 1980; 1985). It is a body of work that is relevant not only to sociological theory, but also to a variety of subfields within sociology. In addition to being wide-ranging, Foucault's work is also dense and subject to multiple interpretations. Further complicating matters is the fact that Foucault is purposely elusive: "Do not ask who I am and do not ask me to remain the same" (1969:17). In fact, Foucault did not remain the same; his work showed important shifts over the course of his career.

Foucault's work also shows a variety of theoretical inputs (Smart, 1985). This variety makes Foucault's work provocative and difficult to handle. Furthermore, the ideas are not simply adopted from other thinkers but transformed as they are integrated into Foucault's unusual theoretical orientation. Thus, Weber's theory of rationalization has an impact, but to Foucault it only is found in certain "key sites," and it is not an "iron cage"; there is always resistance. Marxian ideas (Smart, 1983) are found in Foucault's work, but Foucault does not restrict himself to the economy; he focuses on a range of institutions. He is more interested in the "micro-politics of power" than in the traditional Marxian concern with power at the societal level. He practices hermeneutics in order to better understand the social phenomena of concern to him. Moreover, Foucault has no sense of some deep, ultimate truth; there are simply ever more layers to be peeled away. There is a phenomenological influence, but Foucault rejects the idea of an autonomous, meaning-giving subject. There is a strong element of structuralism but no formal rule-governed model of behavior. Finally, and perhaps most importantly, Foucault adopts Nietzsche's interest in the relationship between power and knowledge, but that link is analyzed much more sociologically by Foucault.

Although a number of theoretical labels fit Foucault, at least in part, we have opted to discuss his work under the general heading of structuralism and more particularly poststructuralism. As we will see, structuralism had a strong influence on Foucault's early work but tended to recede in importance in the later work (hence the label poststructuralist). Not only is Foucault often thought of as a poststructuralist, but he also is included under the heading of "postmodernist." If we associate modernity with such terms as rationality, purpose, totalization, synthesis, and determinacy, then *postmodernity* is a world characterized by such antithetical concepts as irrationality, play, deconstruction, antithesis, and indeterminacy (*Theory, Culture and Society*, 1985). We will see how Foucault looks at the world in such a postmodern way.

Foucault clearly is a theorist to be reckoned with, and his work is likely to continue to attract interest and attention. In this relatively brief section, we can do little more than give the reader a sense of his work by first looking at his conceptual work and then turning to some of his specific studies.

In his early work on methodology, Foucault (1966) is doing an "archaeology of knowledge." His objects of study are bodies of knowledge, ideas, modes of discourse. He contrasts his archaeology of knowledge to history and the history of ideas, both of which he regards as too rational and as seeing too much continuity in the history of knowledge. Alan Sheridan contends that Foucault's archaeology of knowledge involves a search for "a set of rules of formation that determine the conditions of possibility of all that can be said within the particular discourse at any given time" (1980: 48). Here, clearly, we see the influence of structuralism. Foucault wants to study discursive events, spoken and written statements. He is particularly interested in early statements in the history of a field. He wants to uncover the basic conditions that make discourse possible. The unity of these statements, the way that they come to form a science or a discipline, does not come from the subject, but rather from basic discursive rules and practices. More specifically, Foucault was interested in the basic discursive practices that formed the base of scientific discourse, particularly in the human sciences. This highly structural approach in Foucault's early work was later abandoned because it was silent on the issue of power as well as on the link between knowledge and power.

Foucault's (1969) later orientation is best caught by the phrase "genealogy of power." Here he borrows heavily from Nietzsche, who is thought of as a philosopher of power. Foucault is concerned with how people govern themselves and others through the production of knowledge. Among other things, he sees knowledge generating power by constituting people as subjects and then governing the subjects with the knowledge. He is critical of the hierarchization of knowledge. Because the highest-ranking forms of knowledge (the sciences) have the greatest power, they are singled out for the most severe critique. Foucault is interested in techniques, the technologies that are derived from knowledge (especially scientific knowledge), and how they are used by various institutions to exert power over people. Although he sees links between knowledge and power, Foucault does not see a conspiracy by elite members of society. Such a conspiracy would imply conscious actors whereas Foucault is more inclined to see structural relationships, especially between knowledge and power. Looking over the sweep of history, Foucault does not see progress from primitive brutishness to more modern humaneness based on more sophisticated knowledge systems. Instead, Foucault sees history lurching from one system of domination (based on knowledge) to another. Although this is a generally bleak image, on the positive side Foucault believes that knowledge-power is always contested; there is always ongoing resistance to it. Foucault looks at historical examples, but he is primarily interested in the modern world. As he puts it, he is "writing the history of the present" (Foucault, 1979:31).

With this background, let us look at some of Foucault's specific, substantive works. In *Madness and Civilization* (1965), Foucault is doing an archaeology of knowledge, specifically of psychiatry. He begins with the Renaissance, when madness and reason were not separated. However, between 1650 and 1800 (the classical period), distance between them is established, and, ultimately, reason comes to subjugate madness. In other words, he is describing "a broken dialogue" between reason and madness (Foucault, 1965:x). Foucault describes the end result:

> Here reason reigned in the pure state, in a triumph arranged for it in advance over a frenzied unreason. Madness was thus torn from that imaginary freedom which still allowed it to flourish on the Renaissance horizon. Not so long ago, it had floundered about in broad daylight: in *King Lear*, in *Don Quixote*. But in less than a half-century, it had been sequestered and, in the fortress of confinement, bound to Reason, to the rules of morality and to their monotonous nights.
> (Foucault, 1965:64)

There is a clear Weberian, iron-cage imagery here—the "monotonous nights" to be spent by the "mad" (the irrational) in the iron cage constructed by those with reason (rationality).

The scientific psychology of the nineteenth century eventually arose out of the separation of the mad from the sane in the eighteenth century (psychiatry is labeled a "monologue of reason about madness" [Foucault, 1965:xi]). At first, medicine was in charge of the physical and moral treatment of the mad, but later scientific psychological medicine took over the moral treatment." A purely psychological medicine was made possible only when madness was alienated in guilt" (pp. 182–183). Later, Foucault says, "What we call psychiatric practice is a certain moral tactic contemporary with the end of the eighteenth century, preserved in the rights of asylum life, and overlaid by the myths of positivism" (p. 276). Thus, for Foucault psychology (and psychiatry) is a moral enterprise, not a scientific endeavor, aimed against the mad, who are progressively unable to protect themselves from this "help." He sees the mad as being sentenced by so-called scientific advancement to a "gigantic moral imprisonment."

Needless to say, Foucault here rejects the idea that over the years we have seen scientific, medical, and humanitarian advances in the treatment of the mad. What he sees, instead, are increases in the ability of the sane and their agents (physicians, psychologists, psychiatrists) to oppress and repress the mad who, we should not forget, had been on equal footing with the sane in the seventeenth century. The most recent development is that now the mad are less judged by these external agents; "madness is ceaselessly called upon to judge itself" (p. 265). In many senses such internalized control is the most repressive form of control. Clearly, Foucault's archaeology of knowledge leads him to very different conclusions from traditional historians about the history and current status of the mad and their relationship to the sane (and their agents). In addition, he is looking at the roots of the human sciences (especially psychology and psychiatry) in the distinction between the mad and the sane and the exertion of moral control over the mad. This is part of his more general thesis about the role of the human sciences in the moral control of people.

As for Foucault's structuralism in this early work, he argues that madness occurs at two "levels," and at "a deeper level madness is a form of discourse" (p. 96). Specifically, madness, at least in the classical age, is not mental or physical changes; instead, "delirious language is the ultimate truth of madness" (p. 97). But there is an even broader structuralism operating in this early work: "let classical culture formulate, *in its general structure*, the experience it had of madness, an experience which crops up with the same meanings, in the identical order of its inner logic, in both the order of speculation and in the order of institutions, in *both discourse and decree*, in both word and watchword—wherever, in fact, a signifying element can assume for us the value of a language" (p. 116; italics added).

Foucault continues to use a structuralist method in *The Birth of the Clinic* in which he focuses on medical discourse and its underlying structure: "What counts in the things said by men is not so much what they may have thought or the extent to which these things represent their thoughts, as *that which systematizes them from the outset*, thus making them thereafter endlessly accessible to new discourses and open to the task of transforming them" (1975:xiv; italics added).

In *Madness and Civilization*, medicine was an important precursor of the human sciences, and that is an even more central theme in *The Birth of the Clinic*. (As Foucault said, "the science of man . . . was medically . . . based" [1975:36]). Prior to the nineteenth century, medicine was a classificatory science, and the focus was on a clearly ordered system of diseases. But in the nineteenth century, medicine came to focus on diseases as they existed in individuals and the larger society (epidemics). Medicine came to be extended to healthy people (preventive care), and it adopted a normative posture distinguishing between healthy and unhealthy and, later, normal and pathological states. Medicine had become, again, a forerunner of the human sciences that were to adopt this normal-pathological stance toward people.

As yet, however, there was no clinical structure in medicine. The key was the development of the clinic where patients were observed in bed. Here Foucault uses a key term, the *gaze*, in this case a "gaze that was at the same time knowledge" (p. 81). In other words, knowledge was derived from what physicians could see in contrast to what they read in books. As a structuralist, Foucault saw the gaze as a kind of language, "a language without words" (p. 68), and he was interested in the deep structure of that "language." The ability to see and touch (especially in autopsies) sick (or dead) people was a crucial change and an important source of knowledge. Foucault says of the autopsy, "the living night is dissipated in the brightness of death" (p. 146). Foucault sees the anatomo-clinical gaze as the "great break" in Western medicine. Thus, there was not an evolution of knowledge, but an epistemic change. Doctors were no longer playing the same game; it was a different game with different rules. *The* game was that people (patients) had become the object of scientific knowledge and practice (instead of the disease as an entity). In terms of his structuralist orientation, what had changed was the nature of discourse—names of diseases, groupings, field of objects, and so forth (p. 54).

Once again, medicine takes on for Foucault the role of forerunner to the human sciences. "It is understandable, then, that medicine should have had such importance in the constitution of the sciences of man—an importance that is not only methodological, but ontological, in that it concerns man's becoming an object of positive knowledge" (Foucault, 1975:197). Specifically on the medical autopsy, Foucault says, "Death left its old tragic heaven and became the lyrical core of man: his invisible truth, his visible secret" (p. 172). In fact, for Foucault the broader change is the individual as subject and object of his own knowledge, and the change in medicine is but one "of the more visible witnesses to these changes in the fundamental structures of experience" (p. 199).

Many of the same themes appear in *Discipline and Punish* (Foucault, 1979), but now we see more of the genealogy of power and much less on structuralism, discourse, and the like. Here "power and knowledge directly imply one another" (Foucault, 1979:27). Foucault here is concerned with the period between 1757 and the 1830s, a period during which the torture of prisoners was replaced by control over them by prison rules. (Characteristically, Foucault sees this change developing in an irregular way; it does not evolve rationally.) The general view is that this represented a humanization of the treatment of criminals; it had grown more kind, less painful, and less cruel. The reality, from Foucault's point of view, was that punishment had grown more rationalized ("the executioner [in the guillotine] need be no more than a meticulous watchman" [p. 13]) and in many ways impinged more on prisoners. The early torture of prisoners may have made for good public displays, but it was "a bad economy of power" because it tended to incite unrest among the viewers of the spectacle (p. 79). The link between knowledge and power was clear in the case of torture; with the development of rules, that link became far less clear. The new system of rules was "more regular, more effective, more constant, and more detailed in its effects; in short, which increase its effects while diminishing its economic cost" (pp. 80–81). The new system was not designed to be more humane, but "to punish better . . . to insert the power to punish more deeply into the social body" (p. 82). In contrast to torture, this new technology of the power to punish occurred earlier in the deviance process, was more numerous, more bureaucratized, more efficient, more impersonal, more invariable, more sober, and involved the surveillance not just of criminals but of the entire society.

This new technology, a technology of disciplinary power, was based on the military model. It did not involve a single overarching power system, but rather a system of micro-powers. He describes a "micro-physics of power" with "innumerable points of confrontation" (pp. 26–27). Foucault identifies three instruments of disciplinary power. The first is *hierarchical observation*, or the ability of officials to oversee all they control with a single *gaze*. Second is the ability to make *normalizing judgments* and to punish those who violate the norms. Thus, one might be negatively judged and punished on the dimensions of time (for being late), activity (for being inattentive), and behavior (for being impolite). Third is the use of *examination* to observe subjects and to make normalizing judgments about people. The third instrument of disciplinary power involves the other two.

Foucault does not simply take a negative view toward the growth of the disciplinary society; he sees that it has positive consequences as well. For example, he sees discipline as functioning well within the military and industrial factories. However, Foucault communicates a genuine fear of the spread of discipline, especially as it moves into the state-police network for which the entire society becomes a field of perception and an object of discipline.

Foucault does not see discipline sweeping uniformly through society. Instead, he sees it "swarming" through society and affecting bits and pieces of society as it goes. Eventually, however, most major institutions are affected. Foucault asks rhetorically, "Is it surprising that prisons resemble factories, schools, barracks, hospitals, which all resemble prisons?" (p. 228). In the end, Foucault sees the development of a carceral system in which discipline is transported "from the penal institution to the entire social body" (p. 298). Although there is an iron-cage image here, as usual Foucault sees the operation of forces in opposition to the carceral system; there is an ongoing structural dialectic in Foucault's work.

Although Foucault's greater emphasis on power in *Discipline and Punish* is evident in the discussion to this point, he is also concerned in this work with his usual theme of the emergence of the human sciences. The transition from torture to prison rules constituted a switch from punishment of the body to punishment of the soul or the will. This, in turn, brought with it considerations of normality and morality. Prison officials and the police came to judge the normality and morality of the prisoner. Eventually, this ability to judge was extended to other "small-scale judges" such as psychiatrists and educators. Out of this emerged new bodies of scientific penal knowledge, and these served as the base of the modern "scientifico-legal complex." The new mode of subjugation was that people were defined as the object of knowledge; of scientific discourse. The key point is that the modern human sciences have their roots here. Here is how Foucault bitterly depicts the roots of the human sciences in the disciplines: "These sciences, which have so delighted our 'humanity' for over a century, have their technical matrix in the petty, malicious minutiae of the disciplines and their investigations" (p. 226).

One other point about *Discipline and Punish* is worth mentioning. Foucault is interested in the way that knowledge gives birth to technologies that exert power. In this context, he deals with the Panopticon. A *Panopticon* is a structure that allows officials the possibility of complete observation of criminals. It might take the form of a tower in the center of a circular prison from which guards could see into all cells. The Panopticon is a tremendous source of power for prison officials because it gives them the possibility of total surveillance. More important, its power is enhanced because the prisoners come to control themselves; they stop themselves from doing various things because they fear that they *might* be seen by the guards. There is a clear link here among knowledge, technology, and power. Furthermore, Foucault returns to his concern for the human sciences, for he sees the Panopticon as a kind of laboratory for the gathering of information about people. It was the forerunner of the social-scientific laboratory and other social science techniques for gathering information about people. At still another level, Foucault sees the Panopticon as the base of "a whole type of society" (p. 216), the disciplinary society.

Finally, we can look at the first volume of *The History of Sexuality* (Foucault, 1980). Again, the emphasis here is on the genealogy of power. To Foucault sexuality is "an especially dense transfer point for relations of power" (1980:103). He sees his goal as being to "define the regime of power-knowledge-pleasure that *sustains* the discourse on human sexuality in our part of the world" (p. 11). He examines the way that sex is put into discourse and the way that power permeates that discourse.

Foucault takes issue with the conventional view that Victorianism had led to the repression of sexuality in general and of sexual discourse in particular. In fact, he argues the exact opposite position—that Victorianism led to an explosion in discourses on sexuality. As a result of Victorianism, there was more analysis, stocktaking, classification, specification, and quantitative/causal study of sexuality. Said Foucault, "People will ask themselves why we were so bent on ending the rule of silence regarding what was the noisiest of our preoccupations" (p. 158). This was especially the case in schools, where instead of repression of sexuality, "the question of sex was a constant preoccupation" (p. 27). Here is the way that Foucault sums up the Victorian hypothesis and his alternative view:

> We must therefore abandon the hypothesis that modern industrial societies ushered in an age of increased sexual repression. We have not only witnessed a visible explosion of unorthodox sexualities . . . never have there existed more centers of power; never more attention manifested and verbalized . . . never more sites where the intensity of pleasures and the persistency of power catch hold, only to spread elsewhere.
>
> (Foucault, 1980:49)

Once again, Foucault accords a special place to medicine and its discourses on sexuality. Whereas to most, medicine is oriented to the scientific analysis of sexuality, Foucault sees more morality than science in the concerns of medicine. (In fact, Foucault is characteristically hard on medicine, seeing the aim of its discourse "not to state the truth, but to prevent its very emergence" [p. 55]). Also involved in the morality of sexuality is religion, especially Western Christianity, the confession, and the need for the subject to tell the truth about sexuality. All of this is related to the human sciences and their interest in gaining knowledge of the subject. Just as people confessed to their priests, they also confessed to their doctors, their psychiatrists, and their sociologists. The confession, especially the sexual confession, came to be cloaked in scientific terms.

In the West, "the project of the science of the subject has gravitated, in ever-narrowing circles, around the question of sex" (p. 70). Questions aimed at ascertaining who we are have come to be increasingly directed to sex. Foucault sums this all up: "Sex, the explanation of everything" (p. 78).

Instead of focusing on the repression of sexuality, Foucault argues that the scientific study of sex should focus on the relationship between sex and power. Again, that power does not reside in one central source, it exists in a variety of micro settings. Furthermore, as is always the case with Foucault, there is resistance to the imposition of power over sex. Power and the resistance to power are everywhere.

Prior to the eighteenth century, society sought control over death, but beginning in that century the focus shifted to control over life, especially sex. Power over life (and sex) took two forms. First, there was the "anatomo-politics of the human body" in which the goal was to discipline the human body (and its sexuality). Second, there was the "bio-politics of population," in which the object was to control and regulate population growth, health, life expectancy, and so forth. In both cases, society came to see "life as a political object" (p. 145). Sex was central in both cases. "Sex was a means of access both to the life of the body and the life of the species" (p. 146). In the modern West, sex has become more important than the soul (and we know how important that is in Foucault's work) and almost as important as life itself. Through knowledge of sexuality, society is coming to exercise more power over life itself. Yet despite this increase in control, Foucault holds out the hope of emancipation:

> It is the agency of sex that we must break away from, if we aim—through a tactical reversal of the various mechanisms of sexuality—to counter the grips of power with the claims of bodies, pleasures, and knowledges, in their multiplicity and their possibility of resistance. The rallying point for the counterattack against the deployment of sexuality ought not to be sex-desire, but bodies and pleasures.
>
> (Foucault, 1980:157)

Foucault's work, as well as ongoing work in poststructuralism in general, offers an exciting new set of inputs into mainstream sociological theory.

While structuralism and poststructuralism developed outside of sociology, the structural theory to be discussed next is an indigenous development. Beyond that, while structuralists and poststructuralists tend to see structures as invisible theoretical constructs, to structural theorists structures tend to be visible and "real" social phenomena.

STRUCTURAL THEORY

One of the more interesting developments in recent years has been the rebirth of interest in structural theory—that is, a return to the roots of sociology in Emile Durkheim's concept of social facts. This rebirth has been led by many of the leaders of sociology's "old guard," including such people as Robert Merton, Lewis Coser, William Goode, Seymour Martin Lipset, and most important, Peter Blau. Having witnessed their traditional orientations under attack from various sides, they felt the need to reiterate their focus on large-scale structures.

The politics of this revival are interesting and tell us a good deal about structural theory. Lewis Coser (1975a) was particularly upset that many of his colleagues in sociology seemed to have succumbed to "a veritable orgy of subjectivism" in adopting such small-scale theories as phenomenology and ethnomethodology. He argued that the study of large-scale structures is the "cornerstone" of sociology. Sociologists are urged not to give in to the subjectivists, but rather to return to the work of Durkheim, as well as to that of Simmel and Marx, which teaches "us that individual striving is not sufficient to free us from the grip of societal constraints" (Coser, 1975b:210). The ultimate focus of sociology should be on the "stubborn facticity of structural arrangements" (Coser, 1975b:210).

It is not that Coser wanted to focus exclusively on large-scale structures, but rather that he wanted to treat them as the ultimate determinants of the other aspects of social reality. His basic model is that social structures impinge on social processes (for instance, social conflict), which in turn affect individual behavior. Coser exemplified his theoretical approach in terms of the issue of race relations:

> The last ten or fifteen years have seen large-scale changes in the social consciousness, the construction of reality, of both whites and blacks, but these depended not only on underlying structural shifts in the relations between the races, but also on specific conflict strategies and specific mobilization of black militants that helped transform mere potentialities into concrete results.
>
> (Coser, 1975b:212)

The *ultimate source* of all this lies at the level of large-scale phenomena.

The other major "enemy" of the structuralists is the group of sociologists who have focused on the cultural level, on the normative systems of society (Goode, 1975).[3] One of those whom William J. Goode had in mind here must have been Parsons, with his brand of cultural determinism. Goode suggested that, instead of focusing on such nor-

---

[3]Interestingly, Lipset (1975), supposedly operating from a structural perspective, focused on the normative system. He was clearly out of step with the rest of this group.

mative or cultural forces, we focus instead on such structural phenomena as communication systems, authority systems, paths of travel, and the physical layout of housing. Peter Blau (1975a) extended this list by including the following large-scale structures: class structure, structural change, division of labor, associations that structure social relations, status sets and role sets, structural roots of deviance and rebellion, and the interrelationship among the environment, population, and social structure. In addition to this enumeration, he offered a definition: "Social structure refers to the patterns discernible in social life, the regularities observed, the configurations detected" (1975a:3). Blau also defined the antithesis of social structure: "chaos, formlessness, idiosyncratic human behavior that exhibits no regularities and hence is unstructured" (citing Homans, 1975a:3).

Robert K. Merton (1975) clearly supported a large-scale structural approach. He recognized that it is not the answer to all sociological problems, but it is the best we have. Characteristically, Merton wanted structural work to focus on the link between societal and individual levels, although he stated that it is social structure that structures individual alternatives. In discussing deviance, for instance, Merton argued that social structure generates different rates of deviant behavior. However, Merton was generally inclined to take a more balanced approach to the relationship between societal and individual levels. He argued that each new cohort enters a social structure that it never created and by which it is constrained, but it also proceeds to modify that structure. Structures are changeable and, more important, cannot exhaustively explain all of social life.

Not surprisingly, some Marxists, such as Tom Bottomore (1975), were attracted to structural sociology. In fact, Bottomore (citing Macdonald) offered a good description of the structural realities that attract the interest of Marxists:

> I remember once walking in the street and suddenly really *seeing* the big heavy buildings in their obstinate actuality and realizing I simply couldn't imagine all this recalcitrant matter transformed by socialism. How would the street *look* when the workers took it over, how would, how could revolution transfigure the miles and miles of stubborn stone?
>
> (Bottomore, 1975:159)

Bottomore did not see all social structures as rocklike; however, he was unwilling to go to the other extreme and see them as a ceaseless and formless flux of events.

As a Marxist, Bottomore was interested in developing a conception of large-scale structures, but one that allows for conflict and change. In his view, we must describe these structures but in such a way that we do not neglect "the flow of historical action by individuals and social groups which sustains, re-creates, revises, or destructs this order" (Bottomore, 1975:160). What preoccupied Bottomore were the sources of variation in social structures. The first source of variation is the circulation of membership. The new people who enter are never totally socialized into the group so that they construct new subgroups, alter their roles, and so on. Second, the growth in knowledge and the resulting expansion of science and technology lead to continual structural change. Third, the progressive processes of social differentiation lead to changes in social structure. New positions and roles lead to new ideas, mental orientations, social definitions, and social interests. Finally, there is the possibility of change within structures themselves and in their impact on culture and consciousness.

Peter Blau's Structural Theory

The work of Peter Blau (1975b; 1977a; 1977b; Blau and Merton, 1981) is the most important representation of this "reborn" structuralism. Blau offered a rather extreme version of this structural orientation. For one thing, he clearly defined the task of sociology in structural terms: "The most distinctive task of sociology is the structural analysis of various forms of differentiation, their interrelations, the conditions producing them and changes in them and their implications for social relations" (Blau, 1977a:6–7). In this definition, Blau pointedly eliminated cultural- and individual-level variables from sociology. On the cultural issue, Blau stated, "I am a structural determinist, who believes that the structures of objective social positions among which people are distributed exert more fundamental influences on social life than do cultural values and norms" (1977a:x). Blau wanted to look at social structures, but without the cultural and functional connotations of structural functionalism. Furthermore, he was going to ignore the individual levels. From his point of view, the parts of society are groups or classes of people, not actors and their thoughts and actions. "The focus is on structures of differentiated positions and their influences on the relations of human beings, not on the intensive analysis of the sociopsychological processes involved in human relations" (Blau, 1977a:4). Blau recognized the importance of such factors but stated that he would not deal with them. This means that there is an inherent limitation in his approach: "To be sure, these theorems are deterministic only for groups, not for individuals, for whom they are only probabilistic" (Blau, 1977a:7).

Blau also found it necessary to differentiate himself from Lévi-Strauss's brand of structuralism. He examined Lévi-Strauss's claim that in his system the concept of social structure has nothing to do with empirical reality, but rather with theoretical models built about this reality. Blau took the opposite position, arguing that the social structures with which he was concerned were *real social phenomena*. Furthermore, while Lévi-Strauss saw structures as invisible, Blau argued that they are "observable aspects of social life, not theories about it" (1977a:2).

Blau also defined social structure: "population distributions among social positions along various lines—positions that affect people's role relations and social interaction" (1975b:221). There are two key elements of this definition: positions and population. Social positions define social structures. They are, in turn, defined by the various parameters implicit in the social distinctions that people make in their social interaction. Examples of these parameters include age, sex, race, and socioeconomic status. Blau contended that his basic thesis "is that the study of the various forms of differentiation among people, their interrelations, the conditions producing them, and their implications is *the* distinctive task of sociology" (1975b:222).

As implied above, Blau was interested in both the differentiation and interrelationship of social positions. In terms of interrelationships, Blau saw two factors linking social positions: first, the various social associations among people; second, the process of social mobility, which he defined very broadly as *all* movements of people between social positions.

In discussing differentiation, Blau outlined two major types of structural parameters. The first type is *nominal* parameters, which serve to differentiate a population without ranking the different subsets. Each subset has a distinct boundary. Among the nominal parameters that Blau discussed are sex and race. The second type is *graduated* structural parameters, which serve to differentiate people on status dimensions. The differences are stated in terms of gradations, and there are no clear dividing lines between subsets (for example, income and wealth).

Based on his differentiation between parameters, Blau presented two types of social positions, each of which is distinguished by a given structural parameter. A *group* is determined on the basis of nominal parameters, whereas a *status* is determined on the basis of graduated parameters.

Building on parameters and social positions, Blau developed two generic forms of differentiation. The first is *heterogeneity,* which involves the distribution of a population among various groups in terms of nominal parameters. The second is *inequality,* which is determined by status distributions in terms of graduated parameters. We see reflected here Blau's values: there is too much inequality in society, and there can never be too much heterogeneity.

Blau explained in great detail what he meant by parameters of social structure. He did this by explaining what his structural theory does or does not concern itself with. For example, he would not be interested in the ethnic backgrounds of individual actors, but he would be interested in the ethnic heterogeneity of a population. He would not be interested in occupational performance but would be interested in the division of labor. In short, Blau was interested in large-scale structural factors and not in small-scale behavioral and attitudinal factors.

To illustrate his approach, Blau identified several problem areas that would be the focus of structural analyses. One is the issue of social *differentiation and integration.* Unlike Lipset and Parsons, Blau did not believe that such factors as culture, values, and norms produce social integration. Instead, the degree of structural differentiation produces integration among groups and individuals. Blau's parameters, especially nominal parameters, determine the degree of integration. In general, integration occurs when a segment of the population has a high degree of similarity in parameters such as age, sex, race, occupation, and neighborhood. A great deal of heterogeneity tends to produce barriers to social integration. At some point, however, when heterogeneity is too great, the barriers tend to break down. With enough differentiation, people prefer outgroup associates to no associates at all. In fact, in modern society numerous nominal parameters produce multiform heterogeneity, which means that virtually everyone belongs to a multitude of groups and has multiple roles. Such a structure "*compels* people to have associates outside their own groups" (Blau, 1975b:233; italics added). This is the most characteristic form of macrostructural sociology—social structures determining individual action.

Blau (1980) published a "fable" in which he tried to illustrate his theory. He described a fictional spaceship, carrying, among others, two sociologists, that lands on a planet called Stellar 8R. There they encounter "Aytars," or living creatures that Blau described as being "more like people than like protozoa" (1980:777). The Aytars, who live in small villages on an island, are all alike except for two things. First, they come in two colors, blue and green (a *nominal* parameter). Second, they vary in height from ten to thirty inches (a *graduated* parameter). There were no differentiations in sex nor in age, for although time elapsed, it did not change them.

Although the people varied only in these two characteristics, the "research sociologists" found that the villages that the Aytars lived in varied along five dimensions. First, the villages varied in population size from many to comparatively few Aytars. Second, the ratio of blue to green Aytars varied among the villages; some villages were disproportionately blue, others disproportionately green. Third, the villages differed in the average height of the Aytars. Some villages had comparatively tall populations; others had populations that were smaller on the average. Fourth, the differences in height led to inequality in some villages where the population was not homogeneous. "Since size was the only quantitative difference among Aytars, large ones could dominate small ones; they could simply roll over them" (p. 777). Fifth, the villages varied in the extent to which size and color were related. Some villages were dominated numerically by tall green Aytars, others by short blue ones. In sum, although the population differed on only two characteristics, these differences led to major differences in the structure of the villages in which they lived.

Blau's sociologists then discovered that there were other islands on Stellar 8R and that there were more villages on each of these islands. The individuals were the same—that is, varying only in height and color—but these villages could be differentiated along eight dimensions. The first five dimensions were the same as those that differentiated the Aytars on the first island. Sixth, although the ratio of blue to green Aytars on two or more islands might be the same, it could be the result of very different ratios within the villages on each island. Thus, a one-to-one ratio could be the result of a one-to-one ratio within most villages, or it could be the result of great variations between villages that tended to cancel each other out. Seventh, Blau made the same point about height. That is, the average height on an island could come about because all or most villages on the island were similar in height or from the canceling out of some villages dominated by tall Aytars by others dominated by small Aytars. Eighth, the same issue was raised about the relationship between color and size. Again, there could be a similar correlation in most villages, or some villages might be peopled mostly by taller greens and others by smaller blues. Thus, although the demographic characteristics of two islands might be the same, the ecological structures of the villages on the two islands could be very different. Blau's biggest interest was the effect of such ecological (that is, structural) differences on social relationships. As Blau said, "The composition and ecological structure of villages and islands influence the social relations of Aytars independent of their psychological preferences" (p. 780).

Blau began with the assumption that in general people prefer to associate with others like themselves. However, Blau's hypothetical scientists discovered that Aytars of different size and color were sometimes found in each other's company. In their "survey," they uncovered some representative comments: "At least we have the same color, and there is nobody my size around here." "Sure, my friend is green, but to me size is more important than color" (p. 780). Blau argued that the chance of one Aytar having outgroup friends is the product of several structural realities. For example, if one's own kind is a small minority in a village, one is more likely to have outgroup friends. If one exists within small groups, then the chances of outgroup friendships are increased because one will have fewer people with similar characteristics to choose from. Finally, the intersection of parameters tends to inhibit outgroup choices. That is, if size and color are substantially related (if, for example, green Aytars are also likely

PETER M. BLAU: A Biographical Sketch

Peter Blau was born in Vienna, Austria, on February 7, 1918. He emigrated to the United States in 1939 and became a United States citizen in 1943. In 1942 he received his bachelor's degree from the relatively little known Elmhurst College in Elmhurst, Illinois. His schooling was interrupted by World War II, and he served in the United States Army and was awarded the Bronze Star. After the war, he returned to school and completed his education, receiving his Ph.D. from Columbia University in 1952.

Blau first received wide recognition in sociology for his contributions to the study of formal organizations. His empirical studies of organizations as well as his textbooks on formal organizations are still widely cited in that subfield, and he continues to be a regular contributor to it. He is also noted for a book he coauthored with Otis Dudley Duncan, *The American Occupational Structure*, which won the prestigious Sorokin Award from the American Sociological Association in 1968. That work constitutes a very important contribution to the sociological study of social stratification.

Although he is well known for a range of work, what interests us here is Blau's contribution to sociological theory. What is distinctive about it, as reflected in the way in which it has been treated in this book, is that Blau (forthcoming) has made important contributions to two distinct theoretical orientations. As we saw in Chapter 8, his 1964 book *Exchange and Power in Social Life* is a major component of contemporary exchange theory. Blau's chief contribution there was to take the primarily small-scale exchange theory and try to apply it to larger-scale issues. Although it has some notable weaknesses, it constitutes an important effort to theoretically integrate large- and small-scale sociological issues. More recently, Blau has been in the forefront of structural theory. During his term as president of the American Sociological Association (1973–1974), he made this the theme of the annual meeting of the association. Since then he has published a number of books and articles designed to clarify and to extend structural theory.

Blau (forthcoming) described his rationale for switching from a micro-sociological exchange theory to a macro-sociological structural theory:

> One approach is to start with microsociological principles and use these as the foundation for building macrosociological theory. The alternative approach rests on the assumption that different perspectives and conceptual frameworks are necessary for micro and macro theories. . . . I have come to the conclusion that the second approach is the only viable one, at least in this stage of sociological development.

Since 1970 Blau has been professor of sociology at Columbia University, and since 1979 he has simultaneously held the position of distinguished professor at the State University of New York at Albany.

to be short), the intersection of these two factors tends to cause the factors to reinforce each other and make ingroup choices even more likely.

Structural theory includes some old sociological ideas (as, for example, from Simmel and Durkheim) cast in a new form. It remains to be seen how far structural theory can go in sociology, with its exclusive focus on the large-scale structural level of social reality. Although that strict focus might appear to limit its explanatory power, compared to some of the more integrative sociological theories, structural theory appeals to some very basic propensities of sociologists. It will probably prove attractive especially to those sociologists who reject subjective or small-scale factors as primary concerns of sociology.

Blau's theory has led to a number of empirical studies (Blum, 1984; Blau, Beeker, and Fitzpatrick, 1984; Blau, Blum, and Schwartz, 1982). To take one recent example, Terry Blum tested two hypotheses derived from Blau's theory: "(1) ethnic heterogeneity fosters interethnic interactions despite the prevalence of in-group preferences, and (2) religious heterogeneity encourages interreligious interactions despite the prevalence of in-group preferences" (1985:513). Blum's results support Blau's theory and its most general point that "macrosocial structure exerts constraints on interpersonal interaction by providing or limiting opportunities for such interactions" (1985:520–521).

NETWORK THEORY

Another structural approach in modern sociology is network theory. Although it is a type of structuralism, it is less tied to the kinds of external developments discussed earlier and more indigenous to sociology. Thus, although network theorists are interested in "deep structures," the structures are closer to traditional sociological social structures than, for example, to Lévi-Strauss's interest in mental structures. Also in accord with its link to mainstream sociology, network theorists are little interested in philosophizing about structures and much more interested in methodological, even mathematical, rigor and the empirical study of various kinds of networks.

Network analysts take pains to differentiate their approach from what Ronald Burt calls "atomistic" and "normative" sociological approaches (Burt, 1982; see also Granovetter, 1985). Atomistic sociological orientations focus on actors making decisions in isolation from other actors. More generally, they focus on the "personal attributes" of actors (Wellman, 1983). Atomistic approaches are rejected because they are too microscopic and ignore links among actors. As Barry Wellman puts it, "Accounting for individual motives is a job better left to psychologists" (1983:163). This, of course, constitutes a rejection of a number of sociological theories that are in one way or another deeply concerned with motives—symbolic interactionism, phenomenological sociology, existential sociology, Weberian theory, Schutzian theory, and others.

In the view of network theorists, normative approaches focus on culture and the socialization process through which norms and values are internalized in actors. In the normative orientation, what holds people together are sets of shared ideas. Network theorists reject such a view and argue that one should focus on the objective pattern of ties linking the members of society. Here is how Wellman articulates this view:

> Network analysts want to study regularities in how people and collectivities behave rather than regularities in beliefs about how they ought to behave. Hence network analysts try to avoid normative explanations of social behavior. They dismiss as non-structural any explanation that treats social process as the sum of individual actors' personal attributes and internalized norms.
>
> (Wellman, 1983:162)

In this, network theorists reject a large part of structural functionalism, Parsonsian cultural determinism, Durkheimian emphasis on the collective conscience, Simmelian interest in objective and subjective culture, the critical theorist's interest in culture, and so on.

Having made clear what it is not, network theory then clarifies its major concern—the objective pattern of ties linking the members (individual and collective) of society. Let us look at how Wellman articulates this focus:

> Network analysts start with the simple, but powerful, notion that the primary business of sociologists is to study social structure. . . . The most direct way to study a social structure is to analyze the pattern of ties linking its members. Network analysts search for *deep* structures—regular network patterns beneath the often complex surface of social systems. . . . Actors and their behavior are seen as constrained by these structures. Thus, the focus is not on voluntaristic actors, but on structural constraint.
>
> (Wellman, 1983:156–157)

One distinctive aspect of network theory is that it focuses on a wide range of micro to macro structures. That is, the actors to network theory may be people, but they also may be groups, corporations (Clawson, Neustadtl, and Bearden, 1986; Mizruchi and Koenig, 1986), and societies. Links occur at the large-scale, social-structural level as well as at more microscopic levels. Mark Granovetter describes such micro-level links as action "embedded" in "the concrete personal relations and structures (or 'networks') of such relations" (1985:490). Basic to any of these links is the idea that any "actor" (individual or collective) may have differential access to valued resources (wealth, power, information). The result is that structured systems tend to be stratified, with some components dependent on others.

One key aspect of network analysis is that it tends to move sociologists away from the study of social groups and social categories and toward the study of ties among and between actors that are not "sufficiently bounded and densely knit to be termed groups" (Wellman, 1983:169). A good example of this is Granovetter's (1973; 1983) work on "the strength of weak ties." Granovetter differentiates between "strong ties," for example, links between people and their close friends, and "weak ties," for example, links between people and mere acquaintances. Sociologists have tended to focus on people with strong ties or social groups. They have tended to regard strong ties as crucial, whereas weak ties have been thought of as being of trivial sociological importance. Granovetter's contribution is to make it clear that weak ties can be very important. For example, weak ties between two actors can serve as a bridge between two groups with strong internal ties. Without such a weak tie, the two groups might be totally isolated. This, in turn, could lead to a more fragmented social system. An individual lacking in weak ties would find himself or herself isolated in a tightly knit group and lack information about what is going on in other groups as well as in the larger society. Weak ties therefore prevent isolation and allow for individuals to be better integrated into the larger society. Although Granovetter emphasizes the importance of weak ties, he hastens to make it clear "that strong ties can also have value" (1983: 209). For example, people with strong ties have greater motivation to help one another and are more readily available to one another.

Network theory is relatively new and undeveloped. As Burt says, "There is currently a loose federation of approaches referenced as network analysis" (1982:20). But it is growing, as evidenced by the number of papers and books being published from a network perspective and the fact that there is now a journal (*Social Networks*) devoted to it. Although it may be a loose conglomeration of work, network theory does seem to rest on a coherent set of principles (Wellman, 1983).

First, ties among actors usually are symmetrical in both content and intensity. Actors supply each other with different things, and they do so with greater or lesser intensity. Second, the ties among individuals must be analyzed within the context of the structure of larger networks. Third, the structuring of social ties leads to various kinds of nonrandom networks. On the one hand, networks are transitive: if there is a tie between A and B and B and C, there is likely to be a tie between A and C. The result is that there is more likely to be a network involving A, B, and C. On the other hand, there are limits to how many links can exist and how intense they can be. The result is that there are also likely to develop network clusters with distinct boundaries separating one cluster from another. Fourth, the existence of clusters leads to the fact that there can be cross-linkages between clusters as well as between individuals. Fifth, there are asymmetric ties among elements in a system with the result that scarce resources are differentially distributed. Finally, the unequal distribution of scarce resources leads to both collaboration and competition. Some groups band together to acquire scarce resources collaboratively, whereas others compete and conflict over resources. This gives network theory a dynamic quality (Rosenthal et al., 1985) with the structure of the system changing with shifting patterns of coalition and conflict.

EXISTENTIAL SOCIOLOGY

We already have encountered a number of micro-oriented theories in this book that can be grouped together as social definitionism (Ritzer, 1975a; 1975b), creative sociologies (M. Morris, 1977), or sociologies of everyday life (Douglas, 1970; Douglas et al., 1980; Weigert, 1981). Included under all of these similar headings are such theories as symbolic interactionism, phenomenological sociology, and ethnomethodology. Existential sociology can be added to this list. It has not achieved the status of the other social definitionist theories; however, it has been the subject of increasing interest in recent years. It will probably become clear in the next decade whether existential sociology is to occupy a more central position in sociological theory or recede into the background.

First we offer a preliminary definition of existential sociology: "the study of human experience in the world . . . in all its forms" (Douglas and Johnson, 1977:vii; for a similar definition see Fontana, 1984). It is oriented to the study of the way that people live, feel, think, and act. It accords special importance to feelings and emotions as well as the "problematic and situated nature of meaningful experience" (Douglas and Johnson, 1977:xiii). (A relatively new area within the discipline, "the sociology of emotions," is also concerned with these issues. See, for example, Kemper, 1978a,b; 1981.) In accepting such a view, existential sociology rejects any monocausal view of human life. To the existential sociologist, "Man is varied, changeable, uncertain, conflictful, and partially free to choose what he will do and what he will become, because he must be so to exist in a world that is varied, changeable, uncertain, and conflictful" (Douglas, 1977:14). This underscores a dominant theme in existential sociology: people are both free *and* constrained.

This idea as well as many other aspects of existential sociology derive from the work of Jean-Paul Sartre, the French novelist and philosopher. Of particular interest to sociologists was Sartre's effort to relate individual freedom and societal constraints. Sartre sought to fuse his early phenomenological interests and his later Marxian concerns into a dialectical whole. In Ian Craib's (1976) view, Sartre's thought underwent evolution. In his early work, Sartre focused on the individual level, especially on individual freedom. At that point he adhered to the view that people are not subject to or determined by any social laws. In other words, man "cannot justify his actions by reference to anything outside himself" (Craib, 1976:4). However, later in his career, Sartre became more intrigued by Marxian theory and as a result shifted his focus to the "*free* individual situated in a *massive and oppressive social structure* which limits and alienates his activities" (Craib, 1976:9; italics added). Sartre did not simply shift to a societal level of concern, but sought to combine it with his earlier interest in the actor. Craib concluded that later in his career, Sartre succeeded in unifying large- and small-scale theory.

In her analysis of Sartre's work, Gila Hayim (1980) sees continuity between his early and his late work. In *Being and Nothingness*, published in 1943, Sartre focuses more on the free individual and takes the view that "existence is defined by and through one's acts. . . . *One is what one does*" (Hayim, 1980:3). At the same time, Sartre attacks the sociologistic view of "objective structures as completely deterministic of behavior" (p. 5). For Sartre and existentialists in general, actors have the capacity to go beyond the present, to move toward the future. For Sartre, then, people are free; they are responsible for everything that they do; they have no excuses. In some senses, this is a tremendous source of anguish to people, these "staggering responsibilities of freedom" (p. 17). In other senses, this is a source of optimism to people—their fates are in their hands. In the *Critique of Dialectical Reason*, published in 1963, Sartre devotes more attention to social structures, but even here he emphasizes the "human prerogative for transcendence—the surpassing of the given" (Hayim, 1980:16). In this, Sartre is critical of various Marxists (economic determinists, structural Marxists) who overemphasize the role and place of social structure. "Dogmatic Marxists have, by Sartre's view, eliminated the humanistic component of Marx's original idea" (p. 72). As an existentialist, Sartre *always* retained this humanism.

A good illustration of existential sociology was offered by Andrea Fontana, who drew it from George Orwell's short story "Shooting an Elephant":

As soon as I saw the elephant I knew with perfect certainty that I ought not to shoot him. . . . I decided that I would watch him for a little while to make sure that he did not turn savage again, and then go home. . . .

But at that moment I glanced round at the crowd that had followed me. It was an immense crowd. . . . They were watching me. . . . They did not like me, but with the magical rifle in my hands I was momentarily worth watching. And suddenly I realized that I should have to shoot the elephant after all. The people expected it of me and I had got to do it; I could feel their two thousand wills pressing me forward, irresistibly.

(Fontana, 1980:172)

This vignette illustrates several basic components of existential thought. First, the focus is on the actor, in this case the hunter, and his thoughts and actions. Second, there is the situated and problematic character of social life. Left to his own devices, the hunter would not have shot the elephant. However, he found himself in a situation in which he was led to change his course of action. Third, there is the social setting, the crowd, which "forced" the hunter to shoot the elephant. Finally, there is Sartre's theme of "bad faith." The hunter did not have to shoot the elephant, as he claimed. He could have said no to the pressure. This illustrates the political theme of existentialism. Despite the existence of external pressures, one can always say no. The Nazi concentration camp officer is practicing bad faith when he says that he was just carrying out orders; he could have said no.

Although it leads to distinct political conclusions about actions, the basic orientation of existential sociology is not easily differentiated from that of the other social-definitionist theories that allow the actor some autonomy even within certain external constraints. However, the unique characteristics of existential sociology do become clearer when we distinguish it from its closest theoretical neighbor, phenomenological sociology.[4]

Existentialism and Phenomenology

Existential sociology and phenomenological sociology have similar philosophical sources. Both have deep roots in philosophical phenomenology, especially the work of Edmund Husserl. Although phenomenological sociologists have acknowledged this source, existential sociologists have tried to dissociate themselves from both philosophical and sociological phenomenology. For example, Craib (1976) noted that although Sartre was influenced by Husserl, he was not inclined to accept the idea of essences, or invariant structures of consciousness. By excising them from his theory, Sartre left consciousness "empty" of eternal structures; consciousness was to be conceived of as a relationship within the actor and with the outside world.

Herbert Spiegelberg (1967) took great care to differentiate Sartre's existentialism from Husserl's phenomenology. First, phenomenology aspires to be a rigorous science, but existentialism has no similar aspirations. Second, phenomenology brackets, or sets aside, the everyday world in order to get at the essence of consciousness, whereas existentialism focuses on the everyday world. Although existentialists do not focus on consciousness per se, they admit that individual consciousness is a crucial ingredient in the everyday world they study. Third, phenomenologists rely on intuition and description as their methodologies, whereas existentialism eschews a commitment to a single method. Fourth, whereas phenomenologists seek to get at the essence of consciousness, existentialists try to comprehend the larger situation in which thought and action take place. Finally, phenomenologists study all types of beliefs and do not express a preference for any one type, whereas existentialists enunciate a preference for a special mode of existence, one they call "authentic existence." To illustrate this last

---

[4]Some of the earlier work in existential sociology (Tiryakian, 1962; 1965; Manning, 1973) made little effort to do this. In fact, it often seemed that existential sociologists were trying to show how everything was at least to some degree existential.

idea in terms of the earlier example, the elephant hunter was not involved in authentic existence. The objective of the existentialist would be to awaken in the hunter the sense that he was not forced to shoot the elephant.

Andrea Fontana (1980) extended Spiegelberg's differentiation between existentialism and phenomenology. First, Fontana argued that whereas phenomenology aims at making universal statements, existentialism emphasizes a particularistic orientation. Second, whereas phenomenology tends to be abstract and uninvolved, existentialism is concrete and engaged in the real world.

Fontana also made the useful point that the two philosophies are not coterminous with the two sociologies derived from them. For one thing, existential sociology is different from existential philosophy in that the former seeks to discover the systematic structure of everyday life. However, at the same time, it does not deny the situational and problematic character of everyday life. Nor does it lose sight of the fact that its own knowledge of everyday life is itself problematic. In addition, although existential sociology is not limited to any particular method, its adherents have tended to rely on personal observation and participant observation.

Among the differences between existential sociology and phenomenological sociology, Fontana pointed out that because of its basic nature, existential sociology is not as detached from the everyday world as phenomenological sociology. In addition, whereas phenomenological sociologists tend to focus on the routine elements of social life, existential sociologists are not similarly restricted and concern themselves with all facets of everyday life.

Inevitably, comparisons between the theories imply preferences for one or the other. Fontana, for example, seems to prefer the more tangible and more political existential sociology. Spiegelberg (1967) seems to take the opposite position, at least as far as the two philosophies are concerned. He admitted that the two philosophies are comparable, but he criticized Sartrean existentialism for its selective emphasis, its hasty interpretations, and its inadequate descriptions. Spiegelberg concluded, "Existentialism may be on the trail of more vital, more fruitful insights than pure phenomenology. But it has still to learn a few lessons from the older phenomenology, particularly from Husserl" (p. 266).

Primary Concerns

Existential sociology has a deep commitment to the naturalistic study of actors and their thoughts, feelings, and actions. Within this general arena, it emphasizes several phenomena. For one thing, existential sociologists (for instance, P. Manning, 1973; Kotarba, 1979) have a strong interest in feelings, sentiments, and the like, in stark contrast to the propensity of most sociologists, who emphasize the rational aspects of human existence (a notable exception being Kemper, 1978a; 1978b; 1981). Joseph A. Kotarba made clear precisely how important the study of feelings is to the existential sociologist: "Underlying all the work, however, is an emphasis on and a deep commitment to understanding how feelings form the foundations of our lives, as well as the intricate social realities we construct" (1979:350). In other words, our understanding, not only of people but of their social products as well, is made possible by the study of human feelings.

Another crucial concern of the existential sociologist is the *self* (Kotarba and Fontana, 1984), or the "individual's total experience of being." According to Kotarba, "The existential self refers to an individual's unique experience of being within the context of contemporary social conditions, an experience most notably marked by an incessant sense of becoming and an active participation in social change" (1984:225). The self, to the existentialist, cannot be separated from the physical body in which it is found. The relationship between the mental and physical dimensions of life is deemed important and worthy of study (Kotarba, 1977). Furthermore, the self is viewed not as a static structure but as a process, something constantly in a state of becoming (Johnson and Ferraro, 1984). That is, the self is creative and spontaneous, strongly affected by its immediate situation. In this definition, the self is always seen as at least partially problematic and situational.

Future Prospects

What are the future prospects of existential sociology? In order to achieve a more central position, it will need to overcome several problems. First, its practitioners will have to convince a larger number of sociologists that it offers something different from and superior to that which is offered by the other, more established sociologies of everyday life. Second, in spite of Sartre's later work, existential sociology does not yet have much to offer to our understanding of large-scale structures and their relationship to small-scale processes. Third, existentialism will need a better sense of history; it seems to many to be largely ahistorical. Kotarba (1979) sought to deal with this issue directly by arguing that existential sociology is historical, because it leads researchers to be critical of historical documents as "deceitful" products of a particular historical context. In addition, he urged existentialists to use empathic immersion in history as a research strategy.

One final issue bears on the future of existential sociology: it sometimes seems that it was chosen as the favorite of the young, bourgeois intelligentsia only because it spoke to their voguish concerns. In his analysis, Kotarba reinforced this view: "Feelings are more crucial to sociology than ever before. Our society is increasingly marked by the dominance of feelings. This is fairly obvious in the areas of sex, drug use, and violent behavior" (1979:358). The observer is led to wonder whether existential sociology will outlive the voguish concerns of this generation's intelligentsia. Although existential sociology has some strong theoretical roots, its long-term appeal remains to be seen.

SUMMARY

Most of this chapter has been devoted to a variety of theories that are at various stages of acceptance in sociology. Action theory seems to be in decline as a result of its internal contradictions as well as the fact that its basic premises and most useful derivatives have been taken over by more popular theories. Systems theory enjoyed a brief boom, but in the last few years it has declined as a result of attacks for, among other things, showing modest results, being pseudo-scientific, and being ideologically conservative.

We also examined four sociological theories that are currently increasing in popularity—structuralism, structural theory, network theory, and existential sociology. Structuralism constitutes an effort to import into sociology a perspective developed in such fields as linguistics and anthropology. Although structuralism seems to have considerable promise, structuralists have yet to demonstrate the applicability of the theory to a wide range of social issues. However, the work of Michel Foucault is applicable to many aspects of the social world. But Foucault moved beyond structuralism and is seen as a representative of poststructuralism. Structural theory (especially the work of Peter Blau) rejects outright structuralism's interest in invisible structures. Its concern is with visible social structures. Whereas structuralism imported ideas from other fields, structural theory returns to sociology's Durkheimian roots. Another structural approach examined in this chapter is network theory. This theory is also oriented to analyzing underlying social structures, but it is closely tied to mainstream sociology, and much of it is embedded in highly sophisticated empirical studies of social networks throughout the social world. Existential sociology is part of the boom in theories associated with the social-definitionist paradigm, which also includes phenomenology and ethnomethodology. It is not interested in either visible or invisible structures; it has instead a focus on actors, their thoughts and actions. The future of existential sociology is tied to that of social definitionism in general—continuing as part of the boom, being subsumed by either phenomenological sociology or ethnomethodology, or finding itself of declining significance.

CHAPTER TEN
The Emergence of a Central Problem in Contemporary Sociological Theory*

THROUGHOUT this book we have detailed a wide array of sociological theories. It all might seem a bit confused and confusing and, in fact, some sociologists recently have commented on what appears to be a crisis in contemporary sociological theory (Wardell and Turner, 1986b; Wiley, 1985). Although the theories and theorists analyzed throughout this book remain important, it is also a fact that we are witnessing in the 1980s many signs of growing coherence in sociological theory. That coherence centers around the emergence of considerable consensus that the central problem in sociological theory is the study of the relationship between macroscopic and microscopic theories or levels of social reality.

This is not the first effort to contend that the micro-macro problem is a central theoretical issue. Randall Collins has recently contended that work on this problem "promises to be a significant area of theoretical advance for some time to come" (1986a: 1350). However, Collins devotes only a few lines to the issue in the context of a broader discussion of current trends in sociology. In their introduction to a two-volume set of books, one devoted to macro theory (Eisenstadt and Helle, 1985a) and the other

---

*I would like to thank Kenneth Kammeyer for his helpful comments on an earlier draft of this chapter.

(Helle and Eisenstadt, 1985) to micro theory, Eisenstadt and Helle take a similar view and conclude that "the confrontation between micro- and macro-theory belong[s] to the past" (1985b:3).[1]

This emerging consensus has largely escaped notice to this point because it is found in widely different forms, using very different terms, and in the work of extremely divergent theorists. Consensus on a central theoretical problem is to be found, most importantly, in Anthony Giddens's (1984) work on structuration theory, Jurgen Habermas's (1984:343) integration of "action theory and systems theory," Jeffrey Alexander's (1982) call for an integration of action and order (as well as Kreps's [1985:50] effort to analyze disaster using an Alexander-inspired "dialectical relationship between social action and social order," and a similarly oriented paper by Bosworth and Kreps [1986]), Randall Collins's (1981a) attempt to delineate the micro foundations of macro-level phenomena (and related efforts by Knorr-Cetina [1981] and Cicourel [1981]), Michael Hechter's (1983) effort to integrate rational choice theory with more macrosociological issues, the 1979 Symposium on Consciousness, Human Action, and Structure (Secord, 1982), the Symposia on Macro- and Micro-Sociological Analysis at the 1983 World Congress of the International Sociological Association (Eisenstadt and Helle, 1985a; Helle and Eisenstadt, 1985), James Coleman's (1986) effort to integrate a concern with social action with system behavior, Barry Hindess's (1986) analysis of the relationship between actors and social relations and his attempt, in the process, to avoid the extremes of "theoretical humanism" and "structuralism," Richard Emerson's (1981) more integrative exchange theory, Ronald Burt's (1982) structural theory of action, and Raymond Boudon's (1979/1981) "methodological individualism." We will discuss these works in this chapter, but there are many others that we will not be able to deal with even though they point in the same direction.[2]

Although a case will be made in this chapter for an emerging consensus, it would be a great mistake to take this argument too far. Although there *is* an emerging consensus on a central problem, there are, as we will see throughout this chapter, a number of different ways of theorizing about this problem. Furthermore, there are simultaneously

---

[1]However, as we will see below, by creating separate macro and micro volumes, Eisenstadt and Helle have done more to heighten the split than to develop an integrated approach.

[2]The following are other notable works on macro-micro integration: Fararo and Skvoretz's (1986) effort to integrate network theory and the social-psychological expectation states theory, Rossi's (1983) "dialectical conception of structure and subjectivity," Shalin's (1986) dialectical sense of symbolic interactionism, Thomason's (1982:161) effort within the context of an analysis of Schutzian theory to develop a conception of reification based on a "positive bridging of the constructionist/realist divide," Markovsky's (1985) multilevel justice theory, Swidler's (1986) analysis of culture as a "tool kit" of habits, etc., out of which actors construct strategies for dealing with social reality, Hilbert's (1986:15) effort to integrate Durkheim's macro-level theory of anomie with the "reality construction tradition, particularly ethnomethodology," Haines's (1985:70) effort to reorient ecology (inspired by the integrative work of Giddens, Collins, and Burt) away from a macro-level orientation and toward "a relational methodology which views social phenomena as both causes and consequences of individual phenomena," Hayes's (1985) attempt to integrate "causal and interpretive analyses," Hekman's (1983:14) analysis of Weber's ideal-type methodology in which she sees him as having "effected a synthesis between the analysis of subjective meaning and the analysis of structural forms," Podgorecki and Los's (1979) "multi-dimensional sociology," Zurcher's (1985) effort to show that dramaturgical analysis can be used to integrate micro-interactional and more macro-organizational factors in the study of emotions, Perinbanayagam's (1985) general symbolic interactionist case for macro-micro integration, and many others.

very powerful theoretical forces pulling sociology away from this central problem and in a variety of other directions. In other words, concomitant with the emergence of a theoretical consensus is the existence and emergence of theoretical perspectives that are threatening that consensus before it is even solidified. In this category are extremely micro-oriented theories that deny or downplay the existence and significance of macro-level phenomena (for example, Homans's [1967; 1969; 1974] exchange theory; Skinner's [1971] and Baldwin and Baldwin's [1986] behaviorism; Blumer's [1962/1969; 1969] symbolic interactionism) as well as extreme macro-level theories that deny or minimize the role of micro-level phenomena (for example, Parsons's [1966] lapses into cultural determinism, Blau's [1977a; 1977b] structural theory, Mayhew's [1980] structuralism, Foucault's poststructuralist assault on "homocentrism" and the development of a "decentered *man*less world of talkers talking about talk and texts written about texts" [Lemert, 1979:230], some versions of network theory [White, Boorman, and Breiger, 1976], and others).

Another source of caution, as we will see, is the fact that some of the sociologists who articulate a macro-micro problem end up moving in either an extreme micro (Hechter, Collins) or an extreme macro (Alexander) direction. This threat from "within" the group of thinkers supposedly focusing on the macro-micro link is perhaps more serious than the threat posed by either macro or micro extremists.

Also leading us to be cautious is the fact that the emergence of a consensus on the focal significance of the micro-macro link does not constitute something new, but rather a widespread rediscovery of a focal concern that lies at the heart of the work of most of the major thinkers in the history of sociology (Marx, Weber, Simmel, even Durkheim). In spite of its clear centrality, the focus on the macro-micro link was lost. The real issue may not be why so many theorists have come to focus on the macro-micro link in recent years, but rather why the discipline lost that focus for so many years.

Given these caveats, let us turn now to a discussion of the wide array of important recent works that have identified the macro-micro link as the central problem in sociological theory.

THE MACRO-MICRO LINK: THE EMERGENCE OF A CENTRAL THEORETICAL PROBLEM

If we focus on theoretical works published in the late 1970s and 1980s, a strong case can be made for the centrality of the macro-micro link problem. Not surprisingly, it is the younger generation of theorists (Giddens, Collins, Alexander, Hechter, Knorr-Cetina) who have been in the forefront of this type of theorizing, whereas older theorists (Blau, Coser) have tended to continue to adhere to more extreme theoretical positions (Coleman is one exception). This generational difference tends to support the view that in the future we will see less theoretical extremism and more integration.

Before turning to the major theoretical examples of linking micro and macro phenomena, it should be made clear that the author's own work in metatheory (Ritzer, 1979; 1981) has been concerned, at least in part, with the issue of macro-micro integration. (The reader should consult the Appendix for a discussion of this work. Special attention should be paid to Figure A.3, which offers an overview of the author's perspective and will help the reader understand some of judgments rendered in the following discussion.)

Anthony Giddens's Structuration Theory

Perhaps the best known and the most articulated effort to integrate micro and macro concerns is Anthony Giddens's structuration theory. Giddens (1976:8) "introduced" this theory in the 1970s, but it appeared in its most fully developed form in *The Constitution of Society* (Giddens, 1984), a book subtitled *Outline of the Theory of Structuration.* In this work, Giddens goes so far as to say, "Every research investigation in the social sciences or history is involved in relating action to structure . . . there is no sense in which structure 'determines' action or vice versa" (p. 219).

Although highly eclectic, there is a powerful Marxian influence in Giddens's work, and he even sees *The Constitution of Society* as an extended reflection on Marx's (1869/1963:15) inherently integrative dictum: "Men make their own history, but they do not make it just as they please; they do not make it under circumstances chosen by themselves, but under circumstances directly encountered, given, and transmitted from the past" (1869/1963:15).[3]

Giddens directly addresses the macro-micro issue, but he goes to some lengths not to use this terminology. He offers several reasons for this. First, he feels that macro and micro are often pitted against one another by sociologists, and he does not believe that one of them should have priority over the other. Second, even when there is no conflict between macro and micro, there is a tendency for a dysfunctional division of labor to develop among sociological theories. That is, theories like symbolic interactionism tend to focus on the activities of free actors whereas theories like structural functionalism devote their attention to structural constraint. In the end, Giddens concludes that "the micro/macro *distinction* is not a particularly useful one" (1984:141; italics added). The key point here is that a rigid distinction between micro and macro is *not* useful, but their integration is, as Giddens himself demonstrates. We need not use the macro-micro terminology, but we must in Giddens's view deal with that interrelationship.

Giddens begins by differentiating between macro theories like structural functionalism and structuralism and distinguishing them from micro theories like symbolic interactionism and phenomenology.[4] He correctly criticizes the "imperialism" of both types of theories, with macro theories pushing a focus on "social objects" and micro theories emphasizing "the subject." Giddens contrasts structuration theory to these alternatives: "The basic domain of the study of the social sciences, according to the theory of structuration, is neither the experience of the individual actor, nor the exist-

---

[3] This author fully agrees with according Marx such a central place in structuration theory and more generally, theories that integrate macro-micro issues. As this author concluded in his metatheoretical work, Marx's work is the best "exemplar for an integrated sociological paradigm" (Ritzer, 1981:232).

[4] Giddens sees the first set as objective and the second as subjective. From this author's point of view, however, some macro theories are also highly subjective (structural functionalism with its emphasis on norms, values, and culture) and some micro theories are also highly objective (symbolic interactionism's interest in action and interaction). That is, some macro and micro theories have an interest in *both* objective and subjective phenomena.

ence of any form of societal totality, but social practices ordered across time and space'' (p. 2).

Giddens takes as his starting point human activities, but he insists that they be seen as recursive; that is, activities are "not brought into being by social actors but continually recreated by them via the very means whereby they express themselves as actors. In and through their activities agents produce the conditions that make these activities possible" (p. 2). Thus, Giddens's ontological starting point is not consciousness—"the social construction of reality"—nor is it social structure, but rather the dialectic between activities and conditions occurring in time and space. Giddens is concerned with consciousness, or reflexivity, but in being reflexive the human actor is not merely self-conscious, but also monitoring the ongoing flow of activities and conditions. Giddens's time-space ontology allows him not only to deal with the macro-micro distinction, but also with it in a historical, processual, and dynamic way.

Giddens begins with agents (actors) who, as we have seen, continuously monitor their own activities as well as their physical and social contexts. Actors are also capable of "rationalization," or the development of routine processes by which they are able to maintain a continous understanding of the reasons for their actions (pp. 5, 60). Actors also have motivations to act, and these motivations involve the wants that prompt action. Although reflexive monitoring and rationalization are continuously involved in action, motivations are more appropriately thought of as potentials for action. Motivations provide overall plans for action, but most of our action, in Giddens's view, is not directly motivated. Motivations are generally unconscious, but they are significant in human conduct. Also within consciousness, Giddens makes a (permeable) distinction between discursive consciousness (the ability to put things into words) and practical consciousness (what is typically simply done without being able to express it in words). He sees practical consciousness as particularly important to structuration theory, a concern that it shares with micro-subjective theories like symbolic interactionism and phenomenology and that has been ignored by macro theories like structural functionalism and structuralism.

Giddens moves from agents to agency, or the things that agents *do*. Agency does not deal with actors' intentions, but with what actors actually do: "Agency concerns events of which an individual is a perpetrator. . . . Whatever happened would not have happened if that individual had not intervened" (p. 9). Giddens takes pains to separate agency from intentions because he wants to make the point that actions often end up being different from what was intended; in other words, intentional acts often have unintended consequences.

Nevertheless, Giddens links action to power; that is, the actor has the capability of making a difference. Even more strongly, an actor ceases to be an actor if he or she loses the capacity to make a difference. Giddens certainly recognizes that there are constraints in the world, but this does not mean that actors have no choice. To Giddens, power is "logically prior to subjectivity" because action involves power or the ability to transform the situation. Thus, Giddens is opposed to dualistic theories that are inclined to accord power either to the intent of the actor (symbolic interactionism) or to the structure (structural functionalism).

The core of structuration theory lies in the concepts of structure, system, and duality of structure. *Structure* is defined as "the structuring properties [rules and resources] allowing the 'binding' of time-space in social systems, the properties which make it possible for discernibly similar social practices to exist across varying spans of time and space and which lend them 'systemic' form'' (p. 17). *Social systems* are reproduced social practices, or ''reproduced relations between actors or collectivities organized as regular social practices'' (pp. 17, 25). Social systems do not have structures but exhibit structural properties; structure is manifested in social systems (''in reproduced practices embedded in time and space'' [p. 170]) as well as in ''memory traces orienting the conduct of knowledgeable human agents'' (p. 17). Giddens has linked structure (as rules and resources) to both the macro (social systems) and micro (here memory) levels, and he sees this integration as crucial: ''One of the main propositions of structuration theory is that the rules and resources drawn upon in the production and reproduction of social action are at the same time the means of system reproduction (the duality of structure)'' (p. 19).

We are now ready for the concept of *structuration*, which is premised on the idea that ''the constitution of agents and structures are not two independently given sets of phenomena, a dualism, but represent a duality . . . the structural properties of social systems are both medium and outcome of the practices they recursively organize,'' or ''the moment of the production of action is also one of reproduction in the contexts of the day-to-day enactment of social life'' (pp. 25, 26). As we have seen, structure is not external to the actor; it exists in both memory traces and social practices. Moving away from the Durkheimian sense of structure as constraining, Giddens makes the crucial point that structure ''is *always* both constraining and enabling'' (pp. 25, 163; italics added). However, actors can lose control over the ''structured properties of social systems'' as they stretch away in time and space, but such a loss of control is not inevitable.

One of the keys to Giddens's approach is the idea of unintended consequences; peoples' actions continually have unintended consequences that may become unacknowledged conditions of action and feed back into it, conditions that persistently elude efforts to bring them under control. Nevertheless, actors continually strive to bring these unintended consequences under control.

There is a great deal more to structuration theory than we can possibly present here; Giddens goes into great detail about the various components just discussed and outlines many others as well. Along the way he analyzes, integrates, and/or critiques a wide range of theoretical ideas. Unlike many others, Giddens has gone beyond a program statement for macro-micro integration; he has given a detailed analysis of its various elements and, more important, he has focused on the nature of the interrelationship. What is most satisfying about Giddens's approach is the fact that his key concern, structuration, is defined in inherently integrative terms. The constitutions of agents and structures are not independent of one another; the properties of social systems are seen as both medium and outcome of the practices of actors, and those system properties recursively organize the practices of actors.

Jurgen Habermas's Integration of Action and Systems Theory

In his most recent work, Jurgen Habermas (1984) has moved toward a more integrative approach to social theorizing; in fact, this is implied in the book's subtitle, *Reason and the Rationalization of Society.* In Chapter 4, we focused on his work on (reasonable) communicative action. In this, he sees himself as having worked within and extended action theory. Habermas now has turned at least some of his attention to "integrating action theory and systems theory" (1984:343). He differentiates between the life world (a more micro-level world where "participants in communication come to an understanding with one another about something" [p. 337]) and the larger-scale social system and its subsystems. This distinction between life world and social system must be made and the rationalization of the two examined independently. Otherwise, according to Habermas, his efforts at theoretical integration could lead him into the same trap in which Parsons found himself. That is, systems theory could easily absorb and subordinate action theory. Habermas does not want macro-level systems theory to overwhelm action theory and, as a result, develops an approach to integrate the two.

Characteristically, Habermas distinguishes between the rationalization of the social system (society) and the rationalization of the life world. Whereas societal rationalization involves the institutionalization of a normative system, life-world rationalization involves permitting "interactions that are not guided by normatively *ascribed* agreement but—directly or indirectly—by communicatively *achieved* understanding" (p. 340). In other words, the rationalization of the life world requires that people come to agreement freely rather than having agreement determined by external forces.

Having distinguished between rationalization at these two levels, Habermas goes on to argue that in the contemporary world, rationalization has not proceeded at an equal rate; the social system has rationalized more rapidly than the life world. As a result, the life world has come to be dominated by a rationalized social system. Consequently, everyday life has become impoverished, "the life world has become increasingly desolate" (McCarthy, 1984:xxxvii). The solution, in Habermas's view, lies in the societal "decolonization" of the life world, allowing it to rationalize in the manner (freely developed communicative agreement) appropriate to it.

In adding the life world and society to his focus on communicative action, Habermas recently has defined a much more ambitious and integrative task for himself. In so doing, he has had to move far beyond his Marxian and critical theory roots to an engagement with the work of people like Parsons (as the system level) and Schutz (the life world). He now promises even more integration in coming examinations of the work of "Mead with his communicative-theoretic foundation of sociology" and "Durkheim with his theory of social solidarity that interrelates social integration and system integration" (Habermas, 1984:399).

Habermas has worked on integration at both a theoretical and an ontological level. Theoretically, he has sought to link action theory and systems theory. Ontologically, he has grappled with the relationship between the life world and the social system. Habermas is exemplary in dealing with integration at both the theoretical and the ontological levels.

Jeffrey Alexander's Multidimensional Sociology

In the first volume of his heralded (and often criticized) work (*Theoretical Logic in Sociology*), Jeffrey Alexander seeks a "new 'theoretical logic' for sociology" (1982: xv). That new logic affects "sociological thought at every level of the intellectual continuum'' (p. 65). Alexander favors a multi-dimensional sociology involving an ''alternation of freedom and constraint'' (p. 74). That logic is based on two general propositions. The first involves the problem of *action*, or ''the particular nature of norms and motivation'' (p. 70). The second is the problem of *order*, or ''how a plurality of such actions become interrelated and ordered'' (p. 90).

Let us deal with the order problem first because that is most clearly a macro-micro problem. Alexander suggests that there is a macro-micro continuum (''an 'individual' or 'collective' level of analysis'' [p. 93]) in the way in which order is created in society. At the macro end of the continuum, order is externally created and is collectivist in nature (stemming from collective structures). At the micro end, order is derived from internalized forces and is individualistic in nature (stemming from individual negotiation). Action involves a materialist-idealist continuum that also implies a macro-micro dimension. At the idealist (subjective) end, action is described as normative (implying macro subjectivity), nonrational, and affective. At the materialist (objective) end, action is instrumental (implying micro objectivity), rational, and conditional.

Although Alexander does not overtly cross-cut the two continua of action and order, he implies that it can be done in a footnote dealing with the work of Andrew Effrat: ''Effrat's is . . . parallel to the approach to order developed here. Effrat cross-cuts his subjective/objective criterion by the category 'levels of analysis,' which basically corresponds to the individual/collective division'' (p. 211).

Thus, it is possible to depict Alexander's orientation in the following way:

FIGURE 14.1   Alexander's Integrative Model

Although his model is very promising in macro-micro integration, Alexander ends up adopting a very limited position. He specifically rejects all theories (such as symbolic interactionism) that begin at the micro levels with voluntary agency and build toward the macro levels. From his point of view, the problem with these theories is that although they retain notions of individual freedom and voluntarism, they are unable to deal with the unique (*sui generis*) character of collective phenomena. He also rejects theories (such as exchange theory) that begin with rational action and link it to material structures like the economy. Finally, Alexander rejects ''collectivist, rationalist,'' materialist theories (such as economic and structural determinism) that emphasize coercive order and eliminate individual freedom.

Although he (1982:123) wants always to focus on the dialectical relationship among all four levels, Alexander's priority (not surprisingly given his neo-functional sympathies) lies with the "collectivist, normative" position. As he puts it, "the hope for combining collective order and individual voluntarism lies within the normative, rather than the rationalist tradition" (p. 108). Central to this is the view (the faith?) that because the sources of order are internal rather than external, voluntarism is maintained along with order. In addition, in a later essay, Alexander argues that an individualist perspective ends up with "randomness and complete unpredictability" (1985:27) rather than order. Thus, although Alexander is critical of many other theorists for conflating levels of analysis, it would seem that he is guilty of that sin himself. Again, Alexander is quite explicit about this: "the general framework for social theory can be derived *only* from a collectivist perspective" (p. 28; italics added). To him, social theorists must choose either a collectivist or an individualist perspective. If they choose a collectivist theory, they can incorporate a "relatively small" element of individual negotiation. If, however, they choose an individualist theory, they are doomed to the "individualist dilemma" of trying to sneak into their theory supra-individual phenomena to deal with the randomness inherent in their theory. This dilemma can only be resolved "if the formal adherence to individualism is abandoned" (p. 27).

In spite of a number of promising leads, Alexander ends up giving inordinate significance to macro (subjective) phenomena, and, as a result, his contribution to the development of a theory of macro-micro integration is quite limited.

Although he does not directly address Alexander's work, Giddens (1984) comes to a conclusion similar to the one expressed above about *all* work derived from the Parsonsian distinction between action and order. Such work, in his view, inevitably ends up weak at the micro level, especially on "the knowledgeability of social actors, as constitutive in part of social practices. I do not think that *any* standpoint which is heavily indebted to Parsons can cope satisfactorily with this issue at the very core of social theory" (p. xxxvii).[5]

The Microfoundations of Macrosociology

In an essay entitled "On the Microfoundations of Macrosociology," Randall Collins (1981a; see also 1981b) has offered a highly reductionistic orientation toward the macro-micro link question (for a critique see Ritzer, 1985). In fact, despite the inherently integrative title of his essay, Collins labels his approach "radical microsociology." Collins's focus, the focus of radical microsociology, is what he calls "interaction ritual chains," or bundles of "individual chains of interactional experience, crisscrossing

[5]In spite of its limitations, Alexander's work has been influential. For example, in his work on disaster, Kreps (1985; Bosworth and Kreps, 1986) has been heavily influenced by Alexander's distinction between action and order, which are defined as follows: "The problem of action is one of determining how social units are created and sustained by individual thoughts and behaviors. The problem of order is one of determining how individual thoughts and behaviors are shaped and controlled by social units" (Bosworth and Kreps, 1986:299). Although these are defined as unique, they are also seen as being reducible to one another. They see a dialectic here and specifically focus on the relationship between "role-making" (action) and "role-taking" in organizations involved in disasters.

each other in space as they flow along in time'' (Collins, 1981a:998). In focusing on interaction ritual chains, Collins seeks to avoid what he considers to be more reductionistic concerns with individual behavior and consciousness. Collins raises the level of analysis to interaction, chains of interaction, and the ''marketplace'' for such interaction. Collins thus rejects the extreme micro levels of thought and action (behavior) and is critical of the theories (such as phenomenology and exchange theory) that focus on these levels.

Collins also seeks to distance himself from macro theories and their concerns with macro-level phenomena. For example, he is critical of structural functionalists and their concern with macro-objective (structure) and macro-subjective (norms) phenomena. In fact, he goes so far as to say that ''the terminology of norms ought to be dropped from sociological theory'' (p. 991). He has a similarly negative attitude toward concepts associated with conflict theory, arguing, for example, that there are no ''inherent objective'' entities like property or authority; there are only ''varying senses that people feel at particular places and times of how strong these enforcing coalitions are'' (p. 997). His point is that only people do anything; structures, organizations, classes, and societies ''never *do* anything. Any causal explanation must ultimately come down to the actions of real individuals'' (Collins, 1975:12).

Collins seeks to show how ''all macrophenomena'' can be translated ''into combinations of micro events'' (1981a:985). Specifically, he argues that social structures may be translated empirically into ''patterns of repetitive micro interaction'' (p. 985).

Thus, in the end, Collins does *not* seek an integrated approach, but the predominance of micro theory and micro-level phenomena (for a similar critique see Giddens, 1984). As Collins puts it, ''the effort coherently to reconstitute macro sociology upon radically empirical micro foundations is the crucial step toward a more successful sociological science'' (1981b:82).

We can contrast Collins's orientation to that of Karin Knorr-Cetina (1981), who articulated her position in the introduction to a volume in which one of Collins's essays on radical microsociology appeared. Although she too accords great importance to the interactional domain, Knorr-Cetina grants a greater role to both consciousness and macro-level phenomena in her work. Although Knorr-Cetina, like Collins, makes the case for a radical reconstruction of macro theory on a micro-sociological base, she is also willing to consider the much less radical course of simply integrating micro-sociological results into macro-social theory. In addition, she seems to take the position that the ultimate goal of micro-sociological research is a better understanding of the larger society, its structure, and institutions:

> I . . . believe in the seeming paradox that it is through micro-social approaches that we will learn most about the macro order, for it is these approaches which through their unashamed empiricism afford us a glimpse of the reality about which we speak. Certainly, we will not get a grasp of whatever is the whole of the matter by a microscopic recording of face-to-face interaction. However, it may be enough to begin with If we—for the first time—hear the macro order tick.
>
> (Knorr-Cetina, 1981:41–42)

Thus, it seems clear that Knorr-Cetina takes a far more balanced position on the relationship between the macro and micro levels than does Collins.

An even more integrative position is taken by the other editor of the volume mentioned above, Aaron Cicourel (1981). He argues, "Neither micro nor macro structures are self-contained levels of analysis; they *interact* with each other at all times despite the convenience and sometimes the dubious luxury of only examining one or the other level of analysis" (p. 54). There is an implied criticism of Collins here, but Cicourel adopts another position that can be seen as a more direct critique of the kind of position adopted by Collins: "The issue is not simply one of dismissing one level of analysis or another, but showing how they must be integrated if we are not to be convinced about one level to the exclusion of the other by conveniently ignoring competing frameworks for research and theory" (p. 76). To his credit, Cicourel not only understands the importance of linking macro and micro levels, but also that that link needs to take place ontologically, theoretically, and methodologically.

A Rational-Choice Approach to Micro-Macro Relationships

Michael Hechter (1983a) has taken a rational-choice approach to linking micro- and macro-level phenomena. He begins by critically analyzing the two macro-level approaches (focusing on normative and structural phenomena) that narrow or limit individual choice. In his view, no matter how powerful the normative or structural constraint, the actor still has some ability to make choices. Hechter recognizes that norms and structures determine "the constraints under which individuals act" (p. 8). However, these constraints represent limits; they do not determine individual behavior. Thus, we must take into account the consequences and intentions of individual action, but this does not mean that "individual attributes should be given greater weight than structural attributes" (p. 8).

Hechter takes as his micro-level starting point rational-choice theories, which "assume that the individual's ends, or preferences, are given and fixed; that actors must select between alternative choices of action in pursuing these ends; and their selection of a course of action will be rational [i.e. efficient]" (p. 8). Although he proposes an integrated approach based on rational-choice theory, Hechter proceeds to pit that theory against macro theories in order to see which "can offer better explanations of key macrosociological problems" (p. 10).

In a study of group solidarity Hechter comes down in favor of the rational-choice alternative: "Far from being a mystically and normatively produced phenomenon, solidarity can have a basis in the rational action of individuals. On this account the rational-choice theory of group solidarity deserves to be taken seriously" (1983b:50). Hechter is much more intent on making the case *for* rational-choice theory and *against* normative and structural approaches than he is in articulating an integrated approach. In fact, in an essay in Hechter's anthology, Debra Friedman makes precisely this point about Hechter's own essay in the volume (and others): "Previous attempts to account for macrosociological phenomena using rational-choice theories have argued for the merits of these theories as against normative and structural ones" (1983:251). In her own study of strikes, she offers a more integrated approach that combines rational-choice factors such as the workers' calculations about share of rewards and costs of the strike with structural factors like the labor market, profitability of the firm, and the like.

The 1979 Symposium on Consciousness, Human Action, and Structure

Emanating from this conference was a volume edited by Paul Secord entitled *Explaining Human Behavior: Consciousness, Human Action and Social Structure* (1982). In the opening paragraph of his introductory essay, Secord argues that we need to generate explanations of social behavior that articulate a mix of "objective conditions in the physical and social world," "actors' consciousness," and "social structures" (1982a: 13). In his concluding reflections on the papers presented in the conference, Secord attacks the "parochial nature of the various social science approaches," each of which "exaggerates the value of its own position . . . and slights other approaches. . . . Components of the individual/social structure complex that are omitted from consideration are not merely ignored but positively rejected" (1982b:312–313).

Although he recognizes Giddens's (who wrote an essay in the volume) central idea "that structure is reproduced and provides at the same time the enabling conditions for such reproductions,"[6] Secord urges caution about such generalizations. First, he feels that little can be said about such relations in general; such relationships depend upon the specific context. Second, he wonders whether generalizations like those made by Giddens apply only to structures that are not very durable.

Unfortunately, at this conference, psychologists and social psychologists were heavily overrepresented, with the result that many of the essays are slanted in the micro direction and focus on consciousness (Harre, 1982). There are exceptions, however, such as Bhaskar's essay in which he discusses his inherently integrative approach, the "transformational model of social activity," which he describes in terms similar[7] to Giddens's structuration theory: "Society is conceived of both as the ever-present *condition* and the continually reproduced *outcome* of human agency. And human agency is conceived both as work, i.e., (normally conscious) *production*, and as *reproduction* of the conditions of production, i.e., society" (1982:284–285).

The 1983 Symposia on Macro- and Micro-Sociological Analysis

These symposia led to two volumes, one on macro theory (Eisenstadt and Helle, 1985a) and the other on micro theory (Helle and Eisenstadt, 1985), both of which were supposed to be oriented toward dealing with the shift away from micro or macro extremism and toward greater theoretical integration. However, the organization of the symposia and of the volumes reinforced the split between macro and micro theory rather than dealing with their integration. The volume on macro theory had essays that either focused on macro-level phenomena or made the case that the micro levels were to be subordinated to the macro levels. Similarly, the micro volume focused much more on an array of specific micro theories than on their integration with macro theories.

---

[6] For a similar point of view, see Bhaskar (1979; 1982).

[7] Also similar is the position taken by Bourdieu: "Objective structures are themselves products of historical practices and are constantly reproduced and transformed by historical practices whose productive principle is itself the product of the structures which it consequently tends to reproduce" (1977:83).

These symposia and these volumes indicate that in spite of a desire to speak to integration, it is easy to slip back into one or the other mode of theorizing.

James Coleman's Integration of Action and System

In Chapter 9 we discussed Coleman's critique of Parsons's abandonment of action theory and move toward structural functionalism. But Coleman did more than critique Parsons; he attempted to develop his own more integrated action theory. Coleman argues: "The central theoretical problems then come to be two: how the purposive actions of the actors combine to bring about system-level behavior, and how those purposive actions are in turn shaped by constraints that result from the behavior of the system" (1986:1312). He contends that we must not "discard notions of purpose, goal-directedness, and homeostasis (as is true in causal analyses that remain at the social system level), but . . . limit their employment to the level of *actors* in the social system—not positing them for the system itself" (p. 1312). Thus, Coleman seeks to move action theory back to its micro roots and a focus on the actor, although the actor can be "either persons or corporate actors" (p. 1312).

Although clearly articulating the linkage, Coleman does so with the terminology and within the constraints of action theory and structural functionalism. This leads him to several questionable positions. Why, for example, does he restrict his analysis to purposive action? Aren't there other types of action? (If there aren't, why the need to modify action with *purposeful*?) Why the structural-functional terminology, and more important, why does he reduce this to the traditional structural-functional issue? On the latter, Coleman says, "The two problems when taken together provide the elusive result that functional analysis seeks: to characterize the ongoing and sometimes self-equilibrating functioning of a social system" (p. 1312). The reduction of the problem to the concerns and terminology of structural functionalism is quite troubling.

Coleman also illustrates the link by using Weber's Protestant Ethic thesis:

FIGURE 10.2   James Coleman's Integrative Model

Source: Adapted from James Coleman, "Social Theory, Social Research, and a Theory of Action." *American Journal of Sociology* 91(1986).

The heart of action theory in this view is relation 1, but it must be linked to the macro levels in both relations 2 and 3. To Coleman, the main failure in action theory, primarily Parsonsian action theory, has been in relation 3.

Although it is a clear effort to link macro and micro levels, Coleman's diagram illustrates several problems. It offers illustrations but lacks details about the general types of macro- and micro-level phenomena. A glaring omission is the macro-macro link, which Coleman appears to relegate to another theoretical approach. Finally, Coleman's model is generally lacking in feedback loops; it is largely monocausal and insufficiently dialectical.

Ritzer's diagrammatic representation of the macro-micro link (See Appendix, Figure A.3) offers several advantages over Coleman's. Its elements are couched in general terms rather than specific exemplary terms, it is explicitly dialectical, it makes explicit the major differentiations between macro objectivity and macro subjectivity (implicit in Coleman's examples) and between micro subjectivity and micro objectivity (also implicit in Coleman's diagram, but only in relation 3 and omitted from his micro-level concerns). But Coleman's effort has a historical component; change is occurring, whereas Ritzer's appears ahistorical. However, Ritzer takes pains to counter the ahistorical image presented by his diagrammatic representation: "The dynamic quality of the integrated paradigm is related to its inherently *historical* orientation. Instead of looking at static, ahistorical slices of the social world, the integrated paradigm should be interested in the historical roots of contemporary phenomena" (1981:208).

Integrating Humanism and Structuralism

Barry Hindess (1986) sought to avoid the extremes and the obvious weaknesses of "theoretical humanism" and "structuralism." To Hindess, theoretical humanism is defined by its insistence "that social life is to be understood in terms of the constitutive actions of human individuals," whereas structuralism "analyses social life in terms of the functioning of social wholes (totalities) in which necessary effects are seen as produced by the action of the structure" (p. 113). Hindess rejects the micro extremism of theoretical humanism and the macro extremism of structuralism. He sees both as reductionist and offers his own more integrated conception:

> I suggest an alternative approach to social theory, neither structuralist nor humanist. . . . What is involved here is a radical anti-reductionism according to which social phenomena are always dependent on definite and specifiable conditions of diverse kinds. These conditions include the decisions and actions of actors and social conditions that are clearly external to any individual and which are not themselves reducible to any general principle of explanation.
>
> (Hindess, 1986:114)

Hindess does not go into a great deal of detail about his integrated approach, but he makes two key points. First, it is not just human individuals, but also some types of collectivities that can act. Second, although he rejects the idea of social totalities, Hindess argues that various social conditions limit the decisions and actions of actors. Hindess's human actors are creative and constrained, able to change the social world, but not quickly or at will.

Toward a More Integrative Exchange Theory

Richard Emerson and his disciples (especially Karen Cook) have taken the lead in developing a variety of exchange theory that is focally concerned with the macro-micro link. As Emerson himself said: "I am attempting to extend exchange theory and research from *micro* to more *macro* levels of analysis through study of *exchange network structures*" (Cook, forthcoming b). Cook agrees: "The use of the notion, exchange networks, allows for the development of theory that bridges the conceptual gap between isolated individuals or dyads and larger aggregates or collections of individuals (e.g., formal groups or associations, organizations, neighborhoods, political parties, etc.)" (forthcoming b). Emerson and Cook accept the basic premises of micro-level exchange theory. "The exchange approach takes as its first focus of attention the *benefits* people obtain from, and contribute to, the process of social interaction" (Emerson, 1981:31). Emerson outlines three core assumptions of exchange theory:

1. People for whom events are beneficial tend to act "rationally" so that such events occur.
2. People eventually become satiated with behavioral events so that such events come to be of diminishing utility.
3. The benefits that people obtain through social processes are dependent on the benefits that they are able to provide in exchange. This gives exchange theory "its focus [on] the flow of *benefits through social interaction*" (p. 33).

All of this is quite familiar, but Emerson begins to set exchange theory on a different course when he distinguishes between economic and social theories of exchange. Whereas economic theorists focus on isolated, independent transactions among people, social theorists focus on "recurring transactions between interdependent actors," or the "mutually dependent, more or less bonded social relation" (p. 36). In opening this door, Emerson is led to a focus on "very complex social structures of exchange" (p. 36).

Emerson develops his exchange theory by beginning with the psychology of exchange and then moving on to more macro-level phenomena. Interestingly, Emerson begins by criticizing Homans and other exchange theorists for being inadequately psychological, for focusing too much on interaction and too little on psychology. What is needed in particular is more work on what people *value* rather than simply equating it with deprivation; something is of value to people if they have been deprived of it.[8] In addition to deprivation, Emerson argues that value is affected by people's needs, uncertainty about obtaining some reward, and conditioned and generalized reinforcers (see Chapter 7 for a discussion of these). More important, Emerson wants to include within exchange theory a psychology that encompasses both Homans's emphasis on unconscious conditioned choices and the cognitive weighing of alternatives characteristic of rational-choice theory.

Emerson then moves on to two-person exchange. This need not detain us here, although what is interesting is that Emerson concludes that such a focal social phenomenon as power or the potential to exploit others cannot be studied in the isolated dyad:

---

[8] For an effort to deal with value, unfinished at his death but published posthumously, see Emerson, forthcoming.

"We have little to learn about power through the study of dyadic interaction, for power in any sociologically meaningful sense is a social *structural* phenomenon" (pp. 45–46). In an experimental study, Cook and Emerson (1978) demonstrated that power is a function of the position occupied by actors in a larger structure even when the actors occupying the position are unaware of the network structure and their position in it.

Emerson proceeds to the application of exchange theory to a *corporate group* (a collective actor involving two or more people) and a *network* (a set of separate, albeit interconnected actors).[9] The former leads to an examination of interorganizational exchange, whereas the latter leads to a focus on exchange relations among positions within networks. In fact, Cook and her colleagues (1983:277; see also Cook, forthcoming b) in discussing "exchange networks," or social structures made up of two or more connected exchange relations (sets of exchange opportunities that are historically developed and used) between actors, make the point that this concept "has the theoretical advantage of allowing the extension and application of already well developed dyadic conceptions of exchange . . . to more macro . . . levels of analysis" (1983: 277). In addition to its utility in the study of groups and networks, Emerson also sees exchange theory being applicable to stable, long-term social institutions such as marriage.

In fact, Emerson's exchange theory has moved so far in a structural direction that some wonder whether it will be able to retain its micro-level roots. A. M. McMahon (1984) has distinguished Emerson's orientation (and that of others) from the positions of Homans and Blau. The key is that to the latter two thinkers, exchange refers to the psychological processes that lead to structural patterns of interaction, whereas for Emerson, the external structural patterns are given, and the individual chooses courses of behavior that promise short- and long-term benefits. In fact, this work may be moving so far in a macro-structuralist direction that the interpersonal process of exchange threatens to be lost. As McMahon puts it, "As it moves in that direction, however, it is hard to envision that its adherents will be able to retain 'exchange' as a theoretical idea. That individuals give and receive benefits is essentially mandated by the structure and/or motivated by its resource distribution" (p. 131). The challenge to the more integrative exchange theory will be to continue to flesh out its macro-structural orientation while retaining its roots in the psychological and interpersonal aspects of exchange.

A Structural Theory of Action

Ronald Burt (1982) has been in the forefront of network theorists who have sought to develop an integrated macro-micro approach instead of another form of structural determinism. Burt begins by articulating a schism within action theory between the "atomistic" and "normative" orientations. The atomistic orientation "assumes that alternative actions are evaluated independently by separate actors so that evaluations are made without reference to other actors," whereas the "normative perspective is defined by separate actors within a system having interdependent interests as social norms generated by actors socializing one another" (p. 5).

Burt develops a perspective that "circumvents the schism between atomistic and normative action," one that "is less a synthesis of the existing two perspectives on action

---

[9] It is here that Emerson's work on exchange theory ties into network theory discussed in Chapter 9.

than it is a third view intellectually bridging the two views'' (p. 8). Although he admittedly borrows from the other two perspectives, Burt develops what he calls a *structural perspective* that differs from the other two ''in the criterion for the postulate of marginal evaluation. The criterion assumed by the proposed structural perspective is an actor's status/role-set as generated by the division of labor. An actor evaluates the utility of alternative actions partly in regard to his personal conditions and partly in regard to the conditions of others'' (p. 8). He sees his approach as a logical extension of the atomistic approach and an ''empirically accurate restriction'' on normative theory.

The following depicts Burt's structural theory of action:

FIGURE 10.3   Ronald Burt's Integrative Model

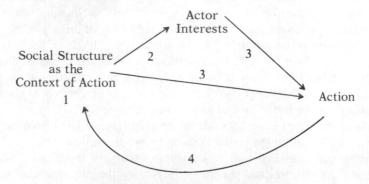

Source: Adapted from Ronald Burt, *Toward a Structural Theory of Action: Network Models of Social Structure, Perception, and Action* (New York: Academic Press, 1982).

Burt describes the premise of a structural theory of action as ''actors are purposive under social structural constraints'' (p. 9) and:

> Actors find themselves in a social structure. That social structure defines their social similarities, which in turn pattern their perceptions of the advantages to be had by taking each of several alternative actions. At the same time, social structure differentially constrains actors in their ability to take actions. Actions eventually taken are therefore a joint function of actors pursuing their interests to the limit of their ability where both interests and ability are patterned by social structure. Finally, actions taken under social structural constraint can modify social structure itself, and these modifications have the potential to create new constraints to be faced by actors within the structure.
>
> (Burt, 1982:9)

Raymond Boudon's "Methodological Individualism"

The contemporary French sociologist Raymond Boudon (1979/1981) has articulated an integrated perspective that he labels (strangely) ''methodological individualism.'' Boudon defines methodological individualism as the principle that:

The sociologist must employ a method which considers the individuals, or individual actors, included in a system of interaction as the logical atoms of his analysis . . . the sociologist cannot be satisfied by a theory which considers an aggregate (a class, a group, a nation) as the most elementary unit to which it will descend . . . an effort being made by the sociologist to analyse the reactions of individual actors to the constraints defined by the system.

(Boudon 1979/1981:36)

Although Boudon emphasizes the individual actor, he clearly implies a more integrated macro-micro relationship.

Boudon goes on to describe *homo sociologicus* and to contrast this model to *homo economicus*. One difference is that homo sociologicus does not always do what he prefers, "but what habit, internalised values, and more generally, diverse ethical, cognitive and gestural conditionings, *force him to do*" (p. 156; italics added). Another is that whereas to the economist, the actor's preferences are given by an assumed philosophical anthropology, *homo sociologicus* assumes that an actors' choices are, at least in part, determined by the structure of the situation and their position in it. Boudon summarizes his position as well as that of classical sociology as conceiving of the actor as "an intentional agent endowed with an autonomy which varies according to the context in which he finds himself" (p. 163).

CONCLUSIONS

We have now reviewed a number of works (almost all of which were published in the 1980s) that have centered in one way or another on the issue of the macro-micro link. Although this problem has been with us since the very beginning of sociology, it tended to be dwarfed by macro or micro extremism. The thesis of this concluding chapter is that in the 1980s, the supporters of theorizing about the macro-micro link, including some of the most important young theorists of this generation, have taken center stage, although the extremists certainly have not been driven from the scene.

In closing this chapter and the body of the book, it would be well to outline some of the continuing issues in micro-macro integration.

1. Although there is a need to continue working on the macro-micro link, additional work is also needed *within* the macro and micro domains.
2. Much of the work that needs to be done on the macro-micro link has to do with specifying in much greater detail the nature of what is at the moment only a very general orientation. Many of those working on this general issue are, in fact, focusing on very different things.
3. Care must be taken to be sure that the still immature effort at macro-micro integration is not overwhelmed by reinvigorated supporters of macro or micro extremism.
4. Perhaps a greater danger lies in the extremists *within* the group working on macro-micro integration. We have in mind here macro-end extremists like Alexander and micro-end extremists like Collins and Hechter. They threaten to tear apart this intellectual development before it has a chance to develop fully.
5. An effort must be made to clarify the relationship between the social world and theories about it in this domain. Some sociologists are interested primarily in

macro-micro integration (Giddens, Ritzer) in the social world, whereas others are more concerned with the integration of different theories. On the latter, some argue against the possibility of theoretical integration (Bhaskar, 1982; Gergen and Gergen, 1982).

In spite of these and other daunting problems, there is promise that sociological theory will continue to develop greater consensus about and knowledge of the problem of the micro-macro link. Although we will not see and should not expect theoretical consensus in sociology, we will see more theorists from an array of different perspectives focusing on the micro-macro relationship. We might even see the emergence of a new sociological paradigm (see Appendix), encompassing one or more sociological theories, that takes the dialectical relationship between microscopic and macroscopic social phenomena as its focal concern. Should it develop, this new paradigm (and its theories) will not supplant extant paradigms (and their theories), but rather supplement their micro- or macro-level foci with a concern for the dialectical relationship between these levels of social reality.

SUMMARY

In this chapter we have reviewed a wide range of work, the vast majority of it published in the 1980s, that focuses in one way or another on the macro-micro link. Particularly notable is Giddens's "structuration" theory, Habermas's integration of action and systems theory, and Alexander's integration of action and order. But this is a wide-ranging effort that encompasses the work of a highly diverse group of sociologists. The issue of macro-micro integration not only defines much of sociological theory in the 1980s, but is likely to concern sociological theorists in the 1990s and beyond.

As this book was about to go into production, a major new contribution to the literature on the macro-micro link was published (Jeffrey Alexander, Bernard Giesen, Richard Munch, and Neil J. Smelser [eds.], *The Micro-Macro Link*. Berkeley: University of California Press, 1987). This anthology is the product of a 1984 conference jointly sponsored by the theory sections of the German and American Sociological Associations. Included in this work are essays by several of the theorists discussed in this chapter (Alexander, Boudon, Coleman, and Collins) as well as a number of other American and German theorists. The merits and contributions of the various essays are yet to be assessed, but it seems clear that this anthology cannot help but contribute further to the emergence of the macro-micro link as the central problem in sociological theory.

APPENDIX
Metatheory and a
Metatheoretical Schema for
Analyzing Sociological Theory

ALTHOUGH it has been played down to this point, this book is based on an underlying organizing schema. Because the primary objective of the text has been to present sociological theory, it was decided to make the organizing schema as unobtrusive as possible. Thus, all chapters as well as the book as a whole can be read without knowledge of the organizing schema that undergirds them. However, some students may be interested in that schema, either early in their reading of the book or after they have finished it. This appendix provides an overview of the book's organizing schema as well as a brief look at the broader field of metatheory of which it is part.[1] Before we get to the specific organizing schema that lies at the base of this book, we need to place that schema in the context of meta-analysis in general and metatheory in particular.

METATHEORY

We can define *meta-analysis* as the study of the underlying principles of some body of already accumulated knowledge. Sociologists are not alone in carrying out meta-analyses. Others who do such work include philosophers (Radnitzky, 1973), psychologists (Gergen, 1973), and historians (White, 1973). Beyond the fact that meta-analysis is found in other fields, it is also the case that various kinds of sociologists, not just

---

[1] This organizing schema is derived from two of my earlier books, *Sociology: A Multiple Paradigm Science* and *Toward an Integrated Sociological Paradigm: The Search for an Exemplar and an Image of the Subject Matter.* The following section on metatheory is based on my essay, "The Current State of Metatheory," *Perspectives: The Theory Section Newsletter* 1986, *10*:1–6.

metatheorists, do such analyses. We can group the various types of meta-analyses in sociology under the heading of *metasociology*, which we can define as the study of the underlying structure of sociology in general as well as of its various components—substantive areas (for example, Hall's [1983] overview of occupational sociology), concepts (Rubinstein's [1986] analysis of the concept of "structure"), methods (*meta-methods*; see Wolf's [1986] *Meta-Analysis*; Hunter, Schmidt, and Jackson's [1982] *Meta-analysis: Cumulating Research Findings Across Studies*; Fendrich [1984], and theories. It is the latter, *metatheory*, or the study of the underlying structure of sociological theory, that will concern us in this section (Fiske and Shweder, 1986).

Metasociology in general, and metatheory more particularly, can be traced back to the very beginnings of sociology. For example, large portions of Durkheim's (1895) *The Rules of Sociological Method* can be thought of as metasociological. However, a good place to start our discussion is with Paul Furfey's *The Scope and Method of Sociology: A Metasociological Treatise* in which he claims: "The term 'metasociology' is a new term introduced by the present writer" (1953/1965:8). Furfey defines metasociology as a science distinct from sociology; that is, sociology takes as its subject matter the social world, "whereas the subject matter of metasociology is sociology itself" (p. 9).[2]

This is very useful, but unfortunately involves a questionable approach to metasociology, one that has been attacked by Turner. Turner (1986) correctly distinguishes between metatheories that seek to lay down the prerequisites for doing theory and metatheories that take developed theories as their subject matter. He argues that in most other fields, metatheory (and, one could add, *all* forms of meta-analysis) is done *after* theories have been developed and seeks to understand their assumptions, strategies, and the knowledge they generate or ignore. However, in sociology, "advocates of meta-theory usually emphasize that we cannot develop theory until we have resolved these more fundamental epistemological and metaphysical questions" (Turner, 1986: 9). Turner concludes, quite rightly in my opinion, that "such meta-theorizing has put the cart before the horse" (p. 9).

Furfey is guilty of undertaking the kind of metasociology critiqued by Turner. Furfey's metasociology does not involve the study of sociology, but is rather prior to, and to be presupposed by, those doing sociology. He begins with the questionable assumption then (and now) that sociology *is* a science and proceeds to argue that metasociology has three tasks to perform for the field of sociology. First, it is to develop criteria for distinguishing scientific from nonscientific sociological knowledge. Second, and reminiscent of Durkheim (but more than a half century later), metasociology is to differentiate between what phenomena are and are not relevant to the field of sociology. Third, "metasociology is to provide practical procedural rules for applying in actual sociological research the two sorts of criteria mentioned" (Furfey, 1953:14).

Furfey's work is dominated by his view that sociology is a science and metasociology is "an auxiliary science which furnishes the methodological principles presupposed by sociology"(1953:17). In Turner's terms, I think Furfey does put the cart before the horse. Metasociology should *not* provide a service to scientific sociology (or antiscientific sociology) but rather should take sociology as a subject of study. Where I

---

[2]Furfey (1953/1965:8) also is cognizant of metatheory which he sees dealing with the "logic of a theory."

part company with Turner is over the latter type of metasociology (particularly meta-theory) that takes sociology as a subject of study. Turner has more sympathy for meta-theory that takes sociological theories as its subject matter, but even here he concludes that "meta-theorizing often gets bogged down in weighty philosophical matters and immobilizes theory building . . . it embroils theorists in inherently unresolvable and always debatable controversies" (1986b:10). Turner's criticisms here rest on practical grounds; metatheorizing prevents us from getting on with theorizing. While this may be the case, it could also be argued that a careful study of extant sociological theories can be a great aid in improving and developing future theories.

In spite of Furfey's position and Turner's critique of that kind of orientation, the fact is that most metasociological and metatheoretical efforts have *not* sought to predefine the field, but rather have studied what actually transpires in the field. This view is very close to Gouldner's (1970) "sociology of sociology," or more specifically his "reflex-ive sociology." Without getting into the "radical" rhetoric that characterizes (and badly dates) *The Coming Crisis of Western Sociology*, we can be satisfied with Gouldner's position that "first and foremost, a reflexive sociology is concerned with what sociolo-gists want to do and with what, in fact, they actually do in the world" (1970:489).

In the next section of the Appendix, I would like to examine metasociology, par-ticularly metatheory, with the goal of defining what has heretofore been a rather ill-defined field as well as analyzing where it ought to go in the near future.

Varieties of Metatheory

There are several rather well-defined metatheories within contemporary sociology, all of which involve the formal or informal study of sociological theory. The first and by far the largest body of work is derived from Thomas Kuhn's (1962; 1970) philosophy of science, and attempts to identify the major paradigm(s) in sociology. Although Kuhn's paradigms encompass both cognitive and communal components, most sociol-ogists working within the Kuhnian tradition have emphasized the cognitive aspects. At a cognitive level, paradigms are sometimes equated with theories (Colclough and Horan, 1983; Effrat, 1973; Friedrichs, 1970; Leinhart, 1977), sometimes with groups of theories (Eisenstadt and Curelaru, 1976; Strasser, 1976), and sometimes with a vari-ety of cognitive components including theories and methods (Albrow's [1974] distinc-tion between the "dialectical" and "categorical" paradigms; Ritzer's [1975a; 1975b] "social facts," "social definition," and "social behavior" paradigms; Platt, [1986]). Efforts to map the cognitive structure of sociological theory are not restricted to those inspired by Kuhn (for example, H. Wagner's [1964] distinction between "structural-functional" and "interpretative-interactional" orientations; D. Wagner and J. Berger's [1985] distinction among theoretical contexts—orienting strategies, unit theories and theoretical research programs), but they are the dominant approaches.

Many of the works discussed above and derived from Kuhn's approach have them-selves spawned considerable thought and research. For example, Ritzer's multiple paradigm schema has elicited a number of empirical tests (Friedheim, 1979; Picou, 1978; Platt, 1986; Snizek, 1976), theoretical extensions (Ritzer, 1981a; Staats, 1976), heated critiques (Eckberg and Hill, 1979), debates (Hill and Eckberg, 1981; Ritzer,

1981b), and so forth. These extensions are as much a part of metatheory as the original works on the cognitive structure of sociology.

The second approach is only partially Kuhnian and emphasizes the communal aspects of various sociological theories. The tendency of this approach is to focus on relatively small groups of theorists who have direct links to one another. There have been various attempts to identify the major "schools" in the history of sociology (Bulmer, 1984; 1986; Harvey, 1987; Tiryakian, 1979; 1985; Wiley, 1979). A related, but more systematic approach, is Mullins's (1973; 1983) effort to use a network approach to identify the major "theory groups" in sociology.

A third approach may be labelled as a "schools of thought approach" (Martindale, 1960; Sorokin, 1928). This is distinguished from a "schools" approach by the fact that a school of thought is a larger, more far-flung group of theorists most of whom have little or no personal contact with one another. They are tied together by a common identity with a particular theory.

These first three metatheoretical approaches tend to be static orientations identifying extant paradigms, schools, or schools of thought. These approaches have been criticized for their static character (Harvey, 1982) and they have led to a fourth approach in which calls are made, and efforts undertaken, to develop a more dynamic approach to the underlying structure of sociological theory (Wagner, 1984; Wagner and Berger, 1985). The focus here is on what causes paradigms, theories, schools and schools of thought to change, grow, decline, etc.

A fifth metatheoretical approach involves shifting from the community to the micro level and focusing on individual theorists and examining, among other things, their training, their institutional affiliations, their career patterns, and their positions within the field of sociology (Gouldner, 1970). The view here is that these and many other experiences shape a sociologist's theoretical orientation.

While this last approach involves a shift from the community to the more micro, individual level, a sixth approach (also suggested by Gouldner) involves shifting to the more macro level to look at the larger society and the nature of its impact on sociological theorizing. Very suggestive in this realm is the work of Michel Foucault (1965; 1975; 1979) and his thoughts on the historical roots of the human sciences (including sociology) as well as the power-knowledge (especially sociological knowledge) linkage (see Chapter 9).

A seventh approach is to look at sociological theories as forms of discourse and to analyze them using an extant array of linguistic tools (Brown, forthcoming). Sociologists in general, and sociological theorists in particular, are seen as using rhetoric in order to persuade others of the adequacy of their approach. Thus, sociological rhetoric, especially sociological theory, can be studied using the same linguistic tools as are used to study everyday forms of discourse. Sociological theory is seen, from this perspective, as *not* being a privileged form of discourse.

An eighth, and very different, approach is to develop a general metatheoretical tool with which to analyze various sociological theories and to develop new theories. Included here would be Alexander's (1982) study of sociological theorists from the point of view of action and order, efforts to deal with "levels" of analysis within sociological theory (Berger and Chaffee, forthcoming; Edel, 1959; Ritzer, 1981), and more specific attempts (discussed in Chapter 10) to work with micro-macro linkages in sociology (Kemeny, 1976).

Given this overview, it is now time to turn to the specific metatheoretical approach that undergirds this book. As will become clear, it involves a combination of the first type of metatheory (identifying major sociological paradigms utilizing a Kuhnian approach) and the eighth type (developing a metatheoretical tool with which to analyze extant theories). We begin with a brief review of the work of Thomas Kuhn and then we examine my analysis of sociology's multiple paradigms. Finally, we review the metatheoretical tool—the integrated sociological paradigm—that is used to analyze sociological theories throughout this book.

THE IDEAS OF THOMAS KUHN

In 1962 the philosopher of science Thomas Kuhn published a rather slim volume entitled *The Structure of Scientific Revolutions*. Because this work grew out of philosophy, it appeared fated to a marginal status within sociology. This seemed especially likely because it focused on the hard sciences (physics, for example) and had little directly to say about the social sciences. However, the theses of the book proved extremely interesting to people in a wide range of fields (for example, Searle, 1972, in linguistics; Stanfield, 1974, in economics; Hollinger, 1980, in history), and to none was it more important than to sociologists. In 1970 Robert Friedrichs published the first important work from a Kuhnian perspective, *A Sociology of Sociology*. Since then there has been a steady stream of work from this perspective (Eckberg and Hill, 1979; Effrat, 1972; Eisenstadt and Curelaru, 1976; Friedrichs, 1972a; Greisman, 1986; Lodahl and Gordon, 1972; D. Phillips, 1973, 1975; Quadagno, 1979; Ritzer, 1975a, 1975b; 1981b; Snizek, 1976; Snizek et al., 1979). There is little doubt that Kuhnian theory dominates metasociology, but what exactly is Kuhn's approach?

One of Kuhn's goals in *The Structure of Scientific Revolutions* was to challenge commonly held assumptions about the way in which science changes. In the view of most laypeople and many scientists, science advances in a cumulative manner, with each advance building inexorably on all that preceded it. Science has achieved its present state through slow and steady increments of knowledge. It will advance to even greater heights in the future. This conception of science was enunciated by the physicist Sir Isaac Newton, who said, "If I have seen further, it is because I stood on the shoulders of giants." But Kuhn regarded this conception of cumulative scientific development as a myth and sought to debunk it.

Kuhn acknowledged that accumulation plays some role in the advance of science, but the truly major changes come about as a result of revolutions. Kuhn offered a theory of how major changes in science occur. He saw a science at any given time as dominated by a specific *paradigm* (defined for the moment as a fundamental image of the science's subject matter). *Normal science* is a period of accumulation of knowledge in which scientists work to expand the reigning paradigm. Such scientific work inevitably spawns *anomalies*, or findings that cannot be explained by the reigning paradigm. A *crisis* stage occurs if these anomalies mount, and this crisis may ultimately end in a scientific revolution. The reigning paradigm is overthrown as a new one takes its place at the center of the science. A new dominant paradigm is born, and the stage is set for the cycle to repeat itself. Kuhn's theory can be depicted diagrammatically:

Paradigm I   →   Normal Science   →   Anomalies   →
Crisis   →   Revolution   →   Paradigm II

It is during periods of revolution that the truly great changes in science take place. This view clearly places Kuhn at odds with most conceptions of scientific development.

The key concept in Kuhn's approach as well as in this appendix is the *paradigm*. Unfortunately, Kuhn is vague on what he means by a paradigm. According to Margaret Masterman (1970), he used it in at least twenty-one different ways. But we will employ a definition of paradigm that we feel is true to the sense and spirit of his early work.

A paradigm serves to differentiate one scientific community from another. It can be used to differentiate physics from chemistry or sociology from psychology. These fields have different paradigms. It can also be used to differentiate between different historical stages in the development of a science. The paradigm that dominated physics in the nineteenth century is different from the one that dominated it in the early twentieth century. There is a third usage of the paradigm concept, and it is the one that is most useful to us here. Paradigms can differentiate among cognitive groupings *within* the same science. Contemporary psychoanalysis, for example, is differentiated into Freudian, Jungian, and Horneyian paradigms (among others)—that is, there are *multiple paradigms* in psychoanalysis—and the same is true of sociology and of most other fields.

We can now offer a definition of paradigm that we feel is true to the sense of Kuhn's original work:

> A paradigm is a fundamental image of the subject matter within a science. It serves to define what should be studied, what questions should be asked, how they should be asked, and what rules should be followed in interpreting the answers obtained. The paradigm is the broadest unit of consensus within a science and serves to differentiate one scientific community (*or subcommunity*) from another. It subsumes, defines, and interrelates the exemplars, *theories* [italics added], and methods and instruments that exist within it.
>
> (Ritzer, 1975a:7)

With this definition we can begin to see the relationship between paradigms and theories. *Theories are only part of larger paradigms*. To put it another way, a paradigm may encompass two or more *theories*, as well as different *images* of the subject matter, *methods* (and instruments), and *exemplars* (specific pieces of scientific work that stand as a model for all of those who follow). An objective of this appendix will be to identify the basic paradigms in sociology.

SOCIOLOGY: A MULTIPLE PARADIGM SCIENCE

The idea that sociology is a multiple paradigm science has received some empirical support (Lodahl and Gordon, 1972), but most of the analyses of the paradigmatic status of sociology have been nonempirical.

In the earliest systematic application of Kuhnian ideas to sociology, Robert Friedrichs (1970) presented two different images of the paradigmatic status of sociology, but both affirmed the idea that sociology was a multiple paradigm science. At one level, Friedrichs argued that despite greater consensus in the past, sociology is split largely between a *system* paradigm (emphasizing societal integration and consensus) and a *conflict* paradigm (emphasizing societal disintegration and coercion) with a wide array of other perspectives as potential paradigms. These paradigms are based on the fundamental images of the subject matter of sociology, but Friedrichs thinks of them as being of secondary importance to two other paradigms that focus on sociologists' images of themselves as scientific agents. These are the *prophetic* and the *priestly* paradigms. Whereas prophetic sociologists perceive themselves as agents of social change, priestly sociologists conceive of themselves as "value-free" scientists. The crucial point for our purposes is that, whether Friedrichs looks at images of the subject matter or images of the sociologists themselves, he concludes that sociology is a multiple paradigm science.

Andrew Effrat (1972) clearly aligned himself with those who see sociology as a multiple paradigm science, although he mistook more specific theories for paradigms. Effrat ended up with a cumbersome list of paradigms, including Marxian, Freudian, Durkheimian, Weberian, phenomenological, ethnomethodological, symbolic interactionist, and exchange theory. As we will see, all of these are best viewed as theoretical components of sociology's multiple paradigms, but Effrat was on the right track in his multiparadigmatic image of sociology.

S. N. Eisenstadt and M. Curelaru (1976) differentiated among discrete, closed-system, and open-system paradigms. They framed their paradigms in terms of the historical development of the field. The earliest is the *discrete paradigm*, in which the focus was on separate concrete entities such as ecological properties, size of groups, or racial and psychological characteristics. Given this image of the world as a set of isolated units, those who operated within this paradigm had difficulty dealing with such relational issues as emergence, innovation, and creativity. This early and primitive paradigm left only a small mark on the development of sociology and persists today in only isolated domains. It was replaced, historically, by the *closed-system model*, whose supporters saw society as composed of separate but interrelated elements. Those who operated within this paradigm tended to see one element as dominant over the others. In Eisenstadt and Curelaru's view (but not this author's), Marx was operating within this paradigm with his emphasis on the economic sector. This paradigm was replaced, in turn, by the *open-system model*, which focuses on the "internal systemic dynamics, interconnections, and continuous feedback processes among the components of the social order" (Eisenstadt and Curelaru, 1976:92). Although the evolution of these paradigms follows "no simple, natural, chronological trend," and there is "considerable temporal and operative overlapping of the several approaches," there is in Eisenstadt and Curelaru's view a long-term trend toward the open-system paradigm.

Charles Lemert (1979) argued that rather than being composed of multiple paradigms, sociology is unified in its *homocentrism*, "the peculiarly nineteenth-century idea which holds that *man* is the measure of all things" (Lemert, 1979:13). Although it is true that sociology is person-centered, it is questionable whether this is really evidence that sociology is unified. One equally plausible conclusion is that there are multiple paradigms in sociology and that the sources of their differences are their varied interpretations *of* humankind. In the author's view, the ideas of homocentrism and multiple paradigms are not mutually exclusive.

Lemert concluded that in spite of their homocentrism, there are important paradigmatic differences among the various modes of sociological discourse. He differentiated among them on a linguistic basis. The first is *lexical sociology*, which is primarily technical in orientation. Second is *semantical sociology*, which focuses on the interpretation of meaning that only people (not animals) are capable of producing. Finally, there is *syntactical sociology*, which is much more political in its orientation to sociology. Thus, for Lemert, there *are* multiple paradigms, at least in contemporary sociology.

Major Sociological Paradigms

Although all the preceding perspectives have some degree of utility, it is my own earlier work on the paradigmatic status of sociology (Ritzer, 1975a; 1975b; 1980) that provides the basis for the metatheoretical perspective that has guided the analysis of sociological theory throughout this book. Like most of those discussed above, I conceive of sociology as a multiple paradigm science. In my view, there are *three* paradigms that dominate contemporary sociology, with several others having the potential to achieve paradigmatic status. I label the three paradigms the *social-facts*, *social-definition*, and *social-behavior* paradigms. Each paradigm is analyzed in terms of the four components of a paradigm outlined in the definition discussed earlier.

THE SOCIAL-FACTS PARADIGM

1. *Exemplar.* The model for social factists is the work of Emile Durkheim, particularly *The Rules of Sociological Method* and *Suicide.*
2. *Image of the subject matter.* Social factists focus on what Durkheim termed *social facts*, or large-scale social structures and institutions. Those who subscribe to the social-facts paradigm focus not only on these phenomena but on their effect on individual thought and action.
3. *Methods.* Social factists are more likely than those who subscribe to the other paradigms to use the interview-questionnaire[3] and historical-comparative methods.
4. *Theories.* The social-facts paradigm encompasses a number of theoretical perspectives. *Structural-functional* theorists tend to see social facts as neatly interrelated and order as maintained by general consensus. *Conflict* theorists tend to emphasize disorder among social facts as well as the notion that order is maintained by coercive forces in society. Although structural functionalism and conflict theory are the dominant theories in this paradigm, there are others that are discussed in this book, including *systems* theory.

THE SOCIAL-DEFINITION PARADIGM

1. *Exemplar.* To social definitionists, the unifying model is Max Weber's work on social action.
2. *Image of the subject matter.* Weber's work helped lead to an interest among social definitionists in the way actors define their social situations and the effect of these definitions on ensuing action and interaction.
3. *Methods.* Social definitionists, although they are most likely to use the interview-questionnaire method, are more likely to use the observation method than those in

---

[3]William Snizek (1976) has shown that the interview-questionnaire is dominant in *all* paradigms.

any other paradigm. In other words, observation is the distinctive methodology of social definitionists.

4 . *Theories*. There are a wide number of theories that can be included within social definitionism: *action theory, symbolic interactionism,* phenomenology, *ethnomethodology,* and *existentialism.*

THE SOCIAL-BEHAVIOR PARADIGM

1. *Exemplar*. The model for sociologists who accept the social-behavior paradigm is the work of the psychologist B. F. Skinner.
2. *Image of the subject matter.* The subject matter of sociology to social behaviorists is the unthinking *behavior* of individuals. Of particular interest are the rewards that elicit desirable behaviors and the punishments that inhibit undesirable behaviors.
3. *Methods.* The distinctive method of social behaviorism is the experiment.
4. *Theories.* Two theoretical approaches in sociology can be included under the heading of social behaviorism. The first is *behavioral sociology,* which is very close to pure psychological behaviorism, and the second, and much more important, is *exchange theory.*[4]

TOWARD A MORE INTEGRATED SOCIOLOGICAL PARADIGM

In addition to detailing the nature of sociology's multiple paradigms, I also sought in my earlier work to make the case for more paradigmatic integration in sociology. Although there is reason for extant paradigms to continue to exist, there is also a need for a more integrated paradigm. Extant paradigms tend to be one-sided, focusing on specific levels of social reality while paying little or no attention to the others. This is reflected in the social factists' concern with macrostructures; the social definitionists' concern with action, interaction, and the social construction of reality; and the social behaviorists' concern with behavior. It is this kind of one-sidedness that has led to what I perceive to be a growing interest in a more integrated approach among a wide range of sociologists. (This is but part of what I see as a growing interest in integration within and even among many social sciences; see especially Mitroff and Kilmann, 1978). For example, Robert Merton, representing social factism, saw it and social definitionism as mutually enriching, as "opposed to one another in about the same sense as ham is opposed to eggs: they are perceptively different but mutually enriching" (1975:30). Among social definitionists, Hugh Mehan and Houston Wood argue that one theoretical component of social definitionism (ethnomethodology) accepts at least one basic tenet of social factism, "the reality of an external and constraining world" (1975:180). Among social behaviorists Arthur Staats (1976) seeks to integrate creative mental processes (a key element of social definitionism) with traditional behaviorism. Calls for a more integrated paradigm are clearly important, but what is necessary is an effort to delineate what such a paradigm might look like.

---

[4]Analyses of Ritzer's paradigm schema include Snizek (1976), Staats (1976), Eckberg and Hill (1979), Friedheim (1979), and Harper, Sylvester, and Walczak (1980).

The key to an integrated paradigm is the notion of *levels* of social reality (Ritzer, 1979; 1981a). As the reader is well aware, *the social world is not really divided into levels.* In fact, social reality is best viewed as an enormous variety of social phenomena that are involved in continuing interaction and change. Individuals, groups, families, bureaucracies, the polity, and numerous other highly diverse social phenomena represent the bewildering array of phenomena that make up the social world. It is extremely difficult to get a handle on such a large number of wide-ranging and mutually interpenetrating social phenomena. Some sort of conceptual schema is clearly needed, and sociologists have developed a number of such schema in an effort to deal with the social world. The idea of levels of social reality employed here should be seen as but one of a large number of such schema that can be, and have been, used for purposes of dealing with the complexities of the social world.

Levels of Social Reality: A Review of the Literature

Although the idea of levels is implicit in much of sociology, it has received relatively little explicit attention. In concentrating on levels here, we are doing little more than making explicit what has been implicit in sociology.

The close of this appendix will offer a conceptualization of the major levels of social reality. To understand adequately that conceptualization some preliminary differentiations must be made. As will be seen, two continua of social reality are useful in developing the major levels of the social world. The first is the *macroscopic-microscopic* continuum (see Chapter 10). Thinking of the social world as being made up of a series of entities ranging from those large in scale to those small in scale is relatively easy, because it is so familiar. Most people in their day to day lives conceive of the social world in these terms. In the academic world, a number of thinkers have worked with a macro-micro continuum (including Blalock and Wilken, 1979; Bosserman, 1968; Edel, 1959; Gurvitch, 1964; Johnson, 1981; Korenbaum, 1964; Wagner, 1964; as well as the many sociologists discussed in Chapter 10). For laypeople and academics alike, the continuum is based on the simple idea that social phenomena vary greatly in size. At the macro end of the continuum are such large-scale social phenomena as groups of societies (for example, the capitalist and socialist world systems), societies, and cultures. At the micro end are individual actors and their thoughts and actions. In between are a wide range of groups, collectivities, social classes, and organizations. We have little difficulty recognizing these distinctions and thinking of the world in macro-micro terms. There are no clear dividing lines between the macro social units and the micro units. Instead, there is a continuum ranging from the micro to the macro ends.

The second continuum is the *objective-subjective* dimension of social reality. At each end of the macro-micro continuum we can differentiate between objective and subjective components. At the micro, or individual, level, there are the subjective mental processes of an actor and the objective patterns of action and interaction in which he or she engages. *Subjective* here refers to something that occurs solely in the realm of ideas, whereas *objective* relates to real, material events. This same differentiation is also found at the macro end of the continuum. A society is made up of both objective structures, such as governments, bureaucracies, and laws, and subjective phenomena, such as norms and values. The objective-subjective continuum is more complicated than the macro-micro continuum, and it is even, as we will see, more complicated than is implied in this introduction. To try to clarify matters and to work toward greater complexity, let us look at a concrete example as well as at the work of a number of sociologists on the objective-subjective continuum.

Consider the purchase of a new automobile. At the micro-subjective level, we would focus on the attitudes and orientations of the individual buyer that influence the kind of car to be purchased. But—and this is the key distinction between the micro-subjective and micro-objective levels of analysis—the buyer may desire (subjective state) a sports car and actually buy (objective act) an economy compact. Some sociologists are interested in subjective mental states, others in objective acts. In many cases it is useful and important to understand the interplay between these two micro levels.

The macro level also has subjective and objective dimensions. For many years most Americans shared a set of preferences for larger and ever more powerful cars. This was a subjective set of attitudes shared by a large number of people. Then a series of objective changes at the societal level had an impact on these shared attitudes. OPEC was formed, oil deliveries to the United States were curtailed, and the government played a more active role in oil-related matters. These and other macro-structural changes led to changes in the shared preferences of large numbers of people. Almost overnight many people came to prize small, fuel-efficient automobiles. This change, in turn, led to a massive alteration in the structure of the American automobile companies. Also affected were the thoughts and actions of many individual Americans. Thus, the purchase of a car as well as most other mundane and extraordinary activities involve the complex interaction of the macro-micro and objective-subjective components of social life.

Now let us turn to the work of several sociologists on the objective-subjective continuum. As we saw in Chapter 1, an important influence on Karl Marx was German idealism, particularly the work of G. W. F. Hegel. The Hegelian dialectic was a subjective process taking place within the realm of ideas. Although affected by this view, Marx and, before him, the Young Hegelians, were dissatisfied with the dialectic because it was not rooted in the objective, material world. Marx, building on the work of Ludwig Feuerbach and others, sought to extend the dialectic to the material world. On the one hand, this meant that he was concerned with real, sentient actors rather than idea systems. On the other hand, he came to focus on the objective structures of capitalist society, primarily the economic structure. Marx became increasingly interested in the real material structures of capitalism and the contradictions that exist among and within them. This is not to say that Marx lost sight of subjective ideas; in fact, notions of false and class consciousness play a key role in his work. It is the materialism-idealism split, as manifest in the work of Marx and others, that is one of the major philosophical roots of the objective-subjective continuum in modern sociology.

We can also find this continuum, although in a different form, in the work of Emile Durkheim (1895/1964). In his classic work on methodology, Durkheim differentiated between material (objective) and nonmaterial (subjective) social facts. In *Suicide*, Durkheim said, "The social fact is sometimes materialized as to become an element of the external world" (1897/1951:313). He discussed architecture and law as two examples of material (objective) social facts. However, most of Durkheim's work emphasizes nonmaterial (subjective) social facts:

> Of course it is true that not all social consciousness achieves such externalization and materialization. Not all aesthetic spirit of a nation is embodied in the works it inspires; not all morality is formulated in clear precepts. The greater part is diffused. There is a large collective life which is at liberty; all sorts of currents come, go, circulate everywhere, cross and mingle in a thousand different ways, and just because they are constantly mobile are never crystallized in an objective form. Today a breath of sadness and discouragement descends on society: tomorrow, one of joyous confidence will uplift all hearts.
>
> (Durkheim, 1897/1951:315)

These social currents do not have material existence; they can only exist within the consciousness of individuals and between them. In *Suicide*, Durkheim concentrated on examples of this kind of social fact. He related differences in suicide rates to differences in social currents. For example, where there are strong currents of anomie (normlessness), we find high rates of anomic suicide. Social currents such as anomie, egoism, and altruism clearly do not have a material existence, although they may have a material effect by causing differences in suicide rates. Instead, they are intersubjective phenomena that can only exist in the consciousness of people.

More recently, Peter Blau (1960) has been in the forefront of those employing an objective-subjective continuum. His differentiation between institutions (subjective entities) and social structures (objective entities) is of this genre. He defined subjective institutions as "the common values and norms embodied in a culture or subculture" (p. 178). Conversely, there are social structures that are "the networks of social relations in which processes of social interaction become organized and through which social positions of individuals and subgroups become differentiated" (p. 178).

It can be argued that the objective-subjective continuum plays a crucial role in the thought of people like Marx, Durkheim, Blau, and many others. But there is a rather interesting problem in their use of the continuum: they employ it almost exclusively at the macroscopic level. However, it also can be applied at the microscopic level. Before giving an example of this, we need to underscore the point that we must deal not only with the macroscopic-microscopic and objective-subjective continua *but also with the interaction between them.*

One example of the use of the objective-subjective continuum at the microscopic level is an empirical study by Mary and Robert Jackman (1973) of what they called "objective and subjective social status." Their micro-subjective concern was "the individual's perception of his own position in the status hierarchy." Micro subjectivity in this study involved the feelings, the perceptions, and the mental aspects of the actors' positions in the stratification system. These are related to various components of the micro-objective realm that include the actor's socioeconomic status, social contacts, amount of capital owned, ethnic group membership, or status as a breadwinner or a union member. Instead of dealing with actors' feeling, these dimensions involve the more objective characteristics of the individuals—the patterns of action and interaction in which they actually engage.

At a more general level, the microscopic aspect of the objective-subjective continuum is manifest in both the social definition and social behavior paradigms, as well as in the differences between them. Although both tend to focus on the micro-objective patterns of action and interaction, they split on the micro-subjective dimension. All of the theoretical components of the social-definition paradigm (for example, symbolic interactionism, ethnomethodology, and phenomenology) share an interest in micro subjectivity—the feelings and thoughts of actors. However, the social behaviorists reject the idea that it is necessary to study the micro-subjective components of social life. This is exemplified by B. F. Skinner's (1971) attack on what he called the idea of "autonomous man." To Skinner, we imply that people are autonomous when we attribute to them such ideas as feeling, minding, freedom, and dignity. People are held to possess some sort of inner core from which their actions emanate. They are able to initiate, originate, and create because of this inner core of micro subjectivity. To Skinner, the idea that people have an inner, autonomous core is a mystical, metaphysical position of the kind that must be eliminated from the social sciences: "Autonomous man serves to explain only the things we are not yet able to explain in other ways. His existence depends on our ignorance, and he naturally loses status as we come to know more about behavior" (p. 12). Although we need to reject this kind of political diatribe, the key point is this: the microscopic level has *both* a subjective and an objective dimension.

Levels of Social Reality: A Model

The most important thinker on the issue of levels of social reality was the French sociologist Georges Gurvitch. While he did not use the same terms, Gurvitch (1964) had a sense of *both* macro-micro and objective-subjective continua. Even more important, he had a profound sense of how these two continua were related. To his credit, he also steadfastly refused to treat the two continua and their interrelationships as static tools but used them to underscore the dynamic quality of social life. But Gurvitch has one major difficulty: his analytical schema is extremely complex and cumbersome. The social world is very complicated and in order to get a handle on it we need relatively simple models.

The simple model we are seeking is formed out of the intersection of the two continua of levels of social reality discussed in the last several pages. The first, the macroscopic-microscopic continuum, can be depicted as in Figure A.1:

FIGURE A.1 The Macroscopic-Microscopic Continuum, with Identification of Some Key Points on the Continuum

The objective-subjective continuum presents greater problems, yet it is no less important than the macro-micro continuum. In general, an objective social phenomenon has a real, material existence. We can think of the following, among others, as objective social phenomena: actors, action, interaction, bureaucratic structures, law, and the state apparatus. It is possible to see, touch, or chart all of these objective phenomena. However, there are social phenomena that exist *solely* in the realm of ideas; they have no material existence. These are sociological phenomena such as mental processes, the social construction of reality (Berger and Luckmann, 1967), norms, values, and many elements of culture. The problem with the objective-subjective continuum is that there are many phenomena in the middle that have *both* objective and subjective elements. The family, for example, has a real material existence as well as a series of subjective mutual understandings, norms, and values. Similarly, the polity is composed of objective laws and bureaucratic structures as well as subjective political norms and values. In fact, it is probably true that the vast majority are mixed types of social phenomena representing some combination of objective and subjective elements. Thus it is best to think of the objective-subjective continuum as two polar types with a series of variously mixed types in the middle. Some of these types may have more objective than subjective characteristics, while others may have the reverse combination. Figure A.2 is the objective-subjective continuum.

FIGURE A.2   The Objective-Subjective Continuum, with Identification of Some Mixed Types

Objective _____ **Subjective**

Actors, action, inter-action, bureaucratic structures, law, and so forth

Mixed types, combining in varying degrees objective and subjective elements; examples include the state, family, work world, religion

Social construction of reality, norms, values, and so forth

Although these continua are interesting in themselves, the interrelationship of the two continua concerns us here. Figure A.3 is a schematic representation of the intersection of these two continua and the four major levels of social reality derived from it.

The contention here is that an integrated sociological paradigm must deal with the four basic levels of social reality identified in the figure and their interrelationships. It must deal with macroscopic objective entities like bureaucracy, macro-subjective structures like values, micro-objective phenomena like patterns of interaction, and micro-subjective facts like the process of reality construction. We must remember that in the real world, all of these gradually blend into the others as part of the larger social continuum, but we have made some artificial and rather arbitrary differentiations in order to be able to deal with social reality. These four levels of social reality are posited for heuristic purposes and are not meant to be accurate depictions of the social world.

FIGURE A.3   Major Levels of Social Reality

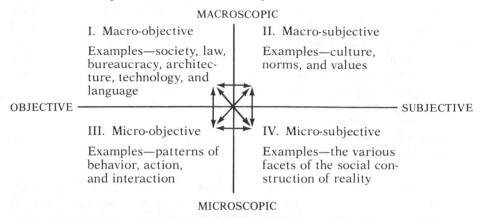

An obvious question is how these four levels relate to the three paradigms outlined in my earlier work as well as to the integrated paradigm. Figure A.4 relates the four levels to the three paradigms.

FIGURE A.4   Levels of Social Reality and the Major Sociological Paradigms

LEVELS OF SOCIAL REALITY	SOCIOLOGICAL PARADIGMS	
Macro-subjective	Social Facts	
Macro-objective		Integrated Sociological Paradigm
Micro-subjective	Social Definition	
Micro-objective		
	Social Behavior	

The social-facts paradigm focuses primarily on the macro-objective and macro-subjective levels. The social-definition paradigm is largely concerned with the micro-subjective world and that part of the micro-objective world that depends on mental processes (action). The social-behavior paradigm deals with that part of the micro-objective world that does not involve the minding process (behavior). Whereas the three extant paradigms cut across the levels of social reality horizontally, an integrated paradigm cuts across vertically. This depiction makes it clear why the integrated paradigm does not supersede the others. Although each of the three existing paradigms deals with a given level or levels in great detail, the integrated paradigm deals with all levels but does not examine any given level in anything like the degree of intensity of the other paradigms. Thus the choice of a paradigm depends on the kind of question being asked. Not all sociological issues require an integrated approach, but it is certain that at least some do.

What has been outlined in the preceding pages is a model for the image of the subject matter of an integrated sociological paradigm. This sketch will need to be detailed more sharply in future years. But that is another task (see Ritzer, 1981a). The goal of this discussion is not the development of a new sociological paradigm, but the delineation of a metatheoretical schema that allows us to analyze sociological theory in a coherent fashion. The model developed in Figure A.3 forms the basis for this analysis.

Each of the sociological theories in the text and the work of the various theorists are analyzed using the four levels of social reality depicted in Figure A.3. This figure provides us with a metatheoretical tool that can be used in the comparative analysis of sociological theories and theorists. It enables us to analyze the concerns of a theoretical perspective and how they relate to the concerns of every other sociological theory.

One thing to be avoided at all costs is the simple identification of a theory or a theorist with specific levels of social reality. Although it is true, given the preceding description of the current paradigmatic status of sociology, that sociological theorists who adhere to a given paradigm tend to focus on a given level or levels of social reality, it often does them an injustice simply to equate the breadth of their work with one or more levels. For example, Karl Marx is often thought of as focusing on macro-objective structures—in particular, on the economic structures of capitalism. But the use of the multiple levels of social reality schema allows us to see that Marx had rich insights regarding all levels of social reality and their interrelationships. Similarly, symbolic interactionism is generally considered a perspective that deals with micro subjectivity and micro objectivity, but it is not devoid of insights into the macroscopic levels of social reality (Maines, 1977).

It is also important for the reader to remember that the use of levels of social reality to analyze any theory or theorist tends to break up the wholeness, the integrity, and the internal consistency of the work. Although the levels are useful for understanding a theory and comparing it to others, one must take pains to deal with the interrelationship among levels and with the theoretical totality of the work of an individual or a school.

In sum, the metatheoretical schema outlined in Figure A.3, the development of which was traced in this appendix, provides the basis for the analysis of the various sociological theorists and theories discussed in this book.

REFERENCES

Abbott, Carroll, Brown, Charles R., and Crosbie, Paul V.
1973   "Exchange as Symbolic Interaction: For What?" *American Sociological Review* 38:504–506.

Aberle, D. F., et al.
1950/1967   "The Functional Prerequisites of a Society." In Nicholas Demerath and Richard Peterson (eds.), *System, Change and Conflict.* New York: Free Press: 317–331.

Abrahamson, Mark
1978   *Functionalism.* Englewood Cliffs, N.J.: Prentice-Hall.

Abrahamsson, Bengt
1970   "Homans on Exchange." *American Journal of Sociology* 76:273–285.

Abrams, Philip
1968   *The Origins of British Sociology: 1834–1914.* Chicago: University of Chicago Press.

Abrams, Philip, Deem, Rosemary, Finch, Janet, and Rock, Paul
1981   *Practice and Progress: British Sociology 1950–1980.* London: Allen and Unwin.

Acker, Joan
1980   "Women and Stratification: A Review of the Recent Literature." *Contemporary Sociology* 9:25–29.

Agger, Ben (ed.)
1978   *Western Marxism: An Introduction.* Santa Monica, Calif.: Goodyear.

Agonito, Rosemary (ed.)
1977   *History of Ideas on Woman.* New York: Putnam.

Akers, Ronald
1981   "Reflections of a Social Behaviorist on Behavioral Sociology." *The American Sociologist* 16:177–180.

Albrow, Martin
1974   "Dialectical and Categorical Paradigms of a Science of Society." *Sociological Review* 22:183–202.

Alexander, Jeffrey
1978   "Formal and Substantive Voluntarism in the Work of Talcott Parsons: A Theoretical and Ideological Reinterpretation." *American Sociological Review* 43:177–198.

1982   *Theoretical Logic in Sociology. Vol. 1, Positivism, Presuppositions, and Current Controversies.* Berkeley: University of California Press.

1984   "The Parsons Revival in German Sociology." In Randall Collins (ed.), *Sociological Theory—1984.* San Francisco: Jossey-Bass: 394–412.

1985a   "The 'Individualist Dilemma' in Phenomenology and Interactionism." In S. N. Eisenstadt and H. J. Helle (eds.), *Macro-Sociological Theory*, Vol. 1. London: Sage.

Alexander, Jeffrey (ed.)
1985b   *Neofunctionalism.* Beverly Hills, Calif.: Sage.

Alexander, Jeffrey, and Colomy, Paul
1985   "Toward Neo-Functionalism." *Sociological Theory* 3:11–23.

Alexander, Jeffrey, Giesen, Bernard, Munch, Richard, and Smelser, Neil J. (eds.)
1987   *The Micro-Macro Link*. Berkeley: University of California Press.

al-Hibri, Azizah
1981   "Reproduction, Mothering and the Origins of Patriarchy." In Joyce Trebilcot
            (ed.), *Mothering: Essays in Feminist Theory*. Totowa, N.J.: Rowman and
            Allanheld: 81–93.

Alt, John
1985–1986   "Reclaiming C. Wright Mills." *Telos* 66:6–43.

Althusser, Louis
1969   *For Marx*. Harmondsworth, Eng.: Penguin.
1977   *Politics and History*. London: NLB.

Althusser, Louis, and Balibar, Etienne (eds.)
1970   *Reading Capital*. New York: Pantheon.

Amin, Samir
1977   *Unequal Development: An Essay on the Social Formations of Peripheral
            Capitalism*. New York: Monthly Review Press.

Amsterdamska, Olga
1985   "Institutions and Schools of Thought." *American Journal of Sociology*
            91:332–358.

Anderson, Margaret L.
1983   *Thinking about Women: Sociological and Feminist Perspectives*. New York:
            Macmillan.

Anderson, Perry
1976   *Considerations on Western Marxism*. London: NLB.

Andreski, Stanislav (ed.)
1974   *The Essential Comte*. New York: Barnes & Noble.

Antonio, Robert J.
1979   "Domination and Production in Bureaucracy." *American Sociological Review*
            44:895–912.
1981   "Immanent Critique as the Core of Critical Theory: Its Origins and Develop-
            ment in Hegel, Marx and Contemporary Thought." *British Journal of Sociol-
            ogy* 32:330–345.
1985   "Values, History and Science: The Metatheoretic Foundations of the Weber-
            Marx Dialogues." In Robert J. Antonio and Ronald M. Glassman (eds.), *A
            Weber-Marx Dialogue*. Lawrence: University Press of Kansas: 20–43.

Antonio, Robert J., and Glassman, Ronald M. (eds.)
1985   *A Weber-Marx Dialogue*. Lawrence: University Press of Kansas.

Appelbaum, Richard
1979   "Born-Again Functionalism? A Reconsideration of Althusser's Structuralism."
            The Insurgent Sociologist 9:18–33.

Archer, Margaret
1985   "Structuration versus Morphogenesis." In S. N. Eisenstadt and H. J. Helle
            (eds.), *Macro-Sociological Theory*. London: Sage: 58–88.

Aronowitz, Stanley
1973   *False Promises: The Shaping of American Working Class Consciousness*. New
            York: McGraw-Hill.

Arthur, Marilyn B.
1976   "Classics." *Signs: Journal of Women in Culture and Society* 2:2:382–403.

Ascher, Carol, de Salvo, Louise, and Ruddick, Sara
1984   *Between Women*. Boston: Beacon Press.

Atkinson, Jane Monnig
1982   "Anthropology." *Signs: Journal of Women in Culture and Society* 8:2:236–258.
Atkinson, J. Maxwell
1984a   *Our Masters' Voices: The Language and Body Language of Politics.* New
                York: Methuen.
1984b   "Public Speaking and Audience Responses: Some Techniques for Inviting Ap-
                plause." In J. Maxwell Atkinson and John Heritage (eds.), *Structures of Social
                Action.* Cambridge: Cambridge University Press: 370–409.
Atkinson, J. Maxwell, and Heritage, John (eds.)
1984   *Structures of Social Action: Studies in Conversation Analysis.* Cambridge:
                Cambridge University Press.
Atkinson, Ti-Grace
1974   *Amazon Odyssey.* New York: Links Books.
Back, Kurt
1970   Review of Robert Burgess and Don Bushell, *Behavioral Sociology. American
                Sociological Review* 35:1098–1100.
Baldwin, Alfred
1961   "The Parsonian Theory of Personality." In Max Black (ed.), *The Social
                Theories of Talcott Parsons.* Englewood Cliffs, N.J.: Prentice-Hall: 153–190.
Baldwin, John D., and Baldwin, Janice I.
1978   "Behaviorism on Verstehen and Erklaren." *American Sociological Review*
                43:335–347.
1986   *Behavior Principles in Everyday Life.* 2nd ed. Englewood Cliffs, N.J.:
                Prentice-Hall.
Ball, Richard A.
1978   "Sociology and General Systems Theory." *The American Sociologist* 13:65–72.
Banner, Lois
1984   *Women in Modern America: A Brief History.* New York: Harcourt Brace
                Jovanovich.
Baran, Paul, and Sweezy, Paul M.
1966   *Monopoly Capital: An Essay on the American Economic and Social Order.*
                New York: Monthly Review Press.
Barbalet, J.M.
1983   *Marx's Construction of Social Theory.* London: Routledge and Kegan Paul.
Barry, Kathleen
1979   *Female Sexual Slavery.* Englewood Cliffs, N.J.: Prentice-Hall.
Bauman, Zygmunt
1976   *Towards a Critical Sociology: An Essay on Commonsense and Emancipation.*
                London: Routledge and Kegan Paul.
Bellah, Robert
1980   "The World Is the World Through Its Theorists—In Memory of Talcott
                Parsons." *American Sociologist* 15:60–62.
Beniger, James R., and Savory, Laina
1981   "Social Exchange: Diffusion of a Paradigm." *The American Sociologist* 16:240–250.
Benston, Margaret
1970   *The Political Economy of Women's Liberation.* New York: Monthly Review
                Press Reprint.
Benton, Ted
1984   *The Rise and Fall of Structural Marxism: Althusser and His Influence.* New
                York: St. Martin's.

Berger, Brigette, and Berger, Peter
1983   *The War Over the Family: Capturing the Middle Ground.* Garden City, N.Y.:
            Anchor.
Berger, Charles R. and Chaffee, Steven H.
forthcoming *Handbook of Communication Science.* Newbury Park, Calif.: Sage.
Berger, Joseph, Wagner, David G., and Zelditch, Jr., Morris
1985   "Theoretical and Metatheoretical Themes in Expectation States Theory." In
            H. J. Helle and S. N. Eisenstadt (eds.), *Micro-Sociological Theories: Perspec-
            tives on Sociological Theory*, Vol. 2. London: Sage: 148–168.
Berger, Peter
1963   *Invitation to Sociology.* New York: Doubleday.
Berger, Peter, and Kellner, Hansfield
1964   "Marriage and the Social Construction of Reality." In Peter Dreitzel (ed.), *Recent
            Sociology, No. 2, Patterns of Communicative Behavior.* New York: Macmillan.
Berger, Peter, and Luckmann, Thomas
1967   *The Social Construction of Reality.* Garden City, N.Y.: Anchor.
Bergeson, Albert
1984   "The Critique of World-System Theory: Class Relations or Division of
            Labor?" In Randall Collins (ed.), *Sociological Theory—1984.* San Francisco:
            Jossey-Bass: 365–372.
Bernard, Jessie
1971   *Women and the Public Interest.* Chicago: Aldine.
1973   "My Four Revolutions: An Autobiographical Account of the American Socio-
            logical Association." *American Journal of Sociology*, 78, 773–792.
1981   *The Female World.* New York: Free Press.
1982   *The Future of Marriage.* 2nd ed. New Haven: Yale University Press.
Bernard, Thomas
1983   *The Consensus-Conflict Debate: Form and Content in Sociological Theories.*
            New York: Columbia University Press.
Bernikow, Louise (ed.)
1974   *The World Split Open: Four Centuries of Women Poets in England and
            America, 1552–1950.* New York: Vintage.
1980   *Among Women.* New York: Harper.
Besnard, Philippe
1983b   "The 'Année Sociologique' Team." In P. Besnard (ed.), *The Sociological
            Domain.* Cambridge: Cambridge University Press: 11–39.
Besnard, Philippe (ed.)
1983a   *The Sociological Domain.* Cambridge: Cambridge University Press.
Best, Raphaela
1983   *We've All Got Scars: What Boys and Girls Learn in Elementary School.*
            Bloomington: University of Indiana Press.
Bhaskar, Roy
1979   *The Possibility of Naturalism.* Atlantic Highlands, N.J.: Humanities Press.
1982   "Emergence, Explanation, and Emancipation." In Paul Secord (ed.), *Explain-
            ing Human Behavior.* Beverly Hills, Calif.: Sage: 275–310.
Bierstedt, Robert
1963   "The Common Sense World of Alfred Schutz." *Social Research* 30:116–121.
1981   *American Sociological Theory: A Critical History.* New York: Academic Press.
Bird, Caroline
1979   *The Two Paycheck Family.* New York: Rawson. Wade.

Birnbauer, J. S., et al.
1965   "Classroom Behavior of Retarded Pupils with Token Reinforcement." *Journal of Experimental Child Psychology* 2:219-235.

Bittner, Egon
1973   "Objectivity and Realism in Sociology." In George Psathas (ed.), *Phenomenological Sociology: Issues and Applications.* New York: Wiley: 109-125.

Blalock, Hubert, and Wilken, Paul
1979   *Intergroup Processes: A Micro-Macro Perspective.* New York: Free Press.

Blau, Peter
1960   "Structural Effects." *American Sociological Review* 25:178-193.
1964   *Exchange and Power in Social Life.* New York: Wiley.
1975a   Introduction, "Parallels and Contrasts in Structural Inquiries." In Peter Blau (ed.), *Approaches to the Study of Social Structure.* New York: Free Press: 1-20.
1975b   "Parameters of Social Structure." In Peter Blau (ed.), *Approaches to the Study of Social Structure.* New York: Free Press: 220-253.
1977a   *Inequality and Heterogeneity: A Primitive Theory of Social Structure.* New York: Free Press.
1977b   "A Macrosociological Theory of Social Structure." *American Sociological Review* 83:26-54.
1980   "A Fable about Social Structure." *Social Forces* 58:777-788.
forthcoming "Microprocess and Macrostructure." In Karen Cook (ed.), *Social Exchange Theory.* Beverly Hills, Calif.: Sage.

Blau, Peter, and Merton, Robert K. (eds.)
1981   *Continuities in Structural Inquiry.* Beverly Hills, Calif.: Sage.

Blau, Peter M., Blum, Terry C., and Schwartz, Joseph E.
1982   "Heterogeneity and Intermarriage." *American Sociological Review* 47:45-61.

Blau, Peter M., Beeker, Caroline, and Fitzpatrick, Kevin
1984   "Crosscutting Social Circles and Intermarriage." *Social Forces* 62:585-606.

Blauner, Robert
1964   *Alienation and Freedom: The Factory Worker and His Industry.* Chicago: University of Chicago Press.

Bleich, Harold
1977   *The Philosophy of Herbert Marcuse.* Washington, D.C.: University Press of America.

Bluestone, Barry, and Harrison, Bennett
1982   *The Deindustrialization of America.* New York: Basic Books.

Blum, Alan, and McHugh, Peter
1971   "The Social Ascription of Motives." *American Sociological Review* 36:98-109.

Blum, Terry C.
1984   "Racial Inequality and Salience: An Explanation of Blau's Theory of Social Structure." *Social Forces* 62:607-617.
1985   "Structural Constraints on Interpersonal Relations: A Test of Blau's Macrosociological Theory." *American Journal of Sociology* 91:511-521.

Blumenstiel, Alexander D.
1973   "The Sociology of Good Times." In George Psathas (ed.), *Phenomenological Sociology: Issues and Applications.* New York: Wiley: 187-215.

Blumer, Herbert
1954/1969   "What Is Wrong with Social Theory?" In Herbert Blumer, *Symbolic Interaction:* 140-152.
1955/1969   "Attitudes and the Social Act." In Herbert Blumer, *Symbolic Interaction:* 90-100.

1956/1969   "Sociological Analysis and the 'Variable.'" In Herbert Blumer, *Symbolic Interaction:* 127–139.

1962/1969   "Society as Symbolic Interaction." In Herbert Blumer, *Symbolic Interaction:* 78–89.

1969a   *Symbolic Interaction: Perspective and Method.* Englewood Cliffs, N.J.: Prentice-Hall.

1969b   "The Methodological Position of Symbolic Interactionism." In Herbert Blumer, *Symbolic Interaction:* 1–60.

1974   "Comments on 'Parsons as a Symbolic Interactionist.'" *Sociological Inquiry* 45:59–62.

1980   Comment: "Mead and Blumer: The Convergent Methodological Perspectives of Social Behaviorism and Symbolic Interactionism." *American Sociological Review* 45:409–419.

Bolton, Charles

1981   "Some Consequences of the Meadian Self." *Symbolic Interaction* 4:245–259.

Bosserman, Phillip

1968   *Dialectical Sociology: An Analysis of the Sociology of Georges Gurvitch.* Boston: Porter Sargent.

Bosworth, Susan Lovegren, and Kreps, Gary A.

1986   "Structure as Process: Organization and Role." *American Sociological Review* 51:699–716.

Bottomore, Tom

1975   "Structure and History." In Peter Blau (ed.), *Approaches to the Study of Social Structure.* New York: Free Press: 159–171.

1983   "Sociology." In David McLellan (ed.), *Marx: The First 100 Years.* New York: St. Martin's.

1984   *The Frankfurt School.* Chichester, Eng.: Ellis Horwood.

Boudon, Raymond

1979/1981   *The Logic of Social Action: An Introduction to Sociological Analysis.* London: Routledge and Kegan Paul.

Boulding, Elise

1976   *The Underside of History.* Boulder, Colo.: Westview Press.

Bourdieu, Pierre

1977   *Outline of a Theory of Practice.* London: Cambridge University Press.

Bourricaud, François

1981   *The Sociology of Talcott Parsons.* Chicago: University of Chicago Press.

Bramson, Leon

1961   *The Political Context of Sociology.* Princeton: Princeton University Press.

Braverman, Harry

1974   *Labor and Monopoly Capital: The Degradation of Work in the Twentieth Century.* New York: Monthly Review Press.

Brawley, Eleanor, et al.

1969   "Behavior Modification of an Autistic Child." *Behavioral Science* 14:87–96.

Breault, K. D.

1986   "Suicide in America: A Test of Durkheim's Theory of Religion, 1933–1980." *American Journal of Sociology* 92:628–656.

Bredemeier, Harry C.

1978   "Exchange Theory." In Tom Bottomore and Robert Nisbet (eds.), *A History of Sociological Analysis.* New York: Basic Books: 418–456.

Brown, Richard
forthcoming   *Society as Text: Essays on Rhetoric, Reason and Reality.* Chicago: University
of Chicago Press.

Brownmiller, Susan
1975   *Against Our Will: Men, Women and Rape.* New York: Simon & Schuster.

Brubaker, Rogers
1984   *The Limits of Rationality: An Essay on the Social and Moral Thought of Max
Weber.* London: George Allen and Unwin.

Bryant, Christopher G. A.
1985   *Positivism in Social Theory and Research.* New York: St. Martin's.

Buckley, Walter
1967   *Sociology and Modern Systems Theory.* Englewood Cliffs, N.J.: Prentice-Hall.

Bulmer, Martin
1984   *The Chicago School of Sociology: Institutionalization, Diversity, and the Rise
of Sociological Research.* Chicago: University of Chicago Press.
1985   "The Chicago School of Sociology: What Made It a 'School'?" *The History
of Sociology: An International Review* 5:62–77.

Burawoy, Michael
1979   *Manufacturing Consent: Changes in the Labor Process under Monopoly
Capitalism.* Chicago: University of Chicago Press.

Burger, Christa
1986   "The Disappearance of Art: The Postmodernism Debate in the U.S." *Telos*
68:93–106.

Burger, Thomas
1976   *Max Weber's Theory of Concept Formation: History, Laws and Ideal Types.*
Durham, N.C.: Duke University Press.
1977a   "Max Weber's Interpretive Sociology, the Understanding of Actions and
Motives, and a Weberian View of Man." *Sociological Inquiry* 47:127–132.
1977b   "Talcott Parsons, the Problem of Order in Society, and the Program of an
Analytical Sociology." *American Journal of Sociology* 83:320–334.

Burgess, Robert, and Bushell, Don
1969a   "A Behavioral View of Some Sociological Concepts." In Robert Burgess and
Don Bushell (eds.), *Behavioral Sociology.* New York: Columbia University
Press: 273–290.

Burgess, Robert, and Bushell, Don (eds.)
1969b   *Behavioral Sociology.* New York: Columbia University Press.

Burris, Val
1979   "Introduction." In "The Structuralist Influence in Marxist Theory and Research." *The Insurgent Sociologist* 9:4–17.

Burt, Ronald
1982   *Toward a Structural Theory of Action: Network Models of Social Structure,
Perception, and Action.* New York: Academic Press.

Bushell, Don, and Burgess, Robert
1969   "Some Basic Principles of Behavior." In Robert Burgess and Don Bushell
(eds.), *Behavioral Sociology.* New York: Columbia University Press: 27–48.

Bushell, Don, Wrobel, Ann, and Michaelis, Mary Louise
1969   "Applying 'Group' Contingencies to the Classroom Study of Behavior of Pre-
school Children." In Robert Burgess and Don Bushell (eds.), *Behavioral
Sociology.* New York: Columbia University Press: 219–230.

Campbell, Colin
1982   "A Dubious Distinction? An Inquiry into the Value and Use of Merton's Con-
             cepts of Manifest and Latent Function." *American Sociological Review*
             47:29–44.
Cameron, Anne
1981   *Daughters of Copper Woman.* Vancouver: Press Gang Publishers.
Canadian Journal of Political and Social Theory
1986   "The Postmodern Scene" (special issue) 10:1–275.
Carden, Maren Lockwood
1974   *The New Feminist Movement.* New York: Russell Sage Foundation.
Carveth, Donald
1982   "Sociology and Psychoanalysis: The Hobbesian Problem Revisited." *Canadian
             Journal of Sociology* 7:201–229.
Carver, Terrell
1983   *Marx and Engels: The Intellectual Relationship.* Bloomington: Indiana Univer-
             sity Press.
Chadwick-Jones, J. K.
1976   *Social Exchange Theory: Its Structure and Influence in Social Psychology.*
             London: Academic Press.
Chafetz, Janet Saltzman
1984   *Sex and Advantage.* Totowa, N.J.: Rowman and Allanheld.
Chafetz, Janet Saltzman, and Dworkin, Anthony Gary
1986   *Female Revolt: Women's Movements in World and Historical Perspectives.*
             Totowa, N.J.: Rowman and Allanheld.
Charon, Joel
1985   *Symbolic Interaction: An Introduction, an Interpretation, an Integration.* 2nd
             ed. Englewood Cliffs, N.J.: Prentice-Hall.
Chernin, Kim
1981   *The Obsession: Reflections on the Tyranny of Slenderness.* New York: Harper.
Chirot, Daniel
1985   "The Rise of the West." *American Sociological Review* 50:181–195.
Chitnis, Anand C.
1976   *The Scottish Enlightenment: A Social History.* Totowa, N.J.: Rowman and
             Littlefield.
Chodorow, Nancy
1978   *The Reproduction of Mothering: Psychoanalysis and the Sociology of Gender.*
             Berkeley: University of California Press.
Chua, Beng-Huat
1977   "Delineating a Marxist Interest in Ethnomethodology." *American Sociologist*
             12:24–32.
Cicourel, Aaron
1974   *Cognitive Sociology: Language and Meaning in Social Interaction.* New York:
             Free Press.
1981   "Notes on the Integration of Micro- and Macro-Levels of Analysis." In
             K. Knorr-Cetina and A. Cicourel (eds.), *Advances in Social Theory and
             Methodology.* New York: Methuen: 51–79.
Clark, Priscilla P. and Clark, Terry Nichols
1982   "The Structural Sources of French Structuralism." In Ino Rossi (ed.), *Struc-
             tural Sociology.* New York: Columbia University Press: 22–46.

Clark, Ronald W.
1971   *Einstein: The Life and Times.* New York: Avon.

Clawson, Dan
1980   *Bureaucracy and the Labor Process: The Transformation of U.S. Industry, 1860–1920.* New York: Monthly Review Press.

Clawson, Dan, Neustadtl, Alan, and Bearden, James
1986   "The Logic of Business Unity: Corporate Contributions to the 1980 Congressional Elections." *American Sociological Review* 51:797–811.

Cohen, Jere, Hazelrigg, Lawrence, and Pope, Whitney
1975   "DeParsonizing Weber: A Critique of Parsons' Interpretation of Weber's Sociology." *American Sociological Review* 40:229–241.

Cohen, Percy
1968   *Modern Social Theory.* New York: Basic Books.

Colclough, Glenna, and Horan, Patrick
1983   "The Status Attainment Paradigm: An Application of a Kuhnian Perspective." *The Sociological Quarterly* 24:25–42.

Coleman, James
1968   Review of Harold Garfinkel, *Studies in Ethnomethodology. American Sociological Review* 33:126–130.
1971   "Community Disorganization and Conflict." In Robert Merton and Robert Nisbet (eds.), *Contemporary Social Problems.* 3rd ed. New York: Harcourt Brace Jovanovich: 657–708.
1986   "Social Theory, Social Research, and a Theory of Action." *American Journal of Sociology* 91:1309–1335.

Colfax, J. David, and Roach, Jack L.
1971   *Radical Sociology.* New York: Basic Books.

Collins, Randall
1975   *Conflict Sociology: Toward an Explanatory Science.* New York: Academic Press.
1981a   "On the Microfoundations of Macrosociology." *American Journal of Sociology* 86:984–1014.
1981b   "Micro-Translation as Theory-Building Strategy." In K. Knorr-Centina and A. Cicourel (eds.), *Advances in Social Theory and Methodology.* New York: Methuen: 81–108.
1981c   "Introduction." In Randall Collins (ed.), *Sociology since Midcentury: Essays in Theory Cumulation.* New York: Academic Press: 1–9.
1986a   "Is 1980s Sociology in the Doldrums?" *American Journal of Sociology* 91:1336–1355.
1986b   "The Passing of Intellectual Generations: Reflections on the Death of Erving Goffman." *Sociological Theory* 4:106–113.

Colomy, Paul
1986   "Recent Developments in the Functionalist Approach to Change." *Sociological Focus* 19:139–158.

Comte, Auguste
1830–1842/ *The Positive Philosophy.* New York: AMS Press.
1974
1851–1854/ *System of Positive Philosophy.* 4 vols. New York: Burt Franklin.
1976

Connerton, Paul (ed.)
1976   *Critical Sociology.* Harmondsworth, Eng.: Penguin.

Cook, Judith, and Fonow, Mary Margaret
1986   "Knowledge and Women's Interests: Issues of Epistemology and Methodology in Feminist Sociological Research." *Sociological Inquiry* 56:1:2–29.

Cook, Karen S. (ed.)
forthcoming a *Social Exchange Theory.* Beverly Hills, Calif.: Sage.
forthcoming b "Emerson's Contributions to Social Exchange Theory." In Karen S. Cook (ed.), *Social Exchange Theory.* Beverly Hills, Calif.: Sage.

Cook, Karen S., and Emerson, Richard M.
1978   "Power, Equity, Commitment in Exchange Networks." *American Sociological Review* 43:721–739.

Cook, Karen S., Emerson, Richard M., Gillmore, Mary R., and Yamagishi, Toshio
1983   "The Distribution of Power in Exchange Networks: Theory and Experimental Results." *American Journal of Sociology* 89:275–305.

Cooley, Charles H.
1902/1964   *Human Nature and the Social Order.* New York: Scribner's.

Coser, Lewis
1956   *The Functions of Social Conflict.* New York: Free Press.
1975a   Presidential Address: "Two Methods in Search of a Substance." *American Sociological Review* 40:691–700.
1975b   "Structure and Conflict." In Peter Blau (ed.), *Approaches to the Study of Social Structure.* New York: Free Press: 210–219.
1977   *Masters of Sociological Thought.* 2nd ed. New York: Harcourt Brace Jovanovich.

Cott, Nancy F.
1977   *The Bonds of Womanhood: Women's Sphere in New England, 1780–1835.* New Haven: Yale University Press.

Cottrell, Jr., Leonard S.
1980   "George Herbert Mead: The Legacy of Social Behaviorism." In Robert K. Merton and Matilda White Riley (eds.), *Sociological Traditions from Generation to Generation: Glimpses of the American Experience.* Norwood, N.J.: Ablex.

Craib, Ian
1976   *Existentialism and Sociology: A Study of Jean-Paul Sartre.* Cambridge: Cambridge University Press.

Culler, Jonathan
1976   *Ferdinand de Saussure.* Harmondsworth, Eng.: Penguin.

Curtis, Bruce
1981   *William Graham Sumner.* Boston: Twayne.

Curtis, C. P., and Homans, G. C.
1934   *An Introduction to Pareto.* New York: Knopf.

Dahrendorf, Ralf
1958   "Out of Utopia: Toward a Reorientation of Sociological Analysis." *American Journal of Sociology* 64:115–127.
1959   *Class and Class Conflict in Industrial Society.* Stanford: Stanford University Press.
1968   *Essays in the Theory of Society.* Stanford: Stanford University Press.

Dallmayr, Fred R.
1973   "Phenomenology and Marxism: A Salute to Enzo Paci." In George Psathas (ed.), *Phenomenological Sociology: Issues and Applications.* New York: Wiley: 305–356.

Daly, Mary
1968   *The Church and the Second Sex.* New York: Harper & Row.
1973   *Beyond God the Father: Towards a Philosophy of Women's Liberation.* Boston:
            Beacon Press.
1978   *Gyn/Ecology: The Metaethics of Radical Feminism.* Boston: Beacon
            Press.
1984   *Pure Lust.* Boston: Beacon Press.
Davis, Kingsley
1959   "The Myth of Functional Analysis as a Special Method in Sociology and An-
            thropology." *American Sociological Review* 24:757–772.
Davis, Kingsley, and Moore, Wilbert
1945   "Some Principles of Stratification." *American Sociological Review*
            10:242–249.
de Beauvoir, Simone
1957   *The Second Sex.* New York: Vintage.
Deckard, Barbara Sinclair
1979   *The Women's Movement: Political, Socioeconomic and Psychological Issues.*
            New York: Harper & Row.
Demerath, Nicholas, and Peterson, Richard (eds.)
1967   *System, Change and Conflict.* New York: Free Press.
de Pizan, Christine
1405/1982   *The Book of the City of the Ladies* (Earl Jeffrey Warren, trans.). New York:
            Persea Books.
Devereaux, Edward C.
1961   "Parsons's Sociological Theory." In Max Black (ed.), *The Social Theories of
            Talcott Parsons.* Englewood Cliffs, N.J.: Prentice-Hall: 1–63.
Dinnerstein, Dorothy
1976   *The Mermaid and the Minotaur.* New York: Harper & Row.
DiTomaso, Nancy
1982   "'Sociological Reductionism' from Parsons to Althusser: Linking Action and
            Structure in Social Theory." *American Sociological Review* 47:14–28.
Ditton, Jason (ed.)
1980   *The View from Goffman.* New York: St. Martin's.
Dobb, Maurice
1964   *Studies in the Development of Capitalism.* Rev. ed. New York: International
            Publishers.
Douglas, Jack
1967   *The Social Meanings of Suicide.* Princeton, N.J.: Princeton University Press.
1977   "Existential Sociology." In Jack D. Douglas et al. (eds.), *Existential
            Sociology.* Cambridge: Cambridge University Press: 3–73.
1980   "Introduction to the Sociologies of Everyday Life." In Jack Douglas et al.
            (eds.), *Introduction to the Sociologies of Everyday Life.* Boston: Allyn and
            Bacon: 1–19.
Douglas, Jack (ed.)
1970   *Understanding Everyday Life.* Chicago: Aldine.
Douglas, Jack, and Johnson, John
1977   "Introduction." In Jack Douglas et al. (eds.), *Existential Sociology.* Cam-
            bridge: Cambridge University Press: vii–xv.
Douglas, Jack, et al. (eds.)
1980   *Introduction to the Sociologies of Everyday Life.* Boston: Allyn and Bacon.

Duncan, O. D., and Schnore, L. F.
1959   "Cultural, Behavioral and Ecological Perspectives in the Study of Social
              Organization." *American Journal of Sociology* 65:132–146.
Durkheim, Emile
1893a/1964   *The Division of Labor in Society.* New York: Free Press
1895/1964   *The Rules of Sociological Method.* New York: Free Press.
1897/1951   *Suicide.* New York: Free Press.
1912/1965   *The Elementary Forms of Religious Life.* New York: Free Press.
1928/1962   *Socialism.* New York: Collier Books.
Dworkin, Andrea
1976   *Our Blood: Prophecies and Discourses on Sexual Politics.* New York: Perigee
              Books.
Eckberg, Douglas Lee, and Hill, Lester
1979   "The Paradigm Concept and Sociology: A Critical Review." *American Socio-
              logical Review* 44:925–937.
Edel, Abraham
1959   "The Concept of Levels in Social Theory." In Llewellyn Gross (ed.), *Sympo-
              sium on Sociological Theory.* Evanston, Ill.: Row Peterson: 167–195.
Edwards, Richard
1979   *Contested Terrain: The Transformation of the Workplace in the Twentieth Cen-
              tury.* New York: Basic Books.
Effrat, Andrew
1972   "Power to the Paradigms: An Editorial Introduction." *Sociological Inquiry*
              42:3–33.
Ehrenreich, Barbara, and English, Deirdre
1978   *For Her Own Good: 150 Years of Experts' Advice to Women.* Garden City,
              N.Y.: Anchor/Doubleday.
Ehrmann, Jacques
1970   "Introduction." In Jacques Ehrmann (ed.), *Structuralism.* Garden City, N.Y.:
              Anchor: vii–xi.
Eisenstadt, S. N., with Curelaru, M.
1976   *The Form of Sociology: Paradigms and Crises.* New York: Wiley.
Eisenstadt, S. N., and Helle, H. J. (eds.)
1985a   *Macro-Sociological Theory: Perspectives on Sociological Theory*, Vol. 1.
              London: Sage.
1985b   "General Introduction to Perspectives on Sociological Theory." In S. N. Eisen-
              stadt and H. J. Helle (eds.), *Macro-Sociological Theory.* London: Sage: 1–3.
Eisenstein, Zillah
1979   *Capitalist Patriarchy and the Case for Socialist Feminism.* New York: Monthly
              Review Press.
Ekeh, Peter P.
1974   *Social Exchange Theory: The Two Traditions.* Cambridge, Mass.: Harvard
              University Press.
1982   "Structuralism, the Principle of Elementarism, and the Theory of
              Civilization." In Ino Rossi (ed.), *Structural Sociology.* New York: Columbia
              University Press: 122–148.
Elster, Jon
1982   "Marxism, Functionalism and Game Theory: The Case for Methodological In-
              dividualism." *Theory and Society* 11:453–482.
1985   *Making Sense of Marx.* Cambridge: Cambridge University Press.

Emerson, Richard M.
1972a   "Exchange Theory, Part I: A Psychological Basis for Social Exchange." In
             Joseph Berger, Morris Zelditch, Jr., and Bo Anderson (eds.), *Sociological
             Theories in Progress*, vol. 2. Boston: Houghton-Mifflin: 38–57.
1972b   "Exchange Theory, Part II: Exchange Relations and Networks." In Joseph
             Berger et al. (eds.), *Sociological Theories in Progress*, vol. 2. Boston:
             Houghton-Mifflin: 58–87.
1976   "Social Exchange Theory." In Alex Inkeles, James Coleman, and Neil
             Smelser (eds.), *Annual Review of Sociology*, vol. 2. Palo Alto: Annual
             Reviews: 335–362.
1981   "Social Exchange Theory." In Morris Rosenberg and Ralph H. Turner (eds.),
             Social Psychology: Sociological Perspectives. New York: Basic Books: 30–65.
forthcoming "Toward a Theory of Value in Exchange." In Karen S. Cook (ed.), *Social Ex-
             change Theory*. Beverly Hills, Calif.: Sage.

Engels, Friedrich
1890/1972   "Letter to Joseph Bloch." In Robert C. Tucker (ed.), *The Marx-Engels
             Reader*. New York: Norton: 640–642.
1884/1970   *The Origins of the Family, Private Property and the State*. New York: Inter-
             national.

Evans, Sara
1980   *Personal Politics: The Roots of the Women's Liberation Movement in the Civil
             Rights Movement and the New Left*. New York: Vintage.

Faghirzadeh, Saleh
1982   *Sociology of Sociology: In Search of . . . Ibn-Khaldun's Sociology Then and
             Now*. Teheran: The Soroush Press.

Faia, Michael A.
1986   *Dynamic Functionalism: Strategy and Tactics*. Cambridge: Cambridge Univer-
             sity Press.

Fararo, Thomas J., and Skvoretz, John
1986   "E-State Structuralism: A Theoretical Method." *American Sociological Review*
             51:591–602.

Farganis, James
1975   "A Preface to Critical Theory." *Theory and Society* 2:483–508.

Faris, R. E. L.
1970   *Chicago Sociology: 1920–1932*. Chicago: University of Chicago Press.

Faught, Jim
1980   "Presuppositions of the Chicago School in the Work of Everett Hughes." *The
             American Sociologist* 15:72–82.

Fendrich, Michael
1984   "Wives' Employment and Husbands' Distress: A Meta-analysis and a Replica-
             tion." *Journal of Marriage and the Family* 46:871–879.

Fine, Gary Alan, and Kleinman, Sherryl
1983   "Network and Meaning: An Interactionist Approach to Social Structure." *Sym-
             bolic Interation* 6:97–110.
1986   "Interpreting the Sociological Classics: Can There Be a 'True' Meaning of
             Mead?" *Symbolic Interaction* 9:129–146.

Fine, William F.
1979   *Progressive Evolutionism and American Sociology, 1890–1920*. UMI Research
             Press (*n.p.*)

Fischer, Norman
1984   "Hegelian Marxism and Ethics." *Canadian Journal of Political and Social Theory* 8:112–138.
Fisher, Berenice, and Strauss, Anselm
1979   "George Herbert Mead and the Chicago Tradition of Sociology—Parts 1 and 2." *Symbolic Interaction* 2,1:9–25; 2,2:9–19.
Fiske, Donald W., and Shweder, Richard A. (eds.)
1986   *Metatheory in Social Science: Pluralisms and Subjectivities.* Chicago: University of Chicago Press.
Fontana, Andrea
1980   "Toward a Complex Universe: Existential Sociology." In Jack D. Douglas et al. (eds.), *Introduction to the Sociologies of Everyday Life.* Boston: Allyn and Bacon: 155–181.
1984   "Introduction: Existential Sociology and the Self." In Joseph Kotarba and Andrea Fontana (eds.), *The Existential Self in Society.* Chicago: University of Chicago Press: 3–17.
Forman, Paul
1979   "The Reception of Acausal Quantum Mechanics in Germany and Britain." In Seymour H. Mauskopf (ed.), *The Reception of Unconventional Science.* Boulder, Colo.: Westview Press: 11–50.
Foucault, Michel
1965   *Madness and Civilization: A History of Insanity in the Age of Reason.* New York: Vintage.
1966   *The Order of Things: An Archaeology of the Human Sciences.* New York: Vintage.
1969   *The Archaeology of Knowledge and the Discourse on Language.* New York: Harper Colophon.
1975   *The Birth of the Clinic: An Archaeology of Medical Perception.* New York: Vintage.
1979   *Discipline and Punish: The Birth of the Prison.* New York: Vintage.
1980   *The History of Sexuality.* Vol. 1: *An Introduction.* New York: Vintage.
1985   *The Uses of Pleasure. The History of Sexuality.* Vol. 2. New York: Pantheon.
Frank, André Gunder
1966/1974   "Functionalism and Dialectics." In R. Serge Denisoff, Orel Callahan, and Mark H. Levine (eds.), *Theories and Paradigms in Contemporary Sociology.* Itasca, Ill.: Peacock: 342–352.
1969   *Capitalism and Underdevelopment in Latin America.* New York: Monthly Review Press.
Frankfurt Institute for Social Research
1973   *Aspects of Sociology.* London: Heinemann.
Freeman, C. Robert
1980   "Phenomenological Sociology and Ethnomethodology." In Jack D. Douglas et al. (eds.), *Introduction to the Sociologies of Everyday Life.* Boston: Allyn and Bacon: 113–154.
Friedan, Betty
1963   *The Feminine Mystique.* New York: Dell.
1981   *The Second Stage.* New York: Summit.
Friedheim, Elizabeth
1979   "An Empirical Comparison of Ritzer's Paradigms and Similar Metatheories: A Research Note." *Social Forces* 58:59–66.

Friedman, Debra
1983   "Why Workers Strike: Individual Decisions and Structural Constraints." In
            Michael Hechter (ed.), *The Microfoundations of Macrosociology*. Philadelphia:
            Temple University Press: 250–283.
Friedman, George
1981   *The Political Philosophy of the Frankfurt School*. Ithaca, N.Y.: Cornell Univer-
            sity Press.
Friedrichs, Robert
1970   *A Sociology of Sociology*. New York: Free Press.
Frisby, David
1981   *Sociological Impressionism: A Reassessment of Georg Simmel's Social Theory*.
            London: Heinemann.
1984   *Georg Simmel*. Chichester, Eng.: Ellis Horwood.
Frye, Marilyn
1983   *The Politics of Reality: Essays in Feminist Theory*. New York: Crossings Press.
Fuhrman, Ellsworth R.
1980   *The Sociology of Knowledge in America: 1983–1915*. Charlottesville: Univer-
            Press of Virginia.
Furfey, Paul
1953/1965   *The Scope and Method of Sociology: A Metasociological Treatise*. New York:
            Cooper Square Publishers.
Gallant, Mary J., and Kleinman, Sherryl
1983   "Symbolic Interaction vs. Ethnomethodology." *Symbolic Interaction* 6:1–18.
1985   "Making Sense of Interpretations: Response to Rawls and the Debate between
            Symbolic Interactionism and Ethnomethodology." *Symbolic Interaction*
            8:141–145.
Gandy, D. Ross
1979   *Marx and History: From Primitive Society to the Communist Future*. Austin:
            University of Texas Press.
Gans, Herbert
1972   "The Positive Functions of Poverty." *American Journal of Sociology*
            78:275–289.
Gardiner, Jean
1979   "Women's Domestic Labor." In Zillah Eisenstein (ed.), *Capitalist Patriarchy
            and the Case for Socialist Feminism*. New York and London: Monthly Review
            Press: 173–189.
Garfinkel, Harold
1963   "A Conception of and Experiment with 'Trust' as a Condition of Concerted
            Stable Actions." In O. J. Harvey (ed.), *Motivations and Social Interaction*.
            New York: Ronald Press.
1967   *Studies in Ethnomethodology*. Englewood Cliffs, N.J.: Prentice-Hall.
1974   "The Origins of the Term 'Ethnomethodology.'" In Roy Turner (ed.), *Ethno-
            methodology*. Harmondsworth, Eng.: Penguin: 15–18.
Gelb, Joyce, and Palley, Marian Lief
1982   *Women and Public Policies*. Princeton: Princeton University Press.
Gergen, Kenneth J.
1973   "Social Psychology as History." *Journal of Personality and Social Psychology*
            26:309–320.
Gerth, Hans, and Mills, C. Wright
1953   *Character and Social Structure*. New York: Harcourt, Brace and World.

Giddens, Anthony
1972   "Introduction: Durkheim's Writings in Sociology and Social Philosophy." In
            Anthony Giddens (ed.), *Emile Durkheim: Selected Writings*. Cambridge: Cam-
            bridge University Press: 1–50.
1976   *New Rules of Sociological Method: A Positive Critique of Interpretive
            Sociologies*. New York: Basic Books.
1979   *Central Problems in Social Theory: Action, Structure and Contradiction in
            Social Analysis*. Berkeley: University of California Press.
1981   *The Contemporary Critique of Historical Materialism*. Berkeley: University of
            California Press.
1982   *Profiles and Critiques in Social Theory.* Berkeley: University of California
            Press.
1984   *The Constitution of Society: Outline of the Theory of Structuration*. Berkeley:
            University of California Press.
Gilbert, Sandra M., and Gubar, Susan
1979   *The Madwoman in the Attic: The Woman Writer and the Nineteenth-Century
            Literary Imagination*. New Haven: Yale University Press.
Gilligan, Carol
1982   *In a Different Voice: Psychological Theory and Women's Development*. Cam-
            bridge: Harvard University Press.
Glenn, Norval, and Weiner, David
1969   "Some Trends in the Social Origins of American Sociologists." *American
            Sociologist* 4:291–302.
Glennon, Lynda M.
1979   *Women and Dualism*. New York: Longman.
Glucksmann, Miriam
1974   *Structural Analysis in Contemporary Social Thought: A Comparison of the
            Theories of Claude Levi-Strauss and Louis Althusser.* London: Routledge and
            Kegan Paul.
Goddard, David
1976   "On Structuralism and Sociology." *American Sociologist* 11:123–133.
Godelier, Maurice
1972a   *Rationality and Irrationality in Economics*. London: NLB.
1972b   "Structure and Contradiction in *Capital*." In Robin Blackburn (ed.), *Readings
            in Critical Social Theory*. London: Fontana: 334–368.
Goffman, Erving
1959   *Presentation of Self in Everyday Life*. Garden City, N.Y.: Anchor.
1961   *Encounters: Two Studies in the Sociology of Interaction*. Indianapolis: Bobbs-
            Merrill.
1963a   *Behavior in Public Places: Notes on the Social Organization of Gatherings*.
            Glencoe, Ill.: Free Press.
1963b   *Stigma: Notes on the Management of Spoiled Identity*. Englewood Cliffs., N.J.:
            Prentice-Hall.
1967   *Interaction Ritual: Essays on Face-to-Face Behavior*. Garden City, N.Y.: Anchor.
1971   *Relations in Public: Microstudies of the Public Order*. New York: Basic
            Books.
1972   *Strategic Interaction*. New York: Ballantine.
1974   *Frame Analysis: An Essay on the Organization of Experience*. New York:
            Harper Colophon.
1977   "The Arrangement between the Sexes." *Theory and Society* 40:3:301–332.

1979   *Gender Advertisements.* New York: Harper & Row.
Gonos, George
1977   "'Situation' Versus 'Frame': The 'Interactionist' and the 'Structuralist'
            Analyses of Everyday Life." *American Sociological Review* 42:854–867.
1980   "The Class Position of Goffman's Sociology: Social Origins of an American
            Structuralism." In J. Ditton (ed.), *The View from Goffman.* New York: St.
            Martin's: 134–169.
Goode, William J.
1960   "A Theory of Role Strain." *American Sociological Review* 25:483–496.
1975   "Homans' and Merton's Structural Approach." In Peter Blau (ed.), *Ap-
            proaches to the Study of Social Structure.* New York: Free Press: 66–75.
1978   *The Celebration of Heroes: Prestige as a Social Control System.* Berkeley:
            University of California Press.
Goodwin, Charles
1979   "The Interactive Construction of a Sentence in Natural Conversation." In
            George Psathas (ed.), *Everyday Language: Studies in Ethnomethodology.* New
            York: Irvington: 97–121.
1984   "Notes on Story Structure and the Organization of Participation." In
            J. M. Atkinson and J. Heritage (eds.), *Structures of Social Action.* Cambridge:
            Cambridge University Press: 225–246.
Goreau, Angeline
1980   *Reconstructing Aphra: A Social Biography of Aphra Behn.* New York: Dial.
Gorman, Robert A.
1975a   "Alfred Schutz: An Exposition and Critique." *British Journal of Sociology*
            26:1–19.
1975b   "The Phenomenological 'Humanization' of Social Science: A Critique."
            British Journal of Sociology 26:389–405.
1977   *The Dual Vision: Alfred Schutz and the Myth of Phenomenological Social
            Science.* London: Routledge and Kegan Paul.
Goudsblom, Johan
1977   *Sociology in the Balance: A Critical Essay.* New York: Columbia University Press.
Gould, Carol C. (ed.)
1983   *Beyond Domination: New Perspectives on Women and Philosophy.* Totowa,
            N.J.: Rowman and Allanheld.
Gouldner, Alvin
1958   "Introduction." In Emile Durkheim, *Socialism and Saint-Simon.* Yellow
            Springs, Ohio: Antioch Press.
1959/1967   "Reciprocity and Autonomy in Functional Theory." In Nicholas Demerath and
            Richard Peterson (eds.), *System, Change and Conflict.* New York: Free Press:
            141–169.
1960   "The Norm of Reciprocity." *American Sociological Review* 25:161–178.
1970   *The Coming Crisis of Western Sociology.* New York: Basic Books.
Gramsci, Antonio
1917/1977   "The Revolution against 'Capital.'" In Quintin Hoare (ed.), *Antonio Gramsci:
            Selections from Political Writings (1910–1920).* New York: International: 34–37.
1932/1975   *Letters from Prison: Antonio Gramsci* (Lynne Lawner, ed.). New York: Harper
            Colophon.
1971   *Selections from the Prison Notebooks.* New York: International.
Granovetter, Mark
1973   "The Strength of Weak Ties." *American Journal of Sociology* 78:1360–1380.

REFERENCES

1983   "The Strength of Weak Ties: A Network Theory Revisited." In Randall Collins (ed.), *Sociological Theory—1983*. San Francisco: Jossey-Bass: 201–233.

1985   "Economic Action and Social Structure: The Problem of Embeddedness." *American Journal of Sociology* 91:481–510.

Grathoff, Richard (ed.)

1978   *The Theory of Social Action: The Correspondence of Alfred Schutz and Talcott Parsons*. Bloomington: Indiana University Press.

Greer, Germaine

1979   *The Obstacle Race: The Fortunes of Women Painters and Their Work*. New York: Farrar, Straus & Giroux.

Greisman, Harvey C.

1986   "The Paradigm That Failed." In Richard C. Monk (ed.), *Structures of Knowing*. Lanham, Md.: University Press of America: 273–291.

Greisman, Harvey C., and Ritzer, George

1981   "Max Weber, Critical Theory and the Administered World." *Qualitative Sociology* 4:34–55.

Griffin, Susan

1978   *Women and Nature: The Roaring within Her*. New York: Harper & Row.

1979   *Rape, The Power of Consciousness*. New York: Harper & Row.

1981   *Pornography as Silence: Culture's Revenge against Nature*. New York: Harper & Row.

1982   *Made from this Earth: An Anthology of Writings*. New York: Harper & Row.

Gurney, Patrick J.

1981   "Historical Origins of Ideological Denial: The Case of Marx in American Sociology." *The American Sociologist* 16:196–201.

Gurvitch, Georges

1964   *The Spectrum of Social Time*. Dordrecht, Neth.: D. Reidel.

Haas, Jack, and Shaffir, William

1982   "Taking on the Role of Doctor: A Dramaturgic Analysis of Professionalization." *Symbolic Interaction* 5:187–203.

Habermas, Jurgen

1970   *Toward a Rational Society*. Boston: Beacon Press.

1971   *Knowledge and Human Interests*. Boston: Beacon Press.

1973   *Theory and Practice*. Boston: Beacon Press.

1975   *Legitimation Crisis*. Boston: Beacon Press.

1979   *Communication and the Evolution of Society*. Boston: Beacon Press.

1984   *The Theory of Communicative Action*. Vol. 1, *Reason and the Rationalization of Society*. Boston: Beacon Press.

Hage, Jerald

1980   *Theories of Organization*. New York: Wiley.

Haines, Valerie

1985   "From Organicist to Relational Human Ecology." *Sociological Theory* 3:65–74.

Halfpenny, Peter

1982   *Positivism and Sociology: Explaining Social Life*. London: George Allen and Unwin.

Hall, Richard

1983   "Theoretical Trends in the Sociology of Occupations." *Sociological Quarterly* 24:5–23.

Hallet, Judith P.

1979   "Sappho and Her Social Context: Sense and Sensibility." *Signs: Journal of Women in Culture and Society* 4:3:447–464.

Hamblin, Robert L., and Kunkel, John H.
1977   *Behavioral Theory in Sociology.* New Brunswick, N.J.: Transaction.
Handel, Warren
1982   *Ethnomethodology: How People Make Sense.* Englewood Cliffs, N.J.:
                Prentice-Hall.
Harding, Sandra, and Hintikka, Merrill B. (eds.)
1983   *Discovering Reality: Feminist Perspectives on Epistemology, Metaphysics,*
                Methodology and Philosophy of Science. Boston: Reidel.
Harper, Diane Blake, Sylvester, Joan, and Walczak, David
1980   "An Empirical Comparison of Ritzer's Paradigms and Similar Metatheories:
                Comment on Friedheim." *Social Forces* 59:513–517.
Harre, Rom
1982   "Psychological Dimensions." In Paul Secord (ed.), *Explaining Human Behav-*
                ior. Beverly Hills, Calif.: Sage: 93–113.
Hartman, Heidi
1979   "Capitalism, Patriarchy and Job Segregation by Sex." In Zillah Eisenstein
                (ed.), *Capitalist Patriarchy and the Case for Socialist Feminism.* New York:
                Monthly Review Press: 206–247.
Harvey, Lee
1987   "The Nature of 'Schools' in the Sociology of Knowledge: The Case of the
                'Chicago School.'" *Sociological Review* 35:245–278.
Hartsock, Nancy
1983   *Money, Sex and Power: Towards a Feminist Historical Materialism.* New York:
                Longman.
Hawkes, Terence
1977   *Structuralism and Semiotics.* London: Methuen.
Hawthorn, Geoffrey
1976   *Enlightenment and Despair.* Cambridge: Cambridge University Press.
Hayes, Adrian
1985   "Causal and Interpretive Analysis in Sociology." *Sociological Theory* 3:1–10.
Hayim, Gila
1980   *The Existential Sociology of Jean-Paul Sartre.* Amherst: University of Massa-
                chusetts Press.
Hazelrigg, Lawrence
1972   "Class, Property and Authority: Dahrendorf's Critique of Marx's Theory of
                Class." *Social Forces* 50:473–487.
Heap, James L., and Roth, Phillip A.
1973   "On Phenomenological Sociology." *American Sociological Review* 38:354–
                367.
Heberle, Rudolph
1965   "Simmel's Methods." In Lewis Coser (ed.), *Georg Simmel.* Englewood
                Cliffs, N.J.: Prentice-Hall: 116–121.
Hegel, G. W. F.
1807/1967   *The Phenomenology of Mind.* New York: Harper Colophon.
1821/1967   *The Philosophy of Right.* Oxford: Clarendon Press.
Hechter, Michael
1983a   "Introduction." In Michael Hechter (ed.), *The Microfoundations of Macrosoci-*
                ology. Philadelphia: Temple University Press: 3–15.
1983b   "A Theory of Group Solidarity." In Michael Hechter (ed.), *The Microfounda-*
                tions of Macrosociology. Philadelphia: Temple University Press: 16–57.

Hekman, Susan
1983   *Weber, the Ideal Type, and Contemporary Social Theory.* Notre Dame, Ind.:
            University of Notre Dame Press.
Held, David
1980   *Introduction to Critical Theory: Horkheimer to Habermas.* Berkeley: Univer-
            sity of California Press.
Helle, H. J., and Eisenstadt, S. N. (eds.)
1985   *Micro-Sociological Theory: Perspectives on Sociological Theory,* Vol. 2.
            London: Sage.
Heritage, John
1984   *Garfinkel and Ethnomethodology.* Cambridge: Polity Press.
Heritage, John, and Atkinson, J. Maxwell
1984   "Introduction." In J. Maxwell Atkinson and John Heritage (eds.), *Structures
            of Social Action.* Cambridge: Cambridge University Press: 1–15.
Heritage, John, and Greatbatch, David
1986   "Generating Applause: A Study of Rhetoric and Response in Party Political
            Conferences." *American Journal of Sociology* 92:110–157.
Heritage, John, and Watson, D. R.
1979   "Formulations as Conversational Objects." In George Psathas (ed.), *Everyday
            Language: Studies in Ethnomethodology.* New York: Irvington: 187–201.
Hewitt, John P.
1984   *Self and Society: A Symbolic Interactionist Social Psychology.* 3rd ed. Boston:
            Allyn and Bacon.
Heyl, John D., and Heyl, Barbara S.
1976   "The Sumner-Porter Controversy at Yale: Pre-Paradigmatic Sociology and In-
            stitutional Crisis." *Sociological Inquiry* 46:41–49.
Hilbert, Richard A.
1986   "Anomie and Moral Regulation of Reality: The Durkheimian Tradition in
            Modern Relief." *Sociological Theory* 4:1–19.
Hill, Lester, and Eckberg, Douglas
1981   "Clarifying Confusions about Paradigms: A Reply to Ritzer." *American Socio-
            logical Review* 46:248–251.
Himes, Joseph
1966   "The Functions of Racial Conflict." *Social Forces* 45:1–10.
Hindess, Barry
1986   "Actors and Social Relations." In Mark L. Wardell and Stephen P. Turner
            (eds.), *Sociological Theory in Transition.* Boston: Allen and Unwin: 113–126.
Hinkle, Roscoe
1963   "Antecedents of the Action Orientation in American Sociology before 1935."
            American Sociological Review 28:705–715.
1980   *Founding Theory of American Sociology: 1881–1915.* London: Routledge and
            Kegan Paul.
Hinkle, Roscoe, and Hinkle, Gisela
1954   *The Development of American Sociology.* New York: Random House.
Hite, Shere
1976   *The Hite Report: A Nationwide Study of Female Sexuality.* New York: Dell.
Hobsbawm, Eric J.
1965   *Primitive Rebels.* New York: Norton.
Hofstadter, Richard
1959   *Social Darwinism in American Thought.* New York: Braziller.

Hollinger, David
1980   "T. S. Kuhn's Theory of Science and Its Implications for History." In Gary Gutting (ed.), *Paradigms and Revolutions*. Notre Dame, Ind.: Notre Dame University Press: 195–222.

Homans, George C.
1950   *The Human Group*. New York: Harcourt, Brace and World.
1958   "Social Behavior as Exchange." *American Journal of Sociology* 63:597–606.
1961   *Social Behavior: Its Elementary Forms*. New York: Harcourt, Brace and World.
1962   *Sentiments and Activities*. New York: Free Press.
1967   *The Nature of Social Science*. New York: Harcourt, Brace and World.
1969   "The Sociological Relevance of Behaviorism." In Robert Burgess and Don Bushell (eds.), *Behavioral Sociology*. New York: Columbia University Press: 1–24.
1971   "Commentary." In Herman Turk and Richard Simpson (eds.), *Institutions and Social Exchange*. Indianapolis: Bobbs-Merrill: 363–374.
1974   *Social Behavior: Its Elementary Forms*. Rev. ed. New York: Harcourt Brace Jovanovich.
1984   *Coming to My Senses: The Autobiography of a Sociologist*. New Brunswick: N.J.: Transaction Books.

Homans, George C., and Schneider, David M.
1955   *Marriage, Authority and Final Causes: A Study of Unilateral Cross-Cousin Marriage*. New York: Free Press.

Hook, Sidney
1965   "Pareto's Sociological System." In James H. Meisel (ed.), *Pareto and Mosca*. Englewood Cliffs, N.J.: Prentice-Hall: 57–61.

Hooks, Bell
1984   *Feminist Theory: From Margin to Center*. Boston: South End Press.

Horowitz, Irving L.
1962/1967 "Consensus, Conflict, and Cooperation." In Nicholas Demerath and Richard Peterson (eds.), *System, Change and Conflict*. New York: Free Press: 265–279.
1983   *C. Wright Mills: An American Utopian*. New York: Free Press.

Huaco, George
1966   "The Functionalist Theory of Stratification: Two Decades of Controversy." *Inquiry* 9:215–240.
1986   "Ideology and General Theory: The Case of Sociological Functionalism." *Comparative Studies in Society and History* 28:34–54.

Huber, Joan
1976   "Sociology." *Signs: Journal of Women in Culture and Society* 1:3:part 1:685–697.

Hunter, J. E., Schmidt, F. L., and Jackson, G. B.
1982   *Metaanalysis: Cumulating Research Findings Across Studies*. Beverly Hills, Calif.: Sage.

Husserl, Edmund
1931   *Ideas*. London: George Allen and Unwin.

Jackman, Mary R., and Jackman, Robert W.
1973   "An Interpretation of the Relation between Objective and Subjective Social Status." *American Sociological Review* 38:569–582.

Jaggar, Alison M.
1983   *Feminist Politics and Human Nature*. Totowa, N.J.: Rowman and Allanheld.

Jaggar, Alison M., and Rothenberg, Paula (eds.)
1984   *Feminist Frameworks.* 2nd ed. New York: McGraw-Hill.
James, Selma, and Costa, Mariarosa Dallacosa
1973   *The Power of Women and the Subversion of Community.* Bristol: Falling Wall Press.
Janeway, Elizabeth
1981   *Powers of the Weak.* New York: Morrow Quill.
Jay, Martin
1973   *The Dialectical Imagination.* Boston: Little, Brown.
1984   *Marxism and Totality: The Adventures of a Concept from Lukács to Habermas.* Berkeley: University of California Press.
1986   *Permanent Exiles: Essays on the Intellectual Migration from Germany to America.* New York: Columbia University Press.
Jefferson, Gail
1979   "A Technique for Inviting Laughter and Its Subsequent Acceptance Declination." In George Psathas (ed.), *Everyday Language: Studies in Ethnomethodology.* New York: Irvington: 79–96.
1984   "On the Organization of Laughter in Talk about Troubles." In J. Maxwell Atkinson and John Heritage (eds.), *Structures of Social Action.* Cambridge: Cambridge University Press: 346–369.
Jessop, Bob
1985   *Nicos Poulantzas: Marxist Theory and Political Strategy.* New York: St. Martin's.
Joas, Hans
1981   "George Herbert Mead and the 'Division of Labor': Macrosociological Implications of Mead's Social Psychology." *Symbolic Interaction* 4:177–190.
Johnson, Doyle Paul
1981   *Sociological Theory: Classical Founders and Contemporary Perspectives.* New York: Wiley.
Johnson, John M., and Ferraro, Kathleen T.
1984   "The Victimized Self: The Case of Battered Women." In Joseph A. Kotarba and Andrea Fontana (eds.), *The Existential Self in Society.* Chicago: University of Chicago Press: 119–130.
Jones, Greta
1980   *Social Darwinism and English Thought: The Interaction between Biological and Social Theory.* Atlantic Richlands, N.J.: Humanities Press.
Kalberg, Stephen
1980   "Max Weber's Types of Rationality: Cornerstones for the Analysis of Rationalization Processes in History." *American Journal of Sociology* 85:1145–1179.
Kando, Thomas
1976   "L'année Sociologique: From Durkheim to Today." *Pacific Sociological Review* 19:147–174.
Kanter, Rosabeth Moss
1977   *Men and Women of the Corporation.* New York: Basic Books.
Karady, Victor
1983   "The Durkheimians in Academe: A Reconsideration." In Philippe Besnard (ed.), *The Sociological Domain.* Cambridge: Cambridge University Press: 71–89.
Kasler, Dirk
1985   "Jewishness as a Central Formation-Milieu of Early German Society." *History of Sociology: An International Review* 6:69–86.

Kasper, Anne
1986   "Consciousness Re-Evaluated: Interpretive Theory and Feminist Scholarship."
              Sociological Inquiry 56:1:30–49.
Kaufman, Debra R., and Richardson, Barbara L.
1982   *Achievement and Women: Challenging the Assumptions.* New York: Free Press.
Keller, Evelyn Fox
1982   "Feminism and Science." *Signs: Journal of Women in Culture and Society*
              7:3:589–602.
Kelly-Godol, Joan
1983   "The Social Relation of the Sexes: Methodological Implications of Women's
              History." In Elizabeth Abel and Emily K. Abel (eds.), *The Signs Reader:
              Women, Gender and Scholarship.* Chicago: University of Chicago Press.
Kemeny, Jim
1976   "Perspective on the Micro-Macro Distinction." *Sociological Review*
              24:731–752.
Kemper, Theodore
1978a   "Toward a Sociological Theory of Emotions: Some Problems and Some Solu-
              tions." *The American Sociologist* 13:30–41.
1978b   *A Social Interactional Theory of Emotions.* New York: Wiley.
1981   "Social Constructionist and Positivist Approaches to the Sociology of Emo-
              tions." *American Journal of Sociology* 87:336–362.
Kent, Raymond A.
1981   *A History of British Empirical Sociology.* Aldershot, Hants, Eng.: Gower.
Kessler, Suzanne J., and McKenna, Wendy
1978   *Gender: An Ethnomethodological Approach.* Chicago: University of Chicago
              Press.
Kitahara, Michio
1986   "Commodore Perry and the Japanese: A Study in the Dramaturgy of Power."
              Symbolic Interaction 9:53–65.
Kittay, Eva Feder
1984   "Womb Envy: An Explanatory Concept." In Joyce Trebilcot (ed.), *Mothering:
              Essays in Feminist Theory.* Totowa, N.J.: Rowman and Allanheld: 94–128.
Knox, John
1963   "The Concept of Exchange in Sociological Theory: 1884 and 1961." *Social
              Forces* 41:341–346.
Kockelmans, Joseph J.
1967a   *Phenomenology: The Philosophy of Edmund Husserl and Its Interpretations.*
              Garden City, N.Y.: Anchor.
1967b   "Some Fundamental Themes of Husserl's Phenomenology." In Joseph J.
              Kockelmans (ed.), *Phenomenology: The Philosophy of Edmund Husserl and Its
              Interpretations.* Garden City, N.Y.: Anchor: 24–36.
Kohn, Melvin L.
1976   "Occupational Structure and Alienation." *American Journal of Sociology*
              82:111–127.
Kolb, William L.
1944   "A Critical Evaluation of Mead's 'I' and 'Me' Concepts." *Social Forces*
              22:291–296.
Korenbaum, Myrtle
1964   Translator's preface to Georges Gurvitch, *The Spectrum of Social Time.*
              Dordrecht, Neth.: D. Reidel: ix–xxvi.

Kotarba, Joseph A.
1977   "The Chronic Pain Patient." In Jack Douglas et al. (eds.), *Existential Sociology*. Cambridge: Cambridge University Press: 257–272.
1979   "Existential Sociology." In Scott McNall (ed.), *Theoretical Perspectives in Sociology*. New York: St. Martin's: 348–368.
1984   "A Synthesis: The Existential Self in Society." In Joseph A. Kotarba and Andrea Fontana (eds.), *The Existential Self in Society*. Chicago: University of Chicago Press: 222–234.
Kotarba, Joseph A., and Fontana, Andrea (eds.)
1984   *The Existential Self in Society.* Chicago: University of Chicago Press.
Kreps, Gary
1985   "Disaster and the Social Order." *Sociological Theory* 3:49–64.
Kuhn, Annette, and Wolfe, Ann Marie (eds.)
1978   *Feminism and Materialism.* London: Routledge and Kegan Paul.
Kuhn, Manford
1964   "Major Trends in Symbolic Interaction Theory in the Past Twenty-five Years." *The Sociological Quarterly* 5:61–84.
Kuhn, Thomas
1962   *The Structure of Scientific Revolutions.* Chicago: University of Chicago Press.
1970   *The Structure of Scientific Revolutions.* 2nd ed. Chicago: University of Chicago Press.
Kurzweil, Edith
1980   *The Age of Structuralism: Lévi-Strauss to Foucault.* New York: Columbia University Press.
Lash, Scott, and Urry, John
1984   "The New Marxism of Collective Action: A Critical Analysis." *Sociology* 18:33–50.
Laws, Judith Long, and Schwartz, Pepper
1977   *Sexual Scripts: The Social Construction of Female Sexuality.* Hinsdale: Dryden.
Layder, Derek
1979   "Problems in Accounting for the Individual in Marxist-Rationalist Theoretical Discourse." *British Journal of Sociology* 30:149–163.
1986   "Social Reality as Figuration: A Critique of Elias's Conception of Sociological Analysis." *Sociology* 20:367–386.
Leach, Edmund
1974   *Claude Lévi-Strauss.* New York: Penguin.
Lefebvre, Henri
1968   *The Sociology of Marx.* New York: Vintage.
Leinhart, Samuel
1977   *Social Networks: A Developing Paradigm.* New York: Academic Press.
Lemert, Charles
1979   *Sociology and the Twilight of Man: Homocentrism and Discourse in Sociological Theory.* Carbondale: Southern Illinois University Press.
Lemert, Charles (ed.)
1981   *French Sociology: Rupture and Renewal since 1968.* New York: Columbia University Press.
Lengermann, Patricia Madoo
1979   "The Founding of the *American Sociological Review.*" *American Sociological Review* 44:185–198.

Lengermann, Patricia Madoo, and Wallace, Ruth A.
1985   *Gender in America: Social Control and Social Change.* Englewood Cliffs,
            N.J.: Prentice-Hall.

Lenzer, Gertrud (ed.)
1975   *Auguste Comte and Positivism: The Essential Writings.* Magnolia, Mass.: Peter
            Smith.

Lever, Janet
1978   "Sex Differences in the Complexity of Children's Play and Games." *American
            Sociological Review* 43:471–483.

Levine, Donald
1981   "Rationality and Freedom: Weber and Beyond." *Sociological Inquiry* 51:5–25.

Levine, Donald, Carter, Ellwood B., and Gorman, Eleanor Miller
1976a   "Simmel's Influence on American Sociology—I." *American Journal of Sociol-
            ogy* 81:813–845.
1976b   "Simmel's Influence on American Sociology—II." *American Journal of Soci-
            ology* 81:1112–1132.

Lévi-Strauss, Claude
1949   *Les Structures Elementaires de la Parente.* Paris: Presses Universitaires de France.
1963   *Totemism.* Boston: Beacon Press.
1967   *Structural Anthropology.* Garden City, N.Y.: Anchor.

Lewis, J. David, and Smith, Richard L.
1980   *American Sociology and Pragmatism: Mead, Chicago Sociology, and Symbolic
            Interaction.* Chicago: University of Chicago Press.

Lilienfeld, Robert
1978   *The Rise of Systems Theory: An Ideological Analysis.* New York: Wiley-
            Interscience.

Lipman-Blumen, Jean
1979   "Jessie Bernard." *International Encyclopedia of the Social Sciences*, Vol. 18.
            New York: Free Press: 49–56.
1984   *Gender Roles and Power.* Englewood Cliffs, N.J.: Prentice-Hall.

Lipset, Seymour M.
1975   "Social Structure and Social Change." In Peter Blau (ed.), *Approaches to the
            Study of Social Structure.* New York: Free Press: 172–209.

Lockwood, David
1956   "Some Remarks on *The Social System.*" *British Journal of Sociology* 7:134–
            146.
1958   *The Blackcoated Worker: A Study in Class Consciousness.* London: George
            Allen and Unwin.

Lodahl, Janice B., and Gordon, Gerald
1972   "The Structure of Scientific Fields and the Functioning of University Graduate
            Departments." *American Sociological Review* 37:57–72.

Lodge, Peter
1986   "Connections: W. I. Thomas, European Social Thought and American Sociol-
            ogy." In Richard C. Monk (ed.), *Structures of Knowing.* Lanham, Md.: Uni-
            versity Press of America: 135–160.

Lorde, Audre
1984   *Sister Outsider: Essays and Speeches.* Trumansburg, N.Y.: Crossings Press.

Lougee, Carolyn C.
1976   *Le Paradis des Femmes: Women, Salons and Social Stratification in
            Seventeenth-Century France.* Princeton: Princeton University Press.

Lucas, Angela M.
1983   *Women in the Middle Ages: Religion, Marriage and Letters.* New York: St. Martin's.

Luckmann, Thomas (ed.)
1978   *Phenomenology and Sociology.* Harmondsworth, Eng.: Penguin.

Lukács, Georg
1922/1968   *History and Class Consciousness.* Cambridge: MIT Press.

Lukes, Steven
1972   *Emile Durkheim: His Life and Work.* New York: Harper & Row.

Luxemburg, Rosa
1971   "Women's Suffrage and Class Struggle." In Dick Howard (ed.), *Selected Political Writings.* New York: Monthly Review Press: 219–220.

Luxenberg, Stan
1985   Roadside Empires: How the Chains Franchised America. New York: Viking.

Lyman, Stanford, and Scott, Marvin
1970   *A Sociology of the Absurd.* New York: Appleton-Century-Crofts.

Lynn, Naomi
1975   "Women in American Politics: An Overview." In Jo Freeman (ed.), *Women: A Feminist Perspective.* Palo Alto: Mayfield: 364–385.

MacIver, Robert
1931   *Society: Its Structure and Changes.* New York: Ray Long and Richard R. Smith.
1942   *Social Causation.* Boston: Ginn.

Mackay, Robert W.
1974   "Words, Utterances and Activities." In Roy Turner (ed.), *Ethnomethodology: Selected Readings.* Harmondsworth, Eng.: Penguin: 197–215.

MacKinnon, Catharine
1982   "Feminism, Marxism, Method and the State: An Agenda for Theory." In Nannerl O. Keohane et al. (eds.), *Feminist Theory: A Critique of Ideology.* Chicago: University of Chicago Press: 1–30.

Maines, David R.
1977   "Social Organization and Social Structure in Symbolic Interactionist Thought." In Alex Inkeles, James Coleman, and Neil Smelser (eds.), *Annual Review of Sociology*, Vol. 3. Palo Alto: Annual Reviews: 259–285.

Manis, Jerome, and Meltzer, Bernard (eds.)
1978   *Symbolic Interaction: A Reader in Social Psychology.* 3rd ed. Boston: Allyn and Bacon.

Mannheim, Karl
1936   *Ideology and Utopia.* New York: Harcourt.

Manning, Peter
1973   "Existential Sociology." *The Sociological Quarterly* 14:200–225.

Manuel, Frank E.
1962   *The Prophets of Paris.* Cambridge, Mass.: Harvard University Press.

Marcuse, Herbert
1964   *One-Dimensional Man.* Boston: Beacon Press.
1969   *An Essay on Liberation.* Boston: Beacon Press.

Markovsky, Barry
1985   "Multilevel Justice Theory." *American Sociological Review* 50:822–839.

Marks, Stephen R.
1974   "Durkheim's Theory of Anomie." *American Journal of Sociology* 82:329–363.

Marsden, Peter V.
forthcoming   "Elements of Interactor Dependence." In Karen S. Cook (ed.), *Social Exchange Theory.* Beverly Hills, Calif.: Sage.

Martin, Wendy
1972   *The American Sisterhood: Writings of the Feminist Movement from Colonial Times to Present.* New York: Harper & Row.

Martindale, Don
1960   *The Nature and Types of Sociological Theory.* Boston: Houghton Mifflin.

Marx, Karl
1842/1977   "Communism and the *Augsburger Allegemeine Zeitung.*" In David McLellan (ed.), *Karl Marx: Selected Writings.* New York: Oxford University Press: 20.
1847/1963   *The Poverty of Philosophy.* New York: International.
1852/1970   "The Eighteenth Brumaire of Louis Bonaparte." In Robert C. Tucker (ed.), *The Marx-Engels Reader.* New York: Norton: 436–525.
1857–1858/   *Pre-Capitalist Economic Formations*, Eric J. Hobsbawm (ed.). New York:
1964   International.
1857–1858/   *The Grundrisse: Foundations of the Critique of Political Economy.* New York:
1974   Random House.
1859/1970   *A Contribution to the Critique of Political Economy.* New York: International Publishers.
1867/1967   *Capital: A Critique of Political Economy*, Vol. 1. New York: International Publishers.
1932/1964   *The Economic and Philosophic Manuscripts of 1844*, Dirk J. Struik (ed.). New York: International Publishers.

Marx, Karl, and Engels, Friedrich
1845/1956   *The Holy Family.* Moscow: Foreign Language Publishing House.

Masterman, Margaret
1970   "The Nature of a Paradigm." In Imre Lakatos and Alan Musgrove (eds.), *Criticism and the Growth of Knowledge.* Cambridge: Cambridge University Press: 59–89.

Masters, William, and Johnson, Virginia
1966   *Human Sexual Response.* Boston: Little, Brown.

Matthews, Fred H.
1977   *Quest for an American Sociology: Robert E. Park and the Chicago School.* Montreal: McGill University Press.

Mauss, Marcel
1954   *The Gift,* Ian Cunnison (trans.). London: Cohen and West.

Mayhew, Bruce
1980   "Structuralism versus Individualism: Part I, Shadowboxing in the Dark." *Social Forces* 59:335–375.
1981   "Structuralism versus Individualism: Part II, Ideological and Other Obfuscations." *Social Forces* 59:627–648.

McCarthy, Thomas
1982   *The Critical Theory of Jurgen Habermas.* Cambridge, Mass.: MIT Press.
1984   "Translator's Introduction." In Jurgen Habermas, *The Theory of Communicative Action.* Boston: Beacon Press.

McLellan, David
1973   *Karl Marx: His Life and Thought.* New York: Harper Colophon.

McLellan, David (ed.)
1971   *The Thought of Karl Marx*. New York: Harper Torchbooks.

McMahon, A. M.
1984   "The Two Social Psychologies: Postcrises Directions." In Ralph H. Turner and James F. Short (eds.), *Annual Review of Sociology*, Vol. 10. Palo Alto: Annual Reviews: 121–140.

McMurty, John
1978   *The Structure of Marx's World-View*. Princeton: Princeton University Press.

McNall, Scott
1979a   Introduction to Part VII, "Biology and Human Behavior." In Scott McNall (ed.), *Theoretical Perspectives in Sociology*. New York: St. Martin's: 397–398.

McPhail, Clark
1981   "The Problems and Prospects of Behavioral Perspectives." *The American Sociologist* 16:172–174.

McPhail, Clark, and Rexroat, Cynthia
1979   "Mead vs. Blumer." *American Sociological Review* 44:449–467.
1980   Rejoinder: "*Ex Cathedra* Blumer or *Ex Libris* Mead?" *American Sociological Review* 45:420–430.

Mead, George Herbert
1934/1962 *Mind, Self and Society: From the Standpoint of a Social Behaviorist*. Chicago: University of Chicago Press.

Meeker, B. F.
1971   "Decisions and Exchange." *American Sociological Review* 36:485–495.

Mehan, Hugh, and Wood, Houston
1975   *The Reality of Ethnomethodology*. New York: Wiley.
1976   "De-Secting Ethnomethodology." *The American Sociologist* 11:13–21.

Meltzer, Bernard
1964/1978 "Mead's Social Psychology." In Jerome Manis and Bernard Meltzer (eds.), *Symbolic Interaction: A Reader in Social Psychology*. 3rd ed. Boston: Allyn and Bacon: 15–27.

Meltzer, Bernard, Petras, James, and Reynolds, Larry
1975   *Symbolic Interactionism: Genesis, Varieties and Criticisms*. London: Routledge and Kegan Paul.

Menzies, Ken
1977   *Tallcott Parsons and the Social Image of Man*. London: Routledge and Kegan Paul.

Merton, Robert K.
1949/1968 "Manifest and Latent Functions." In *Social Theory and Social Structure*. New York: Free Press: 73–138.
1953   Preface to Hans Gerth and C. Wright Mills, *Character and Social Structure*. New York: Harcourt, Brace and World: vii–ix.
1968   *Social Theory and Social Structure*. New York: Free Press.
1975   "Structural Analysis in Sociology." In Peter Blau (ed.), *Approaches to the Study of Social Structure*. New York: Fress Press: 21–52.
1980   "Remembering the Young Talcott Parsons." *American Sociologist* 15:68–71.

Mészáros, István
1970   *Marx's Theory of Alienation*. New York: Harper Torchbooks.

Michaels, James W., and Green, Dan S.
1978   "Behavioral Sociology: Emergent Forms and Issues." *The American Sociologist* 13:23–29.

Miel, Jan
1970   "Jacques Lacan and the Structure of the Unconscious." In Jacques Ehrmann
                (ed.), *Structuralism*. Garden City, N.Y.: Anchor: 94–101.
Miliband, Ralph
1972   "Reply to Nicos Poulantzas." In Robin Blackburn (ed.), *Ideology in Social
                Science: Readings in Critical Social Theory*. London: Fontana: 253–262.
1974   *The State in Capitalist Society*. London: Quartet.
Mill, John Stuart
1867/1980   *The Subjection of Women*, Sue Mansfield (ed.), Arlington Heights, Ill.: AHM
                Publishing.
Miller, David
1981   "The Meaning of Role-Taking." *Symbolic Interaction* 4:167–175.
1982   Review of J. D. Lewis and R. L. Smith, *American Sociology and Pragmatism.
                The Journal of the History of Sociology* 4:108–114.
1985   "Concerning J. David Lewis' Response to My Review of *American Sociology
                and Pragmatism." The Journal of the History of Sociology* 5:131–133.
Miller, Jean Baker
1976   *Toward a New Psychology of Women*. Boston: Beacon Press.
Miller, L. Keith
1970   "A Token Economy for the University Classroom." Paper read at meetings of
                the American Psychological Association, Miami.
Millet, Kate
1970   *Sexual Politics*. Garden City, N.Y.: Doubleday.
Millman, Marcia, and Kanter, Rosabeth Moss (eds.)
1976   *Another Voice: Feminist Perspectives on Social Life and Social Science*. New
                York: Octagon Books.
Mills, C. Wright
1951   *White Collar*. New York: Oxford University Press.
1956   *The Power Elite*. New York: Oxford University Press.
1959   *The Sociological Imagination*. New York: Oxford University Press.
1960   *Listen Yankee: The Revolution in Cuba*. New York: McGraw-Hill.
1962   *The Marxists*. New York: Dell.
Misgeld, Dieter
1983   "Common Sense and Common Convictions: Sociology as a Science, Phenome-
                nological Sociology and the Hermeneutical Point of View." *Human Studies*
                6:109–139.
Mitchell, Jack N.
1978   *Social Exchange, Dramaturgy and Ethnomethodology: Toward a Paradigmatic
                Synthesis*. New York: Elsevier.
Mitchell, Juliet
1975   *Psychoanalysis and Feminism*. New York: Vintage.
Mitroff, Ian, and Kilmann, Ralph
1978   *Methodological Approaches to Social Science*. San Francisco: Jossey-Bass.
Mitzman, Arthur
1970   *The Iron Cage*. New York: Universal Library.
Mizruchi, Mark S., and Koenig, Thomas
1986   "Economic Sources of Corporate Political Consensus: An Examination of
                Interindustry Relations." *American Sociological Review* 51:482–491.
Molm, Linda D.
1981   "The Legitimacy of Behavioral Theory as a Sociological Perspective." *The
                American Sociologist* 16:153–166.

Molm, Linda D., and Wiggins, James A.
1979   "A Behavioral Analysis of the Dynamics of Social Exchange in the Dyad."
            Social Forces 57:1157–1179.
Moore, Wilbert E.
1978   "Functionalism." In Tom Bottomore and Robert Nisbet (eds.), *A History of
            Sociological Analysis*. New York: Basic Books: 321–361.
Moraga, Cherrie, and Anzaldua, Gloria
1981   *This Bridge Called My Back: Writings by Radical Women of Color*. Watertown,
            Mass.: Persephone Press.
Morgan, Robin
1968   *Going Too Far: The Personal Chronicle of a Feminist*. New York: Random
            House.
1970   *Sisterhood Is Powerful*. New York: Vintage.
1982   *The Anatomy of Freedom: Feminism, Physics, and Global Politics*. Garden
            City, N.Y.: Anchor/Doubleday.
Morris, Charles W.
1934/1962   "Introduction." In George Herbert Mead, *Mind, Self and Society*. Chicago:
            University of Chicago Press: ix–xxxv.
Morris, Monica B.
1977   *Excursion into Creative Sociology*. New York: Columbia University Press.
Morse, Chandler
1961   "The Functional Imperatives." In Max Black (ed.), *The Social Theories of
            Talcott Parsons*. Englewood Cliffs, N.J.: Prentice-Hall: 100–152.
Mulligan, Glenn, and Lederman, Bobbie
1977   "Social Facts and Rules of Practice." *American Journal of Sociology*
            83:539–550.
Mullins, Nicholas
1973   *Theories and Theory Groups in Contemporary American Sociology*. New York:
            Harper & Row.
1983   "Theories and Theory Groups Revisited." In Randall Collins (ed.), *Sociologi-
            cal Theory—1983*. San Francisco: Jossey-Bass: 319–337.
Münch, Richard
1981   "Talcott Parsons and the Theory of Action. I. The Structure of the Kantian
            Core." *American Journal of Sociology* 86:709–739.
1982   "Talcott Parsons and the Theory of Action. II. The Continuity of the Develop-
            ment." *American Journal of Sociology* 87:771–826.
Needham, Rodney
1963   "Introduction." In Emile Durkheim and Marcel Mauss, *Primitive Classifica-
            tion* (orig. 1903). Chicago: University of Chicago Press: vii–xlviii.
Nicolaus, Martin
1974   "Foreword." In Karl Marx, *The Grundrisse*. New York: Random House: 7–63.
Nisbet, Robert
1967   *The Sociological Tradition*. New York: Basic Books.
Noble, David F.
1982   *America by Design: Science, Technology, and the Rise of Corporate
            Capitalism*. New York: Knopf.
Oakes, Guy
1984a   "The Problem of Women in Simmel's Theory of Culture." In Guy Oakes
            (ed.), *Georg Simmel on Women, Sexuality, and Love*. New Haven: Yale Uni-
            versity Press: 3–62.

Oakes, Guy (ed.)
1984   *Georg Simmel on Women, Sexuality and Love.* New Haven: Yale University Press.
Oakley, Ann
1974   *Women's Work: The Housewife, Past and Present.* New York: Pantheon.
1981   "Interviewing Women: A Contradiction in Terms." In Helen Roberts (ed.),
                Doing Feminist Research. London: Routledge and Kegan Paul: 30–60.
Oksanen, Ernest H., and Spencer, Bryon G.
1975   "On the Determinants of Student Performance in Introductory Courses in the
                Social Sciences." *American Sociologist* 10:103–109.
Ollman, Bertell
1976   *Alienation.* 2nd ed. Cambridge: Cambridge University Press.
O'Neill, John
1986   "The Disciplinary Society: From Weber to Foucault." *British Journal of Soci-
                ology* 37:42–60.
O'Neill, William L.
1971   *A History of Feminism in America.* Chicago: Quadrangle Books.
Pareto, Vilfredo
1935   *A Treatise on General Sociology.* 4 vols. New York: Dover.
Park, Robert E.
1927/1973   "Life History." *American Journal of Sociology* 79:251–260.
Parsons, Talcott
1934–1935   "The Place of Ultimate Values in Sociological Theory." *International Journal
                of Ethics* 45:282–316.
1937   *The Structure of Social Action.* New York: McGraw-Hill.
1949   *The Structure of Social Action.* 2nd ed. New York: McGraw-Hill.
1951   *The Social System.* Glencoe, Ill.: Free Press.
1954   "Age and Sex in the Social Structure of the United States." In Talcott Parsons
                (ed.), *Essays in Sociological Theory.* New York: Free Press.
1960   "A Sociological Approach to the Theory of Organizations." In Talcott Parsons
                (ed.), *Structure and Process in Modern Societies.* New York: Free Press: 16–58.
1964   "Levels of Organization and the Mediation of Social Interaction." *Sociological
                Inquiry* 34:207–220.
1966   *Societies.* Englewood Cliffs, N.J.: Prentice-Hall.
1970   *Social Structure and Personality.* New York: Free Press.
1970   "On Building Social System Theory: A Personal History." *Daedalus* 99:826–881.
1971   *The System of Modern Societies.* Englewood Cliffs, N.J.: Prentice-Hall.
1974   "Comment on Turner, 'Parsons as a Symbolic Interactionist.'" *Sociological
                Inquiry* 45:62–65.
1977a   "General Introduction." In Talcott Parsons (ed.), *Social Systems and the
                Evolution of Action Theory.* New York: Free Press: 1–13.
1977b   "On Building Social System Theory: A Personal History." In Talcott Parsons
                (ed.), *Social Systems and the Evolution of Action Theory.* New York: Free
                Press: 22–76.
Parsons, Talcott, and Platt, Gerald
1973   *The American University.* Cambridge: Harvard University Press.
Parsons, Talcott, and Shils, Edward A. (eds.)
1951   *Toward a General Theory of Action.* Cambridge: Harvard University Press.
Peel, J. D. Y.
1971   *Herbert Spencer: The Evolution of a Sociologist.* New York: Basic Books.

Perinbanayagam, Robert S.
1981   "Behavioral Theory: The Relevance, Validity, and Appositeness thereof to Sociology." *The American Sociologist* 16:166–169.
1985   *Signifying Acts: Structure and Meaning in Everyday Life.* Carbondale: Southern Illinois University Press.
1986   "The Meaning of Uncertainty and the Uncertainty of Meaning." *Symbolic Interaction* 9:105–126.

Perrin, Robert
1976   "Herbert Spencer's Four Theories of Social Evolution." *American Journal of Sociology* 81:1339–1359.

Petit, Philip
1975   *The Concept of Structuralism: A Critical Analysis.* Berkeley: University of California Press.

Phillips, Bernard
1971   *Social Research: Strategy and Tactics.* New York: Macmillan.

Phillips, Derek
1973   "Paradigms, Falsifications and Sociology." *Acta Sociologica* 16:13–31.
1975   "Paradigms and Incommensurability." *Theory and Society* 2:37–62.

Picou, J. Steven
1978   "Paradigms, Theories, and Methods in Contemporary Rural Sociology." *Rural Sociology* 43:559–583.

Platt, Jennifer
1986   "Functionalism and the Survey: The Relation of Theory and Method." *Sociological Review* 34:501–536.

Podgorecki, Adam, and Los, Maria
1979   *Multi-dimensional Sociology.* London: Routledge and Kegan Paul.

Pollner, Melvin
1979   "Explicative Transactions: Making and Managing Meaning in Traffic Court." In George Psathas (ed.), *Everyday Language: Studies in Ethnomethodology.* New York: Irvington: 227–255.

Pomeroy, Sarah B.
1975   *Goddesses, Whores, Wives and Slaves: Women in Classical Antiquity.* New York: Schocken Books.

Pope, Whitney
1973   "Classic on Classic: Parsons' Interpretation of Durkheim." *American Sociological Review* 38:399–415.

Porpora, Douglas V.
1986   "A Response to Jeffrey Alexander's *Theoretical Logic in Sociology* Concerning the Alleged Unidimensionality of Marxian Theory." *Sociological Quarterly* 27:75–90.

Poulantzas, Nicos
1972   "The Problem of the Capitalist State." In Robin Blackburn (ed.), *Ideology in Social Science.* London: Fontana: 238–253.
1973   *Political Power and Social Classes.* London: Verso.
1974   *Fascism and Dictatorship: The Third International and the Problem of Fascism.* London: NLB.
1975   *Classes and Contemporary Capitalism.* London: NLB.
1976   *The Crisis of the Dictatorships.* London: NLB.

Powers, Charles H.
1986   *Vilfredo Pareto.* Newbury Park, Calif.: Sage.

Prendergast, Christopher
1986   "Alfred Schutz and the Austrian School of Economics." *American Journal of Sociology* 92:1–26.
Procter, Ian
1978   "Parsons's Early Voluntarism." *Sociological Inquiry* 48:37–48.
Psathas, George
1973a   "Introduction." In George Psathas (ed.), *Phenomenological Sociology: Issues and Applications.* New York: Wiley.
1979a   "Organizational Features of Direction Maps." In George Psathas (ed.), *Everyday Language: Studies in Ethnomethodology.* New York: Irvington: 203–205.
Psathas, George (ed.)
1973b   *Phenomenological Sociology: Issues and Applications.* New York: Wiley.
1979b   *Everyday Language: Studies in Ethnomethodology.* New York: Irvington.
Psathas, George, and Waksler, Frances C.
1973   "Essential Features of Face-to-Face Interaction." In George Psathas (ed.), *Phenomenological Sociology: Issues and Applications.* New York: Wiley: 159–183.
Puner, Helen Walker
1947   *Freud: His Life and His Mind.* New York: Dell.
Quadagno, Jill S.
1979   "Paradigms in Evolutionary Theory: The Sociobiological Model of Natural Selection." *American Sociological Review* 44:100–109.
Radway, Janice
1984   *Reading the Romance: Women, Patriarchy and Popular Literature.* Chapel Hill: University of North Carolina Press.
Rapp, Rayna
1979   "Anthropology." *Signs: Journal of Women in Culture and Society* 4:3:497–513.
Radnitzky, Gerard
1973   *Contemporary Schools of Metascience.* Chicago: Henry Regnery.
Rawls, Ann Warfield
1985   "Reply to Gallant and Kleinman on Symbolic Interactionism vs. Ethnomethodology." *Symbolic Interaction* 8:121–140.
Reed, Evelyn
1970   *Women's Liberation.* New York: Pathfinder Press.
Rhoades, Lawrence J.
1981   *A History of the American Sociological Association.* Washington, D.C.: American Sociological Association.
Rich, Adrienne
1976   *Of Woman Born: Motherhood as Experience and Institution.* New York: Bantam.
1979   *On Lies, Secrets and Silences: Selected Prose 1966–1978.* New York: Norton.
1980   "Compulsory Heterosexuality and Lesbian Experience." In Catharine R. Stimson and Ethel Spector Person (eds.), *Women, Sex, and Sexuality.* Chicago: University of Chicago Press: 62–91.
Riley, John, Jr.
1980   "Talcott Parsons: An Anecdotal Profile." *American Sociologist* 15:66–68.
Ritzer, George
1975a   *Sociology: A Multiple Paradigm Science.* Boston: Allyn and Bacon.

1975b   "Sociology: A Multiple Paradigm Science." *American Sociologist* 10:156–167.

1977   *Working: Conflict and Change.* 2nd ed. Englewood Cliffs, N.J.: Prentice-Hall.

1979   "Toward an Integrated Sociological Paradigm." In William Snizek et al. (eds.), *Contemporary Issues in Theory and Research.* Westport, Conn.: Greenwood Press: 25–46.

1980   *Sociology: A Multiple Paradigm Science.* Rev. ed. Boston: Allyn and Bacon.

1981a   *Toward an Integrated Sociological Paradigm: The Search for an Exemplar and an Image of the Subject Matter.* Boston: Allyn and Bacon.

1981b   "Paradigm Analysis in Sociology: Clarifying the Issues." *American Sociological Review* 46:245–248.

1983   "The McDonaldization of Society." *Journal of American Culture* 6:100–107.

1985   "The Rise of Micro-Sociological Theory." *Sociological Theory* 3:88–98.

Ritzer, George, and Bell, Richard

1981   "Emile Durkheim: Exemplar for an Integrated Sociological Paradigm?" *Social Forces* 59:966–995.

Ritzer, George, Kammeyer, Kenneth, and Yetman, Norman

1987   *Introduction to Sociology: Experiencing a Changing Society.* 3rd ed. Boston: Allyn and Bacon.

Roby, Pamela

1972   "Women and American Higher Education." *The Annals of the American Academy of Political and Social Science* 404:118–139.

Rocher, Guy

1975   *Talcott Parsons and American Sociology.* New York: Barnes and Noble.

Rock, Paul

1979   *The Making of Symbolic Interactionism.* Totowa, N.J.: Rowman and Littlefield.

Roemer, John E.

1982   "Methodological Individualism and Deductive Marxism." *Theory and Society* 11:513–520.

Rogers, Mary

1983   *Sociology, Ethnomethodology, and Experience: A Phenomenological Critique.* New York: Cambridge University Press.

Rollins, Judith

1985   *Between Women: Domestics and their Employers.* Philadelphia: Temple University Press.

Rose, Arnold

1962   "A Systematic Summary of Symbolic Interaction Theory." In Arnold Rose (ed.), *Human Behavior and Social Processes.* Boston: Houghton Mifflin.

Rose, Phyllis

1983   *Parallel Lives: Five Victorian Marriages.* New York: Knopf.

Rosenberg, Morris

1979   *Conceiving the Self.* New York: Basic Books.

Rosenberg, Rosalind

1982   *Beyond Separate Sphere: Intellectual Roots of Modern Feminism.* New Haven: Yale University Press.

Rosenthal, Naomi, et al.

1985   "Social Movements and Network Analysis: A Case Study of Nineteenth-Century Women's Reform in New York State." *American Journal of Sociology* 90:1022–1054.

Rossi, Alice

1974   *The Feminist Papers: From Adams to de Beauvoir.* New York: Bantam.

1977	"A Biosocial Perspective on Parenting." *Daedalus* 106:2:1–31.
1983	"Gender and Parenthood." *American Sociological Review* 49:1–19.

Rossi, Ino

1974a	"Intellectual Antecedents of Lévi-Strauss' Notion of Unconscious." In Ino Rossi (ed.), *The Unconscious in Culture: The Structuralism of Claude Lévi-Strauss in Perspective.* New York: Dutton: 7–30.
1974b	"Structuralism as a Scientific Method." In Ino Rossi (ed.), *The Unconscious in Culture.* New York: Dutton: 60–106.
1983	*From the Sociology of Symbols to the Sociology of Signs: Toward a Dialectical Sociology.* New York: Columbia University Press.

Rossi, Ino (ed.)

1982	*Structural Sociology.* New York: Columbia University Press.

Rowbotham, Sheila

1973	*Women's Consciousness, Man's World.* Middlesex, Eng.: Pelican.

Rubin, Gayle

1975	"The Traffic in Women: Notes on the Political Economy of Sex." In Reyna Reiter (ed.), *Towards an Anthropology of Women.* New York: Monthly Review Press.

Rubinstein, David

1986	"The Concept of Structure in Sociology." In Mark L. Wardell and Stephen P. Turner (eds.), *Sociological Theory in Transition.* Boston: Allen and Unwin: 80–94.

Ruddick, Sara

1980	"Maternal Thinking." *Feminist Studies* 6:2:342–367.

Ryan, William

1971	*Blaming the Victim.* New York: Pantheon.

Ryave, A. Lincoln, and Schenkein, James N.

1974	"Notes on the Art of Walking." In Roy Turner (ed.), *Ethnomethodology: Selected Readings.* Harmondsworth, Eng.: Penguin: 265–275.

Sacks, Harvey

1984	"On Doing 'Being Ordinary.'" In J. Maxwell Atkinson and John Heritage (eds.), *Structures of Social Action.* Cambridge: Cambridge University Press: 413–429.

Salamini, Leonardo

1981	*The Sociology of Political Praxis: An Introduction to Gramsci's Theory.* London: Routledge and Kegan Paul.

Salomon, A.

1945	"German Sociology." In Georges Gurvitch and Wilbert F. Moore (eds.), *Twentieth Century Sociology.* New York: Philosophical Library: 586–614.

Sangren, Steven P.

1983	"Female Gender in Chinese Religious Symbols: Kuan Yin, Ma Tsu and the Eternal 'Mother.'" *Signs: Journal of Women in Culture and Society* 9:1:4–25.

Scheffler, Harold

1970	"Structuralism in Anthropology." In Jacques Ehrmann (ed.), *Structuralism.* Garden City, N.Y.: Anchor: 56–79.

Schegloff, Emanuel A.

1979	"Identification and Recognition in Telephone Conversation Openings." In George Psathas (ed.), *Everyday Language: Studies in Ethnomethodology.* New York: Irvington: 23–78.

Schied-Cook, Teresa
1986   "Scientific Advances in the Socio-cultural Sciences." *Sociological Spectrum*
            6:269–287.
Schneider, Louis
1967   *The Scottish Moralists: On Human Nature and Society.* Chicago: University of
            Chicago Press.
Schroeter, Gerd
1985   "Dialogue, Debate, or Dissent? The Difficulties of Assessing Max Weber's
            Relation to Marx." In Robert J. Antonio and Ronald M. Glassman (eds.),
            A Weber-Marx Dialogue. Lawrence: University Press of Kansas:
            2–13.
Schroyer, Trent
1970   "Toward a Critical Theory of Advanced Industrial Society." In Hans
            Peter Dreitzel (ed.), *Recent Sociology: No. 2.* New York: Macmillan:
            210–234.
1973   *The Critique of Domination.* Boston: Beacon Press.
Schutz, Alfred
1932/1967   *The Phenomenology of the Social World.* Evanston, Ill.: Northwestern Univer-
            sity Press.
1962   *Collected Papers I: The Problem of Social Reality.* The Hague: Martinus
            Nijhoff.
1964   *Collected Papers II: Studies in Social Theory.* The Hague: Martinus Nijhoff.
1966   *Collected Papers III: Studies in Phenomenological Philosophy.* The Hague:
            Martinus Nijhoff.
Schutz, Alfred, and Luckmann, Thomas
1973   *The Structure of the Life World.* Evanston, Ill.: Northwestern University
            Press.
Schwanenberg, Enno
1971   "The Two Problems of Order in Parsons' Theory: An Analysis from Within."
            Social Forces 49:569–581.
Schwendinger, Julia, and Schwendinger, Herman
1974   *Sociologists of the Chair.* New York: Basic Books.
Scimecca, Joseph
1977   *The Sociological Theory of C. Wright Mills.* Port Washington, N.Y.: Kennikat
            Press.
Sciulli, David
1986   "Voluntaristic Action as a Distinct Concept: Theoretical Foundations of
            Societal Constitutionalism." *American Sociological Review* 51:743–766.
Sciulli, David, and Gerstein, Dean
1985   "Social Theory and Talcott Parsons in the 1980s." *Annual Review of Sociology*
            11:369–387.
Scott, John Finley
1963   "The Changing Foundations of the Parsonian Action Schema." *American
            Sociological Review* 28:716–735.
Scully, Diana
1980   *Men Who Control Health: The Miseducation of Obstetrician-Gynecologists.*
            Boston: Houghton Mifflin.
Searle, John
1972   "Chomsky's Revolution in Linguistics." *The New York Review of Books*
            18:16–24.

Secord, Paul F.
1982a   "Interfacing the Personal and the Social." In Paul Secord (ed.), *Explaining Human Behavior*. Beverly Hills, Calif.: Sage: 13–34.
1982b   "Epilogue." In Paul Secord (ed.), *Explaining Human Behavior*. Beverly Hills, Calif.: Sage: 311–314.

Secord, Paul F. (ed.)
1982   *Explaining Human Behavior: Consciousness, Human Action and Social Structure*. Beverly Hills, Calif.: Sage.

Seidman, Steven
1983   *Liberalism and the Origins of European Social Theory*. Berkeley: University of California Press.

Selden, Gary
1983   "Frailty, Thy Name's Been Changed: What Sports Medicine Is Discovering about Women's Bodies." In Laurel Richardson and Verter Taylor (eds.), *Feminist Frontiers*. Reading, Mass.: Addison-Wesley.

Sewart, John J.
1978   "Critical Theory and the Critique of Conservative Method." *American Sociologist* 13:15–22.

Shahar, Shulamith
1983   *The Fourth Estate: A History of Women in the Middles Ages* (Chaya Galai, trans.). London: Methuen.

Shalin, Dmitri
1986   "Pragmatism and Social Interactionism." *American Sociological Review* 51:9–29.

Sharrock, Wes, and Anderson, Bob
1986   *The Ethnomethodologists*. Chichester, Eng.: Ellis Horwood.

Sheridan, Alan
1980   *Michel Foucault: The Will to Truth*. London: Tavistock.

Showalter, Elaine
1971   *Women's Liberation and Literature*. New York: Harcourt Brace Jovanovich.

Simon, Herbert
1957   *Administrative Behavior*. New York: Free Press.

Singelmann, Peter
1972   "Exchange as Symbolic Interaction." *American Sociological Review* 38:414–424.

Skinner, B. F.
1938   *The Behavior of Organisms: An Experimental Analysis*. New York: Appleton-Century-Crofts.
1948   *Walden Two*. New York: Macmillan.
1968   *Technology of Teaching*. New York: Appleton-Century-Crofts.
1971   *Beyond Freedom and Dignity*. New York: Knopf.
1983   *Matter of Consequences: Part Three of an Autobiography*. New York: Knopf.

Skinner, Quentin
1985   "Introduction." In Quentin Skinner (ed.), *The Return of Grand Theory in the Human Sciences*. Cambridge: Cambridge University Press: 3–20.

Skocpol, Theda
1979   *States and Social Revolutions*. Cambridge: Cambridge University Press.

Skotnes, Andor
1979   "Structural Determination of the Proletariat and the Petty Bourgeoisie: A Critique of Nicos Poulantzas." *The Insurgent Sociologist* 9:34–54.

Slater, Phil
1977   *Origin and Significance of the Frankfurt School: A Marxist Perspective*. London: Routledge and Kegan Paul.

Smart, Barry
1983   *Foucault, Marxism and Critique.* London: Routledge and Kegan Paul.
1985   *Michel Foucault.* Chichester, Eng.: Ellis Horwood.
Smith, Dorothy
1974   "Women's Perspective as a Radical Critique of Sociology." *Sociological Inquiry* 44:1:7-13.
1975   "An Analysis of Ideological Structures and How Women Are Excluded: Consideration for Academic Women." *Canadian Review of Sociology and Anthropology.* 12:4:353-369.
1978   "A Peculiar Eclipsing: Women's Exclusion from Man's Culture." *Women's Studies International Quarterly* 1:281-295.
1979   "A Sociology for Women." In Julia A. Sherman and Evelyn Torton Beck (eds.), *The Prism of Sex: Essays in the Sociology of Knowledge.* Madison: University of Wisconsin Press.
Smith, Dorothy, and Griffith, Alison
1985   "Coordinating the Uncoordinated: How Mothers Manage the School Day." Presented at annual meeting of the American Sociological Association, Washington, D.C.
Smith, Norman Erik
1979   "William Graham Sumner as an Anti-Social Darwinist." *Pacific Sociological Review* 22:332-347.
Smith, T. V.
1931   "The Social Philosophy of George Herbert Mead." *American Journal of Sociology* 37:368-385.
Snitow, Ann Barr
1979   "Mass Market Romance: Pornography for Women Is Different." *Radical History Review* 20:141-163.
Snitow, Ann, Stansell, Christine, and Thompson, Sharon
1983   *Powers of Desire: The Politics of Sexuality.* New York: Monthly Review Press.
Snizek, William E.
1976   "An Empirical Assessment of 'Sociology: A Multiple Paradigm Science.'" *The American Sociologist* 11:217-219.
1979   "Towards a Clarification of the Interrelationship between Theory and Research: Its Form and Implications." In William Snizek, Ellsworth Fuhrman, and Michael Miller (eds.), *Contemporary Issues in Theory and Research.* Westport, Conn.: Greenwood Press: 197-209.
Snizek, William E., Fuhrman, Ellsworth R., and Miller, Michael K. (eds.)
1979   *Contemporary Issues in Theory and Research.* Westport, Conn.: Greenwood Press.
Snow, David A.
1986   "Frame Alignment Processes, Micromobilization, and Movement Participation." *American Sociological Review* 51:464-481.
Snow, David A., Zurcher, Louis A., and Peters, Robert
1984   "Victory Celebrations as Theater: A Dramaturgical Approach to Crowd Behavior." *Symbolic Interaction* 8:21-42.
Sokoloff, Natalie
1980   *Between Money and Love: The Dialectics of Women's Home and Market Work.* New York: Praeger.
Sorokin, Pitirim
1927   *Social Mobility.* New York: Harper.

1928   *Contemporary Sociological Theories.* New York: Harper.
1937–1941   *Social and Cultural Dynamics.* 4 vols. New York: American Book Co.
1956   *Fads and Foibles in Modern Sociology and Related Sciences.* Chicago: Regnery.
1963   *A Long Journey: The Autobiography of Pitirim Sorokin.* New Haven, Conn.:
              College and University Press.

Speier, Matthew
1970   "The Everyday World of the Child." In Jack Douglas (ed.), *Understanding
              Everyday Life.* Chicago: Aldine: 188–217.

Spender, Dale
1980   *Man Made Language.* London: Routledge and Kegan Paul.
1982   *Women of Ideas (And What Men Have Done to Them).* London: Routledge and
              Kegan Paul.

Spender, Dale (ed.)
1983   *Feminist Theorists: Three Centuries of Key Women Thinkers.* New York:
              Random House.

Spiegelberg, Herbert
1967   "Husserl's Phenomenology and Sartre's Existentialism." In Joseph
              Kockelmans (ed.), *Phenomenology.* Garden City, N.Y.: Anchor: 252–266.
1973   "On the Right to Say 'We': A Linguistic and Phenomenological Analysis." In
              George Psathas (ed.), *Phenomenological Sociology: Issues and Applications.*
              New York: Wiley: 129–156.

Srubar, Ilja
1984   "On the Origin of 'Phenomenological' Sociology." In Kurt H. Wolff (ed.),
              Alfred Schutz: Appraisals and Developments. Dordrecht, Neth.: Martinus
              Nijhoff: 57–83.

Staats, Arthur W.
1976   "Skinnerian Behaviorism: Social Behaviorism or Radical Behaviorism?" *The
              American Sociologist* 11:59–60.

Stacey, Judith, and Thorne, Barrie
1985   "The Missing Feminist Revolution in Sociology." *Social Problems* 32:4:301–316.

Standley, Arline R.
1981   *Auguste Comte.* Boston: Twayne.

Stanfield, Ron
1974   "Kuhnian Scientific Revolutions and the Keynesian Revolution." *Journal of
              Economic Issues* 8:97–109.

Stanley, Liz, and Wise, Sue
1983   *Breaking Out: Feminist Consciousness and Feminist Research.* London:
              Routledge and Kegan Paul.

Stockard, Jean, and Johnson, Miriam
1980   *Sex Roles: Sex Inequality and Sex Role Development.* Englewood Cliffs, N.J.:
              Prentice-Hall.

Stolte, John F.
forthcoming   "Legitimacy, Justice, and Production Exchange." In Karen S. Cook (ed.),
              Social Exchange Theory. Beverly Hills, Calif.: Sage.

Strasser, Hermann
1976   *The Normative Structure of Sociology.* London: Routledge and Kegan Paul.

Strobel, Margaret
1982   "African Women." *Signs: Journal of Women in Culture and Society* 8:1:109–131.

Struik, Dirk
1964   "Introduction." In Karl Marx, *The Economic and Philosophic Manuscripts of
              1844.* New York: International: 9–56.

Stryker, Sheldon
1980   *Symbolic Interactionism: A Social Structural Version.* Menlo Park, Calif.: Benjamin/Cummings.

Swidler, Ann
1986   "Culture in Action: Symbols and Strategies." *American Sociological Review* 51:273–286.

Swingewood, Alan
1975   *Marx and Modern Social Theory.* New York: Wiley.

Symbolic Interaction
1981   Fall. Entire issue devoted to George Herbert Mead.
1983   Review symposium on Lewis and Smith, *American Sociology and Pragmatism* 6:127–174.

Szacki, Jerzy
1979   *History of Sociological Thought.* Westport, Conn.: Greenwood.

Sztompka, Piotr
1974   *System and Function: Toward a Theory of Society.* New York: Academic.

Takla, Tendzin, and Pope, Whitney
1985   "The Force Imagery in Durkheim: The Integration of Theory, Metatheory and Method." *Sociological Theory* 3:74–88.

Tar, Zoltan
1977   *The Frankfurt School: The Critical Theories of Max Horkheimer and Theodor W. Adorno.* London: Routledge and Kegan Paul.

Tarter, Donald
1973   "Heeding Skinner's Call: Toward the Development of a Social Technology." *American Sociologist* 8:153–158.

Theory, Culture and Society
1985   "The Fate of Modernity" (special issue) 2:1–190.

Theory and Society
1986   "Structures of Capital" (special issue) 15:1–309.

Thibaut, John, and Kelley, Harold H.
1959   *The Social Psychology of Groups.* New York: Wiley.

Thomas, William I., and Thomas, Dorothy S.
1928   *The Child in America: Behavior Problems and Programs.* New York: Knopf.

Thomason, Burke C.
1982   *Making Sense of Reification: Alfred Schutz and Constructionist Theory.* Atlantic Highlands, N.J.: Humanities Press.

Thompson, E. P.
1978   *The Poverty of Theory.* London: Merlin Press.

Thompson, Kenneth
1975   *Auguste Comte: The Foundation of Sociology.* New York: Halstead Press.

Thorne, Barrie, Kramarae, Cheris, and Henley, Nancy
1983   *Language, Gender and Society.* Rowley, Mass.: Newbury House.

Thorne, Barrie, and Yalom, Marilyn (eds.)
1982   *Rethinking the Family: Some Feminist Questions.* New York: Longman.

Tiger, Lionel, and Fox, Robin
1971   *The Imperial Animal.* New York: Holt, Rinehart and Winston.

Tilman, Rick
1984   *C. Wright Mills: A Native Radical and His American Intellectual Roots.* University Park, Pa.: Pennsylvania State University Press.

Tinker, Irene (ed.)
1983   *Women in Washington: Advocates for Public Policy.* Beverly Hills, Calif.:
            Sage.
Tiryakian, Edward A.
1962   *Sociologism and Existentialism: Two Perspectives on the Individual and
            Society.* Englewood Cliffs, N.J.: Prentice-Hall.
1965   "Existential Phenomenology and the Sociological Tradition." *American Socio-
            logical Review* 30:674–688.
1979   "The Significance of Schools in the Development of Sociology." In William
            Snizek, Ellsworth Fuhrman, and Michael Miller (eds.), *Contemporary Issues
            in Theory and Research.* Westport, Conn.: Greenwood Press: 211–233.
1981   "The Sociological Import of Metaphor." *Sociological Inquiry* 51:27–33.
1986   "Hegemonic Schools and the Development of Sociology: Rethinking the
            History of the Discipline." In Richard C. Monk (ed.), *Structures of Knowing.*
            Lanham, Md.: University Press of America: 417–441.
Toby, Jackson
1977   "Parsons' Theory of Societal Evolution." In Talcott Parsons, *The Evolution of
            Societies.* Englewood Cliffs, N.J.: Prentice-Hall: 1–23.
Trebilcot, Joyce
1973   "Sex Roles: The Argument from Nature." Paper presented at the meeting of
            the American Philosophical Association, Western Division, April.
Trebilcot, Joyce (ed.)
1984   *Mothering: Essays in Feminist Theory.* Totowa, N.J.: Rowman and Allanheld.
Troyer, William
1946   "Mead's Social and Functional Theory of Mind." *American Sociological
            Review* 11:198–202.
Tucker, Robert C. (ed.)
1970   *The Marx-Engels Reader.* New York: Norton.
Tumin, Melvin
1953   "Some Principles of Stratification: A Critical Analysis." *American Sociologi-
            cal Review* 18:387–394.
Turner, Bryan S.
1974   *Weber and Islam: A Critical Study.* London: Routledge and Kegan Paul.
1981   *For Weber: Essays in the Sociology of Fate.* Boston: Routledge and Kegan Paul.
Turner, Jonathan
1973   "From Utopia to Where? A Strategy for Reformulating the Dahrendorf Con-
            flict Model." *Social Forces* 52:236–244.
1974   "Parsons as a Symbolic Interactionist: A Comparison of Action and Interaction
            Theory." *Sociological Inquiry* 44:283–294.
1975   "A Strategy for Reformulating the Dialectical and Functional Theories of Con-
            flict." *Social Forces* 53:433–444.
1982   *The Structure of Sociological Theory.* 3rd ed. Homewood, Ill.: Dorsey Press.
1985   "In Defense of Positivism." *Sociological Theory* 3:24–30.
1985b   *Herbert Spencer: A Renewed Appreciation.* Beverly Hills, Calif.: Sage.
1986   *The Structure of Sociological Theory.* 4th ed. Homewood, Ill.: Dorsey Press.
forthcoming "Social Exchange Theory: Future Directions." In Karen S. Cook (ed.), *Social
            Exchange Theory.* Beverly Hills, Calif.: Sage.
Turner, Jonathan, and Beeghley, Leonard
1974   "Current Folklore in the Criticisms of Parsonsian Action Theory." *Sociologi-
            cal Inquiry* 44:47–63.

Turner, Jonathan, and Maryanski, Alexandra
1979   *Functionalism.* Menlo Park, Calif.: Benjamin/Cummings.
Turner, Ralph
1968   "The Self-Conception in Social Interaction." In Chad Gordon and Kenneth J. Gergen (eds.), *The Self in Social Interaction.* New York: Wiley: 93–106.
Turner, Roy
1970   "Words, Utterances and Activities." In Jack Douglas (ed.), *Understanding Everyday Life.* Chicago: Aldine: 161–187.
1974a   "Words, Utterances and Activities." In Roy Turner (ed.), *Ethnomethodology: Selected Readings.* Harmondsworth, Eng.: Penguin: 197–215.
Turner, Roy (ed.)
1974b   *Ethnomethodology: Selected Readings.* Harmondsworth, Eng.: Penguin.
Ungar, Sheldon
1984   "Self-Mockery: An Alternative Form of Self-Presentation." *Symbolic Interaction* 7:121–133.
van den Berg, Axel
1980   "Critical Theory: Is There Still Hope?" *American Journal of Sociology* 86:449–478.
van den Berghe, Pierre
1963   "Dialectic and Functionalism: Toward Reconciliation." *American Sociological Review* 28:695–705.
1974   "Bringing Beasts Back In: Toward a Biosocial Theory of Aggression." *American Sociological Review* 39:777–788.
Veltmeyer, Henry
1978   "Marx's Two Methods of Sociological Analysis." *Sociological Inquiry* 48:101–112.
Venable, Vernon
1945   *Human Nature: The Marxian View.* New York: Knopf.
Vetter, Betty M., Baber, Eleanor, and Jensen-Fisher, Susan
1982   *Professional Women and Minorities: A Manpower Resource Service.* Washington, D.C.: Scientific Manpower Commission.
Vidich, Arthur J., and Lyman, Stanford M.
1985   *American Sociology: Worldly Rejections of Religion and Their Directions.* New Haven: Yale University Press.
Vogel, Lise
1984   *Marxism and the Oppression of Women: Towards a Unitary Theory.* New Brunswick, N.J.: Rutgers University Press.
Wagner, David
1984   *The Growth of Sociological Theories.* Beverly Hills, Calif.: Sage.
Wagner, David, and Berger, Joseph
1985   "Do Sociological Theories Grow?" *American Journal of Sociology* 90:697–728.
Wagner, Helmut
1964   "Displacement of Scope: A Problem of the Relationship between Small Scale and Large Scale Sociological Theories." *American Journal of Sociology* 69:571–584.
1983   *Alfred Schutz: An Intellectual Biography.* Chicago: University of Chicago Press.
Wallerstein, Immanuel
1974   *The Modern World-System: Capitalist Agriculture and the Origins of the European World-Economy in the 16th Century.* New York: Academic Press.

1980   *The Modern World-System II: Mercantilism and the Consolidation of the Euro-pean World-Economy, 1600–1750.* New York: Academic Press.

1986   "Marxisms as Utopias: Evolving Ideologies." *American Journal of Sociology* 91:1295–1308.

Wallimann, Isidor
1981   *Estrangement: Marx's Conception of Human Nature and the Division of Labor.* Westport, Conn.: Greenwood Press.

Walum-Richardson, Laurel
1981   *The Dynamics of Sex and Gender.* Boston: Houghton Mifflin.

Wardell, Mark L., and Turner, Stephen P. (eds.)
1986a   *Sociological Theory in Transition.* Boston: Allen and Unwin.
1986b   "Introduction. Dissolution of the Classical Project." In Mark L. Wardell and Stephen P. Turner (eds.), *Sociological Theory in Transition.* Boston: Allen and Unwin: 11–18.

Warner, R. Stephen
1978   "Toward a Redefinition of Action Theory: Paying the Cognitive Element Its Due." *American Journal of Sociology* 83:1317–1349.

Warshay, Leon and Warshay, Diana H.
1986   "The Individualizing and Subjectivizing of George Herbert Mead: A Sociology of Knowledge Interpretation." *Sociological Focus* 19:177–188.

Weber, Marianne
1975   *Max Weber: A Biography* (Harry Zohn, ed. and trans.). New York: Wiley.

Weber, Max
1921/1958   *The Rational and Social Foundations of Music.* Carbondale: Southern Illinois University Press.

Weigert, Andrew
1981   *Sociology of Everyday Life.* New York: Longman.

Weingart, Peter
1969   "Beyond Parsons? A Critique of Ralf Dahrendorf's Conflict Theory." *Social Forces* 48:151–165.

Weinstein, Eugene A., and Tanur, Judith M.
1976   "Meanings, Purposes and Structural Resources in Social Interaction." *Cornell Journal of Social Relations* 11:105–110.

Wellman, Barry
1983   "Network Analysis: Some Basic Principles." In Randall Collins (ed.), *Sociological Theory—1983.* San Francisco: Jossey-Bass: 155–200.

White, Harrison C., Boorman, Scott A., and Breiger, Ronald L.
1976   "Social Structure from Multiple Networks: Parts 1 and 2." *American Journal of Sociology* 81:730–780; 1384–1446.

White, Hayden
1973   *The Historical Imagination in Nineteenth-Century Europe.* Baltimore: The Johns Hopkins University Press.

Whyte, William F.
1961   "Parsons' Theory Applied to Organizations." In Max Black (ed.), *The Social Theories of Talcott Parsons.* Englewood Cliffs, N.J.: Prentice-Hall: 250–267.

Wiley, Norbert
1979   "The Rise and Fall of Dominating Theories in American Sociology." In William Snizek, Ellsworth Fuhrman, and Michael Miller (eds.), *Contemporary Issues in Theory and Research.* Westport, Conn.: Greenwood Press: 47–79.
1985   "The Current Interregnum in American Sociology." *Social Research* 52:179–207.

1986   "Early American Sociology and *The Polish Peasant.*" *Sociological Theory* 4:20–40.

Willer, David, and Anderson, Bo
1981   *Networks, Exchange and Coercion: The Elementary Theory and Its Applications.* New York: Elsevier.

Williams, Robin
1980   "Talcott Parsons: The Stereotypes and the Reality." *American Sociologist* 15:64–66.
1980   "Pitirim Sorokin: Master Sociologist and Prophet." In Robert Merton and Matilda W. Riley (eds.), *Sociological Traditions from Generation to Generation.* Norwood, N.J.: Ablex: 93–107.

Williams, Simon Johnson
1986   "Appraising Goffman." *British Journal of Sociology* 37:348–369.

Wilner, Patricia
1985   "The Main Drift of Sociology between 1936 and 1982." *History of Sociology: An International Review* 5:1–20.

Wilson, Thomas P.
1970   "Normative and Interpretive Paradigms in Sociology." In Jack Douglas (ed.), *Understanding Everyday Life.* Chicago: Aldine: 1–19.

Wiltshire, David
1978   *The Social and Political Thought of Herbert Spencer.* London: Oxford University Press.

Wolf, Frederic M.
1986   *Meta-Analysis: Quantitative Methods for Research Synthesis.* Beverly Hills, Calif.: Sage University Papers.

Wollstonecraft, Mary
1792/1971   *A Vindication of the Rights of Women.* London: Source Book.

Wood, Michael, and Wardell, Mark L.
1983   "G. H. Mead's Social Behaviorism vs. the Astructural Bias of Symbolic Interactionism." *Symbolic Interaction* 6:85–96.

Woolf, Virginia
1928   *A Room of One's Own.* New York: Harcourt Brace and World.
1938   *Three Guineas.* New York: Harcourt, Brace.

Wrong, Dennis
1961   "The Oversocialized Conception of Man." *American Sociological Review* 26:183–193.

Wuthnow, Robert, et al. (eds.)
1984   *Cultural Analysis.* Boston: Routledge and Kegan Paul.

Yamagishi, Toshio
forthcoming "An Exchange Theoretical Approach to Network Positions." In Karen S. Cook (ed.), *Social Exchange Theory.* Beverly Hills, Calif.: Sage.

Zaretsky, Eli
1976   *Capitalism, the Family and Personal Life.* New York: Harper Colophon.

Zeitlin, Irving M.
1981   *Ideology and the Development of Sociological Theory.* 2nd ed. Englewood Cliffs, N.J.: Prentice-Hall.

Zimmerman, Don
1978   "Ethnomethodology." *American Sociologist* 13:5–15.
1979   "Ethnomethodology and Symbolic Interactionism: Some Reflections on Naturalistic Inquiry." Paper presented at the Society for the Study of Symbolic Interaction, Boston.

Zimmerman, Don, and Pollner, Melvin
1970   "The Everyday World as a Phenomenon." In Jack Douglas (ed.), *Under-
            standing Everyday Life*. Chicago: Aldine: 80–103.
Zimmerman, Don, and Wieder, D. Lawrence
1970   "Ethnomethodology and the Problem of Order: Comment on Denzin." In Jack
            Douglas (ed.), *Understanding Everyday Life*. Chicago: Aldine: 285–298.
Znaniecki, Florian
1934   *Method of Sociology.* New York: Farrar and Rhinehart.
1936   *Social Actions.* New York: Farrar and Rhinehart.
Zukin, Sharon, and DiMaggio, Paul
1986   "Preface." In *Theory and Society* 15:1–10.
Zurcher, Louis A.
1982   "The Staging of Emotions: A Dramaturgical Analysis." *Symbolic Interaction*
            5:1–22.
1985   "The War Game: Organizational Scripting and the Expression of Emotion."
            Symbolic Interaction 8:191–206.

NAME INDEX

SUBJECT INDEX

A Note on the Type

The text of this book was set on the Editwriter in a computer version of Times Roman, designed by Stanley Morison for *The Times* (London) and first introduced by that newspaper in 1932.

Among typographers and designers of the twentieth century, Stanley Morison has been a strong forming influence as typographical adviser to the English Monotype Corporation, as a director of two distinguished English publishing houses, and as a writer of sensibility, erudition, and keen practical sense.

About the Author

George Ritzer is the author of numerous books and articles in sociological theory (as well as in other areas of sociology, especially the sociology of work). Among his books are *Sociology: A Multiple Paradigm Science* and *Toward an Integrated Sociological Paradigm*, and he has written articles on sociological theory that have appeared in such journals as the *American Sociological Review*, *Sociological Theory*, *Social Forces*, and the *American Sociologist*. He has been awarded a Fulbright-Hays Fellowship, has been a Fellow in Residence at the Institute for Advanced Studies in the Netherlands, and has been selected a Distinguished Scholar-Teacher at the University of Maryland, where he is currently Professor of Sociology.